Visit us at

www.syngress.com

Syngress is committed to publishing high-quality books for IT Professionals and delivering those books in media and formats that fit the demands of our customers. We are also committed to extending the utility of the book you purchase via-additional materials available from our Web site.

SOLUTIONS WEB SITE

To register your book, visit www.syngress.com/solutions. Once registered, you can access-our solutions@syngress.com Web pages. There you may find an assortment of valueadded features such as free e-books related to the topic of this book, URLs of related Web sites, FAQs from the book, corrections, and any updates from the author(s).

ULTIMATE CDs

Our Ultimate CD product line offers our readers budget-conscious compilations of some of our best-selling backlist titles in Adobe PDF form. These CDs are the perfect way to extend your reference library on key topics pertaining to your area of expertise, including Cisco Engineering, Microsoft Windows System Administration, CyberCrime Investigation, Open Source Security, and Firewall Configuration, to name a few.

DOWNLOADABLE E-BOOKS

For readers who can't wait for hard copy, we offer most of our titles in downloadable Adobe PDF form. These e-books are often available weeks before hard copies, and are priced affordably.

SYNGRESS OUTLET

Our outlet store at syngress.com features overstocked, out-of-print, or slightly hurt books at significant savings.

SITE LICENSING

Syngress has a well-established program for site licensing our e-books onto servers in corporations, educational institutions, and large organizations. Contact us at sales@syngress.com for more information.

CUSTOM PUBLISHING

Many organizations welcome the ability to combine parts of multiple Syngress books, as well as their own content, into a single volume for their own internal use. Contact us at sales@syngress.com for more information.

SYNGRESS®

The Best Damn Server Virtualization Book Period

Kris Buytaert
Rogier Dittner
Juan R. Garcia
Twan Grotenhuis
David E. Hart
Andy Jones
Kenneth Majors
Al Muller

David Payne
Jeremy Pries
Rami Rosen
David Rule Jr.
Paul Summitt
Matthijs ten Seldam
David E. Williams

KEY	SERIAL NUMBER
001	HJIRTCV764
002	PO9873D5FG
003	829KM8NJH2
004	PLTY567AWQ
005	CVPLQ6WQ23
006	VBP965T5T5
007	HJJJ863WD3E
008	2987GVTWMK
009	629MP5SDJT
010	IMWQ295T6T

PUBLISHED BY
Syngress Publishing, Inc.
Elsevier, Inc.
30 Corporate Drive
Burlington, MA 01803

The Best Damn Server Virtualization Book Period

Printed in the United States of America
1 2 3 4 5 6 7 8 9 0

ISBN 13: 978-1-59749-217-1

Publisher: Amorette Pedersen   Page Layout and Art: SPi
Acquisitions Editor: Andrew Williams   Cover Designer: Michael Kavish

For information on rights, translations, and bulk sales, contact Matt Pedersen, Commercial Sales Director and Rights, at Syngress Publishing; email m.pedersen@elsevier.com.

Contributing Authors

Kris Buytaert is Founder and CTO of X-Tend. He is a longtime Linux, Security, and Open Source consultant. He has consulting and development experience with multiple enterprise-level clients and government agencies. In addition to his high-level technical experience, he is also a team leader who likes to deliver his projects on time. He is a contributor to the Linux Documentation Project and author of various technical publications. Kris is a Red Hat Certified Engineer and is currently the maintainer of the openMosix HOWTO Web site. Kris is also a frequent speaker at Linux and OpenSource conferences. He is currently focusing on Linux clustering (both HA and HPC), virtualization, and large infrastructure management.

Rogier Dittner (MCSE NT4, 2000, 2003, MCDBA, MCT, MSF Practitioner) is a consultant at a Microsoft partner offering solutions based on Microsoft technology to customers. As a consultant he supports the sales organization and takes part in planning and designing complex Microsoft-oriented implementations.

Because of his personal interest in Microsoft products and more than 10 years' experience, he has deep technical working knowledge in a broad range of Microsoft products. Within his company he performs the leading role in operations management solutions and training.

He would like thank his wife and children for giving him the time and space to write (Pascalle, bedankt, je bent een schat!)

Juan R. Garcia is a Principal Consultant at Williams & Garcia, LLC. He provides strategic and technical consulting in legacy systems migrations, enterprise architecture, disaster recover planning, and enterprise IT resource consolidation to Williams & Garcia's customers. He specializes in open systems (UNIX/Linux), virtualization technologies (VMware, Xen, and AIX 5L), storage solutions, and RDMBS technologies. Juan's previous positions include Solutions Architect for Bellsouth, Senior Enterprise Architect for John H. Harland Co., and Technical Manager for Sun Professional Services.

v

Twan Grotenhuis (MCT, MCSE NT4, 2000 and 2003, MCSE+messaging 2000 and 2003, CCNA) is a consultant with Sylis Netherlands. He currently provides strategic and technical consulting to several of the Sylis customers in the Netherlands. His specialties include Microsoft Exchange and ISA architecture, design, implementation, troubleshooting and optimization. Twan has been involved in several Virtual Server 2005 projects where virtualization of physical servers was his main focus.

David E. Hart (MCSE#300790, ASE #220919, VCP #4970) is a senior consultant with Callisma. He currently provides senior-level strategic and technical consulting to all Callisma clients in the south-central region of the U.S. His specialties include virtualization technologies, Microsoft Active Directory design and implementation, emerging technology planning, collaboration architecture and design, content delivery design and implementations, enterprise operating systems troubleshooting and optimization, and desktop architecture design and implementation. David's background spans over 15 years in the industry and includes positions at one of the top five consulting firms as the "South Central Microsoft Practice and VMware Lead" for seven years, Microsoft Practice Lead and Senior Microsoft Consultant at a top three telecommunication company for five years, and Desktop Enterprise Practice Lead for a nationwide consulting firm for two years.

Andy Jones (MCSE+I, MCT, CCIA, CCEA, CCI, CCNA, CCDA, MCIW, Network+, A+,) is the Services Director for MTM Technologies, previously known as Vector ESP. He provides comprehensive solutions focused on Citrix and Microsoft technologies for clients ranging from 50 to 50,000 users, focusing mainly on architecting and deploying Access Infrastructure solutions for enterprise customers. One of Andy's primary focuses is in developing best practices, processes, and methodologies surrounding Access Infrastructure that take into consideration and integrate with virtually every part of a customer's infrastructure.

In addition to field work and business development, Andy regularly instructs Microsoft and Citrix courses. Andy holds a master's degree from Morehead State University.

Kenneth Majors (MCSE, MCSA, Project+, VMware VCP, Citrix CCEA, CCA, IBM X-Series Expert, Avaya ACA) is a consultant for Choice Solutions LLC, a systems integrator headquartered in Overland Park, KS. Choice Solutions provides IT design, project management, and support for enterprise computing systems. Kenneth is a key contributor to defining best practices for deployment and implementation of Microsoft technologies, including Windows Server, Virtual Server, and SharePoint; Citrix Presentation Server; VMware ESX; and development of documentation standards. He develops technology solutions and methodologies focused on improving client business processes. These technology solutions touch every part of a system's life cycle from assessment, blueprint, construction, and deployment on projects to operational management and strategic planning for the business process. Kenneth holds a bachelor's degree from Colorado Technical University. He currently resides in Olathe, KS, with his lovely, supportive wife, Sandy, and near their children, Tabitha and Keith, and their grandsons, Wesley and Austin.

Al Muller is a consultant for Callisma, a wholly owned subsidiary of AT&T. He has been in the IT field since 1995, getting his start as a database administrator in the Navy. In 2002 he began using VMware's GSX Server and within a year was involved in his first virtualization project. Since then, he has been an eager proponent of virtualization technology and has worked on a number of different server consolidation and virtualization projects.

He holds a bachelor's degree in English and plans on writing a series of books on the virtual evolution taking place in data centers worldwide and the tools required to leverage and support a virtual infrastructure.

David Payne is an IT enthusiast with a decade of real-world experience in the data center. David is currently CTO of Xcedex, the only U.S.-based professional services firm solely focused on virtualization solutions. David has been key in developing the virtualization practice for Xcedex Professional Services. Specifically over the last four years, David has been engaged in dozens of virtualization initiatives, providing architecture guidance and hands on services for organizations of all sizes across the United States. His practical approach has taken some of the largest US companies in finance, retail, and manufacturing beyond the marketing spin and into real results with today's virtualization technologies. David is a VMware Authorized Consultant (VAC) and a VMware Certified Professional (VCP).

Xcedex is a VMware Premier Partner, joining this invitation-only program as one of the first 10 partners in 2004. Xcedex is recognized nationwide for its professionalism, deep knowledge of virtual infrastructure, and experience in real-world implementations. With a laser focus on virtualization consulting, Xcedex has become one of the top go-to service delivery partners for VMware, Dell, and EMC.

Jeremy Pries is a Virtualization Architect at Xcedex. He has an extensive background in computing infrastructure dating back 10 years, with experience ranging from networking and storage to security and Intel based operating systems. Jeremy's current focus is 100% on virtualization technologies, gaining valuable experience on some of the largest ESX implementations. Jeremy's specialty is filling gaps in management tools to speed project timelines and increase accuracy. His expertise has made him one of the most sought after Xcedex architects. Jeremy is a VMware Authorized Consultant (VAC) and a VMware Certified Professional (VCP).

Xcedex is a VMware Premier Partner, joining this invitation-only program as one of the first 10 partners in 2004. Xcedex is recognized nationwide for its professionalism, deep knowledge of virtual infrastructure, and experience in real-world implementations. With a laser focus on virtualization consulting, Xcedex has become one of the top go-to service delivery partners for VMware, Dell, and EMC.

Rami Rosen (B.Sc, Computer Science, Technion—Israel High Institute of Technology) is working as a Linux and Open Solaris kernel programmer accompanying advanced networking and security projects. His background includes positions in Ethernet switching and Avionic operating system start-ups. His specialities include virtualization technologies and kernel networking internals. His articles are occasionally published in the *Linux Journal* and the lwn.net Web site.

David Rule Jr. (VMware VCP, VAC, MCP, Citrix CCEA, CCA) is a Senior Consultant for Choice Solutions LLC, an Overland Park, KS-based systems integrator that provides IT design, project management, and support for enterprise computing systems. David's primary role is in developing virtualization strategies for Choice Solutions' clients. The strategies include the virtualization of both servers and storage, including the development of best practice and standards documentation. The combination of virtual servers and storage provides systems with enterprise-class stability, performance, and scalability. These technologies are implemented to provide clients with environments that facilitate management of and increase the performance of day-to-day operations while also making them more reliable and cost-effective.

David is currently working toward completing a degree from Park University in Computer Information Systems Management. He resides in Shawnee, KS, with his wife, Kristine, and their two wonderful children, Christian and Collin.

Paul Summitt (MCSE, CCNA, MCP+I, MCP) holds a master's degree in mass communication. Paul has served as a network, an Exchange, and a database administrator, as well as a Web and application developer. Paul has written on virtual reality and Web development and has served as technical editor for several books on Microsoft technologies. Paul lives in Columbia, MO, with his life and writing partner, Mary.

Matthijs ten Seldam (MCSE, CISSP) is a principal consultant with the infrastructure technologies group at Microsoft Consulting Services. His expertise focuses on virtualization, platform management and deployment, security, and networking. One of his specialties is automation of management tasks through various interfaces like WMI and COM using languages like VBScript and C#.

He has developed a technical training on Virtual Server 2005 R2 and delivers this to customers and partners. He currently provides consulting to enterprise customers, delivers technical workshops, and runs early adoption programs of the next generation of virtualization products like Virtual Server 2005 R2 Service Pack 1 and System Center Virtual Machine Manager.

David E. Williams is a principal at Williams & Garcia, LLC, a consulting practice based in Atlanta, GA, specializing in effective enterprise infrastructure solutions. He specializes in the delivery of advanced solutions for x86 and x64 environments. Because David focuses on cost containment and reduction of complexity, virtualization technologies have played a key role in his recommended solutions and infrastructure designs. David has held several IT leadership positions in various organizations, and his responsibilities have included the operations and strategy of Windows, open systems, mainframe, storage, database, and data center technologies and services. He has also served as a senior architect and an advisory engineer for Fortune 1000 organizations, providing strategic direction on technology infrastructures for new enterprise-level projects.

David studied Music Engineering Technology at the University of Miami, and he holds MCSE+I, MCDBA, VCP, and CCNA certifications. When not obsessed with corporate infrastructures, he spends his time with his wife and three children.

Contents

Chapter 1 An Introduction to Virtualization 1

  Introduction 2

  What Is Virtualization? 2

    The History of Virtualization 3

      The Atlas Computer 3

      The M44/44X Project 3

      CP/CMS 4

      Other Time-Sharing Projects 4

      Virtualization Explosion of the 1990s and Early 2000s 5

    The Answer: Virtualization Is 6

  Why Virtualize? 7

    Decentralization versus Centralization 7

    True Tangible Benefits 11

      Consolidation 12

      Reliability 14

      Security 15

  How Does Virtualization Work? 16

    OS Relationships with the CPU Architecture 16

    The Virtual Machine Monitor and Ring-0 Presentation 18

    The VMM Role Explored 19

      The Popek and Goldberg Requirements 19

      The Challenge: VMMs for the x86 Architecture 21

  Types of Virtualization 21

    Server Virtualization 21

    Storage Virtualization 24

    Network Virtualization 25

    Application Virtualization 25

  Common Use Cases for Virtualization 26

    Technology Refresh 26

    Business Continuity and Disaster Recovery 28

    Proof of Concept Deployments 29

    Virtual Desktops 29

    Rapid Development, Test Lab, and Software

      Configuration Management 29

Summary. 31
Solutions Fast Track 31
Frequently Asked Questions 34

Chapter 2 Virtualization Technologies. 37
Hardware Virtualization Software 38
Operating System–Level Virtualization Software. 38
Software Comparison Matrix 39

Chapter 3 Introduction to Microsoft Virtual Server 45
Introduction 46
Microsoft Virtual Server 2005 R2 and Dynamics System Initiative 46
What Is Virtualization, and When Should You Use It? 46
    Advantages of Virtualization 47
        Production Data Centers 47
        Test and Development Data Centers. 49
        Disaster Recovery 49
What Virtualization Tools Are Available? 50
    Third-Party Virtualization Tools. 51
How Does Virtualization Work? 52
Virtual PC versus Virtual Server 2005 52
    Features That Are Found in Both Virtual PC
        and Virtual Server 2005 R2. 53
    Differences between Virtual PC and Virtual Server 2005 R2. 53
        Supported Features in Virtual PC 54
        Supported Features in Virtual Server 2005 R2. 54
            Host Hardware Support. 54
            Virtual Hardware. 54
            Remote Management 54
            Security 54
            Support for Scripting. 54
            WMI Support. 54
            Clustering. 54
    Scenarios for the Use of Virtual PC. 55
        Help Desk. 55
        Training 55
        Testing 55
        Legacy Applications 56
Virtual Server 2005 versus Virtual Server 2005 R2. 56

Summary. 57
Solutions Fast Track 57
Frequently Asked Questions 59

Chapter 4 Installing and Configuring a Virtual Server 61
Introduction 62
Determining the Physical Size of the Server 62
Physical Server Sizing. 62
Evaluating Existing Physical Servers 62
Planning for New Virtual Servers 62
Installing Virtual Server 2005 R2 63
Preinstallation Tasks. 64
Installation Tasks 64
Setting Up a Virtual Server Administration Web Site 74
Virtual Server Administration Web Site Installation. 75
Installing in a Multi-Server Environment 75
Virtual Machine Remote Console 85
Setting Access Permissions for the Virtual Machine Remote Console 86
Setting Default Location and Search Paths. 89
Setting Resource Allocation 92
Summary. 96
Solutions Fast Track 96
Frequently Asked Questions 98

Chapter 5 Virtual Machines 99
Introduction 100
Creating the Virtual Server 100
Using the Administration Web Page. 102
Virtual Machine Configuration 105
General Properties. 106
The Virtual Machine Configuration File 107
Virtual Machine Additions. 109
Memory Properties 110
Hard Disks 112
CD/DVD. 113
SCSI Adapters. 115
Network Adapters 116
Scripts 118
Floppy Disk Drive. 120

COM Ports. 121
LPT Ports 122
Adding Hardware to the Server 123
Building the Host Server 123
Processors 123
Memory 123
Storage Systems 124
Network Cards 124
COM an LPT Ports. 124
USB Ports 125
Installing a Windows OS 125
Loading the Operating System 126
Booting from the Virtual Floppy Disk Drive 128
Starting the Virtual Machine. 130
Navigation 135
Control the Virtual Machine 135
Installing the Operating System 135
Installing Virtual Machine Additions 137
Removing Virtual Machine Additions 142
Installing a Non-Windows OS 143
Creating the Virtual Machine 143
Virtual Machine Additions for Linux. 148
Summary. 163
Solutions Fast Track 164
Frequently Asked Questions 166

Chapter 6 Virtual Networks **169**
Introduction 170
Introduction to Virtual Networks 170
Virtual Networks 170
Viewing the Virtual Networks 172
Virtual Network Properties 175
Using the "Internal Network". 182
Using the Loopback Adapter. 183
Installing the Loopback Adapter 184
Configuring Host-to-Guest Networking and File Sharing. 192
Using the ICS 198
Creating a Virtual Network. 208
Binding a Physical Network Adapter to a Virtual Network. 211
Changing the Binding of a Virtual Network 212

Changing the Virtual Network for a Virtual Machine 216
Using the Virtual Server Network Services 218
Summary. 223
Solutions Fast Track 224
Frequently Asked Questions 226

Chapter 7 Virtual Disks 227
Introduction 228
Removable Virtual Disks. 228
CD/DVD Drive. 228
Floppy Disk Drive 230
Virtual Hard Disks 236
Dynamically Expanding Virtual Hard Disk 237
Compacting. 239
Converting 246
Fixed-Size Virtual Hard Disk. 247
Converting 248
Differencing Virtual Hard Disk 249
Chaining. 253
Merging 254
Summary. 259
Solutions Fast Track 259
Frequently Asked Questions 261

**Chapter 8 Introduction to ADS and
Virtual Server Migration Tool 263**
Automated Deployment Services 264
Rapid Deployment Using ADS 264
What Components Does ADS Use? 265
ADS Controller Service 265
ADS Network Boot Service. 266
ADS Image Distribution Service 266
ADS Host Server Requirements 266
ADS Client-Server Requirements 267
ADS Network and Management Requirements. 267
Installing ADS 268
Installation Options 268
Installation Process 269
Post-Installation: Configuring ADS 281
Automatically Accepting New Clients 281
Enabling Multicast 285

Administration Agent Installing. 287
Adding Hardware Drivers in the Boot OS 292
Editing Using the Sequence Editor. 292
Installing Virtual Server Migration Toolkit onto the
    Virtualization Server. 298
Summary. 303
Solutions Fast Track 303
Frequently Asked Questions 305

Chapter 9 Managing Virtual Server **307**
Introduction 308
The Management Interface. 308
    Configuring a Central Virtual Server Management Site 309
Using the Virtual Server COM API 319
    Using the Virtual Server Programmer's Guide 320
    Connecting to the Virtual Server COM Object 326
Accessing a Virtual Server Using Script 328
    Listing Virtual Server Properties. 329
    Setting Virtual Server Properties 331
Creating a Virtual Machine Using Script. 332
    Creating a Virtual HardDisk 333
    Putting It All Together 334
Creating a Virtual Network Using Script. 337
Retrieving Guest OS Information Using Script. 338
Changing a Virtual Machine State Using Script. 341
    The Virtual Machine State Model 341
Attaching Scripts to Virtual Server Events 344
    Attaching Scripts to Virtual Machine Events 346
    Scripts in Action. 346
Summary. 351
Solutions Fast Track 351
Frequently Asked Questions 353

Chapter 10 Migrating Physical Machines. **355**
Introduction 356
Getting the Virtualization Environment Ready for Usage. 356
    Setting Up the Virtualization tools. 356
    Installing VSMT and ADS Agent on the Virtual Server Host. 357
    Creating the Virtual Network 360
Capturing the Physical Machine 362
    Hardware Inventory 364

Creating the Scripts 367
    Validating Hardware. 367
    Creating Migration Scripts. 368
Data Capture 372
Creating the Virtual Machine on the Virtual Server Host 378
Deploying the Virtual Machine on the Host OS 381
Summary. 385
Solutions Fast Track 385
Frequently Asked Questions 387

Chapter 11 Troubleshooting 389
Introduction 390
Troubleshooting Virtual Server 2005 R2 390
    Troubleshooting Virtual Server Administration Web Site 390
        Troubleshooting LsaLogonUser() failed! 390
        Troubleshooting Internal Server Error 500 397
        Troubleshooting Access Denied Errors 400
        Troubleshooting VMRC Server Disabled Errors 400
    Troubleshooting Virtual Server Settings 401
        Troubleshooting Disappearing Server Settings 401
        Troubleshooting Virtual Network Changes 402
    Troubleshooting Virtual Machine Performance Issues 405
        Disabling TCP Segmentation Offload 406
        Don't Use Network Adapter Auto-Configuration 406
        Use ISOs instead of CDs Whenever Possible 407
        Don't Overallocate Memory. 407
        Use a Separate Disk Controller for Guest Machines. 407
Troubleshooting Automated Deployment Services 407
    Troubleshooting PXE. 407
        Check the DHCP Configuration 408
        DHCP Relay Agent. 408
        Check for Other PXE Servers 409
        Check Your Network Drivers. 410
        Check Your Storage Drivers 410
        Check Your BIOS Clock 410
    Troubleshooting the ADS Services. 410
        Check That the ADS Services Are Running 411
        Confirm the ADS Controller's IP Address 411
        Check the ADS Certificates 411

Troubleshooting the Virtual Server Migration Toolkit. 411
    Troubleshooting the Virtual Network Setup. 411
    Troubleshooting Script Creation 412
    Troubleshooting ADS Integration 412
    Troubleshooting Migration from VMware to Virtual Server. 412
Troubleshooting the Migration Process 413
    Imaging Problems. 413
    IDE Disks Cannot Exceed 127 GB 414
    Converted SCSI Disks Fail to Boot. 414
Summary. 418
Solutions Fast Track 418
Frequently Asked Questions 420

Chapter 12 Introducing Xen 421
Introduction 422
What Is Xen?. 422
    Features of Xen 424
    The XenServer Product Family. 424
Xen's Virtualization Model Explored 427
    Architecture Overview 427
    Processor Architecture. 428
    Paravirtualization with Xen. 428
    Xen Domains. 430
CPU Virtualization. 434
    Exceptions 435
    CPU Scheduling 436
    Time 437
Memory Virtualization 438
    Memory Allocation 439
    Page Tables and Segmentation 441
    Virtual Address Translation 443
I/O Virtualization 445
    Device I/O Rings 447
    Event Channels 448
    Virtual I/O Devices and Split Device Drivers 449
        Network I/O 450
        Block I/O. 451
        Trusted Platform Module and Other Devices 451
    Driver Domains 451
    Software and Hardware IOMMUs. 452

SWIOTLB 453
Grant Tables. 453
The Xenstore. 454
Summary. 458
Solutions Fast Track 458
Frequently Asked Questions 462

Chapter 13 Deploying Xen: Demystifying the Installation **463**
Introduction 464
Determining Which Xen to Choose. 464
System Requirements. 465
Thinking Before You Start 466
Installing Xen on a Free Linux Distribution 468
Fedora Core 6 468
VirtManager. 479
Installing Windows XP 488
Installing the XenServer Product Family 492
What Is XenServer. 492
XenServer Requirements 493
Getting and Installing XenServer. 493
Installing the Host 494
Client Installation 501
Installing an Initial Virtual Machine on XenServer. 505
Other Xen Installation Methods 510
Using the XenSource Binaries and LVM 510
Configuring Xen. 513
Getting Xen on Your Network 515
Summary. 519
Solutions Fast Track 519
Frequently Asked Questions 521

Chapter 14 The Administrator Console and
Other Native Tools **523**
Introduction 524
Native Xen Command-Line Tools 525
The xe Command-Line Interface 525
Installing and Cloning XenVMs 526
Starting Up, Shutting Down, Rebooting, Suspending,
and Resuming XenVMs 526
Shutting Down and Rebooting XenHosts. 526
Query Options for XenHosts. 527

XenServer Administrator Console. 527
    System Requirements for the Administrator Console 527
    Installing the Administrator Console 528
        Installing the Administrator Console on
        Windows (XP/2000/2003) 528
        Installing the Administrator Console on Linux 535
    Using the Administrator Console. 535
        Working with Hosts. 537
            Connecting to a XenHost 538
            Powering Off/Rebooting a XenHost 538
        Deploying and Configuring XenVMs. 539
            Creating Xen Virtual Machines 539
            Cloning XenVMs 540
            Additional XenVM Operations 541
            Performance Monitoring. 542
  Summary. 543
  Solutions Fast Track 543
  Frequently Asked Questions 544

Chapter 15 Managing Xen with
Third-Party Management Tools 545
  Introduction 546
  Qlusters openQRM. 546
    Xen Management with openQRM. 546
        Overview 547
        General Concepts for the Xen/openQRM Mix 548
        Plug-ins and Licensing. 549
    Installing openQRM 552
        System Requirements. 553
        Installing openQRM 3.1.x Server. 554
        Installing the openQRM Xen Plug-in 558
        Managing Xen with openQRM. 560
            How the Xen Plug-in Works 560
            Using openQRM with Xen Integration 561
        Provisioning with openQRM-Pro 565
  Enomalism. 568
    Overview of Enomalism 568
    Installing Enomalism. 569
        System Requirements. 569
        Installation Walkthrough 570
    Using Enomalism to Manage Xen. 570

Project ConVirt and XenMan 574
    Overview of ConVirt. 575
    Installing ConVirt. 575
        System Requirements. 575
        Installation. 576
    Using ConVirt to Manage Xen. 577
        The Dashboard 577
        Server Pool Operations 578
        Server Operations 579
        VM Operations. 579
        The Image Store 581
    Summary. 583
    Solutions Fast Track 583
    Frequently Asked Questions 585

Chapter 16 Deploying a Virtual Machine in Xen 587
    Introduction 588
    Workload Planning and Virtual Machine Placement. 588
        Memory. 588
        CPU 588
        Network 589
    Installing Modified Guests 591
        Installing Red Hat Enterprise Linux 4. 591
    Installing Unmodified Guests 597
        Installing Red Hat Linux Enterprise 5. 598
    Installing Windows Guests 602
        Windows Guest Installation. 602
    Physical-to-Virtual Migrations of Existing Systems 606
        P2V Migration. 607
    Importing and Exporting Existing Virtual Machines. 607
        Exporting XenVMs 609
        Importing XenVMs 610
    Summary. 613
    Solutions Fast Track 613
    Frequently Asked Questions 615

Chapter 17 Advanced Xen Concepts 617
    Introduction 618
    The Virtual Split Devices Model. 618
    Advanced Storage Concepts 619
        High-Performance Solutions for Xen 619

iSCSI Integration with Xen 619
Copy-on-Write 622
DmUserspace 623
UnionFS 623
Advanced Networking Concepts 624
Bridging VLANs 624
Creating Interface Bonds for High Availability
and Link Aggregation 625
Routing, Forwarding, and Other Network Tricks 627
Building a Xen Cluster 628
XenVM Migration 635
XenVM Backup and Recovery Solutions 638
Options for Backing Up Your XenVM 638
Making Xen Part of Your Disaster Recovery Plan 638
Full Virtualization in Xen 639
The New Processors with Virtual Extensions (VT-x and AMD-V) 639
Summary 642
Solutions Fast Track 642
Frequently Asked Questions 644

Chapter 18 Scripted Installation 647
Introduction 648
Setting Up the Scripted Installation 648
Creating the Script 648
Remote Network Installation 655
Summary 656

**Chapter 19 An Introduction to ESX Native Tools
and How to Use Them 657**
Introduction 658
Esxtop 658
Esxtop Overview 658
The Virtual Machine World 660
System World 661
The Service Console World 661
Some Other Helpful Esxtop Metrics 661
%USED 661
%Ready 662
%EUSED 662
%MEM 662

vmkfstools 662
    Viewing Contents VMFS Partition 662
    Import/Export Files. 663
    Adding a New Virtual Disk, Blank Virtual Disk,
        and Extending Existing Virtual Disks 663
    vmware-cmd 664
vmkusage 666
Summary 668

Chapter 20 Scripting and Programming for the
Virtual Infrastructure **669**

Introduction 670
VMware Scripting APIs 670
    What Are the VMware Scripting APIs? 672
    Installing the VMware Scripting APIs. 673
    Putting the VMware Scripting APIs to Work for You 674
        Working with the VmCOM API 674
            VmConnectParams 677
            VmCollection 678
            VmServerCtl 678
            VmCtl 680
            Managing Guests with User-Defined Variables 685
        Working with the VmPerl API 685
            VMware::VmPerl::ConnectParams 686
            VMware::VmPerl::Server 687
            VMware::VmPerl::VM 688
            VMware::VmPerl::Question 690
        Putting It All Together 691
            Example 1: Disconnecting Devices from
                Every Registered VM 691
            Example 2: Simple GUI to List All Virtual Machines 693
            Example 3: Test Automation with VMware 696
VMware Virtual Infrastructure SDK 697
    What Is the VMware Virtual Infrastructure SDK? 698
    The VI SDK Architecture 698
    Overview of the VMware Virtual Infrastructure Web Service 700
        What Are Web Services? 700
        VMware VI SDK Conformance and Web Service Standards 701
    Operations Available Using the Virtual Infrastructure SDK 701
        Operations for Basic Web Service Client Interaction 701

Operations for Element Management. 701
Operations for Virtual Computing 702
Developing with the Virtual Infrastructure SDK 1.1. 703
Preparing the Virtual Infrastructure Web Service 703
Working with the VMware WSDL 706
Virtual Infrastructure SDK 1.1 Concepts and Terminology. 708
Path Hierarchy 708
Terminology 709
Programming Logic for the SDK 711
Data Models and Datatypes 711
Developing Your Management Application 712
The Connection Process 713
Handling SSL Certificates 714
Obtaining with Object Handles 716
Retrieving Items and Performing Operations 719
Updating Interior Nodes 722
Developing with the Virtual Infrastructure SDK 2.0. 723
Features Added to Virtual Infrastructure 2.0. 723
Preparing the Virtual Infrastructure 2.0 Web Service 725
Working with the VMware VI SDK 2.0 WSDLs 727
Virtual Infrastructure SDK 2.0 Concepts and Terminology. 728
Data and Managed Objects 728
Managed Entity Inventory 728
Host Agent versus VirtualCenter Feature Set 729
Data Models and Data Types 730
Programming Logic for the VI SDK 2.0 733
Developing Your Management Application 734
Managed Object Browser and Other Tools 734
The Connection Process 739
Handling SSL Certificates 741
Retrieving Property Information 742
Other Retrieval Mechanisms 746
Performing Advanced Operations 747
Power Operations 748
Virtual Machine Migration. 748
Working with Snapshots. 749
Working with Scheduled Tasks 750
Other VMware SDKs. 751
VMware Guest SDK. 751
VMware CIM SDK 752
Summary. 754

Chapter 21 Building a VM **755**
　　Introduction 756
　　Creation of Virtual Machines Utilizing Command-Line Tools 756
　　　　Creation of a Virtual Machine Configuration File 756
　　　　　　Creating Your Virtual Machine Configuration File 758
　　　　Creation of a Virtual Machine Disk File 762
　　　　Registering Virtual Machines with ESX Server 763
　　Scripting Creation of Virtual Machines in ESX Shell 764
　　Scripting Creation of Virtual Machines in Perl Scripts 770
　　　　Modifying Scripted VM Creation with Perl 777
　　　　Perl Script Components 779
　　　　　　VmPerl Commands 781
　　Cloning Virtual Machines Utilizing ESX Shell Scripts 782
　　Cloning Virtual Machines Utilizing VmPerl Scripts 785
　　Summary 794

Chapter 22 Modifying VMs **795**
　　Introduction 796
　　The Virtual Machine VMDK File 796
　　　　VMDK Components 798
　　　　　　Version=1 798
　　　　　　CID=2af6d34d 798
　　　　　　parentCID=ffffffff 798
　　　　　　file.createType="twoGbMaxExtentSparse" 798
　　　　　　The Size in Sectors Value 799
　　　　　　The Disk Data Base Command 799
　　　　The Virtual Machine Configuration vmx File 801
　　　　vmx File Components 802
　　　　　　config.version = "" 802
　　　　　　Scsi0:0.present = "" 802
　　　　　　Scsi0:0.name = "" 802
　　　　　　Scsi0:0.mode = "" 802
　　　　　　scsi0.present – "" 803
　　　　　　scsi0.virtualDev = "" 803
　　　　　　ethernet0.present = "" 803
　　　　　　ethernet0.connectionType = "" 804
　　　　　　ethernet0.devName = "" 804
　　　　　　ethernet0.networkName = "" 804
　　　　　　Ethernet0.addressType = "vpx" 804
　　　　　　Ethernet0.generatedAddress = "" 804
　　　　　　Ethernet0.virtualDev = "vlance" or "vmxnet" or "e1000" 805

Floppy Drives and CD-ROMs for Virtual Machines 805
Graphics Emulation, Unique Identifiers. 805
Priority, VMware Tools Settings, and Suspend 806
isolation.tools.dnd.disable = "True" or "False". 807
suspend.Directory = "/vmfs/vmhba1:0:83:1" 807
Autostart, Autostop, and Time Sync Options 807
The tools.syncTime Option. 807
Virtual Machine Conversion from IDE to SCSI 808
ddb.adapterType = "buslogic" 808
ddb.adapterType = "lsilogic" 809
Scripted Disconnect of IDE Devices 811
Dynamic Creation of Virtual Machines 814
Summary 822

Chapter 23 Instant Disk: How to P2V for Free 823
Introduction 824
What Is a P2V? 824
P2V Techniques 824
VMware P2V Tool 824
Platespin PowerConvert 825
Barts/Ghost 826
The "Big Secret" of P2V 826
Instant Disk Overview 826
The Bad News. 827
Prepping the ESX Host: Setting Up FTP on ESX Host 827
Prepping the Source Machine: Install the SCSI Driver 830
Installing the SCSI Driver in Windows 2000/2003. 830
Installing the SCSI Driver in Windows NT 838
Continue Prepping the Source Machine: Validate 841
The Linux Rescue CD. 841
Booting the Rescue CD 841
At the Command Prompt. 847
Finding the Hard Drives and Storage 848
Linux and Hardware. 849
Virtual Disk Files on the VMFS 850
Starting the FTP Process 851
Creating a New Virtual Machine and Pointing
It to a New VMDK File 852
Windows VMs 852
Post-P2V. 853
Summary. 854

Chapter 24 Scripting Hot Backups and Recovery for Virtual Machines **855**

Introduction 856
Anatomy of a VM Backup 856
   Limitations. 859
   Layered REDO Logs 860
Hot VM Backup Sample Script. 863
Choosing the Target for VM Backups 866
   NFS. 867
      Attributes of NFS for VM Backups. 867
         Pros 867
         Cons. 867
   CIFS 868
      Attributes of CIFS for VM Backups 868
         Pros 868
         Cons. 868
   FTP. 868
      Attributes of FTP for VM Backups 868
         Pros 869
         Cons. 869
   VMFS 869
      Attributes of Copies to VMFS for VM Backups 869
         Pros 869
         Cons. 870
Existing VM Backup Tools 870
   vmsnap.pl, *vmsnap_all*, and *vmres.pl* 871
   vmbk.pl 871
   Commercial Options 872
VMX File Backups 873
   Incorporating Hot VM Backups into Your Recovery Plan. 876
   Crash Consistent State 878
   Replication 879
   Hot VM Backups as Part of the Recovery Plan 879
      1st Step: Take an Inventory of Your Virtual Machines. 880
      2nd Step: Determine the Recovery Point Objective for Each VM . . . 880
      3rd Step: Determine the Recovery Time Objective for Each VM 881
      4th Step: Apply the Right Backup Job to the Need 881
      5th Step: Document Your Results. 882
   Hybrid Backup Strategy 882
Summary. 885

Chapter 25 The Future of Virtualization 887

Introduction 888
The Unofficial Xen Road Map 888
  Performance and Scalability. 889
    NUMA-Aware Architecture 889
    Multicore Processors 891
    Smart I/O 892
  Operating System Support 893
    Support in Linux Distributions. 894
    Xen and Microsoft. 894
    Other HVM Guests 895
  Beyond the x86 CPU Architecture 895
    IA-64 Feature Sync with x86 895
    Porting to PowerPC. 896
    Porting to the UltraSPARC Architecture 897
  Architecture Enhancements. 898
    Control Tools. 898
    Virtual Hard Disk Images and XenFS. 899
    Virtual Device Enhancements. 899
Virtual Infrastructure in Tomorrow's Data Center 900
  Technology Trends Driving Improvements in Virtualization 901
    Hardware Economies of Scale. 901
    Multicore and Multithreaded Computing 902
  Solutions for Small and Medium-Sized Businesses 904
    Integrated Computing. 904
    Data Center in a Box. 905
  Large Enterprises 906
    Reliability and Availability 906
    Security. 908
    Compliance. 911
The Magic Recipe: Other Hardware and
  Software Virtualization Trends 911
Increasing Density Further with Blade Servers. 912
Storage Virtualization 912
Network Virtualization 912
Summary. 914
Solutions Fast Track 914
Frequently Asked Questions 916

Index 917

## Chapter 1

An Introduction to Virtualization

Solutions in this chapter:

- **What Is Virtualization?**
- **Why Virtualize?**
- **How Does Virtualization Work?**
- **Types of Virtualization**
- **Common Use Cases for Virtualization**

☑ **Summary**

☑ **Solutions Fast Track**

☑ **Frequently Asked Questions**

Introduction

Virtualization is one of those buzz words that has been gaining immense popularity with IT professionals and executives alike. Promising to reduce the ever-growing infrastructure inside current data center implementations, virtualization technologies have cropped up from dozens of software and hardware companies. But what exactly is it? Is it right for everyone? And how can it benefit your organization?

Virtualization has actually been around more than three decades. Once only accessible by the large, rich, and prosperous enterprise, virtualization technologies are now available in every aspect of computing, including hardware, software, and communications, for a nominal cost. In many cases, the technology is freely available (thanks to open-source initiatives) or included for the price of products such as operating system software or storage hardware.

Well suited for most inline business applications, virtualization technologies have gained in popularity and are in widespread use for all but the most demanding workloads. Understanding the technology and the workloads to be run in a virtualized environment is key to every administrator and systems architect who wishes to deliver the benefits of virtualization to their organization or customers.

This chapter will introduce you to the core concepts of server, storage, and network virtualization as a foundation for learning more about Xen. This chapter will also illustrate the potential benefits of virtualization to any organization.

What Is Virtualization?

So what exactly is virtualization? Today, that question has many answers. Different manufacturers and independent software vendors coined that phrase to categorize their products as tools to help companies establish virtualized infrastructures. Those claims are not false, as long as their products accomplish some of the following key points (which are the objectives of any virtualization technology):

- Add a layer of abstraction between the applications and the hardware
- Enable a reduction in costs and complexity
- Provide the isolation of computer resources for improved reliability and security
- Improve service levels and the quality of service
- Better align IT processes with business goals
- Eliminate redundancy in, and maximize the utilization of, IT infrastructures

While the most common form of virtualization is focused on server hardware platforms, these goals and supporting technologies have also found their way into other critical—and expensive—components of modern data centers, including storage and network infrastructures.

But to answer the question "What is virtualization?" we must first discuss the history and origins of virtualization, as clearly as we understand it.

The History of Virtualization

In its conceived form, virtualization was better known in the 1960s as time sharing. Christopher Strachey, the first Professor of Computation at Oxford University and leader of the Programming Research Group, brought this term to life in his paper *Time Sharing in Large Fast Computers*. Strachey, who was a staunch advocate of maintaining a balance between practical and theoretical work in computing, was referring to what he called multi-programming. This technique would allow one programmer to develop a program on his console while another programmer was debugging his, thus avoiding the usual wait for peripherals. Multi-programming, as well as several other groundbreaking ideas, began to drive innovation, resulting in a series of computers that burst onto the scene. Two are considered part of the evolutionary lineage of virtualization as we currently know it—the Atlas and IBM's M44/44X.

The Atlas Computer

The first of the supercomputers of the early 1960s took advantage of concepts such as time sharing, multi-programming, and shared peripheral control, and was dubbed the Atlas computer. A project run by the Department of Electrical Engineering at Manchester University and funded by Ferranti Limited, the Atlas was the fastest computer of its time. The speed it enjoyed was partially due to a separation of operating system processes in a component called the supervisor and the component responsible for executing user programs. The supervisor managed key resources, such as the computer's processing time, and was passed special instructions, or extracodes, to help it provision and manage the computing environment for the user program's instructions. In essence, this was the birth of the hypervisor, or virtual machine monitor.

In addition, Atlas introduced the concept of virtual memory, called one-level store, and paging techniques for the system memory. This core store was also logically separated from the store used by user programs, although the two were integrated. In many ways, this was the first step towards creating a layer of abstraction that all virtualization technologies have in common.

The M44/44X Project

Determined to maintain its title as the supreme innovator of computers, and motivated by the competitive atmosphere that existed, IBM answered back with the M44/44X Project. Nested at the IBM Thomas J. Watson Research Center in Yorktown, New York, the project created a similar architecture to that of the Atlas computer. This architecture was first to coin the term *virtual machines* and became IBM's contribution to the emerging time-sharing system concepts. The main machine was an IBM 7044 (M44) scientific computer and several simulated 7044 virtual machines, or 44Xs, using both hardware and software, virtual memory, and multi-programming, respectively.

Unlike later implementations of time-sharing systems, M44/44X virtual machines did not implement a complete simulation of the underlying hardware. Instead, it fostered the notion that virtual machines were as efficient as more conventional approaches. To nail that notion, IBM successfully released successors of the M44/44X project that showed this idea was not only true, but could lead to a successful approach to computing.

CP/CMS

A later design, the IBM 7094, was finalized by MIT researchers and IBM engineers and introduced Compatible Time Sharing System (CTSS). The term "compatible" refers to the compatibility with the standard batch processing operating system used on the machine, the Fortran Monitor System (FMS). CTSS not only ran FMS in the main 7094 as the primary facility for the standard batch stream, but also ran an unmodified copy of FMS in each virtual machine in a background facility. The background jobs could access all peripherals, such as tapes, printers, punch card readers, and graphic displays, in the same fashion as the foreground FMS jobs as long as they did not interfere with foreground time-sharing processors or any supporting resources.

MIT continued to value the prospects of time sharing, and developed Project MAC as an effort to develop the next generation of advances in time-sharing technology, pressuring hardware manufacturers to deliver improved platforms for their work. IBM's response was a modified and customized version of its System/360 (S/360) that would include virtual memory and time-sharing concepts not previously released by IBM. This proposal to Project MAC was rejected by MIT, a crushing blow to the team at the Cambridge Scientific Center (CSC), whose only purpose was to support the MIT/IBM relationship through technical guidance and lab activities.

The fallout between the two, however, led to one of the most pivotal points in IBM's history. The CSC team, lead by Norm Rassmussen and Bob Creasy, a defect from Project MAC, to the development of CP/CMS. In the late 1960s, the CSC developed the first successful virtual machine operating system based on fully virtualized hardware, the CP-40. The CP-67 was released as a reimplementation of the CP-40, as was later converted and implemented as the S/360-67 and later as the S/370. The success of this platform won back IBM's credibility at MIT as well as several of IBM's largest customers. It also led to the evolution of the platform and the virtual machine operating systems that ran on them, the most popular being VM/370. The VM/370 was capable of running many virtual machines, with larger virtual memory running on virtual copies of the hardware, all managed by a component called the virtual machine monitor (VMM) running on the real hardware. Each virtual machine was able to run a unique installation of IBM's operating system stably and with great performance.

Other Time-Sharing Projects

IBM's CTSS and CP/CMS efforts were not alone, although they were the most influential in the history of virtualization. As time sharing became widely accepted and recognized as an effective way to make early mainframes more affordable, other companies joined the time-sharing fray. Like IBM, those companies needed plenty of capital to fund the research and hardware investment needed to aggressively pursue time-sharing operating systems as the platform for running their programs and computations. Some other projects that jumped onto the bandwagon included

- **Livermore Time-Sharing System (LTSS)**   Developed by the Lawrence Livermore Laboratory in the late 1960s as the operating system for the Control Data CDC 7600 supercomputers. The CDC 7600 running LTSS took over the title of the world's fastest computer, trumping on the Atlas computer, which suffered from a form of trashing due to inefficiencies in its implementation of virtual memory.

- **Cray Time-Sharing System (CTSS)**   (This is a different CTSS; not to be confused with IBM's CTSS.) Developed for the early lines of Cray supercomputers in the early 1970s. The project was engineered by the Los Alamos Scientific Laboratory in conjunction with the Lawrence Livermore Laboratory, and stemmed from the research that Livermore had already done with the successful LTSS operating system. Cray X-MP computers running CTSS were used heavily by the United States Department of Energy for nuclear research.

- **New Livermore Time-Sharing System** (NLTSS) The last iteration of CTSS, this was developed to incorporate recent advances and concepts in computers, such as new communication protocols like TCP/IP and LINCS. However, it was not widely accepted by users of the Cray systems and was discontinued in the late 1980s.

Virtualization Explosion of the 1990s and Early 2000s

While we have discussed a summarized list of early virtualization efforts, the projects that have launched since those days are too numerous to reference in their entirety. Some have failed while others have gone on to be popular and accepted technologies throughout the technical community. Also, while efforts have been pushed in server virtualization, we have also seen attempts to virtualize and simplify the data center, whether through true virtualization as defined by the earlier set of goals or through infrastructure sharing and consolidation.

Many companies, such as Sun, Microsoft, and VMware, have released enterprise-class products that have wide acceptance, due in part to their existing customer base. However, Xen threatens to challenge them all with their approach to virtualization. Being adopted by the Linux community and now being integrated as a built-in feature to most popular distributions, Xen will continue to enjoy a strong and steady increase in market share. Why? We'll discuss that later in the chapter. But first, back to the question… What is virtualization?

Configuring & Implementing…

Evolution of the IBM LPAR—More than Just Mainframe Technology

IBM has had a long history of Logical Partitions, or LPARs, on their mainframe product offerings, from System390 through present-day System z9 offerings. However, IBM has extended the LPAR technology beyond the mainframe, introducing it to its Unix platform with the release of AIX 5L. Beginning with AIX 5L Version 5.1, administrators could use the familiar Hardware Management Console (HMC) or the Integrated Virtualization Manager to create LPARs with virtual hardware resources (dedicated or

Continued

shared). With the latest release, AIX 5L Version 5.3, combined with the newest generation of System p with POWER5 processors, additional mainframe-derived virtualization features, such as micro-partitioning CPU resources for LPARs, became possible.

IBM's LPAR virtualization offerings include some unique virtualization approaches and virtual resource provisioning. A key component of what IBM terms the Advanced POWER Virtualization feature, is the Virtual I/O Server. Virtual I/O servers satisfy part of the VMM, called the POWER Hypervisor, role. Though not responsible for CPU or memory virtualization, the Virtual I/O server handles all I/O operations for all LPARs. When deployed in redundant LPARs of its own, Virtual I/O servers provide a good strategy to improve availability for sets of AIX 5L or Linux client partitions, offering redundant connections to external Ethernet or storage resources.

Among the I/O resources managed by the Virtual I/O servers are

- **Virtual Ethernet** Virtual Ethernet enables inter-partition communication without the need for physical network adapters in each partition. It allows the administrator to define point-to-point connections between partitions. Virtual Ethernet requires a POWER5 system with either IBM AIX 5L Version 5.3 or the appropriate level of Linux and an HMC to define the Virtual Ethernet devices.

- **Virtual Serial Adapter (VSA)** POWER5 systems include Virtual Serial ports that are used for virtual terminal support.

- **Client and Server Virtual SCSI** The POWER5 server uses SCSI as the mechanism for virtual storage devices. This is accomplished using a pair of virtual adapters; a virtual SCSI server adapter and a virtual SCSI client adapter. These adapters are used to transfer SCSI commands between partitions. The SCSI server adapter, or target adapter, is responsible for executing any SCSI command it receives. It is owned by the Virtual I/O server partition. The virtual SCSI client adapter allows the client partition to access standard SCSI devices and LUNs assigned to the client partition. You may configure virtual server SCSI devices for Virtual I/O Server partitions, and virtual client SCSI devices for Linux and AIX partitions.

The Answer: Virtualization Is...

So with all that history behind us, and with so many companies claiming to wear the virtualization hat, how do we define it? In an effort to be as all-encompassing as possible, we can define virtualization as:

> A framework or methodology of dividing the resources of a computer hardware into multiple execution environments, by applying one or more concepts or technologies such as hardware and software partitioning,

time-sharing, partial or complete machine simulation, emulation, quality of service, and many others.

Just as it did during the late 1960s and early 1970s with IBM's VM/370, modern virtualization allows multiple operating system instances to run concurrently on a single computer, albeit much less expensive than the mainframes of those days. Each OS instance shares the available resources available on the common physical hardware, as illustrated in Figure 1.1. Software, referred to as a virtual machine monitor (VMM), controls use and access to the CPU, memory, storage, and network resources underneath.

Figure 1.1 Virtual Machines Riding on Top of the Physical Hardware

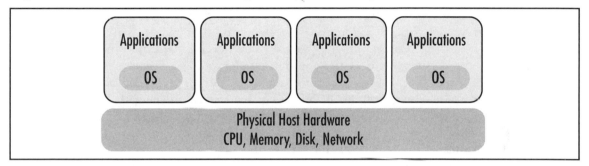

Why Virtualize?

From the mid-1990s until present day, the trend in the data center has been towards a decentralized paradigm, scaling the application and system infrastructure outward in a horizontal fashion. The trend has been commonly referred to as "server sprawl." As more applications and application environments are deployed, the number of servers implemented within the data center grows at exponential rates. Centralized servers were seen as too expensive to purchase and maintain for many companies not already established on such a computing platform. While big-frame, big-iron servers continued to survive, the midrange and entry-level server market bustled with new life and opportunities for all but the most intense use cases. It is important to understand why IT organizations favored decentralization, and why it was seen as necessary to shift from the original paradigm of a centralized computing platform to one of many.

Decentralization versus Centralization

Virtualization is a modified solution between two paradigms—centralized and decentralized systems. Instead of purchasing and maintaining an entire physical computer, and its necessary peripherals for every application, each application can be given its own operating environment, complete with I/O, processing power, and memory, all sharing their underlying physical hardware. This provides the benefits of decentralization, like security and stability, while making the most of a machine's resources and providing better returns on the investment in technology.

With the popularity of Windows and lighter-weight open systems distributed platforms, the promise that many hoped to achieve included better return on assets and a lower total cost of ownership (TCO). The commoditization of inexpensive hardware and software platforms added additional fuel to the evangelism of that promise, but enterprises quickly realized that the promise had turned into a nightmare due to the horizontal scaling required to provision new server instances.

On the positive side, companies were able to control their fixed asset costs as applications were given their own physical machine, using the abundant commodity hardware options available. Decentralization helped with the ongoing maintenance of each application, since patches and upgrades could be applied without interfering with other running systems. For the same reason, decentralization improves security since a compromised system is isolated from other systems on the network. As IT processes became more refined and established as a governance mechanism in many enterprises, the software development life cycle (SDLC) took advantage of the decentralization of n-tier applications. Serving as a model or process for software development, SDLC imposes a rigid structure on the development of a software product by defining not only development phases (such as requirements gathering, software architecture and design, testing, implementation, and maintenance), but rules that guide the development process through each phase. In many cases, the phases overlap, requiring them to have their own dedicated n-tier configuration.

However, the server sprawl intensified, as multiple iterations of the same application were needed to support the SDLC for development, quality assurance, load testing, and finally production environments. Each application's sandbox came at the expense of more power consumption, less physical space, and a greater management effort which, together, account for up to tens (if not hundreds) of thousands of dollars in annual maintenance costs per machine. In addition to this maintenance overhead, decentralization decreased the efficiency of each machine, leaving the average server idle 85 to 90 percent of the time. These inefficiencies further eroded any potential cost or labor savings promised by decentralization.

In Table 1.1, we evaluate three-year costs incurred by Foo Company to create a decentralized configuration comprised of five two-way x86 servers with software licensed per physical CPU, as shown in Figure 1.2. These costs include the purchase of five new two-way servers, ten CPU licenses (two per server) of our application, and soft costs for infrastructure, power, and cooling. Storage is not factored in because we assume that in both the physical and virtual scenarios, the servers would be connected to external storage of the same capacity; hence, storage costs remain the same for both. The Physical Cost represents a three-year cost since most companies depreciate their capital fixed assets for 36 months. Overall, our costs are $74,950.

Table 1.1 A Simple Example of the Cost of Five Two-Way Application Servers

Component	Unit Cost	Physical Cost	Virtual Cost
Server hardware	$7,500.00	$37,500.00	$7,500.00
Software licenses/CPU	$2,000.00	$20,000.00	$4,000.00
Supporting infrastructure	$2,500.00	$12,500.00	$2,500.00
Power per server year	$180.00	$2,700.00	$540.00
Cooling per server year	$150.00	$2,250.00	$450.00
Total three-year costs:		$74,950.00	$16,490.00
Realized savings over three years:	**$58,460.00**		

Figure 1.2 A Decentralized Five-Server Configuration

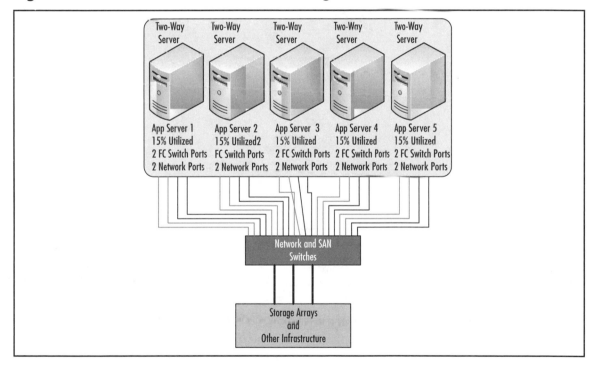

In contrast, the table also shows a similarly configured centralized setup of five OS/application instances hosted on a single two-way server with sufficient hardware resources for the combined workload, as shown in Figure 1.3. Although savings are realized by the 5:1 reduction in server hardware, that savings is matched by the savings in software cost (5:1 reduction in physical CPUs to license), supporting infrastructure, power, and cooling.

Figure 1.3 A Centralized Five-Server Configuration

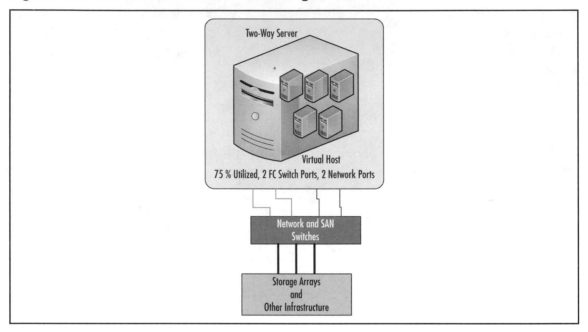

When building the business case and assessing the financial impact of virtualization, be sure not to over-commit the hosts with a large number of virtual machines. Depending on the workload, physical hosts can manage as many as 20 to 30 virtualization machines, or as little as 4 to 5. Spend time upfront gathering performance information about your current workloads, especially during peak hours, to help properly plan and justify your virtualization strategy.

Assuming that each server would average 15-percent utilization if run on physical hardware, consolidation of the workloads into a centralized virtual is feasible. The hard and soft costs factored into the calculations more closely demonstrate the total cost of ownership in this simple model, labor excluded. It is important to note that *Supporting Infrastructure*, as denoted in the table, includes rack, cabling, and network/storage connectivity costs. This is often overlooked; however, it is critical to include this in your cost benefit analysis since each Fibre-Channel (FC) switch port consumed could cost as much as $1,500, and each network port as much as $300. As illustrated in the figures, there are ten FC and ten network connections in the decentralized example compared to two FC and two network connections. Port costs alone would save Foo a considerable amount. As the table shows, a savings of almost 80 percent could be realized by implementing the servers with virtualization technologies.

Designing & Planning…

A Virtualized Environment Requires a Reliable, High-Capacity Network

To successfully consolidate server workloads onto a virtualized environment, it is essential that all server subsystems (CPU, memory, network, and disk) can accommodate the additional workload. While most virtualization products require a single network connection to operate, careful attention to, and planning of, the networking infrastructure of a virtual environment can ensure both optimal performance and high availability.

Multiple virtual machines will increase network traffic. With multiple workloads, the network capacity needs to scale to match the requirements of the combined workloads expected on the host. In general, as long as the host's processor is not fully utilized, the consolidated network traffic will be the sum of the traffic generated by each virtual machine.

True Tangible Benefits

Virtualization is a critical part of system optimization efforts. While it could simply be a way to reduce and simplify your server infrastructure, it can also be a tool to transform the way you think about your data center as a whole. Figure 1.4 illustrates the model of system optimization. You will notice that virtualization, or physical consolidation, is the foundation for all other optimization steps, followed by logical consolidation and then an overall rationalization of systems and applications, identifying applications that are unneeded or redundant and can thus be eliminated.

Figure 1.4 Virtualization's Role in System Optimization

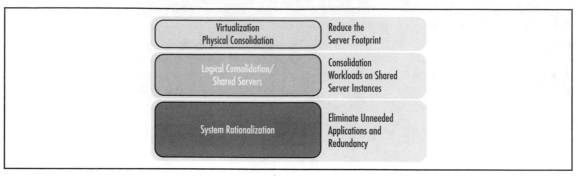

In Table 1.2 you will find a sample list of benefits that often help IT organization justify their movement toward a virtual infrastructure. Although each organization's circumstances are different, you only need a few of these points to apply to your situation to build a strong business case for virtualization.

Table 1.2 Benefits of Virtualization

Category	Benefit
Consolidation	Increase server utilization
	Simplify legacy software migration
	Host mixed operating systems per physical platform
	Streamline test and development environments
Reliability	Isolate software faults
	Reallocate existing partitions
	Create dedicated or as-needed failover partitions
Security	Contain digital attacks through fault isolation
	Apply different security settings to each partition

Consolidation

Three drivers have motivated, if not accelerated, the acceptance and adoption of virtualization technologies—consolidation, reliability, and security. The goal behind consolidation is to combine and unify. In the case of virtualization, workloads are combined on fewer physical platforms capable of sustaining their demand for computing resources, such as CPU, memory, and I/O. In modern data centers, many workloads are far from taxing the hardware they run on, resulting in infrastructure waste and lower returns. Through consolidation, virtualization allows you to combine server instances, or operating systems and their workloads, in a strategic manner and place them on shared hardware with sufficient resource availability to satisfy resource demands. The result is increased utilization. It is often thought that servers shouldn't be forced to run close to their full-capacity levels; however, the opposite is true. In order to maximize that investment, servers should run as close to capacity as possible, without impacting the running workloads or business process relying on their performance. With proper planning and understanding of those workloads, virtualization will help increase server utilization while decreasing the number of physical platforms needed.

Another benefit of consolidation virtualization focuses on legacy system migrations. Server hardware has developed to such levels that they are often incompatible with legacy operating systems and applications. Newer processor technologies, supporting chipsets, and the high-speed buses sought after can often cripple legacy systems, if not render them inoperable without the possibility of full recompilation. Virtualization helps ease and simplify legacy system migrations by providing a common and widely compatible platform upon which legacy system instances can run. This improves the chances that applications can be migrated for older, unsupported, and riskier platforms to newer hardware and supported hardware with minimal impact.

In the past, operating systems were bound to a specific hardware platform. This tied many organizations' hands, forcing them to make large investments in hardware in order to maintain their critical business applications. Due to the commoditization of hardware, though, many of the common operating systems currently available can run on a wide range of server architectures, the most popular of which is the x86 architecture. You can run Windows, Unix, and your choice of Linux distributions on the x86 architecture. Virtualization technologies built on top of x86 architecture can, in turn, host heterogeneous environments. Multiple operating systems, including those previously mentioned, can be consolidated to the same physical hardware, further reducing acquisition and maintenance costs.

Finally, consolidation efforts help streamline development and test environments. Rather than having uncontrolled sprawl throughout your infrastructure as new projects and releases begin or existing applications are maintained, virtualization allows you to consolidate many of those workloads onto substantially fewer physical servers. Given that development and test loads are less demanding by nature than production, consolidation of those environments through virtualization can yield even greater savings than their production counterparts.

Designing & Planning…

More Cores Equal More Guests… Sometimes

When designing the physical platform for your virtualization and consolidation efforts, be sure to take advantage of the current offering of Intel and AMD multi-core processors. Do keep in mind, though, that increasing your core count, and subsequently your total processing power, does not proportionally relate to how many virtual machines you can host. Many factors can contribute to reduced

Continued

guest performance, including memory, bus congestion (especially true for slower Intel front-side bus architectures or NUMA-based four-way Opteron servers), I/O bus congestion, as well as external factors such as the network infrastructure and the SAN.

Carefully plan your hardware design with virtual machine placement in mind. Focus more on the combined workload than the virtual machine count when sizing your physical host servers. Also consider your virtualization product's features that you will use and how it may add overhead and consume resources needed by your virtual machines. Also consider the capability of your platform to scale as resource demands increase—too few memory slots, and you will quickly run out of RAM; too few PCI/PCI-X/PCI-e slots and you will not be able to scale your I/O by adding additional NICs or HBAs.

Finally, consider the level of redundancy and known reliability of the physical server hardware and supporting infrastructure. Remember that when your host fails, a host outage is much more than just one server down; all the virtual machines it was hosting will experience the outage as well.

Always keep in mind the key hardware traits required for any virtualization host:

- Performance
- Flexibility
- Reliability

Reliability

More than ever before, reliability has become a mandate and concern for many IT organizations. It has a direct relationship to system availability, application uptime, and, consequently, revenue generation. Companies are willing to, and often do, invest heavily into their server infrastructure to ensure that their critical line-of-business applications remain online and their business operation goes uninterrupted. By investing in additional hardware and software to account for software faults, infrastructures are fortified to tolerate failures and unplanned downtime with interruption. Doing so, though, has proven to be very costly.

Virtualization technologies are sensitive to this and address this area by providing high isolation between running virtual machines. A system fault in one virtual machine, or partition, will not affect the other partitions running on the same hardware platform. This isolation logically protects and shields virtual machines at the lowest level by causing them to be unaware, and thus not impacted, by conditions outside of their allocations. This layer of abstraction, a key component in virtualization, makes each partition just as if it was running on dedicated hardware.

Such isolation does not impede flexibility, as it would in a purely physical world. Partitions can be reallocated to serve other functions as needed. Imagine a server hosting a client/server application that is only used during the 8A.M. to 5P.M. hours Monday through Friday, another that runs batch processes to close out business operations nightly, and another that is responsible for data maintenance jobs over the weekend. In a purely physical world, they would exist as three dedicated servers that are highly utilized during their respective hours of operation, but sit idle when not performing their purpose. This accounts for much computing waste and an underutilization of expensive investments. Virtualization addresses this by allowing a single logical or physical partition to be reallocated to each function as needed. On weekdays, it would host the client/server application by day and run the batch processes at night. On the weekends, it would then be reallocated for the data maintenance tasks, only to return to hosting the client/server application the following Monday morning. This flexibility allows IT organizations to utilize "part-time" partitions to run core business processes in the same manner as they would physical servers, but achieve lower costs while maintaining high levels of reliability.

Another area that increases costs is the deployment of standby or failover servers to maintain system availability during times of planned or unplanned outages. While capable of hosting the targeted workloads, such equipment remains idle between those outages, and in some cases, never gets used at all. They are often reduced to expensive paperweights, providing little value to the business while costing it much. Virtualization helps solve this by allowing just-in-time or on-demand provisioning of additional partitions as needed. For example, a partition that has been built (OS and applications) and configured can be put into an inactive (powered-off or suspended) state, ready to be activated when a failure occurs. When needed, the partition becomes active without any concern about hardware procurement, installation, or configuration. Another example is an active/passive cluster. In these clusters, the failover node must be active and online, not inactive. However, the platform hosting the cluster node must be dedicated to that cluster. This has caused many organizations to make a large investment in multiple failover nodes, which sit in their data centers idle, waiting to be used in case of an outage. Using server virtualization, these nodes can be combined onto fewer hardware platforms, as partitions hosting failover nodes are collocated on fewer physical hosts.

Security

The same technology that provides application fault isolation can also provide security fault isolation. Should a particular partition be compromised, it is isolated from the other partitions, stopping the compromise from being extended to them. Solutions can also be implemented that further isolate compromised partitions and OS instances by denying them the very resources they rely on to exist. CPU cycles can be reduced, network and disk I/O access severed, or the system halted altogether. Such tasks would be difficult, if not impossible, to perform if the compromised instance was running directly on a physical host.

When consolidating workloads through virtualization, security configurations can remain specific to the partition rather than the server as a whole. An example of this would be super-user accounts. Applications consolidated to a single operating system running directly on top of a physical server would share various security settings—in particular, root or administrator access would be the same for all. However, when the same workloads are consolidated to virtual partitions, each partition can be configured with different credentials, thus maintaining the isolation of system access with administrative privileges often required to comply with federal or industry regulations.

Simply put, virtualization is an obvious move in just about any company, small or large. Just imagine that your manager calls you into the office and begins to explain his or her concerns about cost containment, data center space diminishing, timelines getting narrower, and corporate mandates doing more with less. It won't take too many attempts to explain how virtualization can help address all of those concerns. After realizing you had the answer all along, it will make your IT manager's day to learn this technology is the silver bullet that will satisfy the needs of the business while providing superior value in IT operations and infrastructure management and delivery.

NOTE

Most Virtual Machine Monitor (VMM) implementations are capable of interactive sessions with administrators through CLI or Web interfaces. Although secure, a compromised VMM will expose every virtual machine managed by that VMM. So exercise extreme caution when granting access or providing credentials for authentication to the VMM management interface.

How Does Virtualization Work?

While there are various ways to virtualize computing resources using a true VMM, they all have the same goal: to allow operating systems to run independently and in an isolated manner identical to when it is running directly on top of the hardware platform. But how exactly is this accomplished? While hardware virtualization still exists that fully virtualizes and abstracts hardware similar to how the System370 did, such hardware-based virtualization technologies tend to be less flexible and costly. As a result, a slew of software hypervisor and VMMs have cropped up to perform virtualization through software-based mechanisms. They ensure a level of isolation where the low-level, nucleus core of the CPU architecture is brought up closer to the software levels of the architecture to allow each virtual machine to have its own dedicated environment. In fact, the relationship between the CPU architecture and the virtualized operating systems is the key to how virtualization actually works successfully.

OS Relationships with the CPU Architecture

Ideal hardware architectures are those in which the operating system and CPU are designed and built for each other, and are tightly coupled. Proper use of complex system call requires careful coordination between the operating system and CPU. This symbiotic relationship in the OS and CPU architecture provides many advantages in security and stability. One such example was the MULTICS time-sharing system, which was designed for a special CPU architecture, which in turn was designed for it.

What made MULTICS so special in its day was its approach to segregating software operations to eliminate the risk or chance of a compromise or instability in a failed component from impacting other components. It placed formal mechanisms, called *protection rings*, in place to segregate the trusted operating system from the untrusted user programs. MULTICS included eight of these protection rings, a quite elaborate design, allowing different levels of isolation and abstraction from the core nucleus of the unrestricted interaction with the hardware. The hardware platform, designed in tandem by GE and MIT, was engineered specifically for the MULTICS operating system and incorporated hardware "hooks" enhancing the segregation even further. Unfortunately, this design approach proved to be too costly and proprietary for mainstream acceptance.

The most common CPU architecture used in modern computers is the IA-32, or x86-compatible, architecture. Beginning with the 80286 chipset, the x86 family provided two main methods of addressing memory: real mode and protected mode. In the 80386 chipset and later, a third mode was introduced called virtual 8086 mode, or VM86, that allowed for the execution of programs written for real mode but circumvented the real-mode rules without having to raise them into protected mode. Real mode, which is limited to a single megabyte of memory, quickly became obsolete; and virtual mode was locked in at 16-bit operation, becoming obsolete when 32-bit operating systems became widely available for the x86 architecture. Protected mode, the saving grace for x86, provided numerous new features to support multitasking. These included segmenting processes, so they could no longer write outside their address space, along with hardware support for virtual memory and task switching.

In the x86 family, protected mode uses four privilege levels, or rings, numbered 0 to 3. System memory is divided into segments, and each segment is assigned and dedicated to a particular ring. The processor uses the privilege level to determine what can and cannot be done with code or data within a segment. The term "rings" comes from the MULTICS system, where privilege levels were visualized as a set of concentric rings. Ring-0 is considered to be the innermost ring, with total control of the processor. Ring-3, the outermost ring, is provided only with restricted access, as illustrated in Figure 1.5.

Figure 1.5 Privilege Rings of the x86 Architecture

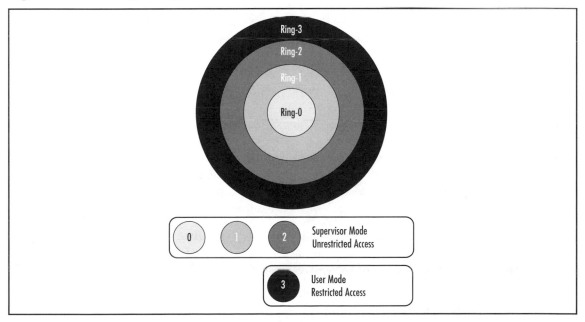

NOTE

The same concept of protection rings exists in modern OS architecture. Windows, Linux, and most Unix variants all use rings, although they have reduced the four-ring structure to a two-layer approach that uses only Rings 0 and 3. Ring-0 is commonly called *Supervisor Mode*, while Ring-3 is known as *User Mode*. Security mechanisms in the hardware enforce restrictions on Ring-3 by limiting code access to segments, paging, and input/output. If a user program running in Ring-3 tries to address memory outside of its segments, a hardware interrupt stops code execution. Some assembly language instructions are not even available for execution outside of Ring-0 due to their low-level nature.

The Virtual Machine Monitor and Ring-0 Presentation

The Supervisor Mode is the execution mode on an x86 processor that enables the execution of all instructions, including privileged instructions such as I/O and memory management operations. It is in Supervisor Mode (Ring 0) where the operating system would normally run. Since Ring-3 is based on Ring-0, any system compromise or instability directly impacts User Mode running in Ring-3. In order to isolate Ring-0 for each virtualized guest, it then becomes necessary to move Ring-0 closer to the guests. By doing so, a Ring-0 failure for one virtualized guest does not impact Ring-0, or consequently Ring-3, of any other guest. The perceived Ring-0 for guests can reside in either Ring-1, -2, or -3 for x86 architectures. Of course, the further the perceived Ring-0 is away from the true Ring-0, the more distant it is from executing direct hardware operations, leading to reduced performance and independence.

Virtualization moves Ring-0 up the privilege rings model by placing the Virtual Machine Monitor, or VMM, in one of the rings, which in turn presents the Ring-0 implementation to the hosted virtual machines. It is upon this presented Ring-0 that guest operating systems run, while the VMM handles the actual interaction with the underlying hardware platform for CPU, memory, and I/O resource access. There are two types of VMMs that address the presentation of Ring-0 as follows:

- **Type 1 VMM**   Software that runs directly on top of a given hardware platform on the true Ring-0. Guest operating systems then run at a higher level above the hardware, allowing for true isolation of each virtual machine.

- **Type 2 VMM**   Software that runs within an operating system, usually in Ring-3. Since there are no additional rings above Ring-3 in the x86 architecture, the presented Ring-0 that the virtual machines run on is as distant from the actual hardware platform as it can be. Although this offers some advantages, it is usually compounded by performance-impeding factors as calls to the hardware must traverse many diverse layers before the operations are returned to the guest operating system.

See Chapter 2 of this book for an overview of several virtualization products and how they accomplish Ring-0 placement.

The VMM Role Explored

To create virtual partitions in a server, a thin software layer called the Virtual Machine Monitor (VMM) runs directly on the physical hardware platform. One or more guest operating systems and application stacks can then be run on top of the VMM. Figure 1.6 expands our original illustration of a virtualized environment presented in Figure 1.1.

Figure 1.6 The OS and Application Stack Managed by the VMM Software Layer

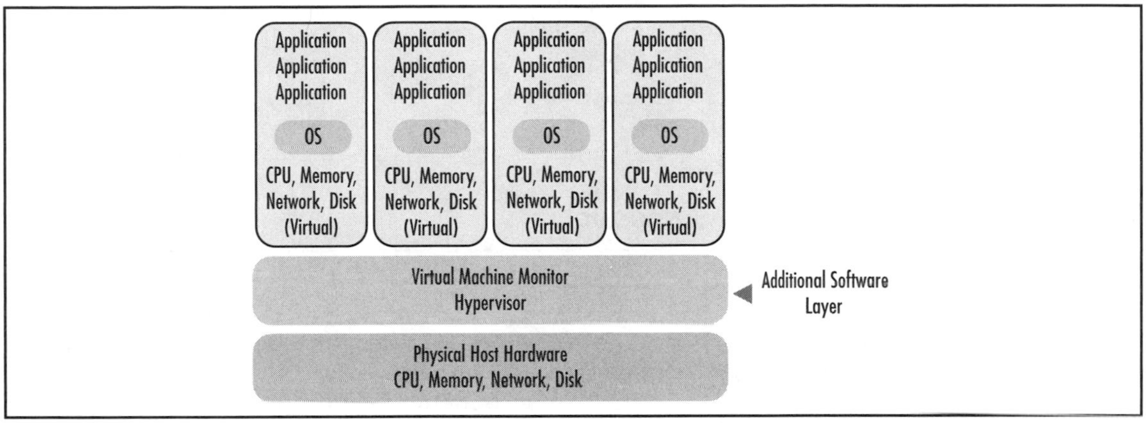

The VMM is the center of server virtualization. It manages hardware resources and arbitrates the requests of the multiple guest operating systems and application stacks. It presents a virtual set of CPU, memory, I/O, and Disk resources to each guest either based on the actual physical hardware or based on a standard and consistent selection of custom hardware. This section further discusses the role of the VMM and design considerations that are used when designing a VMM.

The Popek and Goldberg Requirements

Often referred to as the original reference source for VMM criteria, the Popek and Goldberg Virtualization Requirements define the conditions for a computer architecture to support virtualization. Written in 1974 for the third-generation computer systems of those days, they generalized the conditions that the software that provides the abstraction of a virtual machine, or VMM, must satisfy. These conditions, or properties, are

- **Equivalence**   A program running under the VMM should exhibit a predictable behavior that is essentially identical to that demonstrated when running on the underlying hardware platform directly. This is sometimes referred to as *Fidelity*.

- **Resource Control**   The VMM must be in complete control of the actual hardware resources virtualized for the guest operating systems at all times. This is sometimes referred to as *Safety*.

- **Efficiency**   An overwhelming number of machine instructions must be executed without VMM intervention or, in other words, by the hardware itself. This is sometimes referred to as *Performance*.

According to Popek and Goldberg, the problem that VMM developers must address is creating a VMM that satisfies the preceding conditions when operating within the characteristics of the Instruction Set Architecture (ISA) of the targeted hardware platform. The ISA can be classified into three groups of instructions: privileged, control sensitive, and behavior. Privileged instructions are those that trap if the processor is in User Mode and do not trap if it is in Supervisor Mode. Control-sensitive instructions are those that attempt to change the configuration of actual resources in the hardware platform. Behavior instructions are those whose behavior or result depends on the configuration of resources

VMMs must work with each group of instructions while maintaining the conditions of equivalence, resource control, and efficiency. Virtually all modern-day VMMs satisfy the first two: equivalence and resource control. They do so by effectively managing the guest operating system and hardware platform underneath through emulation, isolation, allocation, and encapsulation, as explained in Table 1.3.

Table 1.3 VMM Functions and Responsibilities

Function	Description
Emulation	Emulation is important for all guest operating systems. The VMM must present a complete hardware environment, or virtual machine, for each software stack, whether they be an operating system or application. Ideally, the OS and application are completely unaware they are sharing hardware resources with other applications. Emulation is key to satisfying the equivalence property.
Isolation	Isolation, though not required, is important for a secure and reliable environment. Through hardware abstraction, each virtual machine should be sufficiently separated and independent from the operations and activities of other virtual machines. Faults that occur in a single virtual machine should not impact others, thus providing high levels of security and availability.
Allocation	The VMM must methodically allocate platform resources to the virtual machines that it manages. Resources for processing, memory, network I/O, and storage must be balanced to optimize performance and align service levels with business requirements. Through allocation, the VMM satisfies the resource control property and, to some extent, the efficiency property as well.
Encapsulation	Encapsulation, though not mandated in the Popek and Goldberg requirements, enables each software stack (OS and application) to be highly portable, able to be copied or moved from one platform running the VMM to another. In some cases, this level or portability even allows live, running virtual machines to be migrated. Encapsulation must include state information in order to maintain the integrity of the transferred virtual machine.

The Challenge: VMMs for the x86 Architecture

Referring back to the IA-32 (x86) architecture, all software runs in one of the four privilege rings. The OS traditionally runs in Ring-0, which affords privileged access to the widest range of processor and platform resources. Individual applications usually run in Ring-3, which restricts certain functions (such as memory mapping) that might impact other applications. In this way, the OS retains control to ensure smooth operation.

Since the VMM must have privileged control of platform resources, the usual solution is to run the VMM in Ring-0, and guest operating systems in Ring-1 or Ring-3. However, modern operating systems have been specifically designed to run in Ring-0. This creates certain challenges. In particular, there are 17 "privileged" instructions that control critical platform resources. These instructions are used occasionally in most existing OS versions. When an OS is not running in Ring-0, any one of these instructions can create a conflict, causing either a system fault or an incorrect response. The challenge faced by VMMs for the IA-32 (x86) architecture is maintaining the Popek and Goldberg requirements while working with the IA-32 ISA.

Types of Virtualization

Many forms of virtualization exist in modern information technology. The most common is server virtualization, which is what most people think of when the term "virtualization" is referenced. However, in addition to server virtualization, IT organizations use other types of virtualization, based on other connotations of the word. Many think of virtualization as meaning "partitioning" a computing resource into multiple entities. Virtualization can also mean just the opposite: presenting multiple entities as a single virtual entity, thus hiding or masking the true computing resources that are performing the work in the background. Many manufacturers and independent software vendors have developed products that utilize the latter approach to virtualization. Of the most common are virtualization products for storage, network, and applications.

Server Virtualization

Server virtualization is the more dominant form of virtualization in use today. Though the concepts we have discussed so far have been about virtualization in general, they are most exhibited in server virtualization products. Implementations of server virtualization exist on, and for all, CPU platforms and architectures, the most popular being the IA-32 or x86. The challenges posed by the x86 architecture's ISA and the Popek and Goldberg requirements have led to several approaches to VMM development. While there are many different implementations of a VMM for x86, they can be summarized into four distinct categories. Table 1.4 provides additional information about each category for server virtualization.

Table 1.4 Types of Server Virtualization

Type of Virtualization	Description	Pros	Cons
Full virtualization	A virtualization technique that provides complete simulation of the underlying hardware. The result is a system in which all software capable of execution on the raw hardware can be run in the virtual machine. Full virtualization has the widest range of support of guest operating systems.	Provides complete isolation of each virtual machine and the VMM; most operating systems can be installed without any modification. Provides near-native CPU and memory performance; uses sophisticated techniques to trap and emulate instructions in runtime via binary patching.	Requires the right combination of hardware and software elements; not quite possible on the x86 architecture in its pure form because of some of the privileged calls that cannot be trapped; performance can be impacted by trap-and-emulate techniques of x86 privileged instructions.
Paravirtualization	A virtualization technique that provides partial simulation of the underlying hardware. Most, but not all, of the hardware features are simulated. The key feature is address space virtualization, granting each virtual machine its own unique address space.	Easier to implement than full virtualization; when no hardware assistance is available, paravirtualized guests tend to be the highest performing virtual machines for network and disk I/O.	Operating systems running in paravirtualized virtual machines cannot be run without substantial modification; virtual machines suffer from lack of backward compatibility and are not very portable.
Operating System Virtualization	This concept is based on a single operating system instance.	Tends to be very lean and efficient; single OS installation for management and updates; runs at native speeds; supports all native hardware and OS features that the host is configured for.	Does not support hosting mixed OS families, such as Windows and Linux; virtual machines are not as isolated or secure as with the other virtualization types; Ring-0 is a full operating

Table 1.4 Continued

Type of Virtualization	Description	Pros	Cons
			system rather than a stripped-down microkernel as the VMM, so it adds overhead and complexity; difficult to identify the source of high resource loads; also difficult to limit resource consumption per guest.
Native virtualization	This technique is the newest to the x86 group of virtualization technologies. Often referred to as hybrid virtualization, this type is a combination of full virtualization or paravirtualization combined with I/O acceleration techniques. Similar to full virtualization, guest operating systems can be installed without modification. It takes advantage of the latest CPU technology for x86, Intel VT, and AMD-V.	Handles non-virtualizable instructions by using trap-and-emulate in hardware versus software; selectively employs accelerations techniques for memory and I/O operations; supports x64 (64-bit x86 extensions) targeted operating systems; has the highest CPU, memory, and I/O performance of all types of x86 virtual machines.	Requires CPU architecture that supports hardware-assisted acceleration; still requires some OS modification for paravirtualized guests, although less than pure paravirtualization.

Designing & Planning…

Hardware-Assistance Enhances Virtualization

To maximize the performance of your x86-based physical platform and the hosted virtual machines, be sure to select processors that support hardware-assisted virtualization. Both Intel, providing Intel Virtualization Technology (Intel VT), and AMD, providing "Pacifica" (AMD-V), offer such technologies in their latest generation of processors available for servers as well as desktops and notebooks.

Hardware-assisting processors give the guest OS the authority it needs to have direct access to platform resources without sharing control of the hardware. Previously, the VMM had to emulate the hardware to the guest OS while it retained control of the physical platform. These new processors give both the VMM and the guest OS the authority each needs to run without hardware emulation or OS modification.

They also help VMM developers design a more simplified VMM. Since hardware-assisted processors can now handle the compute-intensive calculations needed to manage the tasks of handing off platform control to a guest OS, the computational burden is reduced on the VMM. Also, key state information for the CPU and guest OS can now be stored in protected memory that only the VMM has access to, protecting the integrity of the handoff process.

Finally, hardware-assisted processors, all of which support 64-bit processing, now allow the benefits of 64-bit computing to filter up to the guest OS and its hosted applications. This provides virtual machines with greater capabilities, headroom, and scalability.

Storage Virtualization

Storage vendors have been offering high–performance storage solutions to their customers for quite some time now. In its most basic form, storage virtualization exists in the assembly of multiple physical disk drives, or spindles, into a single entity that is presented to the host server and operating system, such as with RAID implementations. This can be considered virtualization because all the drives are used and interacted with as a single logical drive, although composed of two or more drives in the background.

The true storage tier and its components were further masked by the introduction and adoption of storage area network (SAN) technologies. Without any change to the operating system code responsible for managing storage subsystems, IT organizations are now sharing storage components between multiple servers, even though each server thinks it has its own dedicated physical storage, in actuality storage administrators have simply carved out a virtual quantity of drive space and presented it to the hosts for use.

More advanced technologies have begun to hit the market that take storage virtualization to the next level. Products exist that are capable of migrating storage in real time from one storage platform to another in the background based on rules and policies (such as retention policies, age of data, or last-time accessed) without any interruption or impact to the host. Software products exist that trap-and-emulate native SCSI commands and translate them to other storage instructions in the background, making it possible for a disk array to look like a suite of tape drives and tape libraries to back up software and operating systems without any modification.

Network Virtualization

As with storage vendors, manufacturers of network hardware have been in the virtualization arena for some time, although not always recognized as virtualization. The most popular forms of network virtualization are

- **Virtual LAN (VLAN)** Ratified in the IEEE 802.1Q standard, VLANs are a method of creating independent logical networks within a shared physical network. Network administrators incorporate VLANs into their network design to logically segment broadcast domains and control the interaction between devices on different network segments. VLAN technology has evolved and is a common feature in the application-specific integrated circuits (ASICs) of just about all modern-day Ethernet switches. Although multiple devices can be physically connected to the same network switch, VLANs allow network administrators to create multiple virtual networks that isolate each segment from the others. Each segment utilizes a portion of the available resources (CPU, memory, bandwidth, and so on) in the host switch.

- **Virtual IP (VIP)** An IP address that is not connected to a specific computer or network interface in a computer. VIPs are usually assigned to a network device that is in-path of the traversing network traffic. Incoming packets are sent to the VIP but are redirected to the actual interface of the receiving host(s). VIPs are mostly used for redundancy and load-balancing scenarios, where multiple systems are hosting a common application and are capable of receiving the traffic as redirected by the network device.

- **Virtual Private Network (VPN)** A private communication network used to communicate confidentially over a public network. VPN traffic is often carried over highly insecure network mediums, such as the Internet, creating a secure channel for sensitive and confidential information to traverse from one site to another. It is also used as a means of extending remote employees home networks to the corporate network. Although special software is usually needed to establish the connection, once established, interaction with other resources on the network is handled the same way it would be on a true physical network, without requiring any modification of the network stack or operating system.

Application Virtualization

Application virtualization, or software virtualization, is the newest member of the ever-growing virtualization family. It is a new approach to software management. Breaking the paradigm and bond between applications, the operating system, and the hardware hosting the operating system, application virtualization uses virtual software packages to place applications and data rather than conventional installation procedures. Application packages can be instantly activated or deactivated, reset to their default configuration, and thus mitigate the risk of interference with other applications as they run in their own computing space.

Some of the benefits of application virtualization are

- **Eliminates application conflicts**   Applications are guaranteed to use the correct-version files and property file/Registry settings without any modification to the operating systems and without interfering with other applications.

- **Reduces roll-outs through instant provisioning**   Administrators can create pre-packaged applications that can be deployed quickly locally or remotely over the network, even across slow links. Virtual software applications can even be streamed to systems on-demand without invoking a setup or installation procedure.

- **Runs multiple versions of an application**   Multiple versions can run on the same operating system instance without any conflicts, improving the migration to newer versions of applications and speeding the testing and integration of new features into the environment.

Common Use Cases for Virtualization

Now that we have discussed the concept, history, and types of virtualization in depth, the last thing to review before diving into virtualization with Xen's hypervisor, or VMM, is the use cases for virtualization. As mentioned earlier, not every scenario can appropriately be implemented using virtualization technologies. Some workloads are large enough and consistent enough to warranty their own dedicated computing resources. Others are so large it takes a farm of resources just to be able to handle the workload, as is the case with high-performance clusters (HPCs). However, most workloads, regardless of the size of your company, are great candidates for virtualization; and by doing so, you can realize substantial benefits.

If you have not already adopted virtualization technologies as part of your infrastructure strategy, the following are some examples where you can put virtualization to work for you:

- Technology refresh

- Business continuity and disaster recovery

- Proof of concept (POC) deployments

- Virtual desktops

- Rapid development, test lab, and software configuration management

Technology Refresh

Asset life-cycle management is an area that gets many CFOs and CIOs attention because of the cost imposed to the business. As one phase of the life cycle, a technology refresh, or the replacement of older fixed assets with newer ones, can stand out on a department or corporate profit and loss statement, even with the lower prices of technology today. In many cases, it makes more sense to replace them than to pay to maintain aging and often obsolete equipment. But what if you could reduce the cost further?

During a technology refresh, the opportunity to virtualize and consolidate some of your existing workloads is great. There are some basic questions you should ask before undertaking any technology refresh, as represented in Table 1.5. If you could answer to one or more of these questions, then virtualization should be the answer you have been looking for.

Table 1.5 Factors to Consider When Choosing Virtualization for a Technology Refresh

Factor to Consider	How Virtualization Addresses It
Q: Is the server that is being refreshed hosting an application that is still valuable to the company rather than being deprecated or obsolete?	If the application still provides value to the company, then it is a good strategy to make sure the application and operating system are hosted on a reliable, supported hardware environment. Virtualization can help by reducing the costs, both hard and soft, of refreshing your infrastructure.
Q: Is current performance acceptable to the business?	New servers can be several times more powerful than the servers you are planning on refreshing. If you did a physical-to-physical refresh, that would lead to underutilized servers and considerable waste of processing power. If you deem current performance to be satisfactory, then a virtual machine is perfect for your application, especially since virtual machines can often perform at near-native levels.
Q: Is there a trend that shows that additional resources will be needed in the short term?	Upgrading server resources can be a costly and time-consuming effort with considerable downtime. A virtualized environment is flexible, and upgrade can often be performed dynamically on some platforms. For others, it is as simple as taking a few minutes to power down the virtual machine, reconfigure resource allocation, and then power the virtual machine up.
Q: Can legacy applications be migrated easily and cost-effectively to a newer operating system or hardware?	Many legacy operating systems and applications are difficult to migrate to new hardware platforms with substantial modification. The hardware environment presented by the VMM, on the other hand, often has simple hardware with drivers available for all operating systems supported, making migrations much simpler.

Continued

www.syngress.com

Table 1.5 Continued

Factor to Consider	How Virtualization Addresses It
Q: Will there be issues or complications either restoring applications and data to a new server or reinstalling and configuring the applications and data from the ground up?	A process known as physical-to-virtual (P2V) allows you to make an image of your servers and convert them to virtual machines, eliminating the need to restore from backup or possibly reinstall the application from scratch. In some cases, this can happen without any downtime.
Q: Is the application one that requires higher availability and recoverability from failure or some other system compromise?	Features such as live migrations allow single-instance virtual machines to achieve higher availability than on a physical platform. Or if a clustered or load-balanced environment is desired but is not possible because of the hardware investment, making your failover node(s) virtual machines can incur minimal up-front costs that equate to substantial savings down the road.

Business Continuity and Disaster Recovery

Business continuity and disaster recovery initiatives have picked up over the past few years. Customer demand and federal regulations have helped accelerate those efforts and give them the attention they have needed for some time. However, business continuity plans (BCPs) can often require a large investment in standby technology in order to achieve the recovery point and time objectives. As a result, IT disaster recovery can be a slow moving, never-ending process.

Virtualization is an ideal platform for most cases since it eliminates the need to purchase an excessive amount of equipment "just in case." Most software vendors of backup/recovery products support the restoration of operation systems and applications of physical servers to virtual machines. And if you currently use a recovery service provider because hosting your own hot site was too costly, virtualization may make that option more achievable by substantially reducing the investment your company needs to make.

For example, if your company has identified 50 servers that comprise your mission-critical applications and must be brought back online within 72 hours of a disaster, you would need 50 servers available and all the supporting data center and network infrastructure to support them (space, HVAC, power, and so on) at your recovery site. However, establishing your recovery site with virtualization technologies, you could reduce that number to five physical servers, each targeted to host ten virtual machines, a modest quantity based on what most companies achieve currently. That is a 90 percent reduction in acquisition costs for the servers as well as the environment costs to support them. Just think of the space reduction going from 50 to 5 servers!

Proof of Concept Deployments

Business managers often get frustrated with IT's inability to provision an environment to host a proof of concept (POC) for a proposed application that is intended to add value to the business. Most IT organizations do not have spare assets (at least any that are viable) laying around, nor have the time to spend to provision an application that is not associated with an approved "move-forward" project. As a result, most POCs are either set up on inadequate equipment, such as desktops, or not established at all, presenting a risk of missed opportunity for the business.

Virtual machines find their strength in situations such as this. Rapid provisioning, no hardware investment needed, safe, secure, and reliable… all the qualities needed to quickly build a POC environment and keep it running during the time it is needed. Even better, if the POC is successful and you decide to go to production with the application, you can migrate your virtual machine from your test infrastructure to your production virtual infrastructure without having to rebuild the application, saving lots of time in the end.

Virtual Desktops

Companies often have huge investments in client PCs for their user base, many of which do not fall into the category of power users. Similar to server hardware, client PC hardware continues to improve and get more powerful, often being underutilized. If you have users that run a CRM application, e-mail, a Web browser, and some productivity applications such as spreadsheets and word processing, those users are well suited for a virtual desktop environment. Placing a thin client with keyboard, mouse, and monitor on their desk, the computing power can safely and securely be moved into the data center, hosted as a virtual machine on server hardware. In environments requiring desktop hardware encryption, PC firewalls, and other security devices, this can lead to a substantial reduction in complexity and software licensing as well.

If you are planning on rolling out a new wave of PCs for hundreds of call center agents or in a manufacturing environment (just think of how dirty those shiny new, underutilized PCs will get in just a few days on the shop floor), consider instead creating a virtualized desktop infrastructure in your data center and saving your company lots of money while you are at it.

Rapid Development, Test Lab, and Software Configuration Management

Development teams have always been good candidates for virtualization. Whether it's a desktop-based virtualization product or hosting some development servers as virtual machines in the data center, virtualization has proven to be effective in increasing the productivity of developers, the quality of their work, and the speed at which they complete their coding. In the same way, virtualization can speed up the testing cycles and also allow a higher density of automated testing, thus accelerating the time to release or to market.

Virtualization enables companies to streamline their software life cycle. From development and testing, through integration, staging, deployment, and management, virtualization offers a comprehensive framework for virtual software life-cycle automation that streamlines these adjacent yet often disconnected processes, and closes the loops between them. In addition to these obvious benefits, you can creatively design solutions around a virtual infrastructure to help your software development and test teams to:

- Provide remote lab access and desktop hosting for offsite or offshore development resources, minimizing duplication of lab equipment at each site.

- Close the loop between software development and quality assurance—capturing and moving defect state configurations.

- Reproduce and resolve defects on demand.

- Clone or image a production virtual machine and host it in your QA test infrastructure for security patch, service pack, or maintenance release testing.

- Push a staged configuration into production after successful testing is completed, minimizing errors associated with incorrect deployment and configuration of the production environment.

Summary

Virtualization is an abstraction layer that breaks the standard paradigm of computer architecture, decoupling the operating system from the physical hardware platform and the applications that run on it. As a result, IT organizations can achieve greater IT resource utilization and flexibility. Virtualization allows multiple virtual machines, often with heterogeneous operating systems, to run in isolation, side-by-side, on the same physical machine. Each virtual machine has its own set of virtual hardware (CPU, memory, network interfaces, and disk storage) upon which an operating system and applications are loaded. The operating system sees the set of hardware and is unaware of the sharing nature with other guest operating systems running on the same physical hardware platform. Virtualization technology and its core components, such as the Virtual Machine Monitor, manage the interaction with the operating system calls to the virtual hardware and the actual execution that takes place on the underlying physical hardware.

Virtualization was first introduced in the 1960s to allow partitioning of large, mainframe hardware, a scarce and expensive resource. Over time, minicomputers and PCs provided a more efficient, affordable way to distribute processing power. By the 1980s, virtualization was no longer widely employed. However, in the 1990s, researchers began to see how virtualization could solve some of the problems associated with the proliferation of less expensive hardware, including underutilization, escalating management costs, and vulnerability.

Today, virtualization is growing as a core technology in the forefront of data center management. The technology is helping businesses, both large and small, solve their problems with scalability, security, and management of their global IT infrastructure while effectively containing, if not reducing, costs.

Solutions Fast Track

What Is Virtualization?

- ☑ Virtualization technologies have been around since the 1960s. Beginning with the Atlas and M44/44X projects, the concept of time-sharing and virtual memory was introduced to the computing world.

- ☑ Funded by large research centers and system manufacturers, early virtualization technology was only available to those with sufficient resources and clout to fund the purchase of the big-iron equipment.

- ☑ As time-sharing evolved, IBM developed the roots and early architecture of the virtual machine monitor, or VMM. Many of the features and design elements of the System370 and its succeeding iterations are still found in modern-day virtualization technologies.

- ☑ After a short quiet period when the computing world took its eyes off of virtualization, a resurgent emphasis began again in the mid-1990s, putting virtualization back into the limelight as an effective means to gain high returns on a company's investment.

Why Virtualize?

☑ As virtualization technology transitioned from the mainframe world to midrange and entry-level hardware platforms and the operating systems that they ran, there was a shift from having either a decentralized or a centralized computing model to having a hybrid of the two. Large computers could now be partitioned into smaller units, giving all of the benefits of logical decentralization while taking advantage of a physical centralization.

☑ While there are many benefits that companies will realize as they adopt and implement virtualization solutions, the most prominent ones are consolidation of their proliferating sprawl of servers, increased reliability of computing platforms upon which their important business applications run, and greater security through isolation and fault containment.

How Does Virtualization Work?

☑ The operating system and the CPU architecture historically have been bound and mated one to the other. This inherent relationship is exemplified by secure and stable computing platforms that segregate various levels of privilege and priority through rings of isolation and access, the most critical being Ring-0.

☑ The most common CPU architecture, the IA-32 or x86 architecture, follows a similar privileged model containing four rings, 0 to 4. Operating systems that run on x86 platforms are installed in Ring-0, called Supervisor Mode, while applications execute in Ring-3, called User Mode.

☑ The Virtual Machine Monitor (VMM) presents the virtual or perceived Ring-0 for guest operating systems, enabling isolation from each platform. Each VMM meets a set of conditions referred to as the Popek and Goldberg Requirements, written in 1974. Though composed for third-generation computers of that time, the requirements are general enough to apply to modern VMM implementations.

☑ While striving to hold true to the Popek and Goldberg requirements, developers of VMMs for the x86 architecture face several challenges due in part to the non-virtualizable instructions in the IA-32 ISA. Because of those challenges, the x86 architecture cannot be virtualized in the purest form; however, x86 VMMs are close enough that they can be considered to be true to the requirements.

Types of Virtualization

☑ Server Virtualization is the most common form of virtualization, and the original. Managed by the VMM, physical server resources are used to provision multiple virtual machines, each presented with its own isolated and independent hardware set. Of the top three forms of virtualization are full virtualization, paravirtualization, and operating system virtualization. An additional form, called native virtualization, is gaining in popularity and blends the best of full virtualization and paravirtualization along with hardware acceleration logic.

☑ Other areas have and continue to experience benefits of virtualization, including storage, network, and application technologies.

Common Use Cases for Virtualization

☑ A technology refresh of older, aging equipment is an opportune time to consider implementing a virtual infrastructure, consolidating workloads and easing migrations through virtualization technologies.

☑ Business can reduce recovery facility costs by incorporating the benefits of virtualization into the BCP and DR architectures.

☑ Virtualization also gives greater levels of flexibility and allows IT organizations to achieve on-demand service levels. This is evident with easily deployed proof-of-concept, pilot, or mock environments with virtually no overhead to facilitate or manage it.

☑ The benefits of virtualization can be driven beyond the walls of the data center to the desktop. Desktop virtualization can help organizations reduce costs while maintaining control of their client environment and providing additional layers of security at no additional cost.

☑ Virtualization is, and has been, at home in the software development life cycle. Such technologies help streamline development, testing, and release management and processes while increasing productivity and shortening the window of time from design to market.

Frequently Asked Questions

Q: What is virtual machine technology used for?

A: Virtual machine technology serves a variety of purposes. It enables hardware consolidation, simplified system recovery, and the re-hosting of earlier applications because multiple operating systems can run on one computer. One key application for virtual machine technology is cross-platform integration. Other key applications include server consolidation, the automation and consolidation of development and testing environments, the re-hosting of earlier versions of applications, simplifying system recovery environments, and software demonstrations.

Q: How does virtualization address a CIO's pain points?

A: IT organizations need to control costs, improve quality, reduce risks and increase business agility, all of which are critical to a business' success. With virtualization, lower costs and improved business agility are no longer trade-offs. By enabling IT resources to be pooled and shared, IT organizations are provided with the ability to reduce costs and improve overall IT performance.

Q: What is the status of virtualization standards?

A: True open standards for getting all the layers talking and working together aren't ready yet, let alone giving users interoperable choices between competitive vendors. Users are forced to rely on de facto standards at this time. For instance, users can deploy two different virtualization products within one environment, especially if each provides the ability to import virtual machines from the other. But that is about as far as interoperability currently extends.

Q: When is a product not really virtualization but something else?

A: Application vendors have been known to overuse the term and label their product "virtualization ready." But by definition, the application should not be to tell whether it is on a virtualized platform or not. Some vendors also label their isolation tools as virtualization. To isolate an application means files are installed but are redirected or shielded from the operating system. That is not the same as true virtualization, which lets you change any underlying component, even network and operating system settings, without having to tweak the application.

Q: What is the ideal way to deploy virtualization?

A: Although enterprises gain incremental benefits from applying virtualization in one area, they gain much more by using it across every tier of the IT infrastructure. For example, when server virtualization is deployed with network and storage virtualization, the entire infrastructure becomes more flexible, making it capable of dynamically adapting to various business needs and demands.

Q: What are some of the issues to watch out for?

A: Companies beginning to deploy virtualization technologies should be cautious of the following: software costs/licensing from proliferating virtual machines, capacity planning, training, high and unrealistic consolidation expectations, and upfront hardware investment, to name a few. Also, sufficient planning upfront is important to avoid issues that can cause unplanned outages affecting a larger number of critical business applications and processes.

## Chapter 2

Virtualization Technologies

Solutions in this chapter:

- **Hardware Virtualization Software**
- **Operating System-Level Virtualization Software**
- **Software Comparison Matrix**

This book will give an in-depth account of Xen, Microsoft Virtual Server, and VMware. Before we begin, we will take an agnostic look at the different types of server virtualization and other virtual machine software available.

Hardware Virtualization Software

Virtualization software that presents a virtual set of hardware to a guest operating system makes up the majority of server virtualization products available. These virtualization products provide a VMM that either partially or fully virtualizes the underlying hardware, allowing both modified and unmodified guests to run in a safe and isolated fashion.

The most popular of these products, especially for the enterprise, are VMware, Microsoft, and Xen, in order of commercial market share. VMware and Xen are the most mature of the group, offering the richest set of features, such as live migration and bare-metal installation and execution of the hypervisor, as well as the widest array of supported guest operating systems.

Operating System-Level Virtualization Software

Operating system-level virtualization software is either included as part of an operating system, such as Solaris containers, or is installed on top of an operating system, such as Virtuozzo and OpenVZ. These products present an operating system environment that is fully or partially isolated from the host operating system, allowing for safe application execution at native speeds.

> **NOTE**
>
> The key differentiator with operating system-level virtualization software is that, unlike hardware virtualization software, no virtual hardware environment is presented to guests.

In a few ways, operating system-level virtualization software products provide some advantages over hardware virtualization software. First, they can usually run the same operating system that the host is running without having to duplicate every layer and subsystem. This is possible because some of the lower-level functions are shared with the host, thus eliminating the overhead that duplication would cause. Second, it is possible to offer a patch-once approach, allowing administrators to patch the host operating system, which in turn patches subordinate guests. Finally, these products tend to offer the widest array of hardware compatibility, because practically any device that can be used in the host operating system can be used in the guest virtual environments as well.

Software Comparison Matrix

In Tables 2.1 and 2.2, we present you with a comparison of various hardware and operating system-level virtualization software products. These tables are not an exhaustive list of all virtualization software offerings available, but rather a comprehensive comparison of many of the popular products is use today. Both the open-source Xen hypervisor and the commercial XenServer product family from XenSource have also been included in the list.

Table 2.1 List of Hardware Virtualization Software

Name	Creator/Founder	Host CPU	Guest CPU	Host OS	Guest OS (Officially Supported)
Bochs	Kevin Lawton	x86, SPARC, PowerPC, Alpha, MIPS	x86	AIX, BeOS, IRIX, Linux, OS X, Windows	BSD, Linux, Windows
CoLinux	Dan Aloni	x86	x86	Linux, Windows	Linux
Denali	University of Washington	x86	x86	Denali	Ilwaco, NetBSD
KVM	KVM Project	x86	x86	Linux	Linux, Windows
Logical Domains	Sun	UltraSPARC T1	SPARC	Solaris	FreeBSD, Linux, Solaris
Parallels Workstation	Parallels, Inc.	x86	x86	Linux, Windows	FreeBSD, Linux OS/2, Solaris, Windows
QEMU	Fabrice Bellard	x86, IA-64, SPARC, PowerPC, S/390, ARM, M68k	x86, SPARC, PowerPC, MIPS	BeOS, BSD, Linux, OS X, Solaris, Linux	BSD, Linux, Windows
UML	Jeff Dike	x86	x86	Linux	Linux
Virtual Iron	Virtual Iron Software, Inc.	x86	x86	none; bare-metal	BSD, Linux, OS/2, Windows

Continued

Table 2.1 Continued

Name	Creator/ Founder	Host CPU	Guest CPU	Host OS	Guest OS (Officially Supported)
Virtual PC	Microsoft	x86, PowerPC	x86	OS X, Windows	Linux, OS/2, Windows
Virtual Server	Microsoft	x86	x86	Windows	Linux, Windows
VMware Workstation	VMware	x86	x86	Linux, Windows	FreeBSD, Linux, Netware, Solaris, Windows
VMware Server	VMware	x86	x86	Linux, Windows	FreeBSD, Linux, Netware, Solaris, Windows
VMware ESX Server	VMware	x86	x86	None; bare-metal	FreeBSD, Linux, Netware, Solaris, Windows
Xen	University of Cambridge	x86, IA-64, PowerPC	x86	NetBSD, Linux, Solaris	xBSD, Linux, Solaris, Windows
XenServer Family	XenSource	x86	x86	None; bare-metal	Linux, Windows
z/VM	IBM	z/Arch.	z/Arch.	None; z/VM runs directly inside LPAR	Linux for System z, z/OS, z/TPF, z/VSE, z/VM

Table 2.1 Continued List of Hardware Virtualization Software

Name	SMP	Type of Virtualization	License Type	Typical Use	Relative speed	Commercial Support Available?
Bochs	Yes	Emulation	LGPL	Developer, hobbyist	Very slow	No
CoLinux	No	Porting	GPL	Developer, hobbyist	Native	No
Denali	No	Paravirtualization, porting	N/A	Research	Slow	No
KVM	No	In-kernel virtualization	GPL	Developer, hobbyist, server consolidation	Near-native	No
Logical Domains	Yes	Paravirtualization	Free CDDL	Web hosting, server consolidation	Near-native	Yes
Parallels Workstation	No	Full virtualization	Retail	Developer, hobbyist, tester, business workstation	Near-native	Yes
QEMU	Yes	Full virtualization	GPL, LGPL	Developer, hobbyist, server consolidation	Near-native	No
UML	No	Porting	GPL	Developer, hobbyist	Slow	No
Virtual Iron	Yes	Native virtualization	Retail	Developer, tester, server consolidation	Near-native	Yes
Virtual PC	No	Full virtualization	Free Retail	Developer, tester, training	Near-native with VM additions	Yes
Virtual Server	No	Full virtualization	Free Retail	Developer, tester, training, enterprise server consolidation	Near-native with VM additions	Yes

Continued

Table 2.1 Continued

Name	SMP	Type of Virtualization	License Type	Typical Use	Relative speed	Commercial Support Available?
VMware Workstation	Yes	Full virtualization	Retail	Developer, tester, training	Near-native with VM tools	Yes
VMware Server	Yes	Full virtualization	Free Retail	Developer, tester, training, server consolidation	Near-native with VM tools	Yes
VMware ESX Server	Yes	Full virtualization	Retail	Developer, tester, training, enterprise server consolidation	Near-native with VM tools	Yes
Xen	Yes	Paravirtualization with porting, native virtualization	GPL	Developer, tester, training, server consolidation	Near-native	No
XenServer Family	Yes	Paravirtualization with porting, native virtualization	Retail	Developer, tester, training, enterprise server consolidation	Near-native	Yes
z/VM	Yes	Paravirtualization	Retail	Enterprise servers	Native	Yes

Table 2.2 List of Operating System-Level Virtualization Software

Name	Creator	Host CPU	Guest CPU	Host OS	Guest OS (Officially Supported)
Jails	FreeBSD	x86	x86	FreeBSD	FreeBSD
OpenVZ	SWsoft	x86, IA-64, PowerPC, SPARC	x86, IA-64, PowerPC, SPARC	Linux	Linux
Solaris Containers	Sun	x86, SPARC	x86, SPARC	Solaris	Linux, Solaris
Virtuozzo	SWsoft	x86, IA-64	x86, IA-64	Linux, Windows	Linux, Windows
VServer	Open-source project	x86, IA-64, Alpha, PowerPC, SPARC, ARM, S/390, MIPS	same as host	Linux	Linux

Table 2.2 Continued List of Operating System-Level Virtualization Software

Name	SMP	License	Typical Use	Relative Speed	Commercial Support Available?
Jails	Yes	FreeBSD	Web hosting, server consolidation	Native	No
OpenVZ	Yes	GPL	Server consolidation	Native	No
Solaris Containers	Yes	Free CDDL	Developer, tester, enterprise server consolidation, Web hosting	Native	Yes
Virtuozzo	Yes	Retail	Developer, tester, server consolidation	Native	Yes
VServer	Yes	GPL	Developer, Web hosting, server consolidation	Native	No

Products are listed in alphabetical order, and present the following information for each product:

- **Creator/founder**   The products can be placed in two categories, commercial or open source. This column lists either the founder of the open-source project, the project itself, or the commercial (for-profit) company that developed the product.

- **Host CPU**   The CPU architectures upon which the product can run. Note that not all features are available on all architectures.

- **Guest CPU**   Lists the CPU architecture that virtual machines created with the product will see. The most popular architecture is x86.

- **Host OS**   The operating system required to install the virtualization software. Note that some products are bare-metal, meaning that they are distributed and installed from media directly on an empty server.

- **Guest OS (officially supported)**   This is the list of operating systems that can be run inside virtual machines, as indicated by the project's current documentation or by the commercial developer. Although it may be possible to run additional operating systems, such configurations are not supported and not recommended.

- **SMP**   This column indicates whether virtual machines running on the virtualization software support multiple processing (SMP) or not. Note that this is not whether the software supports multiple processors, as all of the products in the list do.

- **Type of virtualization (hardware virtualization only)**   This column indicates the virtualization technique used by the software. Primarily, each product can be broken down into four types: emulation, porting, paravirtualization, full virtualization, and native virtualization. For more information about these types, see Chapter 1.

- **License type**   This indicates the type of license agreement for the use of the product.

- **Typical use**   The common use for the product, although the product can be used for many other uses.

- **Relative speed**   The operating speed of the typical virtual machine as compared with bare metal performance.

- **Commercial support**   Whether paid commercial support is available for the product. In most cases, if support is available, it is through the creator of the product.

## Chapter 3

Introduction to Microsoft Virtual Server

Solutions in this chapter:

- **Microsoft Virtual Server 2005 R2 and Dynamics System Initiative**

- **What Is Virtualization, and When Should You Use It?**

- **What Virtualization Tools Are Available?**

- **How Does Virtualization Work?**

- **Virtual PC versus Virtual Server 2005**

- **Virtual Server 2005 versus Virtual Server 2005 R2**

- ☑ **Summary**

- ☑ **Solutions Fast Track**

- ☑ **Frequently Asked Questions**

Introduction

In recent years the power of servers has grown to huge proportions. In production, the servers perform well but the system is only partially utilized. This makes it fairly impossible to buy a server that is not over-powered.

On the other side, there is the issue with hardware support on that old Windows server that you cannot migrate. These scenarios and a lot more are where virtualization can be a lot of help. There are several virtualization tools available on the market, all of them with specific support and features. We will review the most important ones but our focus will be on the Microsoft Virtualization tool Virtual Server 2005 R2.

Microsoft Virtual Server 2005 R2 and Dynamics System Initiative

The Microsoft Dynamics System Initiative (DSI) was created as a commitment between Microsoft and its partners to create more easily manageable systems that automate many everyday tasks. This will, in effect, streamline IT operations and potentially reduce costs at the same time. Virtual servers play a big part in this initiative by optimizing the way current data centers are run and making them more efficient. Workloads can be optimized by running multiple operating systems and applications on a physical server, which enables it to reach a much higher average utilization. Also, as workloads change over time, virtual machines can be redistributed between other virtual servers to continue to optimize and balance workloads.

DSI applies to all aspects of the application lifecycle. It begins with the design of the application and ends with using applications like SMS and Microsoft Operations Manager (MOM) to manage and monitor the systems. The use of virtualization is key in this design, because it effectively decouples the application workload from its hardware. This enables you to move the workload from one physical server to another as the resource needs of the workload change. Virtualization allows for the rapid deployment of new systems. Without virtualization, as the need develops for new servers, you may not be able to respond quickly enough because you'll need to purchase new hardware for each server needed.

What Is Virtualization, and When Should You Use It?

Virtualization is the concept of taking a single operating system and, instead of installing in on its own dedicated physical hardware, installing it on virtual hardware that is being presented by Microsoft Virtual Server 2005 R2 running on a physical server (see Figure 3.1). The key with virtualization is the isolation of each virtual machine. Each virtual machine is unaware of the other virtual machines that are running on the virtual server. If one virtual machine crashes, it will not crash the other virtual servers. With new processor improvements from Intel and AMD, namely the new dual-core processors, you can consolidate more servers onto a single physical server. With dual-core technology you are able to have a dual-processor server with a total of four processor cores. The jump that both

AMD and Intel made from 32-bit to 64-bit processors has significantly improved the performance of the physical server running Microsoft Virtual server 2005 R2. Consolidation ratios are not going to be the same on every server. They are dependent on the workloads of the virtual machines that are running on the physical server.

Virtual server presents a common set of hardware to every virtual machine. It presents all the key components, such as common NIC, video card, motherboard, SCSI card, hard drives, CD-ROM, etc. The key is that it presents the same common hardware regardless what physical server the virtual servers are running on. This enables you to easily move workloads from one physical server running Microsoft Virtual Server 2005 over to another Virtual Server. The particular devices that are presented to the virtual machine are detailed later in this chapter.

Advantages of Virtualization

There are several scenarios where virtualization has tremendous advantages. We will outline a few scenarios below that may be applicable to your environment.

Figure 3.1 Virtualization Diagram

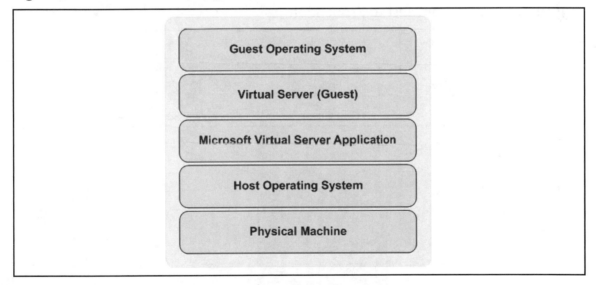

Production Data Centers

Production servers can greatly benefit from virtualization technology, although this is most likely the first environment that you will want to target for virtualization. With any new technology that you are planning on implementing in your environment, it is usually best to implement in a test/pilot/ production method to ensure the stability of production systems (see Figure 3.2). One of the key reasons for virtualization of production is that on average, 90 percent of Windows-based production servers run below 10 percent average utilization. This is a prime reason that virtualization is so prevalent today. You are able to save a great deal of money just by reducing the number of servers purchased. Imagine having a 10-to-1 or greater consolidation ration. You are able to take a data center with 100 servers and consolidate it to 10 servers that can fit in a single server rack. Many clients that we spoke to also look to virtualization of their production systems for other reasons besides consolidation. Some are looking to save on the utility cost from the servers and the cooling for the room. Some have maxed out their power capabilities and are facing an expensive electrical upgrade to continue growing.

Another huge advantage is recoverability. Each virtual server's hard drive is represented by a single file. You are able to take a snapshot of this file for backup. Virtual Server 2005 R1 and later supports vss for snapshots. A prime example of leveraging this technology is in the event of data loss or corruption. For instance, say you are applying the latest service pack to your virtual server and after the automatic reboot the machine comes up with a blue screen. If you took a snapshot of the hard disk that your OS was on, you can within seconds restore that snapshot and go back to before the service pack was applied. This saves you from needing to potentially rebuild the entire virtual server.

Figure 3.2 Phases from Test to Production

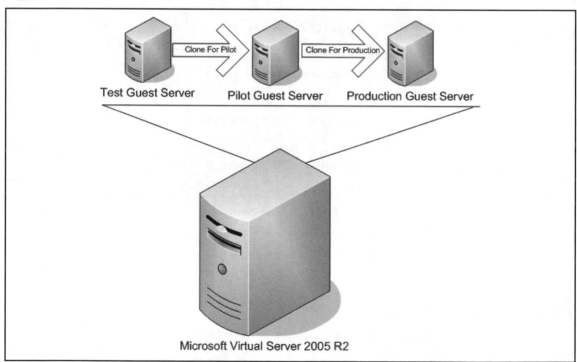

Test and Development Data Centers

One of the main advantages of using virtualization in the test and development areas is the ability to rapidly deploy new virtual serves. You can create a basic Windows Server virtual server and then clone that server any time that a new virtual server is needed. This saves a great deal of time compared to the standard method of loading each OS. You can also create specialty machines, such as specific application servers, Web servers, SQL servers, and so on. By utilizing this, you can prevent diverting needed resources from production servers to spend a great deal of time building test servers.

You can also use the snapshot technology for the test and development system. Because of the nature of the systems, they are constantly having applications installed and uninstalled and having major application changes. By using snapshots you can keep several versions of these systems to help avoid a total rebuild.

Disaster Recovery

Disaster recovery is becoming a critical issue for most companies today. One of the issues with disaster recovery is the potential cost. Without using virtualization as part of the disaster recovery solution, you are faced with replicating the hardware in your production site to the disaster recovery site. By using Microsoft Virtual Server at the disaster recovery location, you are able to significantly reduce the hardware costs. Recoverability and time may be more important to your company. By using Virtual Server you can meet all three objectives above with one solution. There are many ways to implement Microsoft Virtual Server 2005 for use in a disaster recovery site. Figure 3.3 outlines one of the commonly implemented solutions to meet clients' disaster recovery needs. This solution enables clients to reduce their disaster recovery costs considerably. More importantly, they are able to take their server recovery times down from days or weeks to hours and even minutes. The key piece in this solution is the utilization of a Storage Area Network (SAN) at both locations. All the virtual server disk and configuration files reside on the SAN; it is the job of the SAN to replicate the data from the primary site over to the disaster recovery site. Because all the virtual servers' data is being replicated in the event of a disaster, you simply need to power on the virtual servers and their guest operating systems at the disaster recovery site.

Figure 3.3 Disaster Recovery Diagram

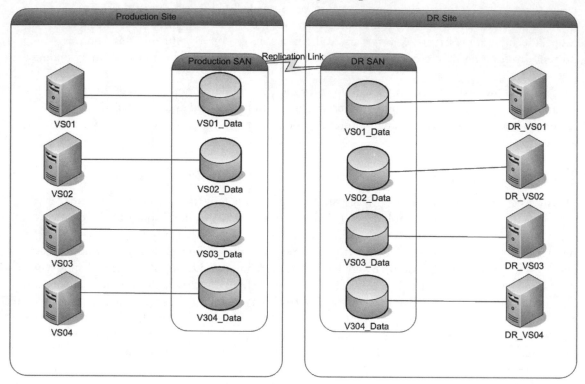

Microsoft Virtual Server 2005 R2
Disaster Recovery Diagram

What Virtualization Tools Are Available?

Virtual Server 2005 Migration Toolkit is a free tool available from Microsoft that enables you to migrate a physical machine to a virtual machine. This is commonly known as the P2V (physical-to-virtual) process. This may be used to make a clone of an existing physical machine for test and development purposes. You may use this as a tool to help move servers off their existing legacy hardware that may be close to failing. This can also be used for creating images of physical machines for disaster recovery purposes as well. This is a list of operating systems that the Migration Toolkit supports:

- Windows Server 2003 (Standard and Enterprise)
- Windows 2000 (Standard and Advanced) SP4 or later required
- Windows NT 4.0 Server (Standard and Enterprise) SP6a required

Third-Party Virtualization Tools

Virtualization technology utilization has exploded in the past few years. As with any product that is seeing this kind of growth, many companies jump on the bandwagon by developing tools to complement or enhance the product. There are still a limited number of third-party tools designed for Virtual Server 2005 R2 today, but as the product grows, many more may become available. One of the companies that specializes in such tools is PlateSpin. They have two main products that help to make the transition from a physical to a virtual environment much easier. The two products described below are PlateSpin PowerRecon and PlateSpin PowerConvert.

PowerRecon is designed to evaluate your current physical environment and to assist you with your server consolidation planning. It is designed to give a complete inventory of your hardware and software and also show the utilization of your servers. This is done by installing a data collector in your environment and then choosing which servers you want to evaluate. One key point is that it does this without the need to install an agent on the server that it is collecting data from. This assessment should be run for a period of at least 30 days to collect the performance characteristics of your environment. The assessment consists of three phases: assess, design, and implement. This assessment is critical to consolidation planning because before you start the consolidation server you need to know how many host machines you need and how large the host server must be to handle the workload.

PowerConvert is used to convert your physical machines into virtual machines. Without a tool to convert your servers from physical to virtual, you would need to build new virtual machines and then transition the applications from the physical server to the virtual server, which would take a great deal of effort and time. PowerConvert accomplishes this by taking an image of the physical server, transferring that image to a virtual machine, and then making the necessary changes so that the machine can boot up as a virtual machine. The other advantage to this is that is does this by not destroying the data on the physical server. So if you need to revert from the virtual machine to the physical machine, it is as simple as turning the physical server back on. PlateSpin PowerConvert also supports V2P (virtual-to-physical) conversions, so if your virtual machine outgrows the resources in the virtual environment, you can convert it to run on its own physical server. It also supports taking an image of either a physical or virtual server and storing it in an image repository for backup or automated deployment purposes.

Designing & Planning…

Evaluate Your Environment

Using tools such as PlateSpin PowerRecon significantly reduces the amount of manual labor needed to evaluate your current server environment. Analyzing the environment before consolidating can be critical to a successful consolidation by accurately sizing the host servers and number of hosts needed.

How Does Virtualization Work?

The basic idea of virtualization is taking a single physical machine and running multiple virtual machines on top of that hardware. This is sometimes related to the concept of partitioning a hard disk into multiple logical drives. Virtualization works by taking the physical components of a machine and presenting virtual hardware instead. Instead of a machine having its own physical hard drive, its hard drive is simply a file residing on the host machine's file system. It also has a virtual NIC, video card, peripheral ports, CPU, and memory. These resources are managed by the Microsoft Virtual Server application that is running on the host machine. The virtualized hardware that is presented to the guest OS is outlined in this section.

- Presents single CPU
- Intel 440BX motherboard
- AMI BIOS
- Up to 3.6 GB RAM
- Up to four virtual IDE devices (CD-ROM or DVD-ROM drives)
- Up to four SCSI controllers
- Emulates Adaptec 7870 SCSI controller
- Emulates S3 Trio64
- Support for up to two virtual floppy disk drives. These can be mapped to a physical floppy disk drive or a virtual floppy disk drive using a floppy image .flp file.
- Up to two serial ports
- One parallel port LPT
- No USB support
- Standard 101-key keyboard
- Microsoft Intellimouse with PS2 interface
- Emulates DEC 21140 Ethernet card

Virtual PC versus Virtual Server 2005

Microsoft Virtual PC 2004 and Virtual Server 2005 are both designed to enable a physical machine to host multiple virtual machines. Both products have a similar architecture and share many of the same features, but they also differ in many ways. Many of the features and the user interface of the Virtual PC were designed with the desktop user in mind. Virtual Server was designed with the system administrator in mind and is useful for hosting Enterprise Server products. It has many advanced features that make its user interface more complex. We will take a closer look at some of the differences and outline some usage scenarios below.

Features That Are Found in Both Virtual PC and Virtual Server 2005 R2

Both products have many of the same core features. They both use the same file architecture; they use .vmc files for their virtual machine configuration file; and their hard disks are .vhd files. They both provide networking for the virtual machines, but Virtual Server adds a number of features that we will look at in the following section. Both products also provide the capability to use advanced disk features such as undoable disk modes.

Differences between Virtual PC and Virtual Server 2005 R2

Along with the many similarities, there are also many differences. The main differences come from the design of the two products. Virtual PC is designed for hosting desktop operating systems and applications and Virtual Server is designed for server operating systems and applications. See Table 3.1 for the OS support matrix.

Table 3.1 OS Support Matrix

	Virtual PC	Virtual Server 2005 R2
Host OS Support	Windows XP Professional	Windows XP Professional
	Windows 2000 Professional	Windows Small Business Server Standard and Premium
		Windows 2003 Server Standard, Enterprise, and Datacenter
Guest OS Support	MS-DOS 6.22	MS-DOS 6.22
	Windows 95	Windows 95
	Windows 98	Windows 98
	Windows 2000	Windows 2000
	Windows NT 4.0	Windows NT 4.0
	Windows XP	Windows XP
	OS/2	OS/2

Supported Features in Virtual PC

Virtual PC offers the following features:

- Sound card support within virtual machines
- Copy/paste functionality from host-to-guest machine
- Folder sharing between the host and guest operating systems
- Shared networking via network address translation

Supported Features in Virtual Server 2005 R2

Virtual Server 2005 R2 supports several host hardware and virtual hardware features. It also supports other features that will be discussed in this section.

Host Hardware Support

Virtual Server 2005 R2 supports up to 32 physical processors. Virtual Server R2 is a multi-threaded application designed to take advantage of all the physical processors.

Virtual Hardware

Virtual Server 2005 R2 supports 3.6 GB memory for each virtual machine. It also supports SCSI disks.

Remote Management

Virtual Server 2005 R2 provides a Web-management interface for remote management of the Virtual Server product and virtual machines. It also provides the Virtual Machine Remote Console (VMRC), which gives console access to the virtual machines.

Security

Virtual Server 2005 R2 provides SSL security for Administrative management Web site and the VMRC. It can be configured to specify what user account on each virtual machine runs under.

Support for Scripting

Virtual Server and the virtual machines running on the Virtual Server can be managed by using COM and API scripting.

WMI Support

WMI counters can be used with Virtual Server 2005 R2 to monitor virtual machines by using Microsoft tools such as Microsoft Operations Manager and by being integrated into third-party management tools.

Clustering

Virtual Server 2005 R2 Enables clustering between two virtual machines for high-availability application.

Configuring & Implementing...

Running the OS on Host Servers

Use the OS on the host server just for running Microsoft Virtual Server 2005 R2 and the virtual machines. Using it to run another application will reduce the amount of resources available to the virtual machines.

Scenarios for the Use of Virtual PC

Both products are very useful, but the key is using each product in the right area. In this section we will discuss some areas where Virtual PC may be the right product to use.

Help Desk

In today's corporate environment, many help desk workers are tasked with supporting a wide variety of operating systems and applications. Without using a Virtual PC, a help desk technician may need to have multiple machines on their desk with all the different operating systems and applications loaded. Or they may need to load dual boot or load multiple operating systems or their PC. This can be very time consuming because you have to wait to reboot the machine to switch between operating systems. By using Virtual PC, you can run multiple operating systems at the same time and switch between them very quickly in order to assist with troubleshooting issues.

Training

For application training purposes, you only need to have a single workstation per student, and then you can run multiple virtual machines on top of that workstation. You can create a full Microsoft infrastructure consisting of domain controllers, Web servers, application server, or whatever else is needed for the training, without the need of multiple machines. You can also keep images of these machines so you can refresh the environment without the need to reload every machine after each class. This can also be done by setting the virtual machine to not save changes made during the class.

Testing

When you need to test a new application, test it in a virtual machine rather than risk creating problems with your workstation by loading an application that may cause conflicts.

Legacy Applications

If you need to run an application that will not work or is not supported under Windows XP, you can run the application within legacy operating systems.

Virtual Server 2005 versus Virtual Server 2005 R2

The core application is much the same between Virtual Server 2005 and R2. R2 is basically a product update to the Virtual Server 2005 release. In this section we outline the following the new additions found in the R2 product:

- **x64 support**   This adds support for 64-bit versions of Windows to be used for the host operating system.

- **Host clustering**   This enables clustering between Virtual Server hosts, which provides for the failover of guest machines.

- **Linux guest OS support**

- **iSCSI support**

- **Improved support for hyper-threading**

- **PXE booting**   The PXE booting support has been enhanced by adding it into the virtual machine network adapter. This will allow for the deployment of virtual machines by using the same methods of network installation used by physical servers.

Summary

Microsoft Virtual Server 2005 R2 is a very versatile application. It has multiple practical applications in today's IT environments. As you have read, Virtual Server can meet your needs whether you need to implement a test, production, disaster recovery site, or all of the above. The main reason for implementing Virtual Server 2005 R2 may be to reduce physical servers and reduce cost. The other advantages, such as OS portability and recoverability, are making it an increasingly popular choice for today's infrastructure needs.

Solutions Fast Track

Microsoft Virtual Server 2005 R2 and Dynamics System Initiative

- ☑ Streamline data center operations
- ☑ Increase server efficiency
- ☑ Improve operating system and application flexibility

What Is Virtualization, and When Should You Use It?

- ☑ To rapidly deploy test systems
- ☑ To consolidate underutilized physical servers
- ☑ To take snapshots to create recovery points
- ☑ To increase disaster recovery potential.

What Virtualization Tools Are Available?

- ☑ PowerRecon automates the process of consolidation feasibility and planning.
- ☑ Consolidation planning is a useful tool in showing the value of virtualization to management.
- ☑ PowerConvert can convert both Windows and Linux physical machines.
- ☑ PowerConvert considerably eases the migration process.

How Does Virtualization Work?

- ☑ Presents standard motherboard to the guest machines
- ☑ Uses up to 3.6 GB of physical RAM on the host
- ☑ Supports physical and virtual CDs
- ☑ Supports porting virtual machines from one host to another

Virtual PC versus Virtual Server 2005

- ☑ Virtual Server supports 3.6 GB RAM per virtual machine.
- ☑ Virtual Server supports 32 processors.
- ☑ Virtual PC supports sound.
- ☑ Virtual PC was designed for desktop operating systems.

Virtual Server 2005 versus Virtual Server 2005 R2

- ☑ x64 support
- ☑ iSCSI support
- ☑ Host-clustering support
- ☑ Enhanced PXE-booting support

Frequently Asked Questions

Q: Can I migrate Virtual PC machines to Virtual Server 2005?

A: Yes, you can move virtual machines from Virtual PC to Virtual Server.

Q: Does Virtual Server 2005 R2 support 64-bit processors and host operating systems?

A: Yes, it enables you the run 64-bit versions of Windows as the host operating system.

Q: Can Virtual Server 2005 R2 run production servers?

A: Virtual Server can run production virtual machines, which makes it a perfect candidate for consolidating underutilized physical machines.

Q: Can I run Linux virtual machines on Virtual Server 2005 R2?

A: Yes, Linux is supported as a guest OS on Virtual Server 2005 R2.

Q: Can I run 64-bit guest operating systems?

A: No, although the host operating system can run a 64-bit operating system, the guests require 32-bit.

Q: Does Virtual Server 2005 R2 support multiprocessor (SMP) virtual machines?

A: No, the virtual machines are uniprocessor.

## Chapter 4

Installing and Configuring a Virtual Server

Solutions in this chapter:

- **Determining the Physical Size of the Server**
- **Installing Virtual Server 2005 R2**
- **Setting Up a Virtual Server Administration Web Site**
- **Virtual Machine Remote Console**
- **Setting Default Location and Search Paths**
- **Setting Resource Allocation**

- ☑ **Summary**
- ☑ **Solutions Fast Track**
- ☑ **Frequently Asked Questions**

Introduction

At this point, we know all about the what, the why, and the when; the next step is the how. The install is very straightforward, as with most Microsoft applications. The installation application is a wizard-based graphical install. The important detail not to overlook is that, before you are able to virtualize servers, you must determine the hardware needed to run your virtual servers' environment and set up the virtual server software.

Running the setup will result in a working server, but when nothing is configured after the installation, only administrators are able to connect to any machine via the console. Configuring your virtual server correctly will provide secure and reliable access while giving the best performance possible.

Determining the Physical Size of the Server

This process of determining the size of the physical server that will host the virtual servers is a critical step that should not be neglected. Adequately planning the size of the physical server will provide a solid foundation from which to run virtual servers. Some of the key things that need to be addressed when planning what physical hardware is needed are the number of virtual machines that will be on the host, and, more importantly, what will be running on these virtual machines. What each virtual machine is running is critical because, for example, a virtual machine that is a basic domain controller may require far fewer resources than that of a virtual machine running SQL or Microsoft Exchange. Refer to Table 4.1 for Virtual Server 2005 R2 system requirements.

Physical Server Sizing

When evaluating the sizing needs of the physical server, the virtual machines that will be running on it will fall into two categories. The first is existing physical servers and the second is new servers that will be in deployed in the environment. The four key performance areas to evaluate are CPU utilization, memory usage, disk I/O, and network I/O. You will also need to determine the disk space requirements of each virtual machine and take this into consideration whether the physical server will utilize internal storage or external storage, such as on a SAN.

Evaluating Existing Physical Servers

Some key reasons for virtualizing existing servers running on physical hardware can be for server consolidation, making clone for test and development, and disaster recovery. In any case, existing servers can be significantly easier to plan for. The main reason for this is that you have a live server to evaluate its current utilization. By determining a server's current utilization you will have a good idea of the resources that it will consume after it is virtualized.

Planning for New Virtual Servers

New servers that will be introduced into the environment are slightly more challenging. There are, however, methods to estimate their resource needs. Most application vendors will publish in the application documentation the particular resource requirements of their application. You can use those requirements in determining what they will require in a virtual server environment. You may also have a similar server running in your environment that you can use to evaluate its resource needs.

Balancing Workloads

To use resources affectively, try to place virtual machines with dissimilar workloads on the virtual server. For example, if some machines are CPU intensive, place them on the same virtual server with machines that are memory or disk I/O intensive.

Table 4.1 lists the system requirements for Virtual Server 2005 R2.

Table 4.1 Virtual Server 2005 R2 System Requirements

Minimum CPU Speed	550 MHz
Number of Processors	Total physical processors supported by the host operating system.
Recommended CPU Speed	At least 1 GHz
Processor Information	Intel and AMD support
Supported Host Operating Systems	Microsoft Windows Server 2003 Standard Edition, Enterprise Edition, or Datacenter Edition
Windows Server 2003 Standard x64 Edition, Enterprise x64 Edition, Datacenter x64 Edition or later	
Windows Small Business Server 2003 Standard Edition or Premium Edition	
Windows XP Professional Service Pack 2 or later	
Minimum RAM	256 MB
Required Available Hard Disk Space	2 GB plus space needed for each virtual machine

Installing Virtual Server 2005 R2

The setup of Microsoft Virtual Server 2005 R2 is much like the installation of other Microsoft software. The wizard-based setup can be run from media downloaded from the Microsoft Web site, or you can order a media CD from Microsoft. The following sections will walk you through the installation of Virtual Server 2005 R2 step by step.

Preinstallation Tasks

1. Acquire Virtual Server software. The software can be downloaded form the Microsoft Web site at **www.microsoft.com/windowsserversystem/virtualserver/software/default.mspx**.

2. Install supported host operating system on physical server.

3. Install IIS on host system.

Installation Tasks

As depicted in Figure 4.1, to begin the installation of Microsoft Virtual Server 2005 R2, simply run the setup.exe file. The software can be obtained from the Microsoft Web site. You can either download the media immediately from the Microsoft Web site or you can also order the Virtual Server software CD from Microsoft.

Figure 4.1 Running Setup

The screen in Figure 4.2 is the initial page that is displayed when running the setup. Click the icon labeled **Install Microsoft Virtual Server 2005 R2**.

Figure 4.2 Microsoft Virtual Serve 2005 R2 Setup

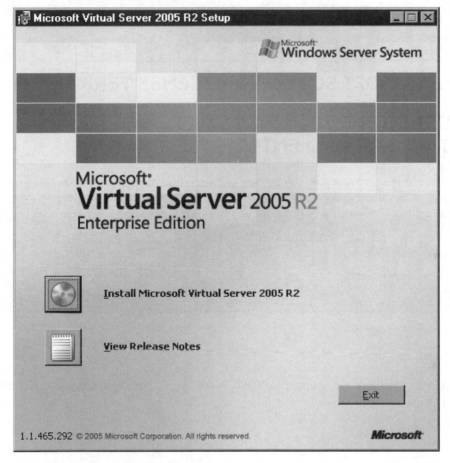

The License Agreement screen appears, as shown in Figure 4.3. Select the **I accept the terms in the license agreement** radio button and then click **Next** to continue.

Figure 4.3 License Agreement

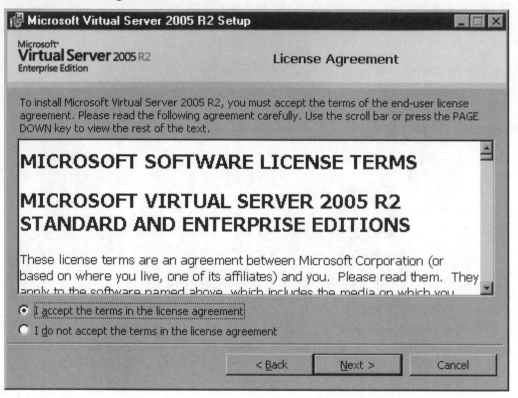

The Customer Information screen appears, as shown in Figure 4.4. Enter your user name and organization information in the appropriate fields. Note that the product key is automatically provided. Click **Next** to continue.

Figure 4.4 Customer Information

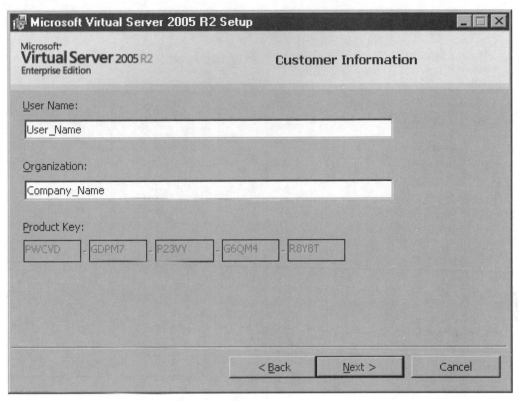

The Setup Type screen appears, as shown in Figure 4.5. Select **Custom** and then click **Next**. This will enable you to select specific components and to choose the desired installation location.

Figure 4.5 Setup Type

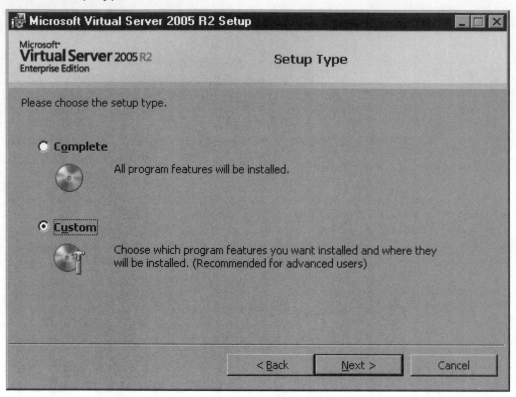

The Custom Setup screen appears, as shown in Figure 4.6. Notice that all components are selected by default. You may choose to install the Virtual Server Web Application on a separate server. This is desirable when implementing more than one Virtual Server 2005 server. From the Virtual Server Web Application you can manager the various Virtual Server 2005 servers. When finished, click **Next**.

Figure 4.6 Custom Setup

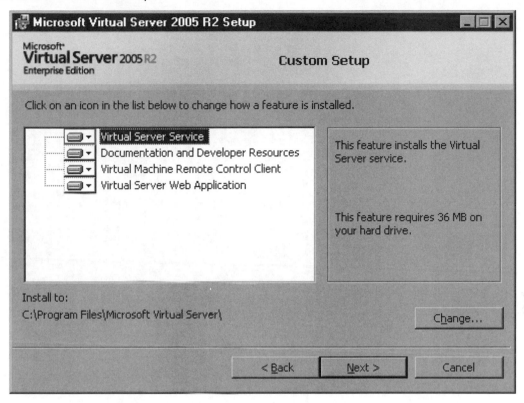

The Configure Components screen appears, as shown in Figure 4.7. You can choose to change the default Web site port. You can also configure whether the Administration Web site will run as the authenticated user (default) or as the Local System account. When finished, click **Next**.

Figure 4.7 Configuring Virtual Server Web Site

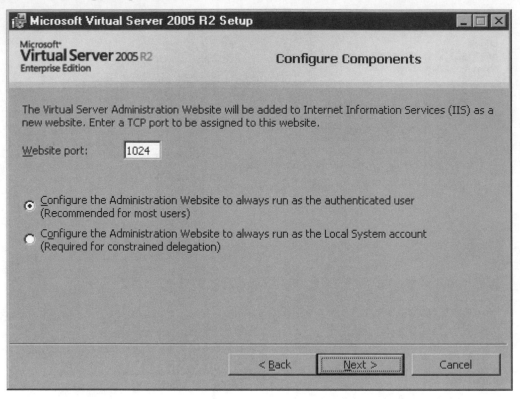

A second Configure Components screen appears, as shown in Figure 4.8. You can choose to have the installation automatically enable Virtual Server exceptions in Windows Firewall. Note: This may not apply if not running Windows Firewall. When finished, click **Next**.

Figure 4.8 Enabling Virtual Server exceptions in Windows Firewall

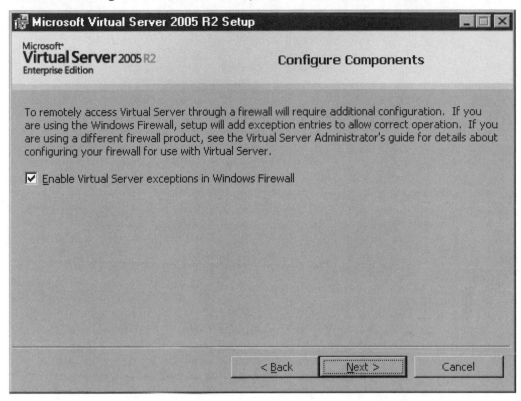

The Ready to Install screen appears, as shown in Figure 4.9. Verify that the installation directory is correct, and then click **Install** to continue.

Figure 4.9 Ready to Install

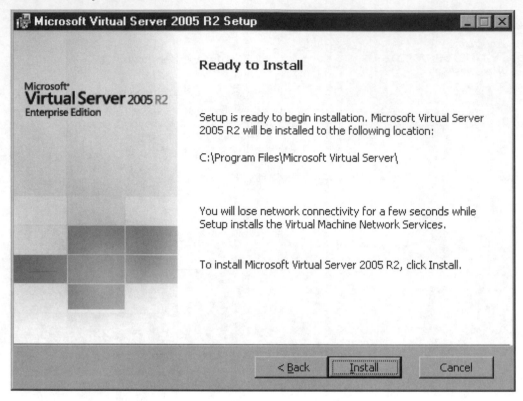

Figure 4.10 shows the installation progress.

Figure 4.10 Installing Microsoft Virtual Server 2005 R2

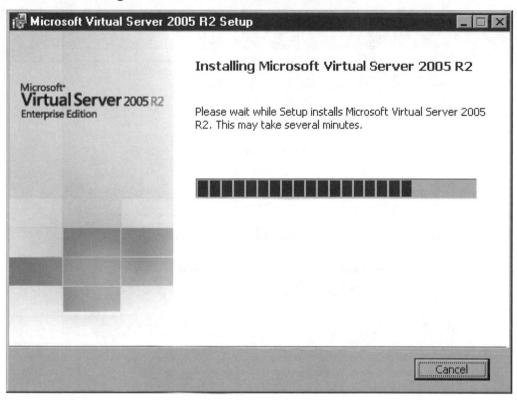

Figure 4.11 shows the post–installation summary. Note the link under "Administration Website." This link will take you to the Administration Web site that is the management interface for Virtual Server.

Figure 4.11 Installation Summary

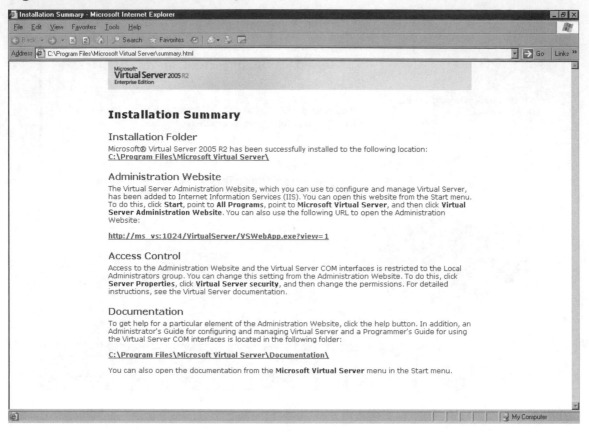

Setting Up a Virtual Server Administration Web Site

The Microsoft Virtual Server Administrative Web site is a Web-based application that is used to manage and configure the virtual server as well as the virtual machines running on the virtual server. The Virtual Server Administrative Web site can be installed in two ways. The first way is to install the Virtual Server Administrative Web site as part of the installation of Virtual Server. The second way is to install the Virtual Server Administrative Web site on its own standalone server. You may want to choose the second option if you plan to have multiple Microsoft virtual servers and want to avoid installing IIS on every host. From a single server running the Virtual Server Administrative Web site you can manage all the Microsoft virtual servers in your environment.

Virtual Server Administration Web Site Installation

The installation of the Virtual Server Administration Web site is part of the standard installation of Microsoft Virtual Server. If you plan to install the Virtual Server Administration Web site on a single server, then you will want to select custom installation during setup.

Installing in a Multi-Server Environment

Additional configuration tasks are required when installing the Virtual Server Administration Web site with the intent to manage multiple machines running Microsoft Virtual Server. If installing in a multi-server environment, you will want to take special note of Figure 4.17, which changes the standard authentication type to enable authentication across multiple servers.

The install the Virtual Server Administrative Web site, you will run the same setup that is used to install Virtual Server.

The screen in Figure 4.12 is the same initial page that is displayed when running the setup. Click on the link labeled **Install Microsoft Virtual Server 2005 R2**.

Figure 4.12 Microsoft Virtual Serve 2005 R2 Setup

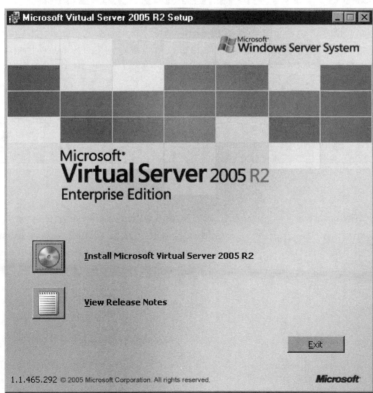

The License Agreement screen appears, as shown in Figure 4.13. Select the **I accept the terms in the license agreement** radio button, and then click **Next** to continue.

Figure 4.13 License Agreement

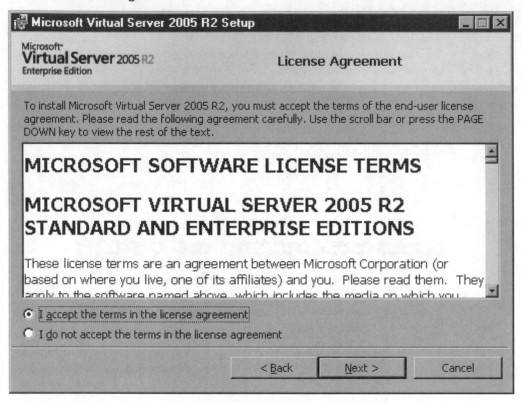

The Customer Information screen appears, as shown in Figure 4.14. Enter your user name and organization information in the appropriate fields. Note that the product key is automatically provided. Click **Next** to continue.

Figure 4.14 Customer Information

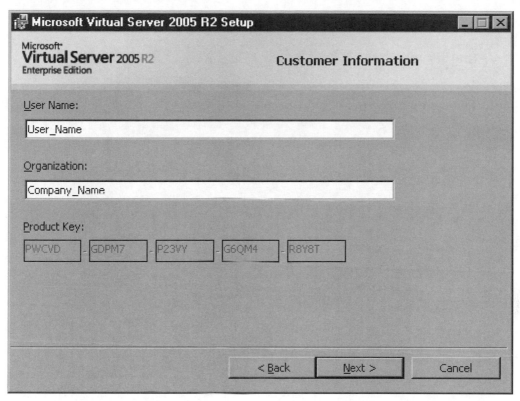

The Setup Type screen appears, as shown in Figure 4.15. Select **Custom** and click **Next**. This will enable you to select specific components and to choose the desired installation location.

Figure 4.15 Setup Type

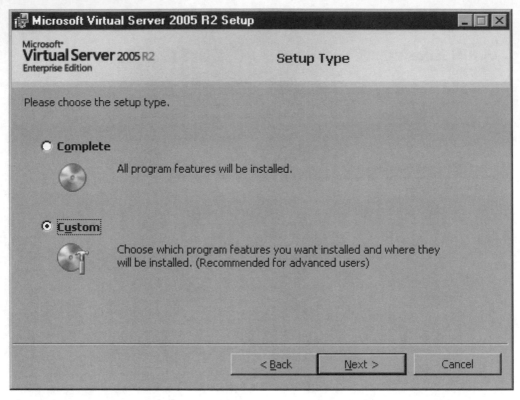

The Custom Setup screen atppears, as shown in Figure 4.16. Deselect all the components except for the Virtual Server Web Application when installing on a standalone server. Click **Next**.

Figure 4.16 Custom Setup

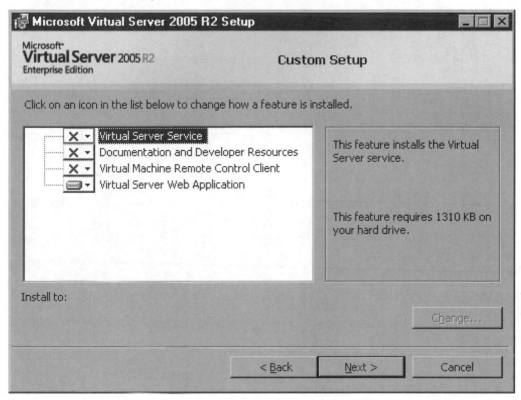

The Configure Components screen appears, as shown in Figure 4.17. You can choose to change the default Web site port. You can also configure whether the Administration Web site will run as the authenticated user (default), or as the Local System account. For managing multiple servers you will want to change the default user that the Web site runs as from authenticated user to have it run as the local system account. Click **Next**.

Figure 4.17 Configuring Virtual Server Web Site

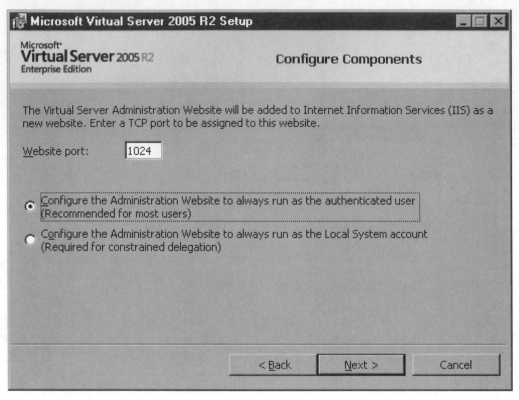

A second Configure Components screen appears, as shown in Figure 4.18. You can choose to have the installation automatically enable Virtual Server exceptions in Windows Firewall. Note: This may not apply if not running Windows Firewall. Click **Next**.

Figure 4.18 Enabling Virtual Server Exceptions in Windows Firewall

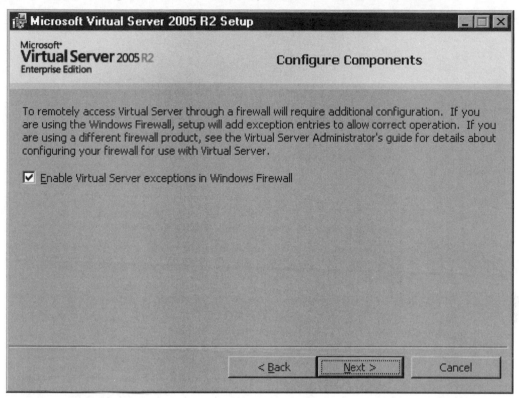

The Ready to Install screen appears, as shown in Figure 4.19. Verify that the installation directory is correct, and then click **Install** to continue.

Figure 4.19 Ready to Install

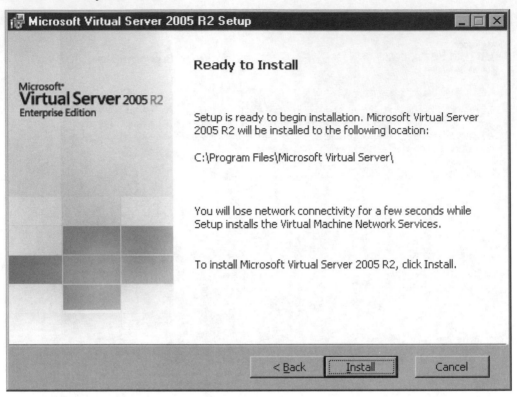

Figure 4.20 shows the post–installation summary. Note the link under "Administration Website." This link will take you to the Administration Web site that is the management interface for Virtual Server.

Figure 4.20 Installation Summary

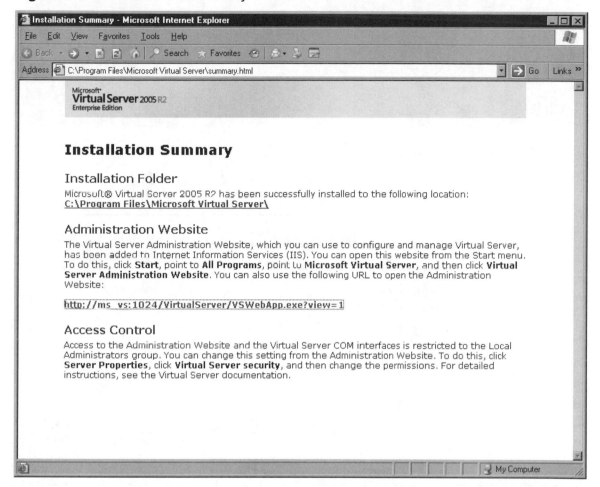

The Specify Virtual Server screen appears, as shown in Figure 4.21. In the **Computer name** field, type the name of the Microsoft virtual server that you are going to administer and then click **Connect** to continue.

Figure 4.21 Connecting to the Virtual Server

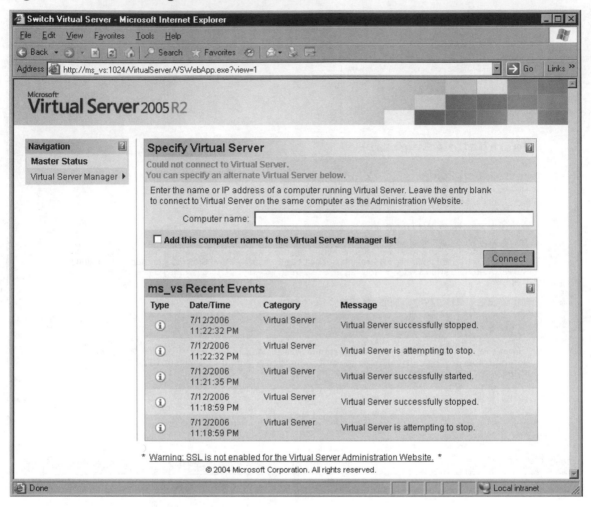

The homepage from which the virtual servers are managed appears, as shown in Figure 4.22.

Figure 4.22 Virtual Server Homepage

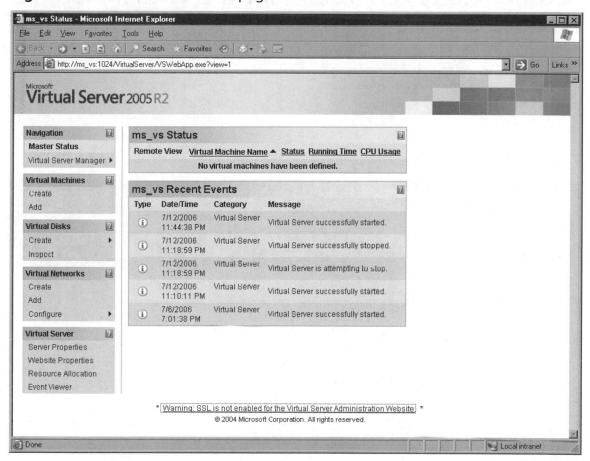

Virtual Machine Remote Console

Because you are unable to attach a monitor, keyboard, and mouse to a virtual machine, Microsoft Virtual Server provides the Virtual Machine Remote Console (VMRC) client. The remote client works much the same way as a physical IP-based KVM. When connecting to a virtual machine by using the VMRC client, you are actually on the console of that specific virtual machine. The VMRC client is used during the initial install of the operating system on the virtual machine, for installing software, and for troubleshooting virtual machine issues. The best practice is to use OS-based remote management like Microsoft Terminal Services or VNC to manage the virtual machines. Using these clients for day-to-day management on the virtual machine takes less of a toll on the resources of the host than using the VMRC.

Setting Access Permissions for the Virtual Machine Remote Console

To set up the VMRC, you will need to follow these steps:

Open the Administration Web site, as shown in Figure 4.23. Click the **Server Properties** link found under the **Virtual Server** section.

Figure 4.23 Virtual Server Home Page

As shown in Figure 4.24, click the link labeled **Virtual Machine Remote Control (VMRC) Server** to enable and configure the VMRC.

Figure 4.24 Virtual Server Properties

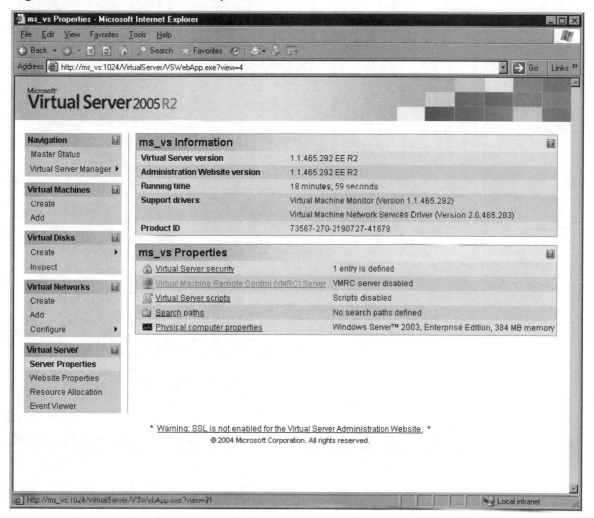

As shown in Figure 4.25, select the **Enable** check box to enable VMRC.

Figure 4.25 VMRC Configuration

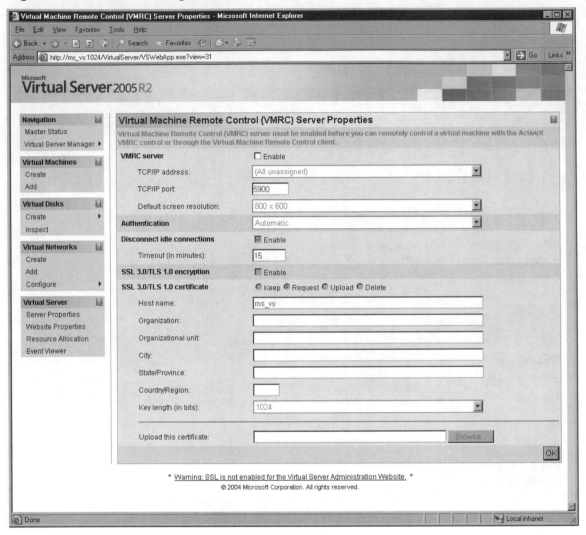

As shown in Figure 4.26, after selecting **Enable**, complete the information on the rest of the page. For additional VMRC security you can also configure it to use SSL to encrypt the connection.

Figure 4.26 Virtual Server Properties

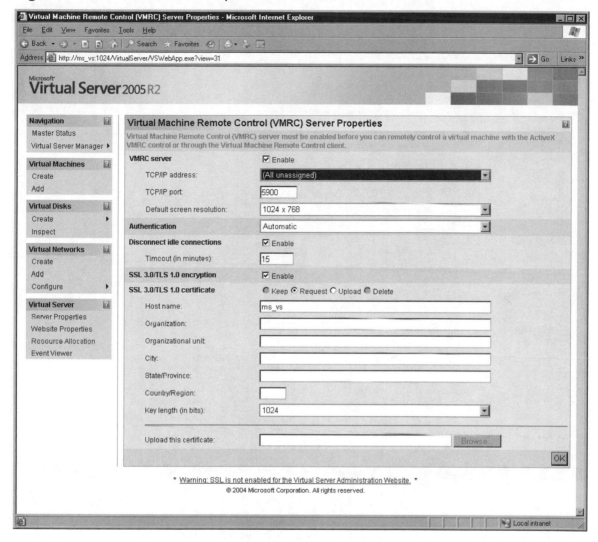

The VMRC is now configured and ready to accept connections.

Setting Default Location and Search Paths

The default location and search path are used to specify where the virtual machine configuration files are placed on the virtual server by default. The next few steps show how to configure the default location and search paths.

1.   To configure the default location and search paths, open the Virtual Server home page, as shown in Figure 4.27.

Figure 4.27 Virtual Server Home Page

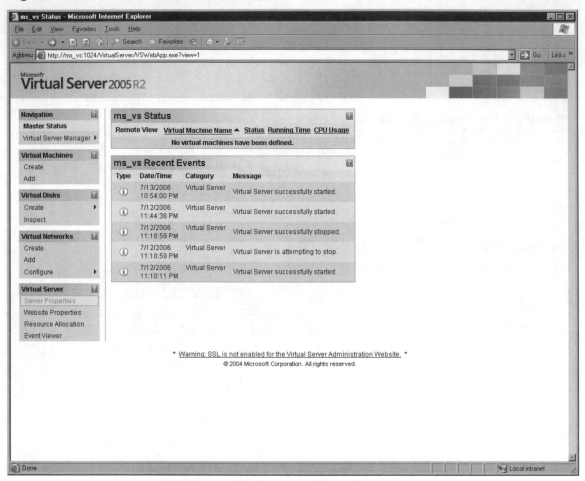

2. From the Virtual Server Properties screen, click **Search paths,** as shown in Figure 4.28.

Figure 4.28 Virtual Server Properties

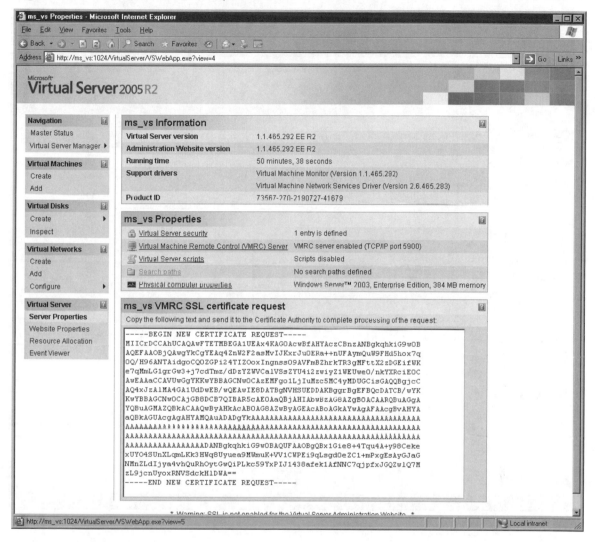

You can specify both the default configuration folder and search path (see Figure 4.29).

Figure 4.29 Virtual Server Properties

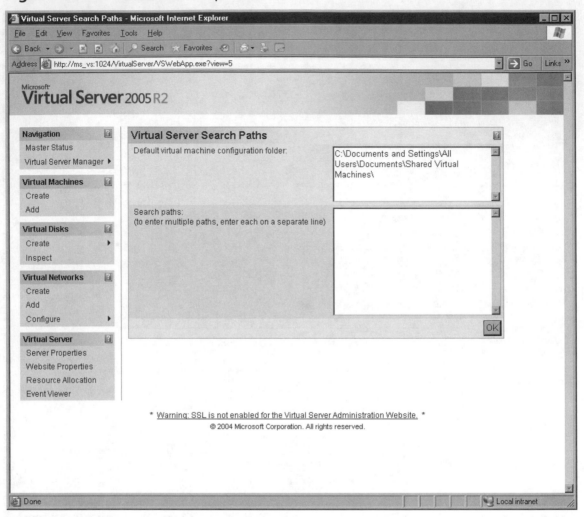

Setting Resource Allocation

Microsoft Virtual Server enables you to customize the resource allocation of the virtual machines. The main resources that you may want to customize are CPU and the amount of memory allocated. The memory allocation is not a dynamic change that can be performed while the virtual machine is running. To change the memory allocation of a virtual machine, you must shut down that particular virtual machine and then either raise or lower the amount of memory allocated. The CPU allocation of the virtual machine is configured as shown in the steps below.

Configuring & Implementing…

Resource Allocation

You can configure the maximum percentage of a CPU that a virtual machine can use to prevent it from negatively affecting other virtual machines. This can be very handy in case of a legacy server that tends to grab all available CPU resources.

To set the resource allocation, connect to the Virtual Server home page, as shown in Figure 4.30.

Figure 4.30 Virtual Server Home Page

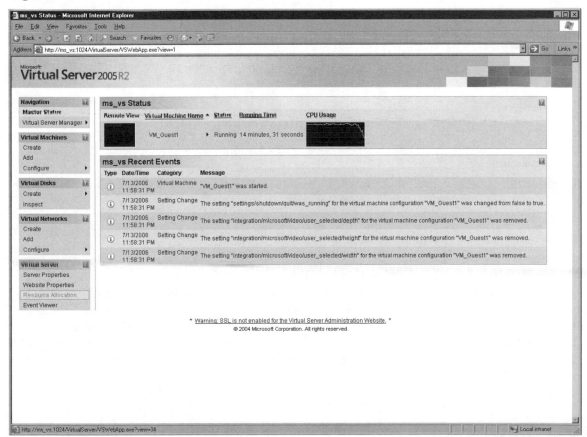

From the Virtual Server Properties screen, click **Resource Allocation** (see Figure 4.31).

Figure 4.31 Virtual Server Properties

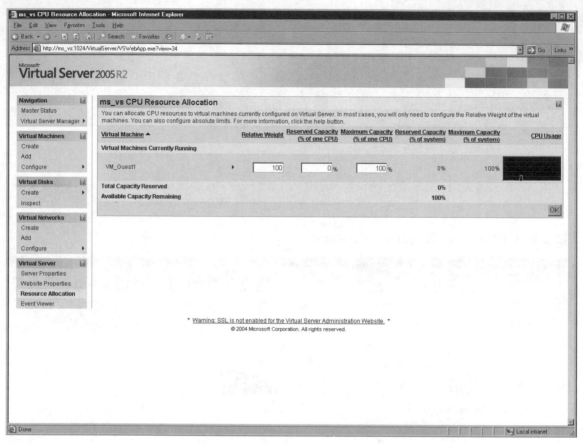

As shown in Figure 4.31, there are three different settings that can be used to set the resource allocation of each virtual machine.

The first field is labeled Relative Weight. This is used to set the priority of this virtual machine compared to the other virtual machines on the host. This is critical if resources are limited on the host and virtual machines start contending with each other for resources. For example, by setting one virtual machine to a relative weight to 200 and leaving the other virtual machines at the default of 100, you can ensure that it gets priority over the other virtual machines for resources. A common configuration is to set production systems to 200 and leave test and development virtual machines at 100.

The second field is labeled Reserved Capacity. By default, all virtual machines are to the 0%. If you want to guarantee that a particular virtual machine always has at least 50 percent of a processor, you can specify that in this field.

The third field is labeled Maximum Capacity. This is where you can specify the maximum percentage of CPU resources that a virtual machine can use. This can be very nice for isolating virtual machines that have processes that tend to run away and use 100% of its CPU. By specifying that it can only use up to a certain amount of CPU resources, you can ensure that it doesn't affect the other virtual machines.

Summary

As you may have noticed, a good deal of planning should go into design and configuration of the virtual server host machines, as well as the virtual machines that will run the host. By adequately planning the size on the host server, you can ensure that there are enough resources the run the desired virtual machines. By planning ahead, you will also be able to identify the method by which you want to implement the Virtual Server Administration Web site. While the default resource allocation settings for relative weight and CPU work great if all the virtual machines are of equal priority, if you have some virtual machines that are more important than others, this can be a critical setting.

Solutions Fast Track

Determining the Physical Size of the Server

☑ Verify the hardware requirements for Microsoft Virtual Server.

☑ Evaluate what will be running in the environment.

☑ Plan adequately for growth of the environment.

Installing Virtual Server 2005 R2

☑ Download the latest media or order media from Microsoft.

☑ Install IIS if you plan to run the Virtual Server Administrative Web site from the host.

☑ Determine if you are going to have a single or multiple virtual server environment.

Setting Up a Virtual Server Administration Web Site

☑ Install IIS before installing the Virtual Server Web site.

☑ Determine whether or not the site will be used to manage multiple virtual servers.

☑ Having a single Virtual Server Administrative Web site can be desirable for security-conscious companies that want to reduce the number of IIS servers in their environment.

Virtual Machine Remote Console

☑ Set the connection timeout to disconnect idle connections.

☑ If using the VMRC through a firewall, ensure that the appropriate ports are open.

☑ Determine whether or not you want to utilize SSL to secure the connection.

Setting Default Location and Search Paths

☑ For consistency, keep the default virtual machine configuration folder the same on each virtual server.

☑ If using a resource on a remote location, ensure that constrained delegating is configured.

☑ Always use fully qualified paths.

Setting Resource Allocation

☑ Utilize relative weight when running virtual machines with different priorities.

☑ Use the reserved capacity setting to guarantee a certain percentage of CPU resources to a virtual machine.

☑ Use maximum capacity setting to prevent a virtual machine from using more than the desired percentage of CPU resources.

Frequently Asked Questions

Q: Should I leave hyper-threading enabled or should it be disabled?

A: Because of the workload on Microsoft Virtual Server, the best practice is to disable hyper-threading.

Q: How many virtual machines can I run on each Microsoft virtual server?

A: This will vary depending on the workload of the virtual machines running on Microsoft virtual server.

Q: What happens if a virtual machine crashes? Does it affect the other virtual machines?

A: Each virtual machine is isolated form the other virtual machines on the host; if one virtual machine crashes it will not effect the other virtual machines.

Q: Can I allocate more memory to a virtual machine on the fly?

A: Although you can't allocate more memory on the fly, you can quickly adjust the amount of memory a virtual machine has by shutting it down and editing its configuration.

Q: How should I connect to the desktop of a virtual machine?

A: You can connect to the desktop by using the VMRC, but the best practice is to use Terminal Services to connect to the desktop when available.

Q: How can I ensure that one machine gets all the resources that it needs?

A: By setting its relative weight higher than the other virtual machines, it will dynamically allocate additional resources as needed from other virtual machines.

## Chapter 5

Virtual Machines

Solutions in this chapter:

- **Creating the Virtual Server**
- **Adding Hardware to the Server**
- **Installing a Windows OS**
- **Installing Virtual Machine Additions**
- **Installing a Non-Windows OS**

☑ **Summary**

☑ **Solutions Fast Track**

☑ **Frequently Asked Questions**

Introduction

A virtual server isn't of any use without any servers deployed on it. Deployment of servers can be done by using the Virtual Server Migration Toolkit, but also by creating a virtual server (virtual hardware) and installing an operating system on it.

Before installing the guest operating system onto the virtual hardware, you need to make the correct decisions about the (virtual) hardware setup. This contains selecting the correct network, choosing the correct disk and controller type. Setting this correctly will give you a fast and flexible (virtual) server.

You need to configure at least one virtual hard disk for the virtual machine to install an operating system. You can have more than one virtual hard disk on a virtual machine if it is needed for separation of data or loading a database or for some other reason. You can configure a virtual machine to boot from a floppy disk or a CD-ROM, but a virtual hard disk is normally required to maintain the operating system and applications of the virtual machine. The four types of virtual hard disk all are saved as .vhd files in the My Virtual Machines folder by default. The four types are:

- **Dynamically expanding**   The actual size of the virtual hard disk expands as it is written. The initial size starts small at less than 100 KB. As data is added, the size expands until it reaches the specified maximum size established when the disk was created. (This is the default type.)

- **Fixed-size**   The actual size of the virtual hard disk is fixed to the maximum size specified when the disk was created. The virtual disk will not grow. If you create a 40 GB fixed-size virtual hard disk, it will immediately use 40 GB of space.

- **Differencing**   A differencing virtual hard disk is a virtual hard disk configured in a parent–child relationship. The differencing disk is the child and the associated virtual disk is the parent. The differencing disk stores a record of all changes made to the parent disk and saves changes without altering the parent disk. It is possible to write-protect the parent virtual hard disk and have several differencing virtual disks share the same parent virtual disk. Changes to the parent virtual disk can be tried with the virtual machines using a differencing virtual disk for testing before committing the changes to the parent virtual disk. A differencing disk can also use a sysprep parent to rapidly deploy multiple virtual machines based on a "golden" image of the operating system.

- **Linked**   A linked virtual disk is a connection to a physical hard disk on the physical computer. This virtual hard disk can have multiple volumes. The virtual hard disk is created with the actual boot partition and partition map from the physical drive on the physical computer. All read and write requests are performed directly on the linked physical hard disk. A linked disk provides a way to convert a physical hard disk to a virtual hard disk. This disk can have multiple volumes. Linked disks are always fixed-size disks that use the entire disk. You must have adequate space on the physical server's disk drives to accommodate this new fixed virtual disk. You cannot use undo and differencing disks with a linked disk.

Creating the Virtual Server

A virtual server can run almost any Intel-based operating system and each can have different amounts of memory, numbers of virtual hard disks, and Com and LPT ports. You must consider some planning steps when making virtual servers. The main thing to remember is that *all* virtual machines are dependant on the physical resources of the Virtual Server 2005 server. The host server must have enough physical resources for memory, disk, CPU, and network bandwidth to handle the number of virtual machines and the allocated resources of each.

Some things to consider are:

- **Virtual Machine filenames**   Each virtual machine must have a unique filename. This filename must be fewer than 150 characters long without any special characters. A descriptive filename is the best practice to avoid confusion later on. An example of a good filename may be EXCH01_Win2003SP1_Exch2003SP2_C.vhd for the C: drive of a server named EXCH01 that is running Windows 2003 Server SP1 with Exchange Server 2003 SP2.

- **Memory**   All running virtual machines require at least enough memory for the host operating system and each guest operating system running on the Virtual Server. The minimum amount of memory for both the host operating system, typically Windows 2003 Server, and the guest operating system for all running virtual machines must be physically present in the host server. The maximum amount of memory in a physical server is dictated by the host operating system. For example if the host server is running Windows 2003 Server R2 Standard, 256 MB is the minimum memory required, and the guest operating system is Windows Small Business Server 2003 Premium, 512 MB minimum memory required, the host server would need at least 768 MB of memory. A maximum of seven of these virtual servers could be run on this host because the maximum memory limit is 4 GB of memory. Of course this limitation can be overcome by using 64-bit servers and using Virtual Server 2005 R2 x64.

- **Hard Disk**   Each virtual machine must have its own virtual hard disk. Any of the four types of virtual hard disk file can be used for the virtual machine. The physical hard disk of the host server also needs to be large enough to accommodate the host operating system and the Virtual Server 2005 R2 software. The virtual server hard disks can use UNC paths and externally connected disk drives but performance can be degraded based on the connection method. Connecting the host server to a Storage Area Network (SAN) is the best method to store virtual hard disks.

- **CD/DVD Drive**   A physical CD/DVD drive may be shared by more than one virtual machine. When a disk is inserted into the drive, the active virtual machine will automatically capture the optical drive. You can manually set other virtual machines to capture the optical drive by using the CD icon on the virtual machine status bar. It is best to configure the virtual servers to start up with the optical drive disconnected. An ISO image of a CD/DVD can also be mounted to the virtual CD/DVD instead of a physical CD/DVD.

- **Floppy Disk**   The physical floppy disk can be used by the virtual machines or a virtual floppy disk can be configured as a .vfd file. To share a virtual floppy disk (.vfd file) between virtual machines, the .vfd file has to be set to read-only. The physical floppy disk will be connected to the first virtual machine that can use it. It is best to configure the virtual servers to start up with the floppy disk drive disconnected or to create a virtual floppy disk for each virtual machine.

- **Com1 or Com2**   All devices attached to a COM port may be used by a virtual machine. Only one virtual machine at a time can access the physical COM ports of the host computer. When connected, the device is not available for use by other virtual machines. After the virtual machine releases the port or is shut down the COM port will become available to other virtual machines. It is best to configure the virtual servers to start up with the COM ports disconnected.

■ **LPT1**   Any device connected to the host computer LPT port can be used by a virtual machine. When the physical LPT port is connected to a virtual machine the device is not available to any other virtual machine or to the host computer until the virtual machine releases the LPT port or is shut down. Physical LPT ports are restricted to I/O address range from 0x378 through 0x37F. It is best to configure the virtual servers to start up with the LPT port disconnected.

Using the Administration Web Page

The administration Web page is the simplest method to use to create your virtual machine. If it is necessary to create several similar virtual machines on multiple host servers, it may be advantageous to use the programmatic functions in the Virtual Server SDK. For most instances you will likely use the administration Web page. Start by opening up your Internet browser and pointing it to http://*servername*/VirtualServer/VSWebApp.exe?view=1 where the *servername* is replaced with the name of the server hosting the administration Web page.

On the left-hand side of the page, select **Create** in the **Virtual Machines** section as shown in Figure 5.1.

Figure 5.1 Selecting the Virtual Machine Section

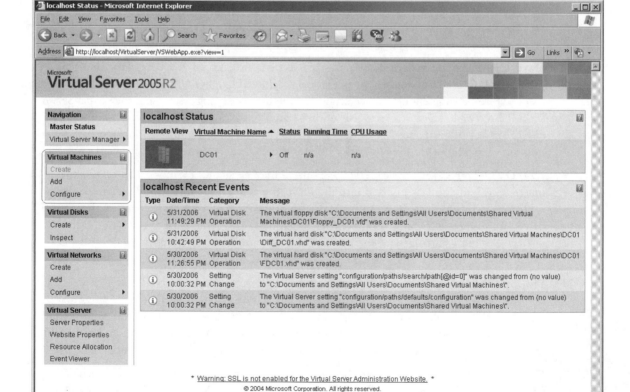

The Create Virtual Machine page appears. This page has all the initial configuration information for the new virtual server. You have several selection options on this page, as shown in Figure 5.2. The main ones are the name of the new virtual server, the virtual hard disk options, and the virtual network adapter.

Figure 5.2 Create Virtual Machine Settings

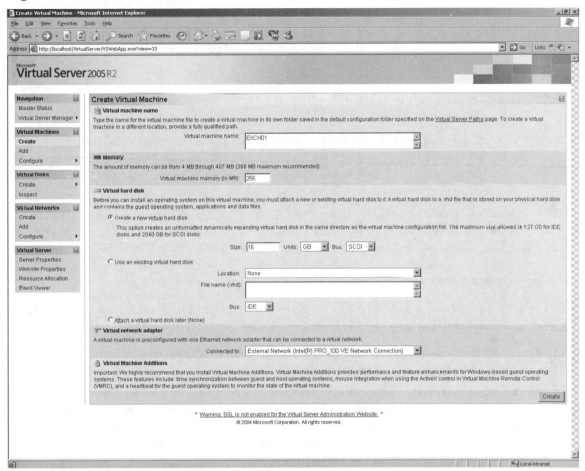

As you can see in Figure 5.2, the Create Virtual Machine page has five settings: Virtual machine name, Memory, Virtual hard disk, Virtual network adapter, and Virtual machine additions. The first thing to do is name the virtual machine. Each virtual machine must have a unique name. Just as you do when naming physical servers, it is best to use some sort of naming convention that makes sense to you.

Next, you need to set the amount of memory that this virtual machine will be allocated. This number is in megabytes (MB). You can be a little stingy on the memory settings if you want. A Windows 2003 Server will run fine on 256 MB of memory and very well on 388 MB. Remember that this memory is taken out of the useful pool of memory for the host server so you don't want to starve it either. You can always go back later and add more to this virtual machine if it really needs it.

The next stage is where you can create a new virtual hard disk or use one that you have already created. You can also elect not to attach a virtual hard disk at this time but a virtual machine must have a virtual hard disk to load an operating system. You have three options under the Virtual hard disk setting:

- **Create a new virtual hard disk**   Asks you to specify a size for the new virtual hard disk. This will create a dynamic virtual hard disk with the same name as the virtual machine name. You can select the size units for the disk drive: your choices are MB or GB. The next option is the bus type. The choices are SCSI or IDE. If SCSI is selected, the virtual hard disk size can be as big as 2040 GB. If IDE is selected, the virtual hard disk is limited to a maximum size of 127 GB.

- **Use an existing virtual hard disk**   Enables you to select a virtual hard disk that was previously created. You can either select one listed in the Location pull-down menu or enter the full path in the **Filename** box. You also need to select a bus type. The same choices and parameters apply.

- **Attach a virtual hard disk later (None)**   This option will create the virtual machine without a virtual hard disk. This may be useful if you are creating virtual machines with different memory and network setting but want to connect to a differential virtual hard disk that has not yet been created. You may also use this option to create the virtual machine before the conversion of a linked virtual hard disk is completed.

The area called Virtual network adapter connects the new virtual machine to one of three network options (virtual networks are covered in more detail in the next chapter):

- **Not Connected**   Means there is no network connected. This will make the virtual machine an island and it will to be able to trade files with any other server.

- **Internal Network**   Each host Virtual Server 2005 server supports an internal network. This will allow virtual machines hosted on this server to communicate with each other but not to any server outside of this host server. This is a good choice for isolation environments where an application must be protected or contained.

- **External Network**   This portion allows the virtual machine to bridge across the host's network interface card (NIC) to access resources on the external network like any other physical server.

After all your choices are entered, click the **Create** button at the bottom of the page. This will create your new virtual machine. Figure 5.3 shows the status page.

The virtual machine status page lists all the different pieces of virtual hardware and the status of the virtual machine. You will notice that the server icon in the upper area of the screen is grayed out. This means the virtual server is turned off. You will also notice that each of the pieces of virtual hardware is also a link to a property page for that piece of virtual hardware.

Figure 5.3 Virtual Machine Status Page

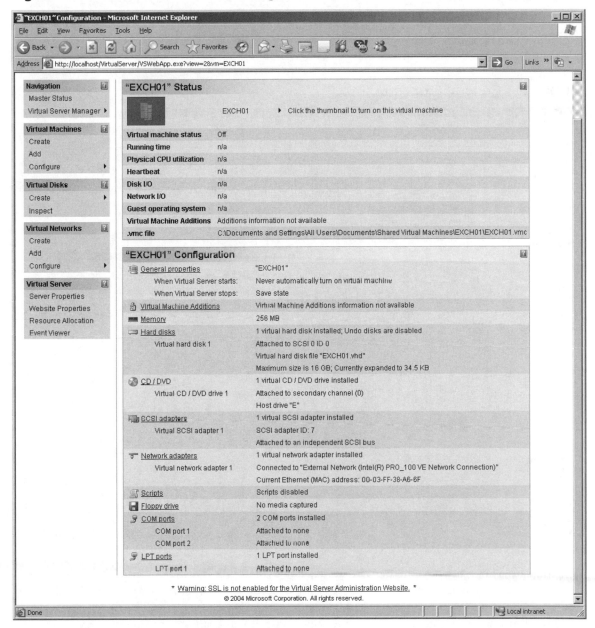

Virtual Machine Configuration

All the details of the virtual hardware are listed on the status page, as seen in Figure 5.3. Each configurable area is accessible from this page. In this section we will look at the different options that are available to us for the virtual machine.

General Properties

The name of the virtual machine and a description of its behavior on Virtual Server 2005 startup or shutdown are contained in this section. Click the **General properties** link. The Properties page will come up for the virtual machine, as shown in Figure 5.4.

Figure 5.4 General Properties

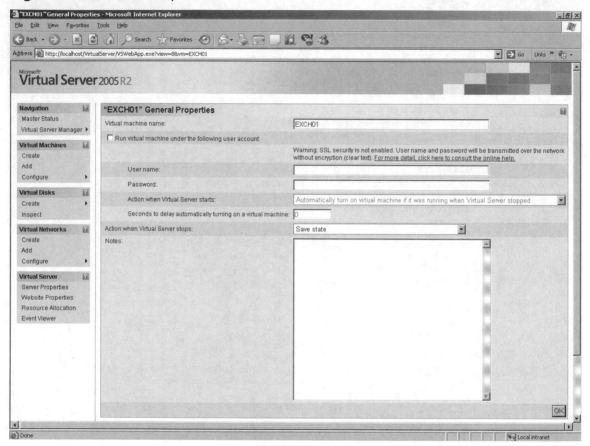

You can change the name of the virtual machine by entering it into the Virtual machine name box. This will not change the node name set in the operating system. This only changes the filename of the virtual machine configuration file. The configuration file is a .vmc file. The folder containing the virtual machine's configuration file is the same name. If you change the name of the virtual server, the configuration filename will change but not the folder containing it.

When the Run virtual machine under the following user account checkbox is checked, it enables the virtual machine to run under a specific user account. A user account must be specified in order for the virtual machine to start up automatically or run scripts based on Virtual Server events. After this box is checked and a user account with sufficient privileges is specified, the pull-down box Action when Virtual Server starts will become active. The options in the pull-down box enable you to:

- **Automatically turn on virtual machine if it was running when Virtual Server stopped**   Will restart the virtual machine if it was running when the Virtual Server was stopped or shut down. If the virtual machine was turned off when the Virtual Server was shut down, it will not be restarted when the Virtual Server starts up again.

- **Always automatically turn on virtual machine**   Will start up the virtual machine when the Virtual Server is restarted. This can be a very handy setting if there are several virtual machines on a Virtual Server computer.

- **Never automatically turn on virtual machine**   Will prevent the virtual machines from starting regardless of their previous state when the Virtual Server was stopped.

The Seconds to delay automatically turning on a virtual machine box will delay the virtual machine startup by the specified number of seconds. If there are several virtual machines on a Virtual Server, this setting will enable you to stagger their startup order. An example of this use would be to start the domain controllers before the file servers. The amount of time to specify depends on your hardware. A common setting is 30 to 60 seconds. The maximum amount of time you can specify is 86,400 seconds, or 24 hours.

The Action when Virtual Server stops drop-down box controls how the virtual machines react when the Virtual Server is shut down. This box presents you with three options:

- **Save state**   Will store the current state of the virtual machine. The virtual machine's memory and running processes are all maintained with this selection. When the Virtual Server is restarted, the virtual machine will return to the same state it was in when the Virtual Server was shut down.

- **Turn off virtual machine**   This option is the same as pushing the power button on a physical server. When the Virtual Server is shut down, the virtual machine is powered off. This is different from shutting down the virtual machines. Powering off a virtual machine could corrupt any open files and lose any unsaved data.

- **Shut down guest OS**   This option forces a controlled shutdown of the virtual machine. This option will close all open files and save data to the virtual hard disk.

The Notes section is a good place for any additional documentation for the virtual machine. This section is a good spot for listing the operating system service packs, network configuration, contact information, or just a good description of the function of this virtual machine.

The final section on this page is the Files Associated with section. This section includes the location information for the configuration file, the virtual hard disk, and the attached virtual network.

The Virtual Machine Configuration File

Each virtual machine has a configuration file associated with it. This file contains all the different setting and a list of the associated virtual hard disks and virtual networks. This file can be read with Notepad and is written in html format. This file can be directly edited with either a script or any text editor. Figure 5.5 shows some of what is contained in this file.

Figure 5.5 Virtual Machine Configuration File

```
13              <serial_number type="string">6160-6017-9286-8677-1579-8978-70</serial_number>
14          </chassis>
15          <cmos
16 type="bytes">00004000002037800 2FFFF0000000000000000000000000031004C0707070703B0FFFF2
17 08580FF00000000200C01800CFC0000000000000000000000000901A32E252580050E999E624010027
18 84004A2080240000000000085AACFE1032547698BAE40000000000000300000000000000000000000000
19 000000000000000000000000000000000000000000000000000000000000000000000000000000000000
20 000000000000000000000000000000000000000000000000000000000000000000000000000000000000
21 0000000000000000000000000000000000000000000000000000000000000000000000</cmos>
22          <time_bytes type="bytes">5200570023000018 0606</time_bytes>
23      </bios>
24              <memory>
25                  <ram_size type="integer">256</ram_size>
26              </memory>
27              <pci_bus>
28                  <ethernet_adapter>
29                      <controller_count type="integer">1</controller_count>
30                      <ethernet_controller id="0">
31                          <ethernet_card_address
32 type="bytes">0003FF38A66F</ethernet_card_address>
33                          <id type="integer">0</id>
34                          <virtual_network>
35                              <id
36 type="bytes">9A3A1C38EEF441D59B7317549651C16B</id>
37                              <name type="string">External Network (Intel(R)
38 PRO_100 VE Network Connection)</name>
39                          </virtual_network>
40                      </ethernet_controller>
41                  </ethernet_adapter>
42          <scsi_adapter>
43              <controller_count type="integer">1</controller_count>
44              <scsi_controller id="0">
45              <adapter_scsi_id type="integer">7</adapter_scsi_id>
46                  <adapter_shared type="boolean">false</adapter_shared>
47                  <id type="integer">1</id>
48                  <location id="0">
49                  <drive_type type="integer">1</drive_type>
50                  <pathname>
51                  <absolute type="string">C:\Documents and Settings\All
52 Users\Documents\Shared Virtual Machines\EXCH01\EXCH01.vhd</absolute>
53                  <relative type="string">.\EXCH01.vhd</relative>
54                  </pathname>
55                  <undo_pathname>
56                  <absolute type="string" />
```

Looking at the *memory* section on line numbers 24 through 27 in Figure 5.5, you can see the configured RAM size is currently 256 MB. By editing this number, you can add or reduce the amount of configured RAM this virtual machine will allocate when it is started. You can also look to see which virtual networks are connected by looking at line numbers 34–39. The virtual network ID is the hex number (line 36) associated to the virtual network name (lines 37 and 38). Do not edit these values unless you have the correct information for the new virtual network.

The most common reason to edit this file besides reallocating memory is to set the location of the virtual hard disk. Line numbers 50–54 give the absolute and relative path for the virtual hard disk. If this virtual machine is moved from the original location where it was created, these lines may need to be edited. Notice the bolded text in these lines because they give the absolute path and filenames associated with the virtual machine. This path must be able to be found on the new Virtual Server when the virtual machine starts up or it will fail to start. This is also why it is recommended to use descriptive names when creating virtual hard disks and virtual machines.

Virtual Machine Additions

Virtual Machine Additions provides additional features for Windows-based guest operating systems (see Figure 5.6). These enhancements include time synchronization between guest and host operating systems, mouse integration when using the ActiveX control in Virtual Machine Remote Control (VMRC), and a heartbeat for the guest operating system to monitor the virtual machine. It also does some kernel-level patching to let the virtual server component run on Ring 0.

Figure 5.6 Virtual Machine Additions Property Page

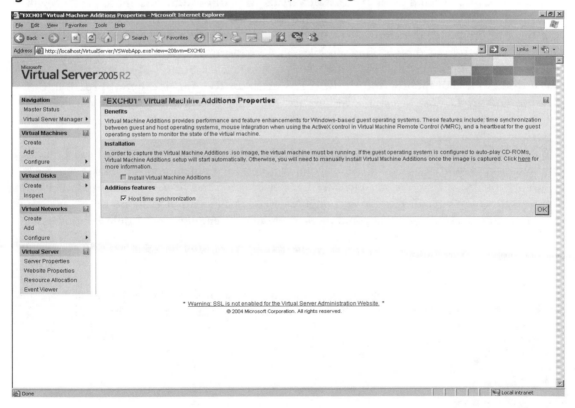

To install Virtual Machine Additions, the target virtual machine must be running with a Windows operating system. The supported Windows server operating systems are:

- Microsoft Windows Server 2003 (all 32-bit versions only)
- Microsoft Windows 2000 Server
- Microsoft Windows NT Server 4.0 with Service Pack 6a (SP6a)

Although desktop operating systems are supported on Virtual Server 2005 R2, they are not intended as a replacement for Terminal Services. Configuring a virtual machine with a desktop operating system is primarily intended for testing and configuration development. There are Virtual Machine Additions provided for the following Windows desktop operating systems:

- Microsoft Windows XP (all 32-bit versions only)
- Microsoft Windows 2000 Professional
- Microsoft Windows Millennium Edition
- Microsoft Windows 98
- Microsoft Windows 95

If the aforementioned operating systems are configured to autorun when a CD is inserted, just start the virtual machine and check the **Install Virtual Machine Additions** checkbox. This will automatically mount and run the Virtual Machine Additions .iso file. If it is necessary to manually install the tools, configure the virtual CD/DVD to use an ISO image file. The Virtual Machine Additions .iso file is located in C:\Program Files\Microsoft Virtual Server\Virtual Machine Additions\VMadditions.iso. After the ISO image is mounted, click **Start | Run** and type **d:\Windows\VirtualMachineAdditions.msi –s –v "/qn Reboot=ReallySuppress"** into the dialog box and press **Enter**. You will need to restart the virtual machine when the installation is finished. You can dismount the VMadditions.iso file from the virtual CD /DVD before restarting the virtual machine.

Checking the Host time synchronization box will synchronize the clock of the virtual machine operating system with the clock of the host computer operating system. You can disable the clock synchronization, by leaving this box unchecked or powering off the virtual machine and unchecking this box. If the guest operating system is configured as a domain controller, the host time synchronization should be disabled. If the guest and the host are in different domains or different time zones, then time synchronization should also be turned off.

Memory Properties

It is easy to adjust the amount of memory assigned to a virtual machine. From the virtual machine **Status** page, select the **Memory** link. The Memory Properties page appears, as shown in Figure 5.7.

Figure 5.7 Memory Properties Page

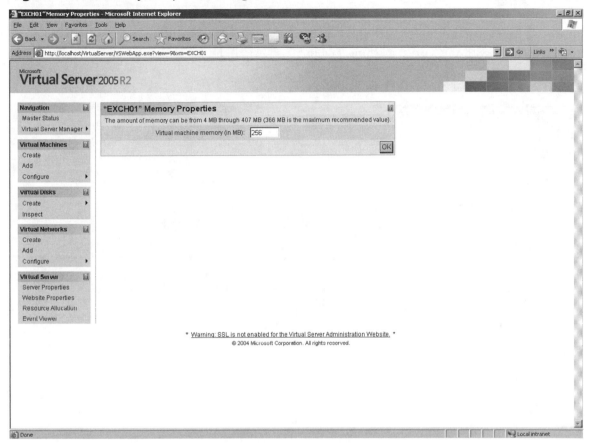

To adjust the amount of memory assigned to a virtual machine, it must be turned off just like a physical machine. Then enter the amount of memory to assign in the **Virtual machine memory (in MB)** box. Each virtual machine must have at least 4 MB of memory assigned but can have up to 3.6 GB. The limitation is tied to amount of memory installed in the host server and the amount of memory the host operating system can support. Click **OK** when you have assigned the memory.

It is important to remember that all virtual machines running on the Virtual Server must share the available memory resources. You cannot assign more memory than what is available for all running virtual machines and the host operating system. You will not be able to start a virtual machine that does not have enough physical memory to allocate to the virtual machine.

Hard Disks

Clicking the Hard Disks link form the virtual machine Status page will list all the attached virtual hard disks associated with this virtual machine. From this page you can add, modify, or remove hard disks associated with this virtual machine. Figure 5.8 shows all the various options.

Figure 5.8 Virtual Hard Disk Properties

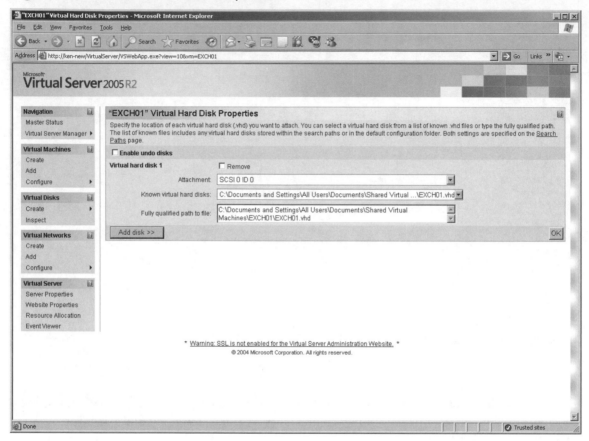

Each virtual machine needs to have a virtual hard disk associated with it. There can be one or more virtual hard disks associated with each virtual machine. Each virtual machine can support either IDE- or SCSI-connected virtual hard disks. To attach a virtual hard disk, the virtual machine must be powered off. Just like a physical server, you cannot connect virtual disk drives to a running virtual machine.

Looking at Figure 5.8 you will notice the available options:

- **Enable undo disk**   This checkbox enables you to create an undo disk. There is more on this feature later, but in short it enables you to load programs and data without writing the changes to the original disk. To enable the undo feature, just check the box for the selected virtual hard disk. To use the undo feature you should make sure there is sufficient storage on the host hard drives to store all the changes.

- **Remove**   This checkbox is fairly self explanatory. It will remove the selected virtual hard disk for the virtual machine. Simply check the **Remove** box for the desired virtual hard disk and then click **OK**. The virtual hard disk will be removed from the virtual machine. The virtual hard disk is not deleted, just removed from this virtual machine.

- **Attachment**   This pull-down box tells where the virtual hard disk will be connected to the virtual machine. There are two IDE interfaces with two connections, primary and slave, each. There is one SCSI bus with six available device IDs. The virtual SCSI bus normally uses ID 7 for itself. The maximum virtual hard disk size that can be used depends on whether it is attached to the virtual IDE or SCSI adapter. The IDE adapter supports virtual hard disks of up to 127 GB, and the SCSI adapter supports virtual hard disks of up to 2 terabytes (TB). Simply select the desired attachment point and click **OK**.

- **Known virtual hard disks**   You can select one of the previously registered virtual hard disks form the pull-down box and click OK to connect it to the virtual machine.

- **Fully qualified path to file**   If your desired virtual hard disk is not "known," just type the full path to the .vhd file in this box. This can be a UNC file path, but the resource must be online and available when the virtual machine starts up. Click **OK** when finished.

- **Add Disk**   This button enables you to attach another virtual hard disk to the virtual machine. You will be asked for attachment and virtual hard disk location information. You can attach several virtual hard disks to a virtual machine.

After all your virtual hard disks are connected and configured, click **OK** to write the configuration information into the virtual machine configuration file, .vmc.

CD/DVD

You can use the virtual CD or DVD drive to access physical media or International Organization for Standardization (ISO) 9660 images. This is a very important feature that will enable you to maintain a collection of .ISO files for the various operating system and program files in a central file share and mount these as needed without physically loading a CD or DVD in a physical drive. It also allows for several virtual machines to be loading software from different files at the same time without having to constantly change a CD or DVD. You change the Capture setting as appropriate to specify either the CD or DVD drive of the physical computer or an ISO image (see Figure 5.9). ISO images can be a maximum file size of 2.2 GB.

Figure 5.9 CD/DVD Drive Properties

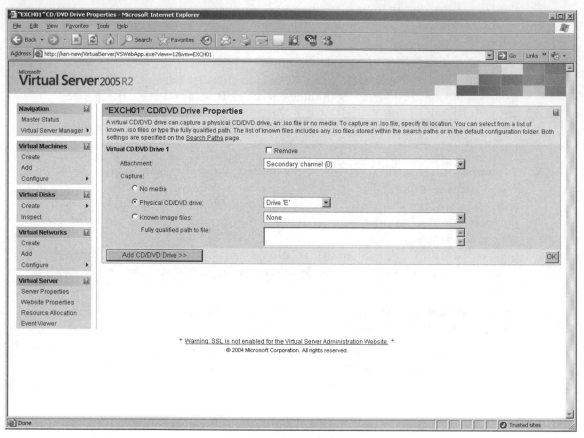

There are several options for the virtual CD/DVD.

Checking the Remove box will remove the virtual CD/DVD from the virtual machine configuration.

All the virtual CD/DVD drives are IDE devices. If you click the down arrow in the Attachment pull-down box, you will see only IDE devices. Available choices will be listed. Because of this restriction you can have only four CD/DVD devices on a virtual machine.

The Capture section tells the virtual machine where the virtual CD/DVD will look for its data files. You can modify the capture properties of the virtual CD/DVD drive while the virtual machine is running. After making your selections, click **OK**. Your choices are:

■ **No media**   This is the best selection if the virtual machine is not using the CD/DVD drive. If No media is selected, the virtual machine does not try to read the drive, so it will increase performance by not continually checking an empty drive. This setting will also prevent starting an installation if the autorun feature is enabled on the virtual machine and a disk is inserted into the physical CD/DVD.

- **Physical CD/DVD drive**   This selection enables the virtual machine to read the physical CD/DVD drive. The drive letter pull-down box will list the drive letters of the physical CD/DVD drives on the host server.

- **Known image files**   This is the selection to use if you want to mount an ISO image file. Click the down arrow on the **Known image files** pull-down box and select the desired image file. If the desired file is not listed, you can enter the fully qualified path into the textbox. This can be a UNC name but the resource must be available to the virtual server.

The Add CD/DVD Drive button enables you to add another virtual CD/DVD drive to the virtual machine. You will have the same options for the additional devices as you have with the initial device. Remember that because you can only use the virtual IDE adapter you are limited to four devices.

SCSI Adapters

SCSI adapters are added to virtual machines to provide additional storage or to cluster virtual machines. As many as four SCSI adapters can be configured on a virtual machine. Each virtual SCSI adapter will support up to seven virtual hard disks. Each virtual hard disk can be of up to 2TB in size.

Enabling a SCSI adapter will also enable the clustering of two virtual machines. You can use server clusters to either test failover between two virtual machines or for training purposes. You *cannot*, however, use server clusters with Virtual Server to fail over between physical computers. Clustering is typically used with Virtual Server in a test or training environment and is *not* intended as a high-availability solution in a production environment.

If you require high availability and want to use Virtual Server, you should consider storing your virtual machines on a SAN and connect additional Virtual Server computers to the SAN. This will enable the rapid recovery of the virtual machine on a different physical computer.

Figure 5.10 shows the SCSI Adapter Properties page.

There are only a few options to configure. Clicking **OK** will apply the setting and update the configuration file for the virtual machine. The options include:

- **Remove**   Checking this box and clicking **OK** will remove the adapter for the virtual machine.

- **Share SCSI bus for clustering**   Checking this box will enable clustering between virtual machines on the same Virtual Server computer. Remember that clustering of virtual machines is only for high availability of the virtual machines. These virtual machines are still dependent on the Virtual Server computer and its resources. Use clustered virtual machines only for training or testing of applications in a clustered environment.

- **SCSI adapter ID**   This pull-down box enables you to set the SCSI device ID for the virtual adapter. This is defaulted to ID 7 but some devices will try to reserve a specific SCSI ID. This setting enables you to change the adapter address as needed. This may also be desirable when setting up a virtual server for clustering. By setting the SCSI adapter ID to something other than ID 7, it will be easy to identify this adapter as the clustered adapter.

Figure 5.10 SCSI Adapter Properties

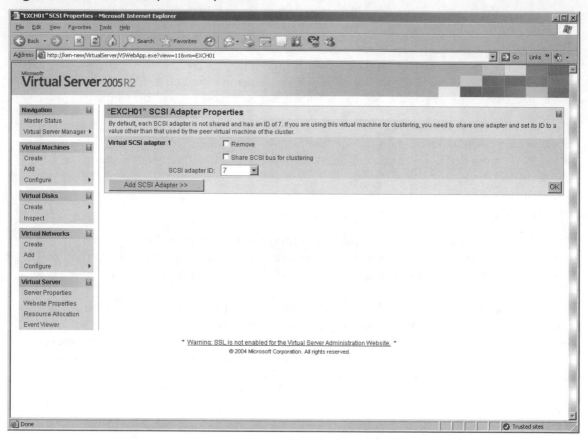

■   **Add SCSI adapter**   Clicking this button adds another virtual SCSI adapter to the virtual machine. You can have up to four virtual SCSI adapters per virtual machine. Each adapter can support up to seven devices with a maximum size of 2TB. That is 56TB per virtual machine!

Network Adapters

From the Network Adapters property page you can add or remove a virtual network adapter or modify the properties of an existing one. Each virtual machine can be configured with up to four virtual network adapters. Figure 5.11 shows the Network Adapter Property page.

This page has a few options. Clicking **OK** will apply the changes and update the virtual machine configuration file. These options are Remove, Connected to, and Ethernet MAC address.

Checking the Remove box will remove the selected virtual network adapter from the virtual machine.

The Connected to pull-down box offers different options for connecting the virtual machine. When a virtual machine is created, it has one virtual network adapter connected to the internal network. You can configure each network adapter to one of the following connections:

Figure 5.11 Network Adapter Properties

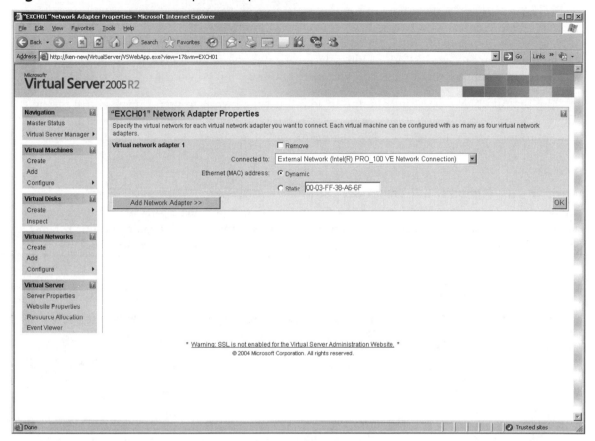

- **Internal** Connects the virtual machine to a virtual network that is available only to other virtual machines on the same Virtual Server computer. This type of network is isolated from the external network of the physical computer.

- **External** Connects the virtual machine to the external network through the network adapter of the physical computer. The virtual machine is visible to all other networked computers in your environment.

- **Microsoft Loopback Adapter** Connects the virtual machine to a virtual network that provides networking between the guest operating system and host operating system. This enables a method of connecting files and transferring data between the Virtual Server computer's disks and the virtual machine.

- **Ethernet MAC address** This setting is the virtual network adapter's Media Access Control (MAC) address. This is the hardware address of the adapter and must be unique for every device on the network. There are two settings for this property: Dynamic and Static. In the Dynamic setting the MAC address will be assigned dynamically by the Virtual

Server when the virtual machine is created. This is the default and for almost all configurations there is no reason to change it. With the Static setting you must supply the MAC address. This setting may be required to gain access to network resources that utilize MAC filtering. If you migrated a physical server to a virtual environment it may be necessary to set this MAC address. Just make sure the physical network adapter from the old computer is not reused on your network or a conflict will exist.

Use the Add Network Adapter button to add a virtual network adapter to your virtual machine. You will be presented with the same options for connection and configuration as before. You can have up to four virtual network adapters per virtual machine.

Scripts

If you have the virtual machine configured to start up under a specific username, scripts can be assigned. You can specify a script or a command-line action to run when a particular event occurs. You can also remove a script that was specified previously. Virtual Server executes command-line parameters or scripts that you specify for a virtual machine event. Figure 5.12 shows the Scripts Properties page.

Figure 5.12 Scripts Properties Page

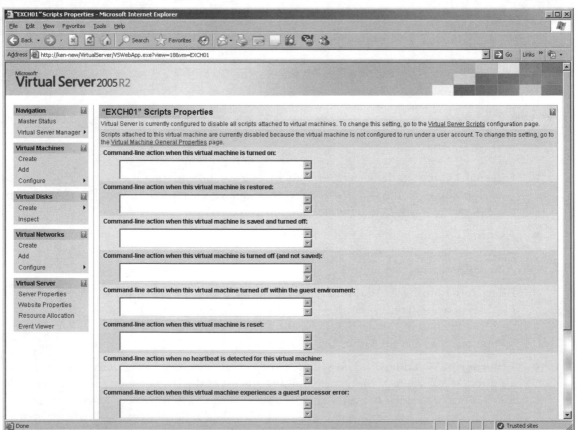

To run a script, the following syntax is used: *script_engine script_name*. You can run a script named Exchange_Start.vbs by using *Cscript* as follows:

```
cscript Exchange_Start.vbs
```

If Virtual Server cannot execute a command, it is recorded in the Virtual Server event log. If the script is executed but results in an error, the error is not recorded in the Virtual Server event log because it only validates that the command line was executed.

Before you can run a script on a virtual machine, you must enable scripting for virtual machines and you must configure a user account for the virtual machine to run under. This user account must have adequate privileges to execute the assigned scripts. There are several types of events that can be used to trigger virtual machine scripts (see Table 5.1).

Table 5.1 Events That Trigger Virtual Machine Scripts

Event	Description
This virtual machine is turned on.	This virtual machine is turned on.
This virtual machine is restored.	This virtual machine is restored from a saved state.
This virtual machine is saved and turned off.	State is saved for this virtual machine.
This virtual machine is turned off.	This virtual machine is turned off without its state being saved.
This virtual machine is turned off within the guest environment.	This virtual machine is turned off because a user shut down the guest operating system.
This virtual machine is reset.	This virtual machine is reset.
No heartbeat is detected for this virtual machine.	A heartbeat for a virtual machine has not been received for three minutes, as follows: One heartbeat per minute is expected. When no heartbeat is detected for more than a minute, Virtual Server prompts the guest operating system for a heartbeat every 10 seconds for two minutes. If no heartbeat is detected at the end of two minutes, this event is generated.
This virtual machine experiences a guest processor error.	Virtual Server receives an error from this virtual machine's processor.
This virtual machine receives a warning due to low disk space on the physical computer.	Virtual Server has received a warning about low physical disk space for the virtual hard disk attached to this virtual machine. This warning is generated when available disk space is at or below 100 MB.
This virtual machine receives an error due to low disk space on the physical computer.	Virtual Server has received an error about low physical disk space for the virtual hard disk attached to this virtual machine. This error means that there is no longer any available disk space. The virtual machine pauses until more disk space is available.

Floppy Disk Drive

Every virtual machine has a single floppy disk drive. This drive cannot be removed and you cannot add floppy disk drives to the virtual machine. You can, like with the virtual CD/DVD, use either the host computer's physical floppy disk drive or an image file for the virtual floppy disk drive. Figure 5.13 shows the properties of the virtual floppy disk drive.

Figure 5.13 Floppy Drive Properties

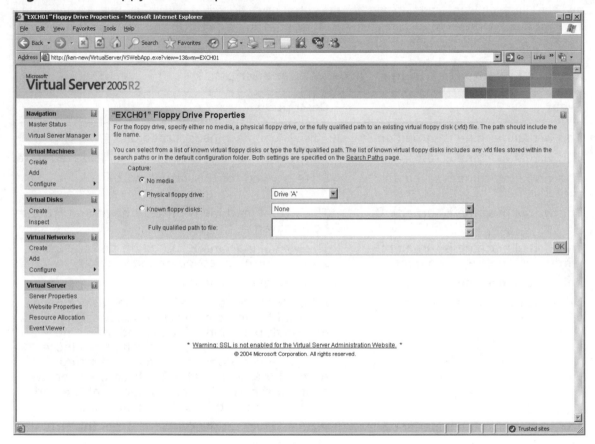

There are only three choices for the Capture property (After making your selection you must click OK to apply):

- **No media**   This choice effectively turns off the virtual floppy disk drive. This can be used to improve performance of the virtual machine by telling it to not check the virtual floppy disk to see if there is media in the drive. This is also the best setting for normal operation of the virtual machine.

- **Physical floppy disk drive**   This selection captures the host computer's floppy disk drive. The pull-down box lists the drive letters of the floppy disk drives on the host computer. This setting should be used when transferring data or starting a program that is on a floppy disk. You should not leave this setting active after you are finished with the floppy disk operation. All virtual machines that capture the host floppy disk drive will see the inserted floppy disk and can access it.

■   **Known floppy disk**   The pull-down box will list the known virtual floppy disk files. These are the .vfd files that are created when building virtual floppy disk files. You can select one of these or enter the fully qualified path to another virtual floppy disk file into the Fully qualified path to file box. You can use UNC file paths for this, but the resource must be accessible to the virtual machine.

You may notice there is no button to add floppy disk drives. Each virtual machine can have only one virtual floppy disk drive.

COM Ports

The COM Port Properties page for the virtual machine configures the COM port properties. A virtual machine can use COM ports for communications between the virtual machine and a device or file. Each virtual machine can configure one or two COM ports. Figure 5.14 shows the Com Port Properties page.

Figure 5.14 COM Port Properties

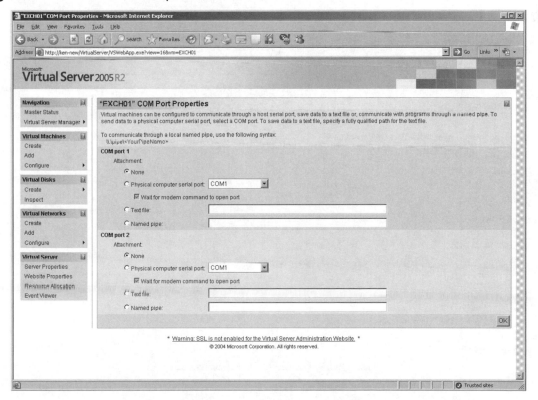

Both COM ports have the same set of properties. The Attachment options are:

■   **None**   The virtual COM port is not connected. This is the default setting and should be the normal configuration unless the virtual machine is actually using the COM port.

- **Physical computer serial port**   Will connect the virtual COM port to the host computer serial ports. The pull-down box will list the configured serial ports on the host computer. There is an additional checkbox to force the COM port to "Wait for a modem command to open port." The virtual machine can only reference COM ports 1 through 4 on the host computer.

- **Text file**   Will write the COM port output to a text file. The text file location is specified by the fully qualified path in the dialog box. When typing paths to folders or files, local file paths reference the computer running the Virtual Server service. You must use a UNC path if the file or folder referenced is on a computer other than the one running the Virtual Server service.

- **Named Pipe**   To use this option you must type the local named pipe to use in the textbox.

LPT Ports

The LPT Port Properties page of the virtual machine enables or disables the parallel port (LPT port). If a parallel device is connected to the physical computer, and you want to make the device accessible to the virtual machine, use this page to specify the port on the physical computer to which the device is attached. Figure 5.15 shows the LPT Port Properties page.

Figure 5.15 LPT Port Properties

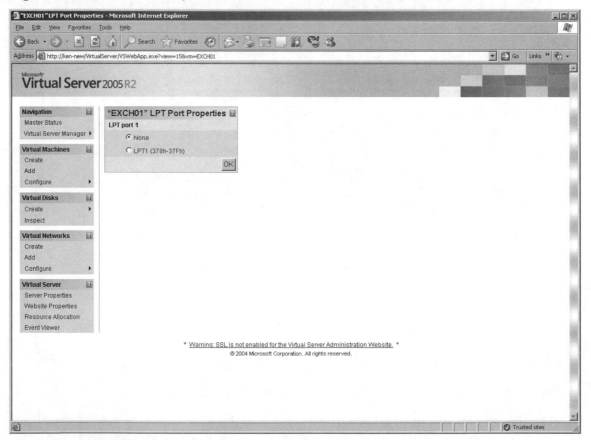

There are only two options on this page to be configured. Clicking OK applies the selection to the virtual machine configuration file.

- **None**   Turns off the virtual LPT port. This is the default for the virtual machines.
- **LPT1 (378h-37Fh)**   This is the physical LPT port on the host computer. If there is more than one LPT port on the physical computer, then there will be multiple choices for an LPT port. It may be necessary for the virtual machine to read the LPT port of the host computer. Direct access to a scanner or a software dongle may be necessary for a virtual machine. Printing is more easily accomplished by using the virtual network and printing to a shared printer.

Adding Hardware to the Server

Adding hardware to your virtual machines is accomplished by modifying the properties of the virtual server. From the Virtual Server Status page as seen in Figure 5.3, you can modify the amount of memory, virtual hard disk, virtual CD/DVD, virtual SCSI adapters, and virtual network adapters. Using these virtual hardware devices it is possible to build very large and advanced virtual machines, but the host computer must have access to the physical resources to support these virtual devices.

Adding hardware resources to the physical computer running the Virtual Server service normally requires shutting down the host computer, thereby making the all the virtual machines also shut down. This is best performed during a scheduled down time for a production host computer. The physical computer must have available expansion slots and be capable of supporting all the physical resources required by the virtual machines. If the host computer cannot access and manage a physical device, then the virtual machines cannot access the device either.

Building the Host Server

We have already covered how to add hardware to our virtual machines, but not how we can maximize the hardware resources of the host computer. This is an important section because the virtual machines cannot take advantage of any resource that the host computer cannot utilize. There are also some limitations of the virtual machines not being able to take advantage of all the possible resources a physical computer could utilize.

Processors

All virtual machines are single-processor computers. That does not mean the host computer is restrained to a single processor. If the host computer operating system can utilize multiple processors, then an overall performance increase can be gained in the virtual machines because there are more physical processors to be shared among the virtual machines. This also means a larger number of physical processors can support more virtual machines than a single processor host computer.

Memory

Although having a large amount of memory in a host computer makes supporting multiple virtual machines possible, there is a limitation on the host computer's supported memory amount. If you are planning to use more than 4 GB of RAM in the host computer, you should consider running the

Enterprise or Data Center edition of Windows Server. Even if you are planning to allocate the bulk of the system memory to the virtual machines, the host operating system must be able to manage all the memory on the host computer. If your host computer hardware can support the x64 version of the host operating system, you can support more memory by using the x64 version of the host operating system.

Storage Systems

The virtual machines are actually large files on the host computer. That means the disk subsystem has to be able to accommodate these files and be able to read and write to them at high speed. The type of disk storage subsystem is transparent to virtual machines. There is no need to support Redundant Array of Inexpensive Disks (RAID) controllers or SAN host bus adapters (HBA) in a virtual machine. They will use the available storage of the assigned virtual disk drives. Where these virtual disk drives physically reside is important only if the host computer cannot access them.

This means that a SAN HBA placed into a host computer can be shared by all the virtual machines to access the SAN storage available to the host computer. This also means the virtual machines (remember these are just large files) can be physically located on the SAN storage. This gives you the capability to run these virtual machines from any of the connected host computers running Virtual Server 2005 R2. This is a very powerful disaster-recovery benefit. It also enables the complete change out or failure of a host computer.

A larger RAID array or SAN storage can be utilized to maintain ISO images of software and operating systems and different virtual floppy disk drive images (.vfd) so they can be mounted to the virtual machine without the need to actually load a CDROM or floppy disk. This capability enables a lights out environment and gives the administrator the ability to manage the virtual machines from anywhere they can access the Virtual Machine Web page.

Network Cards

The host computer can support multiple network interface cards (NIC) to connect it to one or more local area networks (LAN). Each virtual machine can be assigned a virtual network connection running on a specific physical NIC in the host server.

This capability enables better control of the network load distribution to a single LAN or enables connection of the virtual machines to separate LAN segments while running on the same physical host. If all the virtual machines are going to connect to the same LAN, the additional NIC cards can be teamed to provide additional bandwidth to the physical host computer and additional network performance for the virtual machines. Additional information on virtual networks is contained in later chapters.

COM an LPT Ports

Although each virtual machine can access these, they are not commonly used. The virtual machines are limited in the number of attached devices for these host computer resources. In practice, most servers do not have anything attached to these ports and in many cases servers do not even have these ports anymore.

Some software packages require a COM or LPT port for reading a dongle. This dongle is attached to a COM or LPT port on a computer. In these instances it is necessary to configure the virtual machine's virtual COM or LPT port to read the host computer's COM or LPT port.

USB Ports

Although the virtual machines do not have Universal Serial Bus (USB) ports, the host computer can take advantage of these. Attaching disk drives or memory sticks to a host computer's USB ports will enable the host to share the connected disk resources with the virtual machines. This is the only way a virtual machine can access a USB device. The virtual machines must be powered off or restarted when the USB device is connected to the host in order to be seen and utilized by the virtual machine. But the machine has to be turned down when the USB device is inserted. Failure to do so will leave a message that the server cannot find the disk.

Installing a Windows OS

Now that you have your virtual machine built and configured, you must load an operating system before you can use it. The Virtual Server R2 supports all but the Data Center version of Windows Server 2003 (32-bit versions only), Windows 2000 Server Standard and Advanced, Windows NT 4.0 SP6a, and Windows XP SP2 (32-bit versions only).

All these operating systems can be loaded in separate virtual machines running on the same host computer. This capability does *not* mean that Microsoft will support an operating system or other software that has reached its end of life. If you are going to run one of these older operating systems, you should understand the support limitations.

Each virtual machine emulates a specific set of virtual hardware that is supported directly by the supported Microsoft operating systems so there should be no difficulty with drivers or other virtual hardware. Table 5.2 includes a specific list of virtual hardware.

Table 5.2 Virtual Hardware

Component	Emulated Hardware
Basic input/output system (BIOS)	American Megatrends (AMI) BIOS using the Intel 440BX chip set with PIIX4.
Floppy disk drive	Supports a single 1.44 MB floppy disk drive.
Serial (COM) port	Emulates up to two serial ports.
Printer (LPT) port	Emulates a single printer port that maps to the physical parallel port.
Mouse	Emulates a standard PS/2 Microsoft IntelliMouse® pointing device.
Keyboard	Emulates a standard PS/2 101-key Microsoft keyboard.
Network Adapter (multifunction)	Emulates the multi-port DEC/Intel 21140 10/100TX 100 MB Ethernet network adapter with one to four network connections.
Processor	Virtual machines use the CPU of the physical computer. Guest operating systems see only a single CPU.

Continued

Table 5.2 Continued

Component	Emulated Hardware
Memory	Supports 3.6 GB of RAM per virtual machine.
Video card	Emulates the S3 Trio64 graphics adapter with 4 MB of VRAM.
IDE/ATAPI storage	Emulates up to four IDE devices up to 127 MB per IDE channel.
SCSI storage	Emulates the Adaptec 7870 SCSI adapter chip set. Up to four SCSI adapters on a virtual machine with support for up to seven virtual hard disks of up to 2 TB each.

Loading the Operating System

To load a supported Windows operating system from the Virtual Server R2 Administration Web page, select the virtual machine you want to load. Click the **right arrow** next to the server name and select **Edit Configuration** (see Figure 5.16).

Figure 5.16 Virtual Server Administration Web Page

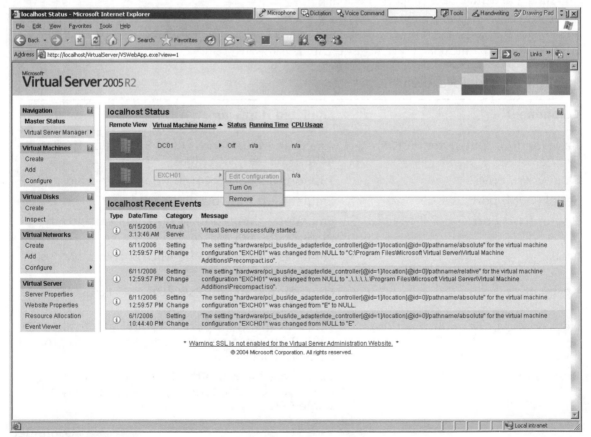

Select the **CD/DVD** section of the virtual machine **Status** page (see Figure 5.17).

Figure 5.17 Selecting the CD/DVD Section of the Virtual Machine Status Page

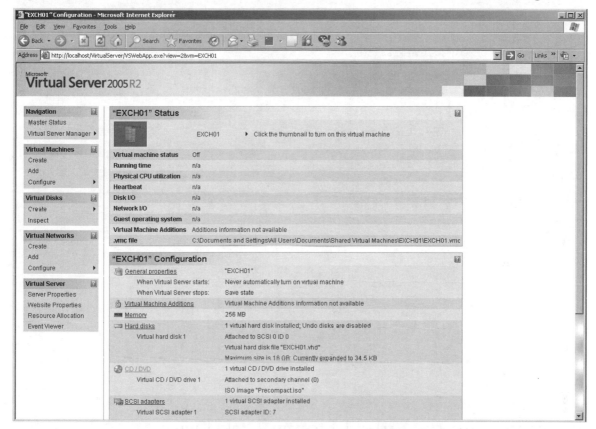

On the **CD/DVD Properties** page, select the source for the operating system files
(see Figure 5.18).

By default, the virtual machine is set to boot from the CD/DVD drive.

- If you are using the host computer's CD/DVD drive, select the **Physical CD/DVD drive** option and the **drive letter** for the selected CD/DVD drive on the host computer. Insert the CD media into the drive.

- If you are using an image file, select the **Known image file** option and select the path from the pull-down box or enter the fully qualified path for the image file in the dialog box. You can use a UNC path for the image file but it must be accessible to the virtual machine.

Click **OK** when finished.

Figure 5.18 Selecting the Source for the OS

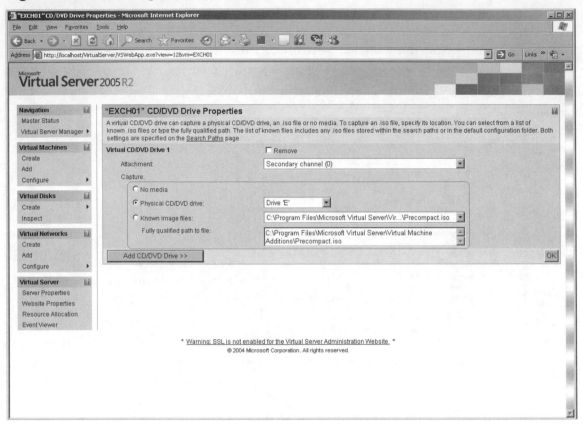

Booting from the Virtual Floppy Disk Drive

Most operating systems today use a bootable CD to start the build process, but Virtual Server 2005 R2 does support booting from the virtual floppy disk drive. If you are trying to load an operating system that uses a boot floppy disk, you will need to configure the virtual floppy disk drive.

From the virtual machine **Status** page, select the floppy disk drive link as seen in Figure 5.19.

Figure 5.19 Selecting the Floppy Disk Drive Link

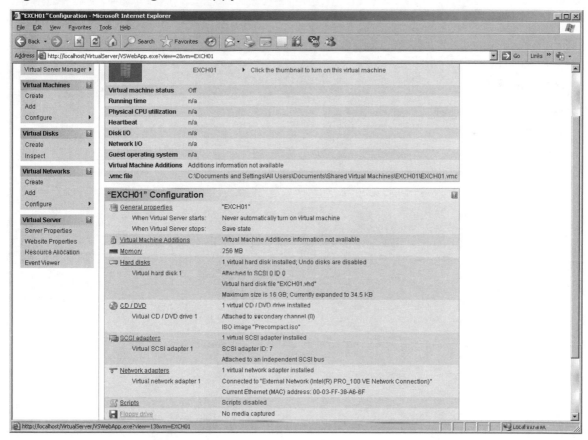

Select the **Physical floppy drive** from the **Capture** section, as shown in Figure 5.20, or select a virtual floppy disk file in the **Known floppy disk** pull-down list. You can also enter the fully qualified path in the textbox for the .vfd file.

Click **OK** when finished.

Figure 5.20 Floppy Drive Properties

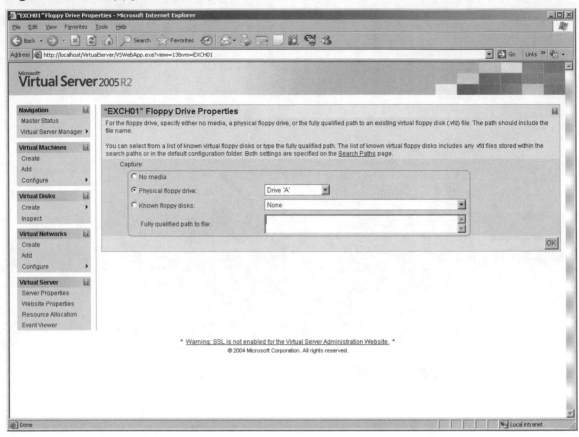

Starting the Virtual Machine

Now that you have your boot media all set up, you are ready to start the virtual machine. Simply go to the Virtual Server Administration Web page, as seen in Figure 5.21.

Figure 5.21 Starting the Virtual Machine

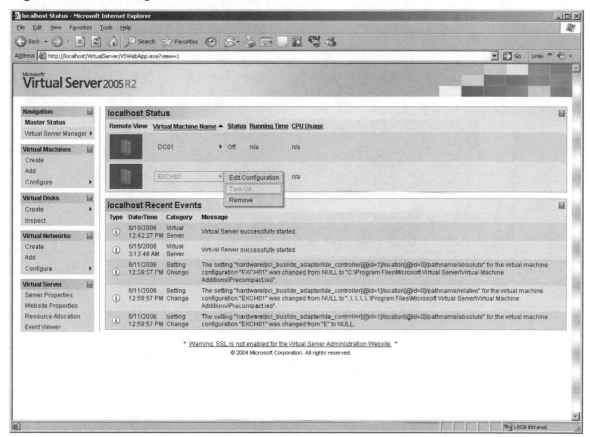

Select the virtual machine you want to start, click the **right arrow**, and then select **Turn On**.
You will notice the picture for your virtual machine will change as it powers up. Click this
thumbnail image to start the remote manager (see Figure 5.22).

Figure 5.22 Virtual Machine Status Page

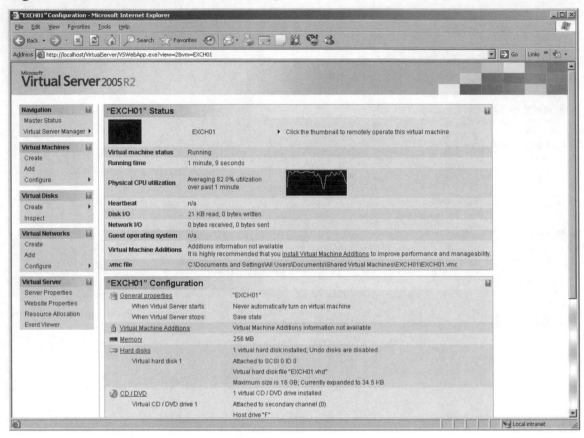

After the remote manager starts, you will see a screen similar to a normal video monitor showing the text portion of the Windows operating system load, as shown in Figure 5.23.

Figure 5.23 Remote Control Screen

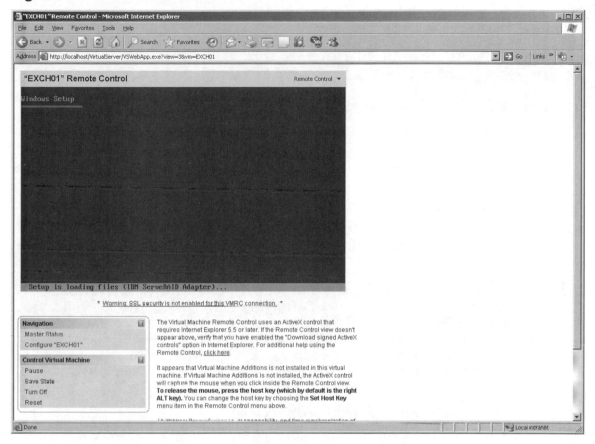

You will notice in the lower-left corner of this screen that there are several controls and instructions to work with the remote console. They are highlighted in a red box to help you identify them. This section is divided into two sections: Navigation and Control Virtual Machine.

You will notice that to pass mouse and keyboard control to the virtual machine, you need to click the remote console screen. To regain control of the keyboard and mouse, you need to press the Right Alt key on the keyboard.

Configuring & Implementing…

Using SCSI in a Microsoft Windows OS

This is the right time to tell the operating system about the SCSI device that can exist in the machine.

Directly after the start, the following text appears: "Press F6 to configure add…." During this message press F6. This will enable you to load the Virtual Server SCSI Shunt driver. If you do not load this driver and your hard disks are based on SCSI, the installation can take anywhere between one to eight hours.

So remember: whenever possible use SCSI as hard disk controller and when you use SCSI, load the Virtual Machine SCSI driver to speed up the installation and performance of the VM.

Using a SCSI Adapter and disk for the virtual machine is the preferred choice for a virtual machine. It enables a larger drive size and can support more virtual hard drives. Although it is possible to load some of the later Windows Server operating systems without loading the SCSI Shunt driver, the setup and formatting of these drives can take a significant amount of time. It is best to use the virtual SCSI Shunt driver found in the Virtual Machine Additions as a virtual floppy disk (.vfd) file. There are drivers for Windows Server 2003, Windows 2000, and Windows XP only.

To use this virtual SCSI Shunt diver:

1. Start your operating system build as normal.

2. When you get to the text portion asking you if you want to add additional hardware ("Press F6 to add…"), press **F6**.

3. In the **Virtual Machine Configuration** Web page, select the **Floppy Drive**.

4. Select **Known floppy disks** in the **Capture** section. Enter the path to the SCSI Shunt Driver.vfd file and click **OK**. This is by default C:\Program Files\ Microsoft Virtual Server\Virtual Machine Additions\SCSI Shunt Driver.vfd.

5. On the virtual machine console page, type **S** and press **Enter**.

6. Select the driver for the guest operating system you are loading and press **Enter**.

7. Continue the rest of the operating system load as normal.

Using this virtual SCSI adapter will greatly speed up the performance of the operating system load and the overall performance of the virtual machine.

If you want to load a virtual machine with Windows NT 4.0, you will need to switch the virtual hard disk to an IDE drive in the virtual machine configuration page. After the operating system is loaded you can load the Virtual Machine Additions and switch the virtual hard disk back to the SCSI adapter.

Navigation

There are two options under the Navigation section. Clicking these navigation options will not stop the virtual machine.

- **Master Status**   Takes you back to the main Virtual Server Administration page.
- **Configure "Virtual Machine Name"**   Takes you to the selected virtual machine configuration page.

Control the Virtual Machine

These options are control functions for the virtual machine. Clicking one these will affect the operation of the virtual server.

- **Pause**   Will temporarily halt a running virtual machine without discarding memory.
- **Resume**   will restart the paused virtual machine.
- **Save State**   Saves the current state of the virtual machine and stops the virtual machine from running. A temporary file is created in the same location as the virtual machine configuration files with a .vsv extension. When the virtual machine is restored from a saved state, it returns to the condition it was in when its state was saved.
- **Turn Off**   Turns off the virtual machine without saving any state information. This has the same effect as pressing the power button on a physical computer.
- **Reset**   Resets the virtual machine. This is the same as pressing the reset button on a physical computer.

Installing the Operating System

Continue to install the operating system as you would on a physical computer. You may notice that this is faster than most physical computers because we are taking advantage of the virtual disk systems.

As the text portion of the install is performed, you may notice that Windows is using hardware that may not be installed in the host computer. Figure 5.24 shows this.

Figure 5.24 Formatting a Virtual Disk

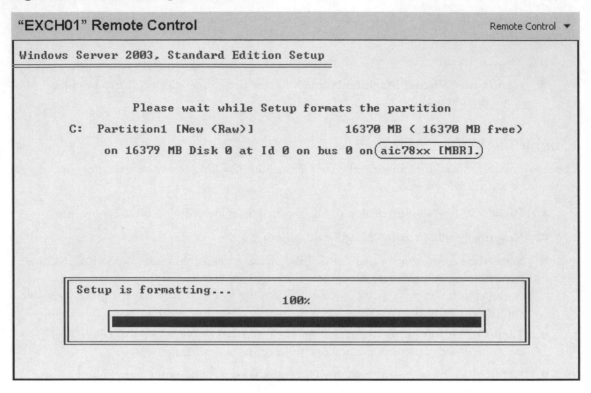

Notice the aic78xx that is circled in Figure 5.24. This is the virtual SCSI bus controller. Continue installing the operating system as normal. When the end of the graphic portion finishes and the last reboot has been performed, your virtual machine is ready.

This might be the time you want to consider using a differential disk for additional virtual machines running the same operating system. These enable you to have a standard operating system build and apply any changes to it for the individual virtual machines. You can also use sysprep or other cloning tools to create multiple copies of this virtual machine to be used as the base for other virtual machines.

Figure 5.25 shows the finished Windows Server 2003 running in a virtual machine.

Figure 5.25 Finished Windows Server 2003 Virtual Machine

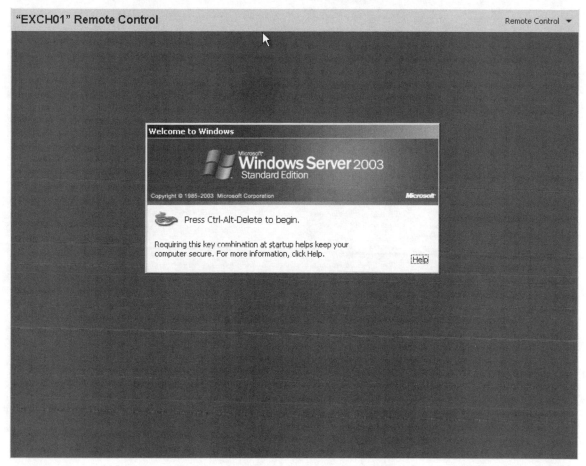

To log on to the virtual machine, press the **Host Key + Delete**. The Host key is the right ALT key on the keyboard.

Installing Virtual Machine Additions

The Virtual Machine Additions are a set of features that improve integration of the host computer and virtual machine operating systems, and the performance of the guest operating system. While these are not required for operation of the virtual machines, it is recommended they be loaded.

To load the Virtual Machine Additions, start at the **Status** page for your virtual machine. Under **Configuration**, click **Virtual Machine Additions**, as shown in Figure 5.26.

Figure 5.26 Configuring Virtual Machine Additions

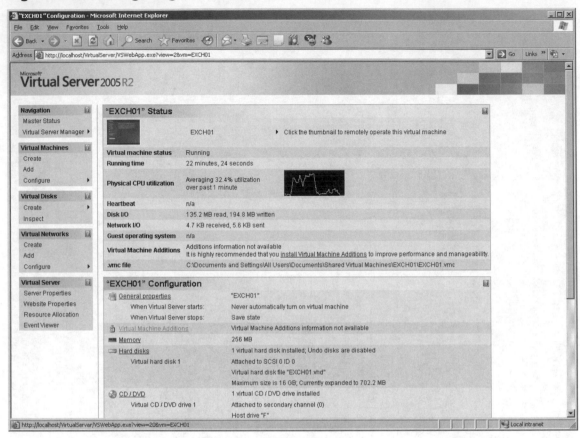

Select **Install Virtual Machine Additions**, as shown in Figure 5.27, and then click **OK**.

Figure 5.27 Install Virtual Machine Additions

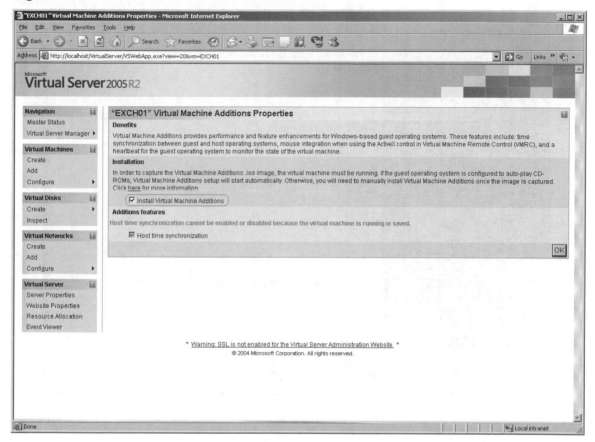

Log on to the virtual machine with an administrative account. You can use either the Administration Web site Remote Control or the Virtual Machine Remote Control client.

When logged on, the Virtual Machine Additions installation wizard will start. Click **Next** (see Figure 5.28).

Figure 5.28 Installing Virtual Machine Additions

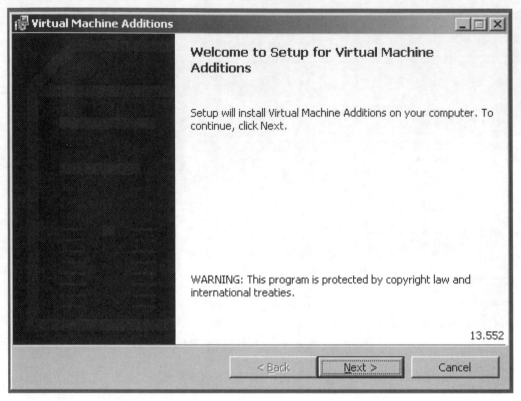

Click **Finish** (see Figure 5.29).

Figure 5.29 Completing the Setup of Virtual Machine Additions

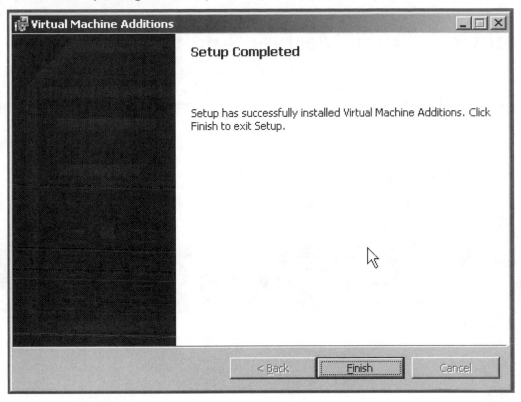

After the wizard is complete, you will be prompted to restart the virtual machine to complete the installation (see Figure 5.30).

Figure 5.30 Reboot Prompt

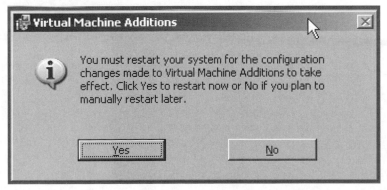

After reboot, you will notice that the keyboard and mouse control is passed by simply locating the mouse over the virtual machine console window.

Removing Virtual Machine Additions

It may be necessary to remove the Virtual Machine Additions. Removing them is just like removing any other piece of software: Select **Settings | Control Panel | Add or Remove Programs**.

Select **Virtual Machine Additions**, and then click **Remove**. Click **Yes** if prompted to confirm removing the Virtual Machine Additions (see Figure 5.31).

Figure 5.31 Removing Virtual Machine Additions

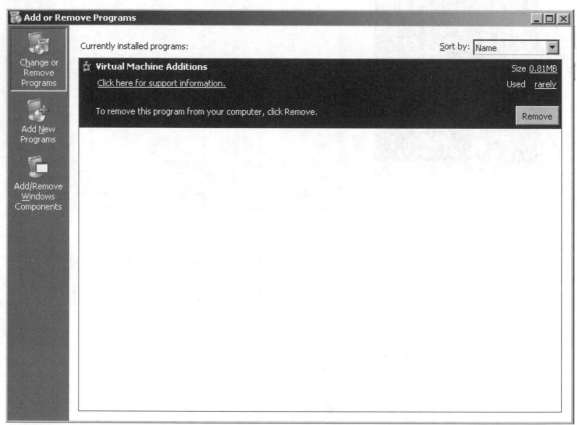

You will need to restart the virtual machine after the Virtual Machine Additions have been removed. Click **Yes** when prompted to restart the virtual machine or click **No** to restart later.

Installing a Non-Windows OS

Virtual Server 2005 R2 does support non-Microsoft operating systems. Although almost all Intel-based operating systems are supported, there are some limitations. The most important is that the operating system must be no more than 32 bit. While Virtual Server 2005 R2 can run on a 64-bit Windows platform, it will only support 32-bit guest operating systems. The most common alternate operating system to Windows is a version of Linux. We will be demonstrating the compatibility with SuSE Linux 10, but almost all of the popular versions will work. Table 5.3 lists the supported versions as of the time if this book. You should check the Microsoft Support site for any additional supported versions.

Table 5.3 Non-Microsoft Operating Systems Supported by Virtual Server 2005 R2

Enterprise Distributions	Standard Distributions
Red Hat Enterprise Linux 2.1 (update 6)	Red Hat Linux 7.3
Red Hat Enterprise Linux 3 (update 6)	Red Hat Linux 9.0
Red Hat Enterprise Linux 4	SuSE Linux 9.2
SuSE Linux Enterprise Server 9	SuSE Linux 9.3
	SuSE Linux 10.0

Remember that just because your version of Linux is not on this table does not mean that it will not work. You will need to try it and see.

Creating the Virtual Machine

You still create the virtual machine just like with a Windows operating system. The big difference is you may not need as much memory or additional resources.

On the **Virtual Server Administration** Web page, in the **Virtual Machines** section, click **Create**. Figure 5.32 shows the virtual machine configuration page.

Figure 5.32 Create Virtual Machine Page

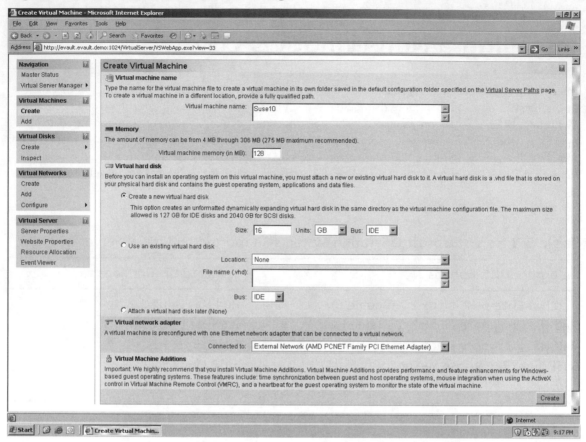

Give the new virtual machine a name and set the other properties as described previously in this chapter. Notice that all the pertinent virtual devices can be configured from this page. When you are finished entering the size and location information, click **Create** to create the new virtual machine (see Figure 5.33).

Figure 5.33 New Virtual Machine Status Page

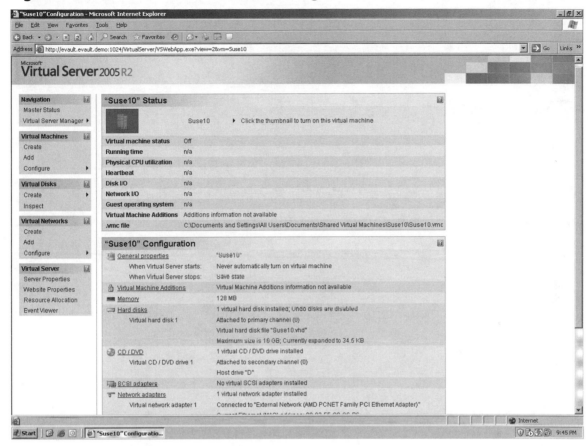

Verify the connection of the virtual CD/DVD or the virtual floppy disk drive by clicking the link and selecting the connection state (see Figure 5.34). Click **OK**.

Figure 5.34 CD/DVD Properties

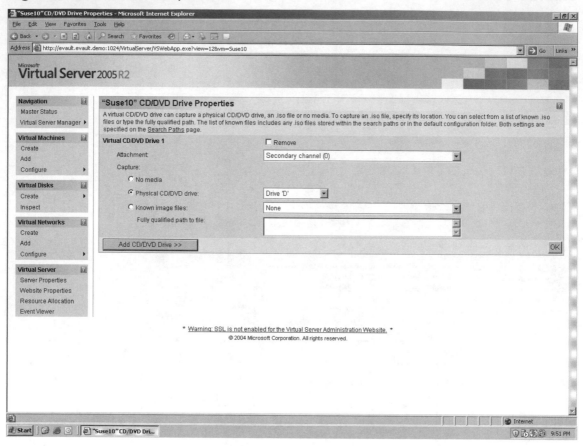

Insert the CD/DVD or boot media and power on the virtual machine. As the virtual machine starts it will begin the setup process. Figure 5.35 shows the startup screen.

Figure 5.35 SuSE Linux Install Screen

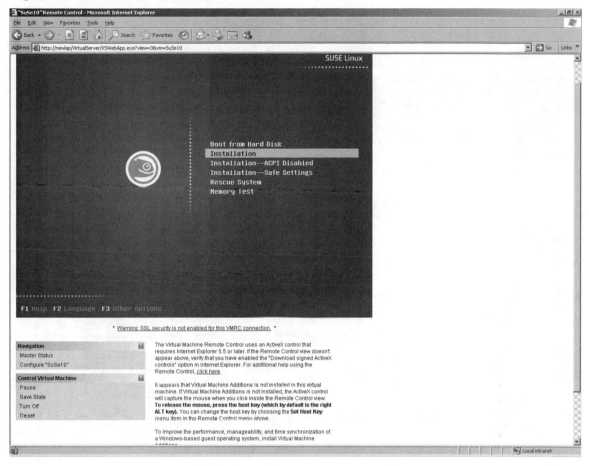

Just follow the prompts and answer the setup questions like you would on a normal installation on a physical computer. As the setup continues, the operating system will find the virtual hardware and configure it for use.

After the installation is complete, you can log on and run the virtual machine just like a physical computer installation. Figure 5.36 shows SuSE Linux 10 running as a virtual machine on a Windows Virtual Server 2005 computer.

Figure 5.36 SuSE Linux 10 Desktop

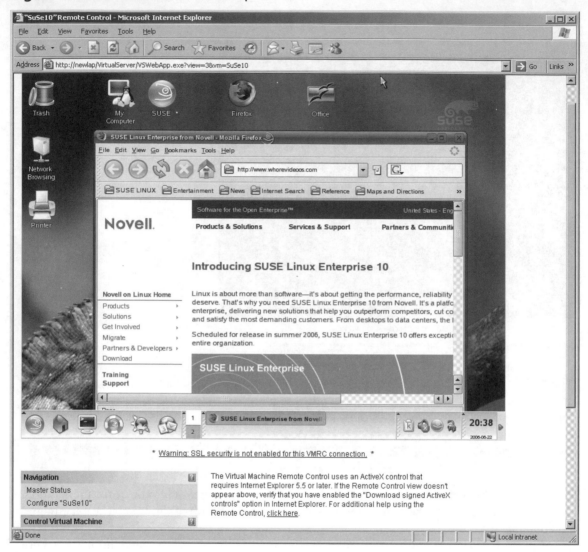

Virtual Machine Additions for Linux

Microsoft has released Virtual Machine Additions for Linux. You may have to register, but they are free additions to your Virtual Server 2005 R2. You can get them at www.connect.microsoft.com/content/content.aspx?ContentID=1475&SiteID=154.

After you have downloaded them, you have to install them on the host computer. Just double-click to install the file (see Figure 5.37).

Figure 5.37 VMAdditions for Linux

Click **Next** (see Figure 5.38).

Figure 5.38 Installation Startup

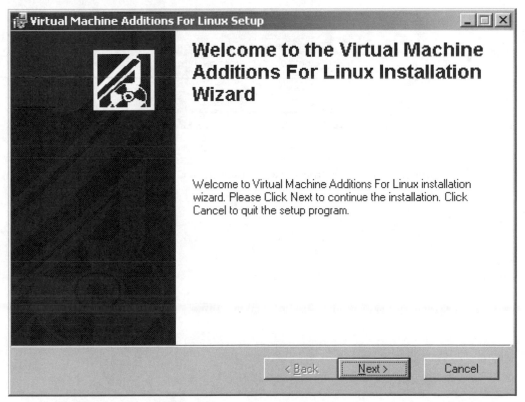

Accept the license agreement and click **Next** (see Figure 5.39).

Figure 5.39 License Agreement

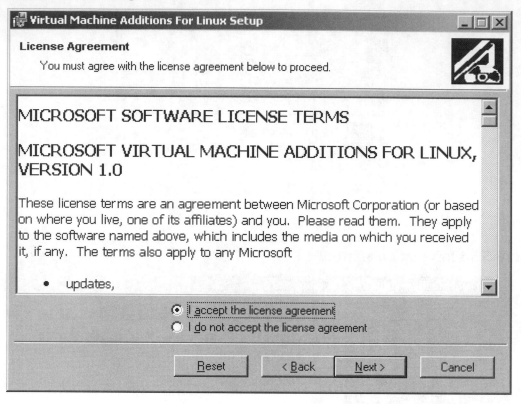

Select the **Destination Folder** for the software installation and click **Next** (see Figure 5.40).

Figure 5.40 Destination Folder

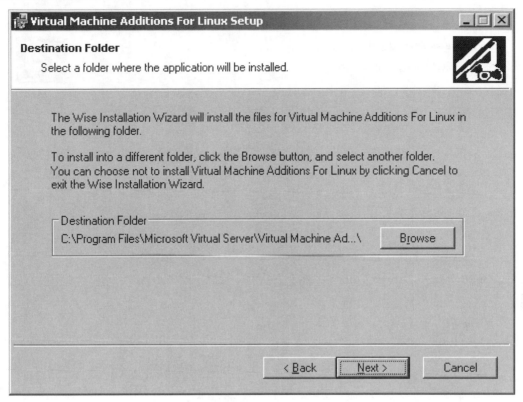

Click **Next** to start the installation (see Figure 5.41).

Figure 5.41 Ready to Install

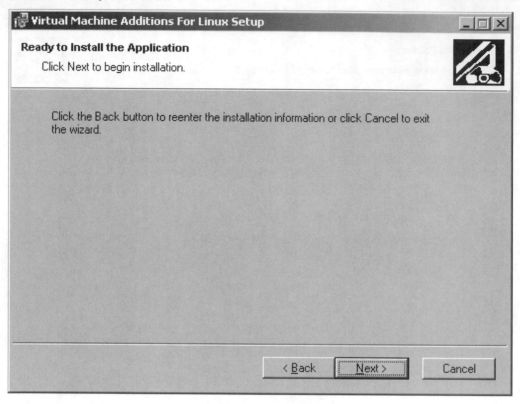

Click **Finish** (see Figure 5.42).

Figure 5.42 Finishing the Installation

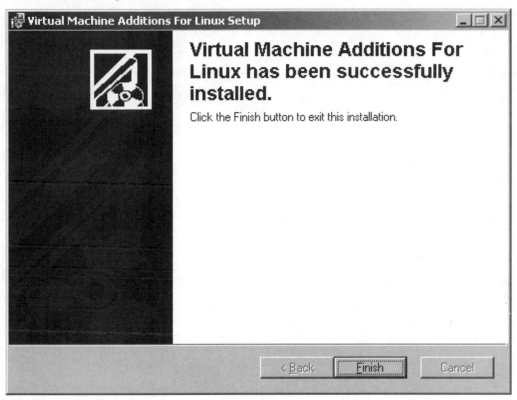

From the Virtual Server Administration Web page, select the Linux virtual machine (see Figure 5.43).

Figure 5.43 Linux Status Page

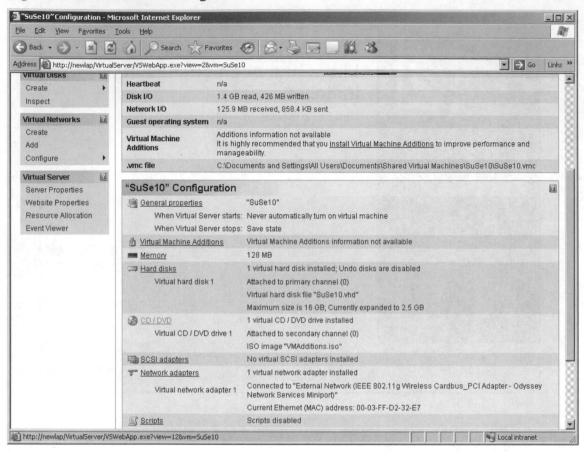

Select **CD/DVD** (see Figure 5.44).

Figure 5.44 CD/DVD Properties

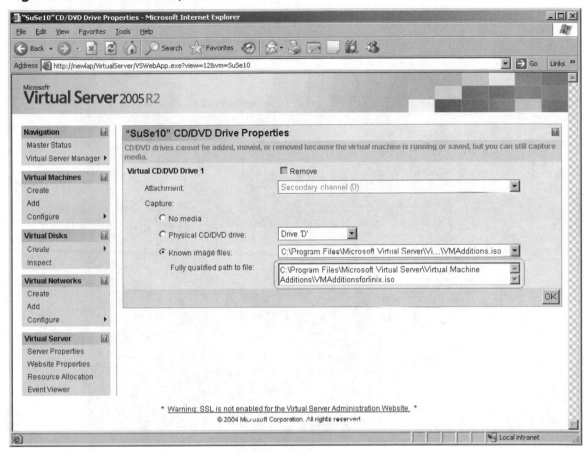

Enter the fully qualified path to the **VMAdditionsForLinux.iso** file. Make sure the virtual machine is running so the .ISO file can be mounted to the virtual machine. Click **OK**.

Click **Open** (see Figure 5.45).

Figure 5.45 Mounting the CD

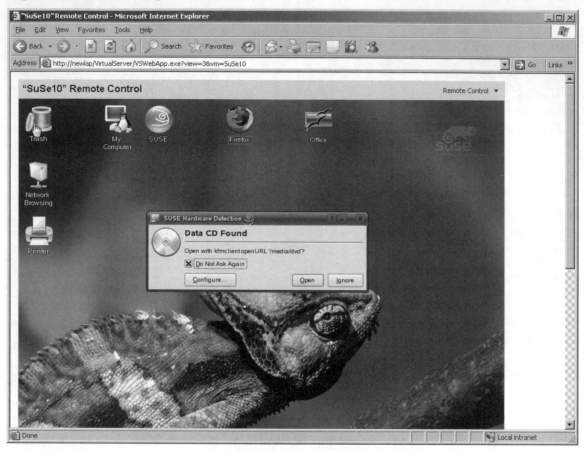

Double-click the **VMAdditionsForLinux** file (see Figure 5.46).

Figure 5.46 Starting the Install

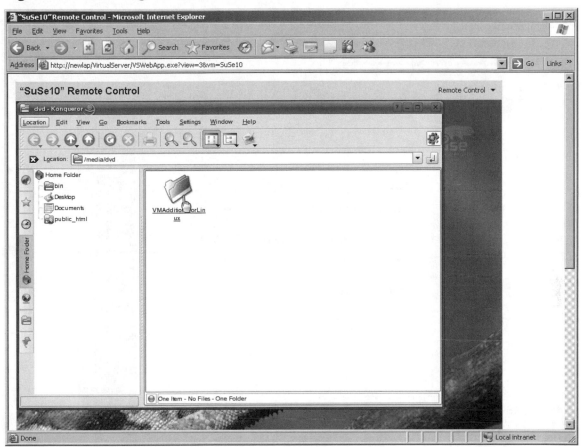

Double-click the **vmadd-full-0.0.1-1.rpm** icon to start the installation of all modules (see Figure 5.47).

NOTICE

Some versions of Linux will not support all the Virtual Machine Additions for Linux. If you experience problems with loading or starting the service, you may want to load the virtual machine additions one at a time. The individual files are shown in Figure 5.47.

Figure 5.47 vmadd-full-0.0.1-1.rpm

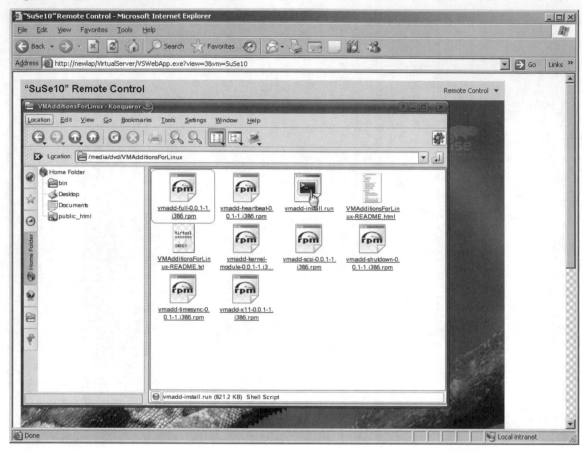

Click **Install Package with YaST** (see Figure 5.48).

Figure 5.48 Installing the RPM Package

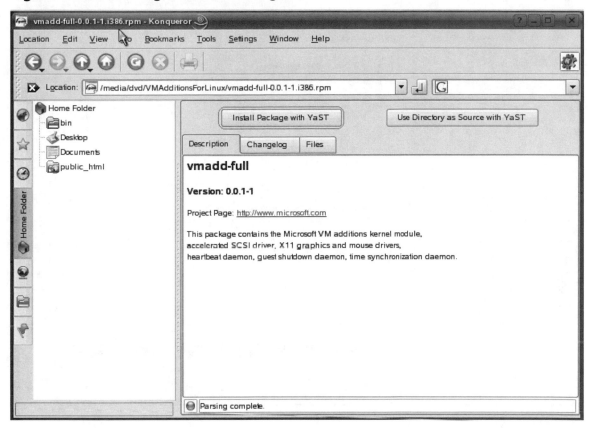

YaST will install the RPM package (see Figure 5.49). After the install is finished, you still must start the services or restart the virtual machine.

Figure 5.49 Installing with YaST

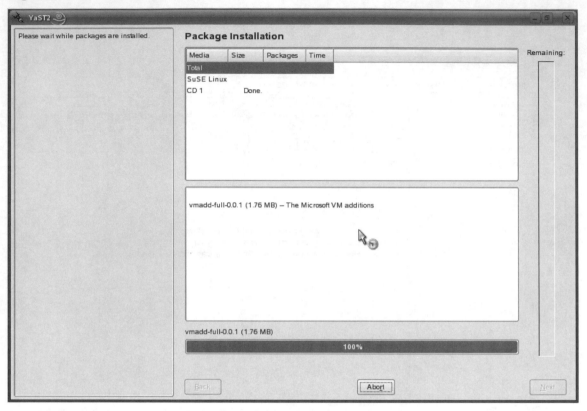

You can now move the control of the keyboard and mouse seamlessly between the virtual machine and the host computer desktop.

Designing & Planning...

Infrastructure in a Box

With Virtual Server's capability to host multiple networks and different operating systems, you have the opportunity to build a complete data center in a single physical server. With just two physical NIC cards you can create a complete virtual infrastructure (see Figure 5.50).

Figure 5.50 Virtual Infrastructure

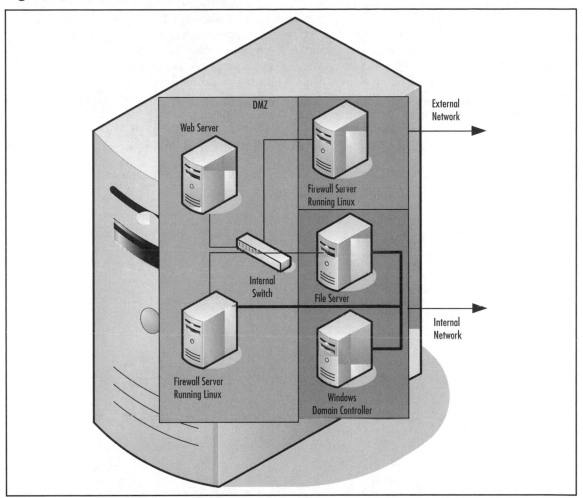

A Linux server running a firewall software package connects to the outside Internet connection. Data is passed back to one of the internal network switches of the Virtual Server. In this DMZ area, the Web server and/or the mail server is running. Another firewall server blocks the internal network from the DMZ. On the internal network, the domain controller and file server connect the local users to their internal resources.

A dual processor server running Windows Server 2003 Standard with 2 to 4 GB of memory and two NIC cards should be sufficient to support the design in Figure 5.50. These specifications are just a guideline and the actual performance and needed resources will vary on your application of the software and demand for the virtual machines.

Continued

This type of solution could be used to deploy a branch office or small office/home office (SOHO). A single host server in a small rack-mounted format can be sent out preconfigured to these locations along with instructions on connecting the computer. Network cables come in multiple colors, so it is easy to designate which cables go into which ports. The fact that the virtual machines can be preconfigured means that they can be set up and tested before sending out to the remote sites.

After they are connected to the network, the virtual server and the virtual machines can be managed remotely. This means the home office doesn't have to send an IT resource to set up the computers at the remote location. There are additional tools on the Virtual Server 2005 Web page from Microsoft to assist in managing multiple virtual servers.

Summary

In this chapter we looked at the different components of the virtual machine and how to create them. Each of the chapter sections showed all the different options and how to add or alter their properties. The creation of virtual machines and the loading of both Microsoft and alternate operating systems were covered along with the use of the Virtual Machine Additions.

There are four different kinds of virtual disks. Each has its own function and by combining the different types is possible to create a basic operating system disk and then apply a differential disk to customize each virtual machine. A fixed disk can be used to reserve all the needed hard drive space for a virtual hard disk. Linked disks can attach a physical partition to a virtual machine to migrate from a physical drive to a virtual drive.

Creating the virtual server along with editing the properties of the virtual components were covered in this chapter. Adjusting the memory, disk, CD/DVD, floppy disk drive, and network adapters all combine to create the virtual server. We discussed adding virtual hardware and connecting a virtual CD/DVD and floppy disk drive to either an ISO image or the physical disk of the host computer. We also looked at the other ports for COM and LPT. We looked at the limitations of a virtual machine and how to stop, pause, and start them. By connecting the virtual hard disks to virtual SCSI adapters and configuring the maximum size virtual hard disk, very large virtual machines can be created very easily and quickly.

Adding hardware to the server can add additional capacity and performance to the host computer. Adding faster processors or additional processors, memory, and NIC cards, and disk subsystems are the primary resources that will increase the capacity of the Virtual Server host computer. All the virtual machines are single-processor machines but a multiprocessor host computer can run many more virtual machines than a single-processor host. Using a host operating system that can support larger memory capacities and multiple processors are good choices for production host computers.

Installing a Windows OS to a virtual machine is very similar to installing on a physical computer. With a common set of virtual hardware, a *golden* image of the installation can be developed. Then using a differential virtual hard drive, applications, service packs, and configurations can be tested before committing to these changes. These images can also be cloned to rapidly deploy new virtual machines without doing a complete install of the operating system.

Installing virtual machine tools enables a better experience with the virtual machines. Versions for both Windows and Linux are available and we have installed both on our virtual machines. These network, SCSI, keyboard, and mouse drivers improve performance and enable a smooth passing of control between the virtual machines and the host computer.

Installing a non-Windows OS was shown. The installation was very similar to a normal installation on a physical computer. Virtual Server 2005 supports the major Linux distributions and provides Virtual Machine Additions for Linux to help improve their performance and operation on the host computer. It is very possible and reasonable to run a mix of operating systems on the same Virtual Server host computer.

Solutions Fast Track

Creating a Virtual Disk

☑ Dynamic virtual hard disks are the default and start small but grow as necessary to the configured size. These are good choices for virtual machines that are newly created and do not require all the disk space at once. As a dynamic disk file grows larger then the physical disk drive can handle, it can be moved to a large physical disk drive or partition.

☑ Fixed virtual hard disks allocate all the configured space at once. This is the method used when a physical disk is migrated to a virtual hard disk. This is best used if a virtual machine requires all the allocated drive space at once.

☑ Linked virtual hard disks are connected to physical partitions and used mainly for migration of physical machines to virtual machines. They are seen as fixed-size disks.

Creating the Virtual Server

☑ Allocate only the amount of memory actually needed. Memory can be increased if necessary but must be available on the host computer before it can be allocated.

☑ Virtual hard disk controllers can be IDE or SCSI. IDE can only support virtual hard disk up to 128 GB in size. The virtual SCSI supports virtual hard disks up to 2TB in size. You can also support more devices on a virtual SCSI than a virtual IDE interface.

☑ The virtual floppy disk and the virtual CD/DVD should be configured to "not connected" state unless you are actually using these devices on the virtual machine. Using image files enables you to manage and configure several different virtual machines without having to load a physical floppy disk or CD/DVD in the host computer.

Adding Hardware to the Server

☑ The hardware in a Virtual Server host computer must be recognized and supported by the Windows version loaded on it.

☑ Processors, memory, and storage subsystems are the most valuable upgrades to the host computer. These are the primary resources used by the virtual machines. Additional network cards can also be used by the virtual machines.

☑ Virtual machines can share host computer resources. This feature makes adding HBA cards, RAID cards, and SAN connections more practical on a Virtual Server host computer. The cost of these devices can be share across all the virtual machines making the return on investment (ROI) easier to justify. Hey, cost is always an object.

Installing a Windows OS

☑ Create the virtual machine from the Virtual Server Administration Web page.

- Configure a new virtual hard disk.

- Connect to an existing virtual hard disk.

- Define the memory for the virtual machine.

☑ Connect the virtual CD/DVD or virtual floppy disk drive to the host computer's CD or floppy disk drive or use an image file.

☑ Start the virtual server and load the operating system like a physical computer.

☑ Use the SCSI Shunt driver to speed up the performance of Windows Server 2003, Windows 2000, and Windows XP virtual machines.

Installing Virtual Machine Tools

☑ Virtual Machine Additions improve the video, mouse, keyboard, and network performance of the virtual machines. They should be loaded on all virtual machines if possible.

☑ Use the checkbox in Virtual Machine Additions Properties page of the virtual machine status to load it. This is an .iso image file that is mounted to the virtual machine when you check the checkbox and click OK.

☑ Remove the Virtual Machine Additions from the virtual machine by selecting **Start | Settings | Control Panel | Add or Remove Software**. This is just like any other software loaded on a physical computer.

Installing a Non-Windows OS

☑ Create the virtual machine from the Virtual Server Administration Web page.

- Configure a new virtual hard disk.

- Connect to an existing virtual hard disk.

- Define the memory for the virtual machine.

☑ Connect the virtual CD/DVD or virtual floppy disk drive to the host computer's CD or floppy disk drive or use an image file.

☑ Start the Virtual Server and load the operating system like a physical computer.

☑ Load the Virtual Machine Additions for the Linux operating system if applicable. These have to be downloaded from Microsoft's Web site. They are installed by connecting the virtual CD/DVD to the .ISO image and running the script or .rpm file.

☑ You must reboot or start the services for the Virtual Machine Additions to work in the Linux-based virtual machines.

Frequently Asked Questions

Q: What operating systems can run Virtual Server 2005 R2?

A: Microsoft Windows Server 2003 Standard, Enterprise, or Datacenter Edition either 32 or 64 versions; Windows XP Pro SP2; and Windows Small Business Server 2003 Standard or Premium Edition can be used as the host operating system. Windows XP Pro SP2 is supported only as a development platform and not as a production environment.

Q: What guest operating systems are supported?

A: Virtually any 32-bit operating system for the Intel platform can be run in Virtual Server 2005 R2. There is a list of supported operating systems on the Microsoft Virtual Server Web site. Basically any version of Windows Server except Datacenter from NT 4 SP6a through Server 2003 R2 can be a guest on the Virtual Server. Windows XP SP2 can also be run as a virtual machine. Almost all the current popular versions on Linux can also be run as a guest operating system.

Q: How many virtual machines can be run on a host server?

A: This depends a lot on the resources of the Virtual Server host. The host must be able to support the needed memory of the guest virtual machine. Processor and disk requirements must also be met by the Virtual Server host computer. Adding processors and storage space along with memory can greatly improve the number and performance of the guest virtual machines. The supported limit is 64 and has a very clear reason: The MAC Address of a virtual machine is based on a manufacturer ID of three bytes (in this case Microsoft), a unique ID one byte and the last two bytes of the host adapter. The unique ID can be anything between 0 and 255. Every virtual machine can have a maximum of four NICs and 256 divided by 4 equals 64. However, besides the hardware specifications, there is no limit on virtual machines, only the number of NICs.

Q: Can Virtual Server 2005 R2 run on a 64-bit operating system?

A: Yes, but all the guest virtual machines must be running a 32-bit operating system. A 64-bit host operating system will enable increased memory support and higher performance of the host computer so additional virtual machines can be supported on the same host computer hardware than on a 32-bit operating system running on the same computer. Regardless of the version of host operating system (32- or 64-bit versions) the supported limit of 64 virtual machines is still in force.

Q: Can I have a 64-bit guest operating system?

A: No, at this time only 32-bit operating systems are supported by Virtual Server 2005 R2. Each guest virtual machine is also limited to a single processor configuration.

Q: How many virtual hard disks can I have on a virtual machine?

A: Each virtual machine can support up to 31 virtual hard disks. Each virtual machine can have up to four SCSI adapters with seven devices on each adapter. Each virtual machine has two IDE channels with two connections on each channel. The CD/DVD drive takes up one so there are three remaining. That is 31 devices. With each SCSI device allowed to be up to 2TB in size, you can make a *very* big virtual machine!

## Chapter 6

Virtual Networks

Solutions in this chapter:

- Introduction to Virtual Networks

- Using the "Internal Network"

- Creating a Virtual Network

- Binding a Physical Network Adapter to a Virtual Network

- Using the Virtual Server Network Services

☑ Summary

☑ Solutions Fast Track

☑ Frequently Asked Questions

Introduction

Building a virtual server park on one machine is one step, creating an entire network infrastructure and logical dividing servers through virtual networks is another.

Using virtual networks opens the possibility to use Virtual Server in your test environment to include test/production scenarios with a demilitarized zone (DMZ). It is even possible to configure Virtual Server in such a way that network users aren't able to connect to the physical server over the network, enabling you to reduce the attack surface even further.

Introduction to Virtual Networks

Each virtual machine can have up to four network adapters, each of which can be configured differently. A virtual network can be configured to support:

- **External resources**   A network that connects the virtual server and the virtual machines to outside resources such as the Internet or other resources on the local area network (LAN). This type of network uses the physical network adapter in the host computer for the virtual network.

- **Internal networks**   An internal network connecting virtual machines only to other virtual machines on the host computer or a connection between the virtual machine and the virtual server host computer. This type of network uses the Microsoft Loopback adapter and does not require any external support or physical network adapter.

Using the different types of virtual networks will enable you to build very sophisticated infrastructures without a large investment in physical servers or network devices. You can also use the features of the virtual network to prototype a network design before investing in physical hardware.

Remote offices can be supported with their own virtual server running all the necessary servers and services to support a secure and robust data center in a box. These can be preloaded and configured at a central location and shipped to the remote office for connection by local non-technical personnel. This saves a business time and money by not tying up their technical resources on installing a remote office and minimizes the cost of deploying server resources to small offices.

Virtual Networks

The virtual networks are managed from the Virtual Server Administration Web page. Figure 6.1 shows the three options available.

Figure 6.1 Virtual Networks Section

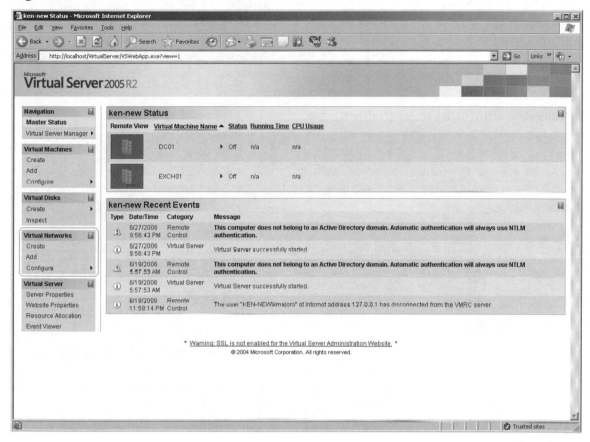

- The *Create* option enables you to create a new virtual network.

- The *Add* option enables you to add a virtual network using an existing configuration file.

- The *Configure* option opens the properties of a virtual network. A virtual network is created for each network adapter on the physical computer. An internal network is created for virtual machines only and is not attached to a network adapter.

If you are using the Remote Control view, the Virtual Network section doesn't show up.

Viewing the Virtual Networks

Because a virtual network is created for each active network interface card (NIC) in the host computer, you can look at these as soon as you load the Virtual Server 2005 R2 software. To view these virtual networks, click **Configure** in the **Virtual Networks** menu of the **Virtual Server Administration Web page** (see Figure 6.2).

Figure 6.2 Configuring Virtual Networks

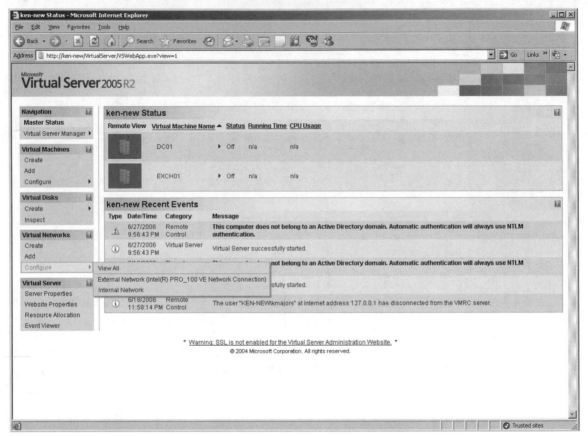

A submenu appears with the option to *View All* virtual networks, to view the *External Network* bound to the host computer's NIC card, or to view the *Internal Network*. Click **View All** (see Figure 6.3).

Figure 6.3 View All Virtual Networks

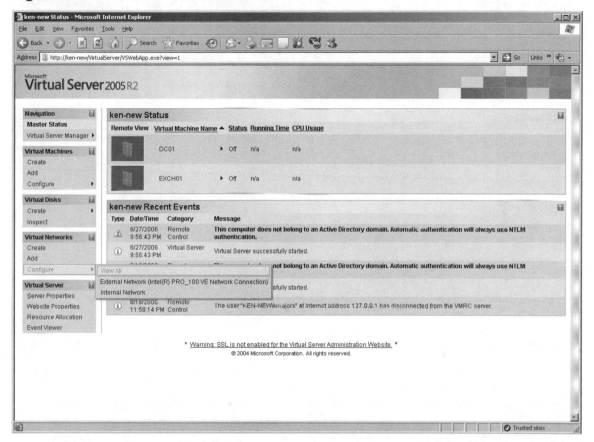

You will see a list of all the different virtual networks configured on the virtual server. You can have an unlimited number of virtual networks with an unlimited number of virtual machines connecting to them. There are some limitations. The virtual machines themselves will support only up to four virtual network adapters. The virtual machines can use only Ethernet adapters. Figure 6.4 shows all the virtual networks.

Figure 6.4 All Virtual Networks

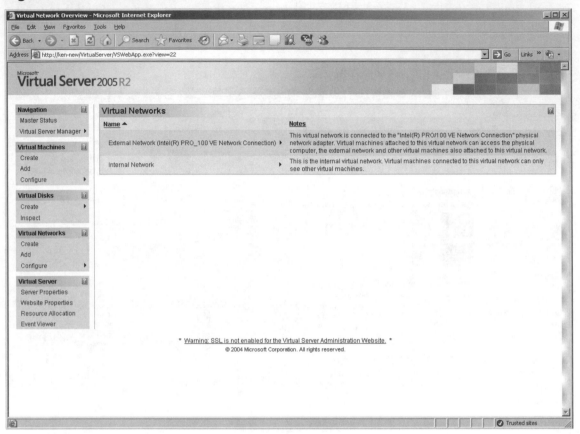

Each External Network is connected to a physical NIC card in the host computer. You are limited only by the number of expansion slots in the host computer. All virtual machines connected to this virtual network can connect to all external servers and computers that can see this network. Other virtual machines sharing this network along with the host computer can communicate with all virtual machines connected to this virtual network.

The Internal Network is a network that is isolated inside the virtual server computer. Only virtual machines contained within the virtual server can communicate with each other. This is a much more interesting feature than it appears at first glance. We will be exploring the Internal Network in greater depth later in this chapter.

Virtual Network Properties

We can view the properties of each virtual network by clicking on the virtual network name and selecting **Edit Configuration** as shown in Figure 6.5.

Figure 6.5 Edit Configuration

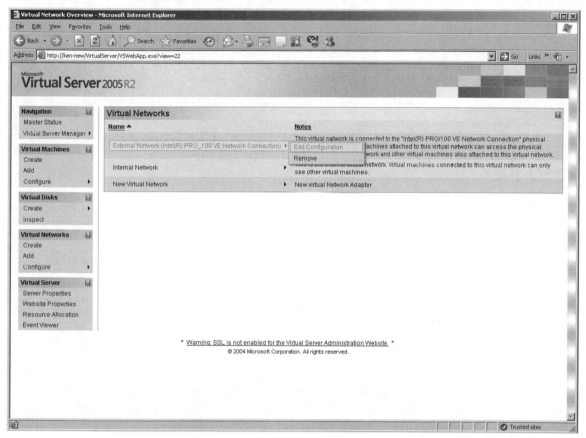

The current properties are displayed for the selected virtual network. Figure 6.6 shows the configuration properties of the External Network inside the red circle.

Figure 6.6 External Network Properties

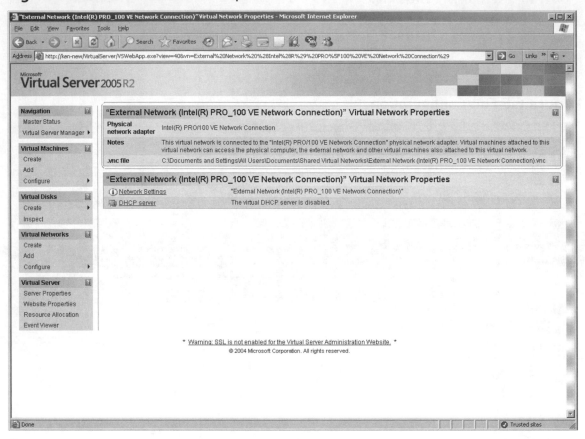

These properties show the physical network adapter associated with this virtual network, any notes associated with this virtual network, and the physical location of the virtual network configuration (.vnc) file.

Each virtual network has two main properties, **Network Settings** and **DHCP server**. Figure 6.7 highlights these with a red circle.

Figure 6.7 Virtual Network Properties

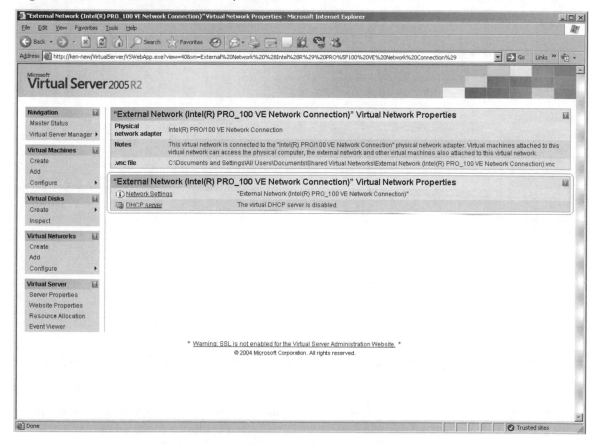

Click the **Network Settings** link (see Figure 6.8).

Figure 6.8 Network Settings

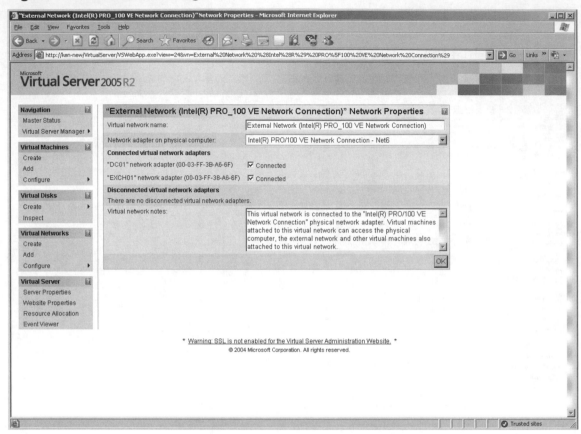

This properties page shows the virtual network name. This name can be anything but is the name of the physical NIC by default. We will look at this more later. A pull-down box lists all the physical NICs in the host computer and a Guests Only choice. Select the physical NIC to connect this virtual network or select **Guest Only** to create an internal network.

In the Connected virtual adapters you can see which virtual machines are using this virtual network. The Connected check box shows if this virtual network is currently connected to the virtual machine. You can disconnect a virtual machine from this virtual network by clearing this box. When you do, the virtual machine will show up in the disconnected virtual network adapters section, as shown in Figure 6.9.

Figure 6.9 Disconnected Virtual Network Adapters

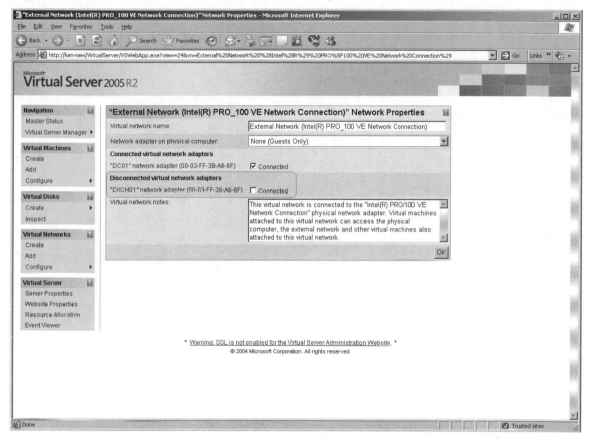

Virtual network notes is a text box for any notes the administrator may want to put on this virtual network. If you are creating several virtual networks, this section can be very helpful for remembering the purpose of this virtual network. Additional notes may be the address range or any other pertinent information. Remember, there is no limit to the number of virtual networks you can create. Click **OK** to apply your changes.

Each virtual network can have a Dynamic Host Configuration Protocol (DHCP) server associated with it. The DHCP server is limited to providing TCP/IP addressing along with default gateway and Domain Name System (DNS) server and Windows Internet Name Service (WINS) server information. Figure 6.10 shows the DHCP Properties page.

Figure 6.10 DHCP Server Properties

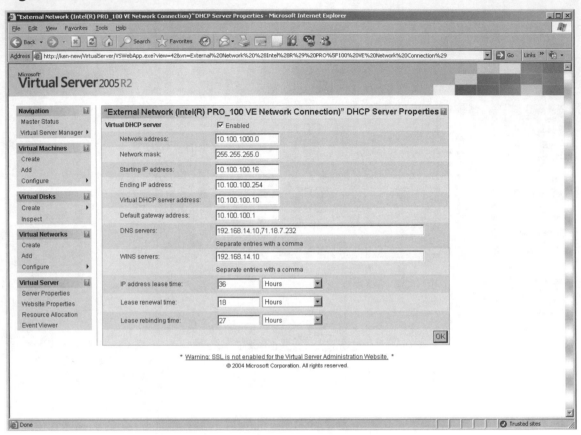

The included virtual DHCP server can be used instead of configuring a virtual machine as a DHCP server. This feature is useful *only* for internal networks because the virtual DHCP server will provide IP addresses *only* to virtual machines and *not* to physical computers. This feature is disabled by default when creating a virtual network.

Designing & Planning...

Internal or External

When planning your virtual networks you should decide which virtual machines need access to LAN resources, which will need access to wide area network (WAN) resources. A physical network interface card (NIC) can have multiple virtual networks associated to it. This means you have a wide variety of addressing possibilities for each physical NIC card.

The physical switch that the physical NIC is plugged into must support all the virtual LANs (VLANs) created by the virtual networks or the external resources cannot connect to the virtual machines. An example of this may be a Web server running on a virtual machine with a virtual network on TCP/IP address 10.100.100.124. This is the address segment for the local office desktop computers. A second virtual network is configured to use the same physical NIC but is for a messaging server in the DMZ between the firewall and the local network. This DMZ network address is 172.17.1.26. The physical switch this physical NIC is connected to must be configured for both the 10.100.100.0 and the 172.17.1.0 VLAN. The network traffic between the virtual machines would have to be routed between the virtual networks for the two virtual machines to exchange data just like two physical servers connected to their respective networks.

Certain network cards such as Intel can utilize advanced features such as VLAN trunking. This advanced option is not supported on Virtual Server 2005 because virtual network services operate on Level 2 of the OSI model only. All VLAN configurations must take place on the network switch device.

You could have two NICs in your virtual server host computer. One could be configured to a classroom network that is not allowed to connect to the Internet or any other resource outside of the classroom. The other could be configured to the normal office network. By managing the connection of the virtual machine's virtual networks you could prepare the server from your desk by connecting the office virtual network. When class was in session you would disconnect the office virtual network and connect the classroom virtual network. These changes do not have any effect on the other virtual machines running on the virtual server host computer.

Using the "Internal Network"

If no physical network adapter is selected, any virtual machine attached to the selected virtual network becomes part of the internal virtual machine network. An internal virtual machine network consists of all virtual machines that are attached to a specific virtual network configured to use no physical network adapter. Each internal virtual network is completely isolated from all other internal virtual networks. This means that all network traffic between virtual machines on an internal network does not interfere or conflict with any other internal virtual network or any external virtual network.

This is a very interesting and significant feature of the virtual server. Groups of virtual machines can be isolated for testing of network applications or operating system configurations or integration without impacting the production network or interfering with any other internal virtual network. Figure 6.11 illustrates this point.

Figure 6.11 Using the Internal Virtual Network

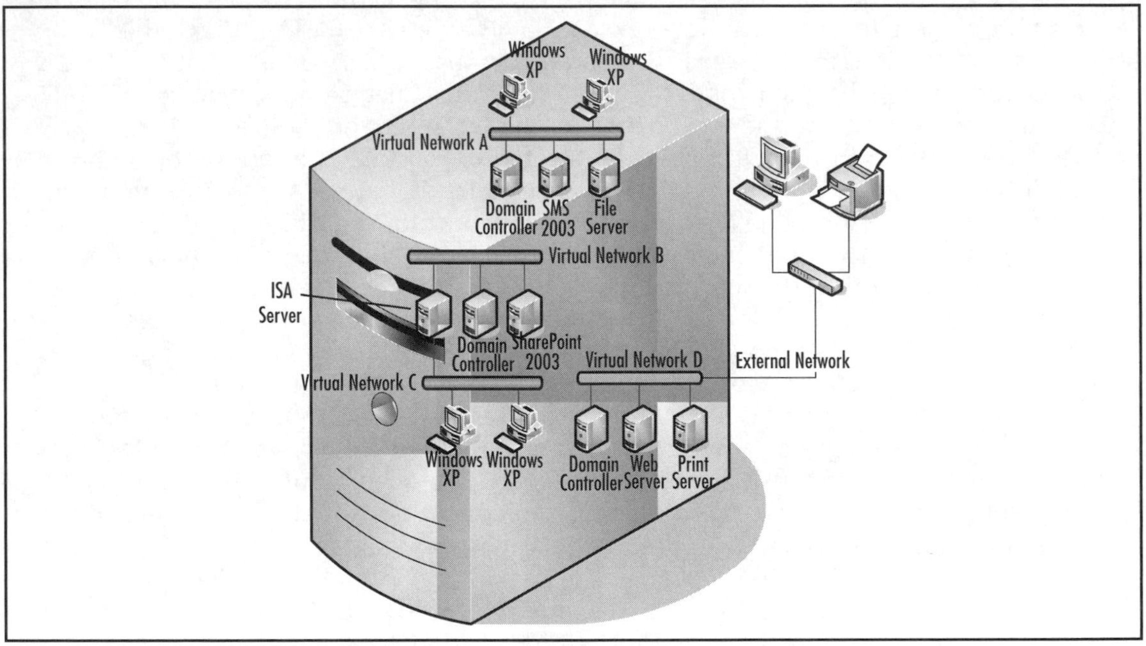

Virtual network A has a complete network including clients. All the necessary elements for testing a System Management Server 2003 deployment are present. Normally, this type of test environment can be difficult to construct because you want the testing environment completely isolated. Using the internal virtual network we accomplish the same goal on our Virtual Server 2005 host computer.

Virtual network B and virtual network C show a simulated Internet application. Client devices on virtual network C are isolated from the servers and the domain on virtual network B by a

Microsoft ISA server connected to both virtual networks. This project is also isolated from the one on virtual network A and is not visible to it.

A set of production servers is also connected to virtual network D. This virtual network is associated to the host computer's NIC card and can access and be accessed by the resources on the production network. The production network will not see the servers connected to the internal networks.

Although this example would require a virtual server with significant resources to support all these virtual machines running at the same time, it is not impossible to create it on a host computer with more modest resources. The virtual machines do not require any resources while in a suspended or powered-off state. In this scenario, the two virtual test environments could be suspended and powered off when not being used. The production servers would remain powered on and active all the time.

Remember the basic guidelines for virtual networks:

- A virtual server can support an unlimited number of virtual networks.

- A virtual network can have an unlimited number of connections from virtual machines.

- A virtual machine can support up to four virtual network adapters.

- Multiple virtual networks can be connected to a physical NIC.

Using the Loopback Adapter

The Loopback adapter is a special internal network that can be used to connect virtual machines to the host computer without using a physical NIC. The Loopback adapter can be configured to:

- Use Internet Connection Firewall (ICF) to protect internal virtual networks. Because the ICF checks all communications traffic that goes across the connection between the virtual network and the Internet and it is selective about which responses from the Internet it allows, a virtual DMZ is created.

- Provide host-to-guest networking and file sharing without having to use an external network. This configuration removes unnecessary data from passing across a shared NIC and provides an easy method of accessing host and guest files.

- Use Internet Connection Sharing (ICS) to provide Network Address Translation (NAT) and share a single connection to the Internet between the host operating system and one or more virtual machines. This method enables a guest operating system to access the Internet without needing to configure any external resources through an external connection.

- Enable the host computer to remove all bindings (client for Microsoft Networks, TCP/IP etc.) except the virtual machine network binding to the physical network adapter. The host computer then becomes invisible to the rest of the network while the hosted virtual machines continue to function normally. The Layer 2 functionality of the virtual networks services enables this type of configuration.

Installing the Loopback Adapter

To install the Microsoft Loopback adapter:

1. In the host operating system, click **Start | Settings | Control Panel**.

2. Click **Add Hardware** as shown in Figure 6.12 to launch the Add Hardware wizard.

Figure 6.12 Control Panel

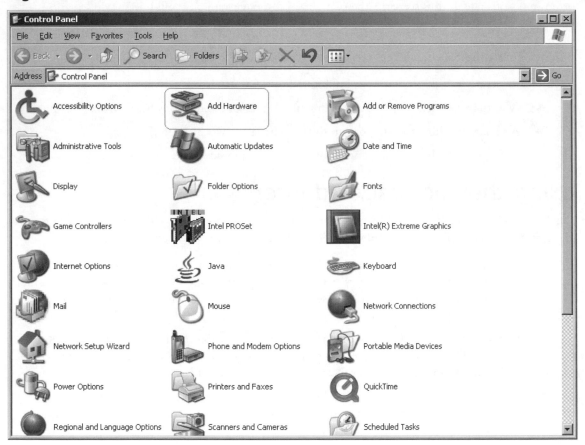

3. In the **Welcome to the Add Hardware Wizard** screen, click **Next** (see Figure 6.13.)

Figure 6.13 Add Hardware Wizard

4. When the **Is the hardware connected?** screen appears, select **Yes, I have already connected the hardware**, and then click **Next** (see Figure 6.14).

Figure 6.14 Hardware Connected?

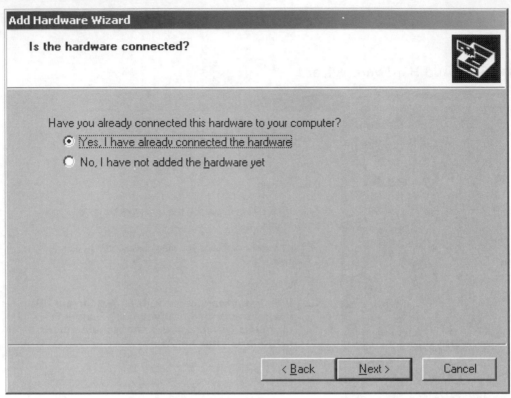

5. In the **Installed hardware** list, scroll to the bottom of the list and select **Add a new hardware device**, and then click **Next** (see Figure 6.15).

Figure 6.15 Add a New Hardware Device

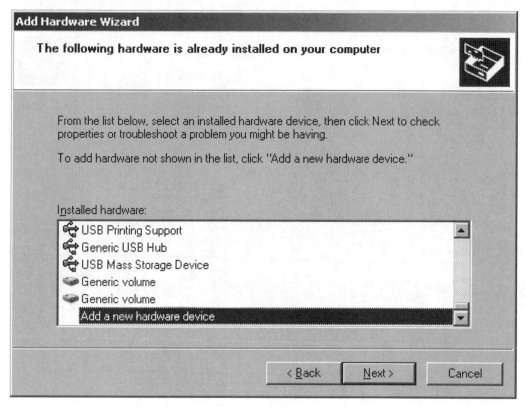

6. In **The wizard can help you install other hardware** screen (see Figure 6.16), select **Install the hardware that I manually select from a list (Advanced)**, and then click **Next**.

Figure 6.16 What Do You Want the Wizard to Do?

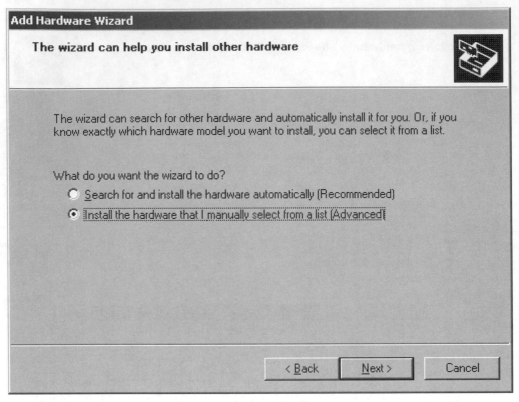

7. In the **Common hardware types** list, select **Network adapters**, and then click **Next** (see Figure 6.17).

Figure 6.17 Common Hardware Types

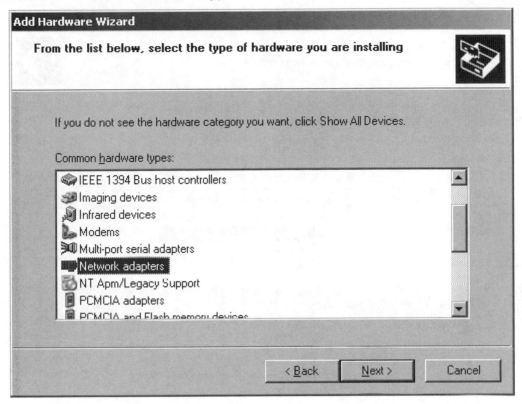

8. In the **Manufacturer** list, click **Microsoft** (see Figure 6.18).

Figure 6.18 Select Network Adapter

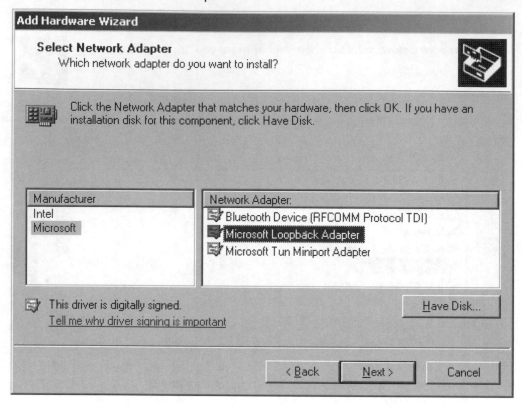

9. In the **Network Adapter** list (see Figure 6.18), click **Microsoft Loopback Adapter**, and then click **Next**.

10. Verify your selection as shown in Figure 6.19, and then click **Next**.

Figure 6.19 Hardware to Install

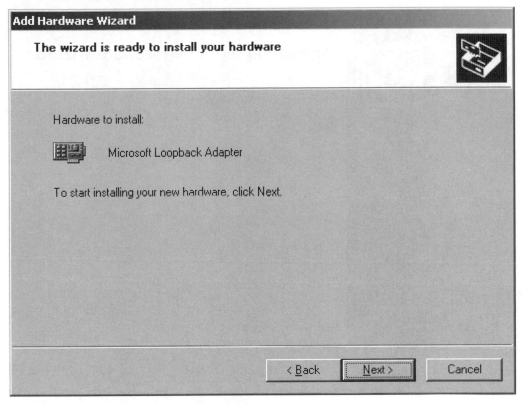

11. If a message about driver signing appears, click Continue Anyway.

12. In the **Completing the Add Hardware Wizard** dialog box, click **Finish** (see Figure 6.20).

Figure 6.20 Completing the Add Hardware Wizard

Configuring Host-to-Guest Networking and File Sharing

Because the host computer and the guest computers do not have to be on the same network or even in the same domain or workgroup, the challenge of moving files between the host and the guest can be a problem. This is what the Loopback adapter is used for. Since the Loopback adapter looks, acts, and is configured just like a physical NIC, it can be used for a virtual network that only the virtual machines and the host computer can use.

To configure the Loopback adapter:

1. On the host operating system, **Click Start | Settings | Control Panel**. In the **Control Panel** screen, double-click the **Network Connections** icon (see Figure 6.21).

Figure 6.21 Control Panel | Network Connections

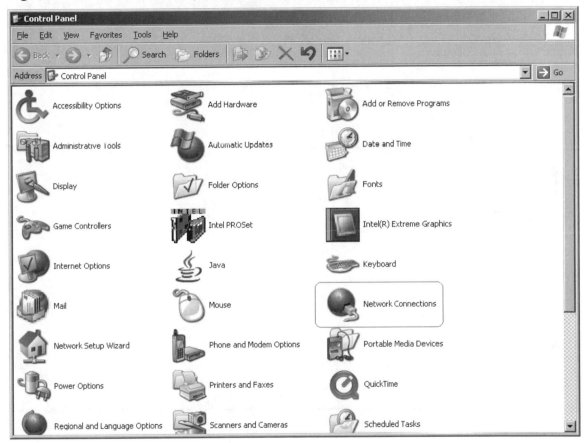

2. Right-click the local area connection for **Microsoft Loopback Adapter**, and then select **Properties** (see Figure 6.22).

Figure 6.22 Network Connections on the Host Computer

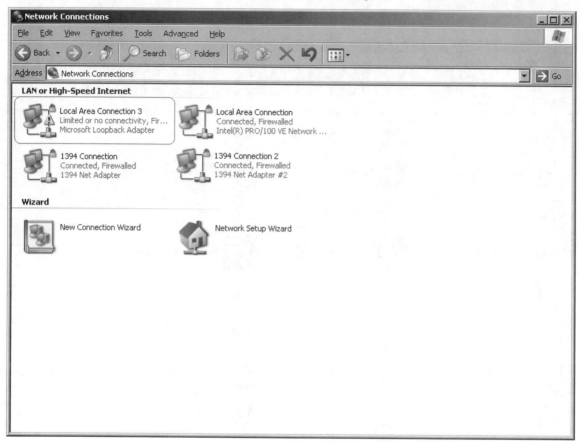

3. In the **Microsoft Loopback Adapter Properties** dialog box, verify that the **Virtual Machine Network Services** check box is selected (see Figure 6.23).

Figure 6.23 Virtual Machine Network Services

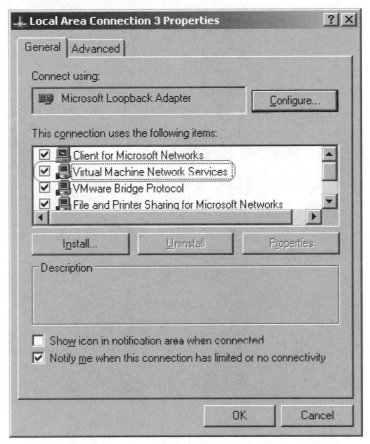

4. Click **Internet Protocol (TCP/IP)**, and then click **Properties** (see Figure 6.24).

Figure 6.24 TCP/IP

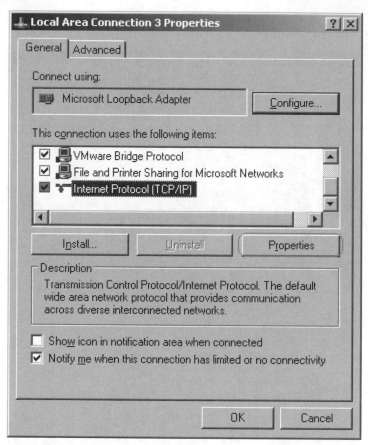

5. On the **General** tab, click **Use the following IP address**, and then type the IP address and subnet mask (such as 10.10.10.2 and 255.255.255.0) as shown in Figure 6.25. Do *not* enter anything for a default gateway. Although you can use any Transmission Control Protocol/Internet Protocol (TCP/IP) address, here it is best to choose one from a reserved range of non-routable TCP/IP addresses that are not in use on your production network. In our example we are using a network address of 10.10.10.X

and a host ID of 2. The virtual machines that are guests on this host computer could use the same network address with a different host ID to communicate with the host and each other.

Figure 6.25 TCP/IP Addressing

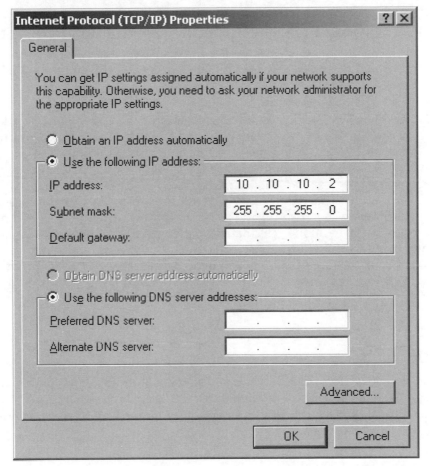

6. Click **OK** then close.

Configuring & Implementing...

Isolating the Connection between the Host and the Guest

You may have several guest virtual machines all running on different networks to isolate them from each other. To maintain this isolation and still enable communication between the host computer and the guest virtual machine, you can assign several different TCP/IP addresses to the host Loopback adapter.

Giving each virtual machine and the host computer a unique network ID and host ID for each virtual network they share will enable you to use your subnetting skills. A subnet mask of 255.255.255.0 will enable 254 hosts to connect to the assigned network ID. If we want only the host and the guest virtual machine to share this virtual network we can assign a subnet mask of 255.255.255.252.

You will need to watch your network addresses to make sure you are assigning the correct numbers. If you can do the math, great, but for those of us that want a little help there is a free subnet calculator online at www.subnet-calculator.com. You might want to write down the assigned virtual networks so you don't forget later. You will want to use a subnet mask that will accommodate the host computer and all the virtual machines that are on the same virtual network.

Using the ICS

What if you are building a new virtual machine and you want it to have access to the Internet but don't really want to configure a virtual network that will connect to the external LAN? You can use the ICS feature of Windows. This will enable your virtual machine to connect to the Internet using the host computer's network connection.

NOTE

This could potentially create a security incident. If you are performing this action on a production network you should check with the security administrator before performing this procedure.

To configure ICS for use with your virtual machines:

1. Install the Microsoft Loopback Adapter as described in this chapter.

2. Start the Network Setup Wizard by clicking **Start | Settings | Control Panel**, and then double-click **Network Setup Wizard** as shown in Figure 6.26.

Figure 6.26 Select the Network Setup Wizard

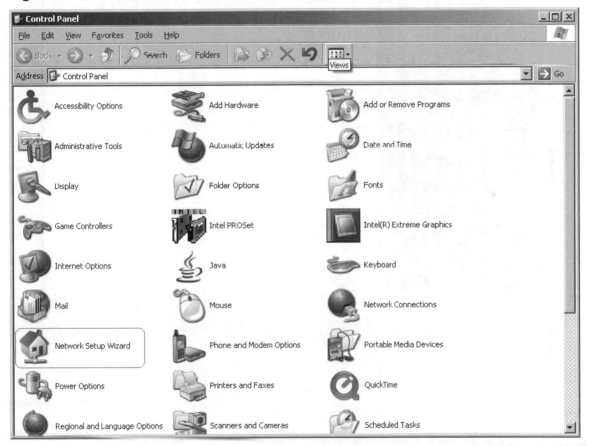

3. On the **Welcome to the Network Setup Wizard** screen, click **Next** (see Figure 6.27).

Figure 6.27 Welcome to the Network Setup Wizard

4. On the **Before you continue** screen, click **Next** (see Figure 6.28).

Figure 6.28 Before You Continue...

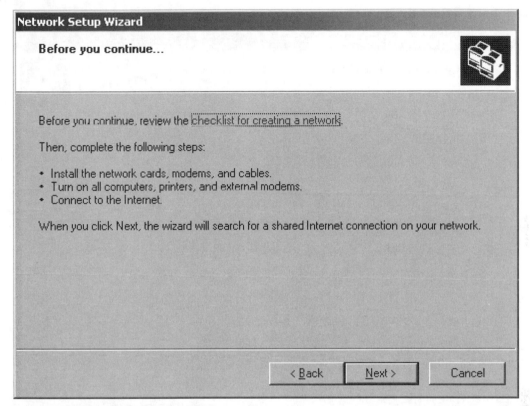

5.   Select **This computer connects directly to the Internet** as shown in Figure 6.29, and then click **Next**.

Figure 6.29 Select a Connection Method

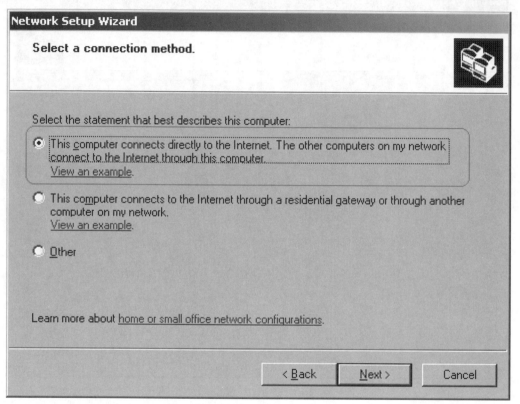

6. Select the host computer's physical NIC that connects to the Internet, as shown in Figure 6.30, and then click **Next**. The wizard will make a selection, so verify that it is the correct network interface card.

Figure 6.30 Select You Internet Connection

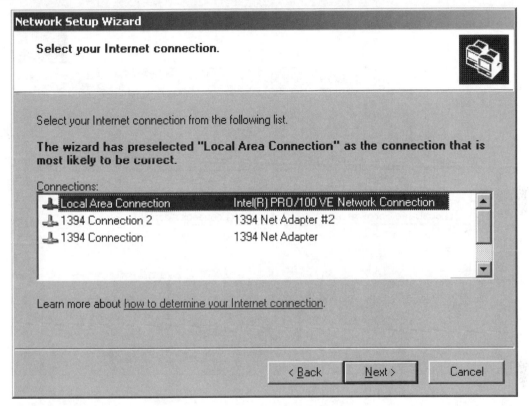

7. Check the box next to the **Local Area Connection** for the Microsoft Loopback adapter, as shown in Figure 6.31, and then click **Next**.

Figure 6.31 Select Your Private Connection

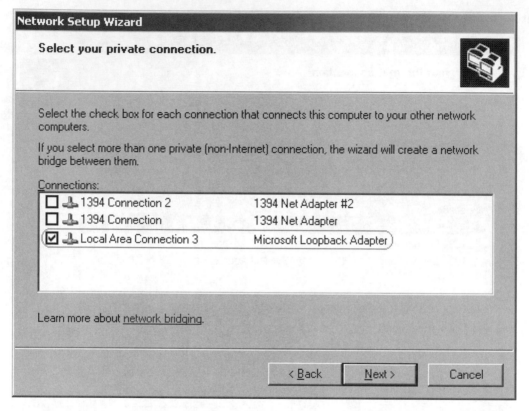

8. Enter a description and name for the computer as shown in Figure 6.32. These will default to the configuration for your host computer. There is no need to change them unless it is required by your Internet service provider or the security officer of your business. Click **Next** when you are finished (see Figure 6.32).

Figure 6.32 Computer Description and Name

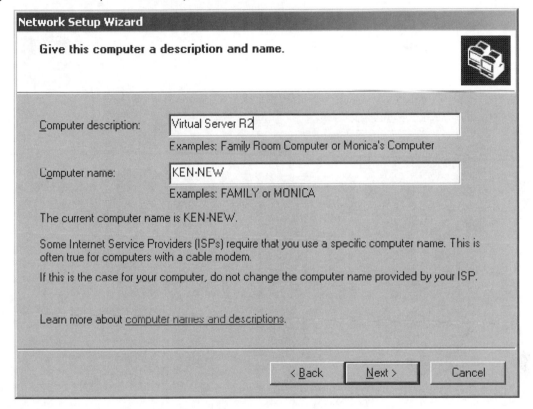

9. Enter a workgroup name as shown in Figure 6.33. You might want to make this a more descriptive name if you have more than one virtual network sharing this connection. Click **Next**.

Figure 6.33 Name Your Network

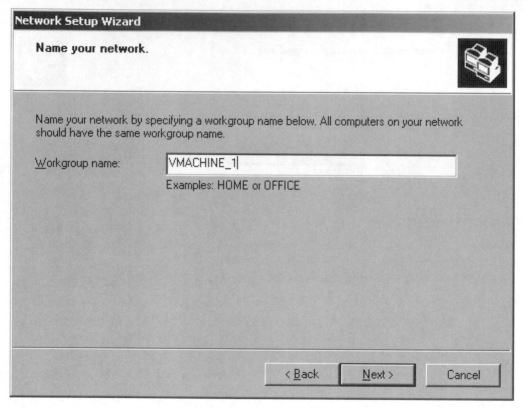

10. Select **Turn on file and printer sharing** if you want to enable your virtual machines to access file shares and printers on the outside network (see Figure 6.34). If you do not want to enable the virtual machines to access file share and printers, then select **Turn off file and printer sharing**. Click **Next** when ready to proceed.

Figure 6.34 File and Printer Sharing

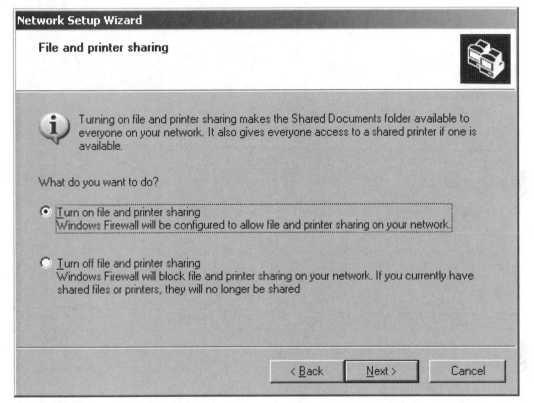

11.   Review the setting as shown in Figure 6.35, and then click **Next**.

Figure 6.35 Ready to Apply Network Settings

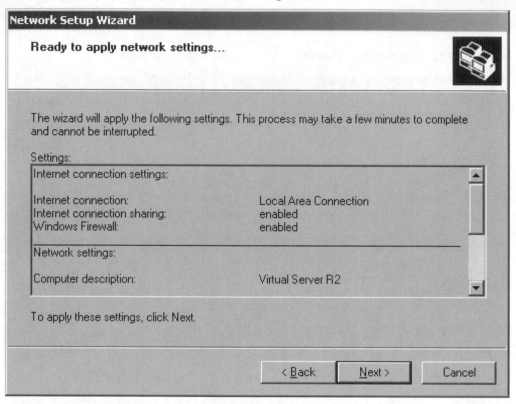

12.   Click **Finish** when the configuration is complete. You may be prompted to restart the host computer.

Creating a Virtual Network

A virtual network is a collection of one or more virtual machines connected to exchange information or provide a service to other virtual machines or computers. Virtual Server 2005 R2 can support an unlimited number of virtual networks. A virtual network can be associated to a physical network adapter or the Loopback adapter or no adapter. More than one virtual network can be associated to either of these choices.

By utilizing one or more physical network adapters along with the internal network and the Loopback adapter, very complex network designs can be incorporated with Virtual Server. A virtual network is created for each physical network adapter in the virtual server host computer by default. Additional virtual networks can be created to fit the needs of the virtual machines.

To create a virtual network:

1. Start by opening the Virtual Server Administration Web page and selecting **Create** from the **Virtual Networks** menu, as shown in Figure 6.36.

Figure 6.36 Virtual Server Administration Web Page

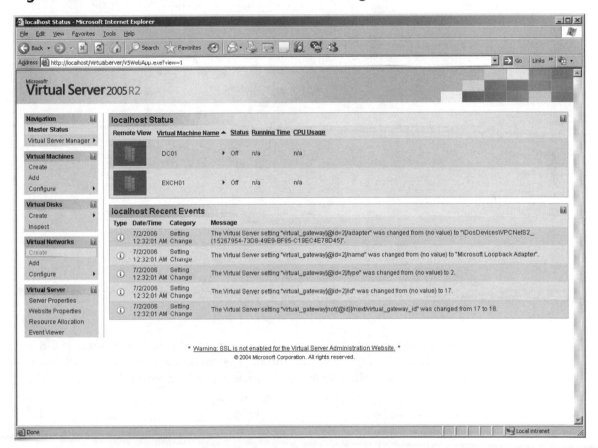

2. Enter the name of the virtual network in the **Virtual network name** box, as shown in Figure 6.37. This name has to be unique to the virtual server and can be almost anything. You should try to make it a descriptive name that will tell you something about the virtual network later.

Figure 6.37 Virtual Network Properties

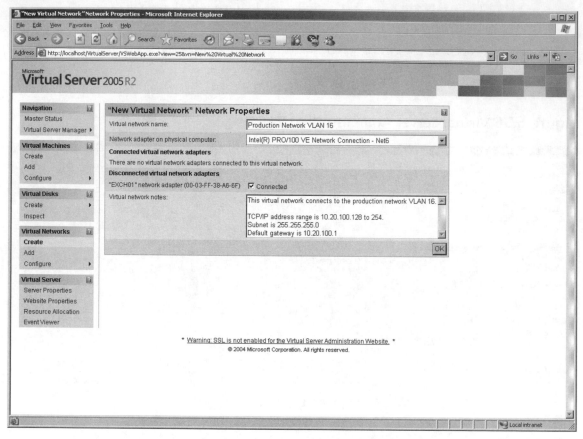

3. Select the network adapter from the **Network adapter on physical computer** pull-down menu. You can select one of the NIC cards in the host computer or the Loopback adapter if you installed it. Selecting None makes this virtual network an internal virtual network.

4. If there are any disconnected virtual network adapters that you want to connect to this virtual network, you can select them by checking the Connected box next to the virtual machine name. If you want to connect a virtual server that does not appear in space, you will need to create a new virtual adapter and connect it to this virtual network.

5. In the Virtual network notes section you can enter any information you want. You might want to put pertinent connection information or other descriptive text about the use and purpose of this virtual network. This box is here to help the administrator remember why the virtual network was created and will make your job much easier after you have several virtual networks.

6. Click **OK** when finished. Figure 6.38 shows the Virtual Network Properties page for the new virtual network.

Figure 6.38 Virtual Network Properties

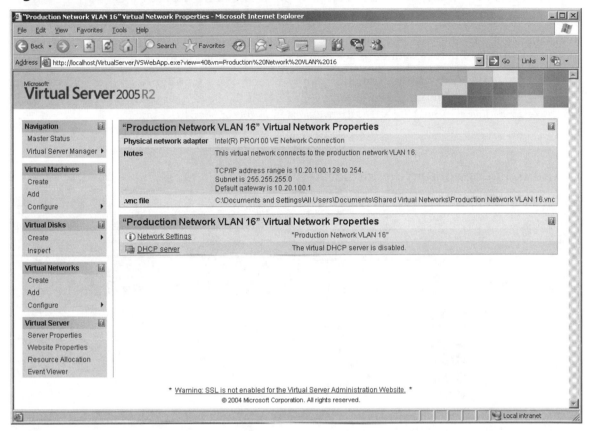

Binding a Physical Network Adapter to a Virtual Network

Even though virtual machines may be portable, virtual networks are not. If a virtual network adapter is connected to a virtual network on one virtual server computer, when the virtual machine is moved to a different virtual server computer the virtual network adapters will all need to be connected to virtual networks on the new virtual server computer. This is one reason why it is recommended that descriptive names and notes be utilized for the virtual networks.

You may want to add another physical network adapter to your virtual server host computer and connect an existing virtual network across this new resource. There may have been a failure or an upgrade and the current NIC card has been replaced with a different one. All these scenarios will require binding a physical network adapter to a virtual network.

Changing the Binding of a Virtual Network

There are many reasons why you would need to change the binding of a virtual network from one physical network adapter to another or change the virtual network from an external virtual network to an internal virtual network. All of these changes are accomplished in the same way.

1. Open the Virtual Server Administration Web page. Select **Configure** from the **Virtual Networks** menu, as shown in Figure 6.39. Select the desired virtual network. We will use *Production Network VLAN 16* that we created in the previous section.

Figure 6.39 Configuring the Virtual Network

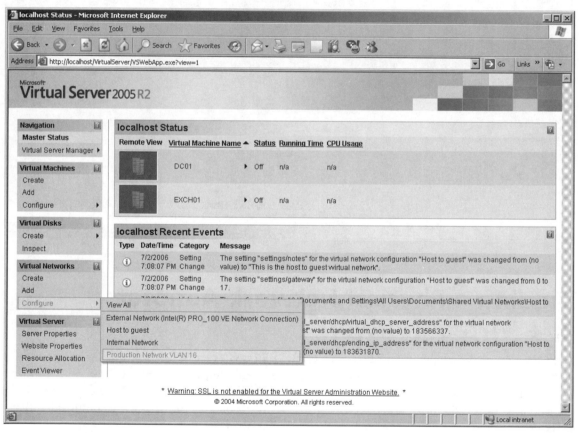

2.   Select **Network Settings**, as shown in Figure 6.40.

Figure 6.40 Network Settings

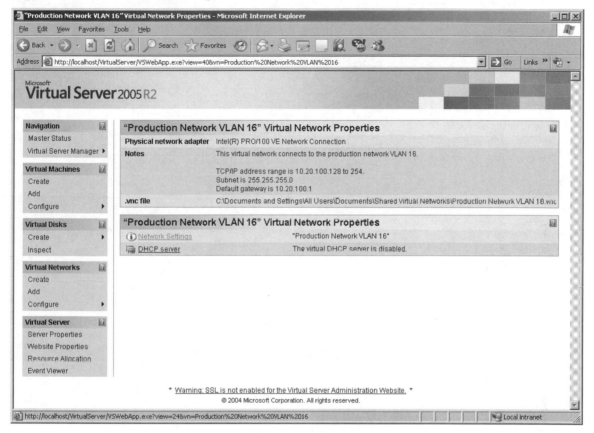

3.   Click the pull-down arrow in the **Network adapter on physical computer** drop-down menu and select the new physical adapter for this virtual network, as shown in Figure 6.41.

Figure 6.41 Selecting a Physical Network Adapter

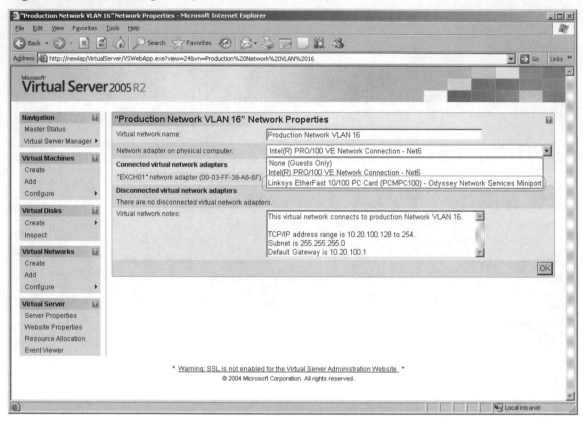

4.   Click **OK** when finished.

All virtual machines connected to this virtual network will now use the new network adapter for their network traffic. You do not need to reconfigure the virtual machines. This can be a very efficient method of managing the network traffic in and out of a virtual server.

Figure 6.42 shows how having multiple network adapters can be used with virtual networks to manage the network traffic.

Figure 6.42 Using Multiple Network Adapters

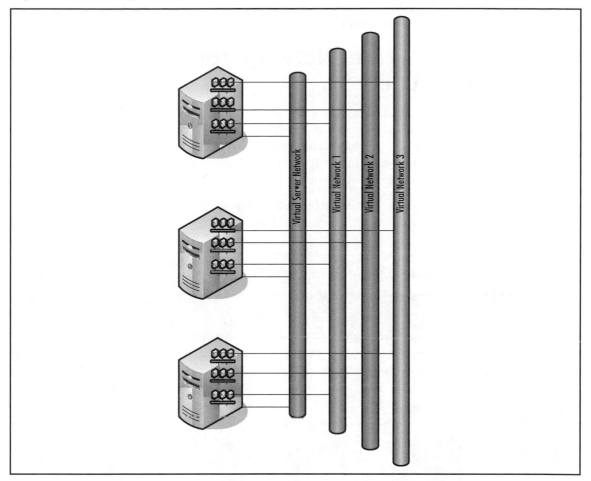

In the example shown, there is a separate network adapter for the virtual server computers. This network manages the network traffic for the host computers. It also enables a direct method of accessing these host systems without using any of the guest computer or virtual network bandwidth. Each of the three virtual networks is connected to a separate physical network adapter in each of the virtual servers. Each virtual server would require this virtual network to be configured and addressed appropriately for the virtual machines to communicate with each other. While it is not required that each virtual network have a dedicated physical network adapter, it is shown this way for clarity. If you do have multiple virtual networks using the same physical adapter, the physical adapter *must* have access to the external networks being used by the virtual networks.

Using these methods will also enable an administrator to quickly disconnect all virtual servers using a virtual network by simply changing the virtual network configuration and selecting the Loopback or None network adapter. The *None* selection makes the virtual network an internal network and isolated from all external network traffic. The *Loopback* adapter, if it is configured, enables network traffic between the host and the virtual machines connected to the virtual network. If you also configure the ICS, the virtual machines will still be able to access the external network by bridging across the host computer's network connection.

Changing the Virtual Network for a Virtual Machine

Now that you have seen how to change the configuration of a virtual network, you may need to change the network connection of your virtual network adapter to use one of these virtual networks. Each virtual machine can support up to four virtual network adapters but it is not necessary to create a new virtual adapter every time you want to connect to a different virtual network. To change the virtual network connection of a virtual machine:

1. From the Virtual Server Administration Web page, select the virtual machine on which you want to edit the configuration, as shown in Figure 6.43.

Figure 6.43 Edit Virtual Machine Configuration

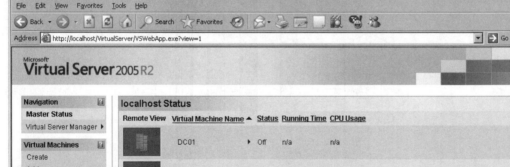

2. Select **Network adapters** from the **Virtual Machine Properties** page, as shown in Figure 6.44.

Figure 6.44 Virtual Machine Properties

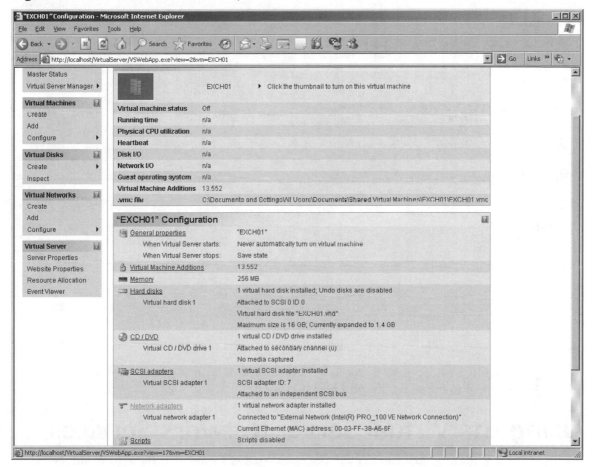

3. Click the pull-down arrow next to the **Connected to** box. The list of available virtual networks is displayed, as shown in Figure 6.45. Select the desired virtual network.

Figure 6.45 *Connected to* List of Virtual Networks

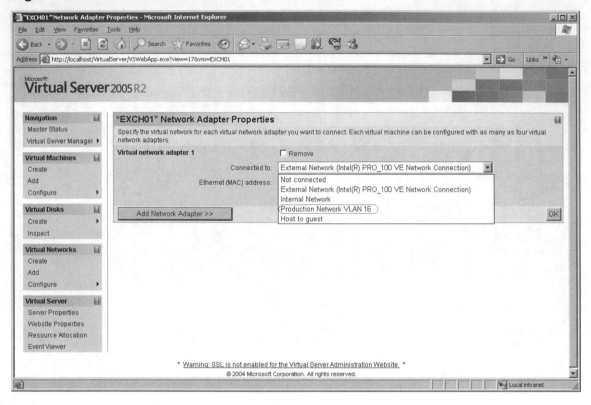

4. Click **OK** to complete the process. The virtual machine's network adapter is now connected to the selected virtual network.

Using the Virtual Server Network Services

Each virtual network also has a virtual DHCP server as part of the configuration. As mentioned earlier, this Dynamic Host Configuration Protocol (DHCP) server is only for the virtual machines on the same virtual server host computer. This DHCP server cannot be used for any other purpose or for any other type of client computer.

Although there are restrictions on its use, it does not mean that this added feature is without merit. You should consider it when setting up internal virtual networks or host–to–guest virtual networks. It can also supply TCP/IP addresses to virtual machines connected to external virtual networks. The assigned address pool must be excluded from the external DHCP address pool or a conflict could occur.

The virtual network DHCP server is disabled by default. To enable and configure it for use:

1. From the **Virtual Server Administration Web page** select **Configure** from the **Virtual Networks** menu. Select the virtual network to configure, as shown in Figure 6.46.

Figure 6.46 Selecting a Virtual Network

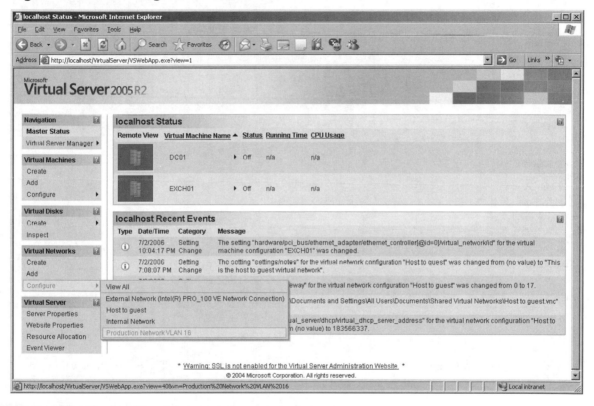

2. Select **DHCP server** from the **Virtual Network Properties** page, as shown in Figure 6.47.

Figure 6.47 Selecting DHCP Server

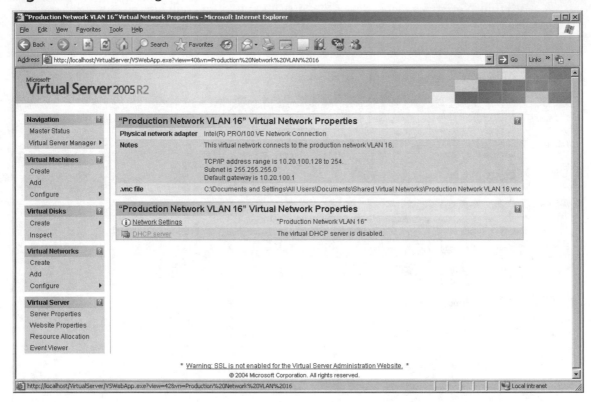

3. Check the **Enable** check box to start the configuration. You will need to enter values in the properties boxes for the virtual DHCP server as shown in Figure 6.48.

Figure 6.48 Virtual DHCP Server Properties

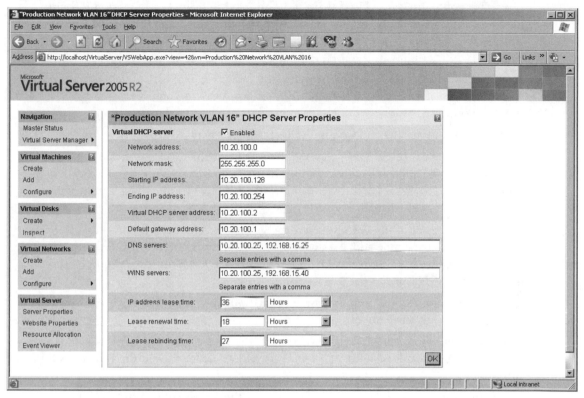

4. Enter the network address for the virtual network in the **Network address** text box. This is the network portion of the TCP/IP address.

5. Enter the subnet mask for this virtual network in the **Network mask** text box. This is the address mask that determines the network portion of the TCP/IP address from the host ID portion.

6. Enter the starting address for the virtual DHCP server address pool in the **Starting IP address** box. This is the first address that the server will assign to a virtual machine on this virtual network.

7. Enter the last address for the virtual DHCP server address pool in the **Ending IP address** box. This will be the last address that can be assigned to virtual machines on this virtual network. If more addresses are requested, they will be denied and the virtual machine will not be able to connect to the virtual network.

8. Enter the address for the virtual DHCP server in the **Virtual DHCP server address** box. Even though this is a virtual service it still requires a TCP/IP address on the virtual network. This should be outside the address pool and not in conflict with any other resource on the virtual network either internal or external to the virtual server.

9. Enter the default gateway address in the **Default gateway address** box.

10. Enter the addresses of any DNS servers the virtual machines can use in the **DNS servers** box. Separate the addresses with a comma. If this is an internal virtual network there may not be any DNS servers on this virtual network. Just leave this box blank if there are no DNS servers for this virtual network.

11. Enter the addresses of any WINS servers the virtual machines can use in the **WINS servers** box. Separate the addresses with a comma. If this is an internal virtual network there may not be any WINS servers on this virtual network. Just leave this box blank if there are no WINS servers for this virtual network.

12. Enter the duration of the address lease in the **IP address lease time** box. Normally just accept the default value for this box.

13. Enter the duration of the lease renewal time in the **Lease renewal time** box. Normally just accept the default value for this box. This value is normally half the IP address lease time value.

14. Enter the duration of the lease rebinding time in the **Lease rebinding time** box. Normally just accept the default value for this box. This value is normally half-way between the IP address lease time and the lease renewal time.

15. Click **OK** when finished.

When the virtual machine is connected to this virtual network the virtual DHCP server will assign all the configured information to the virtual network adapter when the virtual machine is started or the virtual network adapter is connected. Just like a DHCP server running on a physical computer, it will not overwrite settings in the virtual machines that have been entered into the address properties of the virtual network adapter.

If you want your virtual machines to act as a DHCP server to computer on the external network, you have to configure DHCP services for the guest operating system running on the virtual machine. Your virtual machines can also use a DHCP server on the physical network to obtain a network address.

Summary

In this chapter we looked at all the various ways to use the virtual networking features of Virtual Server 2005 R2. The two basic types of virtual network types enable the virtual server administrator to control how the virtual machines can access resources. The external type enables the virtual machines to connect to Internet or other resources directly. This could be useful in building a virtual firewall or Internet Web or message server where outside access is required. Other external networks enable the virtual machines to connect to resources on the LAN. This is a very common design and gives virtual machines access to the LAN to interact like any other physical computer on the LAN. The internal virtual network type isolates the virtual machines on a virtual network that only the virtual machines can access. This is good for building a DMZ or isolating test infrastructures from production virtual machines and networks. Another internal network provides host access for exchanging files between the host computer and the guest virtual machine.

We explored the internal network. We saw how to create internal networks that enabled multiple networking environments to reside on the virtual server without interacting with each other. We also loaded the Microsoft Loopback adapter to enable host-to-guest networking. This type of virtual network enabled the guest to share files and other resources between the guest and the host operating systems. The ICS was also installed to provide for bridging the host network connection to the internal virtual network and the connected virtual machines.

We showed the creation of a virtual network and identified the different properties that can make it an external or an internal virtual network. We showed the connection method of connecting an unconnected virtual network adapter to the new virtual network at the time of creation. We also showed how to change a virtual network adapter from one virtual network to another in the virtual machine properties Web page. We recommended that the virtual network name be descriptive and the notes section be utilized to keep pertinent information on each of the virtual networks.

Multiple virtual networks can be connected to a single physical network adapter and all the virtual networks can be independent of each other as long as the physical network adapter has access to all the configured networks. A virtual server can support an unlimited number of internal virtual networks with an unlimited number of connections on each internal virtual network. All this combined allows for Virtual Server to be very flexible in your infrastructure design. As the need arises or bandwidth load increases, additional physical network adapters can be added to the virtual server host computer. The virtual networks can be reassigned or associated to the physical adapter from the Virtual Network Configuration properties of the Virtual Server Administration Web page. This feature makes it very easy to upgrade to separate the network traffic across different network adapters. This is also important because virtual networks are not portable. They are only valid on the virtual server host computer where they were created. Virtual machines created on one virtual server must have their virtual network adapter reconnected to a virtual network before it can use any network resources.

The last thing we looked at was the virtual DHCP server associated with each virtual network. This service can be used only to provide TCP/IP addressing to the virtual machines on a single virtual server host. This service is disabled by default because the virtual machines can use any available DHCP server on the network. This service is particularly useful for internal virtual networks where there are no outside resources accessible. This feature will avoid the need to configure a DHCP server on one of the virtual machines for the internal virtual network.

Solutions Fast Track

Introduction to Virtual Networks

☑ There are two types of virtual networks: external and internal.

☑ Virtual networks can be combined to form a complete network infrastructure on a single computer.

☑ Virtual networks are not portable. Virtual machines must have their virtual network adapter connected to a virtual network configured on the virtual server hosting the virtual machine.

Using the "Internal Network"

☑ There can be an unlimited number of internal virtual networks each with an unlimited number of connections.

☑ The internal network can be used to isolate a set of virtual machines to form a DMZ or a completely isolated network for testing.

☑ Loading the Microsoft Loopback adapter enables host-to-guest communications. This enables guest virtual machines to share files with the host computer.

Creating a Virtual Network

☑ Virtual networks are created from the Virtual Server Administration Web page.

☑ Use descriptive names for the virtual networks and use the notes section to maintain the pertinent information about the virtual network.

☑ A virtual network is automatically created for each physical adapter in the host computer.

Binding a Physical Network Adapter to a Virtual Network

☑ Multiple virtual networks can be bound to a single physical network adapter. The physical adapter must have access to the VLAN resources the virtual networks are using.

☑ The virtual network can be reassigned to a different physical network adapter from the Virtual Server Administration Web page by clicking Configure in the Virtual Network section and selecting the virtual network to edit.

☑ The Microsoft Loopback adapter is seen as a physical adapter and is used to bridge a virtual machine to the host's network connection.

Using the Virtual Server Network Services

☑ DHCP server is available for every virtual network but is disabled by default.

☑ This service can only be used by the virtual machines on a virtual server and cannot service any outside requests.

☑ It avoids the necessity of loading a DHCP server on a virtual machine using an internal network.

Frequently Asked Questions

Q: Why would I want to use an internal virtual network?

A: The internal virtual network is a good choice for isolating one or more virtual machines for the external network connections. This may be done as part of a DMZ or to isolate a set of virtual servers for testing. The internal network is also very useful for connecting the host and guest virtual machines for sharing files and other resources connected to the host computer.

Q: Can I provide additional network information when using the DHCP service on the virtual network?

A: No. The DHCP server available to the virtual network is a simple service. It can only provide basic addressing information, default gateway, DNS, and WINS server addresses. If you require the capability to provide additional information using DHCP, you should set up a DHCP server on a virtual machine or use an external DHCP server.

Q: What is a practical limit to the number of virtual networks available on a virtual server?

A: Although technically there is no limit, the practical limit is 256 virtual networks on a virtual server. This is calculated as 64 virtual machines, the practical limit of virtual machines for a virtual server times four, the number of virtual network adapters a virtual machine can support. You can have more virtual networks than this but they will not have any connections so they will use any resources.

Q: Do I have to create a new virtual network adapter to connect to a different virtual network?

A: No. A virtual network adapter can be connected to any virtual network by editing the properties of the virtual network adapter and selecting the desired virtual network. You may need to reconfigure the TCP/IP addressing of the virtual adapter when you switch virtual networks. A virtual network adapter can only be connected to a single virtual network at a time.

Q: Can I use a network team adapter set?

A: A teamed set of physical network adapters can be used for a virtual network. The network team must be in place before creating the virtual network. You cannot team virtual network adapters.

Q: What happens if I remove a virtual network without disconnecting the virtual servers connected to it?

A: All the virtual network adapters connected to the removed virtual network will simply become disconnected. You will need to connect the virtual network adapters to another virtual network or you can connect then to a new virtual network when you create it. All connections to the network resources being accessed by the removed virtual network will also be lost. It is best to make sure all virtual machines are removed from the virtual network before removing it to avoid any data loss from the sudden disruption of service.

Chapter 7

Virtual Disks

Solutions in this chapter:

- **Removable Virtual Disks**
- **Virtual Hard Disks**

☑ **Summary**

☑ **Solutions Fast Track**

☑ **Frequently Asked Questions**

Introduction

Virtual machines have many properties that are similar to physical machines. When configuring a virtual machine, the most important properties are memory and disks, because they have the most impact on the host. As with physical machines, virtual machines contain an operating system, applications, and data. Depending on its role, the virtual machine may have one or many virtual hard disks.

Most applications these days are disk I/O intensive. These applications perform many read and write operations from and to the hard disk, so performance is basically determined by the underlying disk I/O subsystem. When they perform heavy disk I/O they are called disk bound.

Disk I/O in a physical machine is basically the slowest I/O compared to processor and memory I/O; therefore, a good performing storage subsystem benefits performance of those applications and, as such, overall performance of the virtual machine.

Removable Virtual Disks

Virtual Server provides its virtual machines with several types of disks. These disks are not physical disks; this would not scale well with many virtual machines and many disks in each virtual machine.

Virtual Server emulates disks, which are called virtual disks. To a guest operating system inside a virtual machine, these virtual disks are the same as those in a physical machine. They behave the same and have the same limitations, determined by their emulated characteristics.

Virtual Server emulates different kinds of disks that are common in today's physical machines. Those can be categorized as either removable disks or hard disks.

Removable disks can be CD/DVD disks or floppy disks. These disks can be used through their emulated disk drive.

CD/DVD Drive

Virtual Server supports the use of removable media such as CD or DVD optical disks. Because a DVD drive also supports CDs, Virtual Server emulates a DVD drive.

The DVD drive in a virtual machine can be captured to the host CD or DVD drive.

Configuring & Implementing…

Virtual Server Terminology

Virtual Server uses the term *attach* to denote a link or connection between a virtual machine and a device. When a CD/DVD drive is attached, this means that the virtual machine contains a CD/DVD drive. The attachment points to the channel and ID the CD/DVD drive exists on. For example, the CD/DVD drive can be attached to the Primary IDE channel with device ID 1.

> Virtual Server uses the term *capture* to denote a link between the virtual machine's CD/DVD drive device and the host. When the CD/DVD drive uses the host's DVD drive, it is said to be captured to the host's drive. If nothing has been captured, the virtual machine still has a CD/DVD drive, but there is nothing in it.

When the CD drive of the host has been captured to the CD/DVD drive in the virtual machine, then the CD/DVD drive is limited to the host drive characteristics. In this case, the host drive can only read CDs and the virtual machine accepts any format the host supports. So despite the fact that Virtual Server emulates a DVD drive, you can capture the host's CD drive.

When the host drive is a DVD drive, the captured CD/DVD drive in the virtual machine accepts any disc format up to any DVD standard. For example, when you put a 4.7 GB DVD+RW disc in the host drive, the virtual machine is able to access the contents. However, you cannot write to the media from within the virtual machine; Virtual Server emulates a read-only DVD drive.

A virtual machine can have up to four CD/DVD drives in a virtual machine. These can all be attached to the host given the condition that the host has four drives of type CD/DVD. You cannot capture the same host drive to more than one CD/DVD drive.

The storage architecture type of a CD/DVD drive is IDE (Integrated Drive Electronics). A virtual machine has two IDE channels: primary and secondary. Each channel supports two drives. This is where the limit of four CD/DVD drives per virtual machine comes from.

NOTE

When using IDE virtual hard disks, the number of CD/DVD drive attachments is limited to what remains of the four IDE device IDs. When using two virtual hard disks attached to IDE, there remain two device IDs for CD/DVD drives.

You are not limited to capturing a host CD or DVD drive. You can capture a so-called image file to a DVD drive. This image file must be in the ISO 9660 format and contain the extension ISO. For Virtual Server 2005, the size limit of the ISO file is 2.2 GB. For Virtual Server 2005 R2, there is no size limit on the ISO image you can attach. Notice that this enables you to use larger ISO images than your host drive supports.

Using ISO images with CD/DVD drives enables you to use CD or DVD "media" in a virtual machine without the need for a physical drive. Because it is a read-only device, you can attach a single ISO to multiple virtual machines. And contrary to capturing multiple DVD drives to the same host drive, you can capture the same ISO image to multiple CD/DVD drives.

To modify the properties of a virtual machine's CD/DVD drive, open the virtual machine's **Properties** page and click **CD/DVD**. The CD/DVD Drive Properties window opens, similar to Figure 7.1.

Figure 7.1 CD/DVD Drive Properties

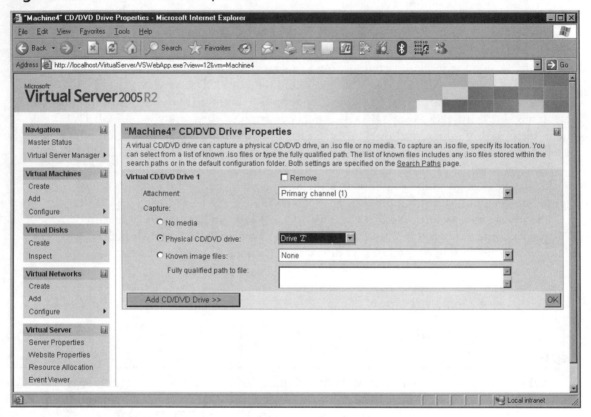

From this window you can modify the virtual CD/DVD drive attachment, its capture status, or you can add another CD/DVD drive.

Floppy Disk Drive

Another type of removable media Virtual Server supports is the virtual floppy disk. Virtual Server emulates a 1.44 MB 3.5" read/write floppy disk drive. This drive supports virtual floppies with sizes of 720 KB, 1.44 MB and 1.68 MB.

Each virtual machine contains one virtual floppy disk drive. This floppy disk drive can be captured to the host floppy disk drive or it can be attached to a virtual floppy image file which has the extension VFD.

To modify the properties of a virtual machine's floppy disk drive, open the virtual machine's **Properties** page and click **Floppy drive**. The Floppy Drive Properties window opens, similar to Figure 7.2.

Figure 7.2 Floppy Drive Properties

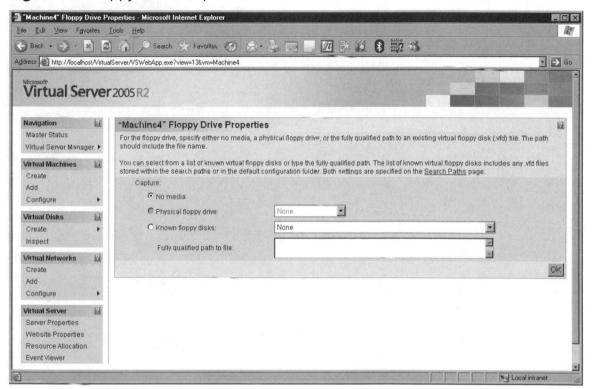

Notice from the figure that there is no attachment property. Every virtual machine contains one floppy disk drive, no more, no less. Also notice that the option to capture a physical floppy disk drive is grayed out; this host does not contain a physical floppy disk drive.

Virtual floppy disks can be created from the Virtual Server interface as follows. From **Virtual Disks**, select **Create**, and then click **Virtual Floppy Disk**. You will be presented with the interface similar to that shown in Figure 7.3.

Figure 7.3 Creating a Virtual Floppy Disk

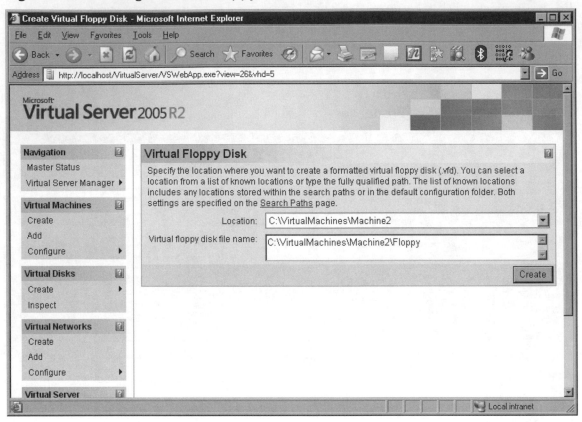

Select the desired location or type the full path and the name of the virtual floppy disk to create. You do not have to type the extension; just the name of the floppy disk suffices.

> **NOTE**
>
> You can also create virtual floppy disks with a shareware product called WinImage. The advantage of WinImage is that you can modify the floppy image's contents from the host. Using Virtual Server you can only modify floppy disk drive contents from within the virtual machine. You can download WinImage from www.winimage.com.

As mentioned earlier, there is always one virtual floppy disk drive in a virtual machine. But when you examine the virtual machine's BIOS configuration, you may have noticed that you can configure two floppy disk drives. See Figure 7.4 for the BIOS Setup screen.

By default, only dive A has been enabled. When you enable drive B as well, the guest operating system detects the drive.

Figure 7.4 Floppy Configuration in the Virtual Machine BIOS

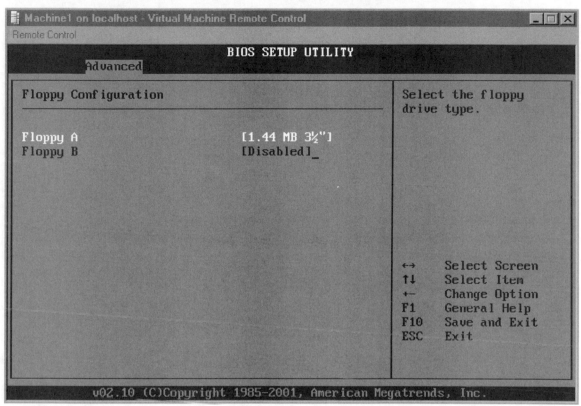

However, you cannot use drive B. Virtual Server supports only one floppy disk drive, which is implicitly attached as the first floppy disk drive. The second floppy disk drive is attached as well, but you cannot capture anything to it.

You should also not modify the drive characteristics; for example, changing the drive option from 3.5 inches to 5.25 inches. The guest operating system detects drive A to be a 5.25-in. drive. However, you can only use the sizes mentioned earlier and only on drive A. Figure 7.5 shows all floppy disk drive options.

Figure 7.5 Floppy Disk Drive Size Options in the Virtual Machine BIOS

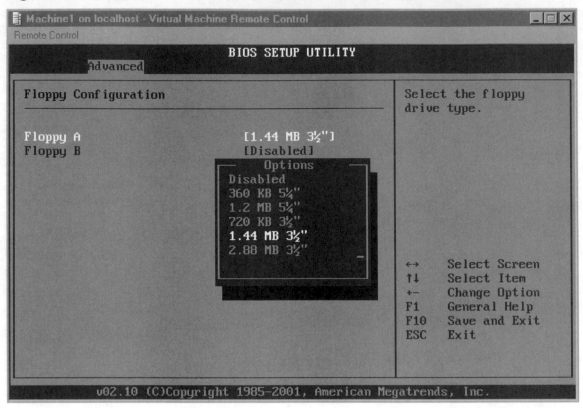

> **NOTE**
>
> When you disable drive A and enable drive B, the power-on self test will fail and report an error. The virtual machine will not boot until you press F1.

A host floppy disk drive can be captured to the virtual floppy disk drive. However, the required format and sizes still apply. This means that 5.25" size host drive or 3.5" with 2.88 MB floppy disks are not supported.

From the previous discussion it should be clear that you should not modify the floppy configuration in the BIOS. There is no need for modification there. If you do not want a virtual floppy *disk,* simply don't attach any in the virtual machine configuration. If you do not want a floppy disk *drive* in the virtual machine, you have to disable drive A.

Virtual Server creates virtual floppy disks read/write by default. Remember that a virtual floppy disk is just a file and that it is created as a *writable* file by Virtual Server. When you want multiple virtual machines to be able to read the same floppy disk, this fails when the floppy disk has not been made read-only. The floppy disk gets locked by the running virtual machine where it is captured.

Recall from the time we all used floppy disks that making a floppy disk read-only meant moving the write-protection tab in the write-protect position. When you did, the tab was moved so the floppy disk had two holes in it (for a 1.44 MB floppy disk). Figure 7.6 symbolically displays the default 1.44 MB floppy disk status after creating a virtual floppy disk called Floppy.vfd.

Figure 7.6 Writable Virtual Floppy Disk

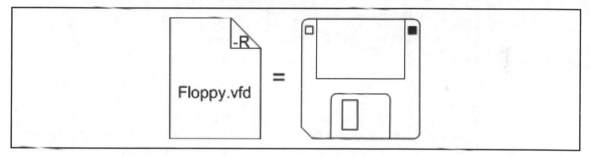

So how do you move the write protection tab on a virtual floppy disk? By making the file read-only. Simply setting the read-only attribute on the file makes it read-only. Then you can have multiple virtual machines capture the same virtual floppy disk. Figure 7.7 symbolically shows the floppy disk status when setting the read-only attribute on the virtual floppy disk called Floppy.vfd.

Figure 7.7 Read-Only Virtual Floppy Disk

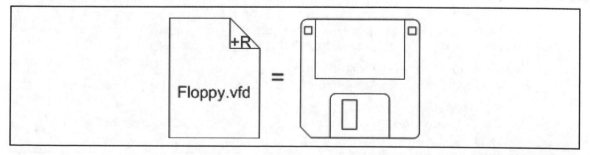

Virtual Hard Disks

The previous paragraphs discussed removable media. Virtual Server supports writing to virtual floppy disks and reading from virtual CD or DVD media. But these media are generally used only for installation tasks or transfer of small files. Installation of an operating system requires a hard disk. And so do applications for retrieving and storing data.

Virtual Server provides virtual machines with hard disks. These disks are not physical disks; therefore, Virtual Server emulates them. To a guest operating system in a virtual machine, however, this is completely transparent. The guest operating system is only aware of the size of the disk and type of storage architecture.

Configuring & Implementing...

Storage Architecture

A virtual hard disk can be attached to two types of storage architecture: IDE (ATA) or SCSI.

Virtual IDE (Integrated Drive Electronics) supports two channels called the primary and secondary. Each channel supports two devices called the master and the slave. In a virtual machine the master is device 0, the slave device 1. The size limit of a virtual hard disk attached to IDE is 127 GB.

Virtual SCSI (Small Computer Systems Interface) supports four buses and 28 devices. Each virtual machine can have up to four SCSI controllers. Each controller can be set to either SCSI ID 6 or 7. The IDs of multiple SCSI controllers may be the same because each controller exists on its own bus. The size limit of a virtual hard disk attached to SCSI is 2 TB. SCSI supports multiple simultaneous disk transactions.

The choice of architecture is determined by several factors.

- Performance
  For best performance you should attach the virtual hard disks to SCSI.

- Maximum number of IDE drives
  Recall that the CD/DVD drive can only be attached to IDE. This leaves three virtual hard disks to be attached to IDE. With SCSI you can have seven virtual hard disks per controller. This gives you much more flexibility in storage and leaves enough options for CD/DVD drives attached to IDE.

- Maximum size of IDE virtual disks
  When the maximum disk size of IDE is a limitation, you must use SCSI.

- SCSI clustering
  Use SCSI clustering when you need to create an MSCS cluster between two virtual machines.

> Besides the storage architectures mentioned above, Virtual Server supports using SAN and iSCSI. But these storage technologies are not available as attachments for virtual hard disks. These can be used from the operating system point of view. However, there is no support for SAN in a virtual machine; you cannot add hardware (HBA) to a virtual machine. Virtual Server emulates storage; it does not virtualize the host's storage. But you can store the virtual disks on a LUN assigned to the Virtual Server host.
>
> You can also use iSCSI with Virtual Server for storing the virtual hard disks. You can use iSCSI within the virtual machines because iSCSI requires only a network adapter. iSCSI must be used in production scenarios for virtual machine clustering and clustering of applications using MSCS.

A virtual hard disk is a file on the host disk. This makes the virtual hard disk storage-architecture-agnostic. In the physical world there is a difference between an IDE and a SCSI hard disk. For Virtual Server these disks are the same, only their attachment makes the difference. You can change the attachment of disks between IDE and SCSI. Notice, however, that Virtual Server will not attach a virtual hard disk larger than 127 GB to IDE.

One property that you cannot change after you have created a virtual hard disk is the size. The size is an internal property of the virtual disk that is set at time of creation. This size is also called the logical size because it has no direct relation with the virtual disk file size.

As with planning a physical machine's storage configuration, you should actually plan even more with virtual machine storage. You should realize that a virtual disk is a file that is stored on the host disk. All reads and writes are done from and to this single file. Rapid access to this file should be as optimal as possible.

Virtual Server contains three types of virtual hard disk. To a guest operating system in a virtual machine, those are all the same. But to you, as an administrator of Virtual Server, the difference is significant and good understanding of each type enables you to create numerous virtual machine scenarios.

The next paragraphs cover the various virtual hard disk types and their usage.

Dynamically Expanding Virtual Hard Disk

When you create a new virtual machine using the Create Virtual Machine page, the Virtual Server Administration Web site defaults to a virtual hard disk of 16 GB in size, attached as the first disk to the Primary IDE channel. This hard disk is of type dynamically expanding.

A dynamically expanding virtual hard disk is a virtual disk that grows as space is needed. To be a bit more precise, it is a file on the host that gets expanded by Virtual Server upon write requests when more storage space is needed on the virtual hard disk and the logical size has not been reached. When necessary, Virtual Server keeps expanding the disk, but only up to its logical size or when the host disk is full.

The advantage of this type should be obvious. It enables you to create any size of virtual disk without allocating the same amount of space on the host. No matter what logical size you choose, a dynamically expanding disk starts as a file of approximately 35 KB in size.

The fact that you can create practically any size of virtual disk without the need of the same amount of available disk space on the host requires planning because the disk may grow beyond the available disk space, thereby creating a "disk full" situation.

Probably the less obvious disadvantage of this type is fragmentation of the file. Because this virtual disk starts as a very small file and grows over time, it is likely to get fragmented. Fragmentation may get worse with multiple virtual hard disks of this type on the same volume. Realize that this file is a *hard disk* of a virtual machine. Many servers these days contain tens of gigabytes of allocated disk space, which would result in a *file* on the host of tens of gigabytes in size.

Virtual Server expands the dynamically expanding disk when necessary. This means that there is some overhead involved with expanding the disk. The overhead may not be noticeable; performance degradation is more likely to occur due to fragmentation. However, even when the virtual disk file is contiguous, there is some overhead.

In what scenario would you use a dynamically expanding disk? For those virtual machines that you don't know how much space their disks will finally take up. In that scenario, you assign a logical disk size large enough to hold its contents.

The final virtual disk size (file disk allocation) on the host is approximately what is actually needed by the guest. If necessary, you can convert the disk to a different type. This is discussed later under "Converting."

You can create the dynamically expanding disk through **Virtual Disks**. Select **Create** and click **Dynamically Expanding Virtual Hard Disk**. See Figure 7.8 for a reference.

The default size in the Virtual Server Administration Web site is 16 GB. Notice from the figure that you do not have to specify the virtual hard disk extension (vhd) in the filename. Consider the

Figure 7.8 Creating a Dynamically Expanding Virtual Hard Disk

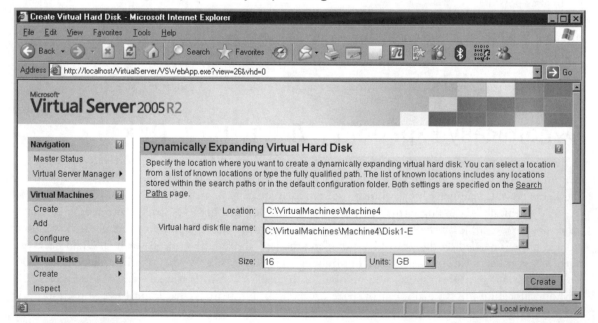

virtual hard disk's storage architecture you plan to use when specifying its size. Anything larger than 127 GB requires SCSI.

Compacting

After you have your virtual machine up and running, you may notice that the current size of the virtual disk file on the host does not correspond to what is allocated in the guest. For example, you may notice a disk file of 8 GB, whereas the guest operating system reports that only 4 GB has been allocated.

In such a situation, files that had obviously been deleted are stored on the virtual disk. These files still exist and allocate space in the virtual hard disk file. The guest operating system can reuse this space for other files. However, Virtual Server had previously expanded the file because there was insufficient disk space but cannot shrink the file because it does not know which files have been deleted.

When a file is deleted, it still exists on the file system. This is a file system aspect and not related to either virtual or physical machines. Files that have been deleted are only marked as deleted, thereby indicating that the space they occupy is available for use. But those files still exist if they have not been overwritten.

Since all files in the guest are actually written in a single file on the host, there needs to be a mechanism for Virtual Server to reclaim space of those deleted files to reduce the virtual hard disk file.

This mechanism is called compaction and is made up of two distinct phases. The first is the so-called pre-compaction phase, which prepares the virtual hard disk for compaction later by Virtual Server. Pre-compaction is run from within the guest operating system. The second phase is the compaction phase, which is run from Virtual Server when the virtual machine is turned off.

So what exactly is pre-compacting? Recall those deleted files on the file system. They are still there but only marked as deleted. You need to enable Virtual Server to reclaim the space (reduce the hard disk file) by zeroing out the sectors they occupy. This is what pre-compaction does; it writes zeroes by writing large files with zeros on the available space. By filling the available space with those large files, it overwrites all files which are marked as deleted. This continues until there is no space left to write. At that point, everything has been zeroed out.

> **NOTE**
>
> Virtual Server 2005 did not come with a pre-compaction tool. This was included with Virtual PC 2004. This has been added to Virtual Server 2005 R2. It is called the Microsoft Virtual Disk Pre-Compactor. If you want, you can use it with Virtual Server 2005 as well. There is no dependence on Virtual Server release, it just was not included.

You run the Microsoft Virtual Disk Pre-Compactor by attaching the Precompact.iso to the CD/DVD Drive. This is an example of a situation where you must have a CD/DVD drive in a virtual machine. To start pre-compaction, perform the following steps. Under **Virtual Machines**, click **Configure <virtualmachine>**, click **CD/DVD**, click **Known image files**, and then select **Precompact.iso**. See Figure 7.9.

Figure 7.9 Attaching Virtual Disk Pre-Compactor ISO to a CD/DVD Drive

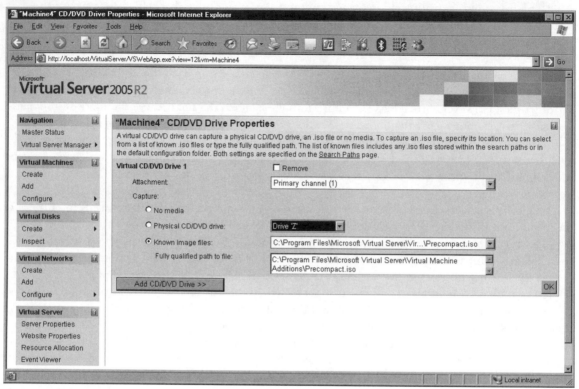

When the virtual machine is running a guest operating system of Windows 2000 or later, the Microsoft Virtual Disk Pre-Compactor will automatically start and show the dialog box shown in Figure 7.10. Notice that it will automatically start only when autorun has not been disabled.

Figure 7.10 Microsoft Virtual Disk Pre-Compactor

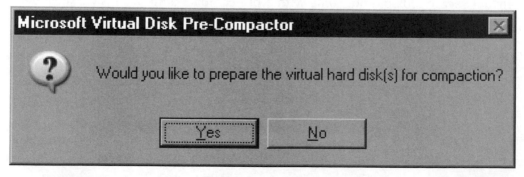

When you click yes, the Virtual Disk Pre-Compactor will perform its write activities on all logical drives. As explained earlier, the Pre-Compactor will write large files to the disk(s). You can see its progress by opening a command prompt in the root of the logical drive. See Figure 7.11, which lists the zeroing files written in the root.

Figure 7.11 Listing the Pre-Compactor Zeroing Files

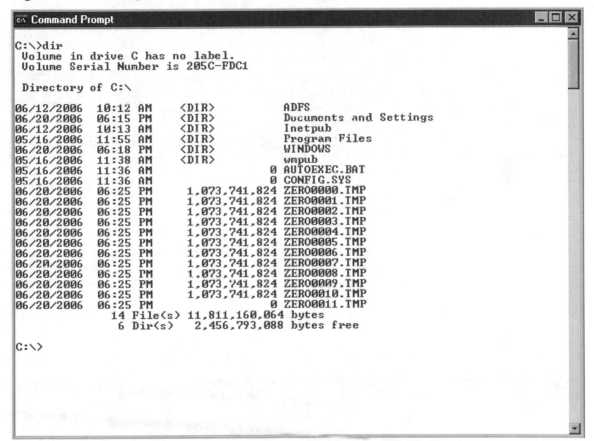

The Microsoft Virtual Disk Pre-Compactor starts writing its first file starting with ZERO0000.tmp. As long as the disk is not full, it keeps writing until the disk is full or the file has reached 1 GB in size. If not full, it continues with the next file, using the last four digits to increase the number.

Configuring and Implementing...

Preparations before Pre-compacting

It is very important to delete any file that can be deleted at this stage. For example, if there are temporary files left by applications, you should delete these, empty the Recycle Bin, delete obsolete files from previous processes, etc. You should basically delete anything that can be deleted before running the Pre-Compactor.

After deleting files, you should run a defragmentation tool to optimize sector occupation of the files that remain. Fragmented files are defragmented, which benefits both performance and compaction. On Windows, you can defragment using Microsoft defrag or you can use commercial products.

Only after these steps have been performed should you run the Pre-Compactor.

When the Virtual Disk Pre-Compactor has finished, you will see a dialog box like the one shown in Figure 7.12. At that point you should shut down the operating system to prevent any unnecessary file modifications on the disk. Notice that the text mentions a Virtual Disk Wizard. This does not exist in Virtual Server; this applies to Virtual PC 2004.

Figure 7.12 Microsoft Virtual Disk Pre-Compactor Completion

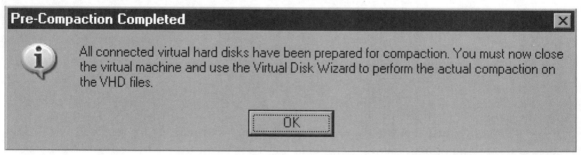

Pre-Compaction Completed

All connected virtual hard disks have been prepared for compaction. You must now close the virtual machine and use the Virtual Disk Wizard to perform the actual compaction on the VHD files.

OK

The Pre-Compactor can also be invoked manually. There are several switches you can provide. You can list all available switches by providing precompact.exe with /? switch. See Figure 7.13.

Figure 7.13 Virtual Disk Pre-Compactor Command-Line Switches

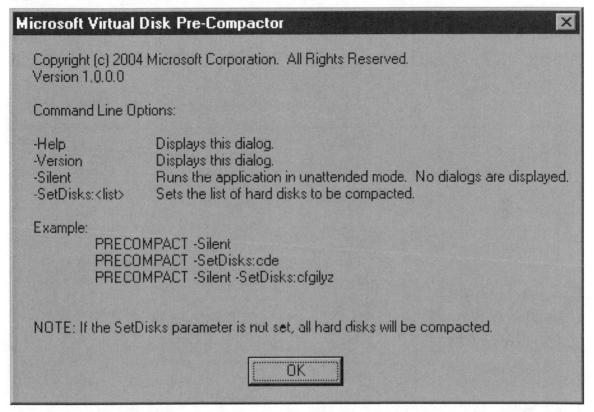

The most important switch is the *setdisks* switch. When you have virtual machines with multiple disks, you may not want pre-compaction to run on all of them but only on a specific one. Or you may be using virtual disks other than the dynamically expanding type on which pre-compaction is useless (see later discussions). The *silent* switch enables unattended operation so that you can automate pre-compaction using script.

After pre-compaction has completed, you should shut down the virtual machine. The next phase is the compaction phase. To compact a virtual disk, perform the following steps. From **Virtual Disks**, click **Inspect**, select the virtual disk to inspect or type the location of the virtual disk, click the **Inspect** button, click **Compact virtual hard disk**, and then click **Compact**.

Figures 7.14, 7.15, and 7.16 show the Virtual Server interfaces along these steps.

Figure 7.14 Inspect Virtual Hard Disk

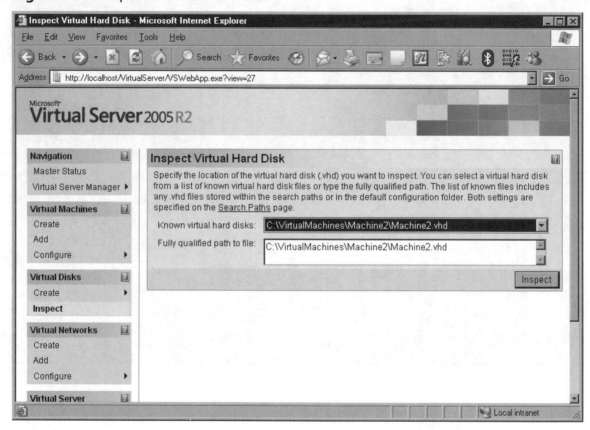

Figure 7.15 Virtual Hard Disk Properties after Inspection

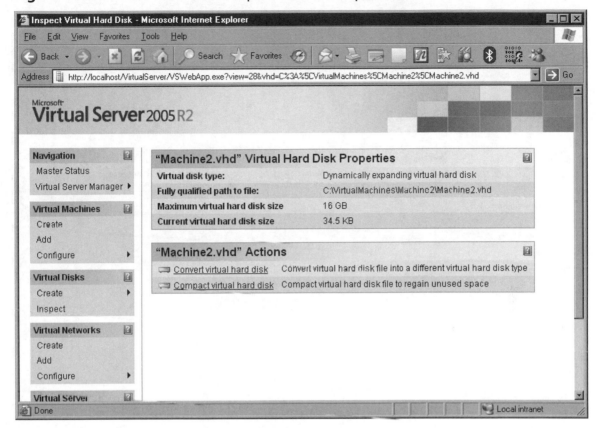

Figure 7.16 Compact Virtual Hard Disk

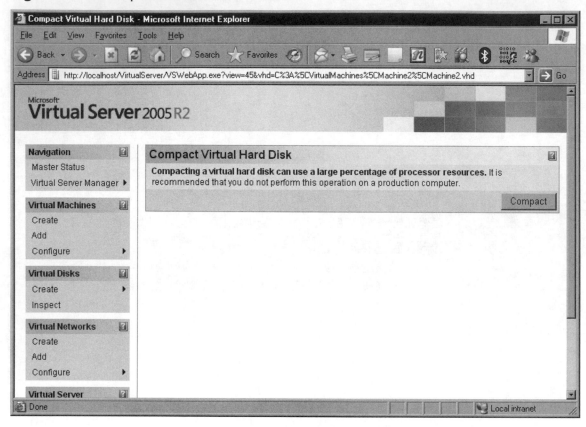

When Virtual Server compacts the virtual disk file, it rewrites the file, ignoring everything that has been zeroed out. After compaction, the size of the virtual disk file should be approximately equal to the amount of allocated space in the virtual machine.

NOTE

The compaction process of Virtual Server has no understanding of a pre-compacted disk. You can run compaction as often as you like without pre-compacting a virtual disk. However, you will find that you do not reclaim much space without the pre-compaction phase.

Converting

The dynamically expanding virtual disk can be converted to a fixed-size virtual disk. That type is covered in the next paragraph. When converting to a fixed-size virtual hard disk, the physical size of the virtual disk image file will be the same as the logical size.

> **NOTE**
>
> Converting the dynamically expanding disk leaves the original disk intact. Technically, you are not converting the disk but migrating to another type.

You can convert a virtual hard disk only when the virtual machine is turned off. The steps are the same as described earlier for compaction. See Figure 7.15 above; instead of **Compact virtual hard disk**, you have to click **Convert virtual hard disk**. This leads to the screen shown in Figure 7.17.

Figure 7.17 Convert Virtual Hard Disk

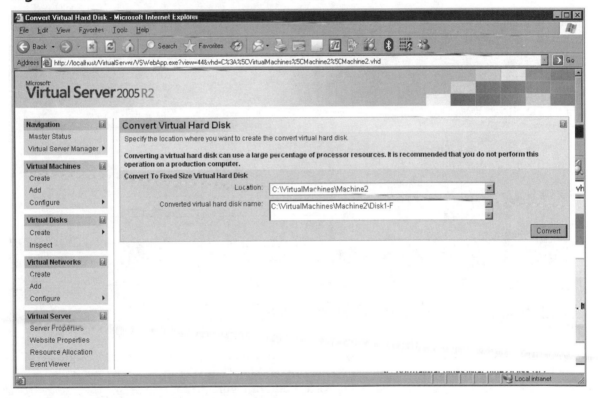

Fixed-Size Virtual Hard Disk

The fixed-size virtual hard disk is exactly the opposite of the dynamically expanding virtual hard disk. Whereas the latter is expanded by Virtual Server as space in the disk is needed, the physical size of the fixed-size disk is at the logical size after creation.

The fixed-size disk is what it is called; fixed in size. This size, however, is the physical size of the disk file and is the same as the logical size. But the logical size is still fixed. The purpose of the fixed-size disk is to allocate the space on the host disk so Virtual Server does not have to "interfere" in an expansion process. This means that there is no overhead when writing to this virtual hard disk type.

The disadvantage should also be obvious; the logical size you choose for this disk will also be the physical size on the host. This requires more planning and capacity management on the host.

When Virtual Server creates this disk, it writes a sparse file filled with zeroes. This way it makes sure the amount of space is pre-allocated on the host disk. From a fragmentation perspective, this type of virtual disk is not likely to get fragmented, assuming that the host disk was defragmented prior to creating the virtual disk and that there was enough space to create a contiguous file.

To create a fixed-size disk through **Virtual Disks**, select **Create** and click **Fixed Size Virtual Hard Disk**. See Figure 7.18 for a screen reference.

Figure 7.18 Creating a Fixed-Size Virtual Hard Disk

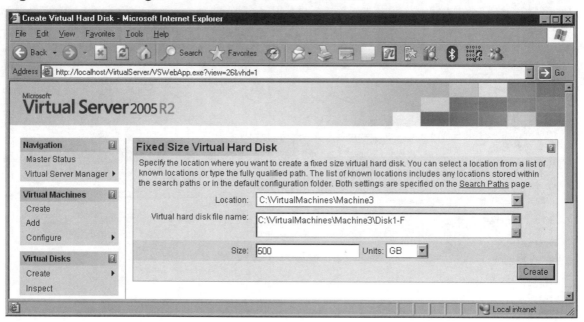

In this window, a fixed-size virtual disk is being configured with name *Disk1-F* and logical size of 500 GB. Recall from the previous discussion that you should consider the type of storage architecture the disk will be attached to. The virtual disk of Figure 7.18 demands SCSI.

Converting

The fixed-size disk can be converted to dynamically expanding. You may want to do this when the disk does not require the amount of space you initially configured. For example, when you have created a 50 GB fixed-size disk but only use 8 GB in the virtual machine, a conversion will result in an 8 GB disk. Notice that its logical size is still 50 GB; that will never change.

Converting the fixed-size disk leaves the original disk intact. Technically, you are not converting the disk but migrating to another type.

The steps required for converting to a dynamically expanding disk are the same as for converting a dynamically expanding disk to fixed size. See the discussion on converting under the section "Dynamically Expanding Virtual Hard Disk."

Differencing Virtual Hard Disk

A rather interesting type of virtual hard disk is the differencing virtual hard disk. Compared to the other virtual disk types, this one is quite different. The dynamically expanding and fixed-size types are basically each other's opposite. This gives you a lot of flexibility when configuring disks for virtual machines. But the differencing disk enables scenarios the other types do not offer.

The differencing disk is a virtual hard disk that contains the differences compared to a reference, called the parent virtual disk. The differencing disk is a "recording" of changes to the parent. Assume the situation as shown in Figure 7.19. A virtual machine is configured with a single virtual disk, Disk1. The virtual disk is a differencing disk with one parent.

Logically, the differencing disk is one virtual disk consisting of a single disk file. A guest operating system in the virtual machine reads from and writes to its "physical" disk because it has no notion of running inside a virtual machine. But physically on the host, Virtual Server divides these operations between two virtual disk files: the write operations to the differencing disk and the read operations from both.

Figure 7.19 Differencing Disk View Points

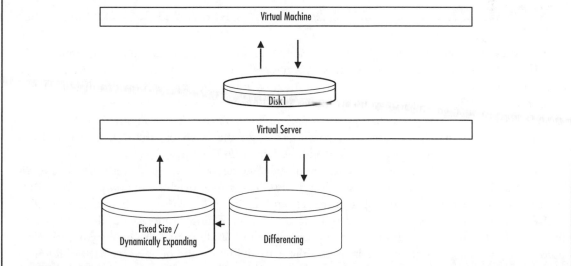

To create a differencing disk, go to **Virtual Disks**, select **Create**, and then click **Create Differencing Virtual Hard Disk**. See Figure 7.20 for a reference.

Figure 7.20 Creating a Differencing Virtual Hard Disk

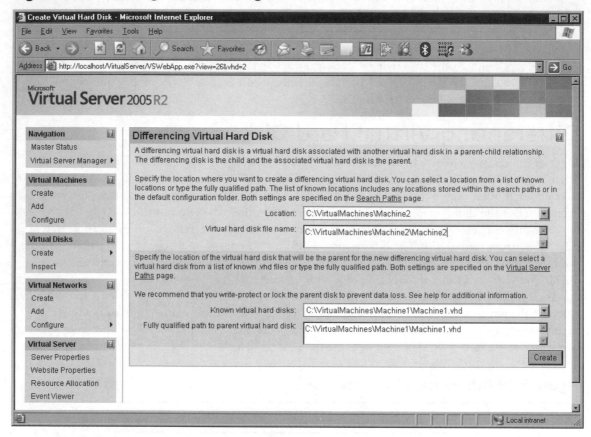

In this figure, a virtual disk Machine2 is created with virtual disk Machine1 as its parent.

When would you use differencing disks? Assume that you have a virtual machine, Machine1, with a disk of type dynamically expanding. You install Windows Server 2003 on this machine (so on the disk). After installation you shut down Windows Server 2003 and create a new virtual machine, Machine2. Then you create a differencing disk for Machine2. See Figure 7.20. You call that disk Machine2.vhd. Finally, you configure Machine2 to use the newly created disk as its first disk. When you turn on Machine2, you notice Windows Server 2003 booting...

The magic behind all this lies in the nature of differencing disks. Virtual Server treats the two disks, the parent and the differencing disk, as one logical disk. The virtual machine has only one disk. But under the hood, Virtual Server manages all reads from both disks and writes to the differencing disk.

Because the parent is treated as read-only, you can create multiple differencing disks using the same parent. Multiple virtual disks can then be used with multiple virtual machines. For example, you could create one parent with 10 children. And these 10 children could be used with 10 different virtual machines. And this scenario requires only a single installation of Windows Server 2003.

NOTE

In the scenario described above, each virtual machine uses differencing disks with the operating system on a parent disk. When these virtual machines are to be used in a network or in a domain, remember to make each operating system unique. Otherwise, you may run into TCP/IP address conflicts, NetBIOS name conflicts, or SID conflicts when used in the same domain.

To create unique Windows virtual machines or unique children, run *sysprep* in the guest operating system of the parent as the last step. This way, each guest operating system in a child will run mini-setup and offer uniqueness in name and SID.

As with the previous virtual disk types, the differencing disk type has some aspects to consider. The differencing disk contains all modifications to its parent. Consecutive modifications are also recorded into this disk. Basically, the differencing disk contains only updates to its parent and can be viewed as a transaction log.

Due to this nature, the differencing disk can only grow. This means that file modifications of file modifications are appended to the virtual disk file. Recall that with the other types, modifications are written to the files themselves and that deleted files' space can be reused. This is not true for the differencing disk, because any modification is recorded, which is yet another append to the file.

When you use the differencing disk in the Windows Server 2003 scenario as depicted above, you will notice that the virtual disk file grows quite quickly. Simply booting the virtual machine can cause a differencing disk of a couple of hundreds of megabytes. This is caused by the fact that once the operating system boots, writes occur to many different files, such as log files and registry files.

However, the differencing disk can be compressed very well. Using NTFS compression, you can dramatically reduce the size of the file on the host. The compression ratio can be enormous, depending on what gets written to the differencing disk. When only updates are recorded, the compression ratio will be much larger than when you have copied compressed files to it.

Configuring and Implementing...

Using NTFS Compression

You might wonder about the performance impact of file system compression on the host CPU. The overhead is a couple of percentages so this should be negligible from CPU perspective.

Continued

You should not consider the impact on CPU load but rather the benefit the extra CPU load gives from a disk I/O perspective.

When files have a good compression ratio, file I/O is much less than without compression. This results in much faster I/O than would be achieved without compression. This is caused by disk I/O that is extremely slow compared to the processing power of the CPU. By leveraging CPU power, you prevent a lot of slow disk I/O.

You should always use NTFS compression on files that really compress well. This increases throughput. Of course, it makes no sense to compress already compressed files; this only increases overhead.

Figure 7.21 shows the result when using NTFS compression on a differencing disk.

Figure 7.21 Using NTFS Compression on a Differencing Virtual Hard Disk File localization

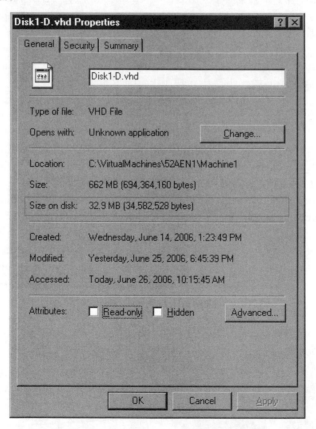

The figure displays the *Size on disk* of the virtual hard disk Disk1–D from virtual machine Machine3. Without compression, this file would take up 662MB. With compression, it takes approximately 33MB.

So here is a tip when using differencing disks: always compress them using NTFS compression.

Since the differencing disk can only grow, it becomes large very quickly. Without NTFS compression the file on the host is likely to get fragmented. It may still get fragmented with compression enabled, but this is usually much less. In both cases, you have to consider fragmentation and schedule defragmentation jobs.

You should also be aware of the fact that the parent may not change once the differencing disk is created. Recall that the differencing disk contains the *differences* relative to the parent. Those differences could become obsolete when the parent's contents were changed. Compare this with a database and its transaction logs; if you change the database before committing the log, this invalidates the changes in the log.

When a differencing disk is created, Virtual Server stores information about the parent in the differencing disk file. Both the header and footer of virtual disks contain information. So does the differencing disk file when it is created. The last modified time as well as the GUID of the parent disk are stored in the differencing disk file. Based on the time stamp, Virtual Server is able to warn you, but not block you, when it detects that the parent's time stamp has been changed. As a best practice, make the parent virtual disk read-only.

The parent's GUID is necessary to create a strong relationship. This relationship can never be changed. But when Virtual Server cannot find the parent virtual disk, you can update the differencing disk through the Virtual Disks interface by inspecting the differencing disk and pointing to the new location of the parent.

> **NOTE**
>
> The relation of a differencing disk with its parent is stored in the differencing disk. Every virtual hard disk contains a GUID, which is used to uniquely identify the parent.
>
> The differencing disk also stores both the relative path and the fully qualified path to its parent. When Virtual Server cannot find the parent using the relative path, it will try the absolute path. Virtual Server will not update the location information when it uses the absolute path. Only when it cannot find the parent will Virtual Server notify in the EventLog. The relation needs to be updated using Inspect and pointing to the parent. When the GUIDs match, Virtual Server updates both relative and absolute location information.
>
> For more information on virtual hard disks, refer to the Virtual Hard Disk Image Format Specification available at www.microsoft.com/windowsserversystem/virtualserver/techinfo/vhdspec.mspx.

The logical properties of the parent are inherited with the differencing disk. For example, the logical disk size is still the same. But the amount of disk space available on the virtual disk is what remained on the parent. Do not expect to extend a disk with a differencing disk when it has become full; the differencing disk will also be full.

Chaining

The fixed-size and dynamically expanding virtual disks can be a parent to a differencing disk. However, this is not the complete story. Actually, any virtual disk type can be a parent to a differencing virtual disk. So can a differencing disk. In such a scenario, there is more than one differencing disk "below" the disk in the virtual machine. There is actually a chain of links from the last differencing disk to the last or top parent; this is called chaining. See Figure 7.22.

Figure 7.22 Chaining Differencing Disks

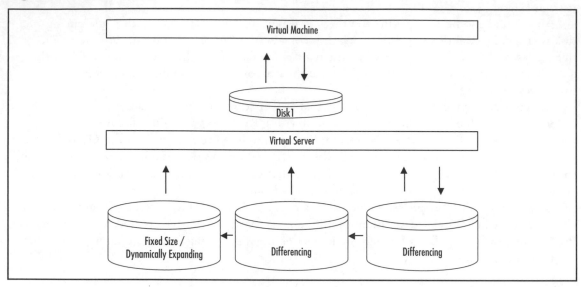

This picture has the same logical view from both virtual machine and Virtual Server as that shown in Figure 7.19. However, the physical disk in the virtual machine is built up of three virtual disks: two differencing disks and one dynamically expanding or fixed-size disk.

With chaining, the same rules apply as with a single differencing disk: all disks in the parent chain are treated as read-only; only the differencing disk attached to the virtual machine is read/write. None of the parents may change, as previously explained. Any change in the parent chain invalidates the differencing disk.

When would you use chaining? When you want to postpone changes to the parent. Let's take an example and see how chaining could enable that.

Suppose you have a Microsoft Exchange Server 2003 server with Service Pack 1. And suppose you want to test Service Pack 2 on the server without making the changes permanent while being able to research its functionality first. You create a differencing disk with the Exchange server's first disk. You create a new virtual machine called ExchangeSP2 and start it with the newly created differencing disk. Then you apply Service Pack 2 and do your research. If you want to revert to the original scenario you can discard this disk and start the original server with Service Pack 1. Or when you are happy with Service Pack 2 and want to keep the changes, you can keep them.

Merging

In the scenario above with the Exchange Server, you could either discard the changes or keep them. The process of applying the changes to your original configuration is called merging.

You have two choices when merging changes: you can merge them into the parent, thereby overwriting the original virtual hard disk, or you can merge them into a new virtual hard disk.

NOTE

There is a fundamental difference in merge scenarios.

When you choose to merge with the parent, all changes are written into the parent and the original parent's content is lost. You end up with the new configuration as if you applied them directly to the parent.

When you choose to merge to a different disk you merge all changes in the chain. So when you have three disks in the chain, you write a new disk that has all updated content from all the disks in the chain.

If you want to merge differencing disks, the virtual machine must be turned off. To merge a virtual disk, go to **Virtual Disks**, click **Inspect**, and then select the virtual disk you want to inspect. Figure 7.23 shows the results after inspection of a virtual disk.

Figure 7.23 Differencing Disk Chain After Inspect

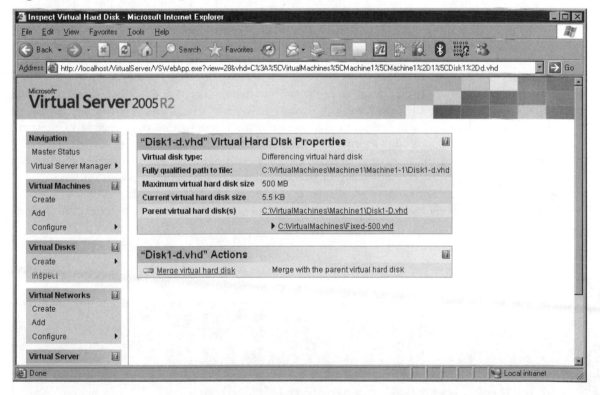

Notice that the results show a chain of disks; C:\VirtualMachines\Fixed-500 is a parent of C:\VirtualMachines\Machine1\Disk1-D, which in turn is a parent of C:\VirtualMachines\Machine1\ Machine1-1\Disk1-D. Also notice the maximum virtual hard disk size, which is 500 MB. This is inherited from the fixed-size disk, Fixed-500. Clicking **Merge virtual hard disk** results in Figure 7.24.

Figure 7.24 Merging Virtual Hard Disks

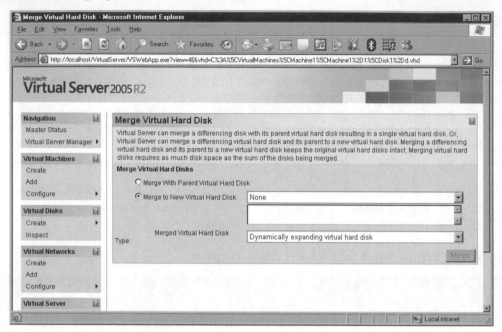

Notice from the figure that you can merge with its parent or merge with a new virtual hard disk. Also notice that along with the merge you can choose the type of virtual disk that will be created.

Using differencing disks is beneficial in test environments where modifications need to be tested frequently and where the starting point needs to be the same for each and every test cycle. Differencing disks enable you to very quickly create a new environment and to easily and quickly restore to that starting point. Basically, using differencing disks saves you huge amounts of time in setting up and configuring your virtual machines because you only have to do that once.

Neither a differencing disk nor a fixed-size disk can be compacted. To reduce their size, you should merge the changes of the differencing disk or convert the fixed-size disk to dynamically expanding.

Configuring & Implementing...

Undo Disks versus Differencing Disks

When you open a virtual machine's disk properties, you can see a check box labeled "Enable undo disks." See Figure 7.25 for a screen reference. When you select this feature, Virtual Server creates an undo disk for each and every virtual hard disk of the virtual machine. Technically, these disks are differencing disks. The difference being that Virtual Server generates them for every disk and that they are enabled on a virtual machine level.

Using undo disks simplifies the process of creating differencing disks for each virtual hard disk in a virtual machine. Another benefit is that when using differencing disks, the undo disk feature delays modifications to even the differencing disks.

Make sure that you have enough storage space when using undo disks. Recall the discussion on differencing disks and their nature of recording updates. These files can become quite large. If you plan to use this feature often, enable NTFS compression on the virtual machine folder.

Figure 7.25 Enable Undo Disks Property

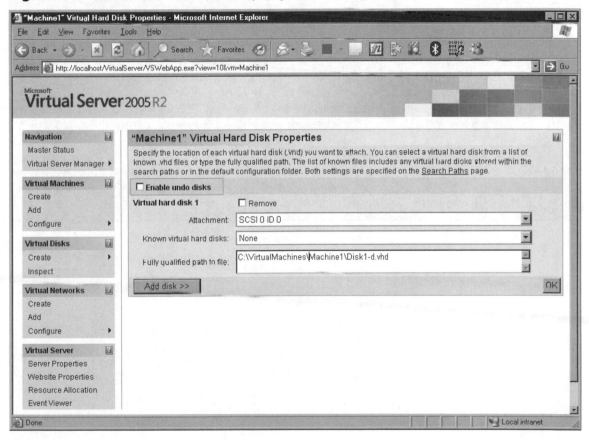

Configuring & Implementing...

Storing Virtual Hard Disks

The demand of an application in a virtual machine finally comes down to the host. If the application is best served with a machine containing two disks, then your virtual machine will have the same. For best performance with disk-bound applications, you should store the virtual disk files separately from the operating system disk on the host and separately from each other. The Virtual Server host is yet another server that serves virtual machines. Very often such a server has a separate disk for the operating system (being either logical or physical) and another disk for things like sources and paging.

Requirements of the host disk I/O subsystem increase with the number of virtual machines and number of virtual disks per virtual machine. Performance of each virtual machine is mainly dependent on the performance of the host disk I/O subsystem.

Always try to separate disk I/O intensive virtual machines by using separate spindles. If you do not want single spindles, then use RAID 0 or RAID 1. If they are mostly intensive readers, you could use RAID 5. Most important is that these virtual machines do not influence each other.

You can also use virtualized storage like SAN or iSCSI. Whatever you choose, always realize that virtual hard disks are very large files so design their storage appropriately.

Use fixed-size disks when fragmentation is an issue or you are designing virtual machines for production use. Production systems generally are decommissioned only once at the end of their lifetime. They should be designed properly and required disk space should be pre-allocated using fixed-size disk.

Summary

Virtual disks enable storage and retrieval in virtual machines. Virtual Server supports a virtual floppy disk drive per machine and multiple virtual CD/DVD drives. Both can be attached to a host drive or can use an image file like a virtual floppy disk or ISO 9660 ISO file.

A Virtual hard disk is virtualized disk storage in a virtual machine. On the host, a virtual hard disk is just a file. Depending on the type of disk, this file has different characteristics.

The dynamically expanding virtual hard disk is expanded as needed; Virtual Server expands the file upon write requests when space in the file is insufficient.

The fixed-size virtual hard disk is a file on the host that is of the same size as the logical size. Advantage is that Virtual Server never interferes to expand. However, you have to plan in advance for disk capacity. There is also no way to reclaim unused space; you have to convert this type first.

The differencing virtual hard disk contains differences compared to content that exists on a parent virtual hard disk. The relationship with the parent is established when the differencing disk is created. The parent can be any type of virtual disk, even a differencing virtual hard disk. This makes chaining possible, with which you can create a hierarchy of disks.

Disks can be converted from fixed size to dynamically expanding and vice versa. differencing disks can be merged with their parent or merged to a new disk.

Performance in general is dependent on that of the disk I/O subsystem. Disk speed, storage architecture, and configuration all determine the final performance and capacity of disk I/O.

Solutions Fast Track

Removable Hard Disks

☑ Virtual Server emulates disks, which are called virtual disks. To a guest operating system inside a virtual machine, these virtual disks are the same as those in a physical machine. They behave the same and have the same limitations, determined by their emulated characteristics.

☑ Virtual Server emulates different kinds of disks that are common in today's physical machines. Those can be categorized as either removable disks or hard disks.

☑ Virtual Server supports the use of removable media such as CD or DVD optical disks. Because a DVD drive also supports CDs, Virtual Server emulates a DVD drive.

Virtual Hard Disks

☑ Dynamically expanding disks are expanded on the host when storage is insufficient and the logical size has not been reached.

☑ Dynamically expanding disks start small and generally grow to the size that is needed in the virtual machine.

☑ Dynamically expanding disks can get fragmented on the host. Heavy fragmentation decreases overall performance.

☑ Fixed-size disks are created at their full size. This requires planning and capacity management on the host.

☑ Differencing disks contain modifications relative to a parent disk's content.

☑ Differencing disks can be created of any type of virtual hard disk; this enables chaining.

☑ The size of a virtual disk is set at creation time and cannot be modified afterwards.

Frequently Asked Questions

Q: Can virtual disks be converted?

A: Yes. Both dynamically expanding and fixed-size virtual disks can be converted to each other's type.

Q: Is it possible to mount a virtual hard disk from outside the virtual machine?

A: No. Virtual Server does not provide this functionality. Virtual Server 2005 R2 Service Pack 1 will support this, however.

Q: Can I change the size of a virtual disk?

A: No. The logical size of the virtual disk is set at time of creation. It is the "physical" size of the disk inside the virtual machine. You cannot change the physical size of a disk. If you need more space you can add another disk or ghost the disk and copy to a larger disk.

Q: Can I modify a parent to update the guest operating system of a virtual machine that uses a differencing disk?

A: Technically you can modify the contents on a parent disk but you should not do that. Modifying the parent will invalidate all modifications recorded in the differencing disk. If you need to update files of a guest operating system, you should update them in the differencing disk.

Q: Can I create multiple differencing disks based on a single parent?

A: Yes. This way you can share the parent's contents among multiple virtual machines using differencing disks. The parent could contain the operating system and base tools and each virtual machine's differencing disk could contain the modifications.

Q: Should I use IDE or SCSI when attaching virtual disks?

A: SCSI allows for multiple concurrent disk I/O. SCSI supports larger disks and more devices. For best performance, even with IDE on the host, you should use SCSI disks in your virtual machines.

Q: Is it possible to compact a differencing disk?

A: No. If you need to reduce its size, you should merge the changes.

Q: Is it possible to move a bootable OS disk from IDE to SCSI?

A: Yes. You need to add a SCSI adapter to the virtual machine. (Re)install the virtual machine additions. Move the disk from IDE to SCSI ID 0.

## Chapter 8

Introduction to ADS and Virtual Server Migration Tool

Solutions in this chapter:

- **Automated Deployment Services**
- **What Components Does ADS Use?**
- **Installing ADS**
- **Post-Installation: Configuring ADS**
- **Administration Agent Installing**
- **Adding Hardware Drivers in the Boot OS**
- **Editing Using the Sequence Editor**
- **Installing Virtual Server Migration Toolkit onto the Virtualization Server**

☑ **Summary**

☑ **Solutions Fast Track**

☑ **Frequently Asked Questions**

Automated Deployment Services

One of the key techniques in the virtualization process is the technique to duplicate the physical environment. With most people, third-party products like Norton Ghost (by Symantec) pop into mind. But in this case we are going to take a look at the Microsoft solution in disk duping land.

Microsoft released Automated Deployment Services (ADS) in 2003. The first version was primarily used for rapid deployment scenarios. At that time, virtualizing needed two separate tools from Microsoft: ADS and the Virtual Server Migration Toolkit (VSMT). After the update on ADS, and lifting the version to 1.1, Microsoft placed VSMT in the ADS software bundle.

Rapid Deployment Using ADS

There is a lot more to do than migrating using ADS. A lot of companies install multiple servers. One of the problems that soon arises is the differences that will exist when installing more that one server by hand. Even when the server is installed using an installation manual, it is very likely that the servers are not the same.

In this situation, ADS can solve your problem. As ADS is able to image your hard disk, it also is able to deploy the same image to multiple servers (of the same type) at once. Combine this feature with the Windows capability called Sysprep, and you have your deployment solution.

In the step 1, you install one server (see Figure 8.1). In step 2 you sysprep and image it using one of the templates given by ADS. In step 3 you hook up several servers and deploy the image to those servers in one action. The servers will reboot and start installing the same way. After the installation is completed, all servers are exactly the same.

Designing & Planning…

Too Much Effort?

It may sound like the effort needed to install three servers is less than the installation of ADS and going through steps 1 to 3. Maybe it is. But the servers are the same. And if you're going to migrate servers, you need the ADS server.

One even better thing is the capability to install ADS on a virtual server. By doing so, you do not have to tear down an entire server to deploy multiple servers. Just install Virtual Server on a supported platform, install ADS on a virtual server, and you're off.

After you're finished, do the following: Delete all images in ADS, defragment the server, run decompactor, and Zip the server. Then burn it to DVD and store it in a safe place to be used the next time.

Figure 8.1 ADS Image and Installation Steps

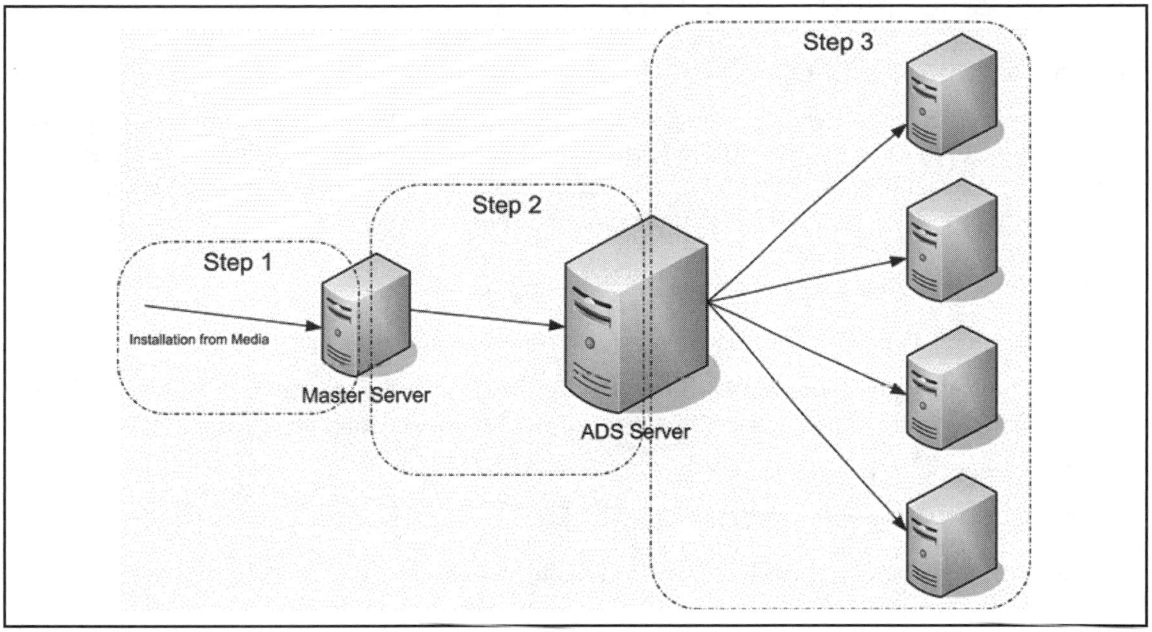

What Components Does ADS Use?

ADS is composed of a set of services, imaging tools, and management agents. At its most basic, ADS contains three discrete services that work in harmony to complete the solution. These services are:

- Controller Service
- Network Boot Service
- Image Distribution Service

Each of these services has specific settings and areas to focus on. In the following chapters we will take a closer look at these services.

ADS Controller Service

The Controller service is the cornerstone upon which all other ADS functionality is built. This service provides for coordination and sequencing of tasks, security and communication with client devices, a centralized database of device data and administrative tasks performed to those devices, and the capability to group devices together to facilitate the management thereof. The Controller service also provides the management of the ADS solution through ADS command-line tools, GUI tools, and WMI-based scripts.

The previously mentioned function of "sequencing of tasks" is one of the most important features because this is the function that allows for a "punch-list" of work to be completed during the deployment of the image-based operating system. For instance, a task sequence may include

BIOS configuration, RAID Controller setup and volume creation, OS image deployment, and post-installation configuration (to name a few).

ADS Network Boot Service

The Network Boot Service (NBS) leverages DHCP to provide ADS boot command authority over the requests of PXE-enabled devices. The PXE-enabled device will receive the location of the NBS as part of its DHCP lease. The NBS is actually two separate services that work together. The first is ADS PXE Service, which sends boot commands to the PXE clients. The second is the ADS Deployment Agent Builder.

The PXE Service is capable of issuing the following commands:

- Download and boot an ADS Deployment Agent created by the Agent Builder Service.
- Download and boot a virtual floppy disk (can be very useful if extensive hardware/BIOS/RAID configuration is warranted prior to the OS image being deployed).
- Ignore the PXE boot request.
- Cease PXE operations and boot to disk (based on the configuration of the BIOS).

The ADS Deployment Agent Builder is a dynamic, device-specific, post-PXE boot service that can perform the following:

- Analyze local hardware on the PXE client and report the findings to the Controller service for recording
- Build a custom "agent" based on the hardware discovered
- Download the agent to execute in the client's local memory

While technically not a component of ADS, a DHCP is required for the NBS part of ADS to function. NBS uses Trivial File Transfer Protocol (TFTP) to send deployments to the agents and the virtual floppy disks to clients.

ADS Image Distribution Service

The Image Distribution Service (IDS) provides for the repository and communications between ADS clients and the images these clients are downloading or uploading. The Controller service facilitates this process and the communications with the client. IDS can deploy images using either a unicast (one-to-one) or multicast (one-to-many) mechanism and has built-in network bandwidth throttling to prevent overloading your network during the deployment process.

The following section will outline the basic requirements to introduce ADS into your environment.

ADS Host Server Requirements

The ADS host servers act as the infrastructure for capturing, deploying, and storing the image-based files for your various Windows server hardware platforms. While all components of ADS could be installed on a single server, in many enterprise-level environments, administrators will choose to separate the various component services that comprise an ADS solution.

The list below is the minimum requirements for a single server ADS solution. For more information on ADS and enterprise ADS solutions, please consult the Microsoft Web site at: www.microsoft.com/windowsserver2003/technologies/management/ads.

- One x86 32-bit computer to host the three basic components of ADS (Controller service, NBS, and IDS)

- 1 GHz or faster processor (x86 32-bit)

- Windows Server 2003 Enterprise Edition in English, Japanese, or German

- 2 GB of hard drive space for ADS setup process *plus* sufficient drive space to store the various images to be distributed (plan ahead for capacity needs because image-based installation can consume copious amounts of disk space)

- 128 MB of RAM (32 GB is the maximum supported and 512 MB is more likely a bare minimum requirement for your host server(s) to function in most small environments)

- 800x600 SVGA or better (mouse and keyboard are optional, because the host server could be treated as a "lights-out" operation for the most part)

- ADS may be installed from local disk, CD/DVD, or network shares

ADS Client-Server Requirements

A "client" server is any Windows Server OS (capable of being managed) that either has the ADS client software installed and configured or is a piece of hardware that meets the requirements for deploying the image-based operating system. The following is a list of the basic requirements to be an ADS client:

- x86 hardware capable of running one of the following operating systems: Windows 2000 Server or Advanced Server with Service Pack 3 or later; Windows Server 2003 Web, Standard, or Enterprise Editions; Windows powered with Service Pack 3 or later

- Network adapter that is Pre-Boot eXecution Environment (PXE) versions 0.99C or later

- BIOS must support booting from PXE and may require an update to support ADS client (consult your hardware manufacturer's documentation to determine eligibility of your hardware to be an ADS client)

ADS Network and Management Requirements

ADS management can occur from the console of the various component servers (or remotely with Remote Desktop). Alternatively, you may choose to install some or all of the management tools on your Windows workstation. In order to remotely manage your ADS environment, you will need to meet the following list of requirements for an x86-based workstation:

- Run an English, Japanese, or German version of the following operating systems: Windows 2000 Professional, Server, or Advanced Server with Service Pack 3 or later; Windows XP Professional with Service Pack 1 or later; Windows Server 2003 Standard or Enterprise Editions.

- All ADS services (and supporting services) must reside in the same multicast domain as the IDS and in the same broadcast domain as the ADS PXE service and DHCP Server.

- All ADS and supporting services must be on the same network.

- A Windows 2000 Server or Windows Server 2003-based DHCP server is recommended and should be on the same network as the clients and ADS services.

NOTE

It is important to note that although Windows Server 2003 Web Edition can be a *client* of ADS, it is not supported as a management end-point of ADS. Additionally, Windows XP Professional and all versions of Windows 2000 first require the .NET Framework 1.1 installed in order to use the Sequence Editor tool.

Installing ADS

The first step in installing ADS is to determine how ADS will be deployed in your environment. ADS may be installed on one, two, or three separate servers to gain flexibility, capacity, and scalability. In all but the largest environments, a one- or two–server install is probably sufficient in terms of scalability and capacity. The questions to ask are:

- How many discrete networks do I need to deploy servers?

- How many images do I need to maintain?

- How quickly do I need to be able to deploy an image?

- What type of database will I be using for the Controller service repository? (MSDE and SQL 2000 SP3 or later are supported)

Installation Options

Prior to beginning installation, the Controller service's repository needs to exist; meaning that the MSDE must be installed on the server that will host the Controller service or the SQL 2000 SP3 or later server must be online and available.

During the installation process you will be presented with the option of "complete" or "custom" installations. For single-server environments, choose "complete." For multi-server environments, or to install the tools and documentation on a separate management workstation, choose "custom." Of the three core services for ADS, the Controller service and NBS are good candidates for installing on the same server in a two-server solution. In both two- and three-server deployments, IDS typically is installed on a separate server with fast disk and network performance. Additionally, if the Controller service and the Image Distribution Service are installed on separate servers, remote management of images is not possible (except through Remote Desktop).

At this point, we are ready to begin the actual installation. Prior to doing that, it is paramount that DHCP be provisioned on the network if images are to be captured or deployed and consideration should be given for the additional network traffic generated by the PXE requests of the clients (and isolated if need be from other PXE solutions, like RIS).

Installation Process

Downloading ADS from Microsoft is the best method to ensure that you have the latest version, which, as of the writing of this book, is version 1.1. As an added bonus, the current version of ADS also includes the VSMT, saving a separate download. Whether you download both of these tools separately or together, they are free for use if you have a Microsoft Windows 2003 Enterprise Edition deployed in your network that is able to host the MSDE database.

The first step is to extract the downloaded files onto your drive. This will give a safety warning because you're about to open a possibly unsafe file (see Figure 8.2). You can safely ignore it and click **Run.**

Figure 8.2 Security Warning on Opening the ADS Source Files

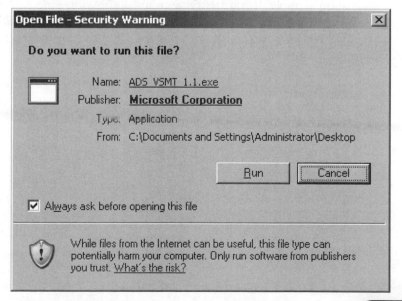

You will be asked to give the location to store the installation files (see Figure 8.3). Remember, you're not installing anything yet; you're just unpacking. Provide a clear path that is easy to find, such as C:\ADSINSTALLATION.

Figure 8.3 Selecting the Unpack Directory

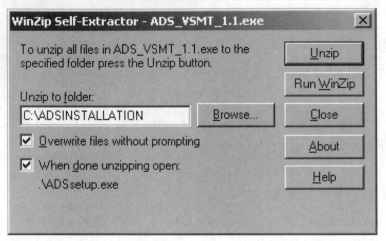

After you have extracted the download, setup should begin automatically. If you do not have a SQL 2000 server available on your network, or intend to use this in a lab or small production environment, the MS SQL Server Desktop Engine (MSDE) option should be fine. Make sure you install the MSDE first if you plan on using it to host the repository for the Controller service in ADS. This is where you need to have the Windows Server 2003 Enterprise Edition server because only then is the MSDE installation available. If you are trying to install the MSDE on a Windows Server 2003 Standard or Web Edition, or MSDE is already installed, the "Install Microsoft SQL Server Desktop Engine SP4 (Windows)" is grayed out (see Figure 8.4). If this is not the case, just click the arrow and the installation will start and complete fully automatic (see Figure 8.5).

Figure 8.4 Grayed-out Installation Option in Case of Windows Server 2003 Standard Edition or It Has Already Been Installed

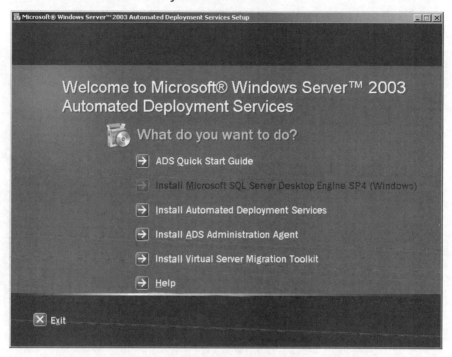

Figure 8.5 Fully Automatic Installation of the MSDE Database

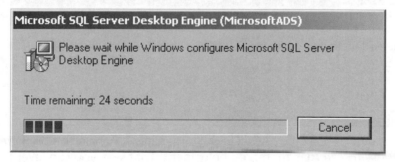

Now that the database is installed, you can start installing ADS. Click the **Install Automated Deployment Services** option to get started (see Figure 8.6).

Figure 8.6 Splash Screen for ADS/VSMT Download

The Automated Deployment Services Setup Wizard will appear (see Figure 8.7).

> **NOTE**
>
> It is a good idea to read the "ADS Quick Start Guide." This gives a brief step-by-step guide on how to use ADS for rapid deployment. That way you can lever the functionality of ADS in a shorter time span.

Figure 8.7 Beginning Installation of ADS

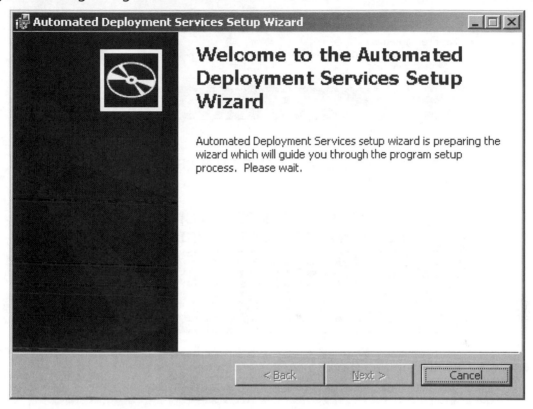

During the installation, you need to accept the license agreement (see Figure 8.8). Reading this will show the need for a licensed copy of Microsoft Windows Server 2003 Enterprise Edition.

In the installation options, you can choose from several installations. For this installation, select the "Full installation" option. If you want to install the management tools only, select the second option, "Administrative tools only." If you're going to distribute the ADS installation among several servers, choose "Custom installation," which enables you to install only the components that are needed. For now, choose **Full installation** (see Figure 8.9). If you would like to change the path to which the application is installed, you need to change it here. However, this does not have to be the location where the images are stored; this can be changed further on in the installation of ADS.

Figure 8.8 Accepting the ADS EULA

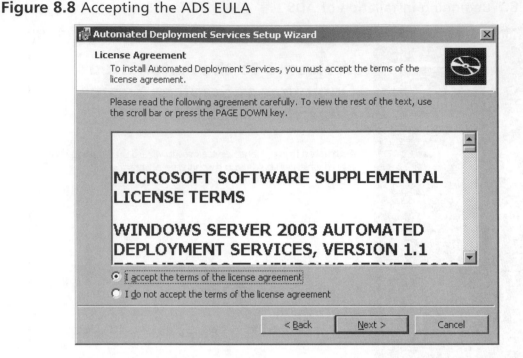

Figure 8.9 Installation Selection for ADS

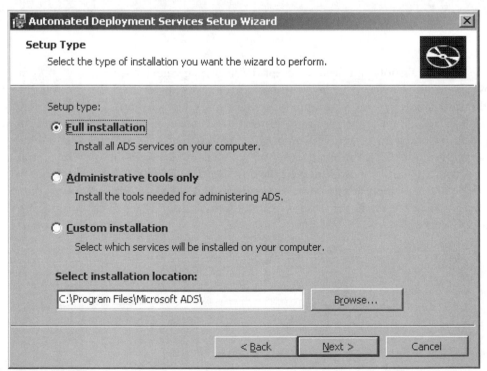

Remember, you are installing a software solution that supports NBS. This means that other network boot solutions can be disrupted. To be sure not to disrupt the other NBS for the cause of virtualization, you can install it on a separate network. Or Install a dedicated DHCP server on the ADS server.

Because of the risk of disrupting the other services, the warning in Figure 8.10 is shown. Check if it is applicable for your situation and click **OK** to resume the installation.

Figure 8.10 ADS PXE Warning

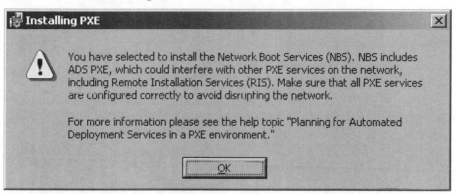

The next step is about the choices for the Controller services. As mentioned before, ADS uses SQL server to store information. This can be locally on the server, but if you like it, it is possible to store it in a full-scale SQL server solution. For a migration server, it is sufficient to store the data in a SQL Server Desktop Edition. If you are rebuilding an ADS server and you have a backup of the old SQL database, you can choose to connect it to the restored one (see Figure 8.11).

Figure 8.11 ADS Controller Service Database Selection and Configuration

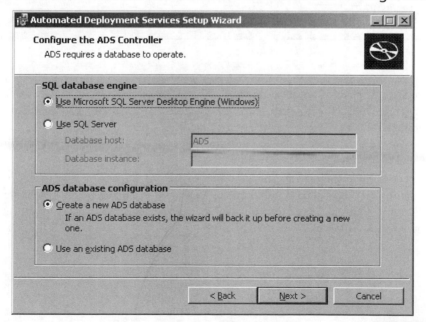

The ADS server needs to be able to reference the setup files, not only to store a copy of these files but also to install the TFTP to be used to download the boot image to the clients. Select the option that is applicable (see Figure 8.12).

Figure 8.12 NBS Path to Windows Setup Files

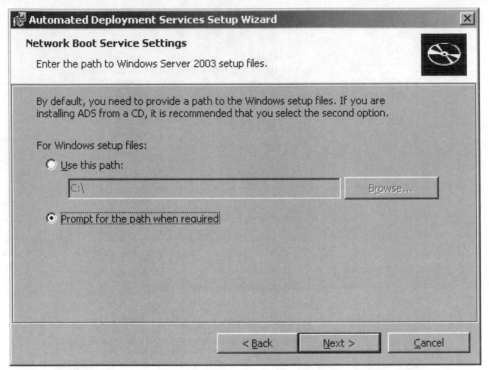

It is possible to use several ways to connect to ADS. One of these ways is by using Windows PE instead of the default Deployment Agent. If you use Windows PE, you're able to give the repository a name and the location of the image or to insert a media if you're prompted. In the case of a virtualization server, there is no need to use Windows PE; you will use the default Deployment Agent of ADS (see Figure 8.13).

Next you need to give the path to the location you like to store the images that are created by ADS (see Figure 8.14). This should be a large disk because the images can grow large during migrations. Remember, you are migrating physical servers to virtual, which means all information on the disks will need to be migrated.

Figure 8.13 ADS Windows PE Repository Location

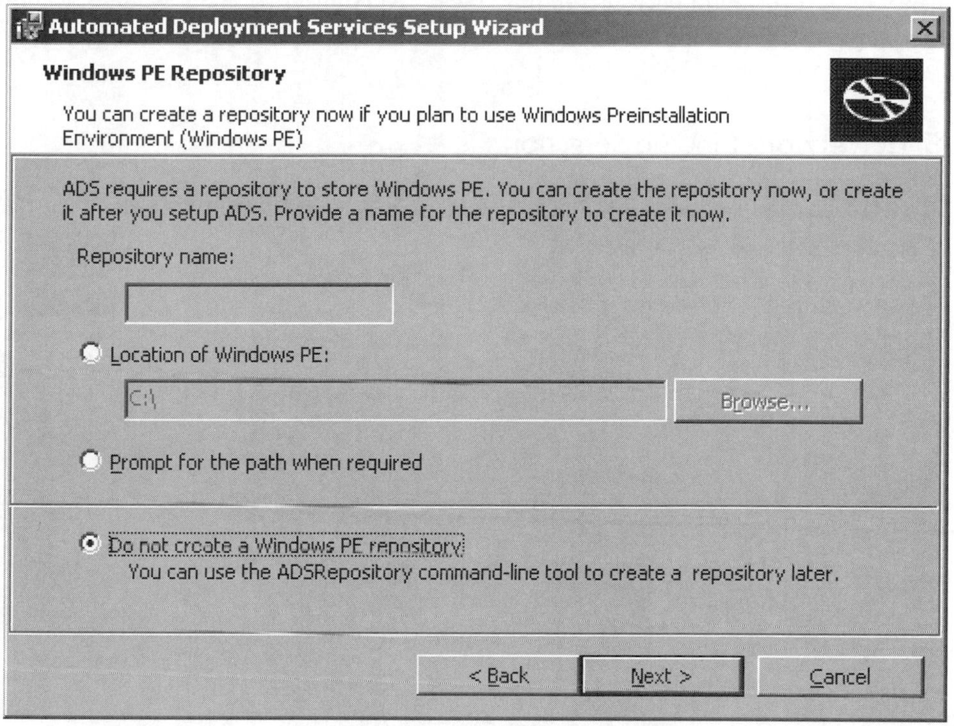

Figure 8.14 Image Distribution Service Image Repository Location

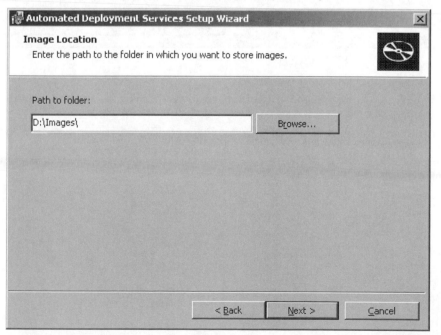

After making the selections on the previous pages, you are ready to install ADS on the server, except when you have a multihomed server. In that case, ADS needs to know where to bind the servers and will provide you with a selection dialog box (see Figure 8.15).

Figure 8.15 Network Binding Selection

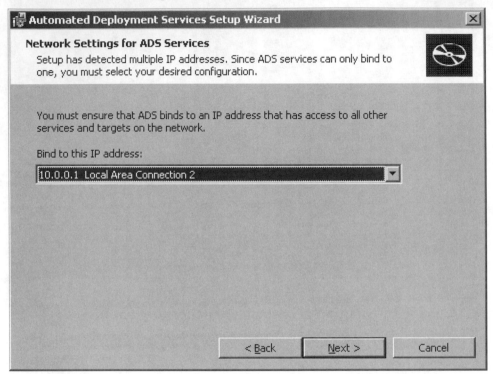

After the previous dialog box, the installation is ready to install. Click **Install** to start the installation (see Figure 8.16).

Just wait patiently to finish the installation (see Figure 8.17).

Figure 8.16 ADS Ready to Install

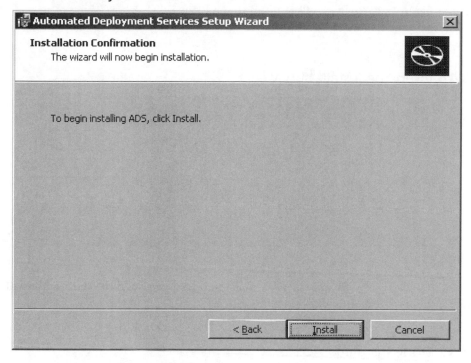

Figure 8.17 Installing ADS

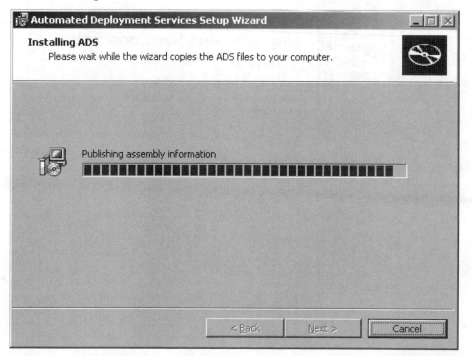

You selected **Prompt for the path when required** on the Network Boot Service Settings dialog box (see Figure 8.12), which will result in the following dialog box asking to provide ADS with the installation media (see Figure 8.18).

Figure 8.18 Insert the Installation Media

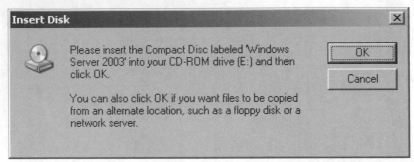

Insert a Windows Server 2003 installation media into the server and the installation will finish (see Figure 8.19). Click **Finish** to end the installation.

Figure 8.19 Done Installing ADS

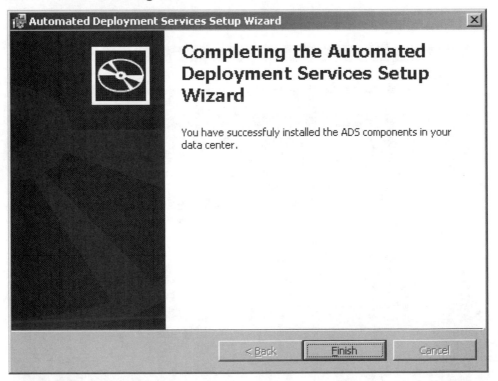

Post-Installation: Configuring ADS

At this point, you have installed ADS. But, as always, installing something will result in a working server but not a configured server. Next, you must configure ADS to do what is necessary with the least amount of administration.

Automatically Accepting New Clients

If there are a lot of clients that need to be installed, it can be handy to automatically insert clients into ADS. You do this by setting the correct parameters in the Controller services. Open the ADS Administrator (see Figure 8.20).

Figure 8.20 ADS Administrator Screen

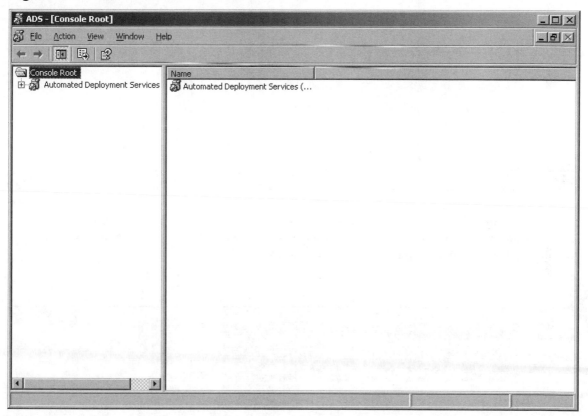

Next you need to expand until your ADS Administrator has the same view as Figure 8.21. Here you can see the several components that make ADS. We are especially interested in the Controller service. This service is responsible for controlling the access and actions of clients.

Figure 8.21 Expanded View of the ADS Administrator Console

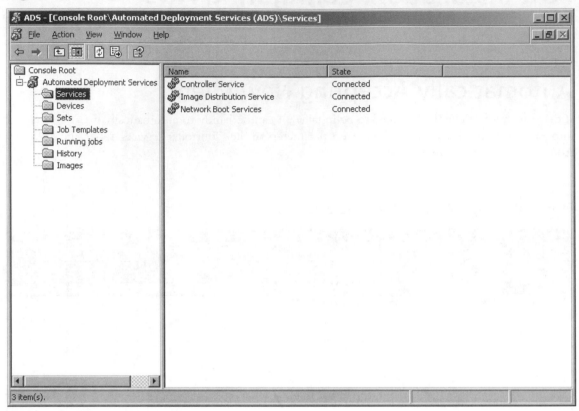

Select **Controller Service**, right–click, and then select **Properties** from the drop–down menu. The Controller Service Properties dialog box appears, as shown in Figure 8.22, where you can see some important information on the network connectivity.

Configuring & Implementing...

Changing the ADS Controller Service IP Address

The IP address is shown and it looks like you're able to change the IP address the ADS server is listening on. However, this is not the case. If you change the IP address here, ADS will stop functioning. To change the IP address of the server, follow these steps:

1. Change the IP address of the server the controller is running on and check connectivity from the new IP address.

2. Open the registry and locate the following key:
   HKEY_LOCAL_MACHINE\SYSTEM\CurrentControlSet\Services\Adsctlr\BMDP\Parameters

3. Change BindExcept to reflect the new IP address.

4. If the server full fills all roles, repeat steps 2 and 3 for the following keys:
   HKEY_LOCAL_MACHINE\SYSTEM\CurrentControlSet\Services\ADSBUILDER\Parameters
   HKEY_LOCAL_MACHINE\SYSTEM\CurrentControlSet\Services\adsimgsvc\Parameters
   HKEY_LOCAL_MACHINE\SYSTEM\CurrentControlSet\Services\ADSPXE\Parameters

5. Go to the ADS Administrator and change the IP address on the tab, as shown in Figure 8.22.

6. Restart ADS Controller, ADS Deployment Agent Builder, ADS PXE Service, and ADS Administration Agent.

7. Check that all services are restarted correctly.

Figure 8.22 ADS Controller Service Properties Dialog Box

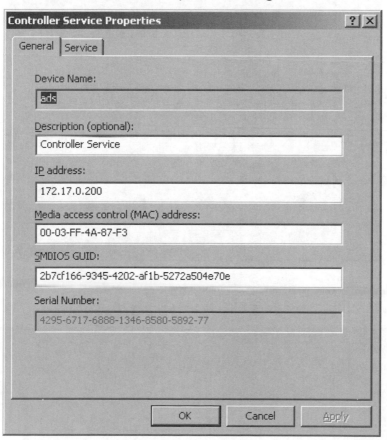

Change to the Service tab to see the important settings. The dialog box in Figure 8.23 is divided into two sections: the first one gives the option to set the default boot method if none is selected. In this case, boot-to-da. In the lower part are the automatic responses in case there is a network boot. ADS is not doing anything unless you take control of the device in ADS. If this is not the case, the client will not boot. If you set the "To PXE action" to Add and click Apply, you will be given a warning (see Figure 8.24).

Figure 8.23 ADS Service Controller Services Default Behavior Configuration

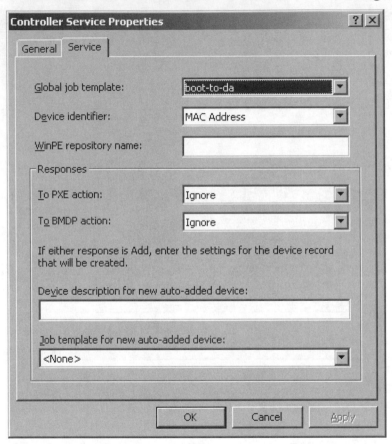

Figure 8.24 Warning Message if PXE Action is Set to Add

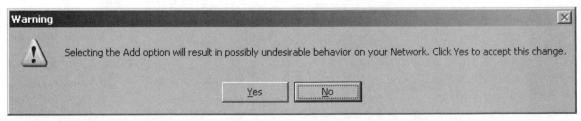

Then you can set the "Device description for new auto–added device" to a recognizable value like "New devise." This way you will spot the new client directly. Of course, you need to tell them what to do the first time they connect to the controller. The options are the same as in the global job template. Typically, you will end up with something similar to Figure 8.25.

Figure 8.25 Typical Setting When Auto Adding Clients

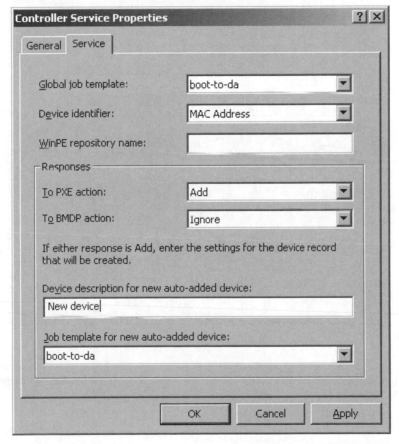

Click **OK** and close the ADS Administrative Panel.

Enabling Multicast

ADS is able to push images with multicast. This makes it possible to install an image on a large number of clients using the same network utilization (from the server) as one. Multicast is enabled by default. If you need to disable it, open the ADS Administrator console and go to the services. Open the Properties of the Image Distribution service (see Figure 8.26).

Figure 8.26 Properties of the Image Distribution Service

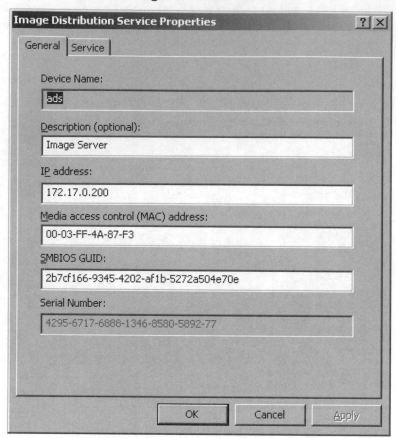

To disable multicast, click the **Service** tab and uncheck **Multicast image deployment** (see Figure 8.27).

Figure 8.27 Image Distribution Service Properties – Service Tab

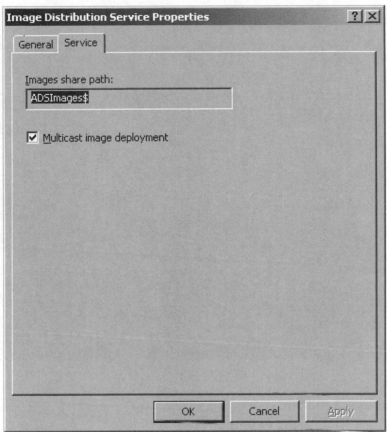

Administration Agent Installing

If you are going to virtualize a physical machine, there is no need for an administration agent. However, if you have ADS running, you might see the ease of use. As the back is running, ADS is waiting for clients to connect to the ADS Controller service.

There are two methods for connecting to the ADS server; booting to PXE and installing the administration agent in the client. In the following steps, you will install the agent. First, open the installation files that you copied from the server. You will get the familiar splash screen (see Figure 8.28). On this screen, select **Install ADS Administration Agent**.

Figure 8.28 ADS Splash Screen

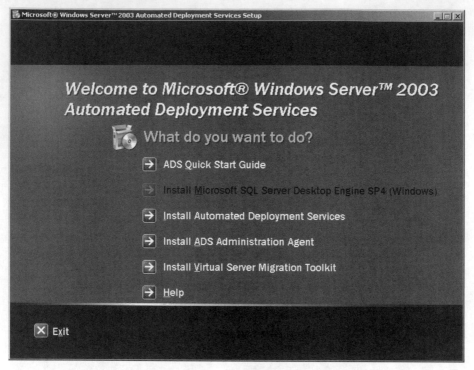

The Administration Agent Setup Wizard will appear (see Figure 8.29). Select **Next** to start the installation.

Accept the license agreement by selecting **I accept the terms of the license agreement** and clicking **Next** (see Figure 8.30).

Figure 8.29 Welcome to the Administration Agent Setup Wizard

Figure 8.30 Agent License agreement

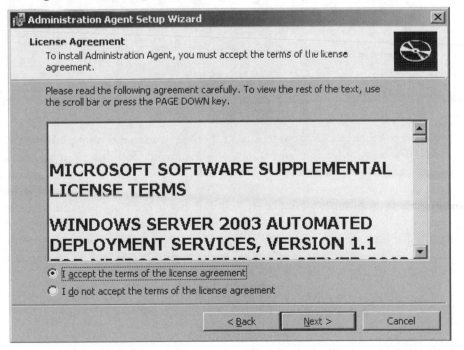

All information transferred between the client and the server is encrypted using certificates (see Figure 8.31). In this screen you need to give the location of the server certificate so you are able to communicate securely with the ADS server. The certificate is stored on the ADS server in *%ADSInstallationpath%* \certificates. There is a certificate called ADSRoot.cer. Copy this file to the server and give the location to the installation program.

Figure 8.31 Certificate Installation Dialog Box

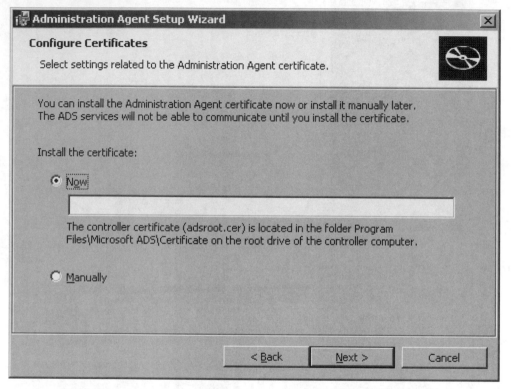

Next, you need to set up the account that ADS is going to use performing jobs on the system (see Figure 8.32). If you like ADS to perform jobs on the domain level, you need to use a domain account. You can use the local system so that you are able to get all information and perform every function on the client.

The final step is to give information about the location where the agent should be installed. This is shown in Figure 8.33. Select the correct location and click **Install** to install the agent.

After the installation is completed, the server is shown in the ADS administrative console and you are able to perform jobs. Sample jobs are provided in the *%ADSInstallationPath%\Samples* directory of the ADS server.

Figure 8.32 ADS Service Account Information

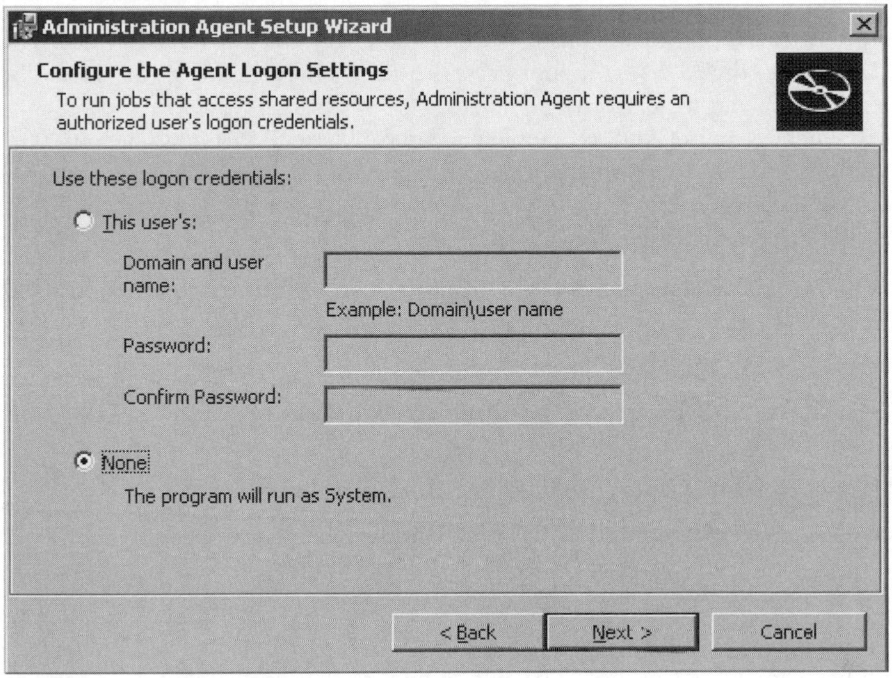

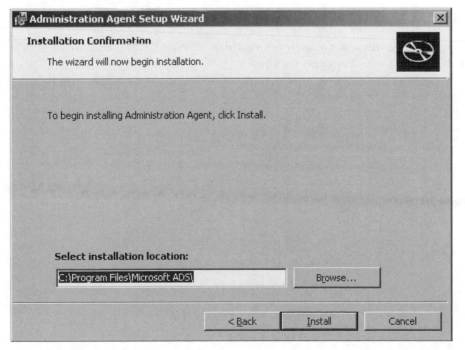

Figure 8.33 Click Install to Start the Agent Installation

Adding Hardware Drivers in the Boot OS

It is common to have multiple server brands within a company. Still, you need to be able to connect the network adapter to the ADS server and access the disks to put the image on. To do this in Windows Server 2003, you use drivers.

The Deployment Agent of ADS is completely compatible with Windows Server 2003. This means that you can use the drivers that you need straight from the Internet or driver CD. The next question is where to put it.

To install the drivers, take the following steps:

1. Copy the **.inf** and **.sys** files into the **Microsoft ADS\nbs\repository\user\PostSystem** directory on the Microsoft ADS server.

2. If the Microsoft ADS console is running, shut it down.

3. Select **Start | All Programs | Administrative Tools | Services**. The Services window opens.

4. Right-click **ADS Deployment Agent Builder**; then click **Stop**.

5. Right-click **ADS Deployment Agent Builder**; then click **Start**.

6. Close the Services window.

7. Start the Microsoft ADS Console.

After you have done this you should be able to boot to the Deployment Agent and access the hard disks in the physical servers.

Editing Using the Sequence Editor

ADS is the tool to use when you're going to virtualize a physical server to a virtual server. But again, that is not the only thing ADS can do for you.

You can use ADS to do mass administration, run scripts, make or deploy images, and so on. Everything is done by ADS through the use of sequence files. These files can be created using the Sequence Editor (see Figure 8.34).

You are able to select several types of commands (see Figure 8.35), and therefore build a controlled series of actions. ADS is able to monitor all actions taken on the client. As the several actions are selected, a sequence file is build. By selecting a client in the ADS administrator console, you are able to select the target computer that performs the sequence. Of course, all sequences can be stored on disk to be used in a later stadium.

Figure 8.34 ADS Sequence Editor

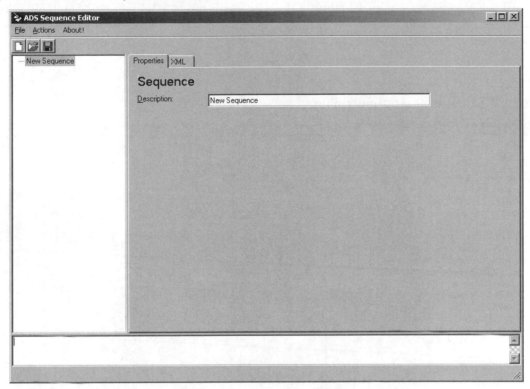

Figure 8.35 Overview of Actions That Can Be Performed Using the Sequence Editor

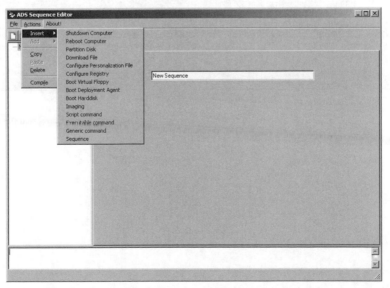

If you select File | Open, you are able to open a sequence file. Samples can be found in the *%ADSInstallationPath%*\Samples directory. In this case (see Figure 8.36), I selected "DA–DEPLOY–IMAGE–DOMAIN," which stands for "deploying a Sysprep image of a server and connecting it to the domain."

Figure 8.36 Sample Sequence File

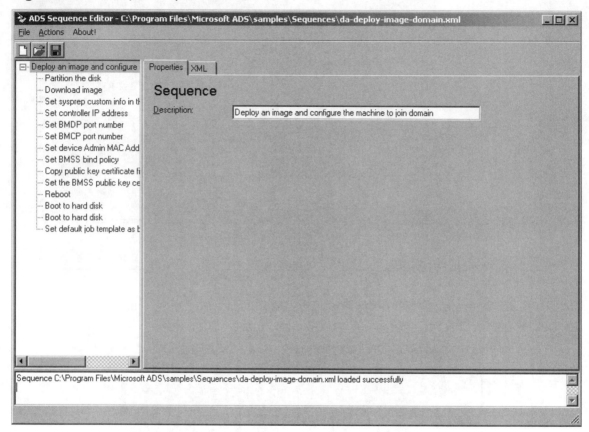

In this sample file, we see several actions, such as partitioning the disk where the image is going to be deployed (see Figure 8.37). The partition is going to be on the first harddisk (or hardware raid device) and it will be the first partition on the disk ("/init"), blowing any existing partitions from the disk. The size is 5 GB and it is made active (/A).

Figure 8.37 Partitioning a Disk

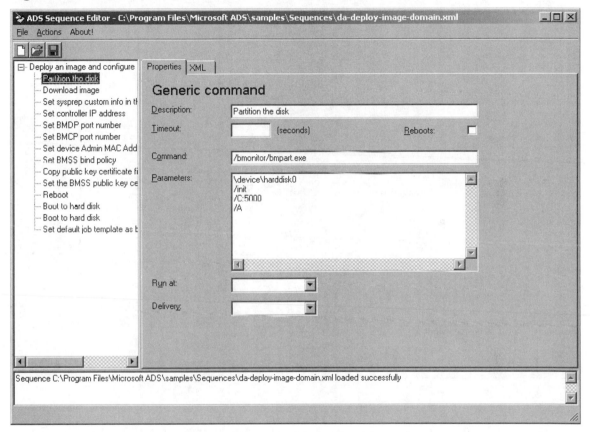

In Figure 8.38, an image is deployed to the server. The image is called "ImageName" and deployed to the first physical disk on the first partition.

Figure 8.38 Deployment of an Image

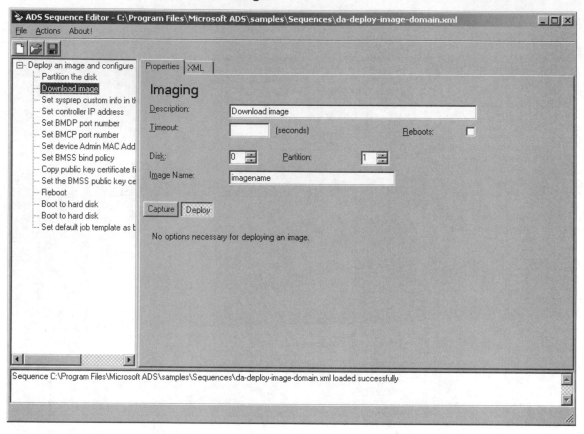

During one of the following stages the server is rebooted (see Figure 8.39). If the server has the network as first boot device, the server will automatically return to the job and continue with the next step, "Boot to hard disk."

Figure 8.39 Reboot to Hard Disk

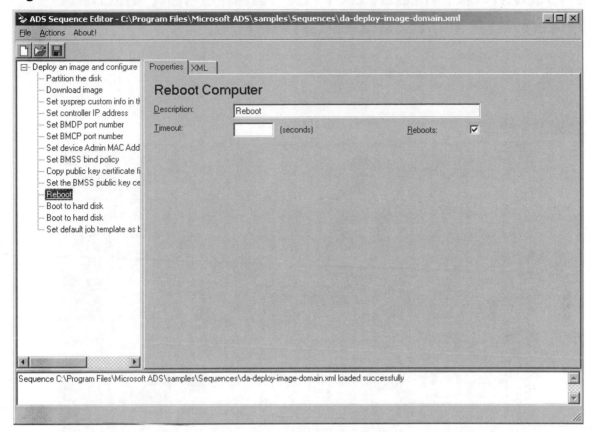

The installation sequence of the servers is as follows:

1. Build the servers in the 19" rack.

2. Connect them to the network.

3. Boot from the network (by setting the network as first boot device) to the Deployment Agent.

4. Deploy an image.

After step 4, the servers are done and you can start installing additional software. So, although previously you could do one or maybe two servers a day, now you're able to do all of them in one day. Let's make things easy....

Installing Virtual Server Migration Toolkit onto the Virtualization Server

The installation of the VSMT starts with the famous splash screen (see Figure 8.40), where you select **Install Virtual Server Migration Toolkit**.

Figure 8.40 Splash Screen ADS Installation

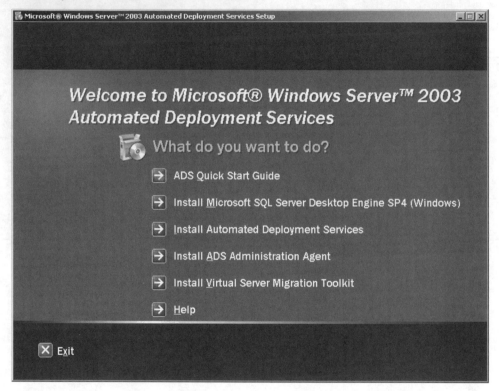

The Setup Wizard will start. Click **Next** to start the installation (see Figure 8.41).

Figure 8.41 Beginning Installation of VSMT

Of course, you need to accept the license agreement (see Figure 8.42) to be able to install VSMT. The next screen enables you to select the type of installation and where to install VSMT. The way it is installed is very important because if the server that is going to host the migrated server is not the one you're using to virtualize, you need to do another installation. In this exercise, select **Full installation** (see Figure 8.43). But if you are going to migrate to another virtual server, install the Tools only (see Figure 8.44). This enables the ADS servers to use scripts to deploy the server. Click **Next** to continue.

Figure 8.42 Accepting VSMT EULA

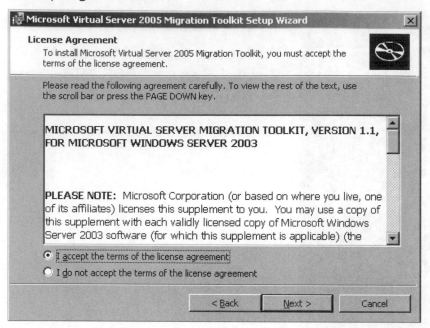

Figure 8.43 VSMT Installation Selection

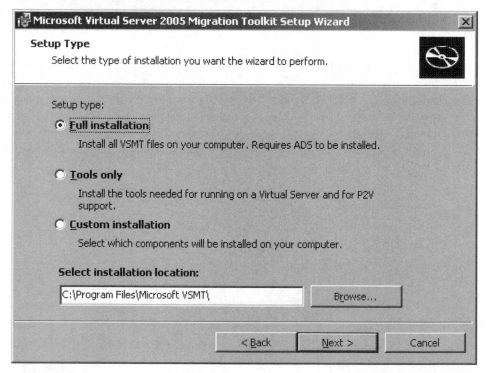

Figure 8.44 VSMT Component Selection

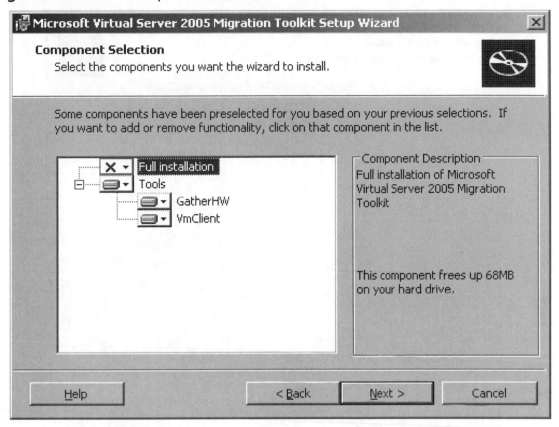

You are ready to start copying files to the installation directory. Click **Install** to start (see Figure 8.45).

When everything goes according to plan, the installations should not take long and the dialog box in Figure 8.46 should be shown.

VSMT is installed. You're ready to start with the migration. For more information on migrating virtual machines, see Chapter 10.

Figure 8.45 Completing the Install of the VSMT

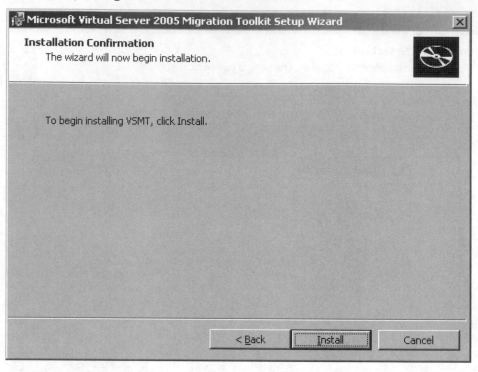

Figure 8.46 VSMT Successful Completion

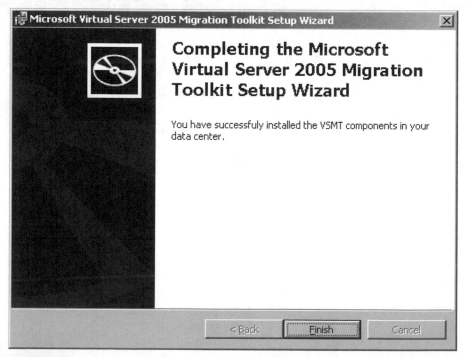

Summary

In this chapter we took a look at the several tools that are involved, besides Virtual Server, during the migration from a physical server to a virtual server. There are two major tools involved: ADS and VSMT. ADS can be used to capture and deploy new servers to maintain a common installation base and enable versioning. This is essential in a large server environment and leverages the reliability of the IT environment. Both are essential for a successful virtualization of the server.

Solutions Fast Track

Automated Deployment Services

☑ Free tool to use on Windows Server 2003 (Enterprise Edition) to capture and deploy servers

☑ Is able to multicast

☑ Can be used to do more than virtualizing

What Components Does ADS Use?

☑ ADS Controller service controls and logs all action done by ADS.

☑ ADS NBS is used to PXE boot to the Deployment Agent.

☑ ADS Image Distribution Service is used to capture and deploy images.

Installing ADS

☑ The Installation files are delivered as one file.

☑ The image directory can be set separately during the installation.

☑ As ADS uses PXE, it is essential to separate the ADS environment from other network boot systems.

☑ ADS integrates with DHCP. If there are multiple DHCP servers, be sure to check for integration on all servers.

Post-Installation: Configuring ADS

☑ After the installation, you can enable the option to automatically add servers to the ADS controller.

☑ Nothing is done to the servers until it is "in control."

☑ Do not attempt to change the IP address only from the Controller service properties, as this results in failure.

Administrative Agent Installing

- ☑ Is needed to be able to run jobs on windows clients.

- ☑ The traffic between the server and the client are encrypted.

- ☑ The certificate used to communicate with the server can be found on the ADS server in *%ADSInstallationPath%\Certificates*.

Editing Using the Sequence Editor

- ☑ The Sequence Editor is a graphical tool to build jobs to use in ADS.

- ☑ There are a lot of sample jobs in the *%ADSInstallationPath%*\Samples directory.

- ☑ Sequence files are stored as XML files and can be reused over and over again.

Adding Hardware Drivers in the Boot OS

- ☑ Every piece of hardware that is supported by Windows Server 2003 is supported by the Deployment Agent.

- ☑ To add new drivers to the boot image, copy the drivers to the "Microsoft ADS\nbs\repository\user\PostSystem" directory and restart the builder service.

Installing Virtual Server Migration Toolkit onto the Virtualization Server

- ☑ The installation of the VSMT needs to be performed on the server that runs ADS.

- ☑ If the server that is going to host the virtual machine is not the one used to virtualize, a "Tools only" installation must be done on that server.

Frequently Asked Questions

Q: Is it possible to use the ADS techniques for deployment of workstations?

A: Maybe, but that's not the intention of the product. It is build for deployment of server operating systems.

Q: I do not have a Windows Server 2003 Enterprise Edition within my company. Can I still install ADS?

A: I am afraid you cannot use ADS, because the license explicitly requires Windows Server 2003 Enterprise Edition.

Q: Is it possible to virtualize the ADS server?

A: Yes; even better, please do. The license constraints of Virtual Server 2005 tells us we don't have to have a license for a server that is not running, so if we need to virtualize, we shut down a production server to be able to run the ADS server. This way there is no license violation.

Q: Does this mean I can do bare metal deployments using ADS?

A: You sure can. I have done this successfully a number of times.

Q: Can I edit the images that I capture without deploying first?

A: Yes, you can mount the images as if it were a drive on the ADS server. That way you are able to add or remove software before deploying the image to the servers.

Q: We already have RIS deployed in our network. Can I deploy ADS alongside?

A: No, not the easy way. Best practices tell us to logically separate the LAN so you do not disrupt the existing RIS installation.

Q: Do you really think this is a cool tool that I should try?

A: Yes, I sure do.

## Chapter 9

Managing Virtual Server

Solutions in this chapter:

- **The Management Interface**

- **Using the Virtual Server COM API**

- **Accessing a Virtual Server Using Script**

- **Creating a Virtual Machine Using Script**

- **Creating a Virtual Network Using Script**

- **Retrieving Guest OS Information Using Script**

- **Changing a Virtual Machine State Using Script**

- **Attaching Scripts to Virtual Server Events**

☑ Summary

☑ Solutions Fast Track

☑ Frequently Asked Questions

Introduction

To manage a virtual server, you use the Virtual Server Administration Web site, available on each and every Virtual Server host. If you do not want to install the Administration Web site on every host or want to automate administration tasks, you have several options to choose from.

The Management Interface

By now you should be familiar with the management interface of Virtual Server. Configuration management of Virtual Server as well as that of each virtual machine from a graphical user interface can only be done from the Virtual Server Administration Web site. As the name clearly implies, this management requires a Web server which, in this case, is Internet Information Services.

NOTE

The next generation of virtualization product, Windows Server Virtualization, no longer requires Internet Information Server. The management interface is completely based on Microsoft Management Console 3.0.

New releases of Virtual Server 2005 R2, of which Service Pack 1 is the next update to be released in 2006, will still require Internet Information Services. However, Microsoft has announced a virtual machine management product called System Center Virtual Machine Manager. This product will be able to manage both Virtual Server 2005 and Windows Server Virtualization installations.

You can install Virtual Server on Windows Server 2003 and Windows XP Professional with Service Pack 2. Windows Server 2003 comes with Internet Information Services 6.0 and Windows XP Professional comes with Internet Information Services 5.1.

NOTE

Virtual Server on Windows XP Professional with Service Pack 2 is not supported for production use. Windows XP is a desktop operating system and not designed for server products.

Depending on the underlying operating system, the Virtual Server Administration Web site is installed on port 1024 for Windows Server 2003 or port 80 for Windows XP. The reason for this is obvious: Internet Information Services on Windows XP supports only a single Web site which, by default, listens on port 80.

Now that you know what is required and what options you have for Internet Information Services, there is not much else to choose from when it comes to managing a single Virtual Server instance. But what if you have multiple Virtual Server hosts? Do you have to install Internet Information Services on each host? Actually, you don't, and the solution lies in a central Virtual Server management site.

Configuring a Central Virtual Server Management Site

A central Virtual Server management site enables you to leverage a single Internet Information Services instance with the Virtual Server Administration Web site for management of all Virtual Server hosts. The Internet Information Services instance may exist on a Virtual Server host, but you can even do without a single installation on any of your Virtual Server hosts.

You can leverage an instance of Internet Information Services that already exists in your environment and place the Virtual Server Administration Web site on that instance. This way you establish a management server for all Virtual Server hosts. The only requirement for this scenario to work is that all Virtual Server hosts are in the same domain as the management server and that the domain is in Windows Server 2003 mode.

Designing & Planning...

Domain Functional Levels and Kerberos Constrained Delegation

Windows Server 2003 supports several domain functional levels. These are Windows 2000 mixed, Windows 2000 native, Windows Server 2003 Interim, and Windows Server 2003.

In all modes except Windows Server 2003, there is only Kerberos Delegation. What does this mean? When a user connects to a Web service, and that service needs to access a resource on yet another server, the Web service impersonates the user. So the Web service accesses the resources on the server as if it were the user accessing the resources.

However, there is no constraint in Windows 2000 to limit the resources the Web service can access on behalf of this user. Once the Web server is trusted for delegation, it is trusted for delegation to any service.

In Windows Server 2003 mode, Kerberos Delegation can be constrained or limited to certain services; hence Kerberos Constrained Delegation (KCD). In the example, the Web server can be trusted for delegation to the specific services only.

With the domain in Windows Server 2003 mode, you configure the Web server's computer account to be trusted for delegation. The steps to be performed are outlined in greater detail later.

NOTE

Only the domain needs to be in Windows Server 2003 mode. You do not need to enable the forest to Windows Server 2003 mode.

When the domain requirement has been met, you can manage any Virtual Server by using a Web browser (Internet Explorer 5.5 or higher) from anywhere within the domain.

To make this work, you have to perform the following steps:

1. Install the Virtual Server Administration Web site on the Internet Information Services instance.

2. Configure the management server to be trusted for delegation.

The steps required to set up a central management server have been documented in both the online product documentation and in a whitepaper called *"Installing the Virtual Server Administration Web Site on a Separate Computer"* (located at www.microsoft.com/downloads/details. aspx?FamilyID=c4dcf45b-72ea-44ed-86aa-1c389ece12f9&displaylang=en). The next paragraph gives a recap of the most important steps based on a fictitious environment. In that environment there is a single-domain forest called *vs.local* and a management server called *webmgmt*. Internet Information Services are already installed on *webmgmt*.

Start the installation of Microsoft Virtual Server 2005. Click **Install Microsoft Virtual Server 2005 R2**. Accept the License Agreement and click **Next**. Enter appropriate information for **Name** and **Organization**, enter the **Product Key**, and click **Next**. You will see the Setup dialog box as shown in Figure 9.1.

Figure 9.1 Virtual Server Custom Setup

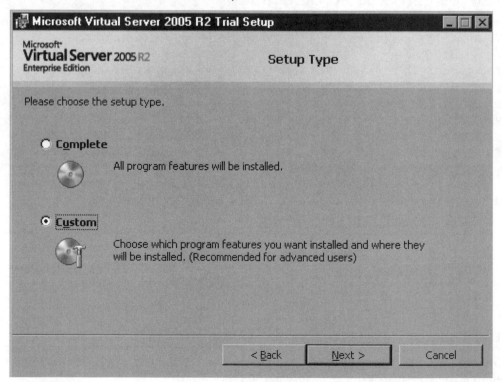

Click **Custom** and then click **Next.**
Deselect all options except the Virtual Server Web Application. See Figure 9.2.

Figure 9.2 Selecting the Virtual Server Features

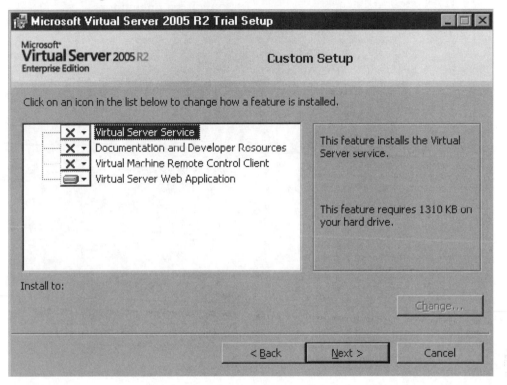

Click **Next**. Now the most important setup dialog is the one in Figure 9.3.

Figure 9.3 Virtual Server Setup Option for KCD

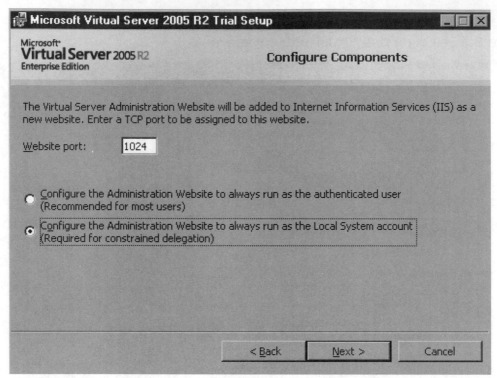

Make sure that you select the second option, which configures the Administration Web site to always run as the Local System account. This is *required* for Kerberos Constrained Delegation. So enter the required port number for the Web site or use the default, select the second option, and then click **Next**. This will bring you to the final setup screen where you have the option to let setup configure exceptions in the Windows Firewall configuration (see Figure 9.4). After that, you have configured everything the way it should be in order to use the management server.

Figure 9.4 Setting Virtual Server Setup Windows Firewall Exceptions

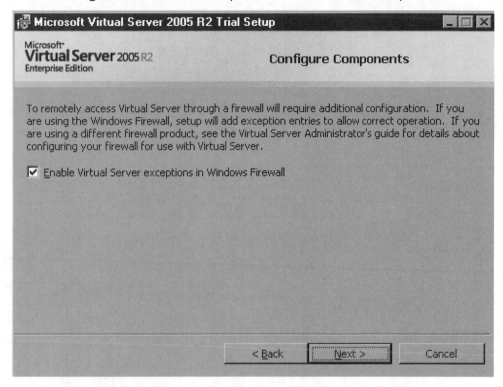

After setup has completed, you are ready for the next and final configuration steps. These should be made on domain level in our fictitious environment *vs.local*.

Open **Active Directory Users and Computers**. You can do this on a domain controller for the domain or on any member server in the domain.

NOTE

By default, you will not find the Active Directory Users and Computers shortcut in the Administrative Tools program group on member servers in the domain. However, the snap-in is available. Simply click **Start | Run**, enter **dsa.msc**, and click **OK**. This will bring up the MMC snap-in.

Find the computer account of the server holding the Virtual Server Administration Web site in the active directory. Select the computer account, Select **Action | Properties**. A dialog box opens, which may look like the one in Figure 9.5.

Figure 9.5 Web Server Properties at Incorrect Domain Functional Level

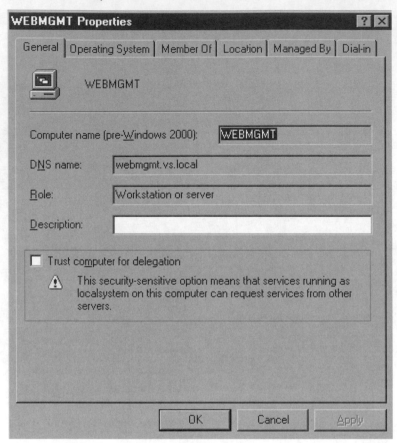

If the Properties dialog box for the computer object *webmgmt* looks like the one in Figure 9.5, then your domain is not operating at the required functional level. You are not able to select any services, so you *must* first raise the domain functional level. To raise the domain functional level, click the domain node and select **Actions | Raise Domain Functional Level…**. Select **Windows Server 2003** and click **Raise**.

NOTE

Changing a functional level, either domain or forest, is irreversible. Functional levels can be raised, but they cannot be lowered. Each functional level enables new functionality but disables backwards compatibility or interoperability.

For a complete overview of all forest and domain functional levels and their characteristics, see the Microsoft Knowledge Base article 322692 at http://support. microsoft.com/kb/322692.

With the proper domain functional level, the Properties dialog box for the computer object *webmgmt* should look like Figure 9.6.

Figure 9.6 Web Server Properties at Correct Domain Functional Level

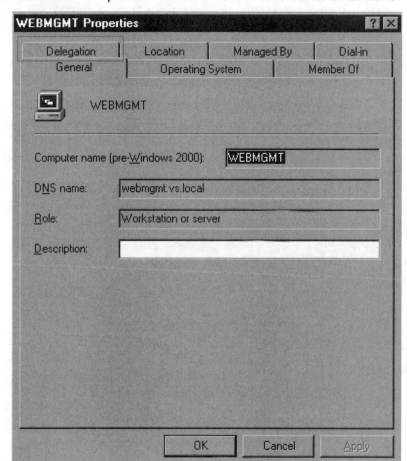

The difference between this and the previous dialog box is the Delegation tab. This existence of this tab indicates that the domain is running at the proper level and that Constrained Delegation can now be configured.

Click **Delegation**, click **Trust this computer for delegation to specified services only**, click **Use any authentication protocol**, and then click **Add...**. Click **Users or Computers...** and enter the names of the virtual server hosts in your domain. You will then see a list of all services registered for those hosts in Active Directory. Select the **CIFS** and **vssrvs** services and click **OK**. Figure 9.6 below shows the results for two virtual server hosts called p01 and p02.

WARNING

When the *vssrvc* service is not listed for a particular Virtual Server host, the Service Principal Name has not been registered. You can verify whether this is the case using the *setspn* command-line tool. *Setspn* is part of the Support Tools package.

When issuing *setspn –l <hostname>* you should see two SPN's registered for the *vssrvc* service on the host: one single label entry and one with the fully qualified name of the host.

When the Virtual Machine Remote Control service has been enabled on the host, you will also see two entries for the *vmrc* service. See Figure 9.7 for output of *setspn –l p02*.

You can use *setspn* to set the required SPN, although we recommend that you investigate the cause that prevents Virtual Server from registering the SPN itself and solve the problem.

Figure 9.7 Registered Service Principal Names

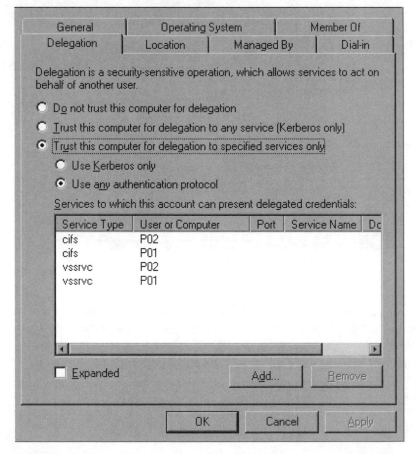

Figure 9.8 Web Server with Constrained Delegation Configuration

```
C:\>setspn -l p02
Registered ServicePrincipalNames for CN=P02,OU=Servers,DC=vs,DC=local:
    HOST/p02.vs.local
    HOST/p02
    vssrvc/p02.vs.local
    vssrvc/p02
    vmrc/p02.vs.local:5900
    vmrc/p02:5900

C:\>_
```

You should now be able to use the management server and connect to the Virtual Server hosts. To connect to the management server, start **Internet Explorer** and type the address (URL) of the management server as follows: **http://<managment server>:<port>/VirtualServer/VSWebapp. exe?View=1**. See Figure 9.9 below for the result of this action to a management server called P03.

Figure 9.9 Connecting to the Management Server

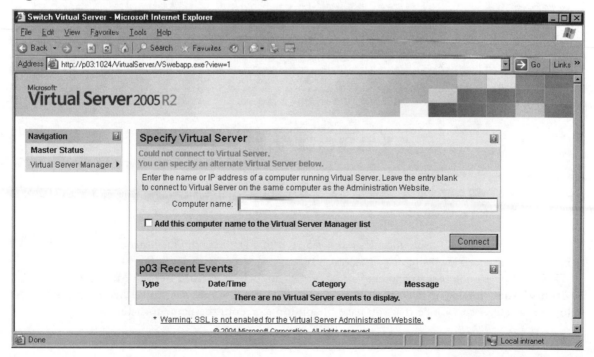

At this stage you are connected to the management server. However, there is no Virtual Server available and none has been specified in the URL. To connect to a Virtual Server, for example P01, type **P01** in the **Computer name** field. You can choose to select **Add this computer name to the Virtual Server Manager list** to record the Virtual Server host name. You can then later select it from a list. Click **Connect** to connect to the Virtual Server host. Figure 9.10 shows the result when connecting to P01.

Figure 9.10 Connecting to the Virtual Server Host from the Management Server

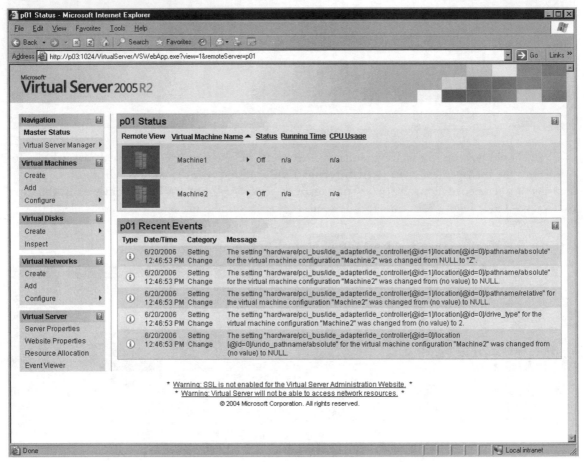

Notice that the URL now includes a *remoteServer=p01* at the end. This instructs the Virtual Server Administration Web site to connect to p01.

If you need to connect to another Virtual Server host, click **Virtual Server Manager,** click **Switch Virtual Server** or select a previously recorded Virtual Server host name. See Figure 9.11 below for a reference. Notice that you have the option to record the name for later use.

Figure 9.11 Specify Virtual Server

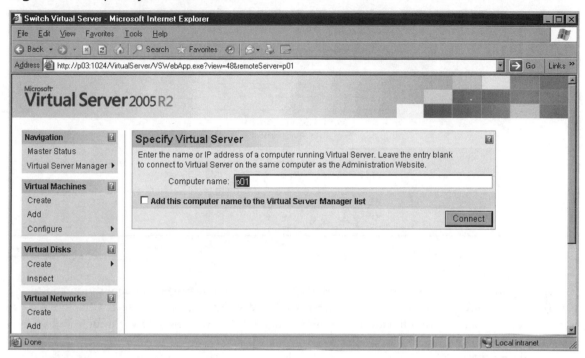

Configuring a central management site was the most advanced topic of Web-based management using the Virtual Server Administration Web site. There are no other means of management by a graphical user interface. However, you can manage Virtual Server by using scripts.

Using the Virtual Server COM API

All management of Virtual Server is performed through the Virtual Server COM API. You can see the whole management picture from the Virtual Server architecture in the Virtual Server Administrator's Guide. From the architecture you can see that the Virtual Server Administration Web site also uses the API. Virtual Server basically exists in a COM (Component Object Model) object. This model abstracts internal functionality to interfaces with which you can interact. Figure 9.12 shows a similar view on the COM interface of Virtual Server.

Figure 9.12 Virtual Server COM Interface

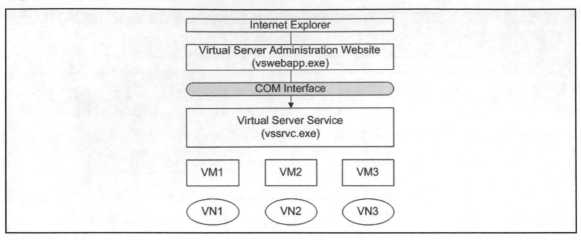

This figure depicts the COM interface as a layer between the management application and the Virtual Server configuration. You can see that Virtual Server is managed from Internet Explorer by using the Virtual Server Administration Web site through COM. By using COM through scripts, you can manage Virtual Server exactly the way you want.

You do not have to be an expert on COM to leverage the API using scripts. You interact with the COM object in a very natural way. You can ask Virtual Server to perform an action like creating a virtual machine or ask which virtual machines are currently running. The way you ask Virtual Server depends on the scripting language you use. You can use any scripting language, like VBScript or Jscript, or any other language that supports COM automation, like C++, VB.Net, or C#.

Since VBScript is the most widely used language of the scripting languages, we will use VBScript in all sample scripts in this chapter. Therefore, you should have some basic knowledge of VBScript, although the samples are kept to minimal complexity to focus more on the API than the language.

Using the Virtual Server Programmer's Guide

The Virtual Server Programmer's Guide is available from the Microsoft Virtual Server program group. When you open that documentation you may notice it is called the Microsoft Virtual Server SDK. That acronym stands for Software Development Kit and usually consists of documentation and tools to enable developers to create a custom solution on top of the product. In the case of Virtual Server, the SDK consists only of the documentation called the programmer's guide.

The base for success on using the API lies in understanding its documentation. You should investigate it to become familiar with navigating through this guide. It may seem cryptic at first, but once you browse and navigate you will quickly be able to find the information you need. To help you get started, the section below covers some steps you can perform to become familiar with its organization.

Click **Start | All Programs | Microsoft Virtual Server**, **Virtual Server Programmer's Guide**. By default, this opens the Microsoft Virtual Server SDK in "collapsed view," as shown in Figure 9.13.

Figure 9.13 Default View of the Virtual Server SDK

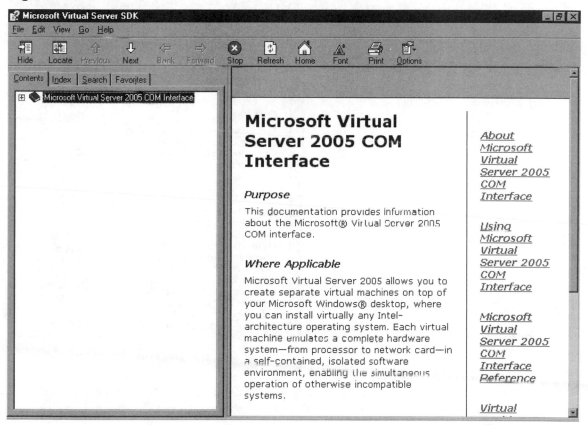

From here you can navigate through the SDK in several ways. You can expand the left node by clicking the + next to the book icon. You can also use the shortcuts on the right pane which leads directly to the chosen section. The shortcuts are more appropriate once you are familiar with the document.

Click on the + sign next to the book to expand its contents. This results in Figure 9.14.

Figure 9.14 Virtual Server SDK Sections

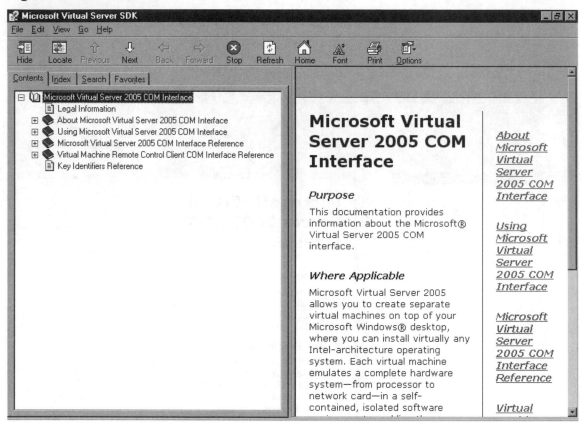

In this figure you can see that there are actually four main sections in the documentation: the "About" section, the "Using" section, and two "Reference" sections. Notice that the right pane's shortcuts correspond to these sections.

You should read all sections, but the most interesting section, and the one you will use most often, is the Microsoft Virtual Server 2005 COM Interface Reference. Open the section by clicking the + sign next to the book. This leads to Figure 9.15.

Figure 9.15 Virtual Server 2005 COM Interface Reference

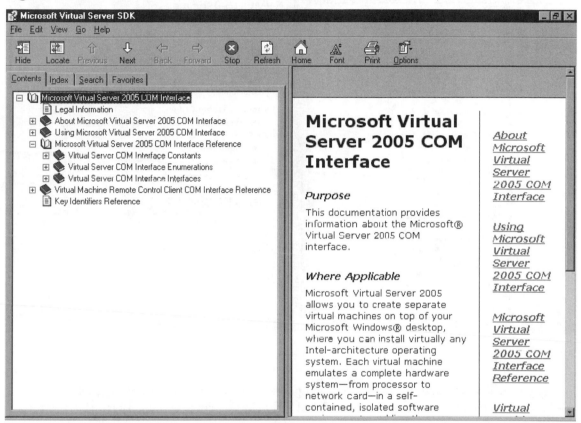

Remember, in the beginning, to navigate using the left pane and use the right pane as the "results" pane. This prevents you from getting confused in navigating. Once you are familiar with the reference, you can use the right pane to quickly go to the referenced locations.

For now, open the Virtual Server COM Interface Interfaces section by clicking the + sign next to the book icon. From there, navigate to the IVMVirtualServer node and expand it by clicking the + sign. The result is displayed in Figure 9.16.

Figure 9.16 Virtual Server Object Reference

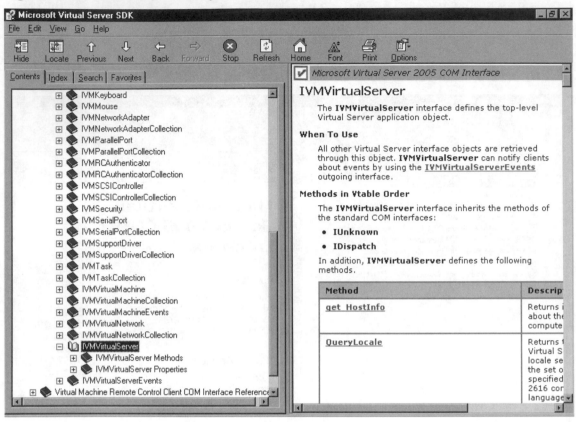

There are several things to notice. First, you probably noticed that you need to scroll down to the IVMVirtualServer node. The nodes are sorted and refer to a corresponding object. Second thing is that all objects start with IVM. This is their internal representation in the COM object. For navigating and using them in VBScript you can ignore the first IVM acronym. Last thing you can see from the figure is that the right pane gives you information on the IVMVirtualServer interface.

NOTE

The IVMVirtualServer interface is the interface to the root of the Virtual Server object. As the right pane states, this is the top-level Virtual Server application object. You connect to this object (using this interface) in all scripts that follow and access all "derived" objects from this object.

To get a good clear overview of the Virtual Server methods and properties it is easier to use the left pane than to use the right pane and browse its contents. When you click on the methods node you will get a screen like that in Figure 9.17.

Figure 9.17 Virtual Server Methods

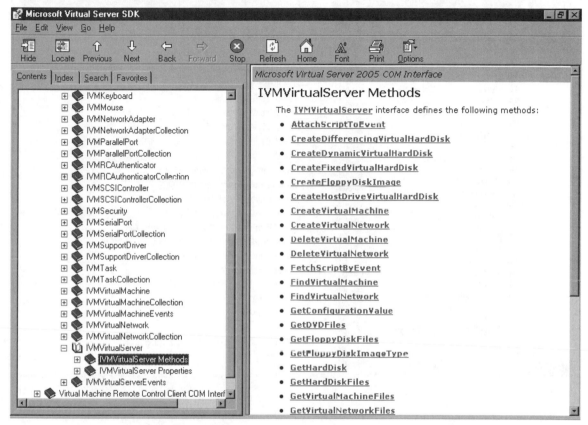

The right "results" pane lists its methods in a more human-readable form. The methods are displayed in sorted order and written in clear English in Pascal notation.

NOTE

In Pascal notation or Pascal casing the first letter is capitalized and each first letter of each concatenated word. For example the method used to create a virtual machine is written as *CreateVirtualMachine*, where the words create, virtual, and machine are concatenated and each first letter capitalized.

Figure 9.18 lists the properties of the Virtual Server object.

Figure 9.18 Virtual Server Properties

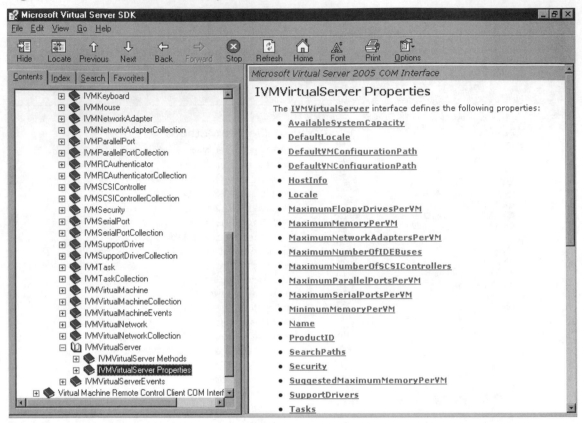

Notice that the meaning of these properties can also be easily understood from their name.

Connecting to the Virtual Server COM Object

The Virtual Server Programmer's Guide has many code samples for C++, Visual Basic, and VBScript. The samples for "Connecting to the Virtual Server COM object" in the guide cover only Visual Basic, C#, and C++. However, you can find the necessary information in the numerous VBScript samples throughout the SDK.

To connect to the COM object from VBScript, type the following:

```
Set objVS = CreateObject("VirtualServer.Application")
```

This is all there is to it to connect to the COM object. This line of code has several parts.

■ Set
    Used with objects to assign an object reference to a variable. The reference here is to the Virtual Server COM object, the variable is *objVS*.

- objVS
  The variable assigned to the Virtual Server COM object. This could be any name you like (within VBScript rules) but the programmer's guide uses *objVS* to denote an **obj**ect variable to **V**irtual **S**erver (*objVS*).

- CreateObject
  CreateObject instantiates a variable to an automation object.

- VirtualServer.Application
  This is the so-called *ProgID* by which the COM object has been registered on the operating system.

The only thing you can change in this single line of code is the name of the variable. If you are happy with the one from the programmer's guide then you can copy this line into your scripts and start using this variable.

Configuring & Implementing...

Setting Up Your Scripting Environment

We highly recommend that you set up your scripting environment prior to writing and testing (executing) your scripts. Your scripts can either run in the Wscript or Cscript host. We recommend that you execute your scripts from the command line and force its output to the console by using the command prompt of either supported operating system and setting the scripting host. You can set the scripting host to cscript by typing:

Cscript //h:cscript

Using cscript enables all output to be directed to the console or command prompt. If you were to output many results in your scripts they would result in a dialog box when using wscript as scripting host. Refer to Figures 9.20 and 9.21 for the difference in output when using cscript and wscript.

Besides the scripting host, make sure you have both the Microsoft Virtual Server SDK and the Windows Script Technologies (Windows Script V5.6 Documentation) open for quick reference. The Windows Script V5.6 Documentation can be downloaded from the Microsoft Download Center at www.microsoft.com/downloads/details.aspx?FamilyID=01592C48-207D-4BE1-8A76-1C4099D7BBB9&displaylang=en

Last but not least, choose a script editor that supports line numbers. There are many free editors available that support even syntax highlighting and other features. Most commercial script editors support more advanced features like debugging and step through.

Cscript has many switches you can use to configure the host or modify its default behavior. Figure 9.19 shows all available switches.

Figure 9.19 Listing Cscript Parameters

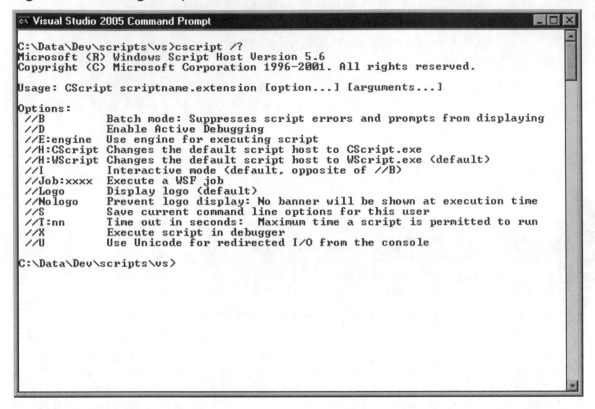

For the scope of this chapter the most important switches are the //H switch to set the script host and the //Logo switch to suppress the banner. Other commonly used but less-frequent switches are the //D switch for active debugging and the //Job switch for running specific jobs when using a Windows Script File, but we will not discuss these switches in this chapter. For more detailed explanation of the switches, please refer to the Windows Server online documentation through Help and Support Center.

Accessing a Virtual Server Using Script

Now that you know what is required to access the Virtual Server COM object and what your scripting environment should look like, you are ready to create your first scripts.

Listing Virtual Server Properties

The Virtual Server COM object has several properties. Many properties are read-only, such as informational and runtime properties. Examples of such properties are *Name*, *Version*, *ProductID*, and *UpTime*. Below is a script that displays the *Name* and *Version* properties of Virtual Server.

```
Set objVS = CreateObject("VirtualServer.Application")
Wscript.echo objVS.Name & ", " & objVS.Version
```

You execute this by executing **cscript <scriptname.vbs>** where scriptname is the name you chose for this script. The output of this script is shown in Figure 9.20.

Figure 9.20 Output of Virtual Server Name and Version

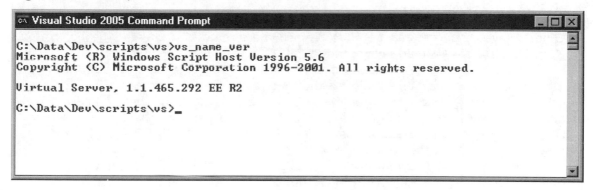

The script separates the Name output from the Version output by a comma. Although not very powerful, the script clearly depicts the ease by which you can retrieve information from Virtual Server. Notice the command that has been used to execute the script. Because cscript has been set as the default scripting host, it is possible to simply enter the script name on the command line without its extension. Figure 9.21 shows the same script results when using wscript as a script host.

Figure 9.21 Output of Virtual Server Name and Version using Wscript

A script that lists runtime information like *UpTime* is similar to the script above. You access the *UpTime* property through *objVS.UpTime*.

```
Set objVS = CreateObject("VirtualServer.Application")
Wscript.echo objVS.Name & ", " & objVS.UpTime
```

Designing & Planning...

Accessing Object Properties and Methods

Objects have properties and methods. Properties are values you can read (get) or write (set). The SDK always marks properties as either read-only or read/write.

Methods are actions you can execute. For example, the *CreateVirtualMachine* method of the Virtual Server object is the function to create a virtual machine.

Methods may require parameters to be able to perform their function. For *CreateVirtualMachine* you must supply the name and path for the virtual machine config file or the fully qualified path. The SDK describes the parameters it expects, their type, and what the method returns.

Methods often have return values. This can be a result code, a Boolean or integer, or even an object. For example, the *CreateVirtualMachine* method returns an object reference to the new virtual machine.

Always read the explanation section on the method and its requirements.

Another script that displays the configuration paths for virtual machines and virtual networks looks like this:

```
Set objVS = CreateObject("VirtualServer.Application")
wscript.echo objVS.DefaultVMConfigurationPath & vbCrLf &
objVS.DefaultVNConfigurationPath
```

The output (Figure 9.22) lists both locations on separate lines. Because the *DefaultVNConfiguratio nPath* is usually long (as the default is often kept) it is better to display each property on its own line. The *DefaultVMConfigurationPath* is read/write. We point this out to you because in most Virtual Server configurations this property is changed to point to a different location. If you want to assign a value by using script, then the only thing you would have to do is assign a value like this:

```
objVS.DefaultVMConfigurationPath="C:\VirtualMachines"
```

Figure 9.22 Output of Virtual Server Configuration Paths

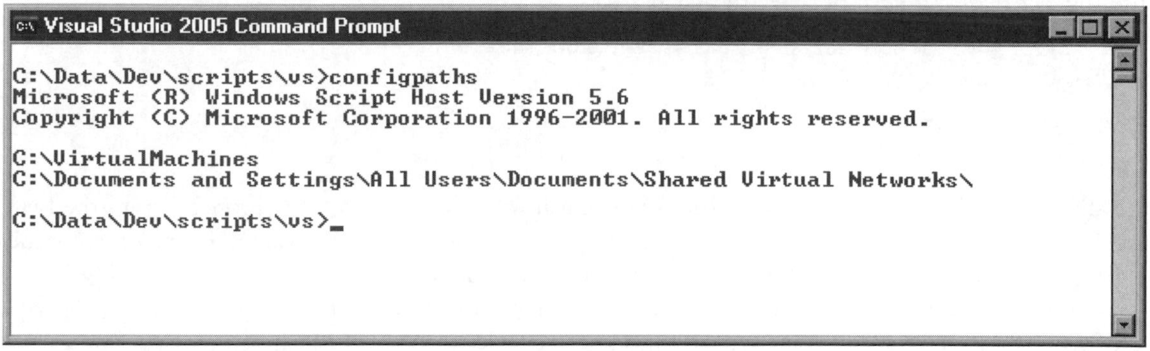

```
Visual Studio 2005 Command Prompt

C:\Data\Dev\scripts\vs>configpaths
Microsoft (R) Windows Script Host Version 5.6
Copyright (C) Microsoft Corporation 1996-2001. All rights reserved.

C:\VirtualMachines
C:\Documents and Settings\All Users\Documents\Shared Virtual Networks\

C:\Data\Dev\scripts\vs>_
```

Setting Virtual Server Properties

In the previous paragraph we accessed the Virtual Server object to list some properties. But some of those properties are likely to be changed right after installing Virtual Server. One such property is the *DefaultVMConfigurationPath* which is the path Virtual Server uses to store virtual machine configuration files. Another property that is likely to be changed is the *SearchPaths* property. This is an array of strings that is being used to search for files like configuration files, virtual floppies, ISO images and such. Setting this property is mainly useful when using the Virtual Server Administration Web site for management. Because it keeps you from having to navigate to those locations, Virtual Server searches the paths and fills the list boxes in the interface. Because you probably use the interface from time to time, it is handy to configure this property from script as well. Here is how you do it:

```
Set objVS = CreateObject("VirtualServer.Application")
objVS.SearchPaths=Array("C:\Media","C:\VirtualDisks","C:\VirtualMachines")
```

> **NOTE**
>
> VBScript has no definition for *safearray*. This type is known in Jscript. When you encounter a property of type *safearray* as with the *SearchPaths* property, you can assign a value to it. However, you cannot simply assign a value like objVS.SearchPaths = "C:\Media" even if you only want to assign a single value. You have to "format" the value using the Array function and then assign it to the variable as outlined in the code sample.

The trick is with the array statement. The *SearchPaths* property is a so-called *safearray* of strings. By using the *array* statement, you assign the *SearchPaths* property a collection of string values.

If you want to list the *SearchPaths* property, you cannot do this by using a single *wscript.echo* statement; the echo method of *wscript* requires a string, not a collection of strings. What should it display from this array? The way to display values in a collection (an array is also a collection) is to use the *For Each … Next* loop. See the script below.

```
Set objVS = CreateObject("VirtualServer.Application")
For Each strPath in objVS.SearchPaths
wscript.echo strPath
Next
```

By using a *For Each* loop, you instruct the script host to walk through the property until the last value is found. So in our example the *SearchPaths* property consists of three values. Every time a value is found it is assigned to the *strPath* variable and echoed to the output.

Another example of setting a Virtual Server property is the *VMRCEnabled* property. This property is of type Boolean (true/false) and setting this to true enables the Virtual Machine Remote Control service. The statement looks like this:

objVS.VMRCEnabled=vbTrue

In this statement the intrinsic constant *vbTrue* is assigned to the property. As with the previous examples you would use this in a Virtual Server configuration script, which would run right after the installation of Virtual Server.

The previous paragraphs were about retrieving and setting Virtual Server properties. Setting Virtual Server properties is probably something you won't do very often; they are concerned with the configuration of Virtual Server and once set they are not likely to change frequently. You only need to retrieve those properties for monitoring or diagnostic purposes.

Most of your scripts will focus on Virtual Server's "data"–like virtual machines and virtual networks. The next paragraphs are about creating virtual machines and virtual networks.

Creating a Virtual Machine Using Script

Creating virtual machines through script saves you lots of time. The process is also more predictable and error free. You develop the script once, test it, and distribute it for repetitive use of creating virtual machines. It will probably start out as a simple script without any error handling, but as you are exploring the Virtual Server SDK, you will probably end with an advanced script that creates all aspects of the virtual machine, like virtual disks. A virtual machine has a lot of properties just like a physical machine. When using the Virtual Server Administration Web site, you will probably create and modify several of them in several steps.

You may wonder how the method *CreateVirtualMachine* requires so few parameters. Notice that you have to supply only name and path or the fully qualified name, which includes the path. The reason for this is that Virtual Server has some default values it assigns to properties like *Memory* and *NetworkAdapters*.

So creating a virtual machine from script is fairly easy, as shown below:

```
Const strVMName="Machine1"
Set objVS = CreateObject("VirtualServer.Application")
Set objVM = objVS.CreateVirtualMachine(strVMName, _
objVS.DefaultVMConfigurationPath & "\" & strVMName)
```

Notice the underscore (_) at the end of the third line. This is to break up long lines of code and tell the script host to continue reading on the next line. If you want a single line of code, delete the underscore and place the fourth line of code after the comma.

You may recall from the "Accessing Object Properties and Methods" sidebar that the method CreateVirtualMachine returns an object. Therefore, we assign the returned object to a variable, which is *objVM* in the code sample. By doing so we can use the *objVM* variable and set its properties. In this example, we could have accomplished the same with this line of code:

```
objVS.CreateVirtualMachine strVMName, _
objVS.DefaultVMConfigurationPath & "\" & strVMName
```

Notice that the parentheses in *CreateVirtualMachine* and the set statement have been removed.

NOTE

Using parentheses in VBScript: When you ran the previous script, you assigned a value to *objVM*, which was returned from the CreateVirtualMachine method. If you modify that line by removing the *"Set objVM ="* part, VBScript will complain with a "Cannot use parentheses when calling a Sub" error message. You can fix this in two ways:

Remove the parentheses (as shown above).

Use a Call statement such as Call objVS.CreateVirtualMachine("strVM.......").

CreateVirtualMachine is a method of the Virtual Server object. Please verify and confirm this from the SDK because it is essential that you understand this. The code further declares a constant for the name of the virtual machine. This constant is used in the method as parameter. Also notice that the property *DefaultVMConfigurationPath* is used as parameter in this method. This way we don't have to retrieve the value separately but "feed" it directly to this method. The concatenation of *DefaultVMConfigurationPath*, the backslash, and the virtual machine name causes the virtual machine configuration file to be created in its own folder. This is to follow best practices where all virtual machine files (configuration, disks, saved state, etc.) are all grouped in the same folder. This also eases ACL administration when configuring access to virtual machines.

Creating a Virtual HardDisk

Although it is perfectly okay to have a virtual machine without virtual disks, you will most often create virtual machines with multiple virtual disks attached to them. Creating a virtual disk is not a virtual machine object method but a Virtual Server method. Again, please verify that several methods exist on the Virtual Server object to create different types of virtual disk.

If not a virtual machine method, why discuss it here? Because another complexity exists with creating a virtual disk that would probably not be understood if it were discussed earlier in this chapter. The default type of virtual disk in the Virtual Server Administration Web site is the Dynamically Expanding virtual disk. The method to create this type of disk is *CreateDynamicVirtualHardDisk*. Please verify from the SDK that this method requires two parameters: the full path to the image file and the size of the disk in megabytes. Also confirm that this method returns an object called a task object, defined as *IVMTask*.

The task object consists of several properties and methods. Some properties of interest are *IsCancelable*, *IsComplete*, and *PercentCompleted*. An interesting method is *Cancel*, which only works if the property *IsCancelable* is true. Creating a virtual disk takes up time. It may be a couple of milliseconds to tens of seconds depending mainly of the type of virtual disk. A dynamically expanding disk is created fairly quickly whereas Fixed Size disk may take some time to be created. Because of this you need to have a way to give Virtual Server time to complete its operation by looping in a wait state and without stressing the CPU.

Let's look at the code of creating a dynamically expanding virtual disk.

```
Const strDisk="C:\VirtualMachines\Machine1\Machine1-disk1.vhd"
Set objVS = CreateObject("VirtualServer.Application")
Set objTask = objVS.CreateDynamicVirtualHardDisk(strDisk,500)
While not objTask.IsComplete
  wscript.sleep 500
Wend
```

The first three lines should be clear by now. The important piece of code, which is different from all previous samples, is the *While Wend* loop. Here we use the property *IsComplete* of the *objTask* object to check whether the operation is complete. If not, we wait for 500 ms before checking again. This way we prevent the script from pegging the CPU continuously.

NOTE

If you use a while loop without a back off like the 500 ms sleep, you will stress the CPU up to 100% because it is basically continuously asking itself if the condition is true. It will do so at the maximum speed possible. During this chitchatting with itself it will not use the time to do things that are actually important.

Putting It All Together

With our knowledge of creating a virtual machine and creating a virtual disk we can create more advanced scripts for virtual machines. The sample shown in Code Listing 9.1 creates a virtual machine, Machine1, with 256 MB of memory, one fixed-size virtual disk of 500 MB attached to a SCSI controller and a DVD drive.

Code Listing 9.1 Creating a Virtual Machine

```
Const strVMName="Machine1"
Const intMemory=256
Const strVMDisk="Machine1-Disk1-F.vhd"
Const intVMDiskSize=500
Set objVS = CreateObject("VirtualServer.Application")
strVMPath=objVS.DefaultVMConfigurationPath
'enable error handling
On error resume next
'echo stage
wscript.stdout.write "Creating fixed disk"
'get a Task object
set objTask = objVS.CreateFixedVirtualHardDisk(strVMPath & "\" & _
    strVMName & "<0x201D> & strVMDisk,intVMDiskSize)
'on success use a loop to check for complete. If not complete echo dot
to show activity.
If err.number = 0 then
  While not objTask.IsComplete
    wscript.stdout.write "."
    wscript.sleep 500
  Wend
  wscript.StdOut.write(" done." & vbCRLF)
'on failure call the error handler sub routine
Else
  Handle(err)
End If
'disable error handling
on error goto 0
'echo stage
wscript.StdOut.write("Creating virtual machine…")
Set objVM = objVS.CreateVirtualMachine(strVMName,strVMPath & "\" _
  & strVMName)
wscript.StdOut.write(" done." & vbCRLF)
If err.number = 0 then
  wscript.StdOut.write("Adding SCSI controller…")
  objVM.AddSCSIController
```

```
  wscript.StdOut.write(" done." & vbCRLF)
  wscript.StdOut.write("Adding SCSI disk 0…")
  'link the hard disk to the virtual machine
  Call objVM.AddHardDiskConnection(strVMPath & "\" & _
strVMName & "\" & strVMDisk,1,0,0)
  If err.number <> 0 then
    handle(err)
  End If
  wscript.StdOut.write(" done." & vbCRLF)
  wscript.StdOut.write("Adding DVDROMDrive…")
  objVM.AddDVDROMDrive 0,1,0
  wscript.StdOut.write(" done." & vbCRLF)
  wscript.StdOut.write("Setting memory…")
  objVM.Memory=intMemory
  wscript.StdOut.write(" done." & vbCRLF)
Else
  Handle(err)
End If
'this is a basic erro handler routine. If anything fails, it logs and quits.
Private Sub Handle(byval error)
  wscript.echo Cstr(hex(error.number)) & ", " & error.description
  wscript.quit
End Sub
Set objVS = Nothing
```

Notice that this script does not introduce new things we have not discussed earlier. What is different is white space, a different way of echoing results (status) to the screen by using the *StdOut.Write* method and a separate error handler for displaying error number and description. Notice the call statement in front of *objVM.AddHardDiskConnection*. This prevents us from having to remove the parenthesis.

Wscript.StdOut.Write echoes or writes to *StdOut* which, in this case, is the console or command prompt window. It does not automatically put a carriage return at the end, so you can display bullets after each other to show that something is happening (see Figure 9.23 for output). The last line of code is also related to VBScript. By setting *objVS* to *Nothing*, we destroy the object and release the memory it had occupied. Strictly speaking, this is not necessary but more a matter of clean programming.

Figure 9.23 Displaying Results to Show Activity

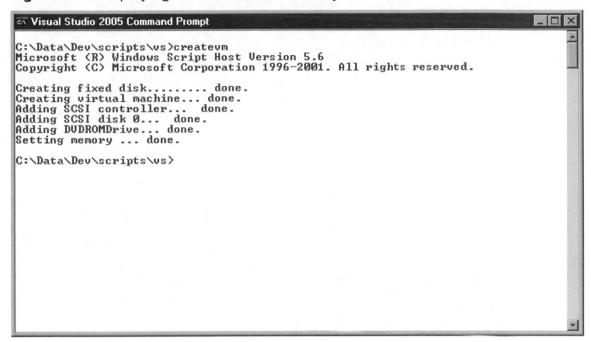

```
C:\Data\Dev\scripts\vs>createvm
Microsoft (R) Windows Script Host Version 5.6
Copyright (C) Microsoft Corporation 1996-2001. All rights reserved.

Creating fixed disk......... done.
Creating virtual machine... done.
Adding SCSI controller...  done.
Adding SCSI disk 0...  done.
Adding DVDROMDrive... done.
Setting memory ... done.

C:\Data\Dev\scripts\vs>
```

Creating a Virtual Network Using Script

Creating a virtual network is very similar to creating a virtual machine. The method to use is a method of the Virtual Server object called *CreateVirtualNetwork*, as shown in Code Listing 9.2. Notice that this method also requires a name and a path, and you can choose how to specify them. As with *CreateVirtualMachine*, it is up to you to specify a name and path or a full path. This method also returns an object to the newly created virtual network. After you have created the network, you can set its properties (it has no methods).

Because the creation of a virtual network is basically the same as for creating a virtual machine, we skip the single line of code. Creating the virtual network itself is not very challenging now that we know how to do that. Simply calling the *CreateVirtualNetwork* method with a name and path results in a Guests Only network.

The more interesting part is configuring the virtual network.

Code Listing 9.2 Creating a Virtual Network

```
Const strVNName="Network1"

Const strNetwork="192.168.150.0"

Const strMask="255.255.255.0"

Const strStartIP="192.168.150.16"

Const strEndIP="192.168.150.32"
```

```
Const strServerIP="192.168.150.1"
Set objVS = CreateObject("VirtualServer.Application")
Set objVN=objVS.CreateVirtualNetwork(strVNName,_
    objVS.DefaultVNConfigurationPath)
Set objDHCP=objVN.DHCPVirtualNetworkServer
objDHCP.IsEnabled=vbTrue
objDHCP.ConfigureDHCPServer strNetwork,strMask,_
    strStartIP,strEndIP,strServerIP
```

This script first sets the network name and *DHCPServer* parameters. Please confirm that when you need to configure the virtual DHCP server of the network that you have to use the *DHCPVirtualNetworkServer* property. Notice that this property returns an object of type *DHCPVirtualNetworkServer*, which has both methods and properties. In the last two lines, the script sets the *IsEnabled* property to true and uses the *ConfigureDHCPServer* method of the *DHCPVirtualNetworkServer* object (*objDHCP*) to configure DHCP scope settings.

Suppose we just ran this script but we wanted to attach this virtual network to the Virtual Server host adapter. Suppose you have a physical host adapter called "Broadcom NetXtreme Gigabit Ethernet." A script that changes the configuration of Network1 would look like this:

```
Const strVNName="Network1"
Set objVS=CreateObject("VirtualServer.Application")
Set objVN=objVS.FindVirtualNetwork(strVNName)
objVN.HostAdapter="Broadcom NetXtreme Gigabit Ethernet"
```

In the third line of code, we retrieve a virtual network object from the collection of objects. Notice that this is a Virtual Server object method. After we have the virtual network object (*objVN*), we can set the *HostAdapter* property to that of the physical host adapter description.

NOTE

The value for the *HostAdapter* property of the virtual network can be retrieved from *ipconfig* using the /all switch. You can then copy the description from the host network adapter.

Retrieving Guest OS Information Using Script

Information from the Guest OS can also be retrieved using script. However, there are some dependencies and restrictions for a successful retrieval of information.

The *GuestOS* is a property of a virtual machine. When you access the property an object is returned. The problem is that the *GuestOS* property exists only when a virtual machine is running. This means that the following script fails when the machine is in saved state.

```
Const strVMName="Machine1"
Set objVS=CreateObject("VirtualServer.Application")
Set objVM=objVS.FindVirtualMachine(strVMName)
Set objOS=objVM.GuestOS
wscript.echo objOS.OSName
```

The resulting output of this script contains an error message like this:

(null): The virtual machine could not be found or is not running.

Another issue with the *GuestOS* property lies with the existence of the Virtual Machine Additions. They must be installed inside the virtual machine for the properties to get values. Without the additions, the properties will stay empty.

So how should you retrieve information properly? Look at the following modified script:

```
Const strVMName="Machine1"
Set objVS=CreateObject("VirtualServer.Application")
Set objVM=objVS.FindVirtualMachine(strVMName)
Set objOS=objVM.GuestOS
If objOS.IsHeartbeating then
  wscript.echo objOS.OSName
End If
```

This script uses the *IsHeartBeating* property of the *GuestOS* object. When this property is true you validate two things:

1. The additions are installed.

2. The virtual machine is running and sending information (*heartbeating*).

The following script lists all properties of the object:

```
Const strVMName="Machine1"
Set objVS=CreateObject("VirtualServer.Application")
Set objVM=objVS.FindVirtualMachine(strVMName)
Set objOS=objVM.GuestOS
On Error Resume Next
If objOS.AdditionsVersion <> "" then
  If err.number <> 0 then
    wscript.echo err.Description
    wscript.quit
  End If
  If objOS.IsHeartbeating then
    With objOS
```

```
    wscript.echo "VM Additions version : " & .AdditionsVersion
    wscript.echo "Operating System Name : " & .OSName
    wscript.echo "HeartBeat percentage : " & .HeartBeatPercentage
    wscript.echo "Is Heart Beating : " & _ BoolToString(.IsHeartbeating)
  wscript.echo "OS can shutdown : " & _ BoolToString(.CanShutdown)
  wscript.echo "Host time sync enabled : " & _ BoolToString(.IsHostTimeSyncEnabled)
    End With
  End If
End If
Function BooltoString(bool)
  If bool = vbTrue then
    booltostring="True"
  Else
    booltostring="False"
  End If
End Function
```

Figure 9.24 displays the output of the script. Note the capital T at the end of Server. It is the Trademark symbol, which cannot be displayed. Also notice the *can shutdown* property. When this property is set to true, you can execute the *GuestOS.Shutdown* method to shut down the virtual machine. This is the operating system shutdown function, which is the same when you interactively select **Start | Shut Down** from the Start Menu.

Figure 9.24 Listing GuestOS Properties

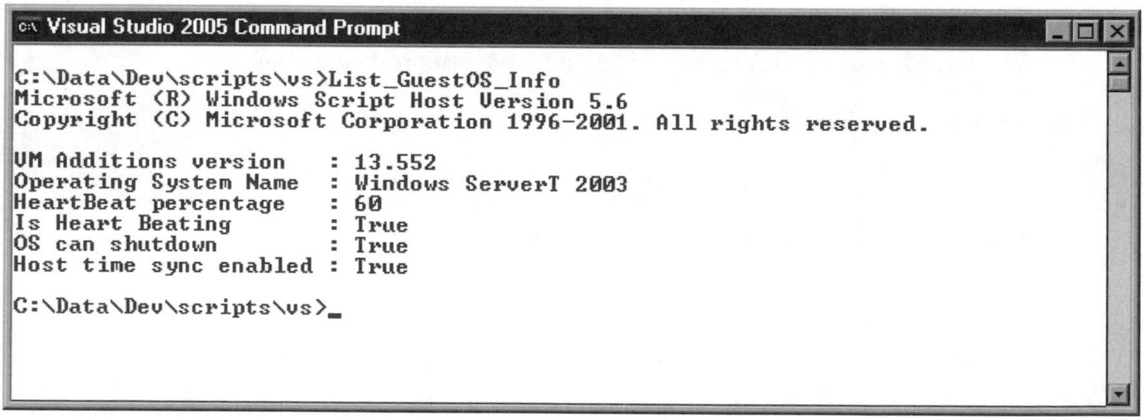

```
Visual Studio 2005 Command Prompt                                     _ □ ×

C:\Data\Dev\scripts\vs>List_GuestOS_Info
Microsoft (R) Windows Script Host Version 5.6
Copyright (C) Microsoft Corporation 1996-2001. All rights reserved.

VM Additions version   : 13.552
Operating System Name  : Windows ServerT 2003
HeartBeat percentage   : 60
Is Heart Beating       : True
OS can shutdown        : True
Host time sync enabled : True

C:\Data\Dev\scripts\vs>_
```

Another method to notice is the *GuestOS.InstallAdditions*. This method also does not have any parameters. When executed, Virtual Server will mount the Virtual Machine Additions ISO (VMAdditions.iso), which in turn results in execution of the Virtual Machine Additions setup, but only if Autorun is enabled on the guest OS.

Changing a Virtual Machine State Using Script

Scripts help out with automating tasks that are either time consuming, error prone, or repetitive. The previous paragraphs all covered retrieving or modifying settings or creating virtual machines and networks. But scripts also have a huge value for operational tasks such as monitoring and control.

For example, if you have a lot of virtual machines on a Virtual Server host, and it's very likely that you will, it can be a very tedious job to save their state or shut them down manually. Suppose that you have to do maintenance on the Virtual Server host, which requires you to shut it down. Touching each and every virtual machine is unrealistic and unnecessary. Scripting is the answer here as well.

From the previous paragraphs we have see there is a *Shutdown* method on the *GuestOS* object. You may need that method from time to time. Very often you may not want to shut down the operating system but want to save the state of the virtual machine. Methods to change virtual machine state exist on the virtual machine object. These methods are:

- *Pause* Puts a running virtual machine on hold. In this state there is no execution, but the machine still has all its resources allocated.

- *Reset* This resets the virtual machine. Compare to a hard power off or unplugging the power.

- *Resume* This resumes a paused virtual machine.

- *Save* This puts a running virtual machine in saved state. In that state the virtual machine releases its resources on the host.

- Startup This starts a virtual machine. If it was in the turned off state it will start. If it was in saved state it will load from the saved state file and continue running.

- TurnOff This has the same effect as reset except that it is kept turned off.

The Virtual Machine State Model

The Virtual Server SDK contains a Virtual Machine State Diagram. This diagram of a State Machine is important when using virtual machines and changing state. The transition of a virtual machine from one state to the other follows a strict path. For example, a virtual machine cannot go from *turned off* to *saved* state. It must enter the *running* state first. Also, the change of state requires time. As with the creation of virtual disks, this depends on the state the virtual machine is in and the state it has to transition to.

Figure 9.25 Virtual Machine States

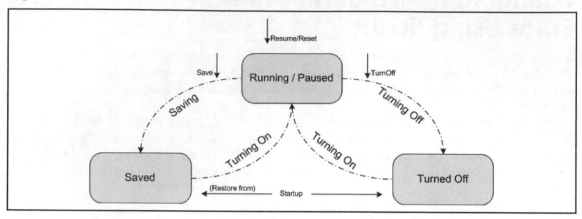

Figure 9.25 shows three virtual finite machine states: *running/paused*, *saved*, and *turned off*. The events or methods are denoted with a vertical arrow. The transition states are shown by dashed lines.

This figure is drawn to clearly depict states, their transition path, and the event that results in a state change. For example, when a virtual machine is in the *running/paused* state, the *save* method causes a transition to *saved* state. The *startup* method can then be used to change the state back to *running*. During these transitions, the machine state is saving and restoring respectively. These states depict a transition. Notice that technically a *saved* virtual machine is *turned off* but in a special state, the *saved* state.

Changing the state of a virtual machine requires a good understanding of each type of virtual machine state and the paths the virtual machine can follow to change into the desired state. In your code you have to retrieve the current state and based upon that decide what you can do. Consider the following script:

```
Const strVMName="Machine1"
Set objVS=CreateObject("VirtualServer.Application")
Set objVM=objVS.FindVirtualMachine(strVMName)
objVM.Startup
```

If we assume for now that machine1 does exist, then the *startup* method may still fail. For example, when the virtual machine is paused, the *startup* method will not make it resume. Therefore, you should add code that complements the method you want to execute.

```
Const strVMName="machine1"
Const vmVMState_Invalidvm = 0
Const vmVMState_TurnedOff = 1
Const vmVMState_Saved = 2
Const vmVMState_TurningOn = 3
Const vmVMState_Restoring = 4
Const vmVMState_Running = 5
Const vmVMState_Paused = 6
Const vmVMState_Saving = 7
Const vmVMState_TurningOff = 8
Const vmVMState_MergingDrives = 9
Const vmVMState_DeleteMachine = 10
Set objVS=CreateObject("VirtualServer.Application")
Set objVM=objVS.FindVirtualMachine(strVMName)
If objVM.State = vmVMState_TurnedOff then
  objVM.Startup
End if
```

This code properly checks the state of the virtual machine prior to calling the *startup* method. Notice the virtual machine state codes. These are defined in the Virtual Server SDK under Virtual Server COM Interface Enumerations. The virtual machine state codes are the values for the VMVMState enumeration, which you will find mentioned under the virtual machine state methods. Using the values as constants makes your code easier to read.

Code Listing 9.3 is a somewhat different script that basically does the same. It uses the state codes differently (in an array) and is more general because it works with command-line arguments.

Code Listing 9.3 Starting Virtual Machines That Are in Turned Off State

```
Option Explicit
Dim objVS, objVM, strVMName, VMStates
VMStates = Array("Invalid", "Turned Off","Saved","Turning On", "Restoring",
"Running", "Paused", "Saving", "Turning Off", "Merging Drives", "Deleting
Machine")
If wscript.Arguments.Count <> 0 then
  Set objVS=CreateObject("VirtualServer.Application")
  strVMName=wscript.arguments(0)
  Set objVM=objVS.FindVirtualMachine(strVMName)
  If err.number = 0 then
   On Error Resume Next
   wscript.echo "Current state of " & strVMName & " _
is " & VMStates(objVM.State)
   if err.number <> 0 then
     Handle(err)
```

```
    end if
    If VMStates(objVM.State) = "Turned Off" then
      objVM.Startup
    End If
  else
    wscript.echo "An error occcurred finding virtual machine " & strVMName
  End If
Else
  wscript.echo "You must supply the name of the virtual machine"
End If
Sub Handle(err)
  wscript.echo Cstr(hex(err.number)) & ", " & err.description
  wscript.quit
End Sub
```

Attaching Scripts to Virtual Server Events

Scripts can be attached to both Virtual Server and virtual machine events. The events for virtual machines are mostly related to virtual machine state changes, loss of heartbeats, and processor- and disk-related conditions of the host. The events for Virtual Server are related to Virtual Server service changes and the previously mentioned events for virtual machines except that these events are for any virtual machine. So events on the Virtual Server level are generic for all virtual machines; those on virtual machine level are virtual machine specific.

Attaching scripts to these events gives you more flexibility in controlling the behavior of Virtual Server. For example, when Virtual Server starts, you may want to be able to control the sequence in which virtual machines are started. Furthermore, you may not only want to start those machines in sequence, but also only start additional virtual machines when specific services like Active Directory are operational. In such a scenario, you could attach a script to the event called *Command-line action when Virtual Server starts*. Let's look at a script that starts two virtual machines but only starts the second when the operating system is running:

```
Option Explicit
Dim objVS, objVM, strVMName, VMStates
VMStates = Array("Invalid", "Turned Off","Saved","Turning On", "Restoring",
"Running", "Paused", "Saving",_ "Turning Off", "Merging Drives", "Deleting
Machine")
Const strVM1="Machine1"
Const strVM2="Machine2"
Set objVS=CreateObject("VirtualServer.Application")
Set objVM=objVS.FindVirtualMachine(strVM1)
If err.number = 0 then
  objVM.Startup
End If
```

```
On error resume next
While not objVM.GuestOS.IsHeartbeating
  wscript.sleep 1000
Wend
Set objVM=objVS.FindVirtualMachine(strVM2)
objVM.Startup
```

Notice that we did not create a *Task* object to track completion. In this case, we use a While Wend loop and check for the IsHeartBeating Boolean. When set to true, the machine has successfully started and the operating system is running.

To attach this script to the Virtual Server event called *Command-line action when Virtual Server starts*, perform the following:

Open the Virtual Server Administration Web site, click **Server Properties**, click **Virtual Server scripts**, and tick the checkbox next to **Enable scripts attached to this server**. See Figure 9.26 for a screen reference.

Figure 9.26 Attaching a Script to a Virtual Server Event

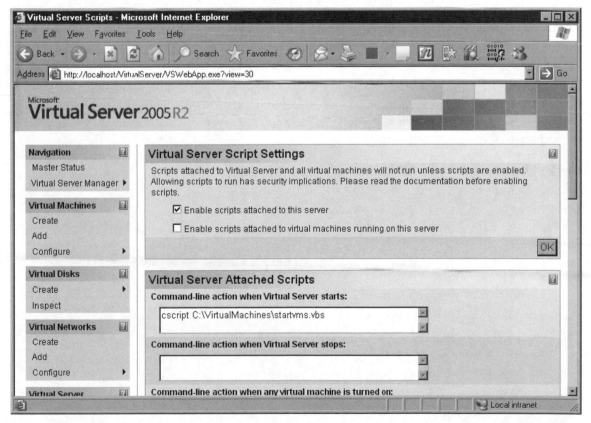

Attaching Scripts to Virtual Machine Events

Attaching a script to a Virtual Server event involves just a few steps. You have to enable scripting in the Virtual Server properties and attach the script to the desired event. If you want to attach a script to a virtual machine, then you have to configure additional settings.

First, you have to enable scripting on the virtual machine level. See Figure 9.19 for the location to enable scripting. To enable scripting, tick the checkbox next to **Enable scripts attached to virtual machines running on this server**. You will not be able to configure scripting on any virtual machine without this setting enabled.

Second, you will have to configure the virtual machine to run under a specific user account. This is for security reasons. By default, the local administrator's security group has full control of Virtual Server. When a virtual machine has not been configured to run under a specific user account, it runs under the account that started it and so would any script that would run as a result of a virtual machine event. Therefore, you must configure each and every virtual machine to run under a specific user account if you want to attach scripts.

The user account can be an account with user privilege. The user needs proper NTFS access to all the objects that belong to the virtual machine or are related due to its configuration. For example, with a virtual machine with a differencing disk and one parent and attached to a virtual network, the account must have read access to the parent virtual disk, read access to the virtual network, and write access to the differencing disk, the virtual machine config file, and any other writeable file. Generally, it is easier to give that account write access to the virtual machine folder. Of course, you must also give that account read access to the script and consider all access requirements as a result of running the script.

Scripts in Action

Code Listings 9.4 through 9.9 are examples of several scripts that you can use in day-to-day operations of Virtual Server. The scripts are focused towards using the COM API and do not deal much with error handling. This is kept to a minimum to keep the scripts small and clear. Code Listing 9.4 shows how to save all running virtual machines.

Code Listing 9.4 Save All Running Virtual Machines

```
Option Explicit
Dim objVS, objVM, objTask, objVMCol, NameLength, MaxNameLength, VMStateCodes
Set objVS = CreateObject("VirtualServer.Application")
VMStateCodes = Array("Invalid", "Turned Off","Saved","Turning On", "Restoring",
"Running", "Paused", "Saving",_ "Turning Off", "Merging Drives", "Deleting
Machine")
Set objVMCol = objVS.VirtualMachines
'Get maximum Name Length for display formatting
For Each objVM in objVMCol
  NameLength = Len(objVM.Name)
  If MaxNameLength < NameLength Then
    MaxNameLength = NameLength
  End If
```

```
Next
'Start up all VMs
Wscript.stdout.write("MACHINE" & Space(MaxNameLength-7) & " - " &
"STATUS" & vbCRLF)
wscript.echo
For Each objVM in objVMCol
  Wscript.stdout.write(objVM.Name & Space(MaxNameLength -
Len(objVM.Name)) & " - " & VMStateCodes(objVM.State) & vbCRLF)
  If VMStateCodes(objVM.State) = "Running" then
    Set objTask = objVM.Save()
      wscript.sleep(500)
      Wscript.stdout.write(Space(MaxNameLength) & " " &
VMStateCodes(objVM.State) & " ")
    While not objTask.IsComplete
      wscript.sleep(1000)
      Wscript.stdout.write(".")
    Wend
    wscript.stdout.write(" " & VMStateCodes(objVM.State))
  End If
  wscript.stdout.write(vbCRLF)
Next
Set objVS = Nothing
```

Code Listing 9.5 Start All Saved Virtual Machines

```
Option Explicit
Dim objVS, objVM, objTask, objVMCol, NameLength, MaxNameLength, VMStateCodes
Set objVS = CreateObject("VirtualServer.Application")
VMStateCodes = Array("Invalid", "Turned Off","Saved","Turning On", "Restoring",
"Running", "Paused", "Saving",_ "Turning Off", "Merging Drives", "Deleting
Machine")
Set objVMCol = objVS.VirtualMachines
'Get maximum Name Length for display formatting
For Each objVM in objVMCol
    NameLength = Len(objVM.Name)
    If MaxNameLength < NameLength Then
      MaxNameLength = NameLength
    End If
Next
'Start up all VMs
Wscript.stdout.write("MACHINE" & Space(MaxNameLength-7) & " - " &
"STATUS" & vbCRLF)
```

```
wscript.echo
For Each objVM in objVMCol
    Wscript.stdout.write(objVM.Name & Space(MaxNameLength -
    Len(objVM.Name)) & " - " & VMStateCodes(objVM.State) & vbCRLF)
    If VMStateCodes(objVM.State) = "Saved" then
        Set objTask = objVM.Startup()
          wscript.sleep(500)
              Wscript.stdout.write(Space(MaxNameLength) & " " &
VMStateCodes(objVM.State) & " ")
    While not objTask.IsComplete
          wscript.sleep(1000)
          Wscript.stdout.write(".")
      Wend
      wscript.stdout.write(" " & VMStateCodes(objVM.State))
    End If
    wscript.stdout.write(vbCRLF)
Next
Set objVS = Nothing
```

Code Listing 9.6 List all MAC Addresses per Virtual Machine

```
Option Explicit
Dim objVS, objVMCol, objVM, objAdap, objAdapCol
Set objVS = CreateObject("VirtualServer.Application")
Set objVMCol = objVS.VirtualMachines
For Each objVM in objVMCol
  Set objAdapCol = objVM.NetworkAdapters
  For Each objAdap in objAdapCol
    wscript.stdout.write("MAC address: " & objAdap.EthernetAddress _
    & ", Virtual machine: " & objVM.Name & vbCRLF)
  Next
Next
Set objVS = Nothing
```

Code Listing 9.7 List all Attached Floppy Images

```
Option Explicit
Dim objVS, objVM, objVMCol, objVF, objVFCol
Set objVS = CreateObject("VirtualServer.Application")
Set objVMCol = objVS.VirtualMachines
On error Resume Next
For Each objVM in objVMCol
```

```
  Set objVFCol = objVM.FloppyDrives
  If objVFCol.Count > 0 then
  For Each objVF in objVFCol
    If objVF.ImageFile <> "" then
      wscript.stdout.write("Machine: " & objVM.Name _
      & " " & objVF.ImageFile & vbCRLF)
    End If
  Next
  End If
Next
Set oVS = Nothing
Option explicit
Dim objVS, objVM
Set objVS = CreateObject("VirtualServer.Application")
If wscript.arguments.count > 1 then
  Set objVM = objVS.FindVirtualMachine(wscript.arguments(0))
  If objVM.DVDROMDrives.Count > 0 then
    Select case objVM.DVDRomDrives.Item(1).Attachment
      case 1 objVM.DVDRomDrives.Item(1).ReleaseImage
      case 2 objVM.DVDRomDrives.Item(1).ReleaseHostDrive
    End Select
    On Error Resume Next
    objVM.DVDROMDrives.Item(1).AttachImage(wscript.arguments(1))
    If err.number <> 0 then
      handle(err)
    End If
    wscript.echo objVM.DVDROMDrives.Item(1).ImageFile & " attached to
    " & objVM.Name
  Else
    wscript.echo "No DVD Drive in virtual machine " & wscript.arguments(0)
  End If
Else
  wscript.echo "Syntax: AttachDVDImage <VirtualMachineName> <FullPathToImageFile>"
End If
```

Code Listing 9.8 Attach DVD Image to Virtual Machine

```
Private Sub Handle(byval error)
  wscript.echo Cstr(hex(error.number)) & ", " & error.description
End Sub
Set objVS = Nothing
```

Code Listing 9.9 List all Registered Virtual Machines

```
Option Explicit

Dim objVS, objVMCol, objVM, VMStateCodes, NameLength, MaxNameLength

Set objVS = CreateObject("VirtualServer.Application")

VMStateCodes = Array("Invalid", "Turned Off","Saved","Turning On", "Restoring",
"Running", "Paused", "Saving",_ "Turning Off", "Merging Drives", "Deleting
Machine")

Set objVMCol=objVS.VirtualMachines

For Each objVM in objVMCol

    NameLength = Len(objVM.Name)

    If MaxNameLength < NameLength Then

      MaxNameLength = NameLength

    End If

Next

wscript.stdout.write "Number of registered VM's: " & objVMCol.Count & vbCRLF

For Each objVM in objVMCol

  wscript.StdOut.write(objVM.Name & space(MaxNameLength - Len(objVM.Name)) & " - ")

  wscript.echo VMStateCodes(objVM.State)

Next

Set objVS = Nothing
```

Summary

This chapter covered the more advanced methods of managing Virtual Server. By setting up a management server, you can manage all Virtual Server hosts using a single instance of the Virtual Server Administration Web site. This way you do not have to install Internet Information Services on each and every Virtual Server installation.

The other method of managing Virtual Server is by using the COM API and programming the actions through your favorite programming environment, whether a scripting environment or any other development language. It does not matter what you choose as long as your language supports the COM object model.

By using scripting with VBScript or Jscript, your code is open to everyone and can easily be shared among all Virtual Server hosts. Scripts can easily be modified and new functionality can be created of them.

Scripting Virtual Server is easy after you understand the Virtual Server COM API. Tasks that require many steps in the graphical user interface can now be automated, which saves time, prevents errors, and makes your Virtual Server configuration tasks more predictable.

Solutions Fast Track

The Management Interface

☑ The Virtual Server management interface is Web based and requires Internet Information Services.

☑ System Center Virtual Machine Manager, to be released in the near future, no longer has this requirement.

☑ Virtual Server hosts in the same Windows Server 2003 domain can all be managed centrally from one Internet Information Services site using the Virtual Server Administration Web site.

Using the Virtual Server COM API

☑ The Virtual Server COM API is documented in the Virtual Server Programmer's Guide.

☑ This guide is really the Virtual Server SDK and installed with the product.

☑ Being able to navigate through the SDK is a requirement for easy and successful programming of Virtual Server.

Accessing a Virtual Server Using Script

☑ You can access Virtual Server properties and methods with a single line of code.

☑ Use the VBScript *CreateObject* function with the Virtual Server *ProgID* to establish the connection.

Creating a Virtual Machine Using Script

- ☑ Create a virtual machine by using the *CreateVirtualMachine* method.
- ☑ You must create machine properties such as virtual disks first.

Creating a Virtual Network Using Script

- ☑ Create a virtual network by using the *CreateVirtualNetwork* method.

Retrieving Guest OS Information Using Script

- ☑ Retrieve guest OS information through the *GuestOS* property of the virtual machine object.
- ☑ Information is only available when the virtual machine additions have been installed and the virtual machine is in the running state.

Changing a Virtual Machine State Using Script

- ☑ Change the state of a virtual machine by using the appropriate state method of the virtual machine object.
- ☑ The state transition of a virtual machine follows a state machine model.

Attaching Scripts to Virtual Server Events

- ☑ You can attach scripts to both Virtual Server and virtual machine events.
- ☑ Attaching scripts gives you more control of the operations.

Frequently Asked Questions

Q: Are Internet Information Services required to manage Virtual Server?

A: No. You can manage Virtual Server any way you like by using the COM API.

Q: Does every Virtual Server installation require Internet Information Services?

A: No. You can manage any Virtual Server using a central management site.

Q: Do sample scripts exist for managing Virtual Server?

A: Yes. You can download Virtual Server script samples from the Microsoft scripting center.

Q: Do I need to be a developer to successfully script Virtual Server?

A: No. You need basic scripting skills and the Virtual Server Programmer's Guide.

Q: Can scripts developed for Virtual Server 2005 be used on Virtual Server 2005 R2?

A: Yes. The COM API has not changed between these versions.

## Chapter 10

Migrating Physical Machines

Solutions in this chapter:

- **Getting the Virtualization Environment Ready for Usage**

- **Capturing the Physical Machine**

- **Creating the Virtual Machine on the Virtual Server Host**

- **Deploying the Virtual Machine on the Host OS**

☑ **Summary**

☑ **Solutions Fast Track**

☑ **Frequently Asked Questions**

Introduction

This is where it all comes together. You're getting ready to duplicate all data from the physical server to your virtualization environment. Now everything comes down to the procedure. There are three stages that the system will pass through, during which you must take several actions. First is preparation: you must retrieve the information of the physical server, check and validate the information, and generate the virtualization scripts, making it possible to capture the physical server. Second is creation: you must create the virtual machine before the captured image can be deployed. Third is deployment: you must deploy the captured data to the virtual machine and perform the post-migration actions.

Getting the Virtualization Environment Ready for Usage

The virtualization environment has to be prepared for the virtualization process. For the virtualization of servers you need three components: Automated Deployment Services (ADS), Dynamic Host Configuration Protocol (DHCP), and the virtual server migration tool. If you already have DHCP or ADS running on your network, you can use these installations.

Setting Up the Virtualization tools

In this chapter you will learn about the additional tools needed for the virtualization process. The first step for preparing our virtualization environment is the installation of an ADS server, which is described in Chapter 8. This server will make the image of the physical server, deploy the image to a virtual machine, and make the necessary changes for the machine to run in a virtual environment. These changes are described later in this chapter.

You will also install the virtual server migration tools on this server. With this installation, you install the tools for gathering information and generating the migration scripts and sources for changing files in the operating system. All this will be described in more detail in following paragraphs.

Designing & Planning…

Planning the ADS Server

It is possible to install ADS (the virtualization server) on the same server as the virtual server. This is the simplest installation and is the best option if you use ADS only for virtual server migration.

If you use ADS for other purposes, such as installing new servers, you can better separate the ADS server from the virtual server by installing it on another server. This eliminates the performance loss that the virtual machines will encounter when you use the ADS server.

ADS uses PXE boot to capture and deploy the images. If you use other PXE services on your network (like Remote Installation Services [RIS]), you have to separate these services from the ADS services.

As mentioned before, you can install ADS on a separate server, but this doesn't necessarily have to be a physical server, it can be a virtual machine. If you install ADS on a virtual machine, you can connect to the virtual machine on a loopback adapter and you can use a second network interface card with a crosslink cable or on a different VLAN for the virtualization process.

Installing VSMT and ADS Agent on the Virtual Server Host

The Virtual Server Migration Toolkit software has to be installed on both the virtualization server and the virtual server host computer. If you run ADS on the virtual server host computer, you don't have to install the ADS Administration Agent.

If you choose to install ADS on a separate server, you will have to install the ADS Administration Agent on the server hosting your virtual machines. Install the agent by launching ADSSetup.exe from the directory where you unpacked the ADS_VSMT_1.1.exe file and selecting **Install ADS Administration Agent** (see Figure 10.1).

Figure 10.1 ADS Setup Splash Screen

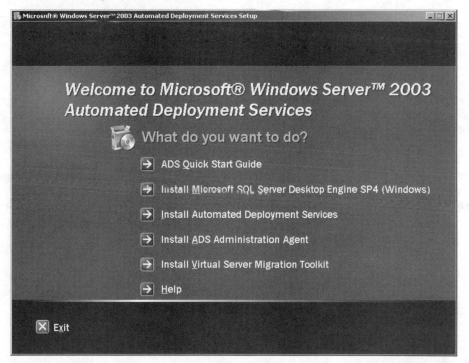

During the installation of the ADS server service, a certificate is created on the ADS server. During setup of the ADS agent, install this ADS certificate so that the client can communicate with the ADS server. The certificate is located in the certificate folder of the ADS installation directory. Normally this is\\ServernameC$\program files\microsoft ADS\certificate\adsroot.cer (see Figure 10.2).

Figure 10.2 ADS Agent Certificate Installation

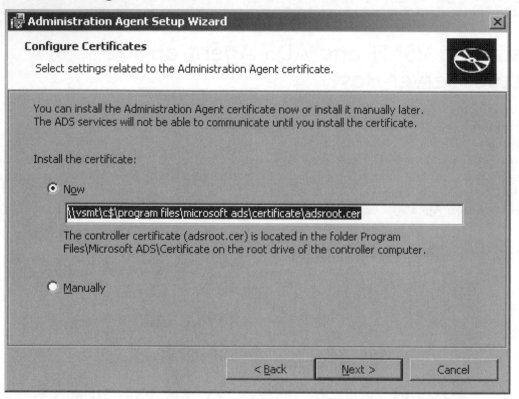

When asked, provide the credentials of a user who can access resources on the Virtual server host and the ADS server (see Figure 10.3). These credentials are used to run the ADS Administration Agent service, which communicates with the ADS server. The credentials that you use must have access rights on the ADS server.

Figure 10.3 ADS Agent Logon Settings

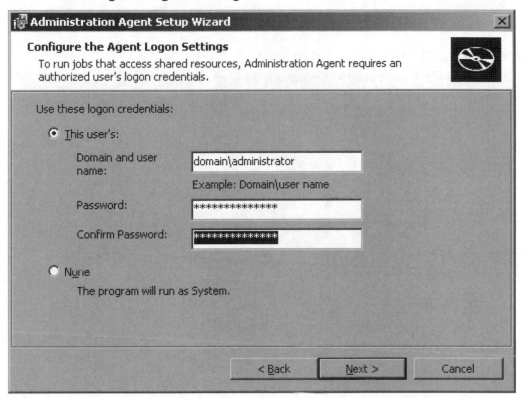

> **NOTE**
>
> If you for some reason chose a wrong account during the installation, you can later change the account by using the *changeagentlogon.exe* program. This program can be found in the bin directory of the folder in which you installed the ADS Administration Agent. By default this is: %systemroot%\program files\Microsoft ADS\bin.
>
> The syntax is: **changeagentlogon** *username* **/password** *password*.

Whether you separated Virtual Server and ADS or you are running them on the same machine, in both cases you need to install VSMT.

The installation of VSMT on a computer running Virtual Server and ADS server is described in Chapter 8.

The following information is the installation of VSMT on the virtual server host computer where ADS is installed on a separate server.

From the directory where you unpacked the ADS_VSMT_1.1.exe file, launch **ADSSetup.exe** (see Figure 10.1) and select **Install Virtual Server Migration Toolkit**.

On the **Setup Type** screen, choose **Tools only** (see Figure 10.4). The only difference between tools only and a full installation are the source directories with patches for all the different Windows versions. These directories are needed only on the computer running the ADS server.

Figure 10.4 VSMT Installation Setup Type

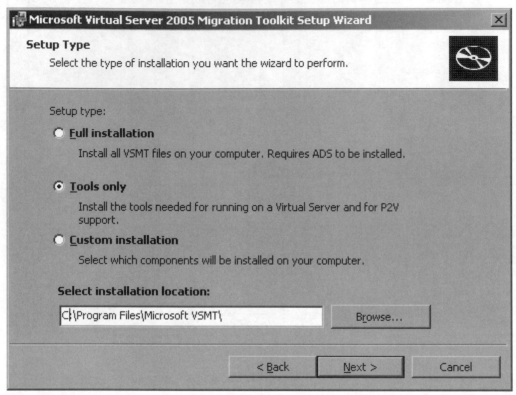

This is the only setup choice you have to make during this installation. On the next page, click **Finish** and you are done.

Creating the Virtual Network

For the creation of the virtualized machines, the Virtual Server Migration Tool (VSMT) uses a virtual network. The default network that is used is VM0 (see Figure 10.6). And it can be created by running a script that is installed with VSMT. The script is located in the installation folder of VSMT in a subfolder called Samples and is called *CreateVirtualNetwork.vbs* (see Figure 10.5).

Figure 10.5 Virtual Network VM0

This script has to be run on the virtual server host computer. It first checks for the installation of Virtual Server and VSMT and then creates the virtual network VM0.

The virtual network VM0 will be connected to the first network interface card of the host server (see Figure 10.6).

Figure 10.6 Virtual Network VM0

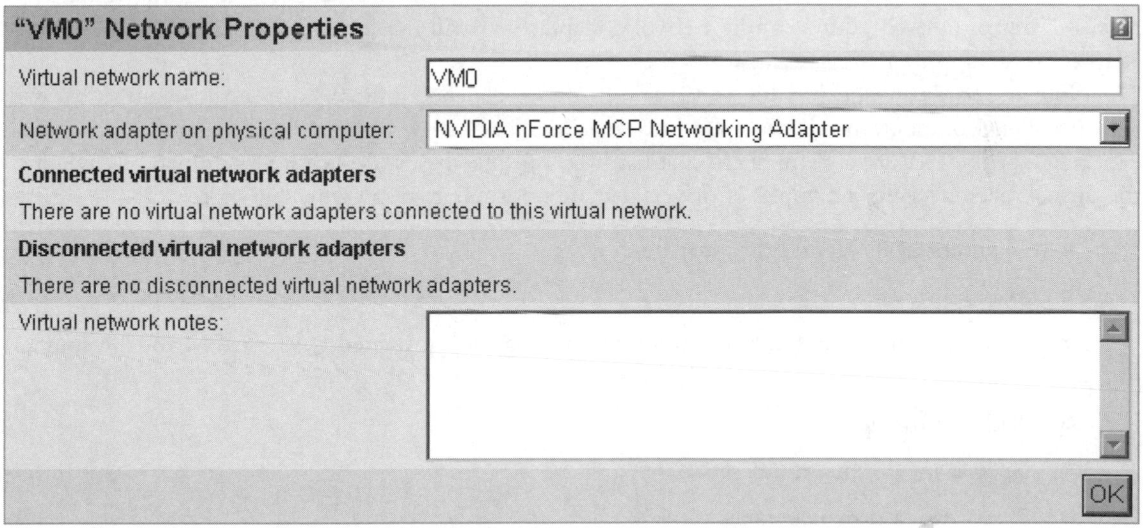

"VM0" Network Properties

Virtual network name:	VM0
Network adapter on physical computer:	NVIDIA nForce MCP Networking Adapter

Connected virtual network adapters

There are no virtual network adapters connected to this virtual network.

Disconnected virtual network adapters

There are no disconnected virtual network adapters.

Virtual network notes:

OK

NOTE

The virtual network can be used during the deployment step and for the creation of the virtual machine. But it is also possible to use another virtual network by default. This is done by editing the Vsmt_initenv.cmd file. It is also possible to specify a different virtual network for one migration by using the *VSHostNet* switch when you generate the migration scripts.

Capturing the Physical Machine

Now that the virtualization environment is complete, it's time to start with the process of capturing the physical machine.

Before you begin the migration, you will have to perform the following tasks to prepare the physical machine: If the machine contains any FAT volumes, you have to convert them to NTFS. VSMT does not migrate FAT volumes. You can convert FAT volumes to NTFS by using a conversion tool such as Convert.exe.

If the machine is running Windows NT Server 4.0 Service Pack 6a, you have to install hotfix 872952 to solve issues with NTFS and you have to install the Windows Management Instrumentation core 1.5. To get a better performance during migration, it's advisable to run *chkdsk* on the Windows NT4 server and defragment drives with fragmentation.

Make sure that the computer is not being managed by ADS. If it is, release control of the device and delete the device record.

When your source computer contains multiple network adapters, make a note of the Media Access Control (MAC) address of the network adapter you will use for the migration. This network adapter must support PXE booting.

Note any hardware-specific drivers. Certain hardware-dependent drivers may not be compatible with the virtual environment. In this case, the virtual machine may fail, perform badly, or cease to function. You can then edit the P2Vdrivers.xml file so that hardware-specific drivers do not start automatically when the virtual machine starts. Examples of drivers that are not supported in Virtual Server are:

- Raid controllers and other storage devices

- Backup devices

- System management and hardware monitoring tools provided by the OEM for the source computer

- Video cards

- Special motherboard chipsets

- Network card management tools

- Tape drives

- Special input devices, such as for a mouse or keyboard

- UPS devices

You can define these specific drivers in the P2Vdrivers.xml file. This file can be found in the Patches folder in the VSMT installation directory.

An example is shown here:

```
<?xml version="1.0" encoding="utf-8" ?>
  <!--
    This file is part of the Microsoft Virtual Server 2005 Migration
    Toolkit Copyright (c) Microsoft Corporation. All rights reserved.
  -->
```

```
<Configuration>
<!-- The services to disable -->
  <Service Name="VMware Tools Service" Start="Disable" />
<!-- drivers to disable -->
  <Driver Name="vmx_svga" Start="Disable" />
  <Driver Name="vmmouse" Start="Disable" />
  <Driver Name="vmscsi" Start="Disable" />
  <Driver Name="amdpcn" Start="Disable" />
  <Driver Name="PCnet" Start="Disable" />
  <Driver Name="cirrus" Start="Disable" />
<!-- storage drivers -->
  <Driver Name="buslogic" Start="Disable" />
  <Driver Name="symc810" Start="Disable" />
  <Driver Name="cpqarray" Start="Disable" />
  <Driver Name="pcntn4m" Start="Disable" />
  <Driver Name="cpqnf3" Start="Disable" />
  <Driver Name="MRaidNT" Start="Disable" />
  <Driver Name="Symc8XX" Start="Disable" />
<!-- VIA chipset drivers -->
  <Driver Name="viaide" Start="Disable" />
  <Driver Name="VIAudio" Start="Disable" />
  <Driver Name="VIAPFD" Start="Disable" />
  <Driver Name="viafilter" Start="Disable" />
  <Driver Name="viaagp" Start="Disable" />
  <Driver Name="viaagp1" Start="Disable" />
<!-- network drivers: Intel(R) PRO/100 -->
  <Driver Name="E100B" Start="Disable" />
  <Program Name="ProMON.exe" Action="Remove" />
<!-- tape drivers -->
  <Driver Name="4mmdat" Start="Disable" />
  <Driver Name="4mmdat-SeSFT" Start="Disable" />
  <Driver Name="SCSIChanger" Start="Disable" />
<!-- The programs in the autorun section to disable -->
  <Program Name="s3tray2" Action="Remove" />
</Configuration>
```

Figure 10.7 Capture Process

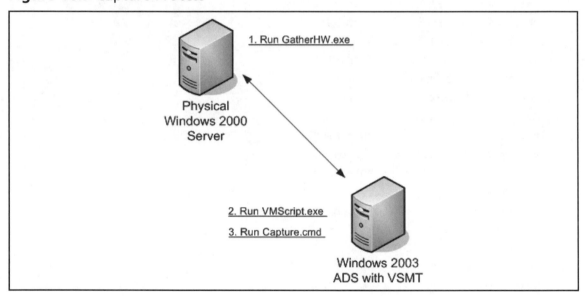

Hardware Inventory

The first step is to gather information about the physical server. To be able to migrate a physical machine to a virtual environment, it is necessary for VSMT to know which hardware and which operating system is used on the source computer. To gather this data, use a program called *GatherHW.exe,* which can be found in the Microsoft VSMT directory.

GatherHW /? shows the available parameters (see Figure 10.8)

Figure 10.8 The *GatherHW* Command Prompt

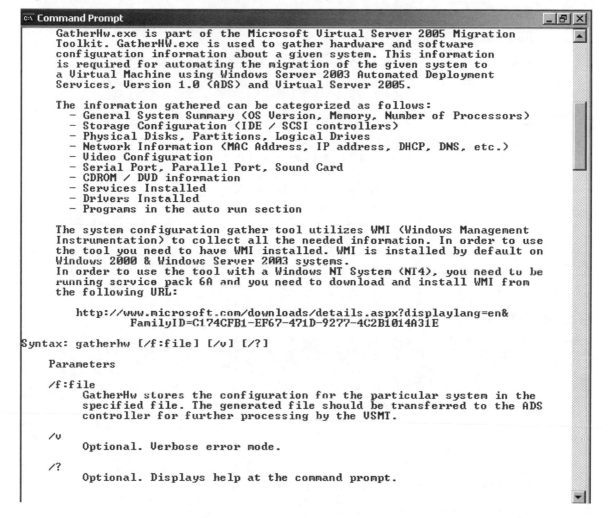

GatherHw.exe is part of the Microsoft Virtual Server 2005 Migration Toolkit. GatherHW.exe is used to gather hardware and software configuration information about a given system. This information is required for automating the migration of the given system to a Virtual Machine using Windows Server 2003 Automated Deployment Services, Version 1.0 (ADS) and Virtual Server 2005.

The information gathered can be categorized as follows:
- General System Summary (OS Version, Memory, Number of Processors)
- Storage Configuration (IDE / SCSI controllers)
- Physical Disks, Partitions, Logical Drives
- Network Information (MAC Address, IP address, DHCP, DNS, etc.)
- Video Configuration
- Serial Port, Parallel Port, Sound Card
- CDROM / DVD information
- Services Installed
- Drivers Installed
- Programs in the auto run section

The system configuration gather tool utilizes WMI (Windows Management Instrumentation) to collect all the needed information. In order to use the tool you need to have WMI installed. WMI is installed by default on Windows 2000 & Windows Server 2003 systems.
In order to use the tool with a Windows NT System (NT4), you need to be running service pack 6A and you need to download and install WMI from the following URL:

    http://www.microsoft.com/downloads/details.aspx?displaylang=en&
        FamilyID=C174CFB1-EF67-471D-9277-4C2B1014A31E

Syntax: gatherhw [/f:file] [/v] [/?]

Parameters

/f:file
    GatherHw stores the configuration for the particular system in the specified file. The generated file should be transferred to the ADS controller for further processing by the VSMT.

/v
    Optional. Verbose error mode.

/?
    Optional. Displays help at the command prompt.

GatherHW generates an XML file from which the migration scripts are generated. By default, this file is written in the same location that GatherHW.exe is run from. This can also be a removable medium, like an FDD or a USB drive. The data in the XML file can be categorized as follows:

- General system information (operating system, number of processors, memory)
- Storage configuration (IDE/SCSI)
- Physical disks, partitions and logical drives
- Network information (MAC, IP, DHCP, DNS, etc.)
- Video configuration
- Ports (serial, parallel, sound)
- DVD/CD information

- ■ Services
- ■ Drivers
- ■ AutoRun information

To gather all this information, the tool uses Windows Management Instrumentation (WMI).

WARNING

WMI is not installed by default on Windows NT4 systems. To be able to use *GatherHW* on NT4 systems, you'll need to have Service Pack 6a installed. You will also have to download and install WMI (wmint4.EXE) from the following URL: http://www.microsoft.com/downloads/details.aspx?displaylang=en&Family ID=C174CFB1-EF67-471D-9277-4C2B1014A31E

Run GatherHW.exe on the source server and get the XML file that contains all the information needed for the migration. You can run this file from a floppy disk, USB disk, or network share (see Figure 10.9).

Figure 10.9 Example XML File

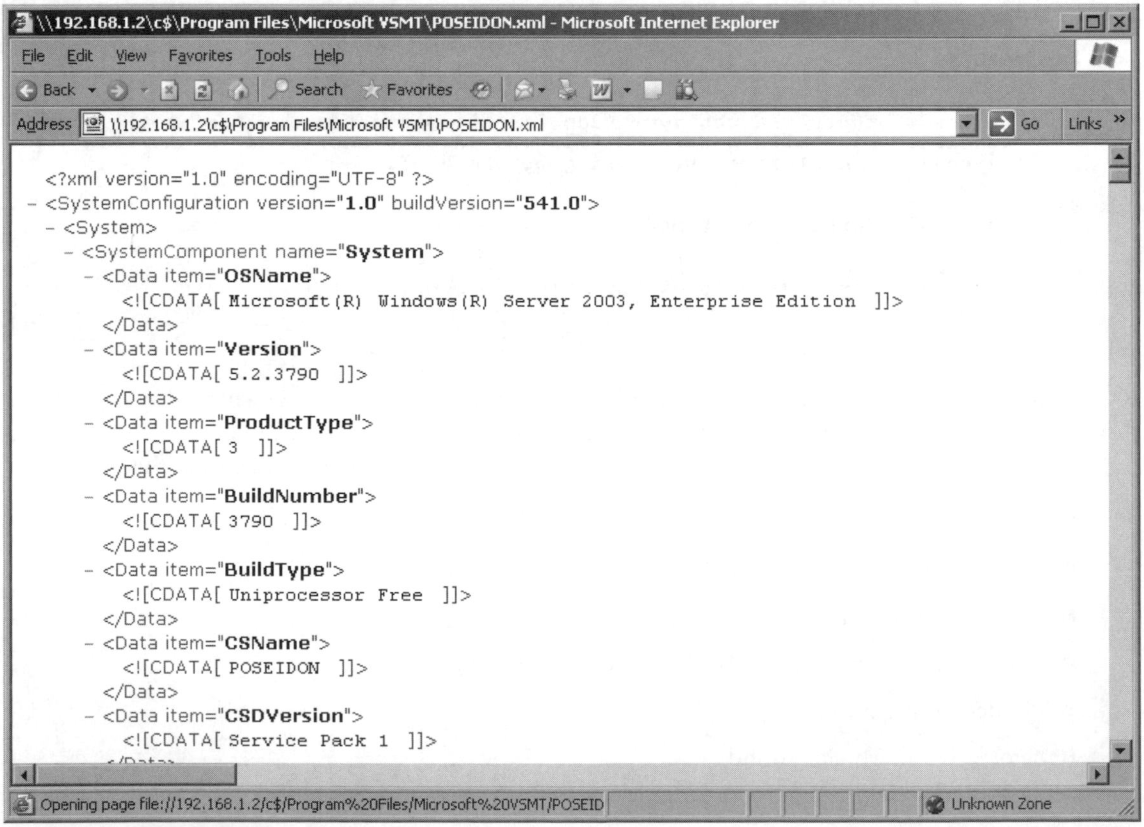

Creating the Scripts

Now that you have gathered all the information about the source system, you can create the migration scripts. You need these scripts to create the virtual hardware in your virtual server environment and to capture and deploy the server.

You create the scripts in two steps. In the first step, you validate the hardware of the source system and in the second step you create the scripts to migrate.

Validating Hardware

Validation is required to check if the source server hardware and operating system configurations are compatible with Virtual server and VSMT. For example, software RAID1 is not supported. You validate the configuration information by running VMScript. VMScript analyzes the configuration information and reports any issues that could prevent a successful migration. If issues are reported, you need to correct them, if possible, and start the process again by gathering and validating the configuration information to verify that no issues remain.

To start with this step, copy the XML file to the VSMT directory of the ADS server and run the following command from within a command prompt in the VSMT directory.

```
VMScript.exe /HWValidate /HWInfoFile:<servername>.xml
```

Where <servername> should be replaced with the name of your XML file.

If everything is okay, you will see the results that are shown in Figure 10.10.

Figure 10.10 Hardware Validation Output

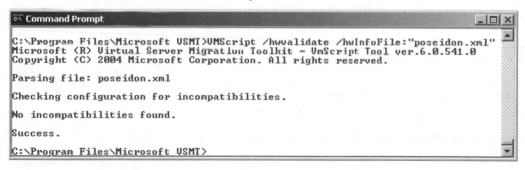

If the output indicates that a required system ("patch") file is missing, you can use the VMPatch tool to load the required file(s) before taking the next migration step.

VMPatch requires only one switch: /s:<path>. Enter the path of the folder that contains the files that are mentioned in the *hwvalidate* output.

If you try to migrate a server that is installed with a service pack that was released after VSMT was released, you will see the output that is shown in Figure 10.11.

Figure 10.11 Hardware Validation Error

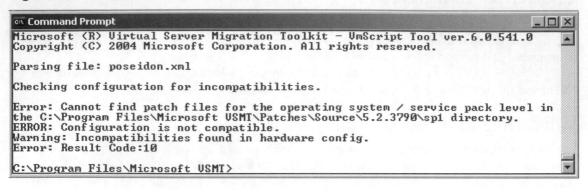

To resolve this issue, use Windows Explorer to navigate to the directory that is mentioned in the warning. If it doesn't exist, create it. Copy the files that are needed (use the files in\Patches\Source\ *OS_NUMBER* as a reference) from the source server, the installation CD, or an extraction of the service pack file to the new directory.

The reason *gatherhw* generates this error is because during the image deployment, VSMT swaps system files for other system files of the same version that support a different type of hardware. This is because the hardware configuration that virtual machines emulate may not be the same as the hardware configuration of the source computer, and some system files depend on hardware configuration. For example, the physical machine is multi-processor and Virtual Server emulates only single-processor machines. In this case, the kernel files have to be replaced by VSMT, so VSMT must have the correct version of the files.

After you copy the necessary files, run *hwvalidate* again to check if the warning is resolved.

Creating Migration Scripts

Time to create the scripts. The scripts are created by using the same *vmscript* tool but with another parameter. You now use the */hwGenerateP2V* parameter.

HwgenerateP2V requires at least the following switches:

- **/hwInfoFile:"<server>.xml"**   States the xml file that is to be used

- **/name:<VM name>**   The name that the server will use within the virtual environment

- **/vmConfigPath:"<vmc Path>"**   The path where the vmc file will be stored on the virtual server

- **/virtualDiskPath:"<vhd Path>"**   The path where the vhd file will be stored on the virtual server

- **/hwDestVS:<VS name>**   The name of the virtual server that will host the virtual machine

The command shown in Figure 10.12 will generate scripts to migrate a server called Poseidon to the virtual server host Hercules. You see that the command creates a subfolder with the server name in the p2v directory of the VSMT program directory and that the filename of all the scripts that are created start with the servername.

Figure 10.12 Migration Script Generation

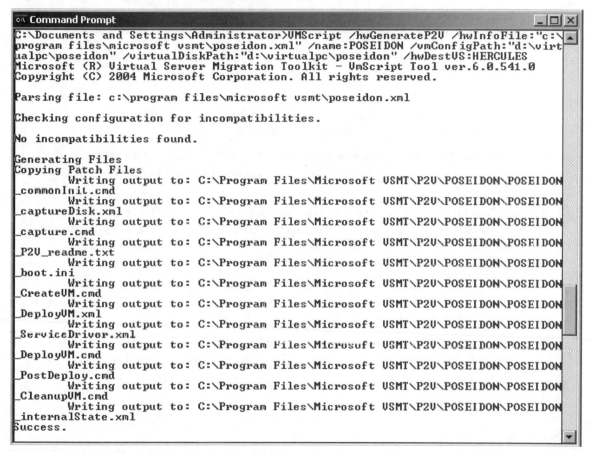

The following switches are optional:

- **/hwTaskSeqPath: "*path*"**   The path of the folder in which to store the generated scripts. The default path is %SYSTEMDRIVE%\Program Files\Microsoft VSMT\P2V.

- **/hwPatchDir: "*path*"**   The path to patch files that are not in the default patch folder.

- **/vsHostNet:*virtual network***   The name of the virtual network to which to attach the machine. The default network is VM0. If you want to change the default setting, you can edit the Vsmt_initenv.cmd file.

- **/virtualDiskDynamic**   Creates all virtual hard disks as dynamically expanding disks. If this is not specified, all are created as fixed-size virtual disks.

- **/adminMac:*MAC address***   If the source device has multiple MAC addresses, the MAC address that is used for PXE booting the device.

- **/virtualMacDynamic**   Specifies that Virtual Server will dynamically assign a MAC address to the network adapter on the virtual machine.

- **/fixHAL:<options>**   *Auto | None | ACPI | NACPI* Specifies the type of HAL to use for the destination virtual machine.

- **/vmMemory:*memory in MB***   The amount of physical memory to be allocated for the virtual machine. If not specified, the allocated memory equals the amount of memory in the source computer.

- **/serviceDriverState:"file path"**   The path to the XML file that specifies services and drivers that are to be stopped during the migration.

- **/suppressVsConsole**   Suppresses the invocation of the Virtual Server Administration Web site. By default, the Administration Web site automatically displays following virtual machine creation.

- **/excludeDrives:logical drive 1**   The logical drive letters to exclude from image capture (for example G:;H:;I:). A drive letter is mapped to a volume. If it is excluded, then the volume is excluded from capture. If all partitions of a hard drive are excluded, then the hard drive is not created.

- **/postDeployAction:0 | 1 | 2**   The action to perform on the virtual machine after deployment is finished. 0 (default) leaves the VM in the ADS Deployment Agent, 1 shuts down the VM, and 2 restarts the VM.

- **/forceGenerate**   Forces VMScript to generate scripts and task sequences, even if the validation phase produced errors. If errors were reported, the generated scripts probably will not work.

! WARNING

A minimum of 96 MB of memory must be allocated to a virtual machine or it will not boot to the ADS Deployment Agent and the migration will fail.

After the task is completed, the following scripts can be found in the directory c:\program files\ microsoft VSMT\:p2v\<servername>\(see Figure 10.13):

Figure 10.13 Migration Scripts

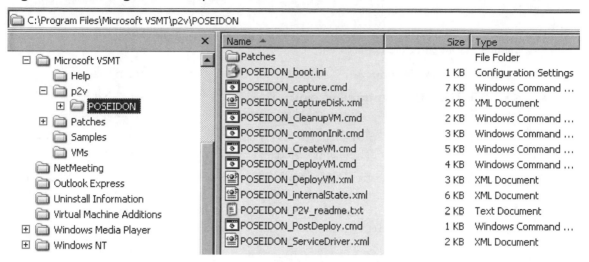

- **<SERVERNAME>_commonInit.cmd**   This file is a script that contains the configuration settings for the virtual machine that you specified when you ran *VMScript* to generate the scripts. Within this script you can change settings like the Mac address that will be used during capture, the name of the virtual machine, etc.

- **<SERVERNAME>_capture.cmd**   This script file captures the disks on the source computer and stores them in ADS image files on the computer running ADS.

- **<SERVERNAME>_CreateVM.cmd**   This script file creates a virtual machine to host the captured disk images. This script calls the *Commoninit* to set common environment variables. It then creates a series of ADS jobs to create the virtual machine.

- **<SERVERNAME>_DeployVM.cmd**   The *deploy* script deploys the image files to the created virtual machine.

- **<SERVERNAME>_PostDeploy.cmd**   This script performs actions on the new virtual machine upon the first logon following migration: The script resets attributes of boot.ini file to System, Hidden, and Read-only. And on computers running Windows NT 4.0 Server SP6a, it runs *fixsetup.cmd* to update the Setup.log file in the winntrepair directory to reflect that the operating system is running on a single-processor computer. Service packs and hotfixes use the information in the Setup.log file to install the appropriate components.

- **<SERVERNAME>_CleanupVM.cmd**   Use this script to clean up the files associated with a failed migration, so that you can reattempt the migration. This script deletes a virtual machine, its resource files, and the ADS devices records associated with it.

- **<SERVERNAME>_internalState.xml**   This XML file contains information about the hardware, file system, and startup.

- **<SERVERNAME>_P2V_readme.txt**   In this file you find the tasks that have to be manually done after the deployment.

- **<SERVERNAME>_boot.ini**   This is the boot.ini file of the source machine.

- **<SERVERNAME>_captureDisk.xml**   This is an ADS task sequence, which is initiated by *Capturedisk.cmd*, which captures the disk partitions on the physical computer.

- **<SERVERNAME>_DeployVM.xml**   This task sequence deploys the captured disk partitions to the virtual machine and is initiated by the *DeployVM.cmd* script.

- **<SERVERNAME>_ServiceDriver.xml**   This task sequence is initiated by *DeployVM. cmd* and configures the start state of specified services and devices for a virtual machine. *VMScript* uses the P2Vdrivers.xml as input to generate this file. You can use the */serviceDriverState* parameter of *VMScript* to change the file that is used as input.

Data Capture

The next step is the capturing of the disks of the physical server. For this step it is necessary to PXE boot the machine. If the machine does not support PXE boot, you must have a compatible NIC to be used by a Remote Installation Services (RIS) boot floppy disk. If your NIC does not support any of these methods, you need to install another NIC and start over.

NOTE

ADS does not encrypt the traffic, because of performance reasons. If you do need to encrypt the traffic between the ADS server and the physical source computer or the virtual target computer. Then delete the nonetencrypt option from the capturedisk. xml and/or the deployVM.xml

On the ADS server, run the script <SERVERNAME>_capture.cmd. This script creates a device and the jobs in ADS and will keep running until the capture process completes (see Figure 10.14).

Figure 10.14 capture.cmd Output

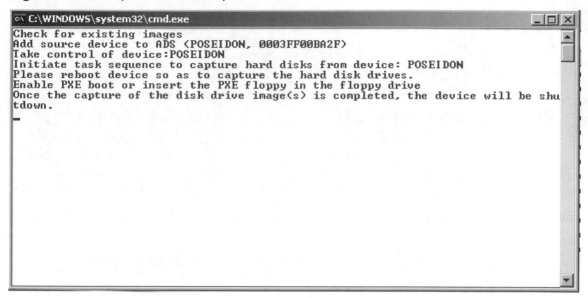

Inside the ADS management console you should now see the physical server as a new device (see Figure 10.15). The identifier of the device is the MAC address of the first network card or the MAC address given with the */adminmac* parameter during script creation.

Figure 10.15 ADS Device

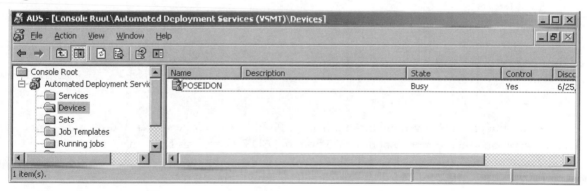

Configuring & Implementing...

MAC Address Adjustment

If your physical server contains more than one network card, make sure you have the network card connected that is used as the device identifier. In the commoninit.cmd file you can check which MAC address will be used (DEVICE_SOURCE_MAC). If it isn't the correct address, you can regenerate the scripts with the parameter /adminmac or edit the DEVICE_SOURCE_MAC value in the commoninit file.

In the ADS management console you can also see the job that is created. See Figure 10.16.

Figure 10.16 ADS Capture Image Job

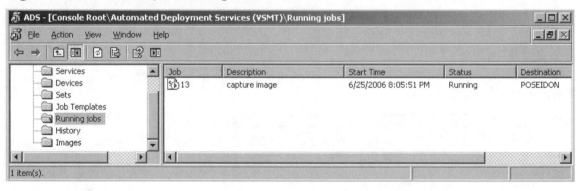

Reboot the physical server and make it boot to PXE. The server gets an IP address from your DHCP server and then obtains a boot image from the ADS server. This boot image is called the Deployment Agent. This agent executes all the tasks that are configured in the job on the ADS server. Figure 10.17 shows the deployment agent while it is running the capture task.

Figure 10.17 Deployment Agent Capture Process

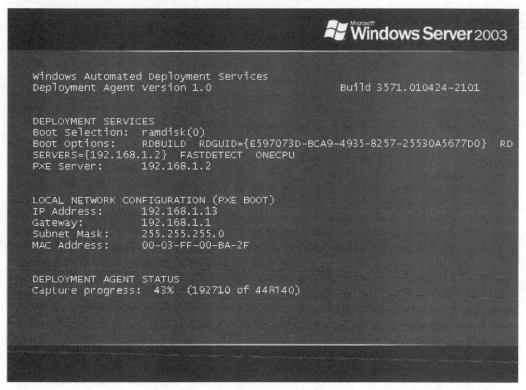

When you double-click the job under running jobs in the ADS management console, you can see the tasks that are completed and the tasks that still have to be executed. You can also see the exact status of each task (see Figure 10.18).

For each directly attached logical disk, an image is captured. Approximately 1 GB of data is captured per minute, depending on your hardware and network settings.

Figure 10.18 Capture Job Details

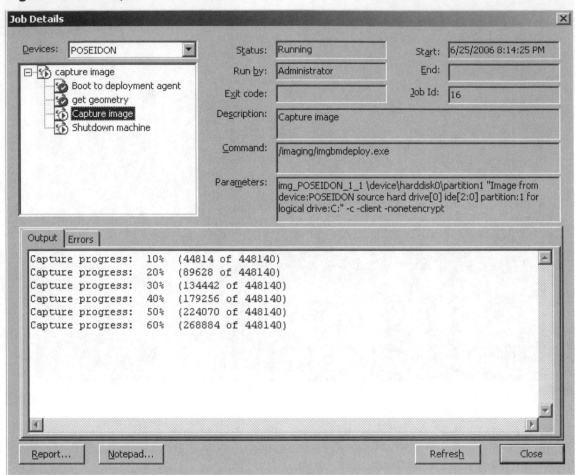

When the capture is completed, the physical server will be shut down, the ADS device object will be released, and this object will be deleted.

Check the job for any errors. You can find the job in the ADS management console under history. If all tasks have run without errors, you will see no text under the error tab and all tasks will be green, like in Figure 10.19.

Figure 10.19 Capture Job Results

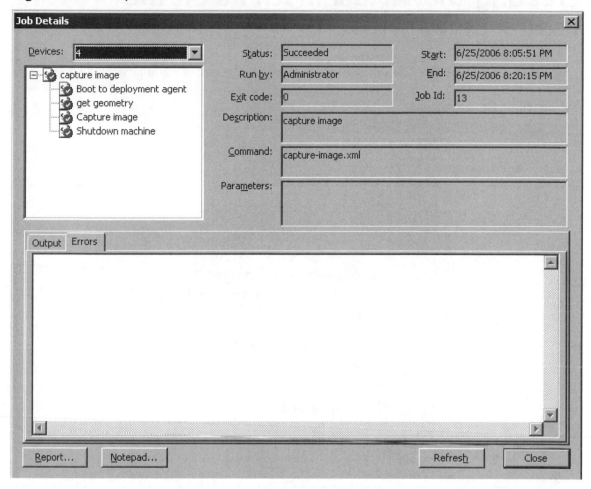

The image file(s) can be found under images like the one shown in Figure 10.20. You are now ready to create the virtual machine.

Figure 10.20 Captured Image File

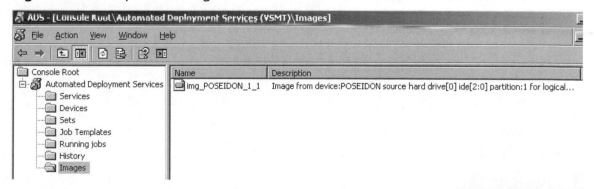

Creating the Virtual Machine on the Virtual Server Host

Now that you have an image and all the information about the system, it is time to create the virtual machine. Use the script called *CreateVM.cmd*. The captured image(s) will later be deployed to this virtual machine.

The next steps are illustrated in Figure 10.21.

Figure 10.21 Deploy Process

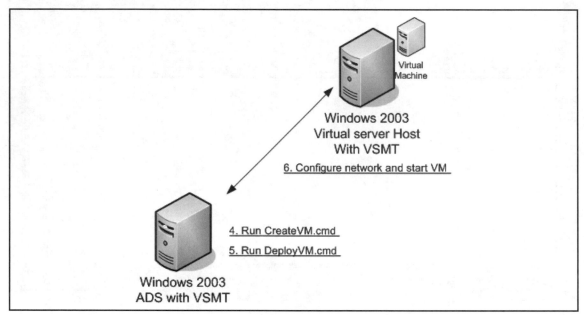

Before you can start with the creation of the virtual machine, add the virtual server host to the devices in the ADS management console so that the script can execute the necessary tasks on the host server. To do this, go into the console, right-click **Devices** and select **Add device**. Enter the name of your virtual server host and enter the MAC address of the network card (see Figure 10.22).

Figure 10.22 Adding Devices

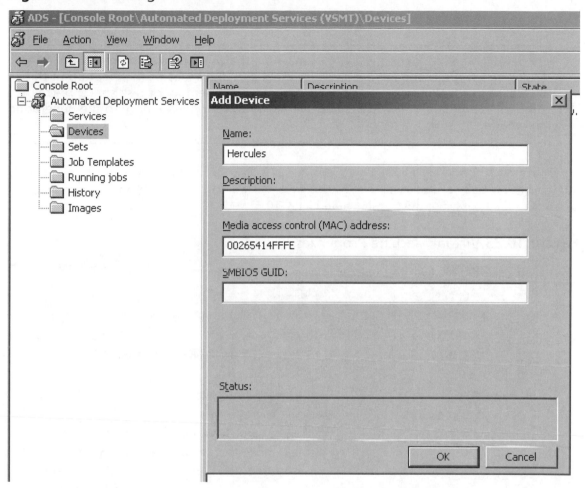

After the device is created, right-click the device and select **Take Control**.

Now run the **CreateVM.cmd** script from the folder containing the generated scripts.

Unless you specify different settings, the virtual machine is created with the same amount of RAM, same number of network adapters (up to four), with the same MAC addresses, and the same disk sizes as the source computer. For more information about customizing settings, see the list of optional switches in the Creating Migration Scripts section earlier in this chapter. The new virtual machine is allocated 100 percent of a single CPU, minus any percentage that the host operating system is using and any percentage that has been allocated to other virtual machines.

It may take several minutes to create the virtual hard disk(s).

The script displays the actions being performed on Virtual Server. You can monitor the creation of the new virtual machine and assignment of properties from the Event Viewer page of the Virtual Server Administration Web site as well as from the ADS Management snap-in.

NOTE

By default, the script creates a virtual machine that is equal to the physical machine. Make sure there is enough available memory and disk space or the creation of the virtual machine will fail. If you do not have enough memory or disk space, re-create the scripts and add the switches */virtualdiskDynamic* or */vmMemory* to the generating command.

When the script completes, the new virtual server is ready for deployment of the disks. The new virtual machine will be attached to the VM0 network and will have the Ris2003.vfd floppy image attached to the floppy disk drive, as shown in Figure 10.23.

Figure 10.23 Virtual Machine Properties

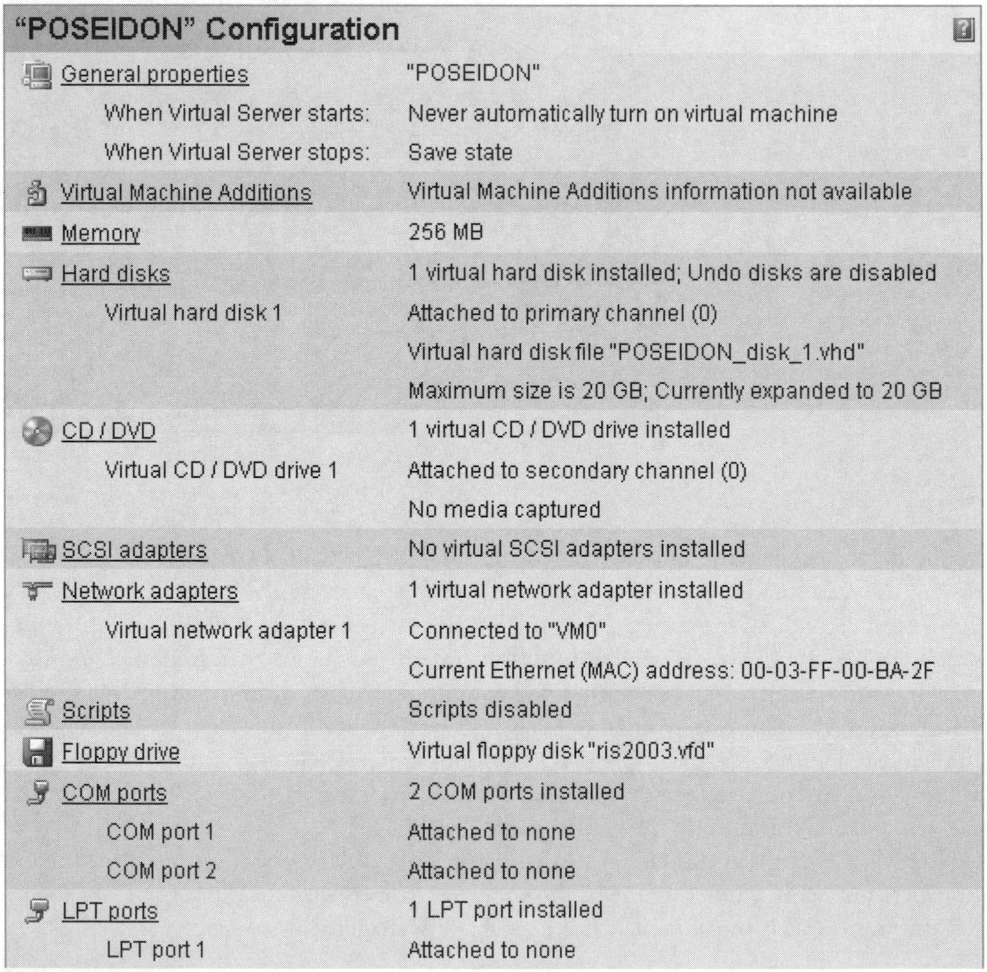

"POSEIDON" Configuration	
General properties	"POSEIDON"
When Virtual Server starts:	Never automatically turn on virtual machine
When Virtual Server stops:	Save state
Virtual Machine Additions	Virtual Machine Additions information not available
Memory	256 MB
Hard disks	1 virtual hard disk installed; Undo disks are disabled
Virtual hard disk 1	Attached to primary channel (0)
	Virtual hard disk file "POSEIDON_disk_1.vhd"
	Maximum size is 20 GB; Currently expanded to 20 GB
CD / DVD	1 virtual CD / DVD drive installed
Virtual CD / DVD drive 1	Attached to secondary channel (0)
	No media captured
SCSI adapters	No virtual SCSI adapters installed
Network adapters	1 virtual network adapter installed
Virtual network adapter 1	Connected to "VM0"
	Current Ethernet (MAC) address: 00-03-FF-00-BA-2F
Scripts	Scripts disabled
Floppy drive	Virtual floppy disk "ris2003.vfd"
COM ports	2 COM ports installed
COM port 1	Attached to none
COM port 2	Attached to none
LPT ports	1 LPT port installed
LPT port 1	Attached to none

In the ADS Management snap-in, a new ADS device object for the virtual machine is also created to perform the image deployment and post-imaging fix-ups or tasks (see Figure 10.24).

Figure 10.24 ADS Device Object

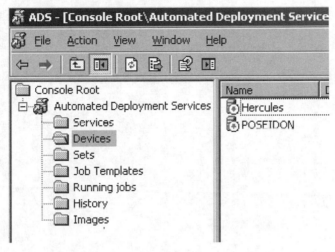

Deploying the Virtual Machine on the Host OS

You're almost there. The next step, and almost last step, is the deployment of the disks. For this step, the newly created virtual machine is booted into the deployment agent by using PXE. So make sure the machine is connected to a network on which the machine can contact the DHCP and the ADS server.

From the folder containing the generated scripts, run the *DeployVM.cmd* script.

The virtual machine that you created turns on. You can view this in the Virtual Server Administration Web site. Because the RIS2003 floppy disk is attached to the virtual floppy disk drive, the virtual machine receives an IP address and PXE boots into the ADS Deployment Agent. Figure 10.25 shows the Deployment Agent when deployment is running.

Figure 10.25 Deployment Agent Deploy Image

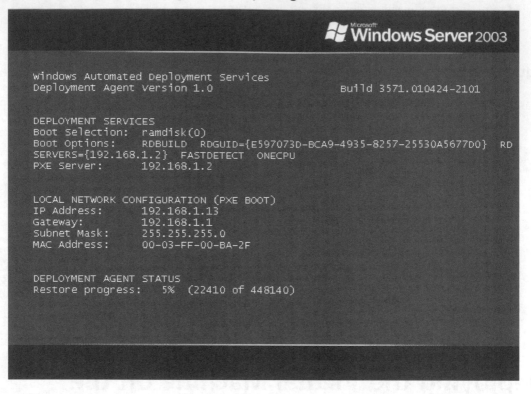

NOTE

If loading of the RamDisk (Deployment Agent) fails, the virtual machine will reboot and try again.

Within the deployment agent, the deployment of the disks is started sequentially. Deployment of the image takes longer than capturing. It also takes more time to deploy an image to a dynamically expanding disk than to a fixed size virtual disk.

After the deployment, some actions are taken, including swapping system files and changing configuration settings (removing the virtual floppy disk and associating the virtual hard disks with the virtual machine). When all is completed, the script exits.

The deployed virtual machine is left in the Deployment Agent screen. To change this behavior, add the switch */postDeployAction* to the command to generate the scripts.

Now that the deployment is completed, there are a few steps left.

First, verify that there are no errors in the virtual server event log. Then let the virtual server reboot: this can be done by sending a reboot command from the ADS console.

Select **Run job** in the ADS console (see Figure 10.26) and select the **Reboot Template**.

Figure 10.26 Add Job to Reboot the Device

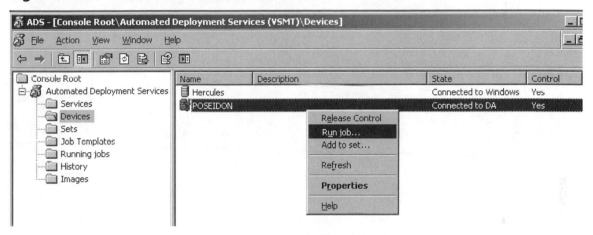

After the virtual machine reboots, release control of it in the ADS management console. To do this, use the Release Control command (visible in Figure 10.26).

When the virtual server is booting, Windows will install drivers and change the necessary configuration settings.

NOTE

The virtual server will not have an IP address configured anymore. If you want the virtual server to boot with the IP address it had when it was still a physical machine, make a reservation in the dhcp scope (you can view the MAC address of the virtual machine under Edit configuration - network cards).

You can follow the progress by viewing the machine within the virtual server management Web site. Finally, when everything is done, the machine will stop at the Windows login.

A few manual tasks have to be done on the virtual machine:

1. Log on to the machine with an administrative account that is a member of the local administrators group.

2. Run the Virtual Machine Additions setup. You can start this setup by clicking on the link in the Virtual Server remote control Web site.

3. Configure the network card and TCP/IP properties.

4. Verify that the machine runs correctly and at last remove the image files from the ADS server.

Summary

Migrating physical servers to a virtual environment is easy to do by following the steps outlined in this chapter. You start with building the environment you need for the virtualization process. This environment consists of an ADS server, your virtual server, and a DHCP server. You then gather the hardware information of the server by running a tool on the physical server. You validate the hardware and generate the migration scripts—these scripts automate the virtualization process. The next step is getting the data to images. You do this by running one of the generated scripts. You then create the target virtual machine by running another one of the generated scripts and finally you deploy the image files to the created virtual machine by running another generated script.

Solutions Fast Track

Getting the Virtualization Environment Ready for Usage

- ☑ The ADS server does not have to be a physical server.

- ☑ DHCP addressing must be available to the device systems. The system hosting the DHCP service can be an existing DHCP server, but it can also be installed on the computer hosting the ADS Controller.

- ☑ If there are existing PXE services in your environment, such as Remote Installation Services (RIS), you need to isolate them from the ADS implementation.

Capturing the Physical Machine

- ☑ The virtualization process is disk intensive. Make sure you use fast disks.

- ☑ The time the capture process needs is about one-half to one and a half minutes per gigabyte.

- ☑ By default, the capture and deploy processes don't use encryption for performance reasons. If you want to encrypt the traffic, delete the *nonetencrypt* parameter from the capturedisk. xml and the deployvm.xml.

Creating the Virtual Machine on the Virtual Server Host

- ☑ The virtual machine that is created will be configured with the same amount of disk space and memory as the physical server had. Make sure you have enough resources available

- ☑ The creation of fixed size disks takes a lot longer than the creation of dynamically expanding disks

- ☑ The created Virtual Machine will be connected to the VM0 virtual network by default. You can change this behavior by adding the /vsHostNet parameter when generating the migration scripts with the vmscript /HWgenerateP2V command.

Deploying the Virtual Machine on the Host OS

☑ To improve performance, don't put the images and the virtual hard disks of the target on the same physical disk or in folders with compression turned on.

☑ Delete or archive the job history in ADS to improve the performance of VSMT.

☑ On a network with a high level of traffic, the deployment of the image may fail because the virtual machine cannot connect to ADS after booting into the Deployment Agent. There is an ADS hotfix, KB 875533, to fix this.

Frequently Asked Questions

Q: Does VSMT support migrating virtual machines to physical machines?

A: No, this is not possible with this tool.

Q: Which operating systems can be migrated with VSMT?

A: Windows NT4 with Service Pack 6a, Windows 2000 SP4, and Windows Server 2003 systems can be migrated with this tool.

Q: What should I do if the migration fails?

A: Turn the physical machine back on. Nothing is changed on the physical server during the migration process.

Q: Is it possible to migrate from one virtual machine to another virtual machine?

A: Yes, VSMT and ADS interact with virtual machines the same way as with physical machines.

Q: Where can I find error messages if one of the steps fails?

A: Error messages can be found either in the ADS job history or in the virtual server log.

Q: Does VSMT require the Enterprise Edition of Virtual Server?

A: No, VSMT works with both the Enterprise and the Standard Editions.

## Chapter 11

Troubleshooting

Solutions in this chapter:

- **Troubleshooting Virtual Server 2005 R2**

- **Troubleshooting Automated Deployment Services**

- **Troubleshooting the Virtual Server Migration Toolkit**

- **Troubleshooting the Migration Process**

☑ **Summary**

☑ **Solutions Fast Track**

☑ **Frequently Asked Questions**

Introduction

Machine setup... OK; Server compatibility... OK; ADS running... OK; everything is running, but still problems come up. That's why we wrote this chapter, to provide you with the information to troubleshoot problems, organized by technique. Enjoy and solve the problems.

Troubleshooting Virtual Server 2005 R2

In this section, we go over troubleshooting for the Virtual Server 2005 R2 itself. While this is not an exhaustive list of problems you may encounter, these tips and tricks should be helpful when dealing with problems in the following areas:

- Virtual Server Administration Web Site
- Virtual Server Settings
- Virtual Machine Performance Issues

Troubleshooting Virtual Server Administration Web Site

The bulk of the administrative functions and troubleshooting you will perform in Microsoft Virtual Server 2005 R2 will be done through the Virtual Server Administration Web site. This section will go over what to do when the Administration Web site *is* the problem.

Troubleshooting LsaLogonUser() failed!

You've got your shiny new Virtual Server loaded and all ready to go and you launch the Administration Web site only to be confronted with the dreaded **LsaLogonUser() failed!** error (see Figure 11.1).

Figure 11.1 LsaLogonUser() failed! Error

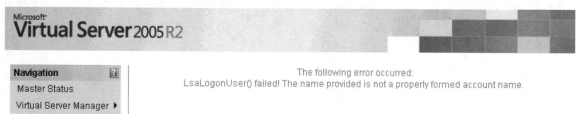

You likely won't see this error unless you've set up your virtual server as a member of a workgroup, rather than as a member of a domain. This error comes from the default settings of the Virtual Server Administration Web site to use Integrated Windows Authentication.

Designing & Planning...

Domains. To Join or Not to Join?

One of the most important decisions you will make when deploying your virtual server is whether or not to join the server to a domain. An even more common question is whether to run your virtual server *on* a domain controller. Table 11.1 lists some of the pros and cons of each scenario.

Table 11.1 Virtual Server Deployment Scenarios

Type of Deployment	Pro	Con
Virtual Server as a stand-alone workgroup server	This is the easiest way to go, since you don't have to worry about too many "what ifs" or "gotchas."	The key drawback to a workgroup server is that you won't have the ability to use Active Directory for user security or group policy. Each user of the virtual server will have to have a separate user account created and maintained on the virtual server host. If this is not a problem, we recommend this route.
Virtual Server as a domain member server	This option is a good middle ground. If you need to be able to administrate users and group policy from within the Active Directory, then this is the best way to go.	There are a couple of reasons to be wary, however, of putting guest machines that are domain controllers on this server: (1) Server Message Block (SMB) signing is a critical part of domain communications in Windows Server 2003, and if you have a virtual domain controller as a guest on a domain member, it won't take long before other domain controllers will confuse communications from the host with communications from the guest domain controller. When this happens, Active Directory replication and authentication can go load haywire rapidly. If you intend to a guest domain controller on a domain member, consider disabling SMB signing on the Virtual Server host. For more

Continued

Table 11.1 Continued

Type of Deployment	Pro	Con
		information on SMB signing, refer to Microsoft's Knowledge Base Article ID 887429 at http://support.microsoft.com/kb/887429/en-us. (2) Another reason to be careful of guest domain controllers is the issue of time synchronization. When you load the Virtual Machine Additions, there is an option to synchronize the guest machine's time with the host. This can be very dicey, when you consider that the host machine could very well be getting its time from the guest domain controller. Make sure that time synchronization is turned off in any guest domain controller. For more information on time synchronization, refer to Microsoft's Knowledge Base Article ID 888746 at http://support.microsoft.com/kb/888746/en-us.
Virtual Server on a domain controller	None.	This option is by far the least attractive and you should avoid it at all costs. SMB signing problems get worse now, since you can't turn off SMB signing on just one domain controller and have any hope of Active Directory replication going on normally. And having one of your guest machines mistaken as the host domain controller when it talks to another domain controller on the network is a very real possibility.
		And if you already have Virtual Server loaded on a system, then upgrade it to a domain controller, expect that every service and setting will break and you will need to just reload Virtual Server.
		We strongly caution against loading Virtual Server on a domain controller.

Fixing the **LsaLogonUser() failed!** error can be tackled in a couple of ways. First, you could go ahead and join the Virtual Server to your domain. This comes with the benefits discussed above, such as centralized administration and pass-through authentication for the Administration Web site, but it also comes with the drawbacks. If you feel comfortable putting your Virtual Server into your domain then, by all means, go right ahead. If you prefer to keep your Virtual Server as a stand-alone host in a workgroup, then follow the procedures below.

First, open the **Internet Information Services (IIS) Manager** by clicking **Start | Control Panel | Administrative Tools | Internet Information Services (IIS) Manager**. Next, browse to the **Virtual Server** Web site, right-click it, and select **Properties**, as shown in Figure 11.2.

Figure 11.2 Virtual Server Web Site Administration

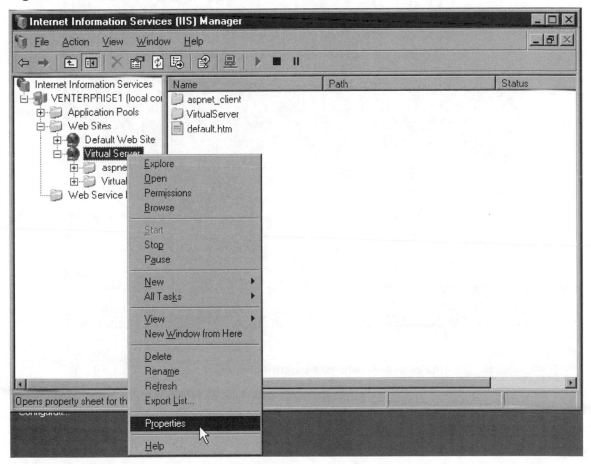

Next, select the **Directory Security** tab and click the **Edit** button, as shown in Figure 11.3.

Figure 11.3 Virtual Server Administration Web Site Directory Security

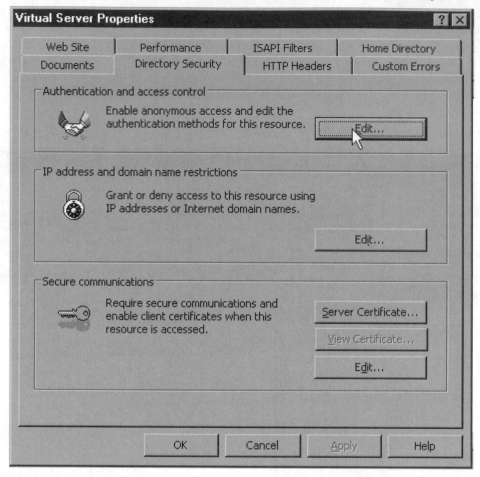

Now, uncheck the **Integrated Windows authentication** check box (see Figure 11.4).

Figure 11.4 Virtual Server Administration Web Site Authentication

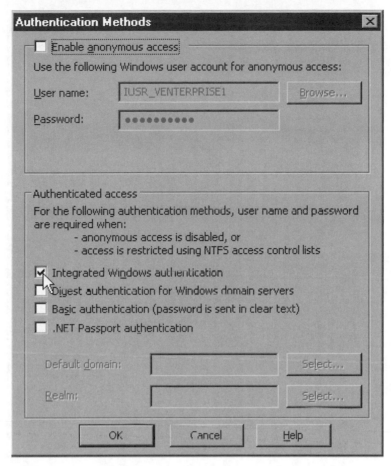

Next, check the **Basic authentication (password is sent in clear text)** box, as shown in Figure 11.5. Click **Yes** to the warning message for basic authentication (Figure 11.6).

Figure 11.5 Changing Virtual Server Administration Web Site Authentication to Basic

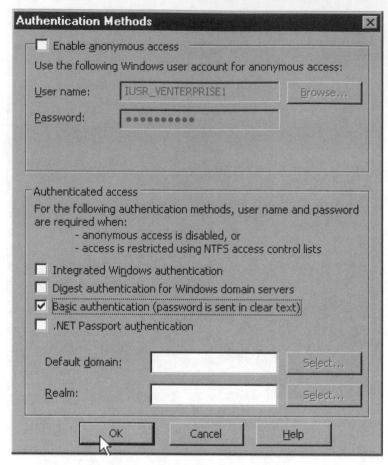

Figure 11.6 Virtual Server Administration Web Site Basic Authentication Warning

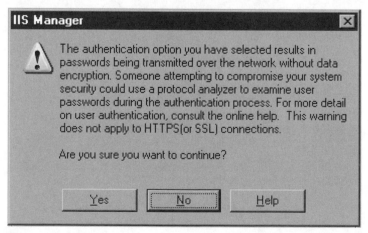

NOTE

If you are concerned about clear text authentication, you can install a digital certificate on the Virtual Server Web site and permit only SSL connections.

The only thing left to do is to restart the Web server. To do this, click **Start | Run** and type **iisreset** as the command to run, as shown in Figure 11.7.

Figure 11.7 Issue the IISRESET Command

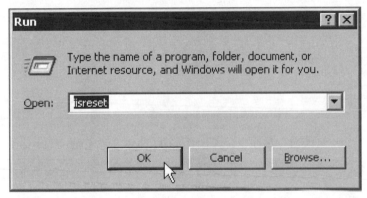

After IIS has finished restarting, go to the Virtual Server Administration Web site and witness your victory: a logon box asking for a username and password (from the local server, of course).

Troubleshooting Internal Server Error 500

Another common error with the Virtual Server Administration Web site is the HTTP 500 – Internal server error, shown in Figure 11.8. This error tends to show up after you attempt to configure constrained delegation, which sounds like a good idea at first, but is not compatible with a workgroup server approach if you installed your Virtual Server as a standalone server and chose **Constrained Delegation** (see Figure 11.9).

Figure 11.8 Administration Web Site HTTP 500 – Internal Server Error

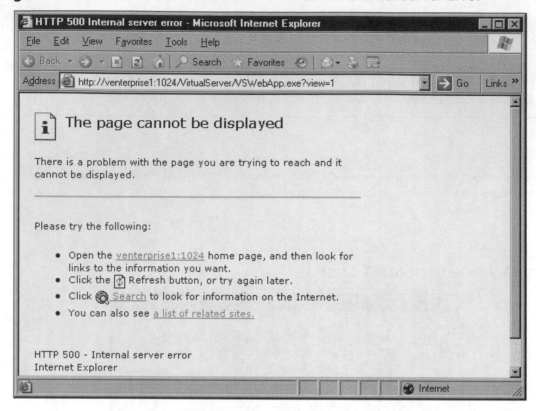

Figure 11.9 Virtual Server Web Site Configuration for Constrained Delegation

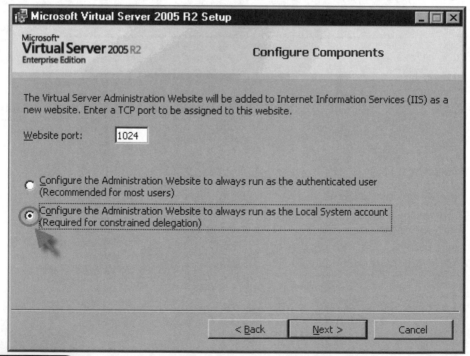

The reason for the HTTP 500 – Internal server error is really quite simple, but is not terribly obvious. In order to use constrained delegation, the product installation needs to register service principal names (SPNs) inside Active Directory, and thus the security delegation fails. In a workgroup mode (or Windows NT 4 domain, for that matter) configuration, there is no Active Directory to register the SPNs with.

As before, there are a couple ways to tackle this error. First, you can join the virtual server to a Windows domain with Active Directory available, or you can disable constrained delegation. Although there is a procedure to generate the SPNs after the installation (See the "Note" below), it is not necessarily the best way to go about it. Since you probably have not installed any virtual machines yet, the better course is to join the virtual server to the domain and then uninstall and re-install Microsoft Virtual Server. It won't take that long and you'll be sure to have created the right SPNs in the right place.

Your other option is to disable constrained delegation, but you'll need to uninstall and re-install Microsoft Virtual Server to this as well. Just make sure that when you are doing the installation, you select **Configure the Administration Website to always run as the authenticated user (Recommended for most users)**, as shown in Figure 11.10.

Figure 11.10 Virtual Server Configuration for Standard Authentication

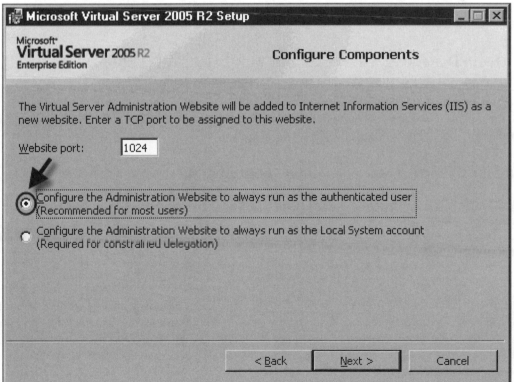

> **NOTE**
>
> In some cases, the SPNs will not be registered correctly even if you do join the Virtual Server to the domain before installation. This happens because the Network Service account of the virtual server fails to generate the appropriate SPNs because of a permissions issue.
>
> For more information on what to do when this happens, or if you want to manually register the SPNs, refer to Microsoft's Knowledge Base Article ID 890893 at http://support.microsoft.com/kb/890893/en-us.

Troubleshooting Access Denied Errors

Your virtual server has been running fine for a while now, but suddenly whenever you go to the Administration Web site, you are presented with "Could not connect to Virtual Server. Access was denied." Did you just install Windows Server 2003 Service Pack 1? Or maybe Windows XP Service Pack 2?

Yes, that's probably what's done you in. The security changes in these service packs break DCOM permissions for the Virtual Server Administration Web site. There are two ways to fix this. First, change them manually, following the steps laid out in Microsoft's Knowledge Base Article ID 891609 at http://support.microsoft.com/kb/891609/en-us.

Alternatively, you can just uninstall and re-install Virtual Server 2005 and let the setup program do all the work for you.

Troubleshooting VMRC Server Disabled Errors

By default, the Virtual Machine Remote Console (VMRC) is turned off. If you try to remotely control a server though the Virtual Server Administration Web site before enabling VMRC, you will be sent to the settings page so that you can enable it (see Figure 11.11). To enable the VMRC, simply click **Enable**, verify the other settings, and click **OK**.

Figure 11.11 Virtual Machine Remote Control (VMRC) Server Properties

Virtual Machine Remote Control (VMRC) Server Properties	?
Virtual Machine Remote Control (VMRC) server must be enabled before you can remotely control a virtual machine with the ActiveX VMRC control or through the Virtual Machine Remote Control client.	
VMRC server ☐ Enable	

Another reason that VMRC may fail is if you are running VNC on your Virtual Server. Both VNC and VMRC run over Port 5900 by default, so in order to resolve the conflict, you can either uninstall VNC from the virtual server or change the ports used by VNC or VMRC.

To change the port used by VMRC, open the Server Properties screen by clicking **Virtual Server | Server Properties** in the Virtual Server Administration Web site. Next, click **Virtual Machine Remote Control (VMRC) Server**, as shown in Figure 11.12.

Figure 11.12 Configuring VMRC in Server Properties

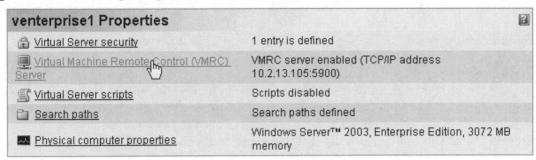

Next, enter a new port number not in use by another network service in the field, as shown in Figure 11.13, and then click **OK**.

Figure 11.13 Changing the VMRC Server Port

Virtual Machine Remote Control (VMRC) Server Properties	
VMRC server	☑ Enable
TCP/IP address:	10.2.13.105
TCP/IP port:	59000

> **NOTE**
>
> To make sure that you don't pick a port that might be used by something else, you can find a listing of well-known ports at www.iana.org/assignments/port-numbers.

Troubleshooting Virtual Server Settings

There are a myriad of individual settings in Microsoft Virtual Server 2005 R2, and maintaining them can be a fulltime chore. It's even harder to maintain them when the virtual server is fighting against you every time you make a change. This section will show you how to deal with the Virtual Server when you make changes and they don't seem to go as planned.

Troubleshooting Disappearing Server Settings

After you have Virtual Server 2005 R2 installed, you will invariably wish to change some of the settings to meet your needs. However, you may find your settings have disappeared on you after a reboot or a system crash. While this is annoying at best, disastrous at worst, it is explainable.

During a normal shutdown of Virtual Server, it attempts to save the current running state of the guest machines. If Virtual Server was not able to finish saving the state of the guest machines during a system shutdown, then it is possible for it to not save any of its settings, thus all your settings are lost. To avoid this problem, always allow your Virtual Server to finish an orderly shutdown.

If the problem persists, even though you're allowing the server to shut down gracefully, it could be one of your guest machines that is causing the problem. A guest machine hanging at shutdown could keep Virtual Server from completing the save of its running state, thus keeping the service from saving your other settings. If this is the case, you will need to use good old process of elimination to find the culprit. Manually shut down one of the guest machines and then reboot the server. Move on to the next guest machine until you are able to get a clean reboot where your changes are saved, at which point you know which guest is the problem and you can go about fixing that one virtual machine.

Troubleshooting Virtual Network Changes

Another thing you may want to change after you have Virtual Server installed and ready to go is your network adapter. Whether you need to add new ones, or just want to update the driver for the Network Interface Card (NIC) that you have already, it is a pretty common thing to change on a network server, so you would think Virtual Server would be able to take it in stride, right? Not so much.

The key thing to remember about your virtual network settings is that they are not dynamically generated, so whenever you make a change to your network cards, you need to make a corresponding change in the network bindings for your virtual networks. Also, bear in mind that this is not just for when you physically add or remove a network card. Oftentimes, if you upgrade the driver for a NIC from the Microsoft-provided driver to one provided by the manufacturer, the adapter name may change, forcing you to update the virtual network setting.

To update your settings, open the Virtual Server Administration Web site, and then select the Virtual Network you want to update by clicking it under **Virtual Networks | Configure**, as shown in Figure 11.14.

Figure 11.14 Configuring Virtual Networks

In the configuration screen for the virtual network, you may be presented with an error as shown in Figure 11.15. This is a sure sign that something has gone awry with your virtual network and it's time to reconfigure it. Also, take note of the .vnc file name; if you can't make changes to the configuration, you may need to remove the virtual network altogether, including deleting the file from the system. We'll talk about that in a minute, but for now let's assume you can get away with a simple reconfiguration and go from there.

Figure 11.15 Virtual Network Properties

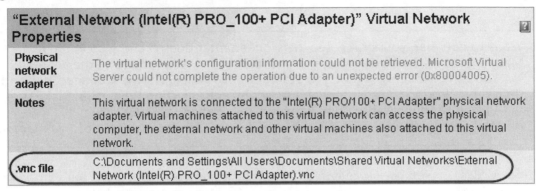

Next, click on **Network Settings**, as shown in Figure 11.16, to modify the virtual network's bindings to the server's physical network connections.

Figure 11.16 Changing Virtual Network Settings

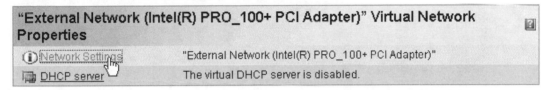

If the Network Settings screen will come up, you will be shown something similar to Figure 11.17. Select the appropriate physical adapter from the drop-down list, and then click **OK**.

Figure 11.17 Selecting the Appropriate Network Adapter

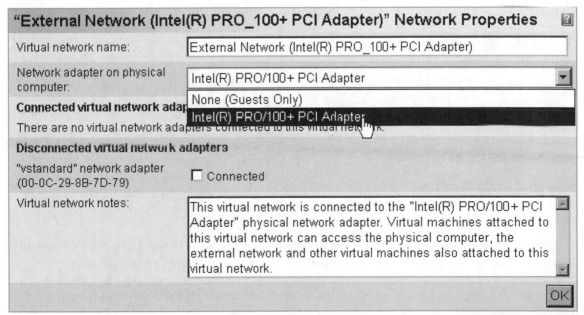

> **NOTE**
>
> What to do when your brand new network adapter doesn't show up in the list? Make sure that the Virtual Machine Networking Service is bound to the adapter.
>
> You can check this by going to **Start | Control Panel | Network Connections** and then right-clicking the adapter you just added and selecting **Properties**. Make sure the **Virtual Machine Networking Service** is checked and click **OK**.
>
> Without this service enabled, the virtual server cannot make use of the adapter.

If the virtual network binding cooperated, then you are done; read no more. If you were unable to open the Network Settings screen, however, it's time for a procedure that's a little bit more involved. From the Virtual Server Administration Web site, open the list of virtual networks by clicking **Virtual Networks | Configure | View All**, as shown in Figure 11.18.

Figure 11.18 Viewing All Virtual Networks

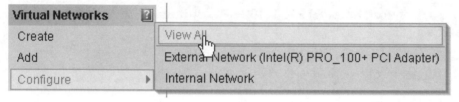

Next, you will be treated to a listing of all of the virtual networks on your virtual server. Click on the virtual network that you want to remove and then select **Remove**, as shown in Figure 11.19.

Figure 11.19 Removing a Virtual Network

Virtual Networks	
Name ▲	**Notes**
	This virtual network is connected to the "Intel(R) PRO/100+ PCI Adapter" physical network
External Network (Intel(R) PRO_100+ PCI Adapter) ▶ Edit Configuration	attached to this virtual physical computer, the
Re̶move	r virtual machines also attached to this virtual network.
Internal Network ▶	This is the internal virtual network. Virtual machines connected to this virtual network can only see other virtual machines.

You're not quite done yet. Remember that .vnc filename back in Figure 11.1? Now it's time to go and manually delete that file from the virtual server. Removing it from the Virtual Server Administration Web site does not remove it from the server. Open Windows Explorer and browse to the file. By default these files are stored on the system drive, under **Documents and Settings |**

All Users | Shared Documents | Shared Virtual Networks. Locate the file with the same name as the errant virtual network and remove it, as shown in Figure 11.20.

Figure 11.20 Deleting the Virtual Network Settings File

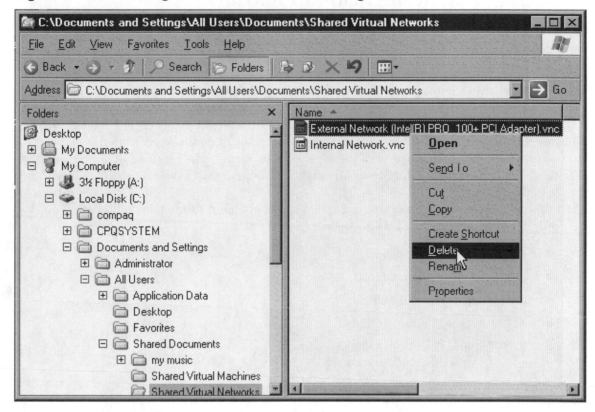

Now, all that's left to do is to create a new virtual network using the correct physical adapter.

NOTE

After you modify the virtual networks, you may need to go back and re-configure the guest machines to use the correct one. To be safe, double-check every virtual machine on the server to ensure that they are connected to the appropriate virtual network, even if you name the new virtual network with the same name. Better safe than sorry.

Troubleshooting Virtual Machine Performance Issues

Performance of your virtual machines is an important thing, especially if you plan to use Microsoft Virtual Server 2005 R2 for more than a test lab. We could write an entire book on optimizing guest machines, but we just didn't have the space! So, here are the quick and dirty ways to optimize your guest machines' performance.

Disabling TCP Segmentation Offload

Most newer server-based network adapters have an option for TCP Segmentation Offload (TSO), which is designed to make the NIC do some of the work of breaking up larger network packets into smaller ones in order to free up CPU cycles. This can also be called large packet offload or TCP offload engine (TOE), depending on the server vendor. In a normal computing environment, this may be a beneficial technology, but in a Microsoft Virtual Server environment, it can bring the network performance of all of your guest machines to a grinding halt.

The reason for this is that the network chipset that Virtual Server emulates to the guest machines does not support TSO, forcing the Virtual Server host machine to do the segmentation *before* the packets get to the NIC. So instead of offloading the packet segmentation to the NIC, you're actually throwing it back on to the Virtual Server host's CPU. Then, after that is done, the NIC still wants to try to do the TSO as well!

In general, any task offloading will cause the same headache, so turn off any offloading features your NIC may support, including the following:

- TCP Segmentation Offload
- IP Receive Checksum Offload
- IP Transmit Checksum Offload
- TCP Receive Checksum Offload
- TCP Transmit Checksum Offload

NOTE

With TSO enabled on your NICs, you're forcing the Virtual Server host to do the segmentation inside the Virtual Server Network Driver Interface Specification (NDIS) driver.

Although NDIS is not bad from a universal compatibility perspective, it is not renowned for being fast, given that it was a new idea back around Windows for Workgroups 3.11. Avoid making the NDIS driver do any more work than it has to by disabling offloading.

For more information about TSO and Virtual Server, see Microsoft's Knowledge Base Article ID 888750 at http://support.microsoft.com/kb/888750/en-us.

Don't Use Network Adapter Auto-Configuration

While it may be nice when you are initially setting up your Virtual Server, network adapter auto-configuration can come back to bite you later. Manually set the speed and duplex for your network adapters. Nothing can cause poor network performance more often then mismatched speed and duplex settings.

Use ISOs instead of CDs Whenever Possible

Using a physical CD-ROM to load software should be a last resort. The performance of the remote CD attachment, or even a CD in the host machine, will pale in comparison to using a local ISO file on the host's disk. Unless you have nothing better to do for the rest of the week, load new guest machines from an ISO image of the software.

Don't Overallocate Memory

Virtual Memory is great, in a pinch, but don't use it unless you're desperate. Make sure that you don't allocate more memory to guest machines than you have physically in the server. If you force the Virtual Server host to swap, the performance hit will be severe and global across all your virtual machines. You can monitor memory usage with Windows Performance Monitor.

Use a Separate Disk Controller for Guest Machines

Not only should you plan on using a different disk partition for your guest machines, just to keep things tidy, you should consider using a completely different set of disks and a second disk controller. The Virtual Server host machine will be cranking away with its own disk needs for basic operating system tasks, so don't weigh that controller down with the job of servicing guest machine disk requests too. If you can, just plan on giving the guest machines their own disk array and disk controller. You'll be glad you did.

Troubleshooting Automated Deployment Services

In this section, we'll show you how to deal with the curveballs that Automated Deployment Services (ADS) will throw at you. If you can't get your systems to show up in ADS, then you're dead in the water when it comes to the Virtual Server Migration Toolkit (VSMT). But wait! Before you walk away from ADS and VSMT to start rebuilding your physical servers in your virtual environment, look here for help.

Troubleshooting PXE

Oftentimes, the problems you will encounter with ADS are not really ADS problems at all; they are related to the way your network is set up. One of the key dependencies of the ADS environment is the Pre-Boot eXecution Environment (PXE, pronounced "pixie"). Whenever you can't get a system to show up in ADS, or it always shows as "disconnected", then it's likely that the PXE setup is your problem. We'll start by looking at these usual suspects:

- DHCP Configuration
- DHCP Relay Agent
- Other PXE Servers

Check the DHCP Configuration

Dynamic Host Configuration Protocol (DHCP) is the network service responsible for handing out IP addresses and PXE server information to the systems managed by ADS. Why is DHCP so important to PXE, you ask? It is the only way that a device that boots into PXE has to "phone home" for startup configuration information. While DHCP is generally your friend here and can make configuration easy, it also has some pesky habits that can make it your biggest foe in getting ADS to work properly.

Check to make sure that your DHCP server is running and assigning addresses. If the DHCP server is a domain member, make sure that it is authorized as well. If your DHCP server is installed on the same server as your ADS, then make sure that the DHCP service has been configured to share the required ports with the Network Boot Service (NBS). To do this, simply issue the *adsdhcpconfig /add* command at the **Start | Run** command line. You can also view the current settings by giving the *adsdhcpconfig /display* command.

DHCP Relay Agent

Remember, DHCP is a broadcast-based protocol, and while this might seem handy, it is not always the best approach to server deployment or virtual migrations. It is definitely not the best approach when one of your mission-critical servers is rebooted and decides that booting into PXE and syncing up to your ADS server is better than starting its local operating system.

Although it is probably best to keep your migration environment separate from your production environment, (see the "Creating Your Migration Environment" sidebar for our recommendations), sometimes this just can't be done. In the event that you feel the need to let PXE run rampant through your environment, make sure you plan around DHCP's broadcast nature.

First, make sure that DHCP has a path across network segments, either through a router or VLAN switch that can handle DHCP forwarding, or by using Microsoft's DHCP relay agent. For more information on how to configure the DHCP relay agent for PXE, view Microsoft's Knowledge Base Article ID 257579 at http://support.microsoft.com/kb/257579/en-us.

> **NOTE**
>
> When you configure your DHCP relay agent, make sure that you include both the DHCP server and the PXE server address. PXE responds to broadcast requests for DHCP options 60, 66, and 67. If your DHCP and PXE servers are not one and the same, then both need to hear the relayed requests. For more on this, check out Microsoft's Knowledge Base Article ID 259670 at http://support.microsoft.com/kb/259670/en-us.

Configuring & Implementing...

Creating Your Migration Environment

Thinking through the way you put your migration environment together is probably the most important part of setting it up. A well-planned environment will head off most of the problems we've talked about. Here are some tips to consider when configuring your migration environment:

- **Place the migration components in an isolated network segment.** If you can, isolate as many of the migration environment components (ADS, DHCP, Virtual Server) onto their own segment. By avoiding the need for a DHCP relay agent, you reduce the complexity of your migrations immensely. Not only do you isolate your production environment from the migration environment, reducing the risk that you might accidentally move a server that is not quite ready to move, but you also keep the imaging traffic from impacting normal operations.

- **Keep your scripts simple.** Don't try to be fancy with your migration environment. The main purpose of it is to get an image off your production server onto a guest machine with minimal change. The only major changes from the physical to the virtual platform should be disk and network drivers, and the VSMT scripts should take care of most of this for you. Anything else just complicates matters.

- **Have all your drivers before you start.** Having the correct drivers is important when you're imaging and deploying servers. Make sure that you have included all the drivers you are likely to run across, otherwise you will spend much of your migration time chasing downloads.

Check for Other PXE Servers

Unlike DHCP, PXE does not have any mechanism to detect other PXE servers on the same network segment. What happens when two PXE servers are listening on the same segment, you ask? Whoever answers first wins.

So, if your device isn't acting right in ADS, check to see if there is another PXE server on the subnet. It could be a RIS server or any other number of third–party PXE servers (Wyse Rapport or Altiris/HP Rapid Deployment to name a few) that is the culprit. Either shut the offender down or move your ADS to a different subnet.

NOTE

If you do move your ADS server, you'll need to remember to take care of a few other things afterwards. First, make sure you change the DHCP and DHCP relay agent settings, if any, to reflect the new location of your ADS server. Second, make sure you change the IP address for the ADS server. Changing the IP address for ADS is not exactly fun (it involves a fair amount of registry work), so try not to have to do it at all. For the exact procedure, take a look at Microsoft's Knowledge Base Article ID 825039 at http://support.microsoft.com/default.aspx?scid=kb;en-us;825039.

Check Your Network Drivers

If your target device boots into PXE, but then fails to identify the network card during the remote floppy boot, check to make sure that you have installed the appropriate network adapter driver. Remember, the remote floppy boot procedure looks only for the first NIC in the system BIOS, so if you have multiple adapters, make sure you've loaded the driver for the first one recognized by the BIOS.

Check Your Storage Drivers

The same goes for your storage drivers. If the remote floppy boot doesn't have drivers for your SCSI controller, then it will have a hard time capturing a disk image. Make sure that there is a driver for each of your disk controllers in the remote boot floppy.

NOTE

Storage and network drivers used in the PXE boot process are stored in C:\Program Files\Microsoft ADS\nbs\repository\User\PreSystem directory.

Check Your BIOS Clock

To make sure it is talking to the right ADS server, the client checks the certificate you installed during ADS setup. In PXE, the clock used is the local system BIOS clock, so if the time is significantly off in the BIOS then your ADS certificate may not be valid yet or expired, depending on which way the clock is off. Make sure that the BIOS clock on the target device is set to the correct time.

Troubleshooting the ADS Services

Now that you're certain that the network setup is not causing your headache, let's talk about the actual ADS services. There are a few key areas to look at when ADS continues giving you fits. This section will lead you through them.

Check That the ADS Services Are Running

First, check to see that the ADS services are running. While it may seem like an obvious step, it's generally the one that most people fly right past. This is also a good place to start because other problems with ADS will keep the services from starting. You can check the state of the ADS services by going to ADS Management Console and confirming that the ADS Controller Service, Image Distribution Service, and Network Boot Services are running. If they show as stopped or disconnected, then take a look at the Windows Event Log to see if there are any errors or if they just need to be restarted.

Confirm the ADS Controller's IP Address

If the device and the Controller aren't talking, check to make sure that the Controller is listening on the right IP address, especially if the controller has multiple NICs. To do this, just type **adsservice /edit /controller /newip** *ipaddress* at the **Start | Run** prompt.

Check the ADS Certificates

ADS makes use of a certificate to make sure that the PXE target device is talking to the correct ADS server. ADS also uses the same certificate to authenticate the Deployment Agent server with the Controller server. If these certificates are not installed properly, ADS will fail.

You can use the **regcert** command to verify and update the appropriate certificate on the Deployment Agent server and the Controller server. To verify the certificate, type **regcert /b /l** at the command prompt of the Deployment Agent server. If the command returns the *No ADS Builder Certificates in registry* message, then you need to install the appropriate certificate. This is done by entering **regcert /b** *certificate* at a command prompt. The default certificate file is stored at **C:\Program Files\Microsoft ADS\Certificate\Adsroot.cer** on the ADS Controller server.

After you have completed these steps, the **regcert /b /l** command should return the following message: *Registered ADS Builder Certificate 'adsroot.cer'*.

Troubleshooting the Virtual Server Migration Toolkit

So, ADS is working as expected and it's time to start using the Virtual Server Migration Toolkit (VSMT). Although most of the processes used by VSMT are similar to the ones used in ADS, they aren't exactly the same, so now you've got to deal with the problems that are unique to Virtual Server migrations. This section is a quick and easy guide to get you through the frequent problems encountered using the migration tool.

Troubleshooting the Virtual Network Setup

One of the first things you should have done when you installed the VSMT was to run the **Createvirtualnetwork.vbs** script. This script creates a new virtual network named **VM0** which is the destination for the migrated images. If your *<virtual machine>_CreateVM.cmd* script fails, check to make sure that **VM0** has been created.

NOTE

Another network configuration item to keep in mind is that the *GatherHW.cmd* script collects the MAC address of the original system. When *<virtual machine>_CreateVM. cmd* is run, it sets the MAC address of the guest machine to the same one that was on the physical server. If both the virtual machine and physical host are on the network at the same time, you may experience intermittent network failures on both.

Troubleshooting Script Creation

The *GatherHW.cmd* script is used to collect information about the target server, but it cannot do its job without a little help from you. If the *GatherHW.cmd* script fails to process, make sure that the target machine has Windows Management Instrumentation (WMI) installed and all of its disk partitions are formatted NTFS. If you are migrating a Windows NT 4.0 server, you will need to install the WMI Core for *GatherHW.cmd* to collect the information it needs.

NOTE

You can download the WMI Core for Windows NT 4.0 at www.microsoft.com/downloads/release.asp?releaseid=18490.

Troubleshooting ADS Integration

The VSMT integrates with ADS through the *<virtual machine>_CreateVM.cmd* file generated by *VMScript.exe*. If the ADS server is offline or disconnected when you execute the *<virtual machine>_CreateVM.cmd*, then the script will fail, but it may leave the job half done. If the migration process fails at any point, the best way to restart it is to go back, delete any reference to the new virtual machine, and start over. If you try the same script again without cleaning up the pieces of the prior attempt, your attempt will only end in disaster.

Troubleshooting Migration from VMware to Virtual Server

If you find yourself needing to move virtual machines from a VMware GSX Server 3 or a VMware Server 1.0 platform, you can use the same process as you would for a physical server. The only difference is in the drivers you need to include in the C:\Program Files\Microsoft ADS\nbs\repository\User\PreSystem directory.

You can download the VMware SCSI driver from the VMware Web site at www.vmware.com/download/server/drivers_tools.html. Also, you need to ensure that the virtual machine you are moving is running the latest version of the VMware Tools before you start the migration, otherwise the SCSI driver you download may not be compatible with the one on the virtual machine.

Troubleshooting the Migration Process

The migration process from physical server to virtual machine is a combination of ADS and VSMT. All of the troubleshooting steps we have already talked about apply during the migration process as well. There are a few more things to cover, though, so read on and we'll show you how to avoid these common pitfalls.

Imaging Problems

The most time-consuming portion of the migration process, other than setting up the migration environment, is the capture of the disk images to be migrated and then their deployment onto the Virtual Server. This section will walk you through the major obstacles and how to overcome them.

Most of the image capture problems will revolve around getting the target device booted properly into PXE with the correct drivers. We won't spend too much time going over what we already covered earlier except to reinforce that if you don't have the correct drivers, you aren't going to get very far with your image capture.

Image deployment is another matter altogether. Here, there are a number of things that can get in your way. Imgdeploy.exe is the executable that handles the capture and deployment of images to the virtual machines, hence the name, but its error messages are not terribly helpful in determining what went wrong. Table 11.2 covers the common errors and what you can do about them.

Table 11.2 Common Imgdeploy.exe Errors

Error Message	Solution
Image *imagename* cannot be added: the directory cannot be removed.	Occurs during image capture operation; this normally indicates that the image storage location has been set up on a FAT volume.
	Move the image storage to an NTFS volume or convert the existing storage volume to NTFS.
The command finishes immediately without any message; image is not captured or deployed.	Occurs during either image deployment or capture; happens when not all files needed for Imgdeploy.exe to function are in the same directory.
	Make sure that Imgdeploy.exe, Imglib.dll, and Adssupport.dll are all in the same folder.
Imgdeploy.exe fails with error 107374180.	Occurs during the image deployment operation; this error normally indicates image corruption. Try capturing a new image and then deploying again.

Continued

Table 11.2 Continued

Error Message	Solution
Network connection was reset (exit code c000105a).	Occurs during image deployment operation; generally indicates that the ADS server is sending the image faster than the virtual server can write it to disk.
	Make sure the speed and duplex of the virtual server's NICs are set correctly. Also ensure that TCP offloading has been turned off.

IDE Disks Cannot Exceed 127 GB

In Virtual Server 2005 R2, the virtual IDE controller is not capable of seeing disks greater than 127 GB. This used to be the upper limit for IDE technology until very recently, and probably shouldn't come as a surprise that virtualization technology still hasn't completely caught up. While this may seem like an almost academic fact, given that most servers will be migrating from SCSI disk technology, it has considerable impact on the migration process.

VSMT and ADS can *read* existing SCSI disks, but when the VSMT generates the virtual machine it defines the target disks as IDE disks, regardless of what kind of disk they were before. So if you are trying to transfer a physical server with a disk larger than 127 GB, stop it. If you are lucky, this is just a data volume and you can migrate the system partition with VSMT and then use a third-party imaging product, such as Symantec Ghost, to migrate the oversized disk. If the disk that is too large is the system partition, then, unfortunately, it's time to break out your ISO images and start building.

Converted SCSI Disks Fail to Boot

Along the same lines as the IDE disk size limit, some real SCSI controllers write their master boot records (MBRs) out in such a way that the virtual IDE controller cannot find where it starts. Hope is not lost, though. Because the imgdeploy.exe will simply lay down a sector-by-sector image of the original disk, your only problem will be once you try to actually boot the newly created guest machine. If your newly migrated server boots to a black screen and hangs, then it's a good guess that this is your problem.

To work around this slight inconvenience, we are going to connect the new virtual disk to a SCSI adapter instead of the IDE adapter created by VSMT.

First, go into the Virtual Server Administration Web site and select the guest machine you are working with and click **Edit Configuration**, as shown in Figure 11.21.

Figure 11.21 Editing the Virtual Machine Settings

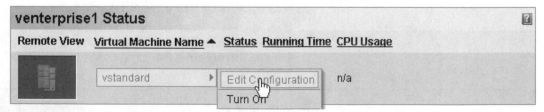

Next, scroll down until you see **SCSI adapters** and click on it (see Figure 11.22).

Figure 11.22 Configuring a New SCSI Adapter

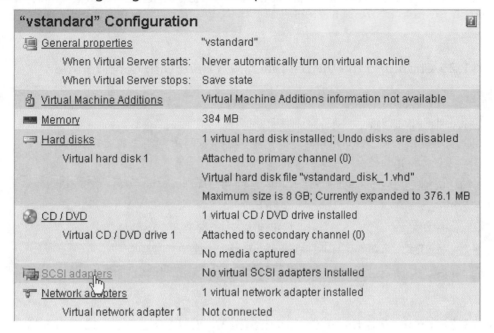

Now you're going to add a SCSI controller to connect your virtual disk to by clicking **Add SCSI Adapter** and then accepting the default settings for the SCSI Adapter and clicking **OK**, as shown in Figures 11.23 and 11.24.

Figure 11.23 Adding a SCSI Adapter to a Virtual Machine

Figure 11.24 Virtual Machine SCSI Adapter Properties

"vstandard" SCSI Adapter Properties

By default, each SCSI adapter is not shared and has an ID of 7. If you are using this virtual machine for clustering, you need to share one adapter and set its ID to a value other than that used by the peer virtual machine of the cluster.

Virtual SCSI adapter 1   ☐ Remove

☐ Share SCSI bus for clustering

SCSI adapter ID: 7 ▼

Add SCSI Adapter >>   OK

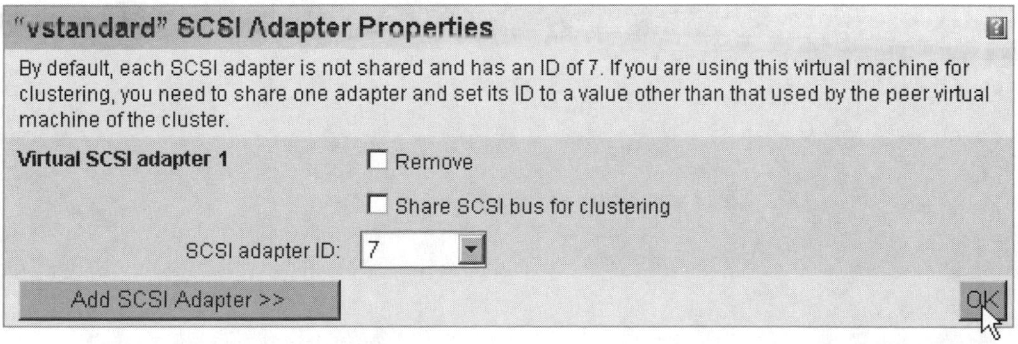

Then click on **Hard disks** (see Figure 11.25) and change the attachment from the IDE channel it is currently on to the appropriate SCSI channel and ID, as shown in Figure 11.26. You should try to mirror the SCSI configuration of the physical server as close as you can here, to ensure that you get the system partition on the right channel.

Figure 11.25 Changing the Virtual Machine's Hard Disk Configuration

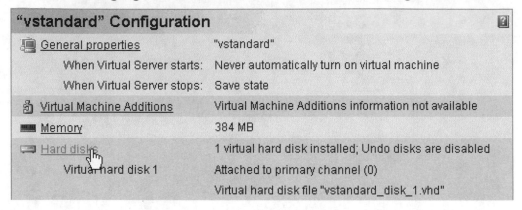

Figure 11.26 Changing the Attachment for Virtual Disks from IDE to SCSI

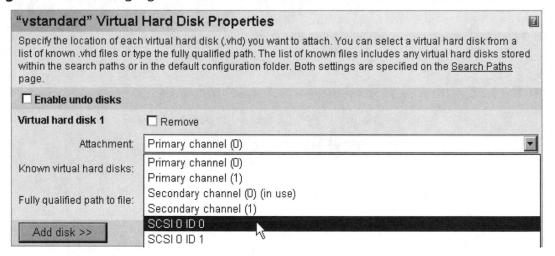

After all your virtual disks are attached to the new SCSI adapter (see Figure 11.27), you're ready to power on the guest machine and finish any other post-migration cleanup you need to do.

Figure 11.27 Virtual Machine Hard Disk Configuration after SCSI Attachment

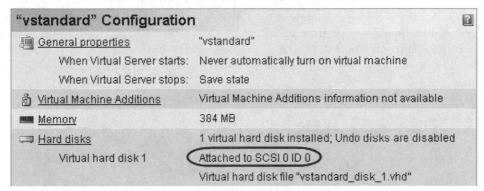

NOTE

From a performance perspective, the virtual SCSI controller is faster than the virtual IDE controller. Because the .vhd files are readable by both virtual controllers, you should convert your disks to using the SCSI controller as a general rule. This will not only smooth out any migration problems from physical SCSI disks, but will also give you a performance gain inside the virtual environment.

Summary

In this chapter, we've tried to help you through some of the most nerve-wracking experiences when dealing with Virtual Server 2005 R2. Whether it's a permissions problem with the Virtual Server Administration Web site or migrating a recalcitrant server to a more pliable guest machine, Virtual Server 2005 R2 can throw some good ones at you. We've tried to give you a head start on most of the common problems and some suggestions on how to avoid them. There will always be new problems to troubleshoot as our environments continue to evolve and change with the virtualization technologies available to us. Remember to use your support resources in the Microsoft Knowledge Base, Technet, and newsgroups, in addition to this chapter, to help you get the most out of your virtual server.

Solutions Fast Track

Troubleshooting Virtual Server 2005 R2

☑ The Virtual Server Administration Web site is very sensitive to the security choices you make during installation. If you choose to use constrained delegation, make sure that you are a member of a domain with Active Directory available. If you make the server a member of a workgroup, turn off Integrated Windows Authentication.

☑ VMRC is disabled by default, so remember to turn it on. Also, remember that it sits on the same port as VNC, so be sure to change ports if you need VNC as well.

☑ Virtual network definition files are not dynamically updated when you change network adapters. If you change NICs, update your virtual networks.

☑ Disable TCP offloading on your network adapters; it can only cause you pain.

Troubleshooting Automated Deployment Services

☑ DHCP and PXE are key components for the correct function of ADS. Check to make sure that your DHCP server and Network Boot Services (NBS) server can be seen by all of the target devices you are planning to migrate.

☑ Storage and network drivers for each target device need to be included in the PXE boot floppy.

☑ The ADS certificate is referenced by the Controller, the Agent, and the Device. If your certificate is not installed properly or your system clocks are not in sync, then ADS is likely to fail.

Troubleshooting Virtual Server Migration Toolkit

☑ Make sure that the VM0 virtual network was created during the VSMT setup. If it's not there, run *Createvirtualnetwork.vbs*.

☑ WMI is an important prerequisite for migration targets to have installed on them. Without WMI, the VSMT cannot get enough information to create the migration scripts.

☑ Don't try to restart a migration job that has failed. Delete any record of it from ADS and VSMT and then start over after you've fixed the problem.

☑ Migrating from VMware GSX Server 3 or VMware Server 1.0 is easy, as long as you are using the VMware SCSI driver in the C:\Program Files\Microsoft ADS\nbs\repository\User\PreSystem.

Troubleshooting the Migration Process

☑ Imgdeploy.exe will be the most frequent source of imaging problems, mainly stemming from network settings, NIC drivers, or disk controller drivers. Also, don't be surprised if the image is corrupted during the capture and you need to recapture it, especially on a busy network.

☑ Virtual Server uses a slightly older virtual IDE controller, which is limited to a maximum capacity of 127 GB per IDE disk. If you are trying to transfer a server with a disk larger than 127 GB, look for an alternative method to migrate it.

☑ The virtual SCSI disk driver is more reliable and has better performance than its IDE counterpart. After the migration process is complete, convert your virtual hard disks to SCSI from IDE to avoid startup and performance problems.

Frequently Asked Questions

Q: Should I load Virtual Server 2005 R2 on a domain controller?

A: Not if you can help it. The problems with time synchronization, SMB signing, and user security probably aren't worth the hassle. If you are in a crunch for hardware, and still need a domain controller, consider loading a virtual domain controller on a standalone virtual server.

Q: You keep coming back to network drivers and disk controller drivers as being the source of migration problems. Is it really smooth sailing once I'm through the drivers?

A: For the most part, yes. That's why we strongly recommend that you download all the drivers you will need and include them, even if you're not sure. It won't hurt to have too many drivers, but you'll be pulling your hair out if you miss one.

Q: My images seem to continuously end up being corrupted. What am I doing wrong?

A: For starters, make sure you have the right drivers. Then check your network settings for duplex and speed. If you're still having problems, consider moving the target and the ADS server onto their own network segment so they don't have to contend with other network traffic during the capture.

Q: Does it matter if my DHCP and ADS services are on the same server?

A: Generally, no, you just need to make sure ADS has made the necessary changes to DHCP; otherwise PXE will not work. So long as you install ADS after DHCP, you should be fine.

Q: I've really fouled things up with my virtual server. What will it hurt if I uninstall and re-install it?

A: None of your virtual machine, disk, or network files are removed during an uninstall. So, as long as you don't delete them, there are still there after a re-install. All you need to do is to define your settings again and you're no worse for the wear.

Q: Is TCP offloading really as big a problem as you make it sound?

A: Yes, absolutely it is. The amount of extra effort that the virtual server has to go through is enormous if TCP offloading is enabled. It can make the network performance of your guest machines so horrible that it will leave even the most ardent fan of virtualization wanting to throw the virtual server out of a third-story window. Friends don't let friends use TCP offloading on a virtual server.

## Chapter 12

Introducing Xen

Solutions in this chapter:

- **What Is Xen?**
- **Xen's Virtualization Model Explored**
- **CPU Virtualization**
- **Memory Virtualization**
- **I/O Virtualization**
- **The Xenstore**

☑ **Summary**

☑ **Solutions Fast Track**

☑ **Frequently Asked Questions**

Introduction

In Chapter 1, we reviewed the origins and theory behind virtualization. Various systems have been developed to subdivide, or virtualize, resources of a single physical computer. These systems exist on a wide variety of platforms. Some are dedicated to a particular hardware platform and guest operating system, while others can be installed on a variety of architecture and support a diverse selection of guests. Their approach varies, but they all share one goal: to assist with high levels of consolidation, increase server utilization, and enable rapid provisioning of partitions to meet your business needs on demand. Xen has been proven to accomplish all that, and has been very successful in doing so.

With its root in open source, and with heavy development still coming from the open-source community, Xen is posed to be one of the most popular and widely used virtual machine monitors (VMMs) for its supported platforms. Many operating systems are integrating Xen's hypervisor into the operating system itself; soon it will not be necessary to even install Xen to begin achieving greater efficiency in your data center. However, Xen is much more than just another free VMM. XenSource, the company currently leading ongoing development efforts of the VMM, has brought Xen into the commercial limelight as a viable solution for the enterprise data center.

This chapter will discuss Xen in detail, including the open-source release as well as the commercial variants from XenSource—XenExpress, XenServer, and XenEnterprise. We will illustrate the underpinnings of the product as well to give you a solid understanding of how Xen works and what to expect. We also review some best practices and tips on how to extract the most benefit from the product as we discuss critical architectural components.

What Is Xen?

Xen is an open-source VMM, or hypervisor, for both 32- and 64-bit processors architectures. It is run as software executing on a host operating system that enables you to run several guest operating systems on top of the host on the same computer hardware at the same time. The virtual machines are executed securely and efficiently with near-native performance.

The Xen project originated as a research project of the Systems Research Group at the University of Cambridge Computer Laboratory. The project was dubbed the XenoServers Project, and was funded by the UK's Engineering and Physical Sciences Research Council (EPSRC). The goal of the project is to provide a public infrastructure that is globally reaching and accessible for purposes of wide-area distributed computing. With a special dedication to systems research, and led by senior researcher Ian Pratt, the project has produced the Xen hypervisor as its core technology.

Xen was released to the public in a two-step approach. First, Pratt and several other original contributors released a paper entitled "Xen and the Art of Virtualization" at the bi-annual Symposium on Operating Systems Principles (SOSP) describing the hypervisor and its approach to bringing virtualization to the x86 CPU architecture in October 2003. At the same time, the first public release, version 1.0, was made available for download. Since then, Xen has grown and matured, playing a key role in many production implementations. Xen is also the base technology for a changing approach to hosting and software as a service (SaaS) models.

Xen development in the open-source community is now led by XenSource, founded by Pratt. Although a channel for commercial enterprise-class solutions based on Xen technology, XenSource is very much committed to the growth of the Xen community, fostering and inspiring developers to take the hypervisor beyond its current state, and dedicating its own resources to the development effort as well. Table 12.1 lists the top 15 contributors to the Xen code base. Note that the majority of the coding is done by XenSource engineering resources, followed by the open-source community. Of the technology partners working with XenSource, IBM and Intel have made the greatest contributions to the project since the release of version 3.0.

Table 12.1 Code Statistics since the 3.0.0 Release of the Xen Hypervisor

Contributor	Aliases	Check-ins	Insertions	% Involved
xensource.com	16	1,281	363,449	64.2%
other	30	189	48,132	8.5%
ibm.com	30	271	40,928	7.2%
intel.com	26	290	29,545	5.2%
hp.com	8	126	19,275	3.4%
novell.com	8	78	17,108	3.0%
valinux.co.jp	3	156	12,143	2.1%
bull.net	1	145	11,926	2.1%
ncsc.mil	3	25	6,048	1.1%
fujitsu.com	13	119	6,442	1.1%
redhat.com	7	68	4,822	< 1%
amd.com	5	61	2,671	< 1%
virtualiron.com	5	23	1,434	< 1%
cam.ac.uk	1	9	1,211	< 1%
unisys.com	3	7	857	< 1%
		Total:	565,991	

TIP

If you are interested in reviewing the source code for Xen, or obtaining the "under-development" version of Xen for the latest in upcoming features, visit http://xenbits.xensource.com.

It is interesting to observe the variety of contributors to the Xen project, ranging from XenSource themselves to technology leaders in the x86 arena for systems and CPU architecture (notably those with the largest budget for x86 research and development) to key Linux distributors. Xen is even contributed to by governmental and educational institutions. With such a wide selection of contributors of diverse backgrounds, Xen has great potential to meet the needs of your organization, regardless of size, budget, or whether it is private or public.

This section reviews the features and requirements of Xen's commercial and open-source versions.

Features of Xen

Xen offers a powerful set of enterprise-class functionality, making it as suitable for larger implementations running mission-critical applications as it is for small and medium-sized businesses. These features include

- Virtual machines with near-native performance
- Full support on x86 (32-bit), x86 (32-bit) with Physical Address Extension (PAE), and x86 with 64-bit extensions
- Support for almost all hardware with Linux drivers available
- Multiple vCPUs supported in each guest machine (Windows and Linux), up to 32-way
- Dynamic resource allocation through hot-plug vCPUs (if the guest operating system supports it)
- Live, zero-downtime migration of running virtual machines between two physical hosts
- Support of hardware-assist processors from Intel (Intel-VT) and AMD (AMD-V), allowing unmodified guest operating systems

Xen supports two modes of virtualization: paravirtualization and full virtualization. For paravirtualization, guest operating systems must be modified and the kernel recompiled to support proper interaction with the Xen VMM. Although this limits the selection of operating systems that can be run in this mode, it offers performance benefits in return. Full virtualization was introduced in version 3.0 with the addition of support for hardware-assisted processor architectures. This mode is only available to physical hosts with Intel-VT or AMD-V processors. Full virtualization enables unmodified guest operating systems to be run, and is the only way to run Microsoft Windows guests, with a minor performance penalty.

The XenServer Product Family

As we discussed earlier, two flavors of Xen are available: open source and the commercial product. Both have roughly the same features, with the commercial product touting a new management tool and being a bit more refined overall. In particular, XenSource's commercial XenServer product family includes the open-source Xen hypervisor with lots of add-ons surrounding it. You can benefit from its following aspects:

- **Ease of use**   XenEnterprise, XenServer, and XenExpress is offered as packaged and supported virtualization. Comprised of three elements, it contains the Xen hypervisor, port of Linux and NetBSD, and management tools that are run in User Mode. XenServer is simple to install on bare metal from a boot CD or across the network. It leverages standard Linux drivers to support a wide and diverse range of network and storage hardware.

- **Robust virtualization**   A highly scalable platform, XenEnterprise can run on up to 64-socket SMP systems and support up to 32 vCPUs in a guest virtual machine. Exceptional performance can be achieved, especially in configurations that can take advantage of hardware virtualization through the latest processors from Intel and AMD. This hardware virtualization also allows XenEnterprise to host Windows and Linux virtual machines, all managed through a single management tool.

- **Powerful management**   Rapid provisioning, performance monitoring, and some trending via the XenServer Administrator Console, physical-to-virtual migrations, and command-line user space tools that can be run locally or remotely make XenEnterprise as efficient to manage and administer as it is to run virtual machines.

Table 12.2 shows a comparison of the XenServer product family, including the open-source release. These features are current as of the XenServer 3.2 and Xen open-source 3.0.4 release.

Table 12.2 The XenServer Product Family

	XenEnterprise Multi-OS Virtualization	XenServer Windows Virtualization	XenExpress On-Ramp to Xen
User Type	Enterprise IT, OEMs	Windows IT Pro	IT Enthusiast/ Developer
Concurrent VMs	No software-imposed limit; limited only by available hardware resources	Eight concurrent VMs	Four concurrent VMs
Physical RAM	Unlimited RAM	8 GB max	4 GB max
Physical CPU	Up to 32 sockets (32-way)	Dual-socket (2-way)	Dual-socket (2-way)
Shared Storage	Yes, Fibre Channel and iSCSI-based SAN	No	No
Windows Guest Support	Windows Server 2003 Windows Server 2003 R2 Windows XP SP2 Windows 2000 SP4	Windows Server 2003 Windows Server 2003 R2 Windows XP SP2 Windows 2000 SP4	Windows Server 2003 Windows Server 2003 R2 Windows XP SP2 Windows 2000 SP4
Linux Guest Support	RHEL 3.6–5.0 SLES 9.2–10.1 Debian Sarge Others via HVM	Windows only	RHEL 3.6–5.0 SLES 9.2–10.1 Debian Sarge Others via HVM

Continued

Table 12.2 Continued

	XenEnterprise Multi-OS Virtualization	XenServer Windows Virtualization	XenExpress On-Ramp to Xen
Physical-to-Virtual Migrations (P2V)	Linux P2V included and via XenSource partners; Windows P2V available from XenSource partners	Windows P2V available from XenSource partners	Linux P2V included and via XenSource partners; Windows P2V available from XenSource partners
Live Migration	Yes	No	No
QoS Resource Controls for vCPU and VIFs	Yes	No	No
VLAN tagging in virtual bridges	Yes	No	No
64-bit guest support	No	No	No
Paravirtualized (PV) drivers included	Yes; signed for Windows	Yes, signed	Yes; signed for Windows
Administration Details	1 or more Xen hosts using Administrator Console	1 or more Xen hosts using Administrator Console	Only support a single Xen host using Administrator Console
Cost of Software License	< $1,000 USD per 2-CPU	< $100 USD per 2-CPU	Free

NOTE

You can learn more about each Xen product and download a free trial (or the full open-source product) at the following locations:

- **Xen 3.0 (open source)** www.xensource.com/xen/xen/
- **XenServer Express** www.xensource.com/products/xen_express/
- **XenServer** www.xensource.com/products/xen_server/
- **XenServer Enterprise** www.xensource.com/products/xen_enterprise/index.html

Xen's Virtualization Model Explored

Although we have been speaking about server virtualization as it relates to the operating system running in a hardware environment (physical or virtual), the focus for any organization that is deploying virtualization technologies for their systems architecture should be on applications. The server platform merely hosts the applications, where the application and data themselves are the intellectual property that actually provides value to the business. Achieving consolidation, optimization, higher availability, and increased flexibility of a company's application portfolio is where virtualization's "sweet-spot" is found, helping customers realize the true business value and benefit of their IT investment.

Architecture Overview

There have been various ways to host multiple applications on a single server, in a shared-services fashion. The most basic method is to host the files and processes for multiple applications on a single instance of the operating system. While it is possible to achieve some level of protection among the different processes using conventional operating systems techniques, the processes are not as well isolated as with dedicated hardware. In fact, a fault experienced by a particular application can not only impact other processes executing on the same operating system, but it can impact the operating system itself, making recovery of all processes difficult if not impossible, as in how configuration requires a delicate balance of privileged mode software (device drivers, operating systems APIs, and so on) and all user mode software, especially those that share common libraries or binaries. More common than fault isolation, however, is the need for performance isolation.

A common issue with "stacked" applications that are co-located and executing on the same operating system instance is the competition for resources. Concurrent processing for CPU, memory, or I/O bound processes can cause the host machine to easily become oversubscribed. Each process believes that it has the cumulative amount of resources to use and will attempt to use them as needed. While it is possible to create containers within a particular operating system to help assure that the processes are getting all the correct resources they have been allocated and no more, this isolation technique has not been shown to provide consistent results or be reliable.

In most cases, enterprise-grade operating systems have, as a minimum process, schedulers that proxy the requests to the operating system for resources. However, when left to its own devices, an application process may be impervious to other processes in the system and "hog" any available resources. Operating systems augment these scheduling limitations by providing resource managers that allow for finer grain control over process resource utilization. These tools, however, are generally complicated to implement and manage, and impose greater administrative overhead when adding new applications.

While dedicating physical server hardware to a single operating system instance provides both the fault and performance isolation desired by most enterprises, it becomes inefficient in cost. The real solution to the issue is server virtualization. As explained in Chapter 1, various types of virtualization technologies are available, each with their own set of strengths and challenges. Xen has been developed as a viable and capable virtual machine monitor for the x86 architecture, taking advantage of paravirtualization (its primary virtualization technique) and full virtualization.

Processor Architecture

Xen currently supports a wide complement of hardware and operating systems. Part of its value proposition is being a commodity VMM for commodity hardware, allowing you to virtualize popular operating systems. Although Xen was originally developed as a VMM project for x86, experimental ports are being developed and tested for additional platforms, including Intel's Itanium and Itanium 2 (IA-64) and IBM's PowerPC. Table 12.3 lists the currently support CPU architectures, as well as the Xen features available for each architecture.

Table 12.3 Xen Features by CPU Architecture

Feature	x86 (no PAE)	x86 (with PAE)	x64 (x86_64)	IA-64	POWERPC
Privileged Domains	X	X	X	X	X
Guest Domains	X	X	X	X	X
SMP Guests	X	X	X	X	
Save/Restore/Migrate	X	X	X	X	
More than 4GB RAM		X	X	X	X
Progressive PV	X	X	X	X	X
Driver Domains	X	X	X		

As of release 3.0.0, Xen also supports the hardware virtualization features provided by the latest processors for Intel and AMD, supporting Intel-VT and AMD-V, respectively. For Intel processors, the feature is called XVM, while AMD processors announce the feature as SVM. In Xen nomenclature, though, both are simply referred to as HVM since they are functionally equivalent and provide the same benefit to Xen. Hardware virtualization allows Xen to host operating systems that cannot be modified and run in a traditional paravirtualized manner. While Intel's and AMD's approaches are different, the net result is the ability to virtualize CPU and memory effectively and efficiently, allowing Xen to run virtually any operating system. Even with HVM, though, special paravirtualization device drivers are available to allow HVM guests to utilize Xen's virtual I/O architecture for maximum efficiency, performance, security, and isolation. For more information on this section, please see Chapter 17.

Paravirtualization with Xen

Xen has an elegantly simple design for a complex architecture. Its architecture was derived from an attempt to account for the idiosyncrasies of the x86 CPU platform as it applies to virtual machine monitors, or hypervisors. One of the main goals of the design was to separate the "how," "when," and "what" (in other words, the policy and the mechanism) as much as possible. Other implementations of x86 VMMs placed the entire burden on the hypervisor; and while offering a great degree of flexibility and success, that led to a sacrifice in performance. However, the developers of Xen believed that an optimal approach to hypervisor design was to let the hypervisor deal with low level complexities, such as CPU scheduling and access control, and not higher-level matters better suited for the guest operating system environments themselves.

As a result of this architecture methodology, the demarcation point, so to speak, in Xen's architecture became a question of control and management. The hypervisor's focus is on basic control operations (the mechanism, or the "how"), leaving the decision making (the policies, or "what" and "when") to the guest operating system. This fits well with the nature of the VMM, where the hypervisor only handles tasks that require direct privileged access. In essence, Xen presents a virtual machine abstraction that is very similar to the hardware platform beneath, without creating an exact copy of it. This technique is at the heart of what is called paravirtualization.

To accomplish this, paravirtualization does require some modification to the guest operating system to make it aware of the underlying virtualization layer, improving its interaction with both the virtual world it has been presented as well as the actual physical world it is running on top of. Although application binaries do not need to be modified as well, operating system modifications facilitate improved performance and support better handling of time-sensitive operations. Paravirtualization does have certain requirements for memory management, CPU, and device I/O, as shown in Table 12.4.

Table 12.4 Paravirtualization Requirements and Considerations

Item Type	Item	Requirements or Special Consideration
Memory Management	Segmentation	Cannot insert privileged segment descriptors and cannot overlap with the top end of the linear address space.
	Paging	Guest operating system has direct read access to hardware-level page tables, but updates are batched or performed individually and validated by the hypervisor.
CPU	Protection	The guest operating system must run at a more restricted privilege level than Xen—in other words, it cannot run in Ring-0.
	Exceptions	The guest operating system must register a table for exception trap handlers.

Continued

Table 12.4 Continued

Item Type	Item	Requirements or Special Consideration
	System calls	The guest operating system may install a handler for system calls, allowing direct calls from an application or the operating system itself. Some of these calls do not need to be handled directly by Xen.
	Interrupts	Hardware interrupts are replaced with a notification event mechanism.
	Time	The guest operating system must be aware and account for both real, wall-clock time as well as virtual time.
Device I/O	Network and Disk	Virtual devices are simple to access. Data is transferred using asynchronous I/O rings, and interrupt-like communication to the guest operating system is handled through event notifications.

Xen Domains

Figure 12.1 illustrates the system structure of a typical full-virtualization VMM for the x86 architecture. While similar in function to other VMMs, Xen has a unique system structure that is broken down into the underlying hardware, VMM (or hypervisor), a control region, and the virtual machines themselves, as illustrated in Figure 12.2. The hypervisor exposes an abstraction layer that contains both Management and Virtual Hardware APIs, including a control interface that allows guests to interact directly and indirectly with the underlying hardware. Interacting with the Management API is a control region that has privileged access to hardware and contains user mode management code. Both the control region and the virtual machines are referred to as domains. At boot time, the system initiates a special domain that is allowed to use the control interface, referred to as Domain-0 (dom0). This initial domain hosts the user mode management software used to administer the Xen environment, whether through command-line tools or using the XenSource Administrator Console. It is also responsible for starting and stopping a less-privileged domain type, guest domains, referred to as Domain-U (domU), via the control interface, as well as control domU CPU scheduling, memory allocations, and access to devices such as physical disk storage and network interfaces. A domU is also referred to as a Xen Virtual Machine, or XenVM.

Figure 12.1 System Structure of the Typical Full-Virtualization VMM for x86

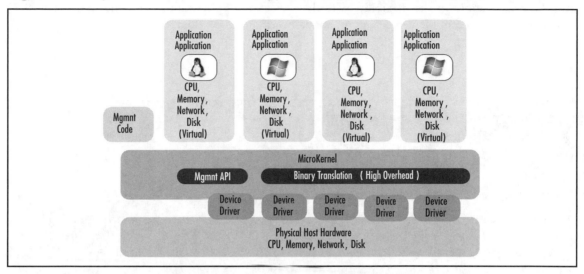

Figure 12.2 System Structure of the Xen VMM

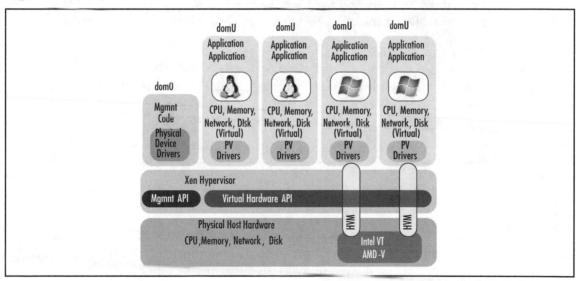

The control domain, dom0, functions like a standard Linux installation. You can run user mode applications, such as those used to manage the Xen environment, as well as install the device drivers needed to support your hardware platform. Because of the ability to compile and run practically any hardware device with available Linux drivers, Xen has a wide array of hardware that it supports. This gives IT organizations greater flexibility with their selection of physical network and storage devices and allows Xen to be implemented on just about any x86 environment.

Configuring & Implementing...

Hardware Compatibility for Domain-0

The following URLs offer a list of supported and tested hardware maintained by the user community. While this does not represent every configuration that will run Xen without issues, it will give you an idea of the type of hardware users have successfully implemented Xen with. For example, if you find an HP, Dell, or IBM server on the list, you can be sure the network interface cards and storage adapters used by the server will work in just about any other server with the same hardware, even though other servers are not listed. You can find the hardware compatibility list at:

http://wiki.xensource.com/xenwiki/HardwareCompatibilityList
or
http://hcl.xensource.com/

If you would like to add your configuration to the list, XenSource offers a XenTest tool that will assess your hardware platform's compatibility and report the results. You can download this tool at the following sites:

HTTP   www.xensource.com/xen/downloads/dl_x30tcd.html

BitTorrent   www.xensource.com/xen/downloads/dl_x30tcd_bt.html

---

WARNING

You should minimize the number of processes running inside Domain-0, or dom0. This domain is a highly privileged domain. As such, any instability or system compromise induced by a running process will impact all guest domains as well. In addition, dom0 shares the same physical hardware that the guest domains are using. As dom0 consumes more resources, fewer will be available to domUs.

The Virtual Hardware API includes a control interface that manages the exposure of physical devices, both creation and deletion, through the following virtual I/O devices:

- Virtual Network Interfaces (VIFs)
- Virtual Firewall and Routers (VFRs)
- Virtual Block Devices (VBDs)

Each virtual I/O device has an Access Control List (ACL) associated with it. Similar to ACLs for a file system or network resource, this ACL contains the information about the domUs that have access to the devices, as well as restrictions and the type of access allowed—for instance, read-only, write, and so on.

The control interface as well as aggregated statistics that profile the state of the Xen system components, are exported to a suite of User Mode management tools run in dom0. These tools can be used to:

- Create and delete domUs
- Create and delete virtual I/O devices
- Monitor network activity
- Migrate live virtual machines from one Xen host to another
- Monitor performance on a systemwide or per-domain level

A complete list of management tools, both native as well as third-party, are discussed in greater detail in Chapters 14 and 15.

The Virtual Hardware API is also responsible for managing the transfer of control interactions between Xen and the overlying domUs. It does so through the use of hypercalls, synchronous calls from the domains to Xen, and events—an asynchronous mechanism to deliver notifications from Xen to the domains.

The hypercall interface allows the guest operating system to perform privileged operations by initiating a trap in the hypervisor. This is done in a manner similar to the system calls that the operating system would perform to underlying hardware, except that they occur from Ring-1 to Ring-0. These CPU- and memory-bound instructions are then carried out by the hypervisor against the physical hardware resources.

Comparatively, Xen communicates with the domains via an asynchronous event mechanism in the same manner the guest operating system would communicate through device interrupts. The control interface takes advantage of this event mechanism to send other important events, such as domain termination requests. Each event is sent as a flag to a particular type of occurrence. The occurrence can be an acknowledgement that a domain request has been completed or be used to notify the domain of a change of state in its operating environment. Though the hypervisor is responsible for updating each domain's queue of pending events, it is the responsibility of the domain itself to respond to event notifications, the deferral of event handling, and to reset the queue. This makes the event mechanism very lightweight from the hypervisor's perspective and accomplishes the objective we discussed earlier, to have the hypervisor share the burden with the guest operating systems themselves.

To better understand Xen's architecture, we will take a behind-the-scenes look at Xen, including the virtual machine abstraction and interfaces. We will reflect on how Xen virtualizes the following compute elements:

- CPU
- Memory Management
- I/O

CPU Virtualization

On the x86 processor architecture, virtualization of the CPU presents several challenges, especially for guest operating systems that assume they are running directly on top of the hardware in Ring-0. While the x86 architecture provides four privileged rings or levels, the typical operating system only uses two: Ring-0 and Ring-3. In a typical VMM for x86, the operating system would coexist with applications in Ring-3. To protect itself, it would run in a completely different and unique address space, indirectly passing control to and from the application via the VMM. This can lead to several isolated inefficiencies that impact performance and flexibility.

An efficient approach to address this issue is to take advantage of the unused privileged levels, Ring-1 and Ring-2. These rings have not been used by an x86 operating system since IBM's OS/2. Any operating system that complies with this arrangement (the use of Ring-0 and Ring-3 only) can, technically, be ported to run on Xen. The operating system would be modified to execute in Ring-1, which still provides isolation and protection from other domUs and keeps it from executing high-privileged Ring-0 instructions, but offers improved isolation from User Mode applications.

Xen paravirtualizes a guest operating system running in a domU by mandating the validation and execution of instructions within Xen. If the domU attempts to execute a privileged instruction, it is trapped and failed by the hypervisor. However, an extended interface is presented to dom0, allowing it to create and boot other domains. This interface also allows dom0 access to high-level control operations such as CPU scheduling. CPU virtualization by Xen must account for exceptions, CPU scheduling, and time. Table 12.5 lists the common hypercalls used in Xen to manage CPU virtualization.

Table 12.5 Xen CPU Hypercalls

Category	Hypercall	Description
Virtual CPU Setup	set_callbacks	Register events callbacks for event processing.
	set_trap_table	Insert entries into the domain's unique trap handler table.
	vcpu_op	Provided for the management of virtual CPUs. Can be used to bring vCPUs up and down to test their current status.
CPU Scheduling and Timer	sched_op_new	Used to request the scheduling of a privileged operation with the hypervisor.
	set_timer_op	Used to request a timer event at a specific system time.
Context Switching	stack_switch	Used to request a kernel stack switch from the hypervisor.
	fpu_taskswitch	Used to facilitate, save, and restore a floating point state, enabling the guest to trap such activity and save/restore the state in a single call.
	switch_vm86	Allows guests to run in vm86 mode.

Exceptions

Xen takes an unique approach to dealing with exceptions. Using a special hypercall, *set_trap_table*, each domain maintains its own unique and dedicated table of trap handlers. Exceptions, such as memory faults and operating system traps, are addressed using trap handlers found in a specialized exception stack frame. This stack frame is identical to that found in the underlying x86 hardware platform, requiring very little modification of the exception process code in the guest operating system. Consequently, exceptions are handled two ways. The first is catered to system calls in the guest operating system and takes advantage of an accelerated exception handler that is registered by each guest and accessed directly by the processor. Although Xen still performs validation to trap privileged instructions, these system calls are carried out at near-native speeds without having to be executed in Ring-0. In other words, Xen does not actually execute the system call on behalf of the guest. The second is for page faults, a difficult and rather impossible exception to address without the involvement of the hypervisor. The technique used for system calls cannot be performed for page faults since they must be carried out in Ring-0 by Xen. Such exceptions are carried out by Xen and the register values stored for retrieval by the guest in Ring-1.

CPU Scheduling

CPU scheduling is critical in server virtualization technology. It is the means in which virtual CPU (vCPU) are carried out by the hypervisor on the underlying CPU architecture. In order to optimize scheduling and allow near-native performance, the scheduling scheme must be efficient and not waste any processing cycles. These types of schemes are referred to as work-conserving; that is, they do not allow CPU resources to go unused. So long as there is capacity enough to execute instructions and there are instructions to be executed, work-conserving schemes will assign trapped guest instructions and assign them to physical CPUs to be carried out. If the workload in not congested, such schemes operate like simple first-in-first-out (FIFO) queuing schemes. However, should the processor queue become congested, the instructions will be queued and will be executed based on the priority and weight set in the scheduling scheme.

In comparison, non-work-conserving queue servicing may allow CPU capacity to go unused. In such cases, there is no advantage to executing instructions sooner than necessary, and downstream physical CPU resources may be spared by limiting instruction execution to the rate at which they can be carried out. It is possible to combine both work-conserving and non-work-conserving schemes in the same hypervisor.

One of the CPU schedulers available in Xen is based on the Borrowed Virtual Time (BVT) scheduling scheme. This is a hybrid algorithm that is both work-conserving and has mechanisms for low-latency dispatch, or domain wake-up, if a domain receives an event notification. The latter is important in a hypervisor to minimize the effect of virtualization on operating system subsystems designed to run in a timely manner. BVT accomplishes its low-latency characteristic by making use of virtual-time warping. This mechanism breaks the rules of "fair-share" and grants early, low-latency favor to domains woken up due to an event. Xen offers two scheduling schemes, Simple Earliest Deadline First (sEDF) and Credit schedulers, and makes it possible to implement a custom scheme of your own through a uniform API for CPU schedulers. The Credit scheduler is optimized for SMP platforms and is the preferred choice. Credit-based scheduling will survive the retirement of sEDF when deprecated in future versions of Xen. BVT is a Credit scheduler.

Scheduling parameters are managed on a per-domain basis using the User Mode management tools running in dom0. While typical credit schedulers running on an SMP host will dynamically move across the physical CPUs in a work-conserving manner to maximize domain and system processor throughput, vCPUs can also be restricted to execute only on a subset of the host's physical CPUs, called pinning. For example, you may want an application server running in a particular domU to only run on CPU 2 and 3 of a four CPU server. Even if CPUs 0 and 1 have free cycles, they will not execute instructions for that domain—hence, the non-work-conserving ability of the hybrid scheduling model.

To view your current sEDF scheduling settings for all domains, run the following command without any parameters:

```
xm sched-sedf
```

To see the credit-based settings, you can execute the *xm sched-credit* with the –d option referencing the target domain ("1" in our example), as follows:

```
xm sched-credit -d 1
```

The output will indicate the cap as well as the relative weight (the default value is 256), as follows. Note that this command gives you the values for a single domain rather than an overall look at all domains, as with the *xm sched-sedf* command.

```
{'cap': 0, 'weight': 256}
```

TIP

Xen provides a command-line interface to manage schedulers. In the following, the first example references the syntax for customizing the sEDF scheduler for a specific domU, while the second is the syntax for customizing the Credit scheduler.
Example #1. sEDF Scheduler Customization:

```
xm sched-sedf <dom-id> <period> <slice> <latency-hint> <extra>
<weight>
```

Example #2. Credit Scheduler Customization:

```
xm sched-credit –d <dom-id> -w <weight> –c <cap>
```

For more information on defining the sEDF scheduler, as well as others available with Xen, visit http://wiki.xensource.com/xenwiki/Scheduling. To learn more about Credit-based scheduling, visit http://wiki.xensource.com/xenwiki/CreditScheduler.

Time

Within a virtual infrastructure, timing becomes critical and can become confusing for guest operating systems. They need to know about both real and virtual time. Real time, referred to as wall-clock time, is managed by the hypervisor; however, virtual time becomes even more important to the guest operating system and for the scheduling of time-sensitive operations. There are several concepts to consider when discussing time in Xen. The following is a list of those concepts and a brief description:

- **System Time**   A 64-bit counter that holds the number of nanoseconds since system boot. At start-of-day, a guest's system time clock represents the time since that domain was created or started.

- **Wall-Clock Time**   This is the time from dom0's perspective, and is maintained by dom0. The time is presented in seconds and microseconds since January 1, 1970, adjusting for leap years. As the key reference of time, it is important that this time be as accurate as possible. One way to do so is to utilize a Network Time Protocol (NTP) client within dom0.

- **Domain Virtual Time**   This time is similar to the system time, but only progresses when the domain is scheduled. Time stops when the domain is de-scheduled. Virtual time is important (as noted in the previous section on CPU Scheduling), because the share of the CPU that a domain receives is based on the rate at which virtual time increases.

- **Cycle Counter Time**   This timer is used to provide a fine-grained reference of time. Cycle counter time is used to extrapolate the other timers, or time references. It is important that the time is synchronized between each physical CPU.

Xen maintains timestamps for both system time and wall-clock time and exports those timestamps through a page of memory shared between Xen and each domain. Xen provides the cycle counter time when each timestamp is calculated, as well as the CPU frequency in hertz (Hz). This allows each guest to accurately extrapolate system and wall-clock times by factoring in the current cycle counter time. Without this extrapolation, the time references would often be inaccurate since the values in the shared page memory may be stale. In addition, the timestamps also have a version number associated with them. This version number is incremented twice for each update of each timestamp. First, it is incremented before updating timestamps, and then a second time after the update completes successfully. The version numbers are compared by the guest by checking to see if the two numbers match. If they do, the guest can assume that the time read is in a consistent state. If not, the guest knows that a timestamp update is in progress and returns to read the time values after the update has completed.

In addition to real and virtual time, Xen incorporate timers to help maintain accurate time in the guest operating system. Xen uses two types of timers. The first is a periodic timer that sends a timer event to the currently executing (awake) domain every 10 ms. A timer event is also sent by the Xen scheduler to a domain when it is scheduled. The guest OS uses these events to make time adjustments while it is inactive. The second type is an intentionally scheduled timer requested by each domain using the *set_timer_op* hypercall. This timer can be used by a guest to implement the timeout concept. For example, if the guest schedules a timed event when making a hypercall to write to virtual memory and the corresponding notification of success has not been received when the scheduled timed event is received, the guest can timeout the original operation.

Memory Virtualization

Memory virtualization is probably the most difficult task that a VMM must perform. Xen is responsible for managing the allocation of physical memory to domains, and for ensuring the safe use of the paging and segmentation hardware. Since several domains share the same memory, care must be taken to maintain isolation. The hypervisor must ensure that no two unprivileged domains, or domUs, access the same memory area. Each page or directory table update must be validated by the hypervisor to ensure that domains only manipulate their own tables. Domains may batch these operations to be more efficient through sequential updates. Segmentation is virtualized in a similar manner, placing the hypervisor in a gate-keeper role to ensure that the domains' segments do not overlap or are invalid in some way or other.

Similar to CPU virtualization, the Xen guest must trap any privileged calls that would require Ring-0 access and pass them to the hypervisor using hypercalls. Table 12.6 highlights the main hypercalls used to manage memory virtualization. To better understand how Xen manages memory, we will discuss memory allocation, virtual address translation, and page tables types and segmentation.

Table 12.6 Xen Memory Hypercalls

Category	Hypercall	Description
Page Table Management	mmu_update	Updates the domain's page table, usually in batch.
	update_va_mapping	Used to update a single page table entry (PTE) for a specific virtual memory address rather than in batch.
	mmuext_op	Used to perform extended memory operations, such as cache flushing, or to reassign page ownership.
	vm_assist	Used to toggle various memory management modes.
Virtual Address Translation	set_gdt	Used to create a new global descriptor table (GDT) for a domain.
	update_descriptor	Used to update either global or local descriptor tables (GDT/LTD).

Memory Allocation

As we have been discussing, in addition to allocating a portion of the physical system RAM for its own private use, Xen also reserves a small portion of every virtual address space. This allocation is dependent on the underlying platform, as Figures 12.3 and 12.4 illustrate.

NOTE

> While the x86 architecture can theoretically support up to 64 GB in PAE mode and up to 8 TB for x64 implementations, only XenEnterprise can utilize the full amount of RAM in such systems. XenServer and XenExpress are limited to 8 GB and 4 GB, respectively.

Figure 12.3 Memory Allocation for 32-bit x86 with and without PAE

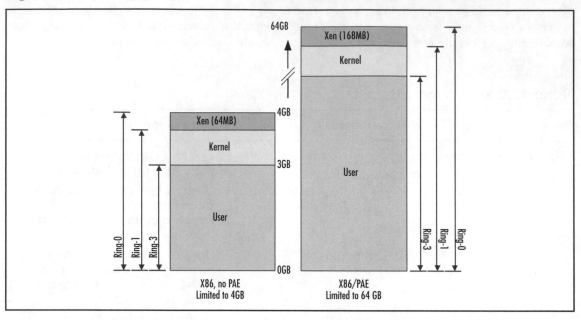

Figure 12.4 Memory Allocation for x64

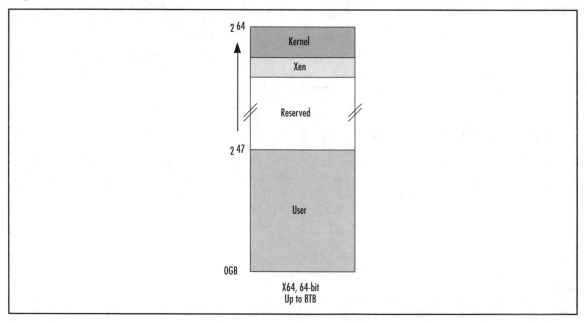

In 32-bit x86 architecture, with and without PAE, segmentation is used to protect the Xen hypervisor from the kernel. The reservation of the 64 MB, or 168 MB respectively, region does not impact the speed at which system calls are serviced. In comparison, the x64 architecture is quite

generous with the reservation allocation to Xen; however, there is no protection from segment limits as in the x86 architecture. This requires Xen to use page-level protection tactics to protect the hypervisor from kernel memory operations.

Focusing on allocations of the domUs, each domain has a maximum and current consumed physical memory allocation. Xen has implemented a balloon driver concept for each domain, enabled independently, that allows the operating system to adjust its current memory allocation up to the maximum limit configured. This allows "unused" allocation to be consumed in other areas, potentially allowing for stable over-commitment of memory resources. Because of this constantly changing memory allocation, combined with the creation and termination of domains, memory is allocated and freed dynamically at a granularity of the page-level. Xen cannot guarantee that a domain will receive a contiguous allocation of physical memory to use. While this breaks the rules of most x86-compatible operating systems, Xen makes up for it with the use of pseudo-physical memory compared to machine, or true physical, memory. Machine memory refers to the total amount of RAM in the physical host, including any reservations made to Xen. Machine memory is made up of 4kB page frames, whether allocated to Xen or to a domU, and is counted in a linear fashion regardless of that allocation. Pseudo-physical memory is the abstraction of those page frames on a per-domain basis.

This is how Xen "fools" each domain into thinking it has a contiguous stretch of memory starting always with frame 0. As machine memory frames leap and skip frame numbers, the pseudo-physical memory continues to represent a consistently numbered, and hence contiguous, page space. This is achieved without any pixie dust, but rather through the use of two tables. The first is readable by the hypervisor and all domains and maps machine page frames to pseudo-physical ones (machine-to-physical). The second is supplied to each domain independently, and maps the inverse, pseudo-physical page frames to machine ones (physical-to-machine). Using both tables, the domain is able to provide the abstraction to facilitate even the pickiest of operating systems.

Page Tables and Segmentation

In the x86 architecture, the memory is divided into three kinds of addresses, logical, linear, and physical. A logical address is a storage location address that may or may not relate directly to a physical location. The *logical address* is usually used when requesting information from a controller. A *linear address* (or a flat address space) is memory that is addressed starting with 0. Each subsequent byte is referenced by the next sequential number (0, 1, 2, 3, and so on) all the way to the end of memory. This is how most non-x86 CPUs address memory. The x86 architecture uses a segmented address space in which memory is broken up into 64KB segments, and a segment register always points to the base of the segment currently being addressed. The 32-bit mode in this architecture is considered a flat address space, but it too uses segments. A *physical address* is an address represented by bits on a physical address bus. The physical address may be different from the logical address, in which case the memory management unit translates the logical address into a physical address.

The CPU uses two units to transform the logical address into physical addresses. The first is called the *segmented unit* and the other is called the *paging unit*, as illustrated in Figure 12.5.

Figure 12.5 Segmented and Paging Units Convert Address Spaces

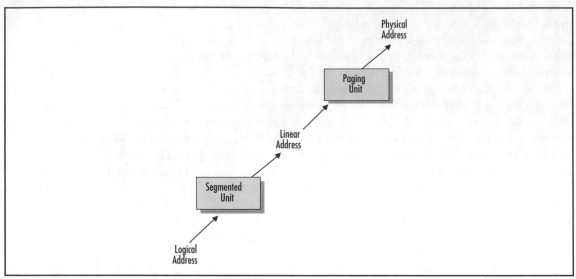

The basic idea behind the segmentation control unit model is that memory is managed using a set of segments. Essentially, each segment is its own address space. A segment consists of two components, the *base address* that contains the address of some physical memory location and the *length value* that specifies the length of the segment. Each segment is a 16-bit field called a *segment identifier* or *segment selector*. x86 hardware consists of a few programmable registers called *segment registers*, which hold these segment selectors. These registers are cs (code segment), ds (data segment), and ss (stack segment). Each segment identifier identifies a segment that is represented by a 64-bit (eight bytes) *segment descriptor*. These segment descriptors are stored in a global descriptor table (GDT) and can also be stored in a local descriptor table (LDT).

Each time a segment selector is loaded onto segment registers, the corresponding segment descriptor is loaded from memory into a matching CPU register. Each segment descriptor is eight bytes long and represents a single segment in memory. These are stored in LDTs or GDTs. The segment descriptor entry contains both a pointer to the first byte in the associated segment represented by the Base field and a 20-bit value (the *Limit* field), which represents the size of the segment in memory.

The paging unit, on the other hand, translates the linear addresses into physical ones as shown in Figure 12.5. A set of linear addresses are grouped together to form pages. These linear addresses are contiguous in nature—the paging unit maps these sets of contiguous memory to a corresponding set of contiguous physical addresses called *page frames*. Note that the paging unit visualizes RAM to be partitioned into a fixed size of page frames.

The data structure that maps these pages to page frames is called a *page table* (*PT*). These page tables are stored in the main memory and are properly initialized by the operating system kernel before enabling the paging control unit.

The translation of linear addresses into their corresponding physical location is a two-step process. The first step converts the address space from a translation table called *Page Directory* (*PD*) to a second

table called the PT. The second step converts the address space from the PT to the required
page frame.

So what does this all mean to Xen?

Xen uses the paging unit more than it does the segmentation unit. Each segment descriptor uses
the same set of addresses for linear addressing, thus minimizing the need to use the segmentation
unit to convert logical addresses to linear addresses. By using the paging unit more than the
segmentation unit, Xen greatly facilitates efficient memory management for the hypervisor and the
guest domains.

Returning to our discussion on memory virtualization, you will recall that the Xen hypervisor has
only one role in this area, which is to validate the page table updates passed via hypercall to ensure safety
and isolation. To aid in this validation effort, Xen associates a type and reference count with each physical
machine page frame. A frame may have any one (and exactly one) of the following types at any point:

- Page Directory (PD)
- Page Table (PT)
- Local Descriptor Table (LDT)
- Global Descriptor Table (GDT)
- Writable (RW)

Since Xen's involvement is only to manage "write" operations, guests can map and access any
of its own page frames without intervention from the hypervisor, regardless of the frame type.
However, a frame cannot be reallocated to another use using the *mmu_update* hypercall until its
reference count is zero. Frames can also be pinned to PD or PT after the hypervisor has completed
the validation of an entry, allowing guests to control the allocation of frames for page-table use.
Through this mechanism, Xen can give the guests the illusion of being able to write to memory
pages directly. When a Xen-aware (or paravirtualized) guest wants to write to a memory page of type
PD or PT, it can request that it be writable by using the *vm_assist* hypercall in conjunction with
mmu_update. Xen then allows the write operation to succeed, but traps it. The page is temporarily
removed from the page table until validated by Xen and reconnected. But again, pinned frames
cannot be reallocated to another frame type until they are unpinned and the reference count zeroed.

While this level of interaction with the hypervisor may appear costly from a resource perspective,
efficiency can be maintained by executing a series of hypervisor calls in batch rather than
performing a single hypercall for each operation. This is done making use of the *multicall* hypercall.
This technique can be used to highly optimize hypercall-intensive actions, such as context switches,
which may require several calls to both CPU and memory virtualization components in the Xen
hypervisor.

Virtual Address Translation

The management of memory is directly impacted by page tables and the Translation Lookaside Buffer
(TLB). The page table is the data structure used by a computer system to store the mapping between
virtual addresses and physical addresses. The TLB is a cache in a CPU that is used to improve the
speed of virtual address translation. It has a fixed number of entries containing part of the page table
that translate virtual memory addresses into physical machine addresses.

The TLB is typically content-addressable memory that uses the virtual addresses as a key that can be given as search input returns the physical address as a search result. If the search returns a match for the virtual memory address—in other words, the translation is successful—the physical address is used to access memory. If the virtual address cannot be found in the TLB, the translation takes an alternate route to identify the physical address via the page table, usually resulting in a longer operation that is costly from a resource perspective. The process can be even longer if the translation tables have been swapped out to secondary storage, such as a page or swap file on the hard drive. Some processor architectures provide a software-managed TLB, in particular RISC architecture such as SPARC, Alpha, and MIPS. However, the x86 CPU architecture does not have a software-managed TLB, relying on hardware to service TLB requests and handle misses. Refer to the sidebar for more information on TLB misses.

Thus lies the challenge for x86-targeted VMMs such as Xen. In order to achieve the highest memory performance possible, all valid translations must be present in the hardware-accessible page table. The x86 architecture does not tag the TLB (a process to indicate mappings that have been used); address space switches (between the hypervisor's and the domains' address spaces) require a complete TLB flush. Placing this burden on the hypervisor or control domains, typically dom0, would be costly. Instead, the developers of Xen opted to tackle this problem in two ways. First, in a manner consistent with other virtualization obstacles, the responsibility is placed on the guest operating systems to allocate and manage the hardware page tables, thus relieving and lightening the load of the hypervisor, whose role is reduced to validation of page table updates to ensure safety and isolation. Second, Xen utilizes a dedicated memory range for itself, avoiding the dreaded TLB flush that occurs when entering and leaving the hypervisor. More is discussed on this in the section titled "Memory Allocation" earlier in this chapter.

Architecture Concepts…

Translation Lookaside Buffer Miss

When a Translation Lookaside Buffer (TLB) miss occurs, two schemes are commonly found in modern architectures. With hardware TLB management, such as the type found in the x86 architecture, the CPU itself walks the page tables to see if there is a valid page table entry for the specified virtual address. If an entry exists, it is loaded into the TLB and the TLB access is retried. This time the access will hit, and the program can proceed normally. If the CPU finds no valid entry for the virtual address in the page tables, it raises a page fault exception, which the operating system must handle. Handling page faults usually involves bringing the requested data into physical memory, setting up a page table entry to map the faulting virtual address to the correct physical address, and restarting the program.

With software-managed TLBs, a TLB miss generates a "TLB miss" exception, and the operating system must walk the page tables and perform the translation in software.

The operating system then loads the translation into the TLB and restarts the program from the instruction that caused the TLB miss. Like with hardware-based TLB management, if the operating system finds no valid translation in the page tables, a page fault has occurred, and the operating system must handle it accordingly.

To illustrate the performance impact of a TLB miss in the x86 architecture, take into consideration the typical hit time of 0.5 to 1.0 clock cycles to find a virtual address in the TLB. If a TLB miss occurs and the CPU resorts to walking the page table to find the virtual address, the miss penalty can range from 10 to 30 additional clock cycles. If the TLB hit rate for a particular system took one clock cycle, a miss took 30 clock cycles, and the TLB miss rate was 10 percent, the effective memory cycle rate would average 3.9 clock cycles per memory access, or almost four times slower than its potential.

Correlating this to CPU selection, a CPU with larger cache can make a substantial performance improvement. Even with the multicore architectures available for x86 and x64 platforms, a larger cache shared by all the cores is better than an individual cache per core. For example, the dual-core Intel Xeon 5050 processor running at 3.0 GHz with 2 MB of L2 cache per core has lower performance than the Intel Xeon 5110 running at 1.6 GHz with 4 MB L2 cache shared between the cores. Though not the only reason for the performance increase, the cache model does contribute. Since both cores can be load-balanced to execute operations, they have a better chance of finding virtual addresses in the shared TLB and can reduce page table walks.

Page table creation is managed by each guest. When a new page table is created, the guest operating system allocates addresses from its own memory reservation and registers it with Xen after initialization. Though residing in its memory space, the guest gives us direct write privileges to the hypervisor, which validates any updates passed to it from the guest through hypercalls. Xen does not guarantee that the page table memory is contiguous, although the guest operating system believes it is; in fact, in most cases, it is not contiguous. In addition, the memory reserved by Xen is not able to be mapped as page-table memory for any guest.

Finally, Xen supports the use of shadow page tables. When using this technique, Xen creates an identical replica of the page tables allocated and initialized by the guest operating system. The guest reads and writes from its resident version of the page tables, while Xen copies all changes in real time to the shadow page table. If a domain commits a page table update that generates a fault, Xen will either send and event notification to the operating system to handle the page fault or, in more serious cases, it will terminate the domain. Either way, the safety and isolation of dom0 and the other domUs is maintained. This technique is useful for operating systems whose CPU and memory operations cannot be paravirtualized, such as Microsoft Windows, and to optimize live XenVM migrations of paravirtualized guests.

I/O Virtualization

Virtualizing I/O devices, such as network interfaces and hard drives, follows a school of thought similar to CPU and memory virtualization. That is, the virtual machine monitor can emulate the underlying hardware or it can work together with modified and highly customized software running in the guest virtual machines to optimize I/O operations for performance, reliability, and security. To be successful at fully virtualizing I/O devices, the VMM must not only look like the underlying hardware but must also be compatible with the software device drivers to be used, as well as emulate things like interrupts, data buses, and resource sharing of the actual physical hardware. This task can often lead to substantial overhead in the VMM and impacted performance.

Waiving any attempt at emulation, the Xen makes use of paravirtualization abstracts to present I/O devices to unprivileged domains containing supported guest operating systems. These abstracts are less complex than the ones for CPU and memory, and they often do not require modification of the guest operating system. Instead, paravirtualization can be accomplished by installing device drivers that are coded to be Xen-aware and interact with the hypervisor APIs (see Table 12.7 for a list of common hypercalls for I/O) that expose the communication to and from the actual physical I/O devices. So while Microsoft Windows and other "closed" operating systems must rely on HVM support to virtualize CPU and memory operations, they can take advantage of the benefits of paravirtualization for I/O. This design is both efficient and meets all requirements for protection and isolation.

Table 12.7 Xen I/O Hypercalls

Category	Hypercall	Description
Event Channels	event_channel_op	Used for all operations on event channels and ports.
Grant Tables	grant_table_op	Used to managed map/unmap, set, dump, or transfer commands against grant tables.
I/O Configuration	physdev_op	Used to set and query IRQ configuration details and other PCI BIOS operations.

I/O data is transferred to and from guest domains and Xen using shared-memory, asynchronous descriptor rings. We will discuss these rings shortly, but note that these rings are key to providing a high-performance mechanism to communicate with Xen when passing buffer information through the system while also providing a means for the hypervisor to perform its validation checks efficiently.

This section will triage the myriad components required to effectively paravirtualize I/O in addition to providing greater insight into the tricks-of-the-trade and up-and-coming techniques available through hardware innovation, including the following:

- Device I/O Rings
- Event Channels

- Virtual I/O Devices and Split Device Drivers
- Driver Domains
- Software and Hardware IOMMUs

Device I/O Rings

With the hypervisor's role of providing an abstraction layer that both protects and isolates guest operating systems from I/O devices, it is important that a means to transfer data be implemented that allows data to move quickly with little overhead. Two factors have led to the design of the mechanism used in Xen: resource management and event notification. The developers of Xen attempted to reduce the amount of work required when processing data in the event an interrupt is received by a device and to thus provide a level of resource accountability. This was accomplished by:

- Managing the asynchronous buffers at a level where the processing time can be correctly accounted for against the appropriate and benefiting domain.

- Reducing crosstalk in I/O buffers by requiring guest operating systems to commit a portion of their memory allocation for device I/O rather than using the shared buffer pool.

- Using the hypervisor to pin the underlying page frames, similar to memory management procedures discussed earlier, to protect data during transfer.

Within the structure of the I/O rings are inbound and outbound queues. These queues do not contain any actual data, but rather act as pointers to I/O buffers allocated by the guest operating systems referenced by I/O descriptors. Working with these queues are pairs of producers and consumers. Each domain has its own producer and consumer used to access the I/O rings, and the Xen hypervisor has a shared producer and consumer that communicates with the domains as well.

Let's step through the process to better understand how this mechanism works. This process is represented in Figure 12.6. As we walk through it, it may help to visualize a round table surface that spins around with the domains and the hypervisor at the outside edge of the perimeter of the ring. Although the table spins like a wheel in a set direction, the domains and hypervisor are static in location. When a domain wants to use an I/O device, it places a request in the requests queue (the spinning wheel) as the *request producer*. This request advances or updates a request pointer that is shared globally among the domains and the hypervisor. Xen then removes these requests for processing as the *request consumer*, advancing an associated request consumer pointer, which is private to Xen. Responses to the requests are also placed on this spinning wheel in the response queue. Xen places each response as the *response producer* on the ring and advances or updates a shared pointer for responses. The appropriate guest then picks up the response and advances or updates its private response pointer as the *response consumer*.

Figure 12.6 The Device I/O Ring

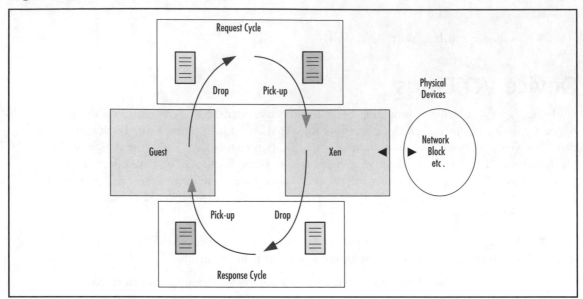

Since the I/O rings are asynchronous, order is not important or required. Each request has a unique identifier associated with it, which Xen uses to mark the corresponding response. There are advantages to the asynchronous nature of this mechanism. First, Xen can reorder the I/O operations efficiently in order to take advantage of scheduling and priority factors when interfacing with the physical devices. This can be particularly effective with block devices, such as mass storage drive arrays. Second, no formal notification or event is sent when a request is made. Xen does not pick up new requests from a domain until the guest sends a hypercall to do so. This allows guests to queue up a series of requests for a similar type of I/O transaction and then send a single hypercall, allowing Xen to pick and service the requests in a more efficient manner. This is particularly effective with network traffic. The same is true with responses. The "fast" transfer nature of BVT allows a domain to be awoken and to retrieve a batch of related responses in a single transaction rather than consuming cycles picking up each response individually. The process is efficient enough to satisfy time-sensitive operations such as certain TCP traffic inside the guest.

In some cases, however, the guest may not want reordering to occur. In such cases, the guest domain can explicitly pass down reorder barriers to prevent the hypervisor from reordering requests in batches. The barriers prevent the elevator scheduler managing the execution of I/O operations from performing its round-robin technique and to execute the operations in the domain's batch in sequence. This can be important in some block device operations, such as write-ahead logs, where the integrity of the data comes at the mercy of the sequence of data arrival.

Event Channels

We previously mentioned the event notification mechanism used by the Xen hypervisor to communicate with guest domains. At the foundation of this mechanism are event channels. Event channels are mediums through which events, the Xen equivalent of a hardware interrupt, are transmitted. The epitome of "the flip of the bit," events are simply a single bit that is transitioned to a value of "1" to trigger that the event has occurred.

Used in a reverse communication from hypervisor to guest, event notifications are received via an upcall (the reciprocal of the hypercall) from Xen. No mechanism exists to track multiple occurrences of the same event, so additional events are masked, or suppressed, until the bit is cleared again, and action must be taken by the guest operating system itself. However, event masking (setting the bit to "1" and leaving it at that value) can be done purposely by the guest to mimic the same functionality as disabling interrupts.

Event channels make use of a variety of commands available in the *event_channel_op* hypercall. These commands are used to set the even channel port to use for communication, to bind and unbind event sessions with domains, and to even bind and unbind event channel ports to specific IRQs. This makes capturing interrupts quite easy and flexible when modifying guest operating systems for paravirtualization in Xen.

Virtual I/O Devices and Split Device Drivers

Instead of providing access to physical devices, Xen offers virtualized views of them. This is not the same as presenting virtual emulation of devices, such as network interfaces or storage devices, but rather devices that guest domains can use to interface with the underlying physical I/O hardware.

When Xen boots and launches dom0, it exports a subset of the devices in the systems to the other domains, based on each domain's configuration. The devices are exported as *class devices*, either as block devices or network devices, but not as a specific hardware model. The interaction with these class devices is based on a translation between domains and the Xen hypervisor via a split device driver architecture. As illustrated in Figure 12.7, this architecture comprises two cooperating drivers: the *frontend driver* which runs in an unprivileged domU, and the *backend driver*, which runs in a

Figure 12.7 The Split Device Driver Architecture

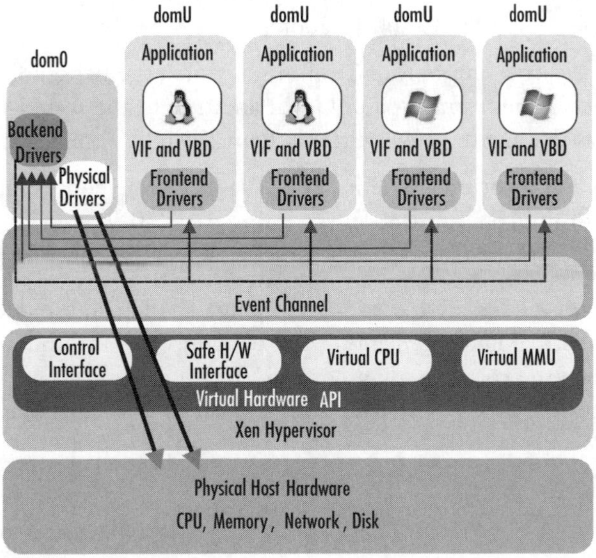

domain with real access to real hardware. While dom0 is usually the only domain that supports the backend drivers, it is possible to create additional privileged domains to fulfill this role.

The frontend driver appears to the domU guest operating system as a real device. The guest can interact with it just as it would any other device for which it had the appropriate drivers installed. It can receive I/O requests from its kernel, but since it does not have direct access to the hardware, it must pass those requests to the backend driver running in dom0. The backend driver, in turn, receiving the I/O requests, validates them for safety and isolation, and proxies them to the real device. When the I/O operation completes, the backend driver notifies the frontend driver that the operation was successful and ready to continue, which in turn reports the I/O completion to the operation system kernel.

The concepts we have discussed previously all come into play to make this happen. Device I/O rings and event channels are central to the virtual I/O architecture, as is one additional component—the Xenstore (which we will discuss in a minute). The Xenstore is used to set up a shared memory frame between the domU frontend and the dom0 backend in each domain.

Network I/O

To facilitate network I/O virtualization, Xen provides an abstraction of a virtual firewall-router (VFR). The VFR has one or more virtual interfaces (VIFs) that logically make up the communication interfaces of the VFR. Each VIF looks and acts like a standard network interface card, containing two I/O rings, one for transmission and the other for reception. The VFR contains the rules, as established by the guest OS, to control the movement data through each VIF in a manner similar to firewall rules.

The two I/O rings handle the payload of the network traffic going to and from the guest domain. The guest places transmission requests on the transmit I/O ring. Xen then makes a copy of the request's header and descriptor, validates it using the VFR rules, and, if all is well, pins the appropriate memory frames in the shared memory frame and performs the actual data transfer to the physical interface mapped to the VIF. The backend driver is responsible for all of this packet handling, which can be summarized as:

- **Validation**   Ensuring that an attempt to generate invalid traffic has occurred. This is done by analyzing the source MAC and IP address.

- **Scheduling**   Using a simple round-robin scheduler, the backend manages the transmission queue from the various running domUs. In addition to the round-robin scheduler, other schemes such as shaping or rate-limiting schemes can be applied.

- **Logging and Accounting**   The backend driver can be coded and configured to log characteristics of the communication traversing each VIF. The logging can be triggered based on network packet data—for example, when a SYN or FIN is received.

To receive data, empty page frames are used as temporary buffers in the guest operating system, just as they would be in a nonvirtual implementation. Xen demultiplexes incoming network traffic and divides the data up between the corresponding domain VIF. Xen again validates it against the VFR rules and, if all is well, exchanges the page buffer with a page frame in the actual shared memory frame.

Block I/O

Similar to network I/O, block devices are only accessible from privileged domains. dom0 has unrestricted access to physical disks, regardless of their type—IDE, SATA, SCSI, Fibre Channel, and iSCSI. Unprivileged domains utilize block device abstractions called virtual block devices (VBDs). A VBD works similar to a physical disk interface. One of the critical components for a high-performing disk subsystem is the ability of a typical operating system to reorder disk I/O requests intelligently and to efficiently retrieve and write data, reducing disk response times. This is possible through advanced scheduling schemes. In the virtual world, Xen has similar abilities, thus a VBD appears to a guest operating system just like a typical physical block device.

The VBD allows competing domains access to portions of a block storage device by using the backend/frontend driver architecture. As a split device driver, a single shared memory frame is used between the frontend and backend drivers for each VBD forming the device I/O ring used to send requests and receive responses. The backend driver has similar responsibilities as with network I/O, particularly in regards to validation, scheduling, and logging and accounting.

Trusted Platform Module and Other Devices

Practically any device can be abstracted and exported to guest domains using the frontend/backend architecture in paravirtualized guest operating systems. An example is the recent addition of Trusted Platform Module (TPM) devices to the supported Xen model. Virtual TPM (VTPM) devices enable domUs to access their own private TPM in a manner similar to built-in, hardware-based TPM devices. Implemented as a split driver, the guest exports a character device, /dev/tmp0, to User Mode application for communicating with virtual TPM, which is identical to the interface of an actual TPM device. The backend driver provides a single interface in the privileged domain, /dev/vtpm, listening for commands from all of the domains. All communication between guest domains and Xen are accomplished using a single I/O ring for sending requests and for sending responses in the opposite direction.

Driver Domains

Up till now, we have talked about an exclusive privileged domain, Domain-0. This domain has access to all hardware devices, and less privileged domains (domUs) perform I/O operations through it. In implementations containing large numbers of virtual machines, or virtual machines that require high levels of I/O utilization, dom0 can become overwhelmed with the burden of supporting the backend drivers for all of the virtual devices, as well as managing the overall Xen system.

Xen provides a way to help offload the burden of extensive consumer load through the creation of driver domains. Driver domains, or isolated driver domains (IDDs), are traditional guest domains that have been granted extended privileges, each with its own devices and consumers, as shown in Figure 12.8. The control interface in the Xen hypervisor allows dom0 to create device-specific guests and assign permissions necessary to directly access the hardware using unmodified device drivers.

While this may seem contrary to the purpose and function of guest domains, it offers a boon in improved and balanced I/O performance. It is assumed that each driver runs inside one and only one drive domain (dom0 or other). This maintains the reliability, maintainability, and manageability provided through driver and fault isolation.

Figure 12.8 User of Driver Domains

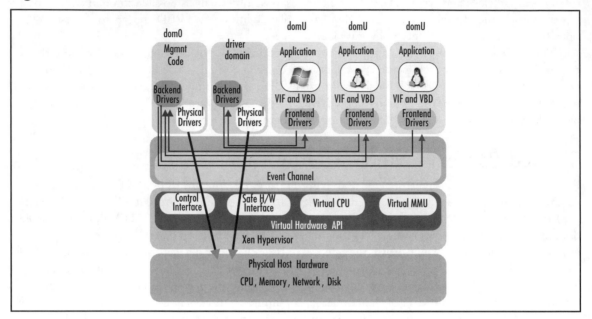

Since IDDs are guest domains themselves, they cannot utilize the conventional mechanisms to interact with other guest domains. They communicate with domUs through device channels, point-to-point communication links that facilitate asynchronous messaging between each side of the channel. dom0 uses the controller interface to introduce the guest operating system and IDD to each other.

One of the key benefits of device-driver domains is fault recovery. Not only are driver faults limited to the domain, and VIFs mapping to that physical interface, but the fault can be detected and the driver restarted. In worse cases, the driver domain itself can be killed and restarted without having to restart the dom0, leaving other virtual environments online and intact.

Software and Hardware IOMMUs

Some new types of devices, however, do not need to utilize the split driver architecture to provide high-performance I/O communication. To understand how this can be accomplished and under what conditions, we will first discuss various I/O Memory Management Units (IOMMUs), hardware constructs that can be emulated in software. IOMMUs provide two main functions, translation and device isolation, as follows:

- The IOMMU translates memory addresses from I/O space to physical space to allow a particular device to access physical memory potentially out of its range. It does this translation by providing an in-range address to the device and either translates the DMA access from the in-range address to the physical memory address on-the-fly or copies the data to the physical memory address.

- Also, IOMMUs can limit the ability of devices to access memory, used for restricting DMA targets.

SWIOTLB

IOMMUs are 32-bit and DMA-capable, and are able to access physical memory addresses higher than 4 GB. They can be programmed so that the memory region appears to be contiguous to the device on the bus. However, remapping can add a performance penalty during data transfers. There are several advantages to this, but the one most important for virtualization is isolation. Although IOMMUs are able to translate memory addresses, the translation must be available for the appropriate device only, but masked from others devices. Therein lies the challenge of IOMMUs in current system architectures.

IOMMUs can be found in two forms: software and hardware. The common forms of software IOMMUs are Software I/O Translation Buffer (SWIOTLB) and grant tables. Xen's implementation of SWIOTLB is based on the standard Linux distribution for IA64 since there are no hardware IOMMUs for that architecture. The Xen team has tweaked the implementation as of version 3.0.0, and runs the IOMMU in dom0. Using SWIOTLB is transparent to the drivers, and it uses DMA mapping in its architecture. The one drawback to this feature is that it requires contiguous blocks of physical memory (based on the DMA requirements), although configurable.

Grant Tables

The second form of software IOMMU, grant tables, provide a memory-sharing approach to I/O management. Grant tables allow pages of data to be shared and transferred between domains. These pages can be read, written to, or exchanged for the sake of providing a fast and secure means for unprivileged domains to receive indirect access to hardware. They support higher performance I/O because the guest operating system can make DMA calls directly into pages in its local memory rather than having to copy or flip pages from a privileged domain to a local memory page. However, as with everything else "Xen," it can only access the pages specified in the grant table, so safety is still maintained. Using the *gnttab_ grant_ foreign_access* hypercall, guest domains can advertise to the hypervisor that a page is available to be shared. Once the sharing is complete and the remote domain has accomplished its work, access is revoked using the *gnttab_end_ foreign_access* hypercall.

Grant tables help resolve the problem of IOMMUs needed to provide both translation and isolation. Working together with SWIOTLB, the two provide not only the translation functionality needed in an IOMMU but also protection by permissions managed at the table level. As CPU manufacturers continue to innovate and develop hardware acceleration into their chips, the translation that SWIOTLB may be replaced with hardware IOMMU equivalents, such as AMD's GART or Intel-VT features, but grant tables will probably last a lot longer.

The Xenstore

Referred to earlier in the chapter, the Xenstore is the primary mechanism for controlling activities such as setting up shared memory regions and event channels, managing notifications of guests of control events, and gathering and reporting status information from guests. The structure of the Xenstore is hierarchical in nature, with a directory-like traversal of a collection of key-value pairs. Each domain has a directory hierarchy containing store information, principally configuration info.

All the information is stored in a database, located at */var/lib/xenstored/tdb*. The store addresses certain key aspects of domain functionality. For example, a Xen bus is provided to facilitate device discovery when drivers are present or during the installation of new drivers. This is critical for plug-and-play functionality inside certain guest operating systems. Also, maintaining the configuration of a domain is as simple as updating references in its store hierarchy. Since domains can only modify the contents of their own directories, they are permitted to register for notifications about changes in their store tree and subtrees and to apply changes in a transactional fashion. For example, if you wanted to switch from using the host's physical CD-ROM drive for a guest domain to using an ISO file, you would use a management tool to update the store of that domain, letting the configuration of the */dev/cdrom* device be reconfigured to map to the ISO file—a change which would take place almost immediately. The contents of the ISO become available for use within the guest operating system without having to tear down and re-create the domain.

Looking at the store hierarchy, three main paths can be used:

- **/vm**   Contains configuration information about the domain.
- **/local/domain**   Stores information about the domain on the local node.
- **/tool**   Contains information about the various User Mode tools.

You can use the information in the store to develop a custom management interface or to perform simple queries within your Xen environment. Although the development of custom code interacting with the Xenstore is beyond the scope of this chapter, it is still worth discussing the type of information that each of the three paths contains, as well as the shell commands used to interact with the store itself.

The daemon spawned by *xend* at boot time, *xenstored*, exposes several commands you can use to manage the store and its contents, including the following:

- **xenstore-chmod**   Permits administrator and developers to manually change the permissions on arbitrary locations in Xenstore.
- **xenstore-list**   Outputs the keys, or categories, stored in the store hierarchical directory tree.
- **xenstore-read**   Outputs the value associated with a specific key in the store.
- **xenstore-write**   Used to change the value of a key within the store.
- **xenstore-exists**   Used to check for the existence of a particular key-value pair.

- **xenstore-ls**   Outputs the entire store hierarchical database tree, including all nodes and key-value pairs.
- **xenstore-rm**   Removes a key from the directory tree

Using a simple shell script, as follows, we can examine the complete store layout for all three paths for each domain, including dom0:

```
#!/bin/sh
function dumpkey() {
  local param=${1}
  local key
  local result
  result=$(xenstore-list ${param})
  if [ "${result}" != "" ] ; then
    for key in ${result} ; do dumpkey ${param}/${key} ; done
  else
    echo -n ${param}'='
    xenstore-read ${param}
  fi
}
for key in /vm /local/domain /tool ; do dumpkey ${key} ; done
```

Narrowing down the output from this script, we will examine a few significant cross-sections, beginning with the */vm* path. In the following output, configuration information for a guest domain is shown. From this output, we can see its UUID, learn that it uses hardware virtualization (HVM), identify the MAC address and VLAN for its VIFs, and determine what features have been enabled, such as ACPI, USB, and the serial console port.

```
/vm/ba2b02b2-7684-432b-b56f-62bf3e573095/image/ostype=hvm
/vm/ba2b02b2-7684-432b-b56f-62bf3e573095/image/kernel=/usr/lib/xen/boot/hvmloader
/vm/ba2b02b2-7684-432b-b56f-62bf3e573095/image/dmargs=-vcpus 1 -serial pty -acpi -
usb -usbdevice tablet -domain-name ba2b02b2-7684-432b-b56f-62bf3e573095 -net nic,
vlan=1,macaddr=00:16:3E:74:33:97,model=rtl8139 -net tap,vlan=1,bridge=xenbr0 -net
nic,vlan=2,macaddr=00:16:3E:A7:D5:EF,model=rtl8139 -net tap,vlan=2,bridge=xenbr1
/vm/ba2b02b2-7684-432b-b56f-62bf3e573095/image/device-model=/usr/lib/xen/bin/
qemu-dm
```

We can also determine uptime using the start_time field and what actions are taken for various events, such as reboot, poweroff, and crash events notifications. We also learn more about the CPU and memory allocations provided to the domain.

```
/vm/ba2b02b2-7684-432b-b56f-62bf3e573095/on_reboot=restart
/vm/ba2b02b2-7684-432b-b56f-62bf3e573095/start_time=1174892778.62
/vm/ba2b02b2-7684-432b-b56f-62bf3e573095/on_poweroff=destroy
/vm/ba2b02b2-7684-432b-b56f-62bf3e573095/on_xend_start=ignore
/vm/ba2b02b2-7684-432b-b56f-62bf3e573095/on_crash=restart
```

```
/vm/ba2b02b2-7684-432b-b56f-62bf3e573095/xend/restart_count=0
/vm/ba2b02b2-7684-432b-b56f-62bf3e573095/vcpus=1
/vm/ba2b02b2-7684-432b-b56f-62bf3e573095/vcpu_avail=1
/vm/ba2b02b2-7684-432b-b56f-62bf3e573095/memory=256
/vm/ba2b02b2-7684-432b-b56f-62bf3e573095/maxmem=256
```

In the following output, we trace the /local/domain path. This is a great place to identify information about a domain's virtual I/O devices. You can identify various configuration information about the frontend and device setup, including which backend device it maps to, the event-channel port, its current state, and statistics since start-of-day.

```
/local/domain/2/device/vbd/768/backend-id=0
/local/domain/2/device/vbd/768/virtual-device=768
/local/domain/2/device/vbd/768/device-type=disk
/local/domain/2/device/vbd/768/state=4
/local/domain/2/device/vbd/768/backend=/local/domain/0/backend/vbd/2/768
/local/domain/2/device/vbd/768/ring-ref=1664
/local/domain/2/device/vbd/768/event-channel=5
/local/domain/2/data/vbd/0/name=hda
/local/domain/2/data/vbd/0/total=8578932736
/local/domain/2/data/vbd/0/used=1998139392
/local/domain/2/device/vif/1/backend-id=0
/local/domain/2/device/vif/1/mac=00:16:3E:A7:D5:EF
/local/domain/2/device/vif/1/handle=1
/local/domain/2/device/vif/1/state=4
/local/domain/2/device/vif/1/backend=/local/domain/0/backend/vif/2/1
/local/domain/2/device/vif/1/tx-ring-ref=1893
/local/domain/2/device/vif/1/rx-ring-ref=1892
/local/domain/2/device/vif/1/event-channel=6
/local/domain/2/device/vif/1/request-rx-copy=1
/local/domain/2/device/vif/1/feature-no-csum-offload=0
/local/domain/2/device/vif/1/request-rx-copy-offset=2
```

Finally, we can see information about the operating system that is running inside the guest domain, such as the OS class, version, IP address, and boot environment.

```
/local/domain/2/attr/PVAddons/Installed=1
/local/domain/2/attr/PVAddons/MajorVersion=3
/local/domain/2/attr/PVAddons/MinorVersion=2
/local/domain/2/attr/PVAddons/BuildVersion=1960
/local/domain/2/attr/os/class=windows NT
/local/domain/2/attr/os/major=5
/local/domain/2/attr/os/minor=2
```

```
/local/domain/2/attr/os/build=3790
/local/domain/2/attr/os/platform=2
/local/domain/2/attr/os/spmajor=0
/local/domain/2/attr/os/spminor=0
/local/domain/2/attr/os/suite=272
/local/domain/2/attr/os/type=3
/local/domain/2/attr/os/boottype=0
/local/domain/2/attr/os/system32_dir=C:\WINDOWS\system32
/local/domain/2/attr/os/hal=hal.dll
/local/domain/2/attr/os/boot_options=FASTDETECT PV
/local/domain/2/attr/os/hotfixes/0/installed=1
/local/domain/2/attr/eth1/ip=192.168.100.180
/local/domain/2/data/os_name=Microsoft Windows Server 2003 Standard
Edition|C:\WINDOWS|\Device\Harddisk0\Partition1
```

Summary

The debate continued on which technique is better for companies large and small—full virtualization or paravirtualization. Full virtualization offers an emulation of the physical server's hardware resources (CPU, memory, disk, and network) through extensive binary translation and trapping techniques at the expense of performance degradation. However, because standard operating system distributions can be used without modification, full virtualization reduces the complexity and administrative overhead of deploying virtual machines.

In comparison, paravirtualization optimizes guest operating systems and makes them hypervisor-aware, making for a more symbiotic relationship between guests and the host's hypervisor. With tweaks for CPU and memory virtualization, responsibility of instruction execution is shared between virtual machines and the host, resulting in a lightweight hypervisor. However, because some guest operating systems cannot be modified, there are fewer compatible choices other than full virtualization.

Regardless of the ferocity of this debate, XenSource continues to lead the charge of Xen's paravirtualization team, consisting of its own development resource as well as developers from IBM, Intel, HP, and the open-source community, and has set out to preach the gospel of Xen and evangelize the open-source virtual machine monitor and its commercial derivatives. Combined with the latest server hardware, Xen continues to provide high-performance virtualization and greater compatibility with operating systems, such as the Microsoft Windows family. The key to its strength is the unique architecture, enabling efficient CPU, memory, and I/O virtualization, while providing a very manageable and intelligent platform for developers and administrators alike.

Solutions Fast Track

What Is Xen?

☑ Xen is a power-packed virtual machine monitor that allows multiple operating systems to run concurrently on the same physical server hardware.

☑ Xen's hypervisor takes its cues from the school of paravirtualization, a technique that presents a software interface that is similar, though not identical, to the underlying hardware.

☑ Xen includes features such as 32- and 64-bit guest support, live migration, and support for the latest processors from Intel and AMD, along with other experimental non-x86 platforms.

☑ The XenServer product family provides a range of virtualization platforms that offer ease of use, robust virtualization, and powerful management.

☑ Xen's hypervisor is available as an open-source release as well as a commercially supported and feature-enhanced suite of offerings, including the XenExpress, XenServer, and XenEnterprise products.

Xen's Virtualization Model Explored

☑ Xen's architecture is currently supported on x86 (with and without PAE) and x64. Limited support is also available for the IA-64 and POWERPC CPU architecture as well.

☑ In Xen's paravirtualization architecture, the hypervisor provides a lightweight support role to the overlying guests, taking the responsibility of access control and resource scheduling while allowing the guest operating systems to maintain accountability and responsibility for higher-level functions. This combination provides high-performance without the expense of the overhead associated with full virtualization.

☑ Xen's approach to paravirtualization is highly focused on maintaining the efficiency of (arguably in order of importance): memory management, CPU, and I/O operations.

☑ Guests are presented in a construct called domains, or the layer of abstraction that lies on top of the physical hardware and the Xen hypervisor and management APIs.

☑ Two types of domains are offered: privileged and unprivileged. Privileged domains, the principle called Domain-0 or dom0, are provided limited access to hardware resources; more important, though, they are granted the ability to create and terminate unprivileged domains, called Domain-Us or domUs, which they have full access to and control over.

☑ The Xen hypervisor executes in Ring-0, thus maintaining full control over all hardware resources. The overlying domains run in Ring-1 of the x86 architecture, providing isolation from one another while avoiding conflict with Ring-3 applications and processes.

☑ Within the user space of dom0 lie all of the management tools used to administer Xen, as well as the ability to interact with the control interface exposed by the hypervisor.

☑ System calls within the operating system are sent to the hypervisor as hypercalls. Communication back to the domains from the hypervisor is sent through an event notification mechanism.

CPU Virtualization

☑ Xen utilizes a trapping mechanism to handle exceptions from faults that occur in guest operating systems.

☑ The Xen hypervisor is responsible for managing the scheduling of guest domain instruction execution with the physical CPUs available in the underlying hardware platform. Several schedulers are available, including a Simple Earliest Deadline First (sEDF) and Credit scheduler optimized for SMP platforms.

☑ Utilizing Borrowed Virtual Time (BVT), Xen favors a work-conserving scheduling scheme while providing a low-latency "fast" dispatch when needed. Xen is able to deliver high levels of CPU performance inside guest domains with minimal overhead in the hypervisor itself.

☑ Xen guests must be aware of both real and virtual time.

☑ Utilizing a calculation of system time, wall-clock time, domain virtual time, and cycle counter time, a guest is able to maintain accurate time, even when idle over an extended period of time.

Memory Virtualization

☑ Memory virtualization is the most difficult and crucial element a virtual machine monitor like Xen must perform.

☑ Safety and isolation are critical to providing a reliable and stable platform for each guest operating system. As a result, Xen must ensure no two unprivileged domains access the same memory area.

☑ Aside from memory reserved to support the guest domains, Xen is allocated a dedicated portion of memory at the top of x86 systems, both with and without PAE. For x86 without PAE, Xen is allocated 64 MB; for x86 without PAE, Xen is allocated 168 MB.

☑ A similar reservation is provided on x64, although it is considerably larger and more generous. However, it does not benefit from segment limits as in the x86 architecture, which relies on page-level protection for the hypervisor from other memory operations.

☑ Although memory can be spread in a fragmented manner across the actual physical machine memory available on the host, Xen uses a construct called pseudo-machine memory to fool guest domains into believing they have a contiguous range of machine memory to use, making memory allocation very operating system friendly.

☑ Page tables, and the TLB, are used to manage memory frames and maintain the performance of memory operations in the guest operating system. Although each guest domain allocates and initializes its own memory space, Xen is responsible for efficient virtual address translation and ensuring the safety and isolation of memory operations.

I/O Virtualization

☑ Xen makes use of I/O rings in a producer-consumer relationship with the guest domains. The rings are asynchronous and allow flexible control of reordering by the guest and hypervisor. Request scheduling is managed by the hypervisor.

☑ Devices are presented as an abstraction class device, rather than an emulated copy of the physical device.

☑ Using an event notification mechanism to replace typical hardware interrupts, event channels facilitate the reverse communication from Xen to the guests. This is how guests know there's data waiting for them to pick up from I/O devices.

☑ To facilitate communication across the rings, Xen uses a bus to bridge data transfer between a frontend device driver installed in the unprivileged domain and a backend driver in the privileged domain.

- ☑ Besides dom0, other domains (still domUs in nature) can be created and granted direct access to physical I/O devices using unmodified drivers. These are called driver domains and can be created and used to improve isolation and performance.

- ☑ Virtual network interfaces (VIFs) and virtual block devices (VBDs) make up the abstraction of the I/O devices and are implemented in Xen along with rules and a shared memory space. They are responsible for validation, scheduling, and logging and accounting via the backend driver.

- ☑ IOMMU implementations in Xen are accomplished in software using SWIOTLB and grant tables. SWIOTLB provides the address translation for I/O operations, while grant tables manage permission, providing the protection that is needed as well.

The Xenstore

- ☑ The Xenstore is the configuration database for each domain, which includes dom0 executing in Xen. The file is located at /var/lib/xenstored/tdb.

- ☑ The store is represented as a hierarchical tree with three paths: /vm, which contains configuration information for the domain; /local/domain, which contains information about the local node; and /tool, which contains information about the tools used.

- ☑ The store enables real-time configuration management of guest domains. Using seven commands exported by xenstored, the store can be read and updated from a command-line or programmatically.

Frequently Asked Questions

Q: Which operating systems can be modified to take full advantage of paravirtualization?

A: At the time of this writing, any Linux distribution based on a 2.6 kernel, NetBSD 3.1 and newer, and Solaris 10 are currently tested and supported for the Xen hypervisor release 3.0 and newer. If you would like to see the most current compatibility list, visit http://wiki.xensource.com/xenwiki/OSCompatibility.

Q: How can I tell if the processor I am using supports HVM?

A: The Xen Wiki maintains a running list of HVM-compatible processors from Intel and AMD at: http://wiki.xensource.com/xenwiki/HVM_Compatible_Processors. If you have a recently released processor that does not appear on the list, check the Intel web site to see if the processor supports Intel-VT, or AMD's Web site for AMD-V support.

Q: I have an HVM-compatible processor, yet Xen won't let me create a full-virtualization domain. Why?

A: Most BIOS implementations give you the ability to disable SVM (AMD) or VMX (Intel) support. In some cases, the default is disabled. Check to make sure you have SVM or VMX enabled. If it is enabled and you still cannot create a full-virtualization domain, be sure Xen recognizes that feature for your processor. You can do this by running "grep vmx /proc/cpuinfo" for Intel or "grep svm /proc/cpuinfo" for AMD and looking for the appropriate flag. If you see the flag, check for the flag in the hypervisor capability set by running "cat /sys/hypervisor /properties/capabilities".

Q: Is it possible to access guest disk images outside of Xen?

A: The answer is both yes and no. Using tools such as iomount and kpartx, you can mount small and large disk images inside dom0 to access data. Be sure the guest is not running, and thus using the disk image, when you mount it, however. Those tools may have issues with some LVM volumes and are meant to work with block devices, not images installed as files.

Q: Do I need a server to run Xen?

A: No. Xen will run on virtually any platform based on the x86 architecture, including desktops and laptops. You must meet the minimum requirements, though. If you have a system with at least a Pentium 4 processor and 1 GB of RAM, you should have sufficient resources to support dom0, and at least a domU, without much suffering. See the Xen Wiki for updated information about requirements for the latest build of Xen.

## Chapter 13

Deploying Xen: Demystifying the Installation

Solutions in this chapter:

- **Determining Which Xen to Choose**
- **System Requirements**
- **Thinking Before You Start**
- **Installing Xen on a Free Linux Distribution**
- **Installing the XenServer Product Family**
- **Other Xen Installation Methods**
- **Configuring Xen**

☑ Summary

☑ Solutions Fast Track

☑ Frequently Asked Questions

Introduction

With Xen's roots in the open-source community, the original users of the hypervisor were skilled Linux experts that new their way around kernel development. As it has grown in popularity, Xen is now widely available to a diverse array of users of various backgrounds. Getting Xen up and running may appear to be a daunting task to newcomers, and taking advantage of every feature nearly impossible—but if you think yourself among the novices, don't worry. The installation really is not that complicated.

In this chapter, we will demystify the installation of Xen. You will learn what kind of machine you need for different Xen installations, walk through various methods for installing Xen, and, even more important, find out how to configure Xen, get connected, and get your first virtual machine up and running.

Determining Which Xen to Choose

When choosing your Xen platform, you should consider a couple of different options. Since Xen started out as an open-source product and most people are running their host platform, domain0 in Xen terminology, on a Linux machine, you can choose between Community, Commercial, or Enterprise Linux Distributions, or a custom Linux platform created by XenSource.

If you choose a Community Linux Distribution, such as Fedora Core, CentOS, Ubuntu, or OpenSuse, you will get a Xen version that is packaged and tested by the community, with a different set of GUI and command-line tools depending on the packager.

Open-source Linux Distributions give you the freedom to do everything yourself and mix and match tools just the way you like them. The disadvantage of this approach is that you need the experience to install, manage, and deploy them, and when you are in trouble, you either need to be able to rely on a local support partner or on the community.

Enterprise Linux Distributions will give you a fully tested version of the hypervisor, which has been certified to integrate seamlessly with existing tools to install and deploy packages. You will also have a support line to call and vent through when things go wrong, but it's going to cost you some money.

Then there is the XenSource platform, a commercial offering of Xen created by XenSource, the creators of Xen, that has one sole goal: making Xen easy. If you are not interested in deploying more Linux machines, this is probably the option you should go for. It's a well-supported platform by the original Xen authors and many OEMs, such as IBM and HP.

While getting Xen to run is for some people as easy as installing two packages on their favorite Linux platform, other people will be performing their very first Linux installation altogether. On the other hand, XenSource markets "Ten minutes to Xen" with their XenServer product family. This chapter will guide you through different ways of installing Xen with the goal of having a minimal virtual machine up and running by the end. We will also show you how to install Xen on a mainstream Linux distribution (Fedora Core 6), how to install the XenEnterprise product from XenSource, and install it as an RPM from XenSource on a general distribution.

In a typical Xen environment, you will be running a host operating system called dom0 and multiple guest operating systems called domUs. We will focus on using Linux as dom0, which is the default dom0 for the XenServer product family as well. Although most people use this configuration, some run dom0 under other Unix-style operating systems such as BSD or Solaris.

System Requirements

Depending on your needs, your system requirements will vary. Xen runs on most x86-compatible hardware that is more recent than the P6, or 686, family of processors. Ports to other architectures such as PowerPC are being worked on, but we will not be covering them. Concerning memory, the default 32-bit Xen supports 4 GB out-of-the-box. As of Xen 3.0, support for the PAE (Physical Address Extensions) has been added so you can address up to 64 GB. Note that on some platforms this feature has been enabled by default, which means you might have problems booting these Xen builds on laptops or older machines.

As general hardware support on driver level, Xen hands all the hardware management over to dom0, this means that all the hardware supported by the average Linux distribution is supported on Xen. Note, however, that Xen was initially developed for server-style hardware, which means that desktop- or even laptop-like features such as suspend and power management were not meant to work, might not have been tested, or may have simply been disabled in the build your distribution ships.

Different types of usage result in different hardware requirements. Let's go over a couple of scenarios.

If you are looking into datacenter virtualization, you will probably need to install as many disks as possible. You should also note the current memory usage of the machines you plan to deploy (or ones similar) and calculate the total sum of these applications, adding a little extra. You don't need to install a graphical interface, and if you are only running Linux, you don't need a VT capable machine. Since your dom0 isn't doing anything besides managing the other machines, it can be really small. If you have small virtual machine instances that can run with a minimal amount of RAM (we often see small servers such as DHCP or DNS server not needing more than 128 or 256 MB RAM), you can easily put 10 to 15 virtual machines in a 2 GB memory machine.

If you are looking at using Xen to run different test platforms, you will need both a graphical interface on your dom0, which requires more memory than your average datacenter dom0. You'll usually give the different environments more memory so you can install their graphical environments as well.

If you are looking at Xen to run Windows on top of your Linux machine, you'll need lots of memory and a VT-capable machine. No, I really meant just a lot of memory.

Windows virtual machines can only be created through full virtualization with support of the Intel-VT or AMD-V CPUs. Most of the new hardware available today have these features. Intel has a good site, www.intel.com/products/processor_number/index.htm, where you can find the CPUs that have VT capabilities. When writing this, most Dual Core processors such as the Xeon MP 7000 series, the Pentium 4 Extreme Edition 955 and 965, Intel Core Duo mobile processors, the Pentium D 9x0, and also Pentium 4 662 and 672 support VT.

Configuring & Implementing…

VT-Support Virtualization on Laptops

The Intel Core duo, which is also used in lots of laptops and the Mac Mini, is VT-capable. The Mac Mini was one of the first machines to support VT. Note, however, that different laptop vendors have disabled VT features, and you either need to enable them in your BIOS or upgrade your BIOS to enable these features. If you want to test your machine to see if it is VT-capable, you can download the Knoppix Xen CD. You can also boot any Linux Live CD and run the following on an Intel machine:

```
[root@macmini ~]# cat /proc/cpuinfo | grep vmx

flags: fpu vme de pse tsc msr pae mce cx8 apic mtrr pge mca cmov pat clflush
dts acpi mmx fxsr sse sse2 ss ht tm pbe nx constant_tsc pni monitor vmx est
tm2 xtpr
```

or

```
[root@box ~] cat /proc/cpuinfo | grep svm

flags: fpu tsc msr pae mce cx8 apic mtrr mca cmov pat pse36 clflush mmx fxsr
sse sse2 ht syscall nx mmxext fxsr_opt rdtscp lm 3dnowext 3dnow pni cx16
lahf_lm cmp_legacy svm cr8_legacy
```

If grep shows you a line like the preceding examples, your CPU is capable of supporting full virtualization. If it comes back empty, you either don't have a VT-capable CPU, or you need to look at your vendors hardware documentation in order to enable the feature.

Thinking Before You Start

Before we start, we must plan how we will be using our disk. What you want to do with your guest operating system determines how you will be using your disk layout. The easiest way to export a disk is to export an actual physical block device (a hard disk or a partition) from dom0 to your virtual machine. This, of course, limits you to the number of disks you have available or the number of partitions you can make on a disk.

"Old-school" virtualization platforms still tend to use files that are images of hard disks. This doesn't scale at all. It is useful if you want to create an image you want to distribute to other people, something to show around. But if you are building an infrastructure, you will limit yourself while paying a big performance penalty.

When you install your software on a loopback device created on a sparse file, which resides on a huge file system next to different other virtual images, chaos will eventually rule. We already know that copying these kinds of files will be slow and that there is no easy way to replicate, grow, or shrink them. When thinking about these kind of problems you realize LVM (Logical Volume Manager) is one of the best ways to solve these issues. LVM gives you the opportunity to manage growing volumes over different physical disks. It gives you the opportunity to take snapshots of those disks (easy for backups) and also solves the issue of a maximum 15 partitions on a SCSI disk.

When using multiple virtual machines on a machine, the problem is not how to manage five partitions on a disk. Since you are managing such a set of partitions for each virtual machine, you need to be able to add virtual machines and, therefore, partitions on-the-fly. Thus, you want to use LVM. It is a way to look at one, or multiple, disks that goes beyond partitions. You gain much more flexibility such as adding, removing, and resizing "partitions" while not having to reboot to reread the partition table.

LVM deals with Physical Volumes (PVs), Volume Groups (VGs), and Logical Volumes (LVs). PVs are the actual physical disk, or partitions, you want to use LVM on. You can combine multiple different partitions in a group. A group doesn't need to have multiple PVs, but it can have them. Within each group, you then can define Logical Volumes. These logical volumes are what you will create a file system on and use in your virtual machines.

Now imagine that you want to deploy a new server. In your average physical setup, you will want different partitions for the operating system, the log files, the data, and so on. If you want to add different actual partitions for each virtual machine, you will end up forgetting if */dev/hda6* was the root partition of your first virtual machine or if it was */dev/hda9*.

A good practice is to create a Volume Group for your virtual machine instances. The following is an example of Virtual Group creation:

```
-bash-3.00# pvs
  PV            VG              Fmt       Attr      PSize     PFree
  /dev/sda8     vm_volumes      lvm2      a-        26.77G    13.90G
-bash-3.00# vgs
  VG            #PV             #LV       #SN       Attr      VSize     VFree
  vm_volumes    1               25        0         wz--n     26.77G    13.90G
```

We then use a consistent naming convention for each of these virtual machines. Thus, a machine called DB2 will have at least a root, a temp, and a swap partition. The following example gives a clear overview of which Logical Volume is being used for which virtual partition.

```
-bash-3.00# lvs
  LV          VG              Attr      LSize     Origin    Snap%     Move Log Copy%
  root-DB1    vm_volumes      -wi-ao    1.17G
  root-DB2    vm_volumes      -wi-ao    1.17G
  swap-DB1    vm_volumes      -wi-ao    128.00M
  swap-DB2    vm_volumes      -wi-ao    128.00M
  tmp-DB1     vm_volumes      -wi-ao    64.00M
  tmp-DB2     vm_volumes      -wi-ao    64.00M
  varlib-DB1  vm_volumes      -wi-ao    4.00G
  varlib-DB2  vm_volumes      -wi-ao    4.00G
```

Another advantage of using LVM is that you can export an LVM partition as a block device to another machine, such as with iSCSI. That's probably a whole lot easier than copying four 3 GB+ files.

So when you are about to install the machine that will serve as a Xen server, don't let the Installer do the partitioning for you. Give it only a limited part of the disk, and then use the rest for LVM. That gives you the freedom to go for both disk images and actual partitions for your virtual machines. Use LVM, do not fully partition, and do not use images.

Of course, you can also choose more advanced methods such as NBD or iSCSI, or even put your root file system on NFS if you prefer to. (Note that putting a loopback file on a remote NFS volume is not advised.)

Installing Xen on a Free Linux Distribution

In this section, we'll discuss how to install Xen on a free Linux distribution.

Fedora Core 6

What is a Fedora? A fedora is a soft felt hat, often in red. When Red Hat decided to build an enterprise distribution, they rebranded the original open-source Red Hat distribution to Fedora Core. The Fedora Project is a Red Hat–sponsored and community-supported open-source project. It is the free as-is, bare Linux version that the new features placed in Red Hat Enterprise Linux will originate from. Fedora can be downloaded from the Internet for free, either via torrents to save bandwidth (from http://torrent.fedoraproject.org/) or via HTTP from http://fedoraproject.org/wiki/Distribution/ Download. You can also often find Fedora Core CD's distributed with magazines at the newsstands.

If you are already running Linux, you can burn the downloaded images to a CD by running the following commands:

```
cdrecord -v dev=ATA:1,0,0 -data FC-6-i386-disc1.iso
cdrecord -v dev=ATA:1,0,0 -data FC-6-i386-disc2.iso
cdrecord -v dev=ATA:1,0,0 -data FC-6-i386-disc3.iso
cdrecord -v dev=ATA:1,0,0 -data FC-6-i386-disc4.iso
cdrecord -v dev=ATA:1,0,0 -data FC-6-i386-disc5.iso
```

You actually only need the first two CDs when you want to do a minimal install of Fedora Core 6. If you are on another platform, the manual with your CD writing software will explain how to burn an ISO image.

Now, it's time for a guided tour, where we show you how to get Fedora Core 6 installed and Xen configured. The following steps will guide you through the process

1. Upon putting your freshly burned CD into the server, press **F10** or the appropriate key combination for your platform to boot from the CD-ROM. Fedora will boot to its initial CD menu. Press **Enter**.

2. The first screen will ask us if we want to check the media we just burned. Feel free to skip the media test.

3. The graphical Fedora Core installer should now launch and show you a welcome screen, after which you will be given the choice of either upgrading or installing a new system (see Figure 13.1). If this is a clean installation, you should select to perform a new install.

Figure 13.1 Choose a Fedora Core Installation Type

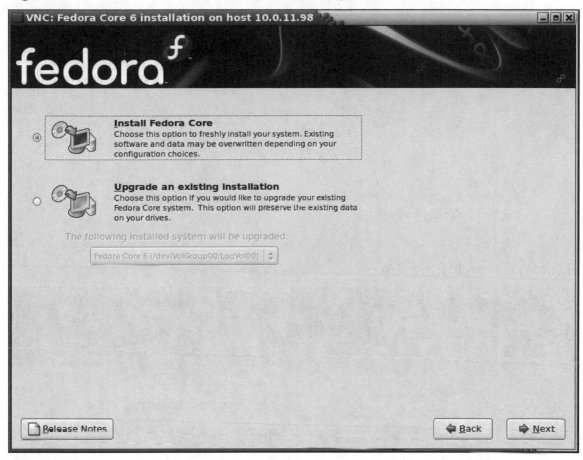

4. The next screen is an important one. A default Fedora Core installation will not give you the Disk Layout you want for a machine that will host different virtual machines. Therefore, I suggest you choose the **Remove All The Partitions From Your Existing Disks** option, and then choose **Review And Modify Partition Layout**.

5. You will be asked to confirm that you want to erase all existing partitions.

6. Fedora will create a boot partition and a Volume Group VolGroup00 where it will create a Logical Volume called LogVol00 (see Figure 13.2) that will take up the whole remaining file system (besides the small boot file systems it creates).

Figure 13.2 Define Your Own LVM Layout

Device	Mount Point/ RAID/Volume	Type	Format	Size (MB)	Start	End
▽ LVM Volume Groups						
▽ VolGroup00				38016		
LogVol01		swap	✓	1984		
LogVol00	/	ext3	✓	36032		

We want a bigger part of that file system for other Logical Volumes that will be used as file systems for virtual machines we will deploy. So we will resize the LogVol00 to about 4 to 6 GB, which should be more than enough for a basic dom0 installation (see Figure 13.3).

Figure 13.3 Modify the Size of Your Root File System

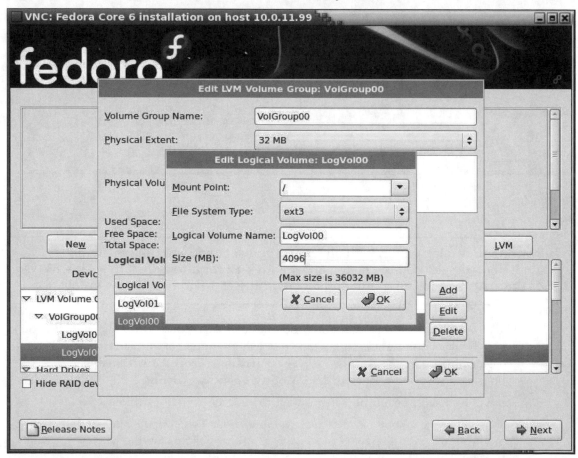

7. The next screen will provide you with the default values for a normal Grub installation. Grub is the bootloader required by Xen.

8. On the Network Configuration screen, configure your network with a static IP address (see Figure 13.4). Unless your DHCP server hands out static IP addresses based on the MAC address of your network card, you don't want to use DHCP for a server since you won't be able to connect to your server again once your DHCP lease changes.

Figure 13.4 Configure Your Network Card

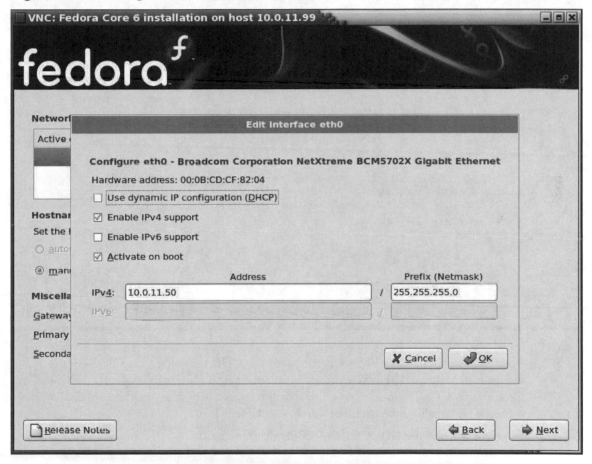

9. Choose the correct Timezone so that when you have to look at log files someday, you will be able to correlate the timestamps with other events on your network.

10. Choose a strong root password for this machine.

11. The next screen will provide you with the choice to install different software packages (see Figure 13.5). A normal Xen server usually does not need anything else besides the tools to manage the virtual machines, so you can disable the Office Tools and Development Tools option. Our goal is to make dom0 as small and lightweight as possible, so a minimal install is sufficient.

Figure 13.5 Choose a Minimal Installation

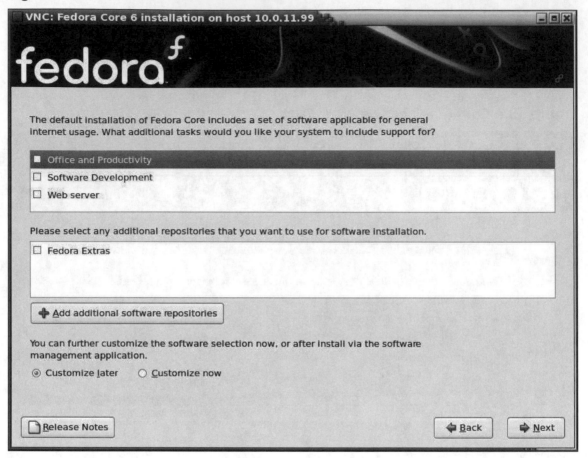

12. After this selection, you will be warned about the CDs you will need to perform the installation. Make sure you have these. If you are doing a minimal install, you only need the first two CDs. The machine will start transferring a basic image to its hard disk and continue by installing the packages you have selected.

13. After you change the CDs, your Fedora installation is ready to be rebooted. Your machine will now boot into your freshly installed Fedora Core 6, and will be ready to ask you the final questions for this installation. Click **Forward** on the Welcome screen.

14. Agree to the License Agreement.

15. For now, disable the firewall feature. It is recommended you re-enable it back after Xen is up and running; however, be sure to keep things simple until you clearly understand the network port and protocol requirements of your applications.

16. Also disable SELinux. SELinux provides you with more fine-grained security constraints such as what a certain process can access or not. Making an SELinux policy to be used with virtual machines is beyond the scope of this chapter.

17. You probably want to enable NTP using either the NTP servers on your internal network or the ones provided by your ISP.

18. Create at least one user so you can log on to the machine while not being root.

19. Since you have disabled both the firewall and SELinux, your machine will now require an additional reboot.

At this point, your Fedora Core 6 is now ready to be used. Our next step will be to install Xen. You can do this either by logging in to the machine remotely on a command line from the login or local desktop, or via the GUI.

Configuring & Implementing…

Building a Local Fedora Core Repository

As of now, we assume your machine has been connected to the Internet and can download packages from a publicly available Fedora Core mirror. If this is not the case, you will need to either reconfigure your network settings so you can access the Internet, or set up a local Fedora Core RPM repository and modify your *yum* configuration accordingly.

An RPM repository is the location where all the RPMs for a distribution and their metadata are stored for later redistribution via the network. Building your own local distribution repository will save you bandwidth and will ensure that if your Internet connection breaks down for some reason you can still continue to deploy new machines while not depending on third-party repositories. You also take the load away from mirrors that are often funding the bandwidth for these repositories out of their own pockets.

Assuming you want to build a local Fedora Core repository, you will need to either copy all the files on the CDs to a directory on your system, such as */data/repository/FC*, and run **yum-arch** in that directory or mount the CD you have on that mount point. In order to have yum use that freshly created repository, you will need to modify the yum configuration. The following is an example of a modified /etc/yum.repos.d/fedora-core.repo:

```
[core]

name=Fedora Core $releasever - $basearch

baseurl=file:///data/repository/FC

#baseurl=http://download.fedora.redhat.com/pub/fedora/linux/core/$releasever/
$basearch/os/

#mirrorl-ist=http://mirrors.fedoraproject.org/mirrorlist?repo=core-
$releasever&ar
```

Continued

```
ch=$basearch
enabled=1
gpgcheck=1
gpgkey=file:///etc/pki/rpm-gpg/RPM-GPG-KEY-fedora file:
///etc/pki/rpm-gpg/RPM-GP
G-KEY
```

You should also modify all the other configuration files in the /etc/yum.repos.d/ directory by changing all the "enabled=1" values to "enabled=0".

The following overview shows you how to install Xen, as well as the accompanying kernel required, via the command line.

```
[kris@mine FC6Install]$ ssh kris@10.0.11.50
kris@10.0.11.50's password:
Last login: Mon Feb 19 20:38:04 2007 from 10.0.11.43
[kris@fc6-xen ~]$ su -
Password:
[root@fc6-xen ~]# yum install xen kernel-xen
Loading "installonlyn" plugin
Setting up Install Process
Setting up repositories
Reading repository metadata in from local files
Parsing package install arguments
Resolving Dependencies
--> Populating transaction set with selected packages. Please wait.
---> Package kernel-xen.i686 0:2.6.19-1.2911.fc6 set to be installed
---> Package xen.i386 0:3.0.3-3.fc6 set to be updated
--> Running transaction check
--> Processing Dependency: libxenstore.so.3.0 for package: xen
--> Processing Dependency: xen-libs = 3.0.3-3.fc6 for package: xen
--> Processing Dependency: bridge-utils for package: xen
--> Processing Dependency: mkinitrd >= 5.1.19.0.2-1 for package: kernel-xen
--> Processing Dependency: libxenctrl.so.3.0 for package: xen
--> Processing Dependency: python-virtinst for package: xen
--> Processing Dependency: libxenguest.so.3.0 for package: xen
--> Processing Dependency: libblktap.so.3.0 for package: xen
--> Restarting Dependency Resolution with new changes.
--> Populating transaction set with selected packages. Please wait.
```

```
---> Package mkinitrd.i386 0:5.1.19.0.2-1 set to be updated
---> Package bridge-utils.i386 0:1.1-2 set to be updated
---> Package xen-libs.i386 0:3.0.3-3.fc6 set to be updated
---> Package python-virtinst.noarch 0:0.98.0-1.fc6 set to be updated
--> Running transaction check
--> Processing Dependency: libvirt-python >= 0.1.4-4 for package: python-virtinst
--> Processing Dependency: nash = 5.1.19.0.2-1 for package: mkinitrd
--> Restarting Dependency Resolution with new changes.
--> Populating transaction set with selected packages. Please wait.
---> Package nash.i386 0:5.1.19.0.2-1 set to be updated
---> Package libvirt-python.i386 0:0.1.11-1.fc6 set to be updated
--> Running transaction check
--> Processing Dependency: libvirt = 0.1.11 for package: libvirt-python
--> Processing Dependency: libvirt.so.0 for package: libvirt-python
--> Restarting Dependency Resolution with new changes.
--> Populating transaction set with selected packages. Please wait.
--- > Package libvirt.i386 0:0.1.11-1.fc6 set to be updated
--> Running transaction check
Dependencies Resolved
```

Package	Arch	Version	Repository	Size
Installing:				
kernel-xen	i686	2.6.19-1.2911.fc6	updates	17 M
xen	i386	3.0.3-3.fc6	updates	1.7 M
Installing for dependencies:				
bridge-utils	i386	1.1-2	core	28 k
libvirt	i386	0.1.11-1.fc6	updates	411 k
libvirt-python	i386	0.1.11-1.fc6	updates	47 k
python-virtinst	noarch	0.98.0-1.fc6	updates	30 k
xen-libs	i386	3.0.3-3.fc6	updates	83 k
Updating for dependencies:				
mkinitrd	i386	5.1.19.0.2-1	updates	438 k
nash	i386	5.1.19.0.2-1	updates	1.1 M
Transaction Summary				

```
Install7 Package(s)
Update 2 Package(s)
Remove 0 Package(s)
Total download size: 20M
Is this ok [y/N]: y
```

```
Downloading Packages:
(1/9): mkinitrd-5.1.19.0.  100% |=========================| 438 kB      00:01
(2/9): libvirt-0.1.11-1.f  100% |=========================| 411 kB      00:01
(3/9): bridge-utils-1.1-2  100% |=========================|  28 kB      00:00
(4/9): kernel-xen-2.6.19-  100% |=========================|  17 MB      01:06
(5/9): xen-libs-3.0.3-3.f  100% |=========================|  83 kB      00:00
(6/9): nash-5.1.19.0.2-1.  100% |=========================| 1.1 MB      00:04
(7/9): python-virtinst-0.  100% |=========================|  30 kB      00:00
(8/9): libvirt-python-0.1  100% |=========================|  47 kB      00:00
(9/9): xen-3.0.3-3.fc6.i3  100% |=========================| 1.7 MB      00:06
warning: rpmts_HdrFromFdno: Header V3 DSA signature: NOKEY, key ID 4f2a6fd2
Importing GPG key 0x4F2A6FD2 "Fedora Project fedora@redhat.com"
Is this ok [y/N]: y
Running Transaction Test
Finished Transaction Test
Transaction Test Succeeded
Running Transaction
  Installing: xen-libs           ####################### [ 1/11]
  Updating : nash               ####################### [ 2/11]
  Updating : mkinitrd           ####################### [ 3/11]
  Installing: bridge-utils       ####################### [ 4/11]
  Installing: kernel-xen         ####################### [ 5/11]
  Installing: xen                ####################### [ 6/11]
  Installing: libvirt            ####################### [ 7/11]
  Installing: python-virtinst    ####################### [ 8/11]
  Installing: libvirt-python     ####################### [ 9/11]
  Cleanup : mkinitrd            ####################### [10/11]
  Cleanup : nash               ####################### [11/11]
Installed: kernel-xen.i686 0:2.6.19-1.2911.fc6 xen.i386 0:3.0.3-3.fc6
Dependency Installed: bridge-utils.i386 0:1.1-2 libvirt.i386 0:0.1.11-1.fc6
libvirt-python.i386 0:0.1.11-1.fc6 python-virtinst.noarch 0:0.98.0-1.fc6
xen-libs.i386 0:3.0.3-3.fc6
Dependency Updated: mkinitrd.i386 0:5.1.19.0.2-1 nash.i386 0:5.1.19.0.2-1
Complete!
```

If you want to use the GUI, choose the **Add/Remove Software** option from the Applications Menu (see Figure 13.6).

Figure 13.6 Choose Add/Remove Software

This will start the Package Manager, which will first update the list of available packages before giving you a screen where you have a Browse, Search, and List tab. On the **Search** tab, search for "xen." From the result set, select the most recent "kernel-xen" and "xen" package. Upon selecting **Apply**, you will see a listing of your selection. Select **Continue** (see Figure 13.7).

Figure 13.7 Confirm Package Selection

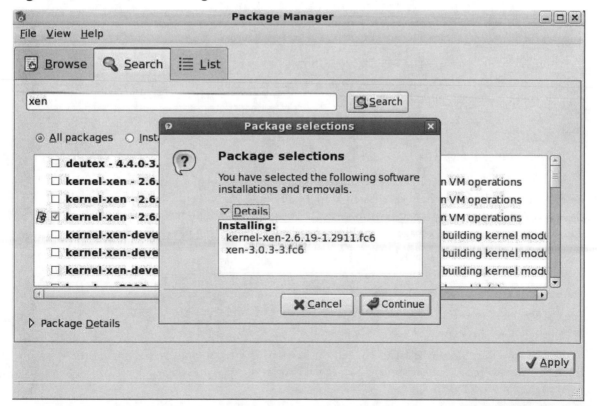

The package manager will now calculate the dependencies for those two packages for you and will ask you to confirm these dependencies before it starts their actual download. Whichever you choose, the next step is to carefully inspect your grub.conf file and find a part similar to the following:

```
[root@fc6-xen grub]# more /boot/grub/grub.conf
# grub.conf generated by anaconda
#
# Note that you do not have to rerun grub after making changes to this file
# NOTICE:  You have a /boot partition.  This means that
#       all kernel and initrd paths are relative to /boot/, eg.
#       root (hd0,0)
#       kernel /vmlinuz-version ro root=/dev/VolGroup00/LogVol00
#       initrd /initrd-version.img
#boot=/dev/hda
default=1
timeout=5
splashimage=(hd0,0)/grub/splash.xpm.gz
hiddenmenu
title Fedora Core (2.6.19-1.2911.fc6xen)
  root (hd0,0)
  kernel /xen.gz-2.6.19-1.2911.fc6
  module /vmlinuz-2.6.19-1.2911.fc6xen ro root=/dev/VolGroup00/LogVol00 no
dmraid rhgb quiet
  module /initrd-2.6.19-1.2911.fc6xen.img
title Fedora Core (2.6.18-1.2798.fc6)
  root (hd0,0)
  kernel /vmlinuz-2.6.18-1.2798.fc6 ro root=/dev/VolGroup00/LogVol00 nodmr
aid rhgb quiet
  initrd /initrd-2.6.18-1.2798.fc6.img
```

In the preceding example, the default boot entry is set to 1, which actually means the second entry, so upon rebooting, the second listed kernel will boot. You will either have to manually change the kernel at boot time by navigating up in the grub menu, or modify this file so the default reads 0. The xen and kernel-xen packages should have installed the following files:

```
[root@fc6-xen ~]# ls /boot/*xen*
/boot/config-2.6.19-1.2911.fc6xen         /boot/vmlinuz-2.6.19-1.2911.fc6xen
/boot/initrd-2.6.19-1.2911.fc6xen.img     /boot/xen.gz-2.6.19-1.2911.fc6
/boot/symvers-2.6.19-1.2911.fc6xen.gz     /boot/xen-syms-2.6.19-1.2911.fc6
/boot/System.map-2.6.19-1.2911.fc6xen
```

Make sure they actually exist and match the versions as listed in your *grub.conf* file. If they are there, it's time to reboot into that new Xen hypervisor, and afterward you will have your first virtual machine up and running.

Yes, the regular Linux version you have just booted into is not running on a regular x86 platform anymore. It is instead running on a Xen Hypervisor. You can check this by running the following command:

```
[kris@fc6-xen ~]$ uname -a
Linux fc6-xen.hs62.be 2.6.19-1.2911.fc6xen #1 SMP Sat Feb 10 16:09:50
EST 2007 i686 i686 i386 GNU/Linux
```

The *fc6xen* tag marks that you are running in a Xen-enabled dom0. If you already started *xend* at boot time, which Fedora does for you, your output of *xm list* should be similar to the following:

```
[root@fc6-xen ~]# chkconfig --list | grep 3:on | grep xen
xend            0:off   1:off   2:on    3:on    4:on    5:on    6:off
xendomains      0:off   1:off   2:off   3:on    4:on    5:on    6:off
[root@fc6-xen ~]# xm list
Name            ID      Mem(MiB)        VCPUs           State           Time(s)
Domain-0        0       1059            1               r-----          38.2
```

NOTE

In other distributions, you still might need to start the xend daemon yourself via: */etc/rc.d/init.d/xend start*

On some distributions and hardware configurations, the creation of a valid *initrd* can fail. The initial RAMDISK is a temporary file system used to load drivers on the platform before the actual root file system will be mounted. This results in a kernel panic proceeded by an error that the kernel cannot mount its root file system. This is caused by some builds of the Xen dom0 kernel insisting on the *initrd* having the most basic kernel modules inserted manually. You can do this by running:

```
mkinitrd /boot/initrd-2.6.19-1.2911.fc6xen.img 2.6.19-1.2911.fc6xen --with-module
mptbase --with-module scsi_mod --with-module sg --with-module mptscsih --with-module
mptspi --with-module ext3 --with-module sd_mod --with-module ide-disk --with-module
dm-mod --with-module jbd --with-module mptctl
```

The version you mention should match both the kernel version you are trying to build an *intrd* for and the directory of modules with the same version that lives in */lib/modules/$version*. You can find the actual list of modules you need to include by running **lsmod** on your active system and including every module listed there that refers to file systems or storage.

VirtManager

As of Fedora Core 6, the distribution provides you with a nice GUI called *virt-manager* which really eases up the installation of guests…Fedora guests, that is. For now, we will use *virt-manager* to install a Fedora guest from which the data will reside in a loopback device. Fedora Core 6's default build only supports XVDX type disks. You cannot easily use a full disk or an LVM volume for your virtual machine storage. We will review how to use LVM later in this chapter when installing the XenSource-provided RPMs.

Of course, the first step is to install the VirtManager package itself, as in the following:

```
[root@fc6-xen ~]# yum install virt-manager
Loading "installonlyn" plugin
Setting up Install Process
Setting up repositories
Reading repository metadata in from local files
Parsing package install arguments
Resolving Dependencies
--> Populating transaction set with selected packages. Please wait.
---> Downloading header for virt-manager to pack into transaction set.
virt-manager-0.2.6-3.fc6. 100% |=========================| 25 kB00:00
---> Package virt-manager.i386 0:0.2.6-3.fc6 set to be updated
--> Running transaction check
--> Processing Dependency: gnome-python2-gnomekeyring >= 2.15.4 for package:
virt-manager
--> Restarting Dependency Resolution with new changes.
--> Populating transaction set with selected packages. Please wait.
---> Downloading header for gnome-python2-gnomekeyring to pack into transaction
set.
gnome-python2-gnomekeyrin 100% |=========================| 3.5 kB      00:00
---> Package gnome-python2-gnomekeyring.i386 0:2.16.0-1.fc6 set to be updated
--> Running transaction check
Dependencies Resolved

=============================================================================
 Package                   Arch      Version            Repository     Size
=============================================================================
Installing:
  virt-manager             i386      0.2.6-3.fc6        updates        553 k
Installing for dependencies:
  gnome-python2-gnomekeyring i386    2.16.0-1.fc6       core           15 k
Transaction Summary
=============================================================================
Install      2 Package(s)
Update       0 Package(s)
Remove       0 Package(s)
Total download size: 568 k
Is this ok [y/N]: y
Downloading Packages:
(1/2): virt-manager-0.2.6 100% |=========================| 553 kB      00:03
(2/2): gnome-python2-gnom 100% |=========================| 15 kB       00:00
```

```
Running Transaction Test
Finished Transaction Test
Transaction Test Succeeded
Running Transaction
  Installing: gnome-python2-gnomekeyring    ######################### [1/2]
  Installing: virt-manager                  ######################### [2/2]
Installed: virt-manager.i386 0:0.2.6-3.fc6

Dependency Installed: gnome-python2-gnomekeyring.i386 0:2.16.0-1.fc6
```

After installing this package, you will once again see a new entry in the Applications | System Tools menu called **Virtual Machine Manager**. Start it. When launched as a non-root user from the menu, you will be prompted for the root password since you will need root privileges to create a virtual machine (see Figure 13.8).

Figure 13.8 Create a New Virtual System

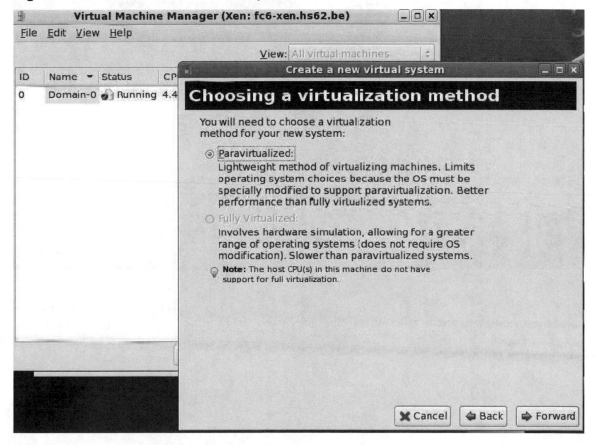

1. Choose to connect to the local Xen Host by clicking **Connect**.
2. Choose **File | New Machine**.
3. Choose a unique and self-explanatory name for your Virtual Machine.

4. Since we are installing a Linux machine, choose to use the Paravirtualized method (see Figure 13.9).

Figure 13.9 Choosing a Virtualization Method

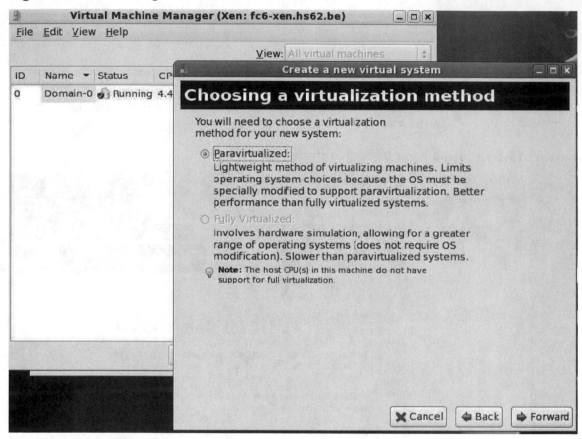

5. Choose a repository where you can install your Guest Virtual Machine, as shown in Figure 13.10.

Figure 13.10 Locating Installation MediaNote

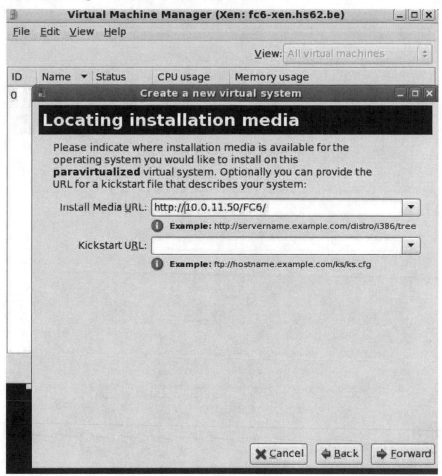

To save on bandwidth and speed up the installation process, make sure you have mounted the DVD, or copied the content of your CDs to a local repository. Also, make sure you can access them via a Web browser. Of course, you can choose a remote Fedora Repository, but that will only slow down the installation.

6.   You can either choose to use a local file or a full file system or LVM partition. Figure 13.11 shows you a dialog box for assigning storage space for your virtual system.

Figure 13.11 Assigning Storage Space

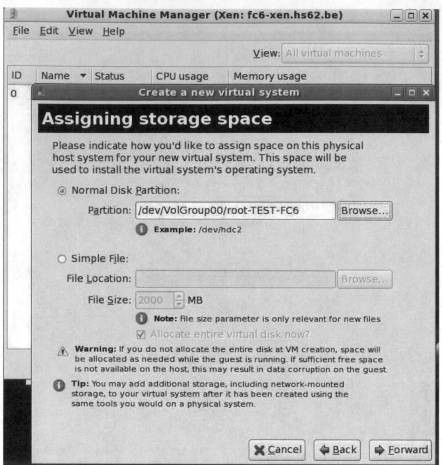

NOTE

You won't be able to mount this LVM partition or disk as a normal file system since Fedora will use this as a full virtual disk. If you don't want this, read on. Later in this chapter we'll discuss how to use actual LVM volumes.

7. After either an empty file has been created or your partition has been chosen, you can also set the default memory parameters. Of course, they depend on how much memory there is in your actual system and how these virtual machines will be used (see Figure 13.12).

Figure 13.12 Allocate Memory and CPU

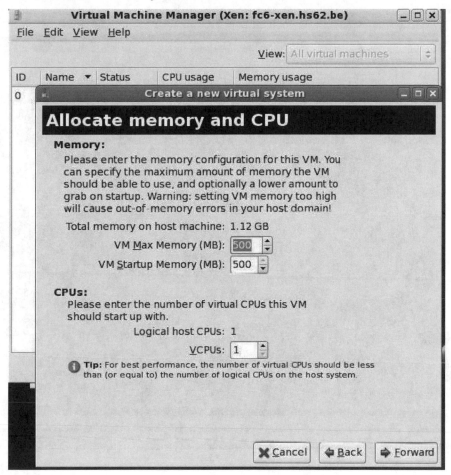

8. By Finishing the Installation Wizard, a configuration file matching your choices will be written into /etc/xen/, and your virtual machine will be started for the first time. You'll recognize the Fedora Core installer again, which you have already used to install this physical machine (see Figure 13.13).

Figure 13.13 Start the Virtual Machine Installation

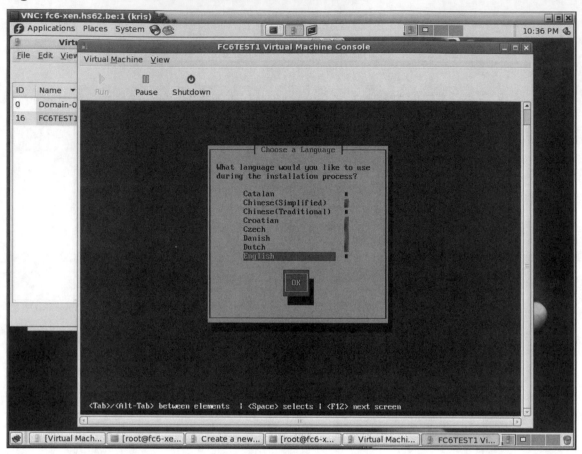

```
[root@fc6-xen xen]# more FC6TEST1
# Automatically generated xen config file
name = "FC6TEST1"
memory = "500"
disk = [ 'phy:/dev/VolGroup00/root-TEST-FC6,xvda,w', ]
vif = [ 'mac=00:16:3e:42:83:34, bridge=xenbr0', ]
vnc=1
vncunused=1
uuid = "f6ebc9f0-8ad4-2868-7297-9822ab6496cd"
bootloader="/usr/bin/pygrub"
vcpus=1
on_reboot = 'restart'
on_crash = 'restart'
```

The preceding config file has been generated by virt-manager for the virtual machine FC6TEST1. It doesn't specify a kernel as it is using pygrub.

NOTE

pygrub is a bootloader that can be used instead of the regular domU kernel for booting. It reads the kernel from the domU's file system rather than from the dom0 file system, enabling reboots of a virtual machine even after it has migrated to another physical machine.

However, it does specify that it will be using the logical volume */dev/VolGroup00/root-TEST-FC6* as a full disk (xvda). It will enable VNC access so you can have a graphical console on the machine. It has one virtual CPU and will have a maximum of 500 MB of RAM.

After the installation of this virtual machine, it will shut down. From there on, you can use the regular Xen *xm* command-line tool to start your virtual machine as follows:

```
xm create FCTEST1
```

In the *virt-man* GUI, you should now see your freshly installed virtual machine listed (see Figure 13.14).

Figure 13.14 A New Host Running in VirtManager

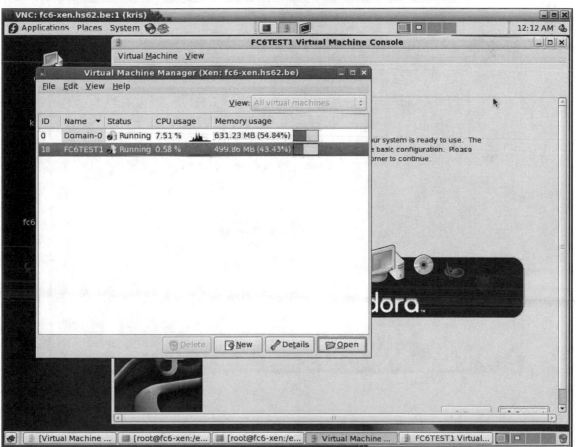

If you select it and then open it, you will be connected to the graphical desktop of that virtual machine, which is waiting for you to finish the installation. From here, you can use either the GUI or the command line to fully manage the virtual machine.

Installing Windows XP

Installing a Windows Virtual machine first of all requires a VT-capable machine. We discussed before in the system requirements how you can test if your machine is VT-capable. Once again, we will be using *virt-manager* to install XP as a virtual machine. The following steps walk you through creating a Windows guest.

1. Rather than choosing Paravirtualization, select **Fully Virtualized** (see Figure 13.15).

Figure 13.15 Choosing a Fully Virtualized Installation Method

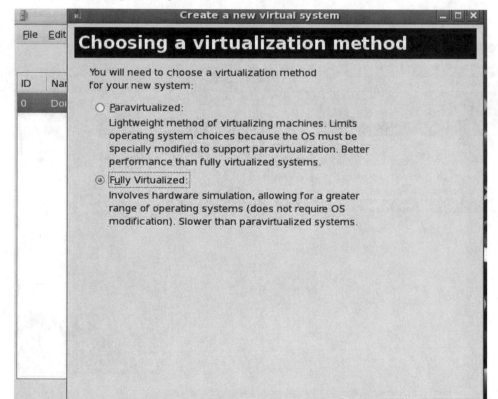

NOTE

If your CPU does not support this feature, you won't be able to select that option and you might need to reboot and modify your BIOS settings or even upgrade to a new BIOS.

2. This time you won't need to select a repository, but you will need to select either a CD mounted in the local CD drive or an ISO image of a CD you have stored somewhere on your file system (see Figure 13.16).

Figure 13.16 Locating Installation Media on CD

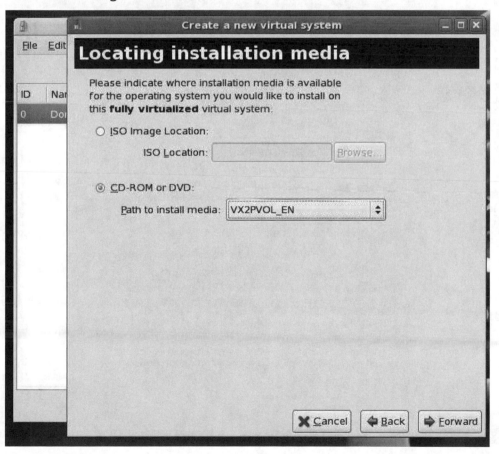

NOTE

You can also use this feature to install Linux distributions not supported by the Fedora installer or other operating systems.

3. Choose a disk or a file image that will host the guest operating system (see Figure 13.17).

Figure 13.17 Adding Storage Space

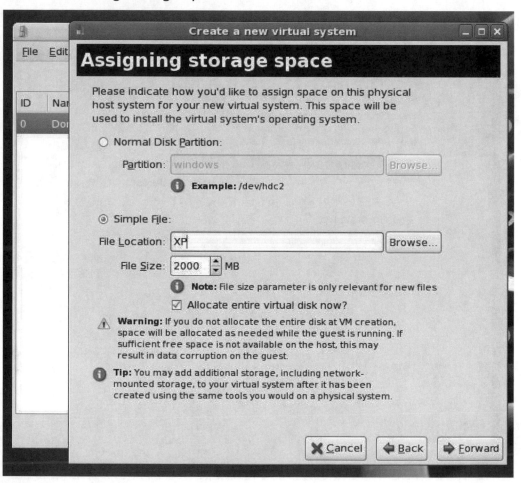

4. Choose the appropriate amount of memory. Be sure to factor in the appropriate amount of memory for the Windows XP operating system and the applications that will run in it.

5. After confirmation of your settings, a virtual machine will be started and will boot the Windows XP installation program from the CD as if it were a regular XP installation (see Figure 13.18).

Figure 13.18 Starting a Fully Virtualized Install

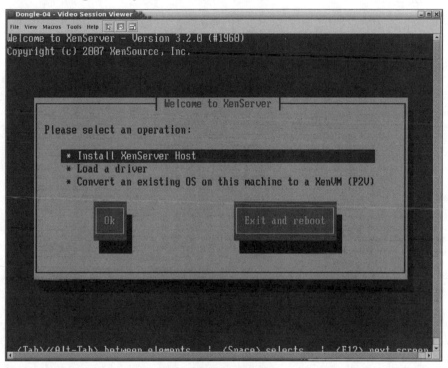

This time, also, a configuration file has been written by VirtManager and you can start the virtual machine after installation by using the *xm* command The following is a sample configuration file.

```
name = "XP"
builder = "hvm"
memory = "1024"
disk = [ 'file:/vhosts/XP.img,hda,w', ]
vif = [ 'type=ioemu, mac=00:16:3e:6d:a4:6b, bridge=xenbr0', ]
uuid = "23a340d1-e82e-da77-6525-4133a9e9e828"
device_model = "/usr/lib/xen/bin/qemu-dm"
```

```
kernel = "/usr/lib/xen/boot/hvmloader"
vnc=1
vncunused=0
apic=1
acpi=1
pae=1
vcpus=1
serial = "pty" # enable serial console
on_reboot = 'restart'
on_crash = 'restart'
```

Notice the different options in the configuration file. The kernel is now the hvmloader, as opposed to a real kernel or pygrub. Since Windows, by default, requires a graphical console, you have two choices. Either you connect to the graphical console by VNC, meaning you will need the vnc=1 parameter, or you want to see the Windows machine booting on the desktop where you launch it, using vnc=0 parameter or replacing it with sdl=1. This way you have the choice between direct output on the screen or connecting via VNC remotely.

We have shown you how to install both a Linux and a Windows virtual machine on a standard open-source Linux distribution. As the stable packages in Fedora Core eventually end up being part of the next Red Hat Enterprise release, you will notice that, with a few cosmetic changes left and right, these instructions will also help you install Xen on a RHEL platform and, therefore, also on a CentOS platform.

In the next section, we describe how to install Xen Enterprise.

Installing the XenServer Product Family

Now let's discuss installing the XenServer product family.

What Is XenServer

XenServer is the commercially supported Xen platform built by XenSource, the authors of Xen. It comes in three different flavors. The first Xen product is XenExpress, which is aimed at the IT Enthusiast or developer. It allows up to four concurrent virtual machines on a dual-socket server with 4 GB of memory. It has support for Linux P2V conversions. It can also run Windows Server 2003, Windows XP SP2, and Windows 2000 SP4. It has templates for different RHEL and Debian releases, and also supports SLES 9.2 through 10.1. From the management console, you can manage a single server, but best of all it is free. Should you decide to use one of the other versions, the process is no more difficult than changing the license key.

The next product in the suite is XenServer, which is aimed at the Windows IT Professional. It allows up to eight concurrent VMs on a dual-socket server with up to 8 GB of memory. It does not support any Linux guests, but it does support all the aforementioned Windows guests and you can manage multiple servers from the management console. It is not free, but for a price of less than $100 per year, it is an interesting platform to get started on.

Finally, there is XenEnterprise, the more expensive alternative of the three but still a lot cheaper than other commercial products in the same field. It is targeted at larger enterprises, with unlimited

VMs and support for as much RAM as your machine is capable of. It has Linux P2V support included and Windows P2V via partner bundles. It supports both Linux and the aforementioned Windows version, and it is the version that supports the more advanced features such as live migration and shared storage first.

Collectively, the XenSource commercial offering is referred to as XenServer, regardless of whether you are talking about XenSource, the Windows-only XenServer, or the flagship XenEnterprise product.

XenServer Requirements

Unlike a Xen installation with Fedora Core, for a XenServer installation you need two machines— one to be installed as the Xen server, and another that will run the XenSource XenServer Administrator Console used to manage the server. The requirements for XenServer are about the same as for a Fedora machine. However, you must take into account the fact that XenServer requires a machine with at least 16 GB of free disk space on the same disk, though more is recommended. In addition, XenEnterprise can use up to 32 CPUs.

XenServer is based on a Centos root file system with a SUSE-based kernel. It is meant to be headless and managed from a remote console. It will install its own two 4 GB LVM partitions for the XenServer host domain and leave the rest free for the virtual machines themselves. As for the virtual machine templates, a minimal Red Hat Enterprise Linux (RHEL)-based install will take a root file system of 4 GB, while the Debian template will take up to 1 GB for its root device and 512 MB for its swap.

The client machine can be almost anything. We will install the client on the Fedora Core, but you can use a Windows XP or 2000 client or any RPM-based Linux machine with about 100 MB of free disk space and a minimum 256 MB. For P2V, you, of course, need a network as fast as possible.

If you compare the feature set of a XenServer with the features of the open-source Xen version, you will see there are a lot fewer features in the XenEnterprise GUI. Many of those features are available under the hood, but not as yet from the GUI. Keep in mind that XenEnterprise was meant to be friendly for the non-Linux savvy public that wants to do bare metal virtualization for Windows virtual machines. Linux experts may still lean towards a fully open-source version of Xen, or an Enterprise Linux version, though the commercial version does provide a support channel as well.

Xen Server is being marketed as "Ten minutes to Xen," and we will show you that that time is about exactly what you'll need to get up and running.

Getting and Installing XenServer

As mentioned before, XenServer comes in different flavors. You can start with a free XenExpress and then upgrade afterwards to other versions. So, after registering or purchasing one of these versions, you will get instructions from XenSource on how to download your install binaries and your license key.

As of XenServer 3.2, Xen now comes as two CDs. One smaller ISO image, which will get you started with a Windows only virtualization platform, and a second larger ISO image if you want to run Linux-based virtual machines. The latter CD contains the basic templates for different Linux distributions. Assuming you downloaded the ISO image to a Linux machine, you can burn the ISO to a CD as root with the following command:

```
cdrecord -v dev=ATA:1,0,0 -data XenServer-3.2.0-install-cd.iso
cdrecord -v dev=ATA:1,0,0 -data XenServer-3.2.0-linux-cd.iso
```

Installing the Host

The first thing to do is install the server. Assuming you have a machine at your disposal that has the preceding specifications, let's install XenEnterprise. We'll be using XenServer Version 3.2.0 Release Candidate, build 1960, for this walkthrough. After you have burned the ISO to a CD, place it in the server you plan to use and power up the server, either your server boots from the CD-ROM by default or you will have to tell it to do so. As the server boots from the CD, it will boot a Xen hypervisor and Xen kernel, and will boot to a text mode install of a Linux system. The installer is based on Anaconda, which is the same installation program used by Fedora Core, Red Hat Enterprise Linux, and other distributions. It is responsible for the basic configuration of your system and also allows you to automate installations via kick start. Since we are installing a server that is not supposed to have a graphical screen, the installation will be in Text mode.

The following steps will guide you through the installation process:

1. The First screen you get after the installer has finished its hardware auto-detection is the KeyMap configuration screen. Choose the keyboard layout you prefer and then press **Enter**.

2. This CD has three functions. The first is to install a XenServer host (see Figure 13.19), which is the option we need now. The second function is to load a network or block device driver for dom0. The third function is used to do a physical-to-virtual machine conversion. Choose **install XenServer** and press **Enter**.

Figure 13.19 Welcome to XenServer

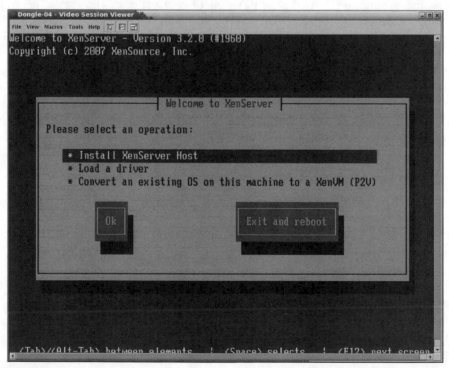

NOTE

Just as with any other regular Linux install in Text mode, you can switch to a different log and a console by using **Alt + F2** for a console, **Alt + F3** or **Alt + F4** for different log files, and **Alt + F1** to go back to the installer.

3. Since you are sure this is the correct machine, click **OK** to continue when warned that XenServer will overwrite data on any drives you select during the install process. Note that you don't need to select all the drives in your server.

4. XenServer asks you to read and Accept the End User License Agreement. Please do so.

5. XenServer might warn you about system requirements you have not met. If you don't have a VT-capable machine, or if you do not have enough memory, XenServer will warn you. You, however, are free to continue installing (see Figure 13.20).

6. The XenServer installer will check if you already have an older version of XenServer installed. If you do, it will ask you if you want to upgrade.

7. Upon detecting multiple hard disks, XenServer will give you the opportunity to choose which disk you want to use and if you want to use and format other disks.

Figure 13.20 System Hardware (VT Detection)

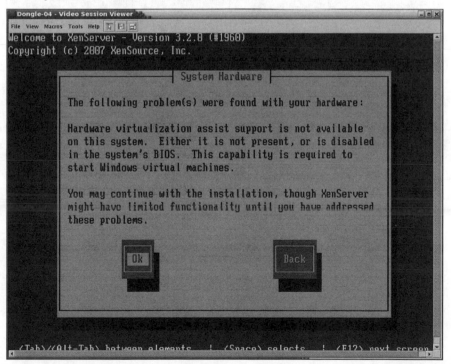

8.   Since we are installing from a CD, choose the **Local media (CD–ROM)** option and click **OK** (see Figure 13.21).

Figure 13.21 Select the Installation Source

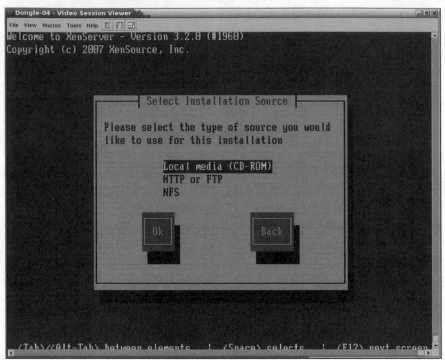

9.   When XenServer thinks your machine is not VT-capable, it will encourage you to add the "Linux pack," which is on the second CD you downloaded and which you will need to bootstrap Linux images from (see Figure 13.22).

Figure 13.22 Adding the Linux Pack

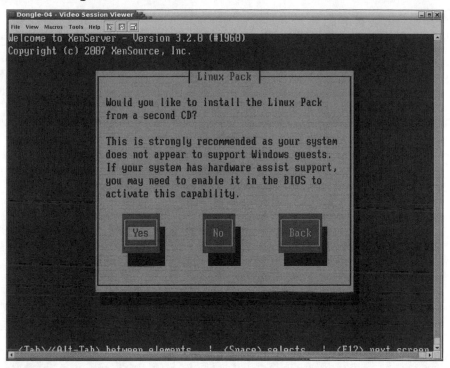

10. If you wish, you can verify whether the CD you created is intact, if you run into problems later during the install, this is worth verifying, but to gain time we can skip the Media Testing for now.

11. XenServer asks you to choose a password, this password can be used to log on to the console of the Xen server and will also be needed to connect to the Xen Server from the Administrator Console. You only need a six-character password, but make sure you choose a strong password you can remember so you don't have to write it down anywhere.

TIP

An easy way to create a strong but easy-to-remember password is to think of a memorable sentence and then use the first letters from each word to compose your password—for example, "Open-Source security is better than security through obscurity!" becomes "OSsibtsto!"

12. Choose the geographical area you are installing the server in. Click **OK**.

13. Choose the city that is in your Time Zone and click **OK**.

14. If you have access to an NTP server, you can use NTP; otherwise, you must do a manual time entry. We will choose to use NTP.

15. An NTP server can be announced by your DHCP server or specified manually. Either your internal network administrator knows which NTP servers can be used or you can use a public one (pool.ntp.org). Figure 13.23 shows a dialog box for an NTP configuration.

Figure 13.23 NTP Configuration

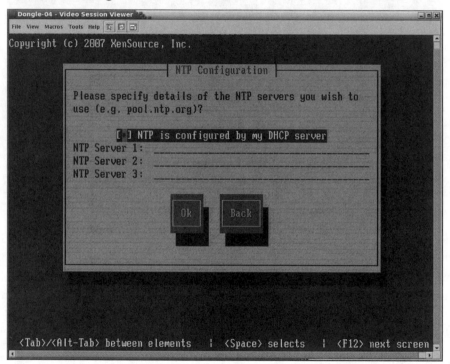

16. The next step is network configuration. Since you are installing a server, you have two options. Either your DHCP server has the MAC address of this server listed and will hand out a static IP address with all the other network configuration parameters, or you will manually configure a fixed IP address. Do not use a dynamic IP address for a server that you can only manage via a remote GUI since when your DHCP lease changes you might end up obtaining another IP address and you wouldn't be able to connect to your XenServer anymore.

17. For each interface in your server, you will now be given the chance to configure the IP address, subnet mask, gateway, and on the second screen, the hostname and the different DNS servers (see Figure 13.24).

Figure 13.24 Hostname and DNS Configuration

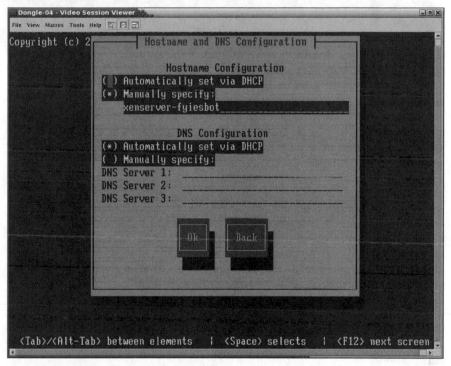

18. You will now get a final warning that all the data on that machine will be destroyed. Click **Install XenServer** if you are sure. *After this leave your XenServer's installer do its work. If you didn't select the extra disk, the next time it will need input from you will be when it is ready to be rebooted. At which time, it will require that you click* **OK** *again.*

19. If you did select the extra disk, after a while the installer will prompt you to insert the second disk (see Figure 13.25).

Figure 13.25 Inserting the Extra Disk

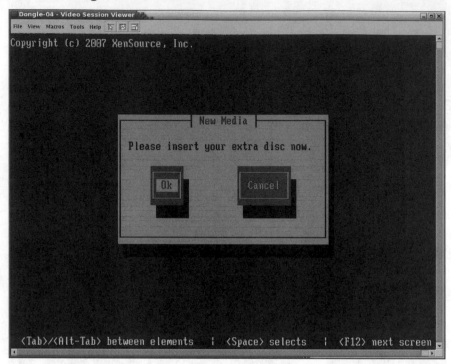

You will also be given the opportunity to verify the new disk, or just go on and skip the verification.

Note that as the second disk is larger, it will take longer to install the second CD compared to the first. After a while, a screen stating "The XenServer installation has completed" will appear. You are now ready to reboot.

Make sure the CD-ROM is not in the drive when the machine restarts again. If everything was installed correctly, you will now see GNU Grub, which will, after a small timeout, boot into Xen. If you need to make changes to the boot parameters (such as giving your dom0 less memory by default), or if want to boot the Xen server in Safe Mode, you can navigate the menu with the **Up-** and **Down-arrow keys** and choose your preferred boot image. If you don't, grub will automatically boot your system and after a few seconds the following message will appear on your screen:

```
XenServer Host 3.2.0-build
System Booted: 2007-03-26 19:40
Your XenServer Host has now finished booting. To manage this server please use the
XenServer Administrator Console application. You can install the XenServer
Administrator Console for Windows and Linux from the XenServer install media.
You can connect to this system using one of the following network addresses:
10.0.11.28
xenserver-lt login:
```

You should now be able to log on as user root using the password you chose earlier in the install. Your Xen server is now ready to be managed. As proof that you actually have a Xen machine up and running, you can try an **xm list**.

```
[root@xenserver ~]# xm list
Name          ID     Mem(MiB)     VCPUs      State      Time(s)
Domain-0      0      121          1          r-----     47.4
```

To be sure your network connection is working, you can now try to ping any machine on your network using the *PING* command.

```
[root@xenserver ~]# ping -c 5 10.0.11.1
PING 10.0.11.1 (10.0.11.1) 56(84) bytes of data.
64 bytes from 10.0.11.1: icmp_seq=0 ttl=255 time=0.227ms
64 bytes from 10.0.11.1: icmp_seq=1 ttl=255 time=0.225ms
64 bytes from 10.0.11.1: icmp_seq=2 ttl=255 time=0.207ms
64 bytes from 10.0.11.1: icmp_seq=3 ttl=255 time=0.246ms
64 bytes from 10.0.11.1: icmp_seq=4 ttl=255 time=0.234ms
```

NOTE

If at a later time you want to modify the hostname or the network configuration of your XenServer host, you won't be able to do so from the command line and you will need to use the regular Linux tools. Since XenServer is based on a Red Hat–style distribution, you must modify the network configuration files located in /etc/sysconfig/network-scripts. The configuration file for your eth0 will be called ifcfg-eth0.

Also, if you first decide you don't need the Linux Pack, but later realize you do need it after all, you can simply mount the Linux install CD and run the install.sh script from the CD.

Client Installation

The XenServer client is a Java-based GUI that can run on either a Linux or Windows platform. It has an installer for both. The Java GUI for Windows resides on the first CD. Just double-clicking the *xenserver-client.exe* will launch the installer, which will guide you through an easy installation. The XenSource XenServer Administrator Console for Linux has been placed on the second Linux CD. In order to install the client on an RPM-based Linux desktop, you need to become root.

```
[user@host ~]$su -
Password:
[root@host ~]#
mount /dev/hdc
[root@host client_install]# df.
```

```
Filesystem          1K-blocks      Used        Available     Use% Mounted on
/dev/hdc            686198         686198      0             100%
/media/XenServer-3.1.0-1332
```

Then install the actual RPM packages.

```
[root@client ~]# cd /media/XenServer-3.1.0-1332/client_install/
[root@client client_install]# rpm -vih xenserver-client*.rpm
Preparing...                    ########################################### [100%]
  1:xenserver-client-jre       ########################################### [ 33%]
  2:xenserver-client-jars      ########################################### [ 67%]
  3:xenserver-client           ########################################### [100%]
```

The client will be installed in */opt/xensource/xenserver-client*, and you can start the client by running:

```
/opt/xensource/xenserver-client/bin/xenserver-client.sh
```

> **NOTE**
>
> If you are running Beryl, the 3D window manager, your xenserver-client will not work and you will get two gray windows rather than readable text. If you switch back to the default metacity window manager, your application will be usable.

Both the Windows and Linux client will go through the following upon first launch.

1. You will be prompted to accept the license agreement.

2. The administration client will ask you to choose a master password. With this password, you will be able to access the management console again so you can manage different servers from the same GUI (see Figure 13.26).

Figure 13.26 The XenSource XenServer Master Login

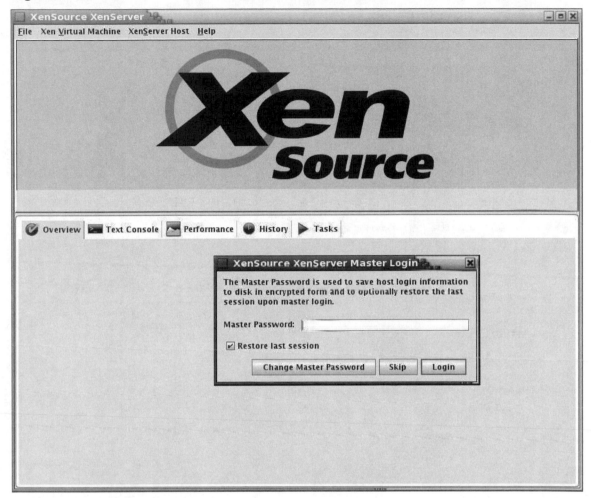

3. The next step is to specify the IP address and the password for the XenServer we just installed.

4. You will now be connected to the management console of a freshly installed and empty XenServer (see Figure 13.27).

Figure 13.27 The XenSource XenServer Dashboard

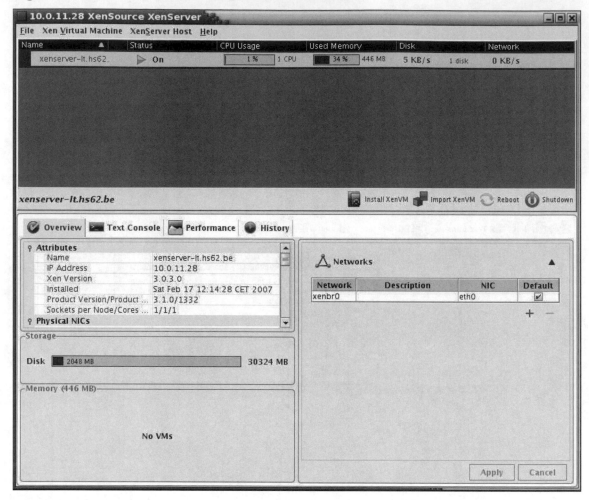

5. The only remaining item is to enable the license key you got from XenSource. From the **XenServer Host** menu, choose **License Key**, then click **...** and select the file in which you saved the license key. Finish by selecting **Apply License** (see Figure 13.28).

Figure 13.28 The XenSource XenServer License Key Installation

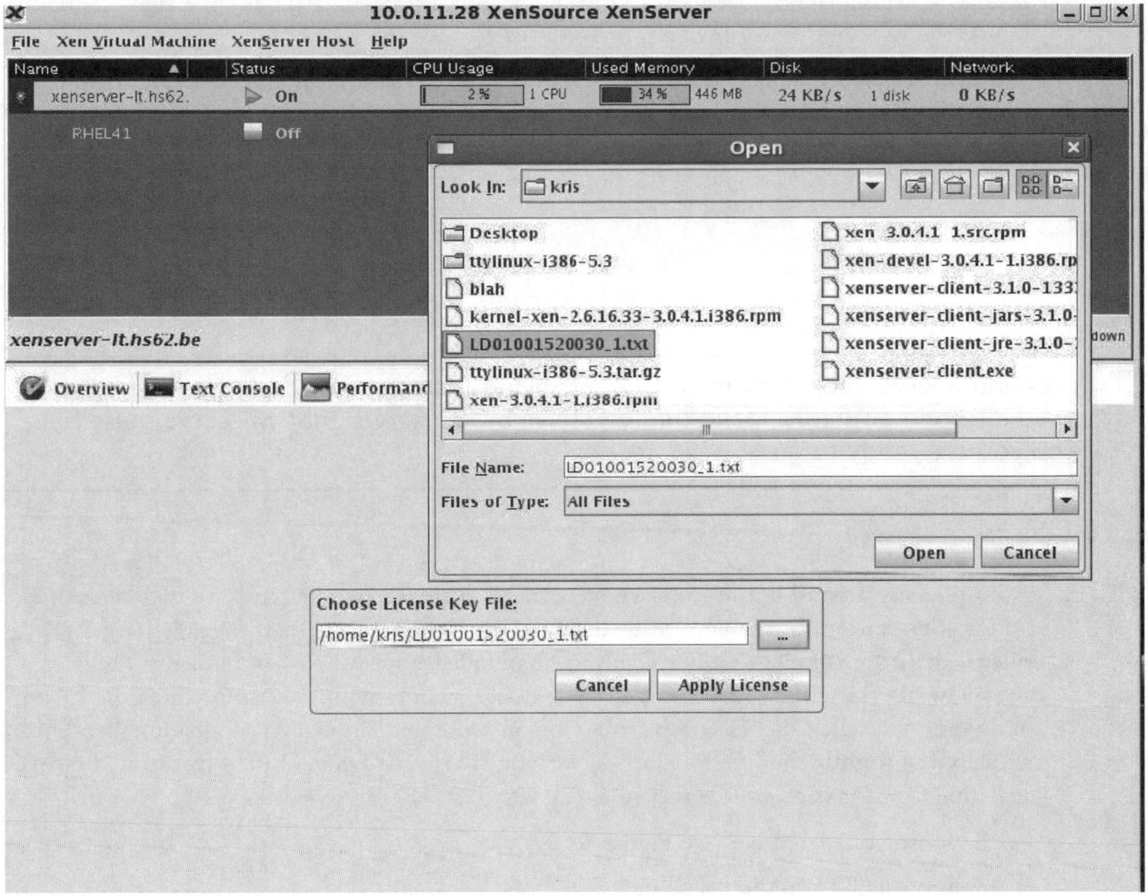

Installing an Initial Virtual Machine on XenServer

Now that we've made it this far, it's time to install our first virtual machine on the XenServer. So if you have already quit the Administrator Console, start it again and log on to our just-installed server.

1. Click the **Install Xen VM** icon in the middle bar.

2. In the lower part, you will now be able to fill in the details about the virtual machine you want to install. Let's start by installing a virtual machine from a Red Hat Enterprise Linux 4.1 repository. First, give it a name and a description. Next, even though you might only have one or two physical CPUs in your machine, you can give your virtual machine more virtual CPUs than you actually have. You, however, cannot give your virtual machine more memory than you actually have. Nevertheless, you can start with a little and grow on-the-fly as you need more memory.

3. On the right hand side you will see the disk and the network configuration. The RHEL 4.1. template has a one 8 GB disk by default. By clicking the + or − signs right below the overview, you can add more disks or remove them.

4. You will also see your network interfaces. Here you can add more interfaces and connect them to different bridges. The default xenbr0 bridges your physical eth0 to the eth0 in your virtual machine. Note that you will need to have access to a RHEL 4.1 repository. One on your local network, of course, is the fastest alternative.

> **NOTE**
>
> Creating a RHEL repository is as easy as copying the content off all the RHEL CDs you have into one directory. Make sure you have a Web server that will serve these files and you are ready to go.

5. After clicking **Install** in the lower-right corner, a virtual machine template will be created and will be started for the very first time. As of this point, you actually already have a virtual machine running—it just needs to be installed now. When you return to the overview, after a while you will see that a virtual machine with the name you chose is "on," and when you click the **Text Console** tab you will see a familiar Anaconda installer. This actually is a slightly modified version of Anaconda that has been adapted to run in a virtual machine. Once it has started, proceed as follows:

1. Choose your language (see Figure 13.29).

2. Choose HTTP as the install media.

Figure 13.29 The XenSource XenServer RHEL Installation

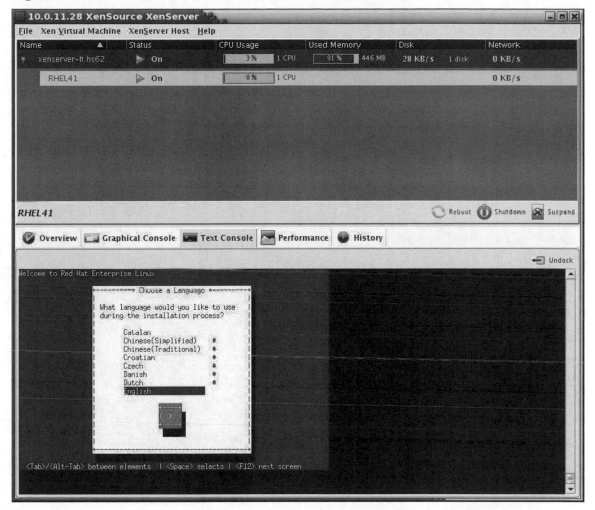

3. Configure your network so you can reach your repository. Test network connectivity by pinging the IP you just configured from a host.

4. Select your repository (see Figure 13.30). Test whether you can use the listed repository by connecting to the IP and the URL you provided with your Web browser.

Figure 13.30 The XenSource XenServer RHEL Repository Configuration

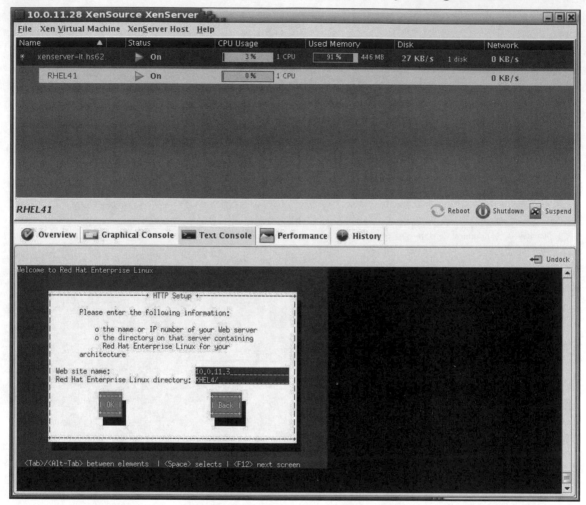

5.   The Red Hat installer will download its initial install images from the network. From here it is just a regular RHEL install. The full RHEL 4 manual, which also documents installation in detail, can be found at www.redhat.com/docs/manuals/ enterprise/RHEL-4-Manual/x8664-multi-install-guide (see Figure 13.31).

Figure 13.31 The XenSource XenServer RHEL Installation Starting

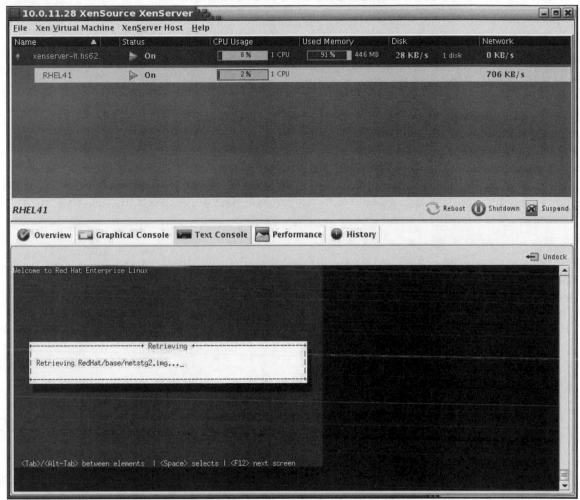

After installation, the Virtual machine will shut down and automatically restart into its freshly installed image. From here, you can use the Xen GUI to stop, start, suspend, and clone as you please.

We just explained how simple it is to install XenServer. You have to agree with us that getting the dom0 up and running is indeed a "Ten minutes to Xen" procedure. The installation of the virtual machines largely is related to the speed of your network. In the following section, we will be documenting how to install the RPMs provided by XenSource on any RPM-based distribution and how to use LVM as a disk backend for your virtual machines.

Other Xen Installation Methods

In this section, we'll discuss other methods for installing Xen.

Using the XenSource Binaries and LVM

You can download the open-source binaries and source code from getxen.org in addition to the XenSource Web site. The getxen.org packages are built by XenSource but are not supported by them; however, they do work on a variety of distributions and often have different features enabled that distributions don't have. One of those features is other disk backends for your virtual machine. Using other backends for your virtual disk means you can download existing images from a distribution and use those on a file system you prepare, rather than having to stick to the tools that a distribution forces you to use.

Jailtime.org provides a variety of distributions you can base your guest virtual machines on. As mentioned earlier, Xen can use both file-backed virtual block devices, which you can create by running:

```
dd if=/dev/zero of=vmdisk bs=1k seek 2048k count=1
```

You can export physical devices (the actual /dev/hda9) or you can use LVM volumes (phy:VolumeGroup/root_volume). We prefer to use Logical Volumes on our machines since they are very flexible to work with. In this section, we will document how to use the XenSource-provided RPM Binaries and how you can build virtual machines with their file systems on an LVM volume.

NOTE

If you are working on the same distribution where you installed virt-manager and the other fedora tools, you will need to uninstall all Xen tools from that distribution first because they will conflict with the XenSource RPMs.

So, the first step is to install the XenSource-provided RPMs on a vanilla machine.

```
[root@fc6-xen kris]# rpm -vih xen-3.0.4.1-1.i386.rpm ker-nel-xen-2.6.16.33-
3.0.4.1.i386.rpm --nodeps
Preparing...      ##########################################       [100%]
  1:kernel-xen ##########################################       [ 50%]
  2:xen         ##########################################       [100%]
```

The Xen RPMs do not modify your grub configuration, so you will need to add a grub entry for your freshly installed kernel yourself.

```
default=0
fallback=1
timeout=5
```

```
splashimage=(hd0,0)/grub/splash.xpm.gz
hiddenmenu
title Fedora Core (XenSource)
  root (hd0,0)
  kernel /xen.gz
  module /vmlinuz-2.6-xen ro root=/dev/VolGroup00/LogVol00 nodmraid xencons=off
  module /initrd-2.6-xen.img
title Fedora Core (2.6.18-1.2798.fc6)
  root (hd0,0)
  kernel /vmlinuz-2.6.18-1.2798.fc6 ro root=/dev/VolGroup00/LogVol00
nodmraid rhgb quiet
  initrd /initrd-2.6.18-1.2798.fc6.img
```

Do not remove the regular Linux kernel since you will need it if anything fails. After modifying that grub entry (take a look at the default kernel and verify it is the kernel you want to boot by default), upon rebooting you should arrive in a Xen-enabled kernel.

```
[root@fc6-xen xen]# uname -r
2.6.16.33-xen_3.0.4.1
```

The XenSource rpm will also have started *xend* and xendomains for you. Thus, the output of **xm list** should also look familiar.

```
[root@fc6-xen grub]# xm list
Name           ID    Mem    VCPUs  State   Time(s)
Domain-0       0     875    1      r-----  89.1
```

Now it's time to install your first virtual machine on an LVM Volume. As we noted earlier, you should still have plenty of space available in the Volume Group you created since you only chose to use 4 to 6 GB of disk for the dom0 file system. So let us create a new virtual machine, this time based on LVM.

```
lvcreate -L4096 -nroot-TEST-FC6 VolGroup00
mkdir -p /vhosts/FC6
mount /dev/VolGroup00/root-TEST-FC6 /vhosts/FC6
```

We usually create a directory */vhosts* where we mount our partitions as they would be mounted in a real machine on our dom0 host. From there, you can install the first FC6 Base packages in a chroot on the actual future root device. First, modify the */etc/yum/repo.d/* files. Uncomment the commented basedir and replace the variables. The beginning of the file should look like:

```
[core]name=Fedora Core $releasever - $basearch
baseurl=http://download.fedora.redhat.com/pub/fedora/linux/core/6/i386/os/
```

You can disable the other repositories for now by modifying the enabled parameter to 0. Start the installation of the Distribution into the chroot with:

```
yum --installroot=/vhosts/FC6/ -y groupinstall Base
```

This installation will take a while depending on the bandwidth you have to the repository as configured in the fedora-core.repo file. After this installation, some small changes are needed to make sure you can open your initial console and log on to your newly created virtual machine.

```
MAKEDEV -d /path/dev -x console
MAKEDEV -d /path/dev -x null
MAKEDEV -d /path/dev -x zero
```

Since we want network connectivity and we want to be able to log on to the virtual machine, you should also create a */etc/sysconfig/network* file, an */etc/sysconfig/network-scripts/ifcfg-eth0* file, and a working */etc/shadow* and */etc/password* file in to the */vhost/FC6* tree in order to be able to log in to the machine once it is booted. Also copy the /lib/modules directory from the dom0, or install the kernel-xen package again with the same install root so the modules will match the appropriate kernel.

We're almost ready. What we still need is the configuration file for this virtual machine. Most of Xen's configuration files live in */etc/xen*. You'll be creating a separate configuration file for each virtual machine you want to deploy on your Xen host. They look like the following example, and if you create a symlink to the */etc/xen/auto* directory, they will even be started at boot time given that you enable the xendomains script at bootup.

```
[root@fc6-xen xen]# more FC6-LVM
kernel = "/boot/vmlinuz-2.6-xen"
#initrd= "/boot/initrd-2.6-xen.img"
name = "FC6-LVM"
memory = "256"
disk = [ 'phy:/dev/VolGroup00/root-TEST-FC6,sda1,w', ]
root = "/dev/sda1 rw"
vif = [ 'mac=00:16:3e:06:3b:80, bridge=xenbr0', ]
```

As you can see, the file system you will use this time is phy:/dev/VolGroup00/root-TEST-FC6—exactly the Logical Volume we just created. The configuration file is rather straightforward, and the Xen packages include examples. You can add multiple Logical Volumes mapped to multiple partitions. We often create a mapping like:

```
disk = ['phy:vm_volumes/root-hostname,sda1,w',
  'phy:vm_volumes/var-hostname,sda3,w',
  'phy:vm_volumes/www-hostname,sda4,w',
  'phy:vm_volumes/swap-hostname,sda2,w',]
```

Make sure you unmount the Logical Volume from */vhosts/FC6* before trying to start the virtual machine. Otherwise, it won't start. You now must start your virtual machine with the command **xm create config file**. If you add a **–c** to that command, you'll see the machine booting and you should get a login prompt within seconds. From there, you can log in and use your virtual machine just like any other machine.

The whole process we've just documented is ideal for managing larger deployments since every step you take can be automated. A paper first presented at the 2005 Hamburg Linux Kongress on Automating Xen Virtual Machine Deployments (which can be found on http://howto.x-tend.be/

AutomatingVirtualMachineDeployment/) documents how you can integrate SystemImager, which is a Large Scale Deployment framework and a couple of simple scripts to automate Xen virtual machine deployment.

If you are interested in Physical 2 Virtual Machine migration tools, the previously mentioned paper, in combination with the golden client framework that SystemImager comes with is perfectly suited to do such migrations for Linux-based physical machines.

Configuring Xen

Most people can get Xen up and running without having to touch any of the configuration files we'll be discussing in the next couple of paragraphs. However, both xendomains and xen have different facets you can tune and tweak.

The main Xen configuration file is xend-config.sxp, which is located in /etc/xen/. If you install the XenSource RPM, it brims with examples and documentation, while other distributions tend to slim down the configuration file and leave you with a preconfigured set of parameters. Note that the commented entries in this file show the default parameters.

Let's have a look at some more important parameters that can be found in these configuration files. A not unimportant feature is logging. If you want to change the location of your log file or the amount of data it is logging, modify the following:

```
(logfile /var/log/xen/xend.log)
(loglevel DEBUG)
```

Xend can be managed via an httpd server which you probably want to disable for security reasons.

```
#(xend-http-server no)
#(xend-port 8000)
```

If you plan on configuring live migration of virtual machines, you will need to enable the xend-relocation-server parameters.

```
#(xend-relocation-server yes)
# Port xend should use for the relocation interface, if xend-relocation-server
# is set.
#(xend-relocation-port 8002)
#(xend-relocation-address '')
```

And as with any daemon, you can restrict the sockets to which xend listens via the following parameters.

```
#(xend-address '')
#(xend-address localhost)
```

A more important section for day-to-day usage is the network configuration portion. Whenever a system is booted in a xen-kernel, it will just have an eth0, just like any other system. This will change when the xend service is started. The xend service will activate bridging and the necessary virtual devices that allow network traffic from outside to the virtual hosts. At first, the current eth0, which is the physical network card, will be changed to peth0. For other network interfaces (eth1, …), the same will happen (peth1, …). From now on, you have to check the link status on device peth0 instead of eth0.

Next, eth0 will be re-created in the same way as on every other virtual host. The virtual host will only see eth0, which has a corresponding VIF interface on dom0. Eth0 on dom0 (which has ID 0) will be mapped to vif0.0, while eth1 of dom0 will be mapped to vif0.1. On a virtual host with ID 3, the eth0 interface will be mapped against vif3.0. In general, you have a unique vifY.X interface on dom0 for every interface of each virtual host. Y indicates the ID of the virtual host and X the number of the interface (eth0, eth1, …).

The connection between the physical interface (peth0) and the interface of the virtual host (vif Y.X) is made by bridging. The amount of bridges and which interface is bounded to which bridge is handled by the Xen configuration.

```
(network-script network-bridge)
# The script used to control virtual interfaces. This can be overridden on a
# per-vif basis when creating a domain or configuring a new vif. The
# vif-bridge script is designed for use with the network-bridge script, or
# similar configurations.
#
# If you have overridden the bridge name using
# (network-script 'network-bridge bridge=$name') then you may wish to do the
# same here. The bridge name can also be set when creating a domain or
# configuring a new vif, but a value specified here would act as a default.
#
# If you are using only one bridge, the vif-bridge script will discover that,
# so there is no need to specify it explicitly.
#
(vif-script vif-bridge)
## Use the following if network traffic is routed, as an alternative to the
# settings for bridged networking given above.
#(network-script network-route)
#(vif-script vif-route)
## Use the following if network traffic is routed with NAT, as an alternative
# to the settings for bridged networking given above.
#(network-script network-nat)
#(vif-script vif-nat)
```

The xend-config.sxp file is also the file where you configure the minimum memory required for a dom0 196, which is more than enough for a dom0. We're mostly running them with only 128 MB of RAM as a minimum. This certainly is enough in a headless environment where the dom0 only serves as a management console for the virtual machines.

```
(dom0-min-mem 196)
(dom0-cpus 0)
```

If you are installing Windows machines as domUs, you can also configure the behavior of a VNC server, or give it a default password.

```
# The interface for VNC servers to listen on. Defaults
#(vnc-listen '127.0.0.1')
# The default password for VNC console on HVM domain.
# Empty string is no authentication.
(vncpasswd '')
```

As mentioned earlier, every configuration file you place or symlink from in */etc/xen/auto* will be started by the rc script xendomains at boot time. Xendomains itself also has a couple of configuration parameters that can be modified in the */etc/sysconfig/xendomains* parameters.

One of the more important configuration parameters in the xendomains config file is the parameter that defines what to do with a virtual machine that has been started by xendomains when the physical machine is being rebooted. By default, a domain will be saved and restarted, unless you modify the configuration parameters. Also, if you want to save a virtual machine, the xendomains config file has a parameter that defines where to store these images:

```
XENDOMAINS_SAVE=/var/lib/xen/save
```

If you leave the preceding line empty, xendomains will not attempt to save the domains and will shut them down before the physical machine goes down. If you leave this config and you run out of disk space, you might run into trouble rebooting afterwards, so be careful.

NOTE

You can also choose to migrate the guests to another physical machine in the event of a shutdown.

Getting Xen on Your Network

As just mentioned, Xen will create a bridge and bind the virtual interfaces of your guest to that bridge. A default bridge configuration will look like

```
[root@tc6-xen xen]# brctl show
bridge name     bridge id            STP enabled     interfaces
xenbr0          8000.feffffffffff    no              vif1.0
                                                     peth0
                                                     vif0.0
```

Configuring & Implementing...

About brctl

As most of you know, a bridge connects two different Ethernet network segments. All protocols go transparently through a bridge as the connection is being made on Layer 2. Linux Bridging has been around since the 2.2 kernel series and is not specifically related to Xen. It has been rewritten by Lennert Buytenhek for 2.4 and 2.6 kernels. The code itself is in the Linux kernel and you'll need the brctl userspace tool to control it.

Creating a bridge is as easy as running.

```
[root@HOST ~]# brctl addbr xenbr1
```

To see the current state of bridges on your system, you can use

```
[root@HOST ~]# brctl show
bridge name       bridge id           STP enabled   interfaces
xenbr0            8000.feffffffffff   no            peth0
                                                    vif0.0
                                                    vif1.0
xenbr1            8000.000000000000   no            can't get port
info: Function not implemented
```

The next thing you need to do is add ports, or interfaces, to that bridge. Such as:

```
[root@HOST ~]#    brctl   addif   xenbr1 peth1
[root@HOST ~]#    brctl   addif   xenbr1 vif0.1
[root@HOST ~]#    brctl   addif   xenbr1 vif1.1
```

Which will then create a bridge for you that looks like:

```
[root@CO-TMS-B ~]#   brctl    show
bridge name       bridge id           STP enabled   interfaces
xenbr0            8000.feffffffffff   no            peth0
                                                    vif0.0
                                                    vif1.0
xenbr1            8000.feffffffffff   no            peth1
                                                    vif0.1
                                                    vif1.1
```

As easy as creating bridge ports is removing them:

```
[root@CO-TMS-B ~]#     brctl   delif   xenbr1 vif1.1
[root@CO-TMS-B ~]#     brctl   delif   xenbr1 vif0.1
[root@CO-TMS-B ~]#     brctl   delif   xenbr1 peth1
[root@CO-TMS-B ~]#     brctl   show
bridge name        bridge id            STP enabled   interfaces
xenbr0             8000.ffffffffffff    no            peth0
                                                      vif0.0
                                                      vif1.0
xenbr1             8000.000000000000    no            can't get port
info: Function not implemented
```

However, before deleting the actual bridge, you must make sure the interface xenbr1 is also down.

```
[root@CO-TMS-B ~]#   ifconfig   xenbr1   down
[root@CO-TMS-B ~]#   brctl     delbr   xenbr1
[root@CO-TMS-B ~]#   brctl     show
bridge name        bridge id            STP enabled   interfaces
xenbr0             8000.ffffffffffff    no            peth0
                                                      vif0.0
                                                      vif1.0
```

If your network requires it, Linux bridging also supports the Spanning Tree Protocol IEEE 802.1d, amongst others, which are responsible for preventing loops in your network. The brctl man page clearly documents its further usage.

If you want to use the eth0 in your machine only for management connections and route all the traffic over other interfaces, nothing can keep you from creating your own xen-network script. You just need to modify the */etc/xen/xend-config.sxp* file to get

```
(network-script my-network-script)
```

Then put your network script in /etc/xen/scripts/. An example might look like:

```
#!/bin/sh
brctl   addbr   xen-br0
brctl   addif   xen-br0   eth1
brctl   addif   xen-br0   vif1.0
brctl   addbr   xen-br1
brctl   addif   xen-br1   eth2
brctl   addif   xen-br1   vif1.1
```

This will actually bind your second and third physical interfaces to your first and second virtual interface. If you want multiple bridges, one bridge per physical interface, you must use a wrapper script. This wrapper script is defined by the xend-config.sxp and will be called when xend is started. The wrapper script will call the original network-bridge script multiple times.

```
[root@XEN-A ~]# grep network-wrapper-bridge /etc/xen/xend-config.sxp
(network-script network-wrapper-bridge)
/etc/xen/scripts/network-wrapper-bridge
#!/bin/sh
/etc/xen/scripts/network-bridge start vifnum=0 netdev=eth0
/etc/xen/scripts/network-bridge start vifnum=1 netdev=eth1
```

Because you will now have multiple bridges, it is not always sure that the correct VIF interface is mapped to the correct bridge. If you want to map each virtual eth0 to the physical eth0, you must write yet another wrapper script, this time for vif-bridge.

```
[root@XEN-A ~]# grep vif-wrapper-bridge /etc/xen/xend-config.sxp
(vif-script vif-wrapper-bridge)
/etc/xen/scripts/vif-wrapper-bridge
#!/bin/sh
if [ $1 = "online" ]
then
  # load some general functions
  dir=$(dirname "$0")
  . "$dir/vif-common.sh"
  # find the bridge number out of the vif interface name
  brnum=$(echo $vif | sed 's/vif.*\.//')
  bridge=xenbr$brnum
  # store the bridgename in xenstore
  bridge=$(xenstore_write "$XENBUS_PATH/bridge" "$bridge")
fi
# load the real vif-bridge script
/etc/xen/scripts/vif-bridge $1
```

This wrapper script will grab the interface number from the VIF interface and use that number for the xenbr. The generated xenbridge name is stored in the xenstore. The vif-bridge script, which is called at the end, will take the correct bridgename out of the Xenstore.

Summary

Creating an environment to deploy virtual machines takes some thinking upfront. We need to make choices about whether we want a Community-supported or Enterprise-supported Linux distribution, or an isolated platform that keeps the Linux system management hidden from us. We need to think about what type of services we want to virtualize and the impact of these choices into CPU selection, disk usage, and memory needs.

Installing Xen, can be done in different ways. In this chapter, you learned how to install Xen and both Linux- or Windows-based virtual machines with either a regular Linux distribution or XenEnterprise on your server, such as Fedora Core, or with the XenSource Enterprise product.

Fedora Core and its successors, including Red Hat Enterprise Linux and CentOS, provide us with an easy-to-install, easy-to-manage platform that eases both the installation and management of Linux and Windows virtual machines. Creating either a Linux or Windows-based virtual machine is just a few clicks away.

XenServer gives you a platform where the Linux management part is hidden from you and you get a well-designed GUI where you can manage different physical and virtual machines. XenServer still is a young product and will gain more features with each release. It is targeted at the Windows IT professional, and though capable, it may not be the product of choice for the seasoned Linux administrator preferring to build and install Xen themselves from a source in their own Linux environment.

Solutions Fast Track

Determining Which Xen to Choose

☑ Choosing your Xen distribution is a matter of deciding between freedom and support, and between virtualizing just Windows, or more.

☑ If you want freedom, go for a community Linux distribution. If you want support, the Enterprise Linux distributions will help you.

☑ XenServer is the obvious product for you if you only plan on virtualizing Windows machines.

System Requirements

☑ Most recent machines you buy already have a VT-capable CPU available. If you plan on virtualizing Windows or other non-modifiable, unsupported operating systems, you will need these capabilities in your CPU.

☑ When buying new hardware, consider the expected disk and memory usage of the virtual machines you plan to deploy. The sum of all of these plus some extra is what your machine should look like.

Thinking Before You Start

- ☑ A regular Linux distribution will not know upfront that you plan on installing virtualization tools. It will not create a disk layout that is suitable to host different virtual machines. Thus, you should modify the default partition layout at install time.

- ☑ LVM is the preferred method of managing virtual machine disk volumes. It gives you both freedom and scalability while hiding complexity.

Installing Xen on a Free Linux Distribution

- ☑ Installing Fedora Core 6 is easy. Use only a minimal install for your domain0 since you will not be running other applications in that domain besides the Xen management tools.

- ☑ VirtManager provides you with an easy GUI that allows you to install both Windows and Linux virtual machines with a couple of mouse clicks.

Installing the XenServer Product Family

- ☑ XenSource provides a "Ten minutes to Xen" framework that allows you to quickly install a host operating system that is ready to have new virtual machines installed.

- ☑ Based on the existing templates, you can install different Linux and Windows distributions from the XenSource client and also manage them from there.

Other Xen Installation Methods

- ☑ Other distributions might not have pre-shipped Xen RPMS, or not have the VirtManager GUI to ease the installation of virtual instances. You can use yum to create installations in chroot environments on different LVM volumes and this way create reproducible Xen installations.

- ☑ Other distributions have similar tools like *yast* and *debootstrap*. Also, frameworks such as *systemImager* allow you to create images of other physical or virtual machines and ease physical-to-virtual machine migration.

Configuring Xen

- ☑ The main configuration files for Xen live in /etc/xen/. This is where all the parameters the *xend* daemon requires and all the different configuration files for the actual virtual machines live. They are usually well documented and example files have been shipped with most distributions.

- ☑ The easiest way of networking Xen is by using the regular Linux bridging tools. Use them to connect the network interfaces of your virtual machines to the appropriate networks on your physical machine.

Frequently Asked Questions

Q: Where do I get Xen?

A: Xen is either included in your distribution already, or you can download either the prebuild RPMS by Xensource from http://getxen.org/ or get the XenExpress Free Starter pack from there.

Q: My machine doesn't boot after installing Xen. What should I do?

A: You most probably are running into a driver problem. The Xen kernel you are trying to boot does not recognize your primary hard disk. If you look carefully at the messages on your screen, you should see an error similar to: Kernel panic: VFS: Unable to mount root fs on sda1. A lot of kernel panics are caused because they can't find the hard disk. This happens because the correct module is not built into the kernel or is not available in the initrd. The xen kernel does not have as many built-in modules as a normal distribution kernel, and the needed modules aren't automatically added in the initrd. The solution is easy: include the needed modules in the initrd. But which module is the correct one? That depends on the hardware in your system. You can start finding the correct modules by reading the dmesg when you boot that system with a working kernel. Creating an Initrd with the matching kernel versions can be done as follows: mkinitrd -v -f –with=ide-generic /boot/initrd-2.6.16.33-xen_3.0.4.1.img 2.6.16.33-xen_3.0.4.1.

Q: Which RPM should I install Xen from? One from my distribution or one from XenSource?

A: Part of that answer depends on what your environment is like. If you are working in an Enterprise Linux environment, you of course will want to use the RPMs that have been shipped with your distribution and will be supported by your vendor. If, however, you are running a Free Distribution, you might want to look at the XenSource RPMs since they have created an RPM with the most features and which has also been created for specific platforms.

Q: Does Xen support my hardware?

A: Xen hardware support is being managed by the dom0 kernel, which means that if your hardware is supported in a general Linux distribution, it will also be supported by Xen. If you are unsure, do not hesitate to contact your local XenSource partner who can help you out.

Q: I got the following error when trying to run xm list: ERROR: Could not obtain handle on privileged command interface (2 – No such file or directory); Error: Unable to connect to xend: No such file or directory. Is xend running?

A: This error usually occurs when you are either running in a non-Xen-enabled environment, or when you haven't started the xend daemon yet. Verify if your kernel is already Xen-enabled by running uname –a, or start your xend daemon by running /etc/init.d/xend start.

Q: I'm running into the following error when trying to start a virtual machine: Error: Device 2049 (vbd) could not be connected. Device /dev/VolGroup00/root-FC6 is mounted in the privileged domain, and so cannot be mounted by a guest. Why?

A: This means one of the virtual disks you have configured for use as a file system in the virtual machine is still being used by another domain. Run df and check the output. It will most probably still be mounted in your dom0. You can solve this by running umount against the volume in question.

## Chapter 14

The Administrator Console and Other Native Tools

Solutions in this chapter:

- Native Xen Command-Line Tools
- XenServer Administrator Console

☑ Summary

☑ Solutions Fast Track

☑ Frequently Asked Questions

Introduction

The sign of an enterprise-ready technology is an efficient tool to manage that technology. Xen is not any different. Many technologies that promised great potential to companies seeking to contain costs and simplify their operations suffered from poor management tools, leading to little, if any, adoption in the enterprise. This has never been more important than with virtualization products, such as Xen. Fortunately, Xen comes with a robust suite of tools, both command-line as well as GUI.

In this chapter, we will review the native management tools that are available. Tool syntax and options will be explored as well as best practices and use cases for each one. In particular, we will thoroughly review the Administrator Console, used to manage XenExpress, XenServer, and XenEnterprise.

Designing & Planning…

Combining XenServer Tools for Enterprise Administration

Whereas the Administrator Console GUI provides a comprehensive set of functions for managing Xen hosts, virtual machines (VMs), and storage, the command-line interfaces (CLIs) complement and expand that functionality.

The xe CLI, which is on all Xen hosts and is installed on the Administrator Console, provides an efficient way to automate functionality by incorporating or "wrapping" the commands within scripting languages. However, the xe CLI does not provide all the functionality of the sm and xm interfaces, present only on the Xen hosts. Additional scripting can be done directly on the Xen hosts to ease administration tasks.

Because there is a choice of tools for different functions, administrators should select a tool based on their operational conditions. For example:

- Creation or modification to a single VM is easiest on the Administrator Console.

- The Administrator Console does not have a scheduler for administrative tasks, so consider using xe-based cron scripts to schedule periodic tasks.

- Live migrations can be done only through the *xm* command on the Xen hosts.

- Certain storage operations can be done only with the sm CLI.

Native Xen Command-Line Tools

All operations that you can perform on XenHosts and XenVMs you can execute through one of the command-line tool interfaces. In particular, three such interfaces are available with Xen distributions:

- The xe tool provides a management interface for both XenHosts and XenVMs. The xe tool is available both on the XenHosts and on the Administrator Console.

- The sm CLI provides a set of additional storage management options not available to the XenHosts Administrator Console. The sm CLI is available only on XenHosts.

- The xm CLI is the traditional Xen tool for management. It is available on the open source Xen as well as the commercial versions (XenExpress, XenServer, and XenEnterprise). The xm interface maintains the original domain nomenclature of dom0 (XenHost) and domU (XenVMs), and all operations are done against domain names or domain IDs. In addition, certain operations, such as XenVM migration, you can do only through the xm interface. The xm interface is available only on XenHosts.

In this section, we will cover only some of the more common xe commands. Chapter 16 contains more in-depth information.

The xe Command-Line Interface

Here is an example of the syntax for the xe CLI:

```
xe command-name [switches] [param=value … param=value]
```

command-name refers to the subcommand that is to be run against a XenHost. Commands are classified under three groups:

- Storage commands
- Host commands
- VM commands

Switches refer to authentication and connection string parameters:

- **–u**   Username on XenHost.
- **–pw**   Password.
- **–pwf**   File containing the username and password (prevents command history or process listing from showing username and password in clear text).
- **–h**   Host (Internet Protocol [IP] address or hostname of XenHost).
- **–p**   Port (if not using the default port).

Installing and Cloning XenVMs

To install a new XenVM, you use *vm-install* with the *xe* command. Here is the syntax:

```
xe vm-install -u USERNAME -pw PASSWORD -h HOSTNAME/IP template-name="TEMPLATE
NAME" -name=VM_NAME auto_poweron=TRUE/FALSE vcpus=1 memory_set=256
```

You can add additional parameters, such as *vif* for network or *vdi* for disk. Upon correct syntax, the output of the command should look something like the following:

```
Adding VIF to install target: host-bridge=xenbr0, MAC=00:16:3E:23:59:32.
Initiating install…
New VM uuid: 5f2852a1-fa96-4e3e-8208-0a05299fc8ed
[DONE]
```

To clone an existing XenVM, use *vm-clone* with the *xe* command. The correct syntax is as follows:

```
xe vm-clone - u USERNAME -pw PASSWORD -h HOSTNAME/IP
vm-name="EXISTING_XENVM" new-name="NEW_VM" new-description="DESCRIPTION FOR
NEW XENVM"
```

Starting Up, Shutting Down, Rebooting, Suspending, and Resuming XenVMs

To boot a XenVM, use the following syntax:

```
xe vm-start - u USERNAME -pw PASSWORD -h HOSTNAME/IP vm-name=XENVM_NAME_HERE
```

To shut down a XenVM, use this:

```
xe vm-shutdown - u USERNAME -pw PASSWORD -h HOSTNAME/IP vm-name=XENVM_NAME_HERE
```

To reboot a XenVM, use this syntax:

```
xe vm-reboot - u USERNAME -pw PASSWORD -h HOSTNAME/IP vm-name=XENVM_NAME_HERE
```

Here is the syntax for suspending a XenVM:

```
xe vm-suspend - u USERNAME -pw PASSWORD -h HOSTNAME/IP vm-name=XENVM_NAME_HERE
```

And here is the syntax for resuming a XenVM:

```
xe vm-resume - u USERNAME -pw PASSWORD -h HOSTNAME/IP vm-name=XENVM_NAME_HERE
```

You need to ensure that the correct information is input for each of the parameters.

Shutting Down and Rebooting XenHosts

To shut down a XenHost, use this syntax:

```
xe host-shutdown - u USERNAME -pw PASSWORD -h HOSTNAME/IP
```

To reboot a XenHost, use this syntax:

```
xe host-reboot - u USERNAME -pw PASSWORD -h HOSTNAME/IP
```

Query Options for XenHosts

Here is the syntax to query a host for existing XenVMs:

```
xe host-vm-list - u USERNAME -pw PASSWORD -h HOSTNAME/IP
```

To query a host for physical network interfaces, use this:

```
xe host-pif-list - u USERNAME -pw PASSWORD -h HOSTNAME/IP
```

To query a host for existing templates, use this:

```
xe host-template-list - u USERNAME -pw PASSWORD -h HOSTNAME/IP
```

And to list vbridges, use this:

```
xe host-vbridge-list - u USERNAME -pw PASSWORD -h HOSTNAME/IP
```

XenServer Administrator Console

The Administrator Console is a remote Java-based application that manages the configuration and operations of XenServer hosts and VMs. The Administrator Console provides a subset of the functionality that is available through the command-line tools. However, this subset encompasses most day-to-day operations, such as creation of XenVMs, power on/off, XenHost reboots, and so on. In addition, the Administrator Console provides basic performance monitoring graphs of CPU, memory, network, and disk utilization for both XenHosts and XenVMs.

System Requirements for the Administrator Console

Table 14.1 outlines the requirements for the Administrator Console.

Table 14.1 Administrator Console System Requirements

Component	Minimum	Recommended
Operating system	N/A	Red Hat Enterprise Linux 4.x
		Novell (SUSE) Linux Enterprise Server 9.x Windows XP
		Windows 2000
		Windows Server 2003
CPU speed	750 MHz	1 GHz or faster
RAM	384 MB	1 GB or better
Disk space	100 MB	N/A
Networking	1 network interface card (NIC)	N/A

Continued

Table 14.1 Continued

Component	Minimum	Recommended
Component	Minimum	Recommended
Operating system	N/A	Red Hat Enterprise Linux 4.*x*
		Novell (SUSE) Linux Enterprise Server 9.*x*
		Windows XP
		Windows 2000
		Windows Server 2003
CPU speed	750 MHz	1 GHz or faster

Installing the Administrator Console

You can deploy the Administrator Console on Red Hat and SUSE, as well as a variety of Windows operating systems. Installation on either Windows or Linux is fairly simple.

Installing the Administrator Console on Windows (XP/2000/2003)

You can find the installation binaries for the Administrator Console on the XenEnterprise installation CD-ROM. The following steps will walk you through the installation process:

1. Insert the XenEnterprise Installation CD into the CD-ROM of the system that will host the Administrator Console.

2. Run the xenserver-client.exe install program from the client_install directory.

3. Click the **Yes button** to continue the installation (see Figure 14.1).

Figure 14.1 XenServer Administrator Console 3.2.0 Setup

4. Click the **Next button** to continue the installation (see Figure 14.2).

Figure 14.2 XenServer Administrator Console 3.2.0 Recommendations

5.   Click **Next** (see Figure 14.3).

Figure 14.3 License Agreement Screen

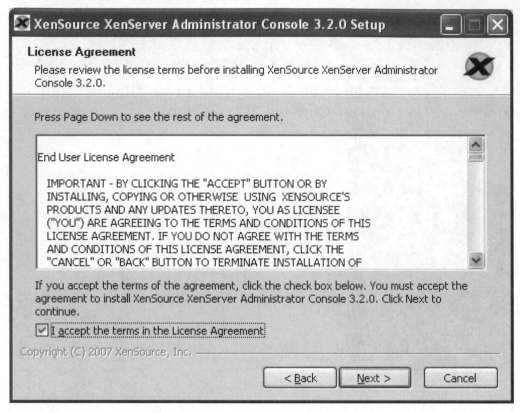

6.   If the destination folder is acceptable, leave the default location; otherwise, enter or browse to your preferred install directory and click **Next** to continue (see Figure 14.4).

Figure 14.4 Installation Location

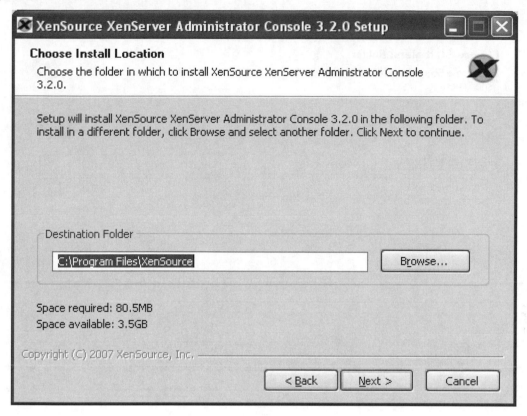

7. To accept the default Start menu folder click the **Install button** (see Figure 14.5). The Show Details button will display the actions of the installer (see Figure 14.6).

Figure 14.5 Start Menu Folder Selection

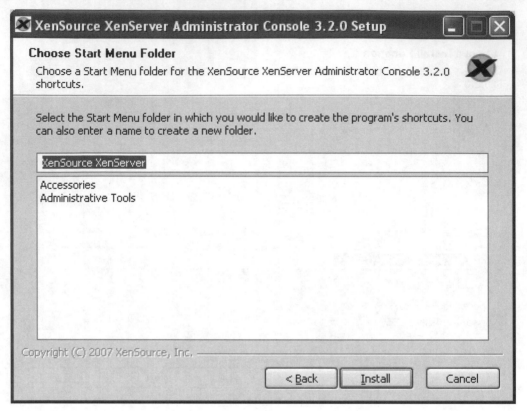

Figure 14.6 Installation Progress

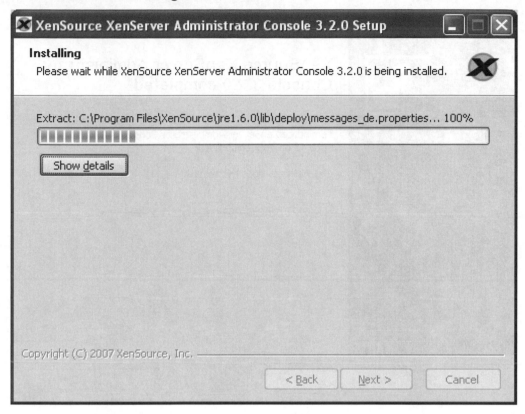

8. To start the Administrator Console, click on the **Run XenServer Administrator Console check box** and then click the **Finish button** (see Figure 14.7).

Figure 14.7 Administrator 3.2 Installation Completed

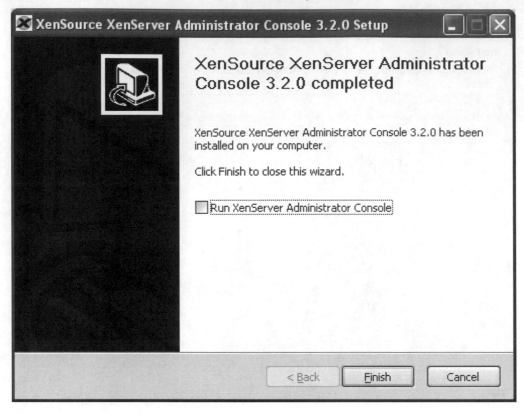

9. The Master Login screen prompts you for your password. This password is used to encrypt host login information locally, such as the XenServer host IP address. Every time you log on to the Administrator Console, you are prompted for the master password. Once you have entered the password, click the **Login button** (see Figure 14.8).

Figure 14.8 Master Login Screen

NOTE

The master password is local to the computer hosting the Administrator Console, and is used only to log into the Administrator Console and encrypt configuration information. The XenServer host password is the password that was given during the installation of the XenServer host, and is used to log the Administrator Console onto the XenServer host.

Installing the Administrator Console on Linux

You can find the installation binaries for Linux on the XenServer Linux Pack CD. To install the Linux Pack, follow these steps:

1. Insert the XenServer Linux Pack CD into the CD-ROM of the workstation to be used to host the Administrator Console

2. *cd* to the client_install directory. The following packages are in the directory:

   - xe-cli-3.2.0-1960.i386.rpm

   - xc-cli-dcbuginfo-3.2.0-1960.i386.rpm

   - xenserver-client-3.2.0-1960.noarch.rpm

   - xenserver-client-jars-3.2.0-1960.noarch.rpm

   - xenserver-client-jre-3.2.0-1960.i386.rpm

3. Install all the packages in the directory, using this command:

```
rpm -ihv *.rpm
```

NOTE

The xe-cli-3.2.0-1960.i386.rpm and xe-cli-debuginfo-3.2.0-1960.i386.rpm packages are not part of the Administrator Console GUI. They provide a CLI to access and control the XenServer host.

Using the Administrator Console

To log on to the Administrator Console on Windows, select **Start Menu | XenSource XenServer | Administrator Console**. On Linux, use the following command:

```
xenserver-client
```

NOTE

Because the Administrator Console is a Java-based GUI application, make sure the Linux distribution has a functional window manager installed.

After launching the application, you will be prompted for the XenServer host IP/hostname and the root password (see Figure 14.9).

Figure 14.9 XenServer Host Login Screen

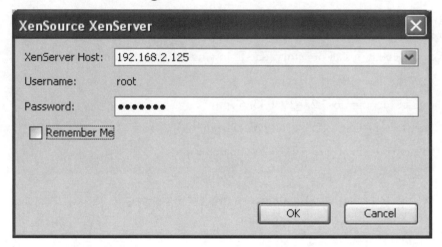

Once you have been authenticated, the Administrator Console screen will appear (see Figure 14.10).

Figure 14.10 The Administrator Console Screen

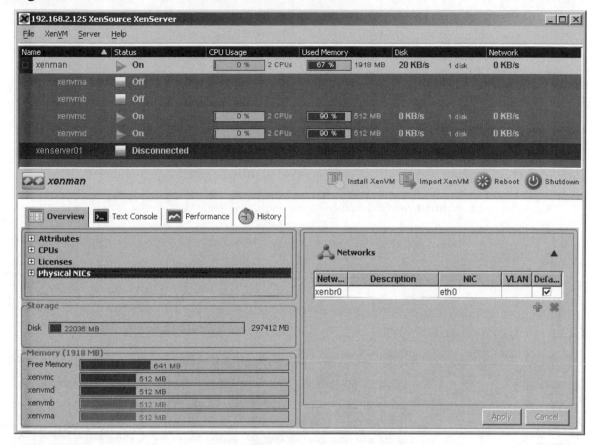

The Administrator Console is functionally divided into three parts:

■ The menu bar

■ A top pane, which contains a listing of XenHosts and XenVMs and several contextual action buttons

■ A bottom pane consisting of multiple tabs for Overview, Consoles, Performance Graphs, and History

You typically can perform actions from the menu bar, from the contextual buttons in the top pane, or within the tabs of the bottom pane.

Working with Hosts

In this section, we'll discuss the steps for connecting to a host and powering off or rebooting a XenHost.

Connecting to a XenHost

To connect to a host click the XenHost and do one of the following:

- Click on the **Connect button** on the top pane.
- Select **Connect** from the **Server menu**.
- Right-click on the **XenHost** and select **Connect**.

Powering Off/Rebooting a XenHost

You can power off/reboot hosts from the Administrator Console by selecting the host and doing one of the following:

- Click on the **shutdown/reboot buttons** on the top pane.
- Select **Shutdown/Reboot** from the **Server menu**.
- Right-click on the host and select **Shutdown/Reboot**.

Figure 14.11 shows the additional host operations from the menu bar.

Figure 14.11 Server Menu

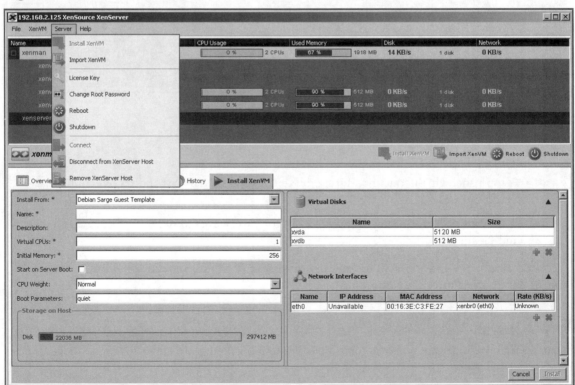

Deploying and Configuring XenVMs

You can use various operations to deploy XenVMs. We explore installing, cloning, exporting, and physical-to-virtual conversions in depth in Chapter 16.

Creating Xen Virtual Machines

Creating VMs in the Administrator Console is a straightforward process:

1. Select the Xen host on which the XenVM will be created.

2. Select **Install XenVM** by clicking the **Install XenVM button**, or by selecting it from the **Server menu**. The lower pane will display the Install XenVM tab (see Figure 14.12).

Figure 14.12 Installing XenVM

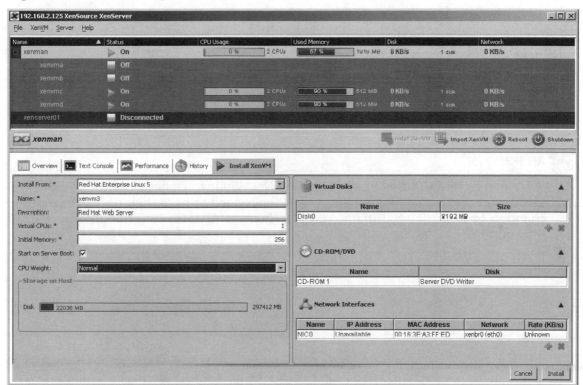

To install XenVM you need to provide information in the following sections of the screen, as shown in Figure 14.12:

■ **Install From:**   Refers to the template to be used for this XenVM. Currently, Xen supports only the Debian Sarge template.

- **Name:** The name of the XenVM (not the OS hostname of the XenVM).

- **Virtual CPUs:** The number of VCPUs that will be presented to the XenVM. This will depend on the type of license being used (only the Enterprise license allows multiple VCPUs).

- **Initial Memory:** The amount of memory allocated to the XenVM.

- **Start on Server Boot:** Whether to start the XenVM automatically after the XenHost is booted.

- **Virtual Disks:** The disk name and size fields are directly editable. You can specify additional virtual disks by clicking on the plus sign.

- **CD-ROM/DVD:** Automatically detects the XenHosts CD/DVD drive. The Disk field is a drop-down menu with additional entries for P2V tools, and Windows XenSource tools.

- **Network Interfaces:** Lists the xenbr0 network. You can select additional networks by clicking the plus sign.

Cloning XenVMs

Another way to create a XenVM is through cloning. Cloning copies the virtual disks and the configuration files of the original XenVM.

WARNING

You need to be careful when cloning XenVMs: Windows clones need to have their SSIDs reset and both Windows and Linux clones need to have their network identity changed to avoid IP or hostname conflicts. Refer to Chapter 16 for additional information.

To create a XenVM clone, follow these steps:

1. Select the XenVM to be cloned.

2. Shut down the XenVM to be cloned.

3. With the powered-off XenVM selected, click on the **Clone button**. The lower pane will ask whether to continue with the cloning process. Click on the **OK button**.

    The cloning process will begin. Notice in Figure 14.13 that the state of the original XenVM (xenvma) is set to cloning, and no information is displayed for the CPU or memory usage (the XenVM is shut down and is not consuming any resources). The new XenVM has the name "Clone of xenvma" and shows a status of "Installing".

Figure 14.13 Cloning Screen

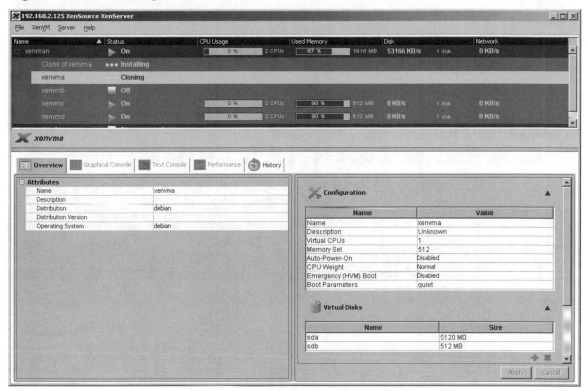

Once you've created the clone, you can modify the fields in the Configuration section of the Overview tab. In addition, you can add virtual disks, but you cannot remove the existing ones.

Additional XenVM Operations

Here is a list of additional XenVM operations:

- Power on/off
- Suspend/resume
- Reboot
- Export
- Force shutdown/reboot
- Uninstall

Performance Monitoring

Although not a comprehensive monitoring platform, the Administrator Console provides basic performance information for both XenHosts and XenVMs (see Figure 14.14). The information displayed is for the most recent 12 minutes and includes data on CPU (percentage), memory (MB), network (bandwidth), and disk utilization (KB/sec).

Figure 14.14 Performance Tab

Summary

Different tools are included with XenExpress, XenServer, and XenEnterprise for managing all components in a Xen implementation. The GUI provides a quick and smart interface for routine operations such as XenVM creation, cloning, and modification, and for XenHost and XenVM power/shutdown and performance monitoring.

The command-line tools provide additional functionality and the ability to automate functionality by creating scripts and using native OS utilities (on the administration workstation and on the XenHosts) to schedule maintenance operations.

The tools are simple to install and use, but be aware of the requirements of the XenVM operating system during creation and cloning activities to avoid potential pitfalls of identity duplication.

Solutions Fast Track

Native Xen Command-Line Tools

- ☑ The Administrator Console, a remote Java-based GUI interface, can manage all XenHosts in an IT environment.

- ☑ xe is a comprehensive command-line tool for managing XenHosts and XenVMs.

- ☑ sm is a command-line tool available on XenHosts for storage management.

- ☑ xm is a XenHost CLI, for the local management of XenHosts, XenVMs, and storage.

XenServer Administrator Console

- ☑ The Administrator Console provides a subset of the functionality that is available through the command-line tools. However, this subset encompasses most day-to-day operations.

- ☑ Through operating system scripting languages and utilities, you can use the different CLIs to extend the functionality of Xen implementations.

- ☑ You can deploy the Administrator Console on Red Hat and SUSE, as well as a variety of Windows operating systems. Installation on either Windows or Linux is fairly simple.

Frequently Asked Questions

Q: When would the Administrator Console be a better choice for administration?

A: The Administrator Console definitely has a role as a first-step tool for XenVM maintenance, such as creation and cloning, as well as power on/off activities. Its performance screen gives a snapshot that can help you to determine hot spots quickly.

Q: Does every tool share the same functionality?

A: No, each tool has a specialized function. The Administrator Console (as of version 3.2 of XenSource's XenServer family), for example, does not have all the functionality of any of the command-line tools. And although the xe and xm interfaces share many capabilities, you can use the xe interface remotely, whereas you can use the xm interface only on the local XenHost.

Q: What do I need to create scripts with the command-line tools?

A: Each operating system supported on the Administrator Console, and with the xe tool, has available scripting languages/shells. Even with only a little experience in scripting, system administrators can extend functionality by creating scripts that automate functionality.

Q: Are other tools available for managing Xen implementations?

A: Yes, a sampling of third-party tools is provided in Chapter 15.

## Chapter 15

Managing Xen with Third-Party Management Tools

Solutions in this chapter:

- Qlusters openQRM
- Enomalism
- Project ConVirt and XenMan

☑ Summary

☑ Solutions Fast Track

☑ Frequently Asked Questions

Introduction

As the popularity of Xen increases, the need to manage all of those Xen installations also goes up. Fortunately, many software companies have come to the rescue and have developed their own management solutions for the Xen Virtual Machine Monitor and its guests. Many of these third-party management tools are available as free, open source alternatives to the existing product line, and others are part of a value-added suite with commercial support and maintenance.

If you have decided to implement a Xen-based virtual infrastructure, or if you already have one but are looking for additional management capabilities in your tool set, this chapter will introduce a few of those that are currently available. Although not an all-inclusive list of available management applications, these products represent some of the more popular choices that Xen administrators have chosen to help keep their implementations under control.

Qlusters openQRM

Qlusters, Inc., is a provider of open source data center provisioning and management software for physical and virtual environments. Its most popular product is openQRM, an open source systems management platform that helps to automate enterprise data centers and keep them running. openQRM is a mature, established product that integrates with existing components in complex data centers to create scalable and highly available infrastructures.

Founded in 2001, Qlusters has grown to be a contender as a data center technology and services provider. openQRM has had a lot to do with the company's success and is currently used by multiple data centers worldwide to improve uptime and reduce operations costs. Qlusters is the founding member of the Open Management Consortium, which creates open source alternatives to proprietary management systems. The company is headquartered in Palo Alto, California, with offices in New York City and Tel Aviv, Israel.

NOTE

For more information about Qlusters and the work going on at the Open Management Consortium, visit www.qlusters.com and www.open-management.org, respectively.

Xen Management with openQRM

Qlusters has recently made available an extension to openQRM that brings advanced virtualization and Xen management capabilities designed to permit simplified deployment, creation, and management of Xen hosts and virtual machines (VMs). This offering bolsters openQRM's capability to provision, manage, and monitor both virtual and bare-metal environments while improving system administrator and hardware efficiencies.

Overview

Once installed, openQRM helps IT professionals rapidly adapt and repurpose their systems to best meet their needs, which includes redeploying or migrating their OS/application environments among various physical and virtual configurations as needed. In addition, the latest version of openQRM helps administrators increase or decrease the memory consumption of a Xen partition on-the-fly while making it possible to add, remove, and assign VMs to specific physical units on any host without having to restart the system.

openQRM is not a tool itself, but is actually a collection of data center management tools that covers many of the areas of systems management. openQRM provides provisioning of the entire software stack, both operating system and installed applications, on physical servers and VMs running on VM monitors such as Xen. openQRM also has a policy engine that allows you to configure resources to be automatically provisioned based on external business needs as well as the requirements of internal organizations.

Out of the box, openQRM includes, but is not limited to, the following functionality:

- Provisioning of physical machines and VMs, or guests
- Monitoring of all major subsystems, including CPU, memory, disk, and network
- High availability through rules and actionable events

You will find that openQRM's provisioning capabilities will be the biggest asset this tool has to offer. openQRM allows for the separation of applications and resources. The application and the operating system are captured in an image and stored on central network storage. You can then deploy the image to a suitable resource, such as a Xen guest. Determining what images to use on which machines is defined by an entity called a virtual environment (VE). The VE definition holds everything necessary to deploy a given image on any range of hardware, including hardware requirements, which images to use, high-availability requirements, and provisioning policies.

When provisioning, the openQRM server selects the appropriate resources from a pool of idle, or unused, resources and assigns them to the VE. The selection is done based on the VE's configuration. The image is then deployed. This deployment triggers the resource to commence running the service that the VE represents. When the VE stops because the service it's running is no longer needed, the resource is de-assigned from the VE/image and is considered idle, waiting to be reallocated elsewhere to host another business-valued service.

openQRM supports several types of deployments, including network-based and local deployments. Network-based deployments include the following:

- PXE with NFS storage
- PXE with software-based Internet Protocol (IP) SAN storage (iSCSI)
- Hardware iSCSI host bus adapters (HBAs)

Local deployments include the following:

- Physical machines or VMs
- Special support for virtual Xen machines

General Concepts for the Xen/openQRM Mix

Conceptually, the formula for an openQRM environment consists of lots of bare-metal physical systems with lots of available resources (CPU, memory, I/O) and boot-from-network support, and the following four additional components:

- A storage server, which can export volumes to your clients such as iSCSI or NFS volumes
- A file system image, captured by openQRM or one that you created from scratch
- A boot image, which the nodes use to network-boot
- A VE, which we discussed earlier in this chapter

openQRM allows you to take any given boot image suitable for your specific hardware (or, as we will discuss shortly, your domU) and combine it with a file system image. Now, the fact that you can mix and combine boot images and file systems makes it extremely interesting. Although this is a novel concept, there are certain idiosyncrasies that you may run into. For example, when adding newer or different hardware types to the VE's pool of resources, you may have to make some minor modifications to your bootstrap environment to account for the differences between the old and new equipment. Though not difficult, it does add another layer of complexity (somewhat unnecessary, at that) to the provisioning process that openQRM facilitates.

This is where provisioning to VMs rather than physical hosts demonstrates the value that virtualization provides. Because the hardware set that Xen presents to hosted guests is identical, regardless of the underlying hardware, you can introduce next-generation hardware into your VEs without having to modify your boot images or file system images. This creates a huge potential for fast provisioning of VMs without having to clone or kick-start a new operating system instance.

With openQRM, you can build a booting environment for Xen guests and physical nodes that works independently of the image that will actually be booted. Unless you are using the Local NFS plug-in, deploying does not mean that you are installing a new operating system on a server, but rather that you are simply booting a guest or physical node and putting it in production. Various kinds of deployments are made possible with openQRM:

- **Single deployment**   One image is run on a single guest.
- **Shared deployment**   The same file system is run on multiple machines. In this deployment scenario, you can define pools of resources for each file system with the intent of load-balancing between those instances.
- **Partitioned deployment**   Instead of using dedicated hardware for a booted node, you can partition the physical host into multiple VMs, even using the same file system images.

Once you boot your nodes from the network, they arrive in an idle state. When you tell openQRM you need a new virtual platform, one of the idle nodes then gets promoted to a production node based on existing resources and the matching requirements from the metadata in a VE.

Plug-ins and Licensing

openQRM itself is a freely distributed open source application licensed under the Mozilla Public License (MPL). This license includes the following plug-ins:

- **DHCP**   This plug-in is a Dynamic Host Configuration Protocol (DHCP) server used to manage the nodes and give them the capability to network-boot and receive their IP addresses. DHCP is optional because you can use your own DHCP server; however, you need to take certain steps to configure your existing DHCP server.

- **iSCSI**   This plug-in installs iSCSI-enabled kernels for use with openQRM, allowing you to store your file system images on an external storage array that supports the iSCSI storage protocol.

- **LDAP**   This plug-in allows user authentication through a centralized Lightweight Directory Access Protocol (LDAP) server instead of using internal user credentials stored on each server.

- **TFTP**   If you do not have an existing Trivial File Transfer Protocol (TFTP) server, this plug-in provides one that allows managed openQRM nodes to boot from the network.

- **Windows**   This plug-in gives openQRM the capability to manage Microsoft Windows systems, including the capability to monitor the nodes and perform start/stop operations.

In addition to these, the open source community has made several other plug-ins available, including the following:

- **SSHLogin**   This plug-in allows administrators to establish an SSH connection to managed openQRM nodes directly from the Web-based GUI.

- **VNCLogin**   Similar to SSHLogin, this plug-in allows administrators to connect to nodes using VNC.

- **WedminDHCP**   This plug-in provides a graphical interface to manage openQRM's DHCP server plug-in or any external DHCP server that openQRM is configured to use.

- **Nagios**   This plug-in allows tight integration with Nagios, including management of the services Nagios will use to monitor each VE. It also allows administrators to view both openQRM and Nagios management GUIs from the same console.

- **Xen**   This plug-in gives openQRM the capability to be Xen-aware and allow openQRM's partitioning process to integrate smoothly with the Xen VM monitor.

Although there is a Xen community plug-in, it is important to note that Qlusters announced in March 2007 that it is supporting Xen officially through its commercially licensed suite of plug-ins. The openQRM extension for Xen management adds substantial functionality needed to support Xen in small, medium, and large deployments. In addition to the core functionality discussed earlier, some of the added functionality in the latest extension release (3.1.4) includes:

- Live migrations of guest domains from one Xen host to another

- An intuitive and dynamic network interface and virtual interface (VIF) for guests and hosts, including adding or removing additional network cards and configuring through which physical network card on the Xen host traffic should be routed

- Extending a handed-over Logical Volume Manager (LVM) device from the Xen host to the partition without restart, useful for on-the-fly increases to Xen guests on virtual hard disks

In addition to Qluster's Xen plug-in, the following plug-ins are also available to enhance your Xen-based virtual infrastructure to make it more robust, flexible, and available:

- **QRM-HA**   This plug-in adds a high-availability option to the openQRM server. In essence, you can cluster multiple openQRM servers in an active-passive configuration, allowing passive openQRM to take over should the active openQRM fail or become unavailable. The running nodes and environments will be unaffected by such a failover.

- **Power Management**   Using technologies available through the IPMI standard (mostly used in Dell and IBM x86 hardware) and HP's Integrated Lights-on (iLO) management which ships with each ProLiant server, openQRM can power-off physical nodes when they are not needed, reducing the overall power consumption in your data center. When the demand necessitates the powered-off nodes, openQRM will power them back on automatically.

- **Provisioning Portal**   The Provisioning Portal is a set of plug-ins which provides an integrated Web portal for the "end users" of the data center to commit their requests for systems and services. The portal makes provisions for new requests, approvals (or denials), and automated provisioning based on the parameters outlined in the original request.

Although you can install all of the components (the openQRM server, MySQL database, and all the plug-ins) on the same management server, it is recommended that you separate some of the roles to their own dedicated server, as illustrated in Figure 15.1. Note that the figure also illustrates the QRM-HA plug-in for high availability.

Figure 15.1 An Advanced openQRM Deployment Scenario

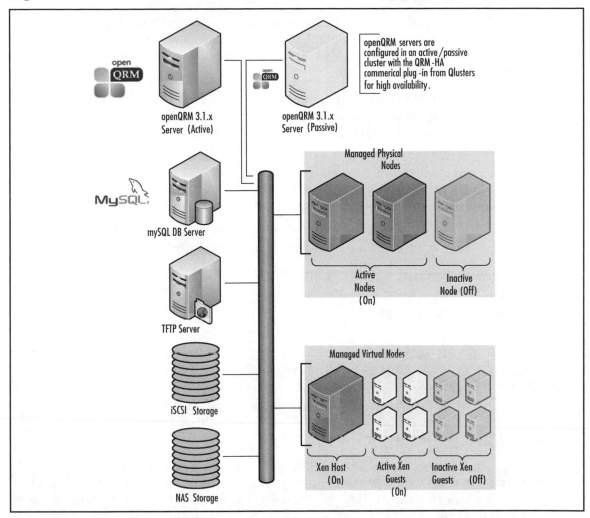

As more and more organizations utilize virtualization technologies as the foundation of their network infrastructure, Qlusters is striving to become your choice for Xen management by continuing to develop and extend openQRM's capabilities to meet the growing needs of the data center.

Installing openQRM

This section will review the steps you can take to install and configure openQRM and the Xen extension. We will base our installation of both the openQRM server and the extensions we will discuss on the latest releases available at the time of this writing. There are three ways you can get openQRM 3.1:

- Use the openQRM-Pro trial package. This package includes a complete set of components and a super-simple installation script that makes sure you have everything preconfigured and ready to work. If you want to quickly evaluate openQRM-Pro, this is the route for you.

- Download the RPMs from SourceForge. These packages allow you to install and use the base openQRM and configure it yourself. If you are a more advanced user and would like to configure openQRM for your needs, this is the route for you.

- Download the sources and build it yourself. If you want to use openQRM on your favorite distribution of Linux and you are an advanced user, this may be the route for you.

Configuring & Implementing...

Evaluating openQRM

There are two ways to evaluate openQRM for your environment. First, the Avastu team working in cooperation with the openQRM team has released a virtual appliance to get you up and running quickly. This appliance is based on CentOS and the 3.1.2 release of openQRM Server. It is fully functional and will not time-expire.

Qlusters also offers a trial package of its openQRM Provision (openQRM-Pro) version. openQRM-Pro is the open source openQRM management application combined with the commercial Provisioning Portal plug-in. By downloading this package, you can easily set up and test openQRM's functionality in minimal time. The package contains a simple and preconfigured install script that will set up all components for you.

You can find the virtual appliance at:
www.openqrm.org/openqrm-virtual-appliance.html
You can find more information about the openQRM-Pro trial package at:
www.openqrm.org/provisioning-use-case/openqrm-provision-use-case-details.html

System Requirements

Before beginning with our installation walkthrough, you need to ensure that you have met all of the prerequisites and requirements for a successful installation. openQRM has many dependencies that you can install either separately or via specially configured packages included with openQRM. We will install all of the requirements on the same server for simplicity's sake. In a production environment, you should spread the roles around to maximize the robustness and reliability of your openQRM deployment.

To install all components on the same machine, you should meet the system requirements outlined in Table 15.1.

Table 15.1 openQRM System Requirements

Requirement Category	Details

Hardware	x86 or x64 system with:
	    At least a 1 GHz processor
	    512 MB of RAM
	    500 MB of hard disk space available

Storage	Access to NFS or NAS-based shared storage for network boot file system images. If you plan to install the iSCSI plug-in, you will need access to a properly configured IP SAN. All managed nodes must have access to the shared storage.

Software (OS)	openQRM has been officially tested on the following operating systems:
	    Red Hat Enterprise Linux 3 (RHEL 3)
	    Red Hat Enterprise Linux 4 (RHEL 4)
	    SUSE Linux Enterprise Server 10 (SLES 10)
	Note: Other distributions may work, but are not officially supported.

Software (openQRM)	Download the following RPM packages:
	    openqrm-core-base
	    openqrm-plugin-tftpd
	    openqrm-plugin-dhcpd
	    openqrm-extras-local_nfs
	    openqrm-extras-mysql
	    openqrm-plugin-xen
	You can download the packages or source binaries at:
	http://sourceforge.net/project/showfiles.php?group_id=153504
	Note: Although the Xen plug-in may not be part of a typical install, it is needed for our purposes in terms of managing Xen with openQRM.

Continued

Table 15.1 Continued

Requirement Category	Details
Networking	One or two separate Ethernet adapters. For testing purposes, you will need a minimum of one 100BaseT (Fast-Ethernet) adapter. However, for production, it is recommended that you have two gigabit adapters in the openQRM server: one for the openQRM interface (to handle management traffic to the nodes) and the other for the public local area network (LAN) interface to the rest of the world.
Managed nodes	All managed nodes must have PXE-enabled network adapters that support PXE 2.1. The adapter's BIOS must be enabled and the managed node's BIOS must be configured appropriately to allow network/PXE boot in the system's boot order before hard drive. Although the managed node can work with a single network adapter, it is recommended that it have two: one for network boot and one for LAN access.

NOTE

Although version 3.1.4 is the most recent at the time of this writing (released March 30, 2007), version 3.1.3 was the last release to be posted with prepackaged Red Hat RPMs. Debian packages and openQRM source are available, though.

Installing openQRM 3.1.x Server

With all of your preparation ready, you are now ready to install openQRM. Begin by getting the RPMs listed in Table 15.1 installed. If you choose to install and use NFS as a local image repository on your openQRM server, you may want to also install the NFS utilities. You can accomplish this by running:

```
yum install nfs-utils
```

MySQL is also a requirement for openQRM. You may decide to install MySQL separately or let the openQRM installer assist you in downloading the package and installing it.

Configuring & Implementing...

New and Existing MySQL Installations

You do not need to have MySQL installed for openQRM. Both the MySQL Server and the MySQL Client are installed as part of the openqrm-core-base installation package. However, if you plan to use an existing MySQL Server installation from the package distributed with Red Hat or CentOS (MySQL 4.1 or higher), be sure to complete the following steps after running it.

You may receive the following error when attempting to start openQRM after installation and configuration (see the next section) when using a default MySQL install (non-openQRM):

```
668 FATAL [ContainerServices] (main:Initial TX) openQRM server does not
support REPEATABLE READ transaction isolation level. Please check your
database configuration.
```

If you receive this error message, modify your TRANSACTION ISOLATION LEVEL to READ COMMITTED by running the following command:

```
mysql> SET GLOBAL TRANSACTION ISOLATION LEVEL READ COMMITTED;
```

If this resolves your problem, commit the change permanently by editing /etc/my.cnf and adding the following under the *[mysqld]* directive:

```
[mysqld]
transaction-isolation = READ-COMMITTED
```

Be sure to save the file and restart both MySQL and openQRM (in that order) by running:

```
service qrm-server start
service mysqld start
```

Once you have all of the packages we identified for our walkthrough installed, your next step is to install and configure openQRM with the installation procedure. The core RPM has placed all the files that you need in /opt/qrm. Proceed with the following steps:

1. Launch the installation and configuration script by running */opt/qrm/qrm-installer -i -c*. This will bring you to the openQRM Installer, as shown in Figure 15.2.

Figure 15.2 The openQRM Installer

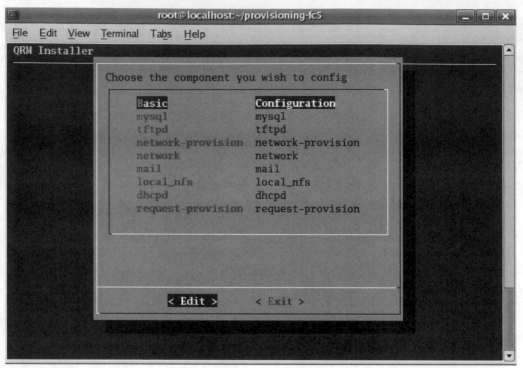

2. Configure each item, following the on-screen instructions and editing the default values, where applicable, to match your test or production environment. The most critical item is "Basic Configuration," as this has the parameters for network communication, directory paths, and database connection items. Note that some plug-ins cannot be configured at this point; they are configured using the openQRM Web console once they are installed and running. When all items have been configured, select **Exit**.

3. Upon exiting, the installer then goes through a series of "sanity checks," checking for MySQL, the qrm-core binaries, and the binaries for all of the plug-ins that you selected as part of the installation process and configured in step 2.

4. MySQL will prompt you to restart. Select **y**.

5. You are then brought to a license prompt. If you are installing the MPL-licensed open source version (no commercial components), just press **Enter**. If you have a license for any commercial components, follow the on-screen prompts.

6. You will then be prompted to initialize the system entities. Select **y**. This will configure the PXE server and create the default boot image, based on the kernel and using a default initrd. Note that if you need to customize the initrd, you can find it at /opt/qrm/etc/templates/initrd-qrm.tgz.

7. qrm-init script will then run, finishing the installation of the qrm-core plug-in.

8. Follow the instructions for the remaining plug-ins.

When the installation has successfully completed, you should see the following:

```
###########################################################################
 Installation finished
Plugins with status SUCCESS : mysql qrm-core tftpd dhdcp iscsi local_nfs
Plugins with status ERROR :
###########################################################################
```

You should confirm at this point that no plug-ins failed (are listed with status ERROR). For more information about the *qrm-installer* optional switches and for another sample walkthrough, visit www.openqrm.org/installation-guide/openqrm-3.0-installation-guide—installer-options.html.

At this point, you should have a functioning openQRM system, if everything installed correctly. Navigate to the openQRM Web console by browsing to http://youropenqrm:8080. The default username and password are both *qrm*. You should see the openQRM Dashboard, as shown in Figure 15.3.

Figure 15.3 The openQRM Dashboard

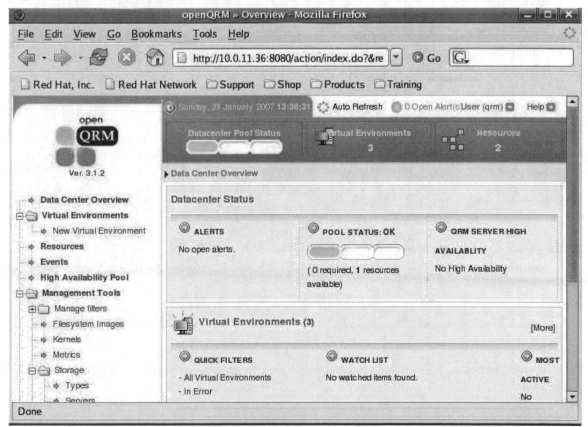

Installing the openQRM Xen Plug-in

With openQRM Server and the core plug-in installed (at a minimum), we will now focus on getting the Xen community plug-in installed and configured for use. This section explains in detail how to gain further efficiencies in Xen system management with openQRM with Xen integration.

To begin, you should download the version of the Xen plug-in that matches your openQRM Server version. For most Red Hat distributions, the latest version as of the time of this writing is 3.1.3. You can download and install it by running the following command:

```
rpm -iHv qrm-xen-plugin.rpm
```

Optionally, you can visit Sourceforge.net to download the source binaries and compile and install them manually. This is often the only option, depending on which Linux distribution you are working with, as Debian, Red Hat, and Solaris packages are usually the ones available prepackaged for download.

Configuring & Implementing...

Building the Xen Plug-in

To build the Xen plug-in, download the Xen plug-in source package from Sourceforge. net and unzip it in your openQRM source directory. Change to the ../src/plugins/xen directory and run:

```
make clean && make && make install
```

This will compile the components for the Xen plug-in, including the Xen hypervisor, the Xen tools, and the special Xen Linux kernel for your domain-0. If compilation fails, be sure that you have the latest compiler and kernel headers installed on your build system, and that they are properly referenced. A common issue with compiling software on some distributions with a kernel of 2.6.20 or higher is that one of the kernel headers, config.h, has been renamed to autoconf.h. If the compiler complains about missing files, be sure they actually exist.

For the "config.h renamed to autoconf.h" issue, the easiest solution is to create a symlink in your kernel source directory. You can do this with the following:

```
cd /usr/src/kernels/$(uname -r)*/include/linux
ln -c autoconf.h config.h
```

The next step is to register the Xen plug-in within the openQRM Server by running the following:

```
/opt/qrm/bin/qrm-plugin -u qrm -p qrm xen register
```

Once it's registered, you can configure the plug-in by performing the following steps:

1. Launch the openQRM configurator by running */opt/qrm/qrm-configurator*.

2. Select the plug-in menu item and be sure that the Xen plug-in is selected (enabled).

3. Return to the main configuration menu and select the menu item to configure the plug-in.

4. Select **Xen** and follow the wizard's instructions.
   As you work through the wizard, you will need to provide the IP address for the source system being used to create a Xen host file system image, a logical name for the storage server, the full path to the file system image directory, and its regular and management IP addresses. For the storage type, the default is NFS, although you can specify iSCSI if you have that plug-in installed. You will also need to provide the IP address of the default gateway in your network. Table 15.2 provides a sample configuration for the Xen plug-in.

Table 15.2 Sample Configuration of Xen Plug-in

Configuration Item	Value
Source Xen host's IP address	192.168.1.10
Storage server name	nfs-server
Storage server path	/diskimages/Xen-Hypervisor
Storage server IP address	192.168.1.100
Storage server management IP address	192.168.1.101
Storage server type	NFS
Default gateway	192.168.1.1

5. Run the following commands to install and enable the Xen plug-in on the openQRM Server. The installation procedure creates the boot image, *Xen-Hypervisor*; the storage server, NFS server; and the file system image, *Xen-Hypervisor*.

```
/opt/qrm/bin/qrm-plugin -u qrm -p qrm xen install
/opt/qrm/bin/qrm-plugin -u qrm -p qrm xen run_once
```

6. Restart the openQRM Server by running:

```
/etc/init.d/qrm-server restart
```

TIP

File system image creation can be time-consuming and very I/O-intensive on the live Xen server. If possible, migrate all running VMs with the *xm migrate* command to another Xen host or hosts with sufficient resources. If this is not possible, create the file system image during hours of low utilization to not impact business processes that rely on applications hosted in its guest domains.

7. In the Virtual Environment (VE) view of the openQRM Server, you can create a new VE from the previously listed components. Choose a name and configure the VE to use Xen partitioning. Also, select it to be a **Multi-server**. Figure 15.4 shows a Xen VE in an unstarted, or inactive, state. The VE is called XenDom0.

Figure 15.4 A Xen VE in the openQRM Console

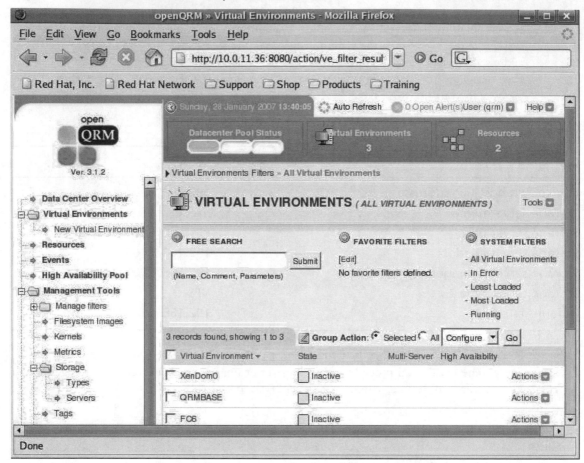

Managing Xen with openQRM

In this section, we will discuss how to manage Xen with openQRM.

How the Xen Plug-in Works

To remote-boot a Xen server, a special assignment/de-assignment procedure is needed. For this purpose, the Xen plug-in registers an **event listener** that listens to both assignment and de-assignment in the openQRM Server while creating and using the special Xen PXE-Linux configuration files generated an assignment utility attached to the event listener. The Xen event listener also takes care of the de-assignment of the Xen VE, which restores the original PXE-Linux configuration for network boot.

The tricky thing about booting a Xen host on openQRM is that it generally does not have any IP or network boot information in its /proc/cmdline, even if it is configured in its PXE-Linux configuration file. This is because the kernel that initially boots on a Xen host is the Xen hypervisor, not a traditional Linux kernel. The Linux kernel is started, or bootstrapped, as dom0 after the hypervisor loads. To have this special boot mechanism conform with openQRM, the Xen assignment process triggered via the event listener creates the correct /proc/cmdline by appending parameters for the Xen host in the PXE module configuration for the dom0 kernel.

Once a Xen host has been provisioned and booted by openQRM's network boot functionality, it still needs to be managed. You can do this by sending administrative commands to the Xen host via *qrm-execd* from the openQRM server. These commands control start guest, stop guest, create guest, and delete/destroy guest (or in openQRM lingo, *partition*) actions on the Xen host. Each partition has a separate configuration file created by the qrm-xen-manage utility on the Xen host. The configuration files are stores as /var/lib/xen/VirtualMachines/[mac-address]/[mac-address].xen.

The regular Xen control tool, xm, is used to manage each openQRM-provisioned domU. IP addresses for each domU are gathered by DHCP on the Xen host on behalf of the guest's Media Access Control (MAC) address which then assigns them to the guests via the Xen configuration file. The *create* procedure for the Xen guests also configures a /proc/cmdline conformant to openQRM so that they are able to boot the regular *initrd*.

Using openQRM with Xen Integration

Now that we have everything installed, we are ready to start managing our infrastructure with openQRM. To begin, though, we need to make sure that we have resources available to boot into our Xen image. Figure 15.5 illustrates the resources view of the console. You will notice that there are two nodes, called Node 1 and Node 2. The console will list the resources available in each node, in particular the CPU count and speed, amount of memory, and amount of disk storage in gigabytes.

Configuring & Implementing...

Networking Tips for Xen Host Virtual Environments

It is a best practice to have a minimum of two network adapters in a Xen host managed by openQRM. One adapter is used for network boot and network volume or iSCSI traffic. The other adapters would be used as bridges for guest network traffic as well as dom0 traffic for native Xen management purposes. Although the first adapter (often eth0) will grab an IP from the DHCP server to PXE boot and TFTP sessions, it is recommended that the Xen host image contain a valid network configuration for the other adapters (eth1, eth2, etc.) to avoid having to manually intervene and configure the VE after it has been provisioned.

The simplest approach to this would be to configure each adapter to use DHCP to obtain its IP configuration. If you want to ensure that each VE has a particular IP address, you can take advantage of lease reservations in your DHCP configuration, because you will know network adapter MAC addresses ahead of time.

Figure 15.5 Available Resources Shown in the openQRM Console

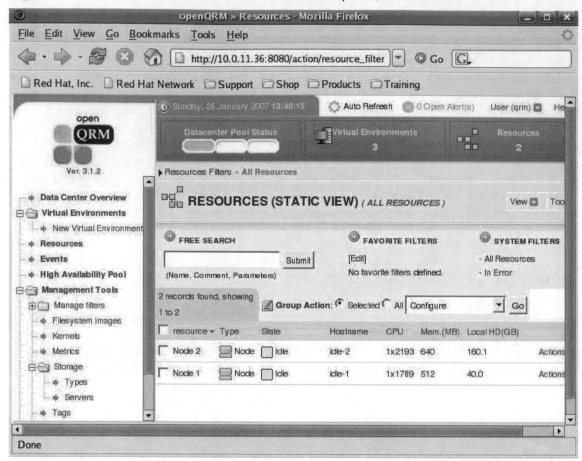

Once you have identified the physical systems on which you want to start the Xen host VE, you can assign those systems as new VEs. When the Xen host VE starts, it will initiate the Xen hypervisor and the special Xen Linux kernel, Xen-Hypervisor in our example. Just as with any Xen host installation, the kernel will boot and become domain-0 (dom0) with all of the standard control tools available to you. You can determine whether everything is working correctly by logging onto the Xen host and running the following Xen command:

```
xm list
```

This should return a list of the current active Xen guest domains, and chances are you will see only dom0 because we have not created any guests yet.

If you are having problems starting dom0, you may need to rebuild the Xen plug-in using the kernel binaries from your Linux distribution rather than using a downloaded precompiled package. Refer to the sidebar "Building the Xen Plug-in," earlier in this chapter, for additional information.

With your Xen host VEs image-provisioned and booted on a physical resource, we will now review how to use openQRM to manage guest domains, or domUs. In openQRM terminology, guests are referred to as *partitions*, and the act of creating a guest is called *partitioning the resource*. To create a new partition, follow these steps:

1. Click on the resource used for the Xen host VE and find the partition tab added by the Xen plug-in. A configuration page for creating partitions opens when you click on it. Here you can assign things such as the number of virtual CPUs and the amount of RAM, and even set up physical CPU affinity to control which CPUs the guest can be scheduled against (see Figure 15.6).

Figure 15.6 Creating a Partition's Profile

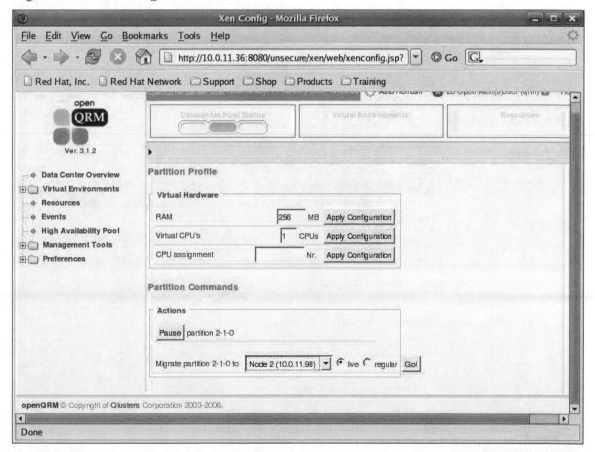

2. Configure the parameters to start one partition by using one CPU with, for example, a 700 MHz CPU speed and 256 MB of RAM. Ensure that the amount of RAM configured for the partition does not exceed the available memory on the Xen host, which needs about 120 MB of RAM itself.

3. Pressing **create** creates and starts the partition on the Xen host VE. It will become available, though idle, in the resource view as a new Xen resource.
   The available Xen partitions created and started can now be used as a resource for any VE in the openQRM managed network.

4. To start a VE on a Xen partition, go to the partition's configuration page and select **Xen partition**.
   This causes the openQRM server to choose a free Xen partition to start the VE.
   No further changes are required. Figure 15.7 shows an active partition running and FC6 image and an inactive partition available for provisioning.

5. Manage your VE running on Xen partitions in the usual way using the **Actions** menu.

Figure 15.7 Xen Partitions in the openQRM Console

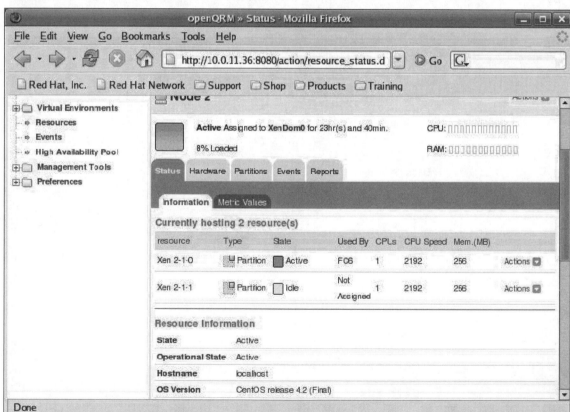

Provisioning with openQRM-Pro

If you are interested in having some business processes wrapped around your openQRM management, you may want to consider the commercial Provisioning Portal plug-in. This component adds a provisioning request and approval mechanism to openQRM. The tool is deployed as a separate servlet, allowing you to grant access to users without having to expose the openQRM Administrator Console.

As mentioned before, a simple way to test openQRM-Pro functionality is to download the trial package available on the openQRM Web site. Once you've installed it, you can navigate to the Provisioning Portal login screen (see Figure 15.8) and manage request activities. We have included some screen shots to further introduce you to the possibilities of the Provisioning Portal. The process workflow and automation present the real value-add to the commercial products, providing functionality such as submitting new requests (see Figure 15.9), approving or denying requests (see Figure 15.10), and managing provisioning schedules for approved requests (see Figure 15.11). The documentation that is included with the trial package download provides additional information.

Figure 15.8 Login Page for the Provisioning Portal

Figure 15.9 Submitting a New Request

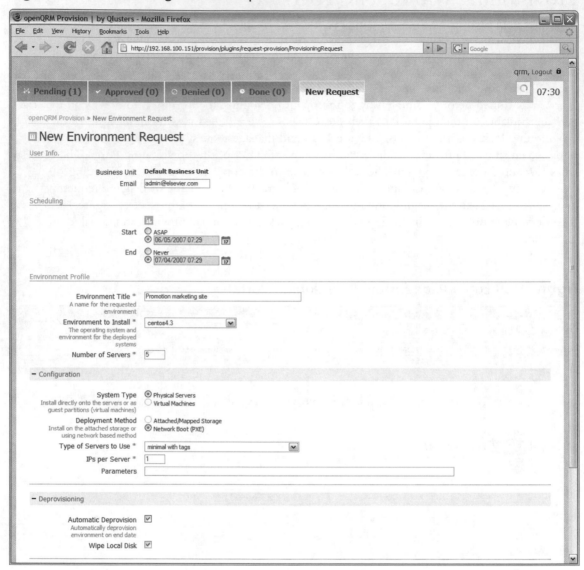

Figure 15.10 Pending Requests Waiting for Approval or Denial

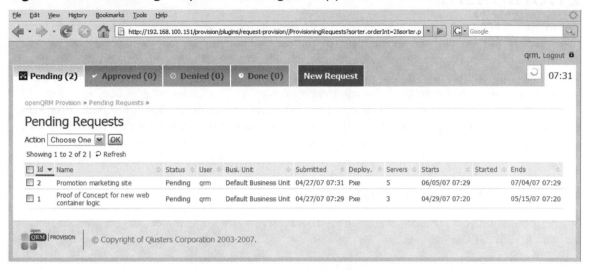

Figure 15.11 Managing Approved Requests

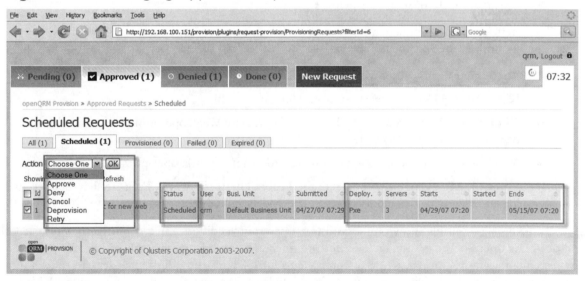

Enomalism

Enomalism was founded in November 2005 by Enomaly Inc., an open source consulting firm located in Toronto. Enomaly has been focusing on solving the challenges of cost and complexity for enterprises that run large technical server infrastructures. As a result, it has combined industry-proven open source components with its experience in designing and operating large-scale, mission-critical software systems, resulting in the Enomalism management application.

Enomalism is an open source, Web-based, virtual server management application built specifically for the needs of a flexible hosted application environment. It was designed to answer the challenges of fragmented hosting environments by providing an interface to provision concurrent isolatedservers using the Enomalism Virtualized Grid (EVG) environment and the Elastic Computing Platform (ECP).

Overview of Enomalism

With Enomalism, you can manage multiple physical servers as a single server using a specialized tool set which includes the following:

- Centralized user provisioning system
- Virtualized server creation wizard and templates which facilitate virtual server configuration
- Application deployment mechanism
- Integration into third-party applications via a Web services API
- Centralized LDAP user management

The latest release of Enomalism, version 0.7, builds upon several open source applications, including, but not limited to, the following:

- **Turbogears**   A Python Web application framework.
- **Kid**   An XHTML frontend templating engine.
- **CherryPy**   Middleware that allows you to program Web applications by writing event handlers that return data to templates.
- **MochiKit**   A JavaScript library to make programming in JavaScript more Python-like.
- **OpenLDAP**   Originally requiring the Fedora Directory Server, Enomaly has replaced the dependency with this more common and widely used directory service.

Enomalism is available in two versions: a free, open source edition, and a commercial enterprise edition. The open source edition includes features such as a control center dashboard, resource management, infrastructure-as-a-service components for ISVs, real-time disk management tools, an SSH client, a Web service-based API, and a virtual appliance management system for running VMs as virtual appliance packages. The enterprise edition adds to the open source edition by including multiserver migration for enhanced workload management, enhanced disk management, an enhanced serial console called Twisted, and the ability to create and package VMs as virtual appliances.

Enomalism is distributed under the GNU Lesser Public License (LGPL), because it relies on GPL libraries but does not modify any of that code.

Installing Enomalism

This section will review the requirements and general steps that you can follow to install your own Enomalism management system. The installation is actually modularized into several smaller installations for the various core components upon which Enomalism functions.

System Requirements

To begin, Enomalism requires the Fedora Core 6 distribution. Any hardware that meets the requirements for FC6 installation will suffice for installing Enomalism. Enomaly has stated that Ubuntu Edgy 6.10 or the recently released 7.04 version may work, but they are not officially supported.

From a software perspective, you must have the following installed prior to installing Enomalism:

- GCC.
- Python 2.4 or newer.
- Openssl.
- Apache with mod_ssl. This is optional, but strongly recommended for production deployments.

Other modules discussed earlier in this section will be detected (if installed) or deployed by the Enomalism installation process itself.

WARNING

Since version 0.63, Enomalism can manage only those systems that are running the XenSource 3.0.4 hypervisor or newer. Enomalism cannot manage versions 3.0.3 and older. We mention this because as of the time of this writing, many common distributions, including Fedora Core 6, Red Hat Linux 5, and SUSE Linux Enterprise Server 10.2, include Xen as an integrated package, but the hypervisor is at the 3.0.3 release. In order to manage those Xen deployments, you may need to uninstall the package that came with the distribution and install the latest release from source.

Also, if you plan to manage XenSource's commercial XenServer product family, keep in mind that version 3.1 is based on the 3.0.3 hypervisor. You will need to upgrade to the latest release, version 3.2, to manage XenServer with Enomalism, as it is based on the 3.0.4 hypervisor.

If you need to download the open source Xen 3.0.4 binaries, visit www.xensource.com/download/index_3.0.4.html.

Installation Walkthrough

To install Enomalism, follow these basic steps:

1. Download the latest release at http://sourceforge.net/project/showfiles.php?group_id=164855.

2. Untar the downloaded file into /opt.

3. If you are upgrading from a previous version of Enomalism, be sure to back up the entire /opt/enomalism directory, and then simply untar the new release on top of the original.

4. For new installs and upgrades, go to /opt/enomalism and run the install script, preinstall.py. It's that simple!

NOTE

You must install to /opt/enomalism. Do not try to place the Enomalism binaries in another directory or path.

Because Enomalism requires Xen, if you have not already done so, be sure to install Xen 3.0.4 or newer along with the Xen kernel before starting any Enomalism processes. For assistance with installing Xen, see Chapter 13.

Using Enomalism to Manage Xen

With everything installed and configured, you can now administer your Xen environment. Because Enomalism is installed in the dom0 of the Xen host, there is no need to register or point the management tool to a Xen environment to manage. You simply need to browse to the Enomalism Web GUI at http://yourxenhost:24514, as shown in Figure 15.12.

Figure 15.12 The Enomalism Login Screen

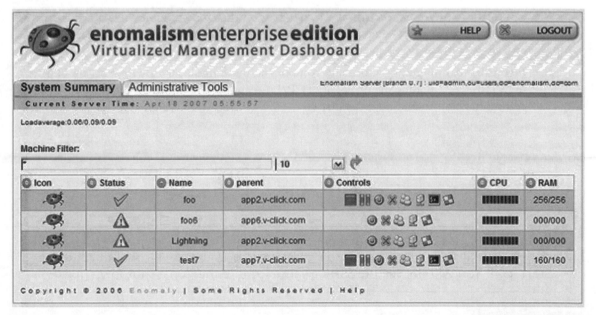

After logging in, you will see the Virtualized Management Dashboard, as illustrated in Figure 15.13. It is through this dashboard that you can monitor and perform a variety of actions against your Xen guests. The dashboard itself is divided into two tabs. The first tab, System Summary, provides you with information regarding the status, name, parent (or Xen hostname), and CPU and memory utilization for each domU. As shown in Figure 15.14, you also have point-and-click control over the domUs for the following activities:

Figure 15.13 The Virtualized Management Dashboard

Figure 15.14 Controls for domU Management

1. **Shutdown** This will power-off the domU, invoking any shutdown processes for the operating system running inside the guest. Note that shutdowns may not be graceful.

2. **Pause** This will suspend the running domU. If the domU is already paused, this icon is replaced with a green arrow icon to "unpause" the guest.

3. **Destroy** This is a hard shutdown, the equivalent of pulling out the power cable of a physical server.

4. **Delete** This performs the "Destroy" activity followed by removing the guest's configuration, files, and references in Enomalism.

5. **Permissions** This will open a new window to allow you to administer permission to the guest for enrolled users and groups.

6. **Resources** This will open a new window with two tabs. The first is used to control the hard drive(s) for the guest, including changing its sizes. The second tab allows you to configure various components of the guest, including the amount of memory, the number of virtual CPUs, setting the VNC password, enabling or disabling VNC and USB, and configuring the virtual serial console.

7. **SSH, VNC, or AJAX Terminal** Depending on the configuration, this will allow you to interact with the guest's operating system using the integrated SSH client, an AJAX-based terminal, or the VNC client.

8. **Firewall** An interesting and useful component, the firewall allows you to set up basic firewall rules, including the protocol (TCP/UDP/both) and ports allowed for network communication to and from the guest.

NOTE

The control icons visible to you depend on the state of the Xen guest. For example, if a guest is already shut down, you will not see the Shutdown icon, but rather the Start icon. You will not see the SSH or Pause icons, either, on a shutdown guest.

The other dashboard tab, Administrative Tools, will present you with four icons and tools to administer your Enomalism environment. As shown in Figure 15.15, you have tools to administer users, provision new domUs, export or migrate domUs, and gain access to the VMCast appliance feed.

Figure 15.15 The Enomalism Administrative Tools

User administration will be straightforward for those used to LDAP, though it may prove to be challenging for those not experienced with directory services when setting up diverse organizations, containers, and users. Provisioning is also straightforward, and should provide you with the ability to rapidly deploy new guests and virtual appliances. Export and migration tools are very useful for moving guests around and, in the enterprise edition, creating your own virtual appliance that can be applied to a farm of Enomalism-managed hosts.

That leads us to the appliance feed tool. This is a unique concept from the Enomaly team, and it really shows the power that virtualization will bring to IT organizations for internal and external use. Tied to Enomaly's VMCasting initiative, the appliance feed provides you with Web access to a catalog of available virtual appliances, making it easy to find one that meets your needs, download it, and deploy it. Unlike other mechanisms currently available to deploy virtual appliances, this Web tool eliminates the need to manually download, register, and run appliances on your virtual host. Figure 15.16 illustrates a feed with two available images, a Debian 3.1 image and a Fedora Core 6 image. Enomaly and the open source community promise more images, which promises to change the whole paradigm on systems management and deployment.

Figure 15.16 Enomalism Appliance Feed for VMCasting

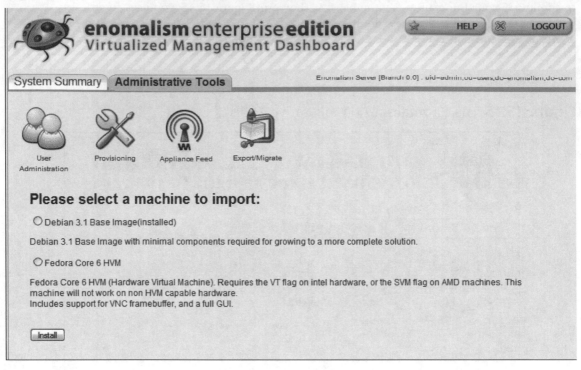

For more information about Enomalism, VMCasting, and the GeoElastic alliance, visit Enomaly's Web site, at www.enomaly.net.

Project ConVirt and XenMan

Project ConVirt is an active, open source project with the goal of tackling the administrative and infrastructure management challenges that adoption of virtualization platforms presents to the traditional data center. The XenMan Administrator Console is Project ConVirt's first release.

XenMan is a graphical management tool aimed at operational life cycle management for the Xen virtualization platform. XenMan should be helpful to you regardless of whether you are a seasoned Xen administrator or are just seeking an introduction to Xen virtualization. With XenMan's secure, multinode administration, performance management, and provisioning capabilities, you can manage your entire environment from a single, centralized console. Most common administrative tasks, such as starting, stopping, monitoring, and provisioning VMs (or domUs), typically involve just a few mouse clicks with XenMan. You can also use this point-and-click style to perform system management operations such as scanning operating system configurations or preparing individual servers for maintenance.

XenMan is distributed under the GNU General Public License (GPL).

Overview of ConVirt

ConVirt is a very active project and, as such, XenMan is under constant development release and change. The features, however, are still focused on the following:

- **Multiserver management**   Use XenMan to manage all of your Xen hosts and their guest domains.

- **Centralized view**   Use a single console to monitor and view what is happening across your virtual infrastructure, including resource utilization, guest deployments, task status, and configuration of both hosts and guests.

- **Security**   Based on the SSH tunneling approach, XenMan enhances, if not surpasses, the security provided with the core Xen control tools.

- **Repository of images**   Use XenMan to maintain a store of images for rapid domU deployment. You can also automate deployments using the Image Store SDK.

- **Remote server operations**   Manage your virtual infrastructure from "virtually" anywhere that you have access to the XenMan console.

Currently, XenMan allows both single and multiple host administration and image provisioning. It does not provide a mechanism for live migrations, centralized user administration (via LDAP, for example), or extensibility and automation through common Web protocols, such as SOAP and XML-RPC (similar to what XenSource, openQRM, and Enomalism provide). The console is not Web-enabled yet, but all of these features are included in the development road map for the product.

Installing ConVirt

XenMan is distributed as both a source/binary tarball as well as an RPM package for various Red Hat distributions. Community packages for Debian, SUSE, and others are also available.

System Requirements

Regardless of which deployment option you choose, you must meet some basic system requirements. For the management server running XenMan's server components, you must have Xen 3.0.2 installed and running, and the SSH daemon must be running. For the client system, Xen must be installed, although you do not need to be booted into the Xen kernel with xend running. You also need to have X server functioning (because XenMan is a GUI-based application), be able to connect to the management server via SSH2, and have the Paramiko library installed.

The Paramiko library is a Python module that implements the SSH2 protocol for secure connections to remote machines. Note that this library is also distributed under LGPL.

> **NOTE**
>
> The Paramiko library also has its own prerequisites—in particular, Python, version 2.3 or higher, and Pycrpyto, version 1.9 or higher. The library has been tested as stable with Red Hat FC 1 and higher, RHEL 3 and 4, Debian Sarge 3.1, and Ubuntu Edgy 6.10. So although you can compile XenMan successfully on other distributions, you will be limited to those that support this library.
>
> If you need to install this library, you can download it and learn more about the project at www.lag.net/paramiko.

Installation

To deploy from the tarball, follow these steps:

1. Download and extract the source tarball from https://sourceforge.net/project/showfiles.php?group_id=168929. The latest release is xenman-0.6.tar.gz.

2. Make sure your environment fulfills XenMan's prerequisites, as listed earlier.

3. If you haven't already, deploy python-paramiko in your environment.

4. Execute the default configuration script if you see one for your distribution. For example, if you are running SUSE, you would run configure_defaults-suse.sh located in ./distros/suse/.

5. If you see a default configuration file for your distribution in the same directory, rename it to xenman.conf and copy it to the top of the installation directory. For example, if you were running Fedora Core, you would run the following command:

```
cp ./distros/fedora/xenman.conf ./xenman.conf
```

> **NOTE**
>
> If you do not see a default configuration file specific to your distribution, XenMan will create one for you upon startup.

6. Create a local copy of the image store by running the following command. This will create the image store at /var/cache/xenman/image_store.

```
sh ./mk_image_store
```

7. Make sure XenMan has execute permissions by running:

```
chmod 0755 ./XenMan
```

8. Once you have finished the installation, you can run XenMan by simply running *XenMan*.

To deploy from RPM, download the appropriate package for your distribution, if available. For example, if you are running SUSE, you would download the RPM for SUSE and run the following command. Once it's installed, follow step 8 as outlined in the steps for tarball installation.

```
rpm -Uvh xenman-0.6-1.suse.noarch.rpm
```

> **W**ARNING
>
> If you have an earlier version of XenMan installed, you must uninstall it first. If it was installed via RPM, simply run the command *rpm -e xenman*.

Using ConVirt to Manage Xen

Once your environment is set up and configured, you can use XenMan immediately to start managing your Xen-based virtual infrastructure. The following sections are a summary of common operations you can perform as outlined in the XenMan documentation for the following:

- The XenMan dashboard
- Server pool operations
- Server operations
- VM operations
- The image store

The Dashboard

The XenMan Dashboard is a consolidated listing of all known managed servers along with critical performance, availability, and configuration metrics for each host. It provides the user the ability to view the state of the entire Xen environment at a glance. The following are common administrative tasks:

- **Launch**   The Dashboard is the default screen when the XenMan GUI is launched, but you can return to it by selecting **Server Pool** in the navigator on the left and then clicking on the **Summary tab** on the right-hand side.
- **Operations**   Left-clicking a row in the Dashboard selects the associated managed server. You can then perform the following actions:

- **Double-click** Connect to the managed server and drill down into a more detailed view. This selects the server's node in the navigator on the left-hand side and brings up the Summary tab for the server on the right.

- **Right-click** Context-sensitive menu. Most server operations can be executed directly from here.

- **Sort** Clicking on the column header will re-sort the listing based on the clicked column (not available for all columns).

- **Data** Each row in the Dashboard corresponds to a managed server, as shown in Figure 15.17. The fields are:

  - **Server** The name of the managed server.

  - **Connection** Connectivity status to the managed server (i.e., whether XenMan has an active connection to the server).

  - **VM Summary** A compact listing of VM status on the server.

  - **VM CPU(%)** Aggregate processor usage by VMs running on the server. This does not include the dom0's processor usage.

  - **VM Mem(%)** Aggregate memory usage by VMs running on the server. This does not include the dom0's memory usage.

  - **Server CPU(s)** Number and clock speed of the physical processors on the managed server, if available.

  - **Server Mem** Total, usable physical memory installed on the managed server, if available.

  - **Version** The version string being reported by Xen at the managed server.

Server Pool Operations

XenMan shows a Server Pool node to refer to a collection of managed Xen hosts. XenMan supports only a single server pool in the current release. The local Xen installation is automatically added to the pool, and you can add additional Xen hosts to the pool for centralized management. The following are some common server pool tasks that you can confirm in the XenMan console:

- **Add Server** You can add additional remote managed servers by using the Add Server operation. You will need to provide the information regarding the hostname, Xen port (usually 8005), and credentials for the connection.

- **Remove Server** You can remove a server from the list by selecting it and choosing Remove Server.

Figure 15.17 XenMan Dashboard and Metrics

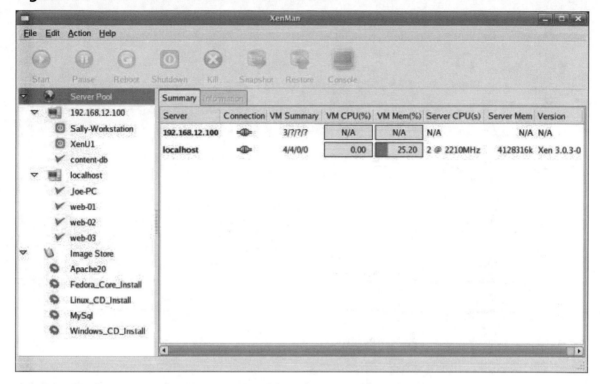

Server Operations

The following is a list of all operations that you can perform against a specific Xen host:

- **Start All VMs**   Start all VMs on a selected server.

- **Shutdown All VMs**   Shut down all VMs on a selected server.

- **Kill All VMs**   Kill all VMs on a selected server.

- **Provision VM**   Allows you to create a new VM with very few parameters.

- **Open VM Config File**   Allows you to add a new VM file to the list, which you can then edit using the Settings context menu or start using the Start button.

VM Operations

The following is a list of all operations that you can perform against a specific Xen guest (domU), as shown in Figure 15.18:

Figure 15.18 VM Operations Available in the XenMan GUI

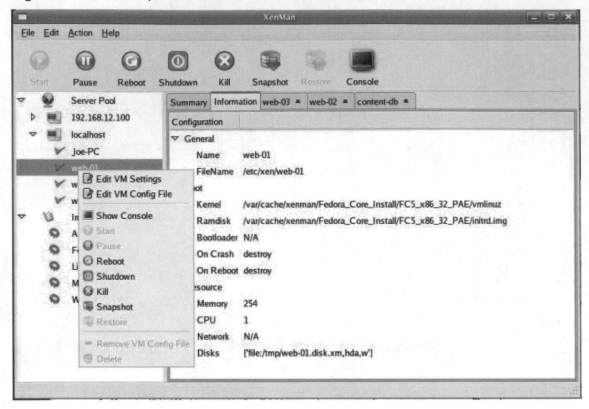

- ■ **Edit VM Settings**   Change the configuration settings for the selected VM.
- ■ **Edit VM Config File**   Edit the VM's configuration file directly.
- ■ **Show Console**   Launch a text or graphical console of the guest operating system.
- ■ **Start**   Start the selected VM.
- ■ **Pause**   Toggle button to pause/resume running of the VM.
- ■ **Reboot**   Reboot a selected VM.
- ■ **Shutdown**   Shut down a running VM.
- ■ **Kill**   Hard–kill a VM.
- ■ **Snapshot**   Save the state of a running VM to a file.
- ■ **Restore**   Restore a VM from a stored snapshot.
- ■ **Remove VM Config File**   Remove the VM filename from the list of VMs registered to XenMan.
- ■ **Delete**   Delete the VM file and associated Virtual Block Devices (VBDs) or LVMs.

The Image Store

XenMan allows administrators to define their images and create VM configurations from them. For example, you may have a scenario where you need to frequently deploy four different types of machines: RHEL 4, CentOS, SUSE, and Ubuntu. You can configure XenMan to point to kernel and RAMDisk images of each distribution and deploy many VMs using predefined images. This collection of images is referred to as the *image store*. XenMan ships with a default image store containing a few useful provisionable images. You may also construct your own image descriptions and provisioning schemes and add them to the image store.

The following is a review of some of the operations you can perform to manage the image store:

- **Location**   The image store is listed in the navigator. Clicking or expanding the Image Store node results in a listing of the available, provisionable images.

- **Image Operations**   Use these operations to manage a specific image:

  - **Click**   Selects the image and displays useful information about it in on the right-hand side. When creating an image, you can place important information which can be viewed at this point that gives a brief description of the image, prerequisites, and deployment instructions, as shown in Figure 15.19.

Figure 15.19 Summary Information Displayed for a Provisionable Image

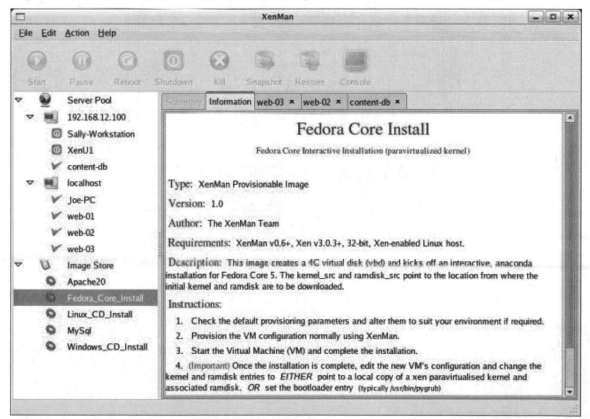

- **Right-click** Brings up a context menu with various image-specific tasks. These include Provision to start the provisioning process (see Figure 15.20), Edit Settings to alter the definition of the image, Edit Script to alter the mechanism used to provision VMs using this image, and Edit Description to modify the description associated with this image.

Figure 15.20 Setting Parameters for VM Provisioning

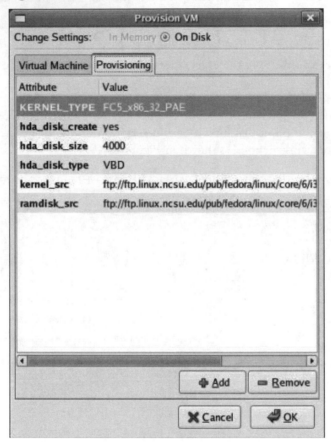

Summary

Xen's adoption in data centers of all sizes has led a diverse range of use cases in development, test, and production environments. As administrators have begun to reap the benefits of virtualization with Xen, they have also begun to feel some pain in the management of Xen hosts and their guest domains. Although the native management tools do provide some efficient ways to manage aspects of a Xen-based virtual infrastructure, only the XenServer Administrator Console available with the commercial XenSource offering has the convenience of graphical administration. However, even this tool is limited in functionality and compatibility, as you cannot use it to manage open source Xen deployments.

Fortunately, many companies have recognized the challenges that administrators faced and have presented tools to address the issues of monitoring, provisioning, and overall systems management. Most are open source, and many are freely distributed, making little (if any) impact on an organization's budget. Others offer an even more robust set of features for a nominal cost that even the tight budget can still support.

Although there are many offerings, we have taken the time to review three of the most popular in use today: Qlusters openQRM, Enomalism from Enomaly, and XenMan, part of Project ConVirt. These applications show that you can achieve great value through virtualization if you manage it with the right tool.

Solutions Fast Track

Qlusters openQRM

- ☑ openQRM offers a wide range of systems management features for both physical and virtual environments, making it a one-stop shop for your systems and resource management needs.

- ☑ Administrators can manage their entire workload across both physical and virtual resources through policies that dynamically interact with partitions and nodes to ensure that service levels and business processes proceed with impact.

- ☑ openQRM offers a unique way to provision guests, or partitions, without having to install or deploy a new operating system instance. It is also the only tool in the group that manages Windows and Linux servers, both physical and running inside a Xen domU.

- ☑ Most of the functionality is available in the free, open source edition, although advanced plug-ins such as QRM-HA and the Provisioning Portal are available only through commercial offerings from Qlusters.

- ☑ Although offering lots of functionality, openQRM does expose an API for programmatic interaction with the QRM server.

Enomalism

- ☑ Bringing the concept of geographic computing to the common data center, Enomalism provides a unique, if not elastic, approach to Xen management.

☑ Using a centralized dashboard, administrators can view their Xen environment and control activities manually or in an automatic and dynamic way to meet business and workload needs in real time.

☑ You can manage system users as well as the systems themselves through a central LDAP directory service. Administrators can assign and control system resource parameters and reassign resources as needed.

☑ Enomalism features the Enomalism Virtual Appliance package management interface that automates the processes of installing, upgrading, configuring, and removing software packages using the VMCasting system, based on RSS feed technology.

☑ An open and accessible API enables easy third-party integration with other management products, while supporting industry standards such as SOAP.

Project ConVirt and XenMan

☑ XenMan provides an intuitive interface for managing and administering multiple Xen systems. Through XenMan, administrators can manage host and guest performance and utilize its robust provisioning capabilities.

☑ XenMan gives you complete control of hosts and guests. Through a series of clicks, you can start, stop, deploy, and configure your VMs and their hosts.

☑ Utilizing a unique approach to image repository management, XenMan employs an image store to store, define, and provision images to managed systems.

Frequently Asked Questions

Q: We want to create a policy that prohibits anyone, including administrators, from interactively logging into a Xen host. If I use these tools, will we ever have to use the native management tools?

A: Although all three products discussed in this chapter offer an extensive feature set and functionality, they are not a direct replacement for the native tools. There may be occasions when you will need to use the control tools available in dom0—for example, when the host is not available on the network. Also, future releases of the tools may not keep pace with the functionality introduced by Xen in upcoming versions, in which case you will either need to delay your upgrades or make sure that your administrative processes still let you manage hosts locally.

Q: My data center has a mixture of virtualization technologies. I would like to minimize the number of tools that I have to use and maintain. Which tool best fits my need?

A: Although all three offer great management capabilities, only openQRM allows you to manage VMware and Xen hosts in a single console. On top of that, you can also manage your physical hosts, running either Windows or Linux.

Q: Can I receive support for any of these tools?

A: Yes and no. Only openQRM and Enomalism offer a commercial package that adds functionality and support to the equation. However, all three tools are widely used around the world to manage Xen environments, and as such, they have a strong user base that is willing to help you in user forums accessible online. In most cases, you can have your questions answered by posting to these forums.

Q: My company is using XenSource's XenEnterprise. Should I use these third-party tools to manage my VMs?

A: In most cases, the answer is yes. These tools supplement the functionality available in the XenServer Administrator Console. Many features have been included that are not even available in the Administrator Console, making them valuable to your organization. With that said, you should exercise caution when implementing changes to your hosts. Installing additional packages onto a XenServer host may void any support agreement with XenSource, and its CentOS-based dom0 has been minimized and meets certain criteria of functionality and resource consumption.

Q: I need help deploying my Xen hosts as well as Xen guests. Which tool fits my need?

A: openQRM allows you to create a "golden image" of a Xen host and provision that to available physical resources as needed or desired. Although the other two are more focused on VM provisioning, other tools are available which we did not cover in this chapter that will help you with Xen host deployments.

Chapter 16

Deploying a Virtual Machine in Xen

Solutions in this chapter:

- **Workload Planning and Virtual Machine Placement**

- **Installing Modified Guests**

- **Installing Unmodified Guests**

- **Installing Windows Guests**

- **Physical-to-Virtual Migrations of Existing Systems**

- **Importing and Exporting Existing Virtual Machines**

☑ Summary

☑ Solutions Fast Track

☑ Frequently Asked Questions

Introduction

Understanding the interaction between XenVMs and Xen Hosts requires that administrators understand their workloads. Once they understand their workloads for every application, they can decide which XenVMs work well together and which ones will contend for resources.

Once the Xen Hosts are installed, administrators will have to create the XenVMs. Xen provides different techniques for provisioning XenVMs. Users can create a new XenVM by installing from media or network shares, they can clone a XenVM, they can export a XenVM and use it as a template, or they can convert the OS on a physical host to a "virtualized" XenVM.

Workload Planning and Virtual Machine Placement

As discussed in previous chapters, the appeal of virtualization includes the ability to maximize the utilization of IT assets, reduce administrative overhead, and accelerate provisioning times, among others. At first glance, virtualization is mostly about CPU and memory utilization, but as most of us that have been implementing virtualization technologies for years can attest, both network and disk I/O can also have a major impact in workload combination decisions.

To accomplish an optimal workload mix, thorough research has been done on current physical server utilization and an understanding of the additional horsepower impact of newer servers and I/O subsystems. To help with this task, both commercial and open source products are available that can assist in mapping physical-to-virtual workloads.

Memory

Memory is one of the most expensive system components, and one that should not be underestimated. Xen allows administrators to reserve a minimum amount of memory specific to each virtual machine (VM) upon startup.

Understanding physical server memory utilization is a paramount factor in VM placement. If a Xen host is oversubscribed, the XenVMs can run into physical memory contention, creating a potential performance impact and, in some cases, causing processes and VMs to crash.

CPU

One of the areas where server consolidation has the most impact is CPU utilization. With CPU processing power doubling every couple of years, it is possible that when analyzing the physical server CPU speed, coupled with the power of those processors in comparison with current ones, a huge opportunity for workload consolidation exists.

Make sure that systems with similar high demands on processor resources will not cause contention hot spots as XenVMs running on the same Xen Host.

WARNING

Make sure you understand multicore processor technology. On Intel and AMD multicore processors, increasing the number of cores does not provide a linear increment in processing power, even with dedicated cache and multiple buses.

Designing & Planning...

Modeling CPU Consolidation

A simple rule of thumb when modeling load on an existing physical server to a newer processor platform is to multiply the utilization of the processors by the speed (clock cycles) and number of processors:

Number_of_Processors x Old_Processor_Speed x %_Utilization = Total_ consumed_ processor_speed

For example:

4 processors × 1 GHz × 40% = 1.6 GHz

This last example only illustrates a straightforward number of cycles of processing used. And although other factors in workload processing consolidation, such as concurrency and context switching, result in a more complex equation, from experience this rule of thumb has served well as the foundation for VM placement and consolidation.

Network

The network is probably the most overlooked resource when migrating physical servers to VMs. With today's increasing bandwidth at the network infrastructure, it is easy to overlook the cumulative demands of physical servers on the network.

Understanding that total network usage for all the VMs will now be exceeding the physical interface(s) of the Xen Host is paramount to successful migration.

Design & Planning...

High Availability, Replication, and Backups

Every IT organization has requirements in terms of system availability and data protection. Most solutions that meet these requirements have to move data between systems in the form of a network-based backup, via clustering, or by logically replicating the data from one system to another.

These solutions can have different demands on networks: steady streams of low-impact or periodic bursts, or, in the case of network-based backups, steady, high-impact streams.

- **High availability**   High-availability solutions, such as clustering technologies, often require different networks for different functions. In most cases, a minimum of two networks are required: a public network through which clients can communicate with the servers, and a private network that is used for heartbeats, or messaging, between cluster nodes. In addition, most clustering solutions best practices include redundant networks or alternative networks, which would limit the available networks to other XenVMs.

- **Replication**   *Replication* refers to the transport of data from one application to another. Different application types, such as RDMBS and e-mail systems, use proprietary methods to accomplish replication, but the result is that either a subset or all of the data in the original has to be transported to the replica. All of this traffic occurs over the network (whether virtual or physical), and may be synchronous or asynchronous. In either case, either a steady stream of data or a periodic burst will occur on the network, and may impact the performance of all VMs on a specific Xen Host.

- **Backups**   Although administrators can back up XenVMs using cloning or exporting techniques (we won't discuss the merits and constraints of those techniques here), it is still highly recommended that you back up using traditional network-based methods in which a network server is attached to the media (tapes, disks, virtual tapes, etc.) and to which clients send copies of files and data.

- Backup applications will take advantage of any available bandwidth to accomplish the backups in as little time as possible. So, cohabiting XenVMs that have high data volumes and frequent data changes will impact the performance of those VMs during backup periods.

Also, be sure to take into consideration how much data needs to be backed up and how frequently it changes.

In addition to the issue of bandwidth, network isolation due to security might also be required, and taking into account that the XenVM's virtual network interface cards (NICs) and the Xen Host's physical NICs are on the same subnet, and that any Xen Host can have, at most, three NICs, users might find themselves in situations that limit where they can place the XenVMs.

Installing Modified Guests

Modified guests are guest operating systems that are optimized by replacing the kernel with a Xen-aware version and providing Xen-optimized disk and network drivers that "understand" the underlying virtualization layers.

The process of installing modified Linux guests is different in that it requires an "exploded" network share of the installation binaries (not the ISOs of the CD-ROMs/DVDs). Although it is not necessary to have a boot server (the XenVM will boot and then prompt for the network share), having one allows for fully automated deployments of Linux XenVMs.

In the following subsection, we will discuss how to install Red Hat ES 4 from a network share.

Installing Red Hat Enterprise Linux 4

Red Hat ES 4 installation requires the use of a network share. The network share can be run on the NFS, FTP, or HTTP protocol, depending on the user's preference and\or existing solutions. In addition, each protocol has a list of requirements and dependencies that need to be met, including connectivity, binaries, and security considerations.

To install a Red Hat ES 4 XenVM, follow these steps:

1. Log on to the **Administrator Console**.

2. Select the **Xen Host** on which to deploy the Red Hat ES 4 XenVM.

3. Click on the **Install XenVM button**. The Install XenVM tab will appear in the bottom pane, as shown in Figure 16.1.

Figure 16.1 The Install XenVM Tab in Red Hat ES 4

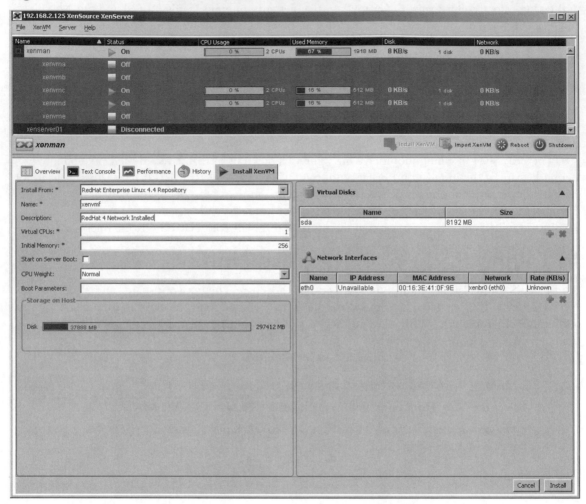

The Install XenVM pane consists of the following fields and sections:

- **Install From**   A pull-down menu that allows you to select the operating system template that will be used for the XenVM. This template does not contain OS images, but rather produces a default configuration for the components in this type of XenVM (the number of virtual CPUs, disks and disk sizes, NIC definitions, etc.).

- **Name**   The unique alphanumeric identifier for the XenVM (this is not the hostname of the resulting operating system).

- **Description**   A nonmandatory field that allows you to identify the function or other characteristics of the XenVM.

- **Virtual CPUs**   The number of virtual CPUs that will be presented to the XenVM.

- **Initial Memory**   The amount of dedicated memory for the XenVM.

- **Start on Server Boot**   A check box that indicates whether to start this XenVM when the Xen Host boots.

- **CPU Weight**   A drop-down menu that allows you to select the relative CPU resource allocation for this XenVM. The values in the menu are Low, Normal, and High. You also can define more granular CPU weight distributions from the command-line interface (CLI).

- **Storage On Host**   A display of the storage allocation to the Xen Host.

- **Virtual Disks**   Displays the virtual disks to be used for this XenVM. To add or remove virtual disks click on the plus (+) or delete (X) symbol. A new virtual disk will appear, or the selected virtual disk will be removed.

- **CD-ROM/DVD**   Allows you to select the media device to present to the XenVM.

- **Network Interfaces**   Presents you with the default NIC for the XenVM. Clicking the plus or remove symbol will add NICs or remove the select NIC from the screen. If more than one network is defined on the Xen Host, the network column becomes a drop-down menu allowing you to select the correct network for that interface.

4. Once you have filled in all of the mandatory fields, click on the **Install button** in the bottom pane. The Red Hat pseudographical install screen will appear (see Figure 16.2). At this point, you have not indicated where the install files are located, or a boot server from which to boot. This boot image is actually provided by the Xen Host, and is selected based on the Installation Type field shown in Figure 16.2.

Figure 16.2 The Red Hat Install Screen

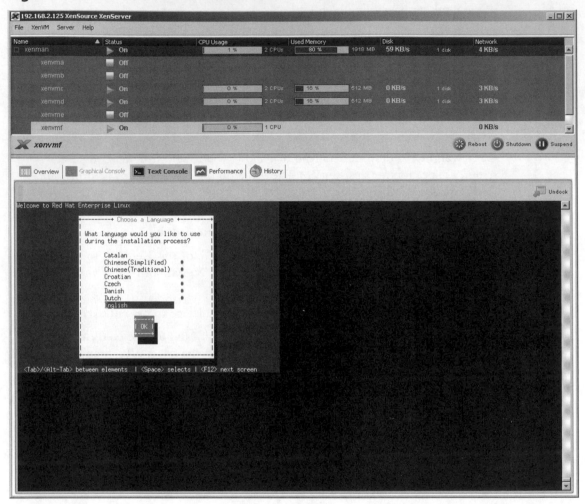

5. Select the appropriate language and tab to the **OK button**. Once the OK button is highlighted, press the **Enter key**. The screen will change, and the installer will prompt for the location of the media, as shown in Figure 16.3.

Figure 16.3 Network Install Media Location

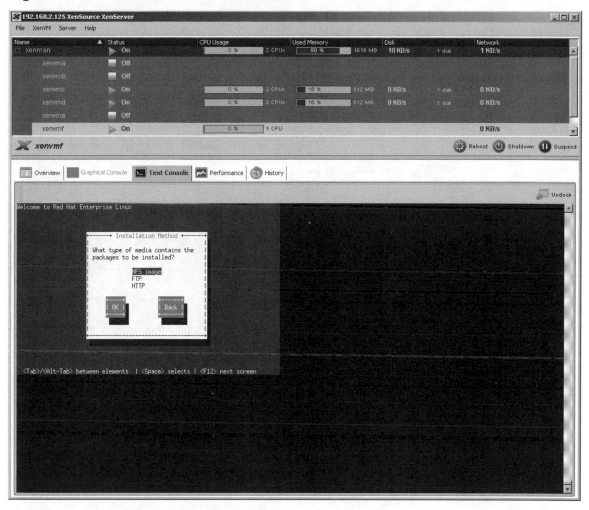

6. Select the type of media to be used by using the up/down arrows. Then tab until the OK button is highlighted and press **Return**. The new Red Hat ES 4 XenVM will request a network identity from the network (tftpboot/dhcp servers), as shown in Figure 16.4.

Figure 16.4 Searching for Hostname and Domain Information

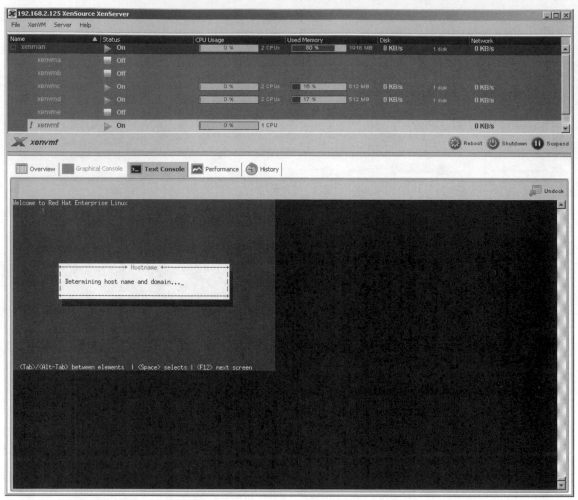

7. If no DHCP/TFTPBOOT server can be found, the installer will ask for network information to be entered manually.

8. After you supply the network information and click the **OK button**, the installer will prompt you for information on the network share to use:

   - If you selected **NFS** as the media type, the installer will prompt for the hostname/IP address of the NFS server, and the installation directory, as shown in Figure 16.5.

   - If you chose **HTTP**, the installer will prompt for the URL of the server, including the path to the installation files.

   - If you selected **FTP**, the installer will prompt for the hostname/IP address of the server along with the authentication credentials to be used.

Figure 16.5 Entering Media Share Network Information

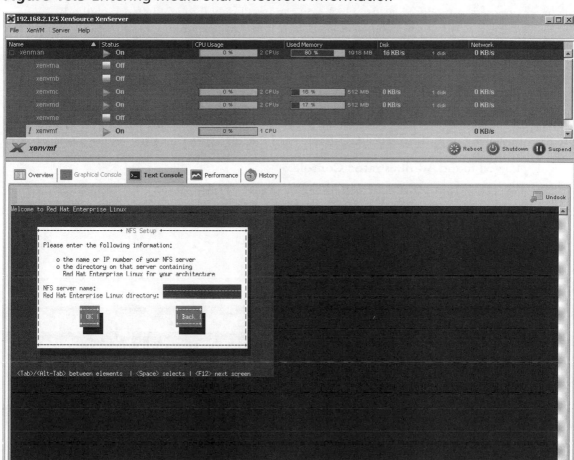

9.   Once you've entered the share information, tab to the **OK button** and press **Enter**. At this stage, the installation will commence, and the installer will prompt you for all the configuration information. Refer to the Red Hat Enterprise Linux documentation for complete installation instructions.

Installing Unmodified Guests

Support for installing unmodified guests is available only for Red Hat Enterprise Linux 5, SUSE Linux Enterprise Server 10 SP1, and Windows XP/2003 (Windows XP and Windows 2003 installations are covered in the section "Installing Windows Guests," later in this chapter).

One of the characteristics of unmodified hosts is that you can install them directly from vendor media, as opposed to modified guests, which you can install only through network methods.

As discussed earlier in this book, *unmodified guests* refers to operating systems that can actually run in emulated mode. And although unmodified guests can run permanently, they use more resources because they use emulation drivers instead of the Xen-provided drivers.

Installing Red Hat Linux Enterprise 5

You can install Red Hat 5 either from vendor media or via a network share. We will discuss the process of installing from the original CD-ROMs and then paravirtualizing the resulting XenVM.

1. Log on to the **Administrator Console**.

2. Select the **Xen Host** on which to deploy the Red Hat 5 XenVM.

3. Click on the **Install XenVM button**. The Install XenVM tab will appear in the bottom pane, as shown in Figure 16.6.

Figure 16.6 The Install XenVM Pane

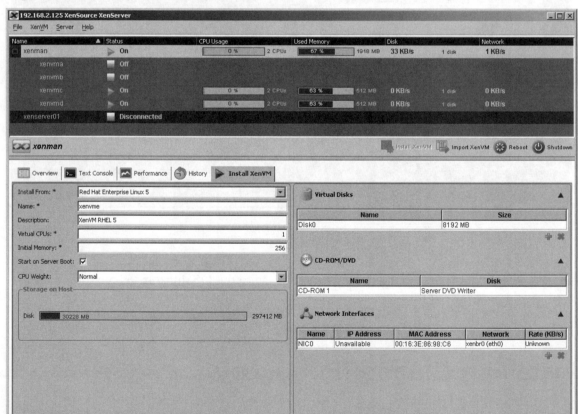

4. Once you have filled in all of the mandatory fields (★), click on the **Install button** at the bottom of the Administrator Console window. The History tab in the lower pane will indicate the progress of the install.

5. The Overview tab in the bottom pane will display the characteristics of the newly created XenVM; however, the XenVM will not be powered on, as indicated in the upper pane in Figure 16.7.

Figure 16.7 Installed XenVM

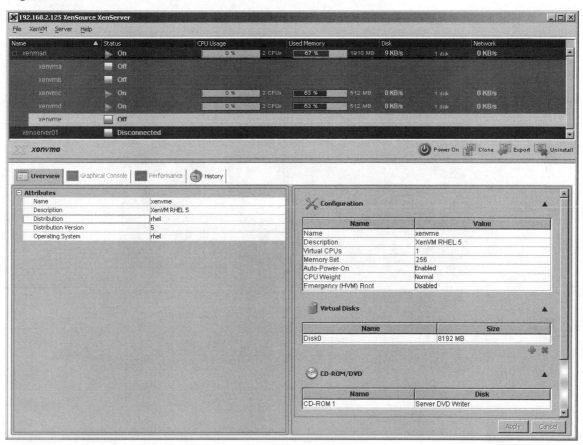

6. Insert **Disc1** of the Red Hat Enterprise Linux 5 distribution into the CD-ROM/DVD of the Xen Host.

7. Boot the **XenVM** by selecting it from the upper pane and clicking the **Power On button**. The new XenVM will go through its boot sequence from CD-ROM/DVD. Figure 16.8 shows the Red Hat install splash page in the XenVM's Graphical Console tab.

Figure 16.8 Booting the New XenVM from Vendor Media

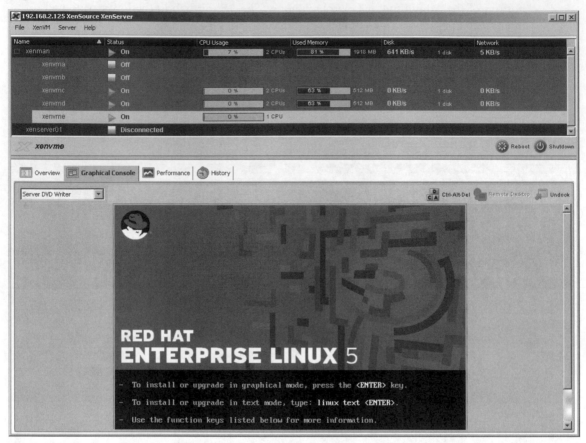

8. Click inside the lower pane to get TTY control. To continue the install in graphical mode, press **Enter**. The boot sequence is displayed on the Graphical Console tab, as shown in Figure 16.9.

Figure 16.9 The Boot Sequence for XenVM

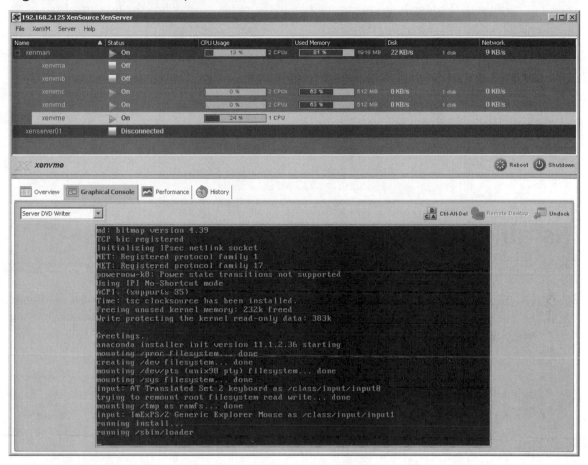

9. The installation will prompt for user-defined parameters. Make sure to refer to the Red Hat documentation for installation details.

10. Once the installation is complete, the installer will prompt you to eject the CD-ROM/DVD from the Xen Host's bay and click on the **Reboot button**. The Graphical Console will display the reboot process.

11. When the XenVM has rebooted completely, it is ready for use. At this point, however, the XenVM has not been paravirtualized, and as such, it is not performing to capacity. Select the **XenSource Linux P2V tools CD** from the CD-ROM/DVD pull-down. This will make the ISO image available for the XenVM to use, but will not mount it.

12. Mount the ISO image with the following command:

    ```
    # mount -t iso9660 /dev/hdd /cdrom
    ```

13. Copy the contents of the mounted ISO image to a separate location. This is required because the Vendor Install media must be in the physical bay when the paravirtualization script is called. When the copy command is complete, enter *unmount /cdrom*:

    ```
    # cp -ra /cdrom /"$TEMP_AREA"
    ```

14. Insert the **Red Hat Enterprise Linux 5 Disc1** into the Xen Host's CD-ROM/DVD.

15. Run the xen-setup tool:

    ```
    # $TEMP_AREA/xen-setup/xen-setup
    ```

16. After the xen-setup script completes successfully, reboot the XenVM. After the reboot, verify that the kernel for the XenVM has been paravirtualized:

    ```
    # uname -a
    ```

Installing Windows Guests

Finally, Windows guests are supported in Xen. This is a much-anticipated event, as Windows operating systems have the lion's share of installations worldwide.

Much like Linux unmodified guests, you can install Windows guests from vendor media and they are unmodified upon first installing the XenVM. However, a quick run around the resulting operating system will show that paravirtualization is absolutely necessary for any semblance of performance.

It's important to understand what happens under the covers:

- First, the Xen Host provides the Windows installer with an emulated IDE and NIC drivers, just to allow the installation to complete.

- After the installation has completed, you will need to install the XenPV tools for Windows, which replace those drivers with optimized versions.

Windows Guest Installation

In this section we will discuss the steps for installing a Windows guest.

1. Insert the **Windows CD-ROM** in the Xen Host on which you want to deploy.

2. Log on to the **Administrator Console**.

3. Select the **Install XenVM button**, after selecting the desired **Xen Host**. The Install XenVM tab appears, as in Figure 16.10.

Figure 16.10 The Install XenVM Windows Tab

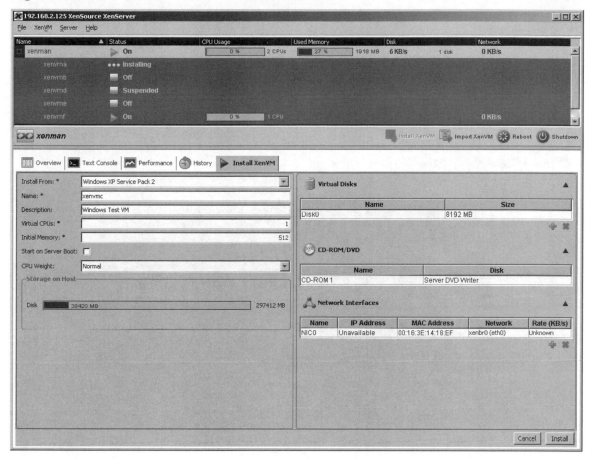

4. After entering the appropriate information to identify the XenVM (and selecting the **Server DVD Writer**), click on the **Install button** in the lower pane. The lower pane will be switched to the Graphical Console for the new XenVM, as shown in Figure 16.11, and the Windows Installer screen will appear.

Figure 16.11 The Windows Installer Screen

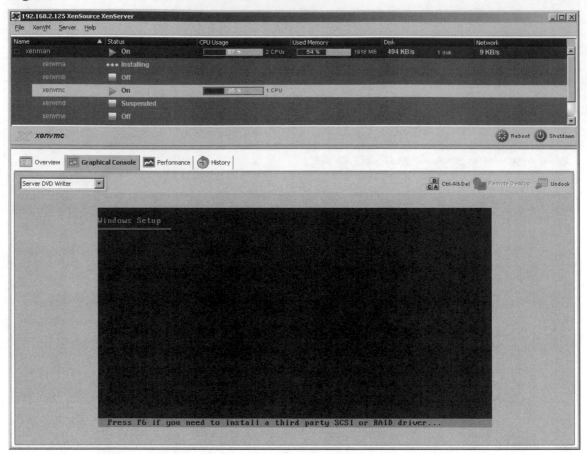

5. After you work your way through the Windows installation, the OS will be booted completely. In the lower pane, the Media drop-down menu will appear. Select the PV Tools for windows option from the menu (see Figure 16.12).

Figure 16.12 The Xen PV Tools from Media Drop-Down

6. The End User License Agreement (EULA) will appear on the screen (see Figure 16.13).

Figure 16.13 The Xen PV Tools EULA

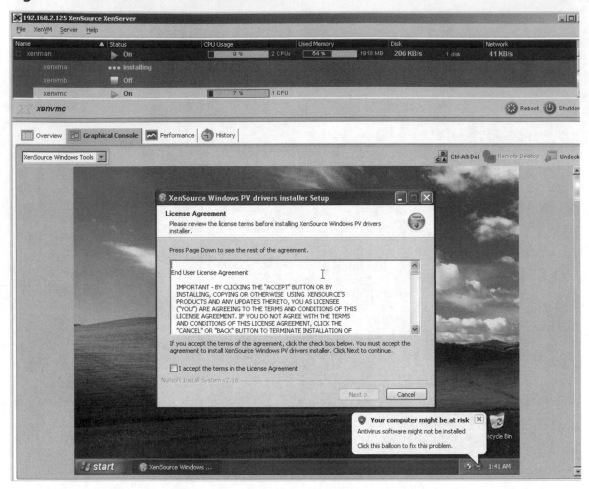

7. Click on the **Accept the terms of the License Agreement check box** and then click on the **Next button**.

8. Follow the installation instructions. To finalize, the installer will reboot the Windows XenVM. At this point, the resulting XenVM is fully paravirtualized and ready to use.

Physical-to-Virtual Migrations of Existing Systems

Physical-to-virtual (P2V) migrations consist of copying and modifying the operating system files of a physical server to either a logical volume on a Xen Host or a network share. Once the files have been copied, the result is a bootable XenVM.

P2V migrations are now industry-standard, as one of the main advantages of virtualization is the ability to reduce the physical data center footprint. Xen provides a P2V tool in the installation media, but third-party vendors have developed extended-functionality products to assist companies with their migrations.

The P2V tool provided by Xen works only on Linux physical hosts, and then only on those with PAE support. You cannot migrate Windows physical servers with Xen's provided P2V tool; however, several third-party vendors support Windows migrations.

P2V Migration

To migrate a physical server to a XenVM, follow these steps:

1. Boot the **physical server** from the Xen installation media.

2. At the **Welcome to Xen screen**, tab to the **OK button** and press **Return**.

3. After the installer has reviewed the server components, two choice will appear. Select the **P2V option**, then tab to the **OK button** and press **Return**.

4. Click the **OK button** on the **Welcome screen**.

5. The next screen requires the networking information for the resulting XenVM. You can choose to either allow the Dynamic Host Configuration Protocol (DHCP) for all interfaces, or manually configure them. Once completed, tab to the **OK button** and press **Return**.

6. After the installer has verified that the physical host is running a supported version of Linux, tab to the **OK button** and press **Return**.

7. Enter a **name** and **description** for the XenVM. This is not the hostname as registered in the operating system, but rather the name displayed on the Administrator Console or through the CLI.

8. Enter the **desired size of the root disk**, or accept the defaults, and then select **OK** and press **Return**.

9. Select the **target location** for the resulting file system. The options are Xen Host or an NFS server. Once you've made your selection, tab to the **OK button** and press **Return**.

10. Enter the **IP address** of the Xen Host, tab to the **OK button**, and press **Return**.

11. Enter the **root password** for the Xen Host, and select **OK**.

12. After the progress bar has completed, select **OK**. The physical server will eject the Xen Installation CD-ROM and reboot the server. Make sure to take out the media before the reboot.

13. You can verify that the installation completed by launching the **Administrator Console** and selecting the **XenVM name** given in step 7.

Importing and Exporting Existing Virtual Machines

Exporting is a mechanism for copying a XenVM. You can then use the copied XenVM as a template (like a clone) to create similar XenVMs with the characteristics of the original. In addition, you can import the exported XenVM to a different Xen Host (a mechanism that you can use to increase XenVM availability, or in disaster recovery solutions).

The process involves copying the virtual disks (VDIs) of the exported XenVM along with an XML document describing the configuration, as shown in Figure 16.14. The files are copied from the Xen Host to the Administrator Console. The Administrator Console will need enough disk space to store the VDI images.

NOTE

The VDI images will be compressed and are usually smaller than the actual size of the disk.

Figure 16.14 Sample XML of Exported XenVM

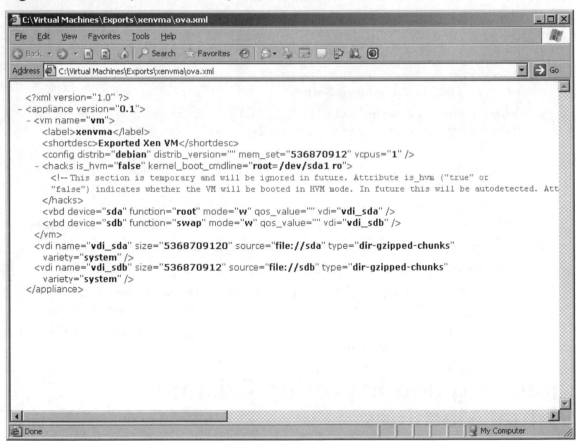

Exporting XenVMs

Before starting the export process, administrators need to ensure that the Administrator Console server has enough disk space to store the exported XenVM files:

1. Log on to the **Administrator Console**.

2. Select the **XenVM** that will be exported. You must shut down the XenVM in order to export it. If the XenVM is still running, click on the **Power Off button**.

3. Once you've shut down the XenVM, click on the **Export button**. Figure 16.15 shows the Export tab that appears.

Figure 16.15 The Export XenVM Tab

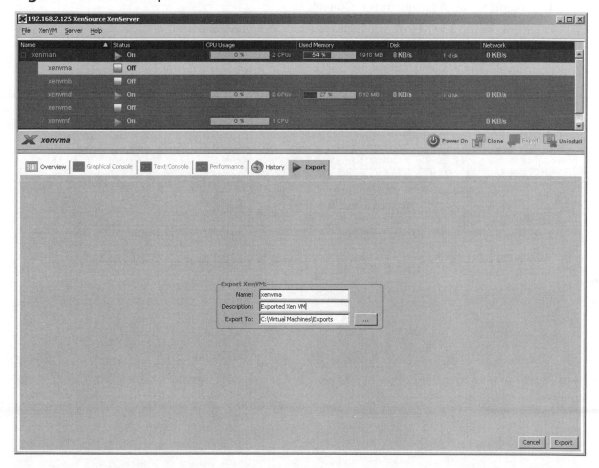

Three fields appear:

- **Name**

- **Description**

- **Export To**   The directory on the Administrator Console in which to save the exported XenVM.

4. Click on the **Export button** to begin the process. The lower pane will switch to the History tab for the XenVM and a progress bar will appear showing the status of the export. Export can take a long time, depending on the number and size of the virtual disks and the network bandwidth available between the Xen Host and the Administrator Console.

Importing XenVMs

Importing a XenVM consists of moving the exported XenVM's files to a Xen Host. The process is the reverse of the export operation; copying the VDI files and XML file from the Administrator Console to the Xen Host.

To import a previously exported XenVM, follow these steps:

1. Log on to the **Administrator Console**.

2. Click on the **Xen Host** to which the XenVM will be imported.

3. Click on the **Import XenVM button**, and the Import XenVM tab appears in the lower pane. Figure 16.16 illustrates the Import XenVM tab.

Figure 16.16 The Import XenVM Tab

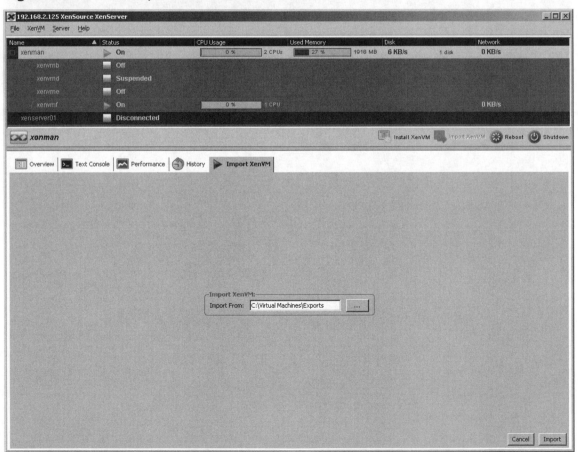

4. In the **Import From: field**, enter the location of the export XenVM directory, and then click the **Import button**. The lower pane will immediately change to the History tab for the imported XenVM. The import process may take awhile, as the VDI files are being copied over the network and then reassembled on the Xen Host.

Design & Planning...

Export/Import XenVM As an Enterprise Tool

The ability to "transport" a XenVM via export/import is one of Xen's most powerful yet underrated features. In today's IT landscape, where business demands are progressively greater and budgets are lower, having a flexible tool that can decrease provisioning times, increase overall availability, and reduce disaster recovery costs is indeed a necessity.

Exporting a XenVM allows administrators the flexibility of moving XenVMs from one physical Xen Host to another. Downtime for XenVM migrations due to hardware maintenance and hardware migrations can be reduced. In addition, administrators can export XenVMs and use them as templates for creating additional XenVMs on other Xen Hosts, cutting down on provisioning times.

However, exporting and importing XenVMs can be time-consuming, and this is something to consider if you are planning to use this mechanism as a way to migrate XenVMs among Xen Hosts.

In addition to exporting and importing XenVMs, Xen provides an interface to "migrate" XenVMs from one Xen Host to another. From a high level, live migrations consist of moving the active memory pages and the NIC definitions (along with Internet Protocol [IP] address and ARP tables) for a XenVM between Xen Hosts. In addition, both Xen Hosts involved in the operation require simultaneous access to the VDI definitions of the XenVM and the same local area network (LAN).

Currently, the XenSource Administrator Console does not have an interface for performing live migrations of XenVMs. However, the XM CLI provides a mechanism to accomplish live migrations:

```
xm migrate --live XenVM_NAME XEN_HOST_NAME
```

This command will move the XenVM named *XenVM_NAME* to the *Xen_HOST_NAME* physical server from its current Xen Host.

Continued

Although you can move a XenVM with either mechanism, both have benefits and constraints:

■ As discussed earlier, exporting requires that the XenVM be powered off. In contrast, live migrations move the XenVM between Xen Hosts in "real time" (depending on the application, the XenVM might need to be quiesced).

■ However, live migrations require shared storage, which adds a cost to the infrastructure. Exporting XenVMs doesn't require such costs, but takes significantly longer to accomplish.

■ You can use exported XenVMs as templates to create additional XenVMs, whereas live migrations don't actually copy the XenVMs files; they just move control of the VDIs to another physical host.

Summary

XenVM deployment is at the heart of Xen's functionality. In most cases, administrators will start by creating some test XenVMs from either the Administrator Console or the CLI. As users get more comfortable, additional deployment techniques such as cloning or exporting/importing are employed. And after the value of Xen has been tested and proven, users will start using physical-to-logical migrations as an indispensable tool.

Soon, administrators will discover that not all XenVMs can be placed together, as they contend for any or all of the resources on the Xen Host. At that stage, exporting the XenVMs to a different Xen Host allows administrators to balance the workload more evenly.

At a more developed stage, administrators understand that moving XenVMs from one Xen Host to another needs to be more streamlined and dynamic. Enter live migrations, which allow administrators to reduce and even eliminate the downtime associated with moving the XenVMs to another physical host, but for which the IT group has to make additional investments in infrastructure.

Solutions Fast Track

Workload Planning and Virtual Machine Placement

☑ Understanding physical application requirements is paramount to planning the workload for a virtual environment.

☑ You determine workloads by measuring the use of CPU, memory, network, and disk I/O on either the physical host or the XenVM.

☑ With today's enterprise infrastructure components, disk I/O and the network are usually simpler to consolidate.

☑ CPU and memory are often the most critical components in workload balancing, and usually they are the most expensive resources on the physical servers.

Installing Modified Guests

☑ Modified guests refer to operating systems that are "paravirtualized" during the installation process, such as Red Hat Enterprise Linux 4.*x* and SUSE 9.*x*.

☑ You can install modified guests only from a network share. Supported protocols for installation network shares are NFS, HTTP, and FTP.

Installing Unmodified Guests

☑ Unmodified guests are based on operating systems that do not need to be paravirtualized in order to run as a XenVM.

☑ Operating systems that support unmodified guests include Red Hat Enterprise Linux 5, SUSE 10.1, and Windows XP/2003, and they require the use of processors with virtualization extensions built in, such as the Intel-VT and AMD-V.

☑ In contrast to modified guests, you can install unmodified guests from vendor media, such as CD-ROM or DVD.

☑ Although you can deploy unmodified guests without being paravirtualized, it is highly recommended that you modify them once installed, as performance will improve dramatically.

Installing Windows Guests

☑ Windows guests are installed as unmodified guests. Administrators then have to paravirtualize them.

☑ Windows XP, 2000, and 2003 are supported.

☑ In order to run Windows XenVMs, the Xen Host has to have a processor with virtualization extensions. Currently, only physical hosts with the Intel-VT or the AMD-V processors are supported.

Physical-to-Virtual (P2V) Migrations of Existing Physical Servers

☑ P2V migrations are accomplished by booting the physical servers from the Xen install CD and copying and modifying the contents of the boot disk to the Xen Host.

☑ Although you can convert all operating systems supported in XenVMs from physical to logical, only Linux operating systems are supported with the Xen installation media. Windows operating systems require third-party tools to be converted.

☑ P2V migrations allow administrators to minimize the impact of converting physical servers. In addition, P2V migrations also minimize risk by keeping the original server intact.

Importing and Exporting Existing Virtual Machines

☑ Exporting an existing VM involves copying the virtual disk definitions from the Xen Host to the Administrator Console. In addition, an XML definition file is copied and is used to "reproduce" the identity of the XenVM.

☑ You can use XenVM exports to move the VM from one physical host to another. You also can use exports as a way to create templates and simplify deployments.

☑ You import a XenVM when the resulting files from an export are moved from the Administrator Console to a Xen Host.

☑ Export and imports of XenVMs can take a relatively long time, depending on the size of the VDIs and the network bandwidth available between the Xen Host and the Administrator Console.

Frequently Asked Questions

Q: What are the pitfalls of migrating a physical server to VMs indiscriminately?

A: Not all workloads perform well together. Take into consideration the resource requirements of each physical server before deciding which Xen Host to migrate it to, and even whether migration is a viable option at all.

Q: Why can some Linux operating systems be installed directly from media, whereas others require a network-based install?

A: Hardware virtualization is a relatively new development in the x86 arena. Older operating systems are not "virtualization-aware," so they will not run as an unmodified XenVM. In contrast, the latest batch of Linux from Red Hat and SUSE "understands" virtualization.

Q: Is export/import a viable technique for implementing workload balancing?

A: It really depends on the availability requirements of the underlying application. Exports and imports can require long periods of time to complete, as the data from the XenVM is transported to and from the Administrator Console over the network. If the application can be down for those periods, export/import may be a viable technique.

Q: Are live migrations quicker than export/import?

A: Yes, they are; however, live migrations require higher technical and financial commitments. Live migrations reduce downtime greatly when you're trying to achieve workload balancing; however, they require higher-bandwidth network and shared storage (SAN). These requirements increase the environment's complexity and create additional administrative overhead.

## Chapter 17

Advanced Xen Concepts

Solutions in this chapter:

- **The Virtual Split Devices Model**
- **Advanced Storage Concepts**
- **Advanced Networking Concepts**
- **Building a Xen Cluster**
- **XenVM Migration**
- **XenVM Backup and Recovery Solutions**
- **Full Virtualization in Xen**

☑ **Summary**

☑ **Solutions Fast Track**

☑ **Frequently Asked Questions**

Introduction

Xen is an advanced virtualization solution that encapsulates three layers of virtualization: devices, memory, and CPU. Due to these types of virtualization, which are sophisticated and difficult to implement, you can achieve very good performance results with Xen.

In this chapter, we will discuss advanced Xen concepts like storage and networking, live migration, clustering, and backup solutions. Various solutions exist in these areas, and we will discuss the pros and cons of some of them.

The Virtual Split Devices Model

In Xen, I/O is performed by Virtual Split Devices, which have a FrontEnd layer and a BackEnd layer. The idea behind this is safe and efficient hardware isolation. The BackEnd layer is part of domain 0 (dom0). It is the only layer that has direct access to the hardware devices in a default Xen installation. Note that it is possible to configure domUs with hardware access, too—something called "driver domains." Also note that work is done to enable domUs to access hardware devices (such as infiniband) without usage of driver domains—for example, there is ongoing research about VMM-bypass for I/O access using infiniband for VM environments (see http://nowlab.cse.ohio-state. edu/publications/conf-papers/2006/usenix06.pdf). Each unprivileged domain has a FrontEnd layer of itself. Access from the FrontEnd to the BackEnd and backwards is performed by event channels and shared memory. Each domain can have up to 1024 event channels on i386 machines, and up to 4096 event channels on x86_64 machines. The FrontEnd and BackEnd share memory pages for communication, which is controlled by a grant tables mechanism. Figure 17.1 illustrates the Split Devices mechanism.

Figure 17.1 Split Devices Diagram

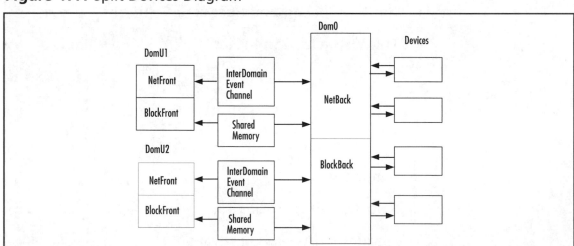

Advanced Storage Concepts

A variety of storage methods can be used in Xen. The main reason for employing the Copy-On-Write method is to save disk space. When thinking about sharing storage—a mandatory requirement in many cases—iSCSI storage is one of the available solutions. We discuss the various storage solutions in the following sections.

High-Performance Solutions for Xen

Disk access is done in Xen by a virtual block device (VBD). Any block device that can be accessed from the block backend can be exported as a VBD. This includes Network Block Devices (NBDs), iSCSI, Logical Volume Manager (LVM) devices, Global Network Block Devices (GNBDs), and more. The disk = […] entry in the domain configuration file shows the mapping between the device node and the VBD. The VBD is a split device, (as explained earlier in this chapter), and messages that pass between the BlockFront and the BlockEnd can be of two types: READ or WRITE.

When you work with a physical device, you should have a disk = ['phy:…'] entry in the domain configuration file; and when you work with a file, you should have a disk = ['file:…'] entry in that configuration file. When working with iSCSI devices, this entry can be: disk = ['phy:…'], and if you have the block-iSCSI script installed, it can also be: ['iscsi:…']—for example, disk = ['iscsi: iqn.2001-04.com.example:diskarrays-sn-a8675309', hda, w']. More details on this option later in the chapter.

In certain cases, you should have some type of shared file system or clustered file system—for example, when performing live migration, or when you have a Xen-based cluster. Live migration only handles the transfer of memory pages; file systems are not transferred. As a result, a shared file system is needed, so an application that performs I/O will be able to continue to run as before. When working in a cluster, multiple clients can access shared storage. In such cases, you should not use an ordinary file system because of the risk of data corruption. Thus, you must use a cluster file system, which has a locking mechanism to avoid data corruption. Also, in some cases, you may want to use a Copy-on-Write image, because it needs less disk capacity.

iSCSI Integration with Xen

iSCSI is a transport protocol that works on top of TCP (see RFC 3720). You do not have to buy expensive equipment to use it and it is quite simple to deploy. In RedHat Fedora Core, the storage is called "iscsi-target" and the client is termed "iscsi-initiator." In SUSE, the storage is named "iscsi-server," and the client is termed "iscsi-client." The iSCSI storage can have one or more logical units that process client commands. Logical units are assigned identifying numbers called logical unit numbers (LUNs) iSCSI is a block-level protocol that encapsulates SCSI commands into TCP/IP frames. After an iSCSI client logs in to an iSCSI server, a session is held between them. The iSCSI target can be configured to require authentication for login. The iSCSI session is in layer 5 (session layer) of the OSI seven-layer model. In most cases, the performance of iSCSI is worse than Fibre Channel due to the overhead added by using the TCP/IP protocol. However, employing technologies that become more and more popular, like Gigabit and 10 Gb/s network cards or network cards with TCP Offload Engine (TOE), may reduce this overhead. An iSCSI initiator can be a software initiator or a hardware-based iSCSI initiator

(Host Bus Adapter, HBA). HBA is in fact an extended network interface card. In addition to performing all regular network card functions, it also processes iSCSI protocol commands and iSCSI TCP commands, thus freeing the system CPU from doing iSCSI processing.

TIP

You can download an open-source implementation of iSCSI from SourceForge.net. To build an iSCSI target, download the iSCSI Enterprise Target (iET) at http://iscsitarget.sf. net. You can also download and install an iSCSI initiator supported on Linux from www.open-iscsi.org (see Figure 17.2).

Figure 17.2 iSCSI Initiators and an iSCSI Target

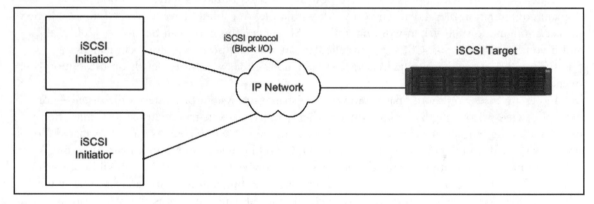

Configuring & Implementing…

Setting Up an iSCSI Initiator

In order to set up an iSCSI initiator on your Xen host to access iSCSI-based storage, you must configure the initiator using user space tools. Here is an example of a three-step process.

1. First, send a SendTargets message from the initiator to get a list of available iSCSI targets using the following command:

```
iscsiadm -m discovery -type sendtargets -p 192.168.0.190:3260
```

2. **Then, in order to show discovered targets, perform the following:**

```
iscsiadm -m node

(192.168.0.190:3260,1 iqn.2001-04.com.example:storage.disk2.sys1.xyz)
```

3. **To log in to that target, use**

```
iscsiadm -m node -T iqn.2001-04.com.example:storage.disk2.sys1.xyz -
p 192.168.0.190 -l
```

4. **You can log out from a target by using**

```
iscsiadm -m node -T iqn.2001-04.com.example:storage.disk2.sys1.xyz -
p 192.168.0.190 -u)
```

The target replies to the *SendTargets* command by returning a list of all iSCSI nodes it knows about.

We should mention here that you may also encounter queries to an Internet Storage Name Server (iSNS). This server allows iSCSI targets to register with a central point.

You can see by tail /var/log/messages which device was assigned to the target (sda, sdb, and so on). /var/log/messages is the kernel log file. Alternatively, you can use fdisk –l to detect new, added devices or use a utility called lsscsi to view your scsi devices and detect which device was added. You can download lsscsi from http://sg.torque.net/scsi/lsscsi.html.

Next, you can add the device in the domU configuration file by either setting the *disk =* *['phy: …]* entry to point to that device or by using a script to accomplish the same.

TIP

If you want to implement a script to facilitate iSCSI storage for Xen, the block-iscsi script created by Kurt Garloff from SUSE R&D is a great example to follow. You can download Kurt's script at: www.suse.de/~garloff/linux/xen/scripts/block-iscsi.

To modify the script to meet your needs, adjust the disk entry as follows, where the iqn is the node you discovered and want to use.

```
disk = [ "iscsi: iqn.2001-04.com.example:diskarrays-sn-a8675309', hda, w" ]
```

Using iSCSI storage this way does not require anything special to configure in domU; the disadvantage of using iSCSI storage in this manner is its slowness. A better way is to use iSCSI storage directly from domU: perform the login to iSCSI targets from domU and mount them from domU. This requires some configuration on domU (for example, for automatic iSCSI login to the iSCSI targets).

> **NOTE**
>
> Every initiator and target node must have a single name defined for it. This name is used as part of all sessions between iSCSI targets and initiators. iSCSI names are of two types.
>
> *iqn* stands for iSCSI qualified name. iSCSI devices, or nodes, must be allocated unique names. The iqn is the preferred standard. Its format is "iqn" plus a date field plus the reverse DNS name with unique qualifiers. For example: iqn.2001-04.com. example:diskarrays-sn-a8675309.
>
> The other type is Enterprise Unique Identifier (*eui*). Its format is "eui" plus 16 hex digits. For example, eui.02004567A425678D.

Copy-on-Write

Copy-on-Write (CoW) is an optimization technique for storage. The premise is that when multiple clients want to modify their copy of the resource, the operating system hands all of the clients' pointers to the same resource. When a client wants to modify its copy of the resource, a true copy is created to prevent making changes to that copy, which is owned by the other clients.

A variety of CoW solutions can be used for Xen, including the following:

- Blktap

- DmUserspace

- UnionFS

Blktap is a user space toolkit that provides user level disk I/O. It consists of a kernel module and some user space libraries. It uses the asynchronous calls of Linux libaio. It is already included as part of the Xen project. You can create a qcow disk using a utility called qcow-create, which is a utility that is part of Xen blktap tools. qcow is one of the formats supported by the QEMU processor emulator open-source project, which Xen uses. It represents a fixed-size block device in a file. Since a qcow image has an asynchronous backend, the performance when working with blktap with qcow images is good. It also supports AES encryption and transparent decompression. You can use it in domU by using the tap:qcow option for a QCOW image in the configuration file of the guest domain, such as in the following sample:

```
disk = [ 'tap:qcow:/server/qcow.img,xvda,w' ]
```

> **NOTE**
>
> Blktap has utilities for qcow conversion. *img2qcow* converts a raw disk or file system DomU image into a qcow image, and *qcow2raw* converts a qcow image into a raw file system or disk image.

DmUserspace

DmUserspace provides Copy-on-Write behavior by user space control over the device mapper. It exists as a patch to Xen and as a standalone module with user space tools. It is in the process of being integrated into the Linux kernel device mapper. Its use is simple. If you use the patch version, you just need to adjust the disk entry in the domU configuration file. For example, instead of:

```
disk = [ `phy:/dev/vols/os,hda1,w' ]
```

It should be something like:

```
disk = [ `dmu:dscow:/work/os.dscow: /dev/vols/os,hda1,w' ]
```

When the domain starts, all changes made to the disk will be stored in `/work/os.dscow`; the base image `/dev/vols/os` will not change.

If you don't use the patched version, you will need to first create a Copy-on-Write dscow image with the *dscow_tool* by running the following command:

```
dscow_tool -c /tmp/mydom.dscow /tmp/base.img
```

Then, start `cowd,` the user space daemon, to create a pseudo device called `myblockdev` as follows:

```
cowd -p dscow myblockdev /tmp/mydom.dscow
```

This will create a device named `/dev/mapper/myblockdev`, which will behave as a block device and will have Copy-on-Write semantics. All writes will be saved in /tmp/mydom.dscow. The base image, `/tmp/base.img`, will not change. DmUserspace also includes qcow support.

NOTE

DmUserspace was written by Dan Smith of the IBM Linux Technology Center. For more information, see http://static.danplanet.com/dm-userspace.

UnionFS

UnionFS is a stackable file system that enables you to manage a set of directories as a single unified view. Each directory is called a branch and has a priority and can be either read-only or read-write. When the highest priority branch is read-write, UnionFS provides you with copy-on-write semantics for read-only branches. You can use UnionFS in Xen by initrd—for example, see http://wiki. xensource.com/xenwiki/GinoUnionCOW. It can be done also without initrd (for example, see http://wiki.xensource.com/xenwiki/InstructionsFrom.MichaelLang). UnionFS is currently not part of the Linux kernel, but it is in Andrew Morton's mm tree and is in the process of being integrated into the Linux kernel. For more information about UnionFS, see: http://www.fsl.cs.sunysb.edu/project-unionfs.html.

NOTE

UnionFS is used in LiveCD projects like Knoppix, SLAX, Clusterix, and more. For more information, visit www.am-utils.org/project-unionfs.html.

Advanced Networking Concepts

Xen has two primary networking architecture options: bridging and routing. The default is bridging. In order to change it to routing, change the network-script entry in /etc/xen/xend-config.sxp from network-bridge to network-route, and the vif-script entry from vif-bridge to vif-route. Whenever working with bridging, when xend starts it runs the /etc/xen/scripts/network-bridge script. First, it renames the eth0 interface to peth0. Than it creates a bridge named xenbr0, and two interfaces are added to this bridge: peth0 and vif0.0. You can attach other interfaces to the bridge using `brctl xenbr0 addif interfaceName`. You can also see which interfaces belong to the bridge via `brctl show` and create new bridges in dom0 by using `brctl add`. The vif-bridge script is called for the unprivileged domains virtual interfaces.

Apart from the networking scripts mentioned previously, there are also scripts for configuring a NAT—and for more complex network settings, you can add scripts of your own. All of the scripts are located under /etc/xen/scripts.

Bridging VLANs

VLAN stands for virtual LAN. It is a method for creating independent networks within a LAN. It is implemented by tagging the Ethernet frame using the IEEE 802.1Q tagging protocol. Using VLAN improves overall performance, because multicasts and broadcasts from VLANs are kept within the VLAN (broadcast domain). You can also configure VLAN for security. VLANs can be defined in software using the vconfig utility. For more information on VLAN, go to http://linux-net.osdl.org/index.php/VLAN.

Configuring & Implementing...

VLAN Creation

Suppose you want to create a VLAN from dom0 and add to it eth0 from dom0 and a virtual interface from domU. To do this, create VLANs from domain 0 using the following process:

1. Load the VLAN kernel module:

```
modprobe 8021q
```

2. Run the following commands, which add eth0 to a VLAN that has a VID of 45 (the number was chosen arbitrarily):

```
vconfig add eth0 45
ifconfig eth0.45 up 192.168.0.1 netmask 255.255.255.0
```

Verify the configuration by running ifconfig –a in dom0. This should show you that eth0.45 is among the other interfaces of this domain.

In order to configure an interface to be in a VLAN in domU, do the following:

1. Create the file: /etc/sysconfig/network-scripts/ifcfg-eth0:45. In this file, add the following lines:

```
DEVICE=eth0:45
BOOTPROTO=static
IPADDR=192.168.0.2
NETMASK=255.255.255.0
ONBOOT=YES
TYPE=Ethernet
VLAN=yes
```

2. Bring up the interface.

WARNING

Do not try to use the NetworkManager utility when working with bridging in Xen. It won't work properly, and other network control programs may not work correctly either.

Creating Interface Bonds for High Availability and Link Aggregation

Bonding is a Linux driver for aggregating multiple network interfaces into a single logical interface. By doing this, you can achieve high availability. The bonding module detects link failures and reroutes the traffic to a different interface. With bonding, you can assign two or more network cards the same IP address.

Configuring & Implementing...

Bonding Example

Suppose you have three network cards: eth0, eth1, and eth2, and you want to create a bond between eth1 and eth2 in dom0. The following are the steps you must take to accomplish this:

1. In /etc/modprobe.conf, add the following lines:

   ```
   alias bond0 bonding
   options bond0 miimon=100 mode=0
   ```

   Then, we will create the following configuration file: /etc/sysconfig/network-scripts/ifcfg-bond0.

   It will have the following data:

   ```
   DEVICE=bond0
   BOOTPROTO=none
   ONBOOT=no
   ```

2. Change the entries in two files under the /etc/sysconfig/network-scripts directory so both eth1 and eth2 will work with bonding. This can be done by using the following code:

   ```
   /etc/sysconfig/network-scripts/ifcfg-eth1 will be:
   DEVICE=eth1
   BOOTPROTO=none
   ONBOOT=no
   MASTER=bond0
   SLAVE=yes
   /etc/sysconfig/network-scripts/ifcfg-eth2 will be:
   DEVICE=eth2
   BOOTPROTO=none
   ONBOOT=no
   MASTER=bond0
   SLAVE=yes
   ```

3. Restart the interfaces by using

   ```
   service network restart
   ```

4. Create a bridge in dom0, named xenBondBridge, by running the following:

```
brctl addbr xenBondBridge
```

5. Disable arp and multicast as follows:

```
ip link set xenBondBridge arp off
ip link set xenBondBridge multicast off
ip link set xenBondBridge up
ip link set xenBondBridge address fe:ff:ff:ff:ff:ff
ip link set xenBondBridge arp off
ip link set xenBondBridge multicast off
```

6. Add the bond to the bridge you created and start the bond:

```
brctl addif xenBondBridge bond0
ifup bond0
```

WARNING

Trying to add bond0 to a bridge without disabling arp and multicast will result in an error that reads "Can't add bond0 to the bridge."

Routing, Forwarding, and Other Network Tricks

When working with routing, starting xend will call the network-route script, which enables IP forwarding by setting /proc/sys/net/ipv4/ip_forward in dom0 to a value of 1. When a guest domain starts, the vif-route is called. It copies the address of eth0 into vif<id#>.0 (id# is the ID of domU when it starts).

TIP

You can use the ebtables filtering tool to filter traffic in the bridge (see http://ebtables.sourceforge.net). Using ebtables, you can perform packet filtering based on the Link Layer Ethernet frame fields. You can also alter MAC addresses. Ebtables is part of the Linux kernel.

Building a Xen Cluster

Xen is an ideal candidate Virtual Machine Monitor (VMM) for a high-performance computing (HPC) paravirtualization system given its performance metrics and its large-scale development efforts. Lawrence Livermore National Laboratory (LLNL) did some interesting research on the performance impact of Xen using current HPC commodity hardware. The results show that usually the Xen solution poses no statistically significant overhead over other OS configurations currently in use at LLNL for HPC clusters, except in very specific cases. (See "Paravirtualization for HPC Systems" by Rich Wolski *et al.* at www.cs.ucsb.edu/~ckrintz/papers/ISPA-XenHPC.pdf.)

Several deployments come to mind for Xen-based clusters—for example, a single computer that acts as a complete cluster, running several Xen guests. Another deployment configuration can be a cluster where each node runs some domU guests. These guests may run on every node of the cluster. Should a crash occur, this guest may start on a different node in a very short time. You can use live migration of domains for maintenance and for load balancing in such a deployment configuration. This illustrates some of the benefits of deploying a Xen-based cluster.

Possible solutions for building a Xen cluster can be RedHat Cluster Suite (see http://sourceware. org/cluster) or Oracle Real Application Cluster (RAC) (see www.oracle.com/technology/products/ database/clustering/index.html). The nodes will be Xen domUs.

When choosing a file system for the cluster, two options are recommended: GFS (or GFS2) and OCFS2. GFS, the Global File System from Red Hat, is a shared storage file system available for clusters. It has a distributed lock manager (dlm), which enables the secured sharing of files using a locking mechanism. GFS is part of the Linux kernel. GFS2 is an improved version of GFS and is part of version 2 of the Red Hat Cluster Suite.

OCFS2 (Oracle Cluster File System) is a cluster file system. It has many similarities to ext3 and has a distributed lock manager that is implemented differently than GFS dlm. It was integrated into the version 2.6.16 of the Linux kernel. It is posix-compliant and is a journaling file system. It supports direct I/O and asynchronous I/O. OCFS2 has its own kernel space cluster membership service and heartbeat functions. It comes with two in-memory file systems: configfs and ocfs2-dlmfs. OCFS2 uses configfs to communicate with the in-kernel heartbeat thread and the in-kernel node manager; ocfs2_dlmfs, on the other hand, is used by OCFS2 tools to communicate with the in-kernel dlm OCFS2 for releasing or taking dlm locks. OCFS2 is not compatible with OCFS1. It also uses debugfs, an in-memory file system developed by Greg Kroah-Hartman. It helps in the debugging process as it lets code in kernel space export data easily to userspace.

Fencing, or I/O Fencing, is a mechanism for removing a malfunctioning node from a cluster, thus preventing it from causing data corruption. Fencing supports two operations: removal of a node and recovery of a node. When heartbeat detects that a node fails, the cluster manager directs the fencing system to remove that node from the cluster. The most effective way to do this is known as STONITH (an acronym that stands for "Shoot The Other Node In The Head"). It forces the system on that node to power off or reboot.

When setting up an RAC, you will need shared storage for the Oracle Cluster Registry (OCR) and for Database files. Apart from this, you will need shared storage for the Xen environment, which can be for example iSCSI or block devices. You also need at least two interfaces, one for private use (cluster interconnect) and one as a public interface (intranet).

NOTE

If you want a shared GFS/OCFS2 partition, you will need to add "w!" to the physical device ID in the domain configuration file. For example, disk=['phy:/dev/vg1/xenstore, sda2,w!'].

The following example shows how to set a Xen-based cluster using the RedHat cluster suite (see Figure 17.3). Two nodes, host1 and host2, will run dom0 Xen, in which two domUs will run. Host3 and host4 will be the nodes for storage. On each of the storage nodes, host3 and host4, you will install and run Distributed Replicated Block Device (DRBD). Heartbeat service will run between host3 and host4.

Figure 17.3 A Xen Cluster

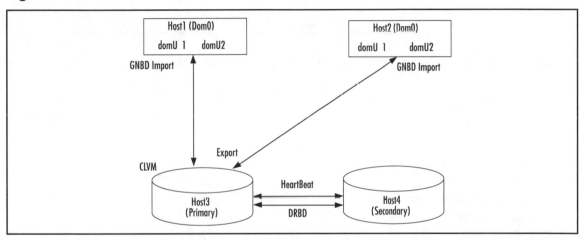

DRBD is a block device mirroring technique that is designed to build high-availability clusters. This is done by mirroring a whole block device via network TCP connection. You could think of it as a network RAID1.

First, you will install drbd-8 by performing the following actions:

```
wget http://oss.linbit.com/drbd/8.0/drbd-8.0.1.tar.gz .
tar xvzf drbd-8.0.1.tar.gz
cd drbd-8.0.1
make KDIR=/work/src/xen-3.0.4_1-src/linux-2.6.16.33-xen
make install && make tools && make install-tools
```

Then, you should configure the /etc/drbd.conf file.

An example of a drbd.conf for two nodes—node3 and node4—follows:

```
resource cluster {
protocol C;
handlers {
   pri-on-incon-degr "echo '!DRBD! pri on incon-degr' | wall ; sleep 60; halt -f";
      }
startup {
  degr-wfc-timeout 120;
}
disk {
  on-io-error detach;
}
net {}
syncer {
  rate 5M;
}
on node3 {
   device /dev/drbd0;
   disk /dev/vg1/cluster;
   address 192.168.0.73:7788;
   meta-disk internal;
}
  on node4 {
   device /dev/drbd0;
   disk /dev/vg1/cluster;
   address 192.168.0.74:7788;
   meta-disk internal;
  }
}
```

As you have probably noticed, the "disk /dev/vg1/cluster" entry refers to a storage device you have not yet created. Now you will create it. To create storage partitions, first install the lvm2-cluster; this is the cluster extensions for userspace logical volume management tools. It runs a daemon called clvmd, which distributes LVM metadata updates around a cluster. All nodes in the cluster must run the clvmd daemon. You do this by downloading the code from ftp://sources.redhat.com/pub/lvm2 and building it.

Suppose /dev/sda5 is the partition you intend to use for DRBD replication. If so, you must create logical volumes with the *same size* on all storage nodes. (By the way, when using software RAID1, there is a similar size equality constraint.)

NOTE

Protocol C in the configuration file, drbd.conf, specifies that write IO is reported as completed if it has reached both local and remote disk. Two other valid protocol specifiers exist: B and C.

Protocol A specifies that write IO is reported as completed if it has reached the local disk and local TCP send buffer, while protocol B specifies that write IO is reported as completed if it has reached the local disk and remote buffer cache.

```
pvcreate /dev/sd5a
vgcreate vg1 /dev/sda5
lvcreate -L 10G -n cluster vg1
```

pvcreate initializes PhysicalVolume for later use by the Logical Volume Manager (LVM), and *vgcreate* creates a volume group named vg1. Subsequently, *lvcreate* creates a logical volume in the volume group we created, vg1. This logical volume is 10G in size and is named "cluster."

NOTE

Without the –n (name) option, a default name of "lvol#" will be generated where # is the LVM internal number of the logical volume.

The drbdadm is the administration tool for DRBD. The first time you want to activate the nodes, run "drbdadm create-md resourceName" to initialize the metadata storage.

The command *drbdadm up* is a shortcut for attach and connect.

Now perform the following two commands on both nodes:

```
drbdadm create-md cluster
drbdadm up all
```

Both nodes started as Secondary and Inconsistent, as you can see by running cat /proc/drbd. Choose one host to be the primary, and on that host run

```
drbdadm -- --overwrite-data-of-peer primary all
```

> **NOTE**
>
> In previous versions of DRBD, setting a node to be primary is done by using
> `drbdadm -- --do-what-I-say primary all`
> The `-- --overwrite-data-of-peer` flag replaced `-- --do-what-I-say` flag for more clarity.

You can create an OCFS2 file system on /dev/drbd0 by using

```
mkfs.ocfs2 -L ocfs2_cluster /dev/drbd0
```

-L dictates that the volume label for this file system will be ocfs2.

Install the RedHat cluster suite and apply the following two patches. (See www.redhat.com/archives/cluster-devel/2006–June/msg00162.html.)

```
wget ftp://sources.redhat.com/pub/cluster/releases/cluster-1.02.00.tar.gz
tar xvzf cluster-1.02.00.tar.gz
cd cluster-1.02.00
./configure --kernel_src=/work/src/xen-3.0.4_1-src/linux-2.6.16.33-xen
make install
```

Load the gnbd module using

```
modprobe gnbd
```

Create a configuration cluster file for the cluster: /etc/cluster/cluster.conf. This is an XML file.

The following is a simple example of cluster.conf; the cluster has four nodes. host3 and host4 are the storage backend, which export a block device via gnbd. For the sake of simplicity, use empty fence tags.

```
<?xml version="1.0"?>
<cluster name="xencluster" config_version="1">
<clusternodes>
  <clusternode name="host1">
    <fence>
    </fence>
  </clusternode>
  <clusternode name="host2">
    <fence>
    </fence>
  </clusternode>
  <clusternode name="host3">
    <fence>
    </fence>
```

```
  </clusternode>
  <clusternode name="host4">
     <fence>
    </fence>
  </clusternodes>
<fencedevices>
</fencedevices>
</cluster>
```

The same cluster.conf should be on every node on the cluster.

The ccsd is a daemon that must be run on each node that wishes to join a cluster.

Start the ccsd daemon by using

```
ccsd
```

Afterwards, each node should join the cluster by running

```
cman_tool join
```

When you want to leave the cluster, run

```
cman_tool leave
```

You can see the status of the cluster and the membership information of its nodes by running the *clustat* command. For example, after adding two hosts to the cluster—host3 and host4—and running *clustat*, you get

```
Member Status: Quorate

Member Name                        ID Status
------ ----                        -- ------
host3                              1 Online, Local
host4                             2 Online
```

You need to export GNBD devices from storage backend. This is done by using

```
gnbd_serv
```

gnbd_serv will start the gnbd server daemon (gnbd_serv). Then use

```
gnbd_export -e clusterfs -d /dev/drbd0
```

(The -e specifies the gnbd export device: it will be /dev/gnbd/clusterfs.)

Import the GNBD storage device from storage backend by using

```
gnbd_import -i ipAddress
```

Install ocfs2-tools with the following:

```
wget http://oss.oracle.com/projects/ocfs2-tools/dist/files/source/v1.2/ocfs2-tools-
1.2.3.tar.gz.
tar xvfz ocfs2-tools-1.2.3.tar.gz
cd ocfs2-tools-1.2.3
./configure && make && make install
```

o2cb.init is the init script for ocfs2-tools. After installation, copy vendor/common/o2cb.init to /etc. init/o2cb. The o2cb was originally written for SLES and RHEL4, but it also supports other distributions like Fedora and others.

> **NOTE**
>
> The initial release of OCFS supported *only* Oracle database workloads, whereas OCFS2 provides full support as a general-purpose file system.

Prepare the configuration file /etc/ocfs2/cluster.conf. An exact copy of this file should be copied to all cluster nodes.

The following is an example of /etc/ocfs2/cluster.conf:

```
node:
  ip_port = 7777
  ip_address = 192.168.0.71
  number = 0
  name = host1
  cluster = xencluster
  ip_port = 7777
  ip_address = 192.168.0.72
  number = 1
  name = host2
  cluster = xencluster
node:
  ip_port = 7777
  ip_address = 192.168.0.73
  number = 2
  name = host3
  cluster = xencluster
node:
  ip_port = 7777
  ip_address = 192.168.0.74
  number = 3
  name = host4
  cluster = xencluster
cluster:
  node_count = 4
  name = xencluster
```

If a new node is being added to the cluster, all existing nodes must have their "cluster.conf" updated *before* mounting the ocfs2 partition from the new node. Moreover, changes to this file must be propagated to the other nodes in the cluster. Also, changes in cluster.conf require that the cluster be restarted for the changes to take effect. The node name should match the hostname of the machine.

TIP

You can perform initial setup of OCFS2 using the ocfs2console graphical tool. Using this tool you can configure OCFS2 cluster nodes, propagate configuration to other nodes, and more.

Then you can mount the ocfs2 file system by running the following commands:

```
modprobe ocfs2
/etc/init.d/o2cb load
/etc/init.d/o2cb configure (For setting a configuration for OCFS2)
/etc/init.d/o2cb online xencluster
mount -t ocfs2 /dev/gnbd/clusterfs /mnt/cluster
```

You can get info about the ocsf2 modules with /etc/init.d/o2cb status, and unload the modules using /etc/init.d/o2cb unload. You can tune OCFS2 with the tunefs.ocfs2 utility, which enables you to increase the number of node slots (to increase the number of nodes that can concurrently mount the volume), change the volume label, and increase the size of the journal file.

Every cluster node imports the GNBD device, which is exported by the storage hosts and mounts it. OCFS2 is the cluster file system used in this GNBD device.

You can use heartbeat between the cluster storage nodes as a high availability solution. First, install the heartbeat service using

```
yum install heartbeat
```

Then you should configure three files: /etc/ha.d/ha.cf, /etc/ha.d/haresources, and /etc/ha.d/authkeys. DRBD installation creates a file named /etc/ ha.d/resource.d/drbddisk. Configure it according to your needs; it is called when a DRBD host becomes primary. Afterwards, start the heartbeat service on both storage hosts, host3 and host4. For more on how to configure these files and on the heartbeat high availability solution, see www.linux-ha.org.

XenVM Migration

Live Migration enables us to transfer unprivileged domains between hosts on the same subnet. When performing live migration, the downtime is very low and reaches about 50 to 300ms.

In order to minimize downtime, live migration is done in stages. First, the source domain sends a request to a destination domain. The source domain cannot be domain 0. The destination domain verifies that it has enough resources for the request. This stage is called *Reservation*. If the destination host has enough resources, proceed to the second stage, where all memory pages are copied using a

TCP socket. This stage is also called *Iterative Pre-copy*. Some iterations occur in this stage when in each iteration you copy the pages dirtied while the previous iteration occurred. Then at some edge, when there is a relatively small number of dirtied pages in each iteration, you stop the source domain and copy the remaining pages. This stage is called *Stop and Copy*. When this stage finishes, resume the VM on the destination host. This stage is called *Activation*.

To enable live migration, first edit the /etc/xen/config.sxp file and uncomment the following two lines:

```
#(xend-relocation-port 8002)
#(xend-relocation-address '')
```

The first line is for setting Xen to listen on TCP port 8002 for incoming migration requests. The second line permits connections from any host.

Run live migration from dom0 by using the following command:

```
xm migrate --live sourceDomain destinationDomain
```

You can view which domains are running on each machine by running xm list.

Figures 17.4 and 17.5 demonstrate live migration of domU4 from Host A to Host B:

Figure 17.4 Live Migration Stage A (Before Migration Started)

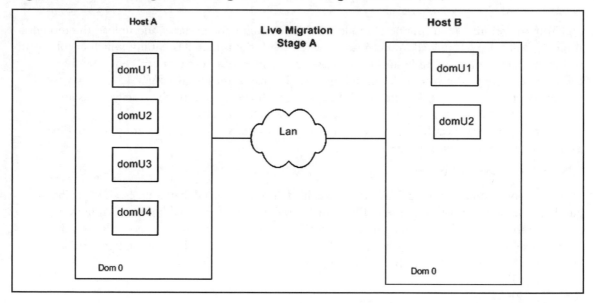

Figure 17.5 Live Migration Stage B (after domU4 Was Transferred from Host A to Host B

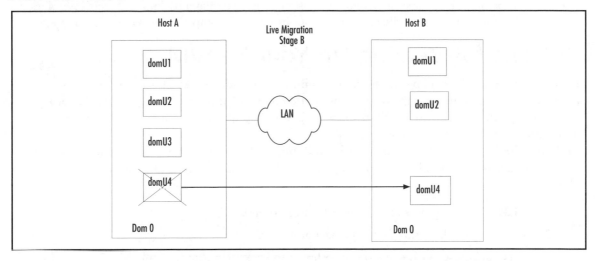

There is another type of migration, non-live migration, that pauses the source domain, copies the memory pages to the host, and resumes its operation on the host. The downtime when using non-live migration naturally is much longer. Non-live migration is done by issuing the same *xm migrate* command but omitting the *--live* flag.

> **NOTE**
>
> It is important to notice that live migration does not transfer the file system from the source to the destination. It is assumed that both domains, source and destination, share the same file system, by means of a Fibre-Channel or iSCSI SAN or NFS, for example, or any other shared storage method.

You can use live migration as a solution for load balancing or a disaster recovery plan, or for taking down physical machines for maintenance without stopping the VM running on them, or for managing a pool of VMs running on a cluster.

Another method of migration is called "self migration." In self migration, the unprivileged domain being migrated handles the migration itself. For more on live migration and self migration, visit www.cl.cam.ac.uk/research/srg/netos/papers/2005-migration-nsdi-pre.pdf.

Currently migration of Windows-based domUs is not supported in Xen. Supposedly, in near-future releases of Xen, live migration of Hardware Virtual Machine (HVM) domains will be supported.

XenVM Backup and Recovery Solutions

One of the most important tasks of system administrators is preparing a backup and recovery solution. With that in mind, we will next discuss some solutions for the backup and recovery of Xen guests.

Options for Backing Up Your XenVM

In a configuration where all block devices in domUs are provided by LVM, you can use lvm-snapshots. You can mount a snapshot in dom0 and then use a backup tool, such as *rsnapshot* or *rdiff-backup* or *duplicity*, to perform a backup. *rsnapshot* is a backup utility based on rsync. For more information, see www.rsnapshot.org.

If you don't have LVM, you can shut down domU and then back it up using some backup utility.

If you have domUs inside a DMZ and you don't have backup agents on them, you can do the following:

1. Make LVM snapshots of these domUs from dom0.

2. Block attach these snapshots to a backup server.

3. The backup server mounts the snapshots and backs them up the same way it backs up a local file system.

4. The backup server unmounts the snapshots.

5. The snapshots are block-detached.

6. The snapshots are discarded.

Block-attach and block-detach are subcommands of the *xm* command. They allow you to hotplug/unplug a block device to a domU. Block-list shows the list of block devices attached to a domain. An example for the preceding series of actions could be:

```
lvcreate -L1G -s -n mydomU sata/mydomU-snapshots
xm block-attach amandaserver phy:sata/mydomU-snapshots
blkid=$(xm block-list amandaserver| tail -n 1| awk '{ print $1; }')
xm block-detach amandaserver $blkid
lvremove -f sata1/mydomU-snap
```

Making Xen Part of Your Disaster Recovery Plan

You can install Xen with Software RAID1, or disk mirroring. The following example demonstrates the installation of Xen on /dev/md0, which uses a RAID set comprised of sda2 and sdb2. All writes are performed to both disks. Should the Xen host experience a disk failure, the other disk can replace it. See www.freax.be/wiki/index.php/Installing_Xen_with_RAID_1_on_a_Fedora_Core_4_x86_64_SMP_machine for more information.

A different strategy for disaster recovery could consist of the following: suppose you want a disaster recovery for a Xen-based server. If the server does not contain data, like a Web server (apache for example), you can perform "xm save" once a week or once a month, copy the saved image to a disaster recovery server, and then perform "xm restore" on the Web server since "xm save" stops the domain. If some disaster occurs (a motherboard or hardware failure, for example), run "xm restore" on the recovery disaster server, fix the fault on the problematic server, and migrate that domU back to the server. If the server is a database server, however, you should also back up the file system using common backup methods like LVM snapshot.

Full Virtualization in Xen

On x86 processors, when running in protected mode, there are four privilege levels. The operating system kernel executes in privilege level 0 (also called "supervisor mode") while applications execute in privilege level 3. Privilege levels 1 and 2 were not used, except in rare cases (for example, in OS/2). Certain special instructions to the processor are only allowed in privilege level 0 since they affect the whole systems behavior. When the processor detects such an instruction at a level other than privilege level 0, it generates a general-protection violation.

Virtualization is essentially of two types: full virtualization and paravirtualization. Paravirtualization is based on a principle of making some sections of the operating system aware that it's running on top of a virtual machine monitor, actually known as the hypervisor. The hypervisor will manage the different virtual machines (also known as guests)—for example, letting each guest run for a certain amount of time and then the next guest for another set amount of time, thus allowing the guests to appear to run simultaneously (similar to the way the operating system deals with multiple applications). Part of the modification to the operating system is to shift all privilege level 0 code into privilege level 1, which means the code will occasionally cause a general protection fault that ends up inside the hypervisor, which helps the hypervisor track and control what the guest is doing.

The New Processors with Virtual Extensions (VT-x and AMD-V)

Full virtualization (a.k.a., unmodified guests) is based on no changes to the operating system source-code, and is very difficult to achieve without hardware extensions in the processor. Hardware manufacturers like Intel and AMD have begun to recently (starting in 2005) develop processors with built-in virtualization extensions. With these new processors, you can run an unmodified guest operating system.

Naturally, many will prefer a situation where the guest operating system code need not be modified, especially in the case of a closed-source operating system like Windows or operating systems with a small user-base that makes the effort of modifying the operating system source-code prohibitively expensive.

Intel has developed the VT-x technology for the x86 processor. This technology provides hardware virtualization extensions. With Intel's VT-x, the VMM runs in "VMX root operation mode" while the guests (which are unmodified OSes) run in "VMX non-root operation mode." While running in this mode, the guests are more restricted, and some instructions, like RDMSR, WRMSR, and CPUID, will cause a "VM exit" to the VMM. VM exit is a transition from non-root operation to root operation. Some instructions and exceptions will cause a "VM exit" when the configured conditions are met. Xen handles the VM exit in a manner that is specific to the particular exception.

To implement this hardware virtualization, Intel added a new structure called VMCS (Virtual Machine Control Structure), which handles much of the virtualization management functionality. This structure contains the exit reason in the case of a VM exit. Also, ten new instruction opcodes were added in VT-x.

These new opcodes manage the VT-x virtualization behavior. For example, the VMXON instruction starts VMX operation, while the VMREAD instruction reads specified fields from the VMCS, and the VMWRITE instruction writes specified fields to the VMCS. When a processor operates in VMX root operation mode, its behavior is much like when it operates in normal operating mode. However, in normal operating mode, these ten new opcodes are not available.

Intel also published its VT-d (Intel(r) Virtualization Technology for Directed I/O). VT-d enables I/O devices to be directly assigned to virtual machines. It also defines DMA remapping logic that can be configured for an individual device. There is also a cache called an IOTLB which improves performance. For more details on VT-d, see Intel's documentation at http://download.intel.com/technology/computing/vptech/Intel(r)_VT_for_Direct_IO.pdf.

In AMD-V—a.k.a., SVM (Secure Virtual Machine)—there is something quite similar, but the terminology is a bit different: You have Host Mode and Guest Mode. The VMM runs in Host Mode and the guests run in Guest Mode. In Guest Mode, some instructions cause VM EXIT, which is handled in a manner that is specific to the way Guest Mode is entered.

AMD added a new structure called the VMCB (Virtual Machine Control Block), which handles much of the virtualization management functionality. The VMCB includes an exit reason field which is read when a VM EXIT occurs. AMD added eight new instruction opcodes to support SVM. For example, the VMRUN instruction starts the operation of a guest OS, the VMLOAD instruction loads the processor state from the VMCB, and the VMSAVE instruction saves the processor state to the VMCB. The VMCB contains a set of bits to indicate to the processor which particular instructions are to cause a VMEXIT and which can flow freely in the guest.

For more details, see the *AMD64 Architecture Programmer's Manual*, Volume 2: System Programming, Chapter 15, titled "Secure Virtual Machine," which is available at http://www.amd.com/usen/assets/content_type/white_papers_and_tech_docs/24593.pdf.

AMD also had published its I/O virtualization technology specification (IOMMU).

The AMD IOMMU technology intercepts devices' access to memory. It finds out to which guest a particular device is assigned, and decides whether access is permitted and whether the actual address is available in system memory (page protection and address translation). You can think of AMD IOMMU as providing two facilities for AMD processors: the Graphics Aperture Remapping Table (GART) and the Device Exclusion Vector (DEV). In the AMD IOMMU, there is optional support for IOTLBs. For more details, see AMD I/O virtualization technology (IOMMU) specification Rev 1.00 at http://www.amd.com/usen/assets/content_type/white_papers_and_tech_docs/34434.pdf.

Since AMD and Intel are similar in many ways, a common API called HVM (Hardware Virtual Machine) was developed. For example, HVM defines a table called hvm_function_table, which is a structure containing functions common to both Intel VT-x and AMD SVM. These methods are implemented differently in the VT-x and AMD SVM trees.

With Xen running in paravirtualized mode, there is a device model based on Backend/Frontend virtual drivers (also called "split drivers"). See the introduction to this chapter. The Backend is in domain 0, while the Frontend is in the unprivileged domains. They communicate via an interdomain event channel and a shared memory area (using the sharing mechanism of grant tables).

Only domain 0 has access to the hardware through the unmodified Linux drivers. When running on VT-x or SVM, you cannot use this IO model because the guests run unmodified Linux kernels. So Both VT-x and SVM use the emulated device subsystem of QEMU for their I/O. QEMU runs in Xen as a userspace process. Using QEMU has a performance cost, so, in the future, it is possible that QEMU will be replaced by a better performing solution. It is, however, important to understand that an IOMMU layer, even one built according to the new AMD or Intel specs, cannot in itself be a replacement for QEMU, because the same device may need to be shared between multiple domains.

It is possible for an unmodified guest to use paravirtual (Frontend) drivers in the same way as paravirtualized mode, but drivers must be developed for the particular OS being used as a guest.

As mentioned earlier, Intel VT-x and AMD SVM have much in common (like usage of QEMU and the common API which HVM abstracts). However, some differences do arise—for example:

- The AMD SVM uses a tagged TLB; this means they use an ASID (Address Space Identifier) to distinguish between host-space entries from guest-space entries. By using this identifier, you don't have to perform a TLB flush when there is a context switch between guest and host. This significantly reduces the number of TLB flushes. A TLB flush slows the system because after a TLB flush occurs, subsequent accesses to memory will require a full page table lookup.

- Intel's VTX doesn't support real-mode. In order to boot an Intel VT-x machine, you need a special piece of code called VMXassist which uses VM86-mode to simulate real-mode. Using a Linux loader to load a guest OS starts in real mode. AMD SVM, on the other hand, supports real-mode for guests, so it does not need the VM86 mode of the VMXassist.

Next-generation processors with virtualization extensions from both AMD and Intel will probably have new, exiting features that improve performance and functionality; one new feature will probably be IOMMU support, which was discussed briefly earlier. Another feature is multilevel translation in hardware; this feature will improve the process of the domU virtual addresses translation process. There is already some support for this feature in the unstable version of Xen—it is called hap (hardware assisted paging). (In AMD processors, this feature is called "nested paging.")

In conclusion, we can see many similarities between Intel VT-x and AMD SVM when running Xen, sometimes the terms are even similar (like VM Entry/VM Exit). In addition, performance slowdown due to QEMU is common to both. Moreover, next generation processors will probably also have some similar features.

For more information about the new processors with virtualization extensions from AMD and Intel, see http://wiki.xensource.com/xenwiki/XenIntro.

Summary

Xen provides support in several advanced areas, like storage and networking. You can integrate Xen with advanced storage methods like iSCSI or various CoW solutions. You can also apply various networking solutions like using VLANs, bonding, routing, and more. You have seen that Xen can be integrated easily into a cluster in various deployment configurations—for example, in the RedHat cluster suite or Oracle Real Application Cluster (RAC). Overall, Xen is an interesting virtualization project that evolves dynamically and seems to support many highly advanced features in various areas.

Solutions Fast Track

The Virtual Split Devices Model

☑ Xen uses virtual split device drivers for virtual I/O with Frontend and Backend layers. The Frontend drivers are used in unprivileged guests, domUs, while Backend drivers are used in dom0.

☑ It is possible to create additional domains, domUs, with unmodified drivers for the unlerlying I/O devices. These domains are referred to as "driver domains."

☑ The Frontend and Backend use shared memory pages for communication. Access is controlled through the use of grant tables.

Advanced Storage Concepts

☑ All devices exported via iSCSI will be presented as SCSI disks, regardless of their type.

☑ CoW (Copy-on-Write) is an optimization technique for storage.

☑ For Xen, there is a variety of CoW solutions: blktap, DmUserspace, UnionFS, and more.

☑ iSCSI is a transport protocol that works on top of TCP.

Advanced Networking Concepts

☑ Xen has two primary networking architecture options: bridging and routing.

☑ By default, Xen starts with bridging.

☑ You can define VLANs in software using the vconfig utility.

☑ Bonding is a Linux driver for aggregating multiple network interfaces into a single logical interface.

☑ VLAN is a method for creating independent networks within a LAN.

Building a Xen Cluster

- ☑ Two file systems that are candidates for clusters are GFS and OCFS2.

- ☑ Both are included in the Linux Kernel.

- ☑ domUs are the nodes of the cluster.

- ☑ DRBD are used for network block-device mirroring.

XenVM Migration

- ☑ Live migration is the transfer of unprivileged domains between hosts on the same subnet.

- ☑ Live migration is performed using xm migrate –live sourceDomain destinationDomain.

- ☑ Live migration does not transfer the file system of the source to the destination.

- ☑ The downtime when using nonlive migration is much longer than the downtime when using live migration.

XenVM Backup and Recovery Solutions

- ☑ "xm save" stores an image of the domain; it can be used for recovery upon disaster.

- ☑ "xm restore" starts a domain from a saved image.

- ☑ Block-list shows the list of domains attached to a domain.

- ☑ Block-attach and block-detach allow you to hotplug/unplug a block device to a domU.

Full Virtualization in Xen

- ☑ There are two general approaches to virtualization: full virtualization and paravirtualization.

- ☑ New processors with virtualization extensions were developed to support running unmodified operating systems as guests. Intel had developed the VT-x and AMD had developed the AMD-V (a.k.a., SVM).

- ☑ A common API called HVM (Hardware Virtual Machine) was developed in Xen to support common functionality of the new processors with virtualization extensions.

- ☑ Some instructions and exceptions will cause a "VM exit" that will be handled in Xen in a manner specific to the particular exception.

Frequently Asked Questions

Q: What is the maximum number of interfaces I can add in domU?

A: The maximum number of interfaces is restricted to three.

Q: I need to set a MAC address for a domain instead of a random address.

A: In the domain configuration file, use mac= … in the vif directive.

Q: How can I see which bridges are in dom0 and what they consist of?

A: Run *brctl show* from dom0.

Q: I see "STP disabled" when I run *brctl show*. What does "STP" stand for?

A: STP stands for Spanning Tree Protocol, a networking protocol for finding shortest paths and avoiding loops.

Q: How can I change the bridge name from xenbr0 to mybr0?

A: In xend-config.sxp, set the network-script to be (network-script 'network-bridge bridge= mybr0).

Q: What is fencing?

A: Fencing is a mechanism for removing a malfunctioning node from a cluster.

Q: I want to install a Xen-based cluster. Which open-source file systems are available for me?

A: You can use GFS of RedHat or OCFS2 from Oracle.

Q: Why other file systems are not suitable for such a cluster?

A: You need a locking mechanism against simultaneous writes from different clients.

Q: I saw that in some domU configuration files, the disk = […] entry includes the "ioemu" directive. What is it for?

A: When using full virtualization, you can use the "ioemu" directive, it tells Xen to use its patched QEMU driver for the device.

Q: What does GNBD stand for?

A: Global Network Block Device.

Q: What does the exclamation mark in the "disk" entry of the domU configuration file denote?

A: The exclamation mark notes that the storage device may be shared.

Q: What does DRBD stand for?

A: Distributed Replicated Block Device.

Q: And what does DRBD do?

A: It provides mirroring for block devices over a network TCP connection.

Q: What does STONITH stand for?

A: Shoot The Other Node In The Head.

Q: What does HVM stand for?

A: HVM is the acronym for Hardware Virtual Machine. This is the common API for the new processors in Xen.

Q: What is the main benefit of full virtualization when compared with paravirtualization?

A: You can run an unmodified operating system with full virtualization, whereas when working with paravirtualization you must work with modified operating systems.

Q: What is the difference between full virtualization and paravirtualization in regards to the device driver model?

A: When working with paravirtualization, you use the split devices model. When working with full virtualization, you use the emulated device subsystem of QEMU for I/O.

Chapter 18

Scripted Installation

Solutions in this chapter:

- **Setting Up the Scripted Installation**
- **Remote Network Installation**

☑ **Summary**

Introduction

If you are setting up your virtual infrastructure or plan on scaling it out and will be building ESX host servers, this chapter is a must for you. The scripted installation method is a fast, efficient, and sure way to provision ESX hosts, and you'll be amazed at how simple it is to set up. We'll also review the Kickstart file so you fully understand how this install method works, and touch on the remote network install procedure as well.

Setting Up the Scripted Installation

Setting up the scripted installation correctly will make the process run smoothly and provide you with a very satisfactory experience. As a result, you'll likely choose this method over any other for setting up ESX hosts that have similar configurations. You'll set up the script—a Kickstart configuration file—based on parameters you would normally select during an ESX server install. If you want the exact configuration of the ESX server where you are setting up the Kickstart file, then make the same choices you made when you built it originally. (You did document that, right?)

After you have set up the Kickstart file, you have two options for building new ESX servers: 1) From the new ESX server, insert the ESX Server installation CD in the local CD-ROM; or 2) install ESX Server across the network from installation files hosted on another ESX server. This second option is convenient if your data center or server room is geographically remote or just a pain to get to.

Additionally, the scripted installation method can run unattended. However, like any unattended install of software, if something goes wrong, you'll be prompted to respond, and the install will hang until you do so.

Creating the Script

So to begin, as a prerequisite for the scripted installation method, you need to have an ESX server built and ready to perform the setup for the scripted installation. Some of the unique parameters you will be setting include the following:

- **Installation Type**   Two types are available: 1) *Initial Installation* (for a new install), and 2) *Upgrade* (if you are upgrading an existing ESX server such as an ESX Server 2.5 host).

- **Root Password**

- **Time Zone**

- **IP Address Information**   It is recommended you statically set your ESX server IP address.

- **Disk Partition Information**

- **Licensing Data**   This is a new "feature" in ESX 3.0.

You can choose DHCP if you want, but it is a good idea to have the IP information at hand, and it's recommended that your ESX server have static IP addresses.

To create the script, log on to the prebuilt ESX Server via a Web browser. You will be presented with the Web page shown in Figure 18.1.

Figure 18.1 The VMware ESX Server 3.0 Welcome Web Page

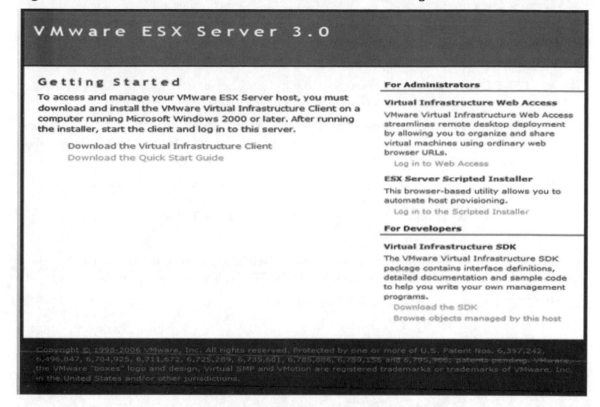

From this page, click the **Log In To The Scripted Installer** link under the ESX Server Scripted Installer heading. You will then be presented with the Scripted Install Web page, as shown in Figure 18.2.

Figure 18.2 The Scripted Install Web Page

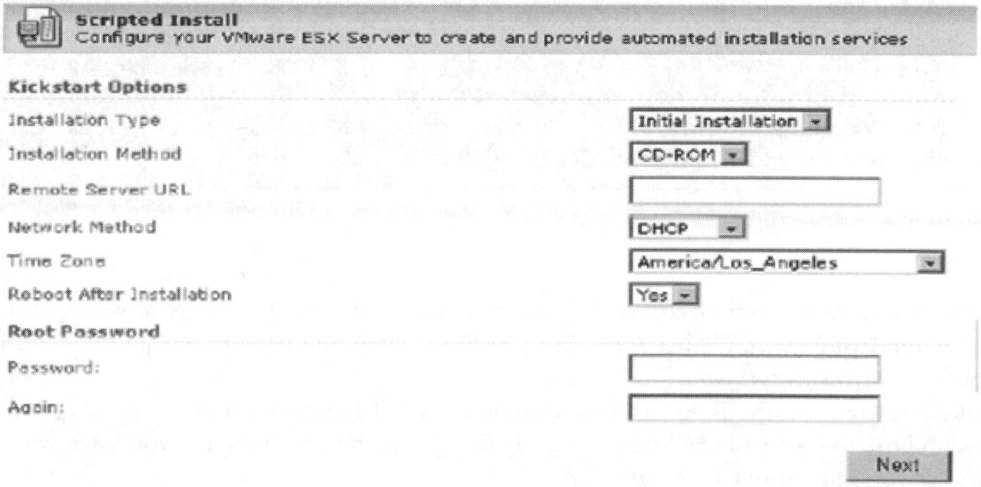

You must now input the information you want for the Kickstart script. In this example, the Installation Type field is set to Initial Installation, which means that this Kickstart file will be for new servers. If you want to have a script for upgrading existing ESX servers, you would change the install type to **Upgrade**.

In the Installation Method box, you can select one of the following three methods:

- **CD-ROM**   This method allows you to install ESX Server from the CD-ROM of the new server itself. This method may require physical access to the server itself.

- **Remote**   This method allows you to install ESX Server from a remote server that contains the ESX Installation files. If you choose this method, you will also need to include the URL and port number of the remote server.

- **NFS**   This method allows you to use an NFS mount point. In the **Remote Server URL**, you would input the hostname of the NFS server and the mount point. For example, **esx01:loadesx**, where **esx01** is the server name and **loadesx** is the mount point.

In the **Network Method** section, you can choose **DHCP** if you want to give your ESX server a dynamic IP address. Alternatively, you can select **Static IP** if you want to set your ESX server with a static IP.

Swiss Army Knife...

Modifying IP Information

As mentioned earlier in this chapter, it's recommended that you give your ESX server a static IP address, although you can use DHCP to provision new ESX servers from the same Kickstart file. If you choose this method, it's a good idea to go back and statically set the IP information and change the hostname, or to create multiple Kickstart files with different hostnames and statically set the IP information.

In the **Time Zone** section, choose the time zone you would like your ESX server to be in. In the **Reboot After Installation** field, select **Yes** so your ESX server will reboot itself after the installation is complete.

Make sure you give the Root account a strong password and click **Next**.

If you chose to give your ESX server a static IP address, the next window you'll see will concern networking options (see Figure 18.3).

Figure 18.3 The Networking Options Page

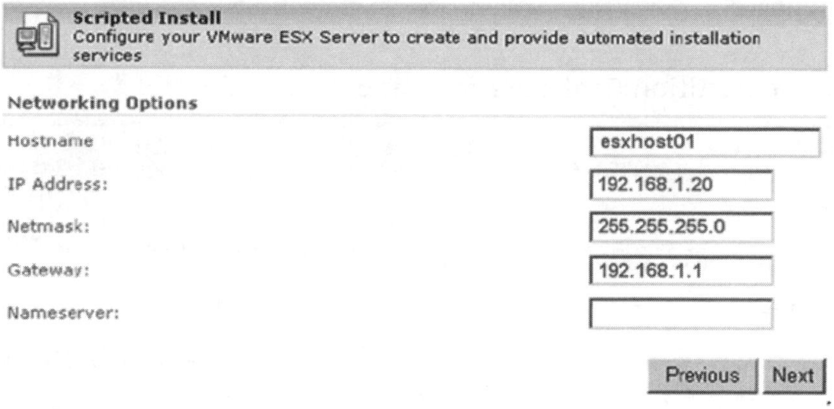

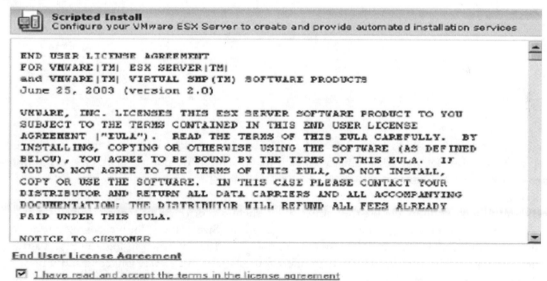

Next, input all of the IP information needed. Enter the specific information for your new ESX server, including the hostname and IP address, the subnet mask in the Netmask field, the gateway, and the nameserver (DNS). Use fully qualified domain names if you are running domains such as esxhost01.domian-name.net. Select which network device you would like the service console to run on and click **Next**.

The End User License Agreement (EULA) windows will appear (see Figure 18.4).

Figure 18.4 EULA

Of course, read the EULA and check the **I Have Read And Accept The Terms In The License Agreement** checkbox, then click **Next**.

The Partition Configuration page should appear. It's here that you select how your ESX server's disk will be partitioned. A basic example can be seen in Figure 18.5.

Figure 18.5 The Partition Configuration Page

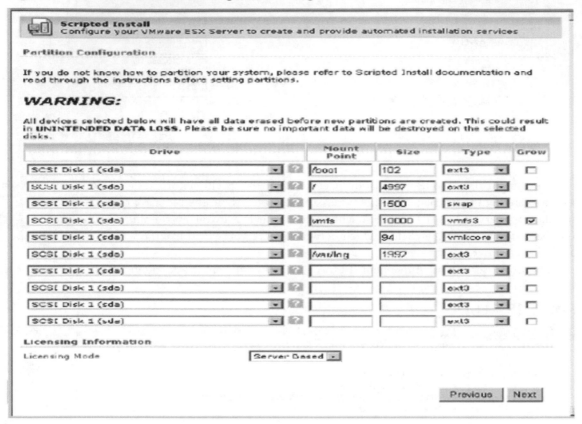

If you modify this, which surely you will, make sure you give it at least the minimum required space to do so. Also, be aware that some SCSI card manufacturers do not use SDA, employing instead other devices, such as Compaq (HP)'s CCISS.

From the Drive list, choose a drive such as SDA, IDE (use /dev/hda), CCISS, or one of many others. In the next column, choose the mount point, such as root (/), boot (/boot), vmfs (vmfs3), swap (swap), and so on. Give each mount point a size in the Size column (in megabytes, but do not use MB as a suffix, such as in 102 MB; use only the number 102, as shown in Figure 18.5). Lastly, provide the type in the Type column, which offers four choices: ext3, swap, vmkcore, and vmfs3.

New to ESX 3.0 is the Licensing Mode. Thus, you must select the appropriate mode for your installation:

- **Server Based**   This mode allows you to obtain a license automatically from your license server, which may have been set up on your VirtualCenter server.
- **File Based**   This mode allows you to upload a license file.
- **Post Install**   This mode allows you to configure your licensing after the install is complete.

Once you have completed the partitioning information and licensing mode, click **Next**.

In the preceding example, Server Based Licensing was chosen, so the next page that appears is that for Server Based Licensing Information, as shown in Figure 18.6. You will add your license server information on this page.

Figure 18.6 The Server Based Licensing Information Page

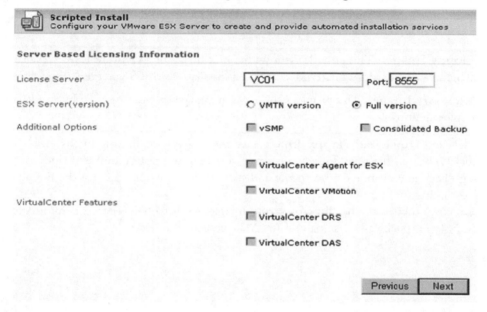

Fill in the License Server information, including its port number—for example, 8555. In the **Additional Options** section, you may select **vSMP** (virtual symmetric multi-processing) and/or **Consolidated Backup**.

Additionally, you can select any VirtualCenter options as well. Click **Next** when you have finished.

If you chose File Based licensing, you'll be presented with the page shown in Figure 18.7.

Figure 18.7 The File Based Licensing Information Page

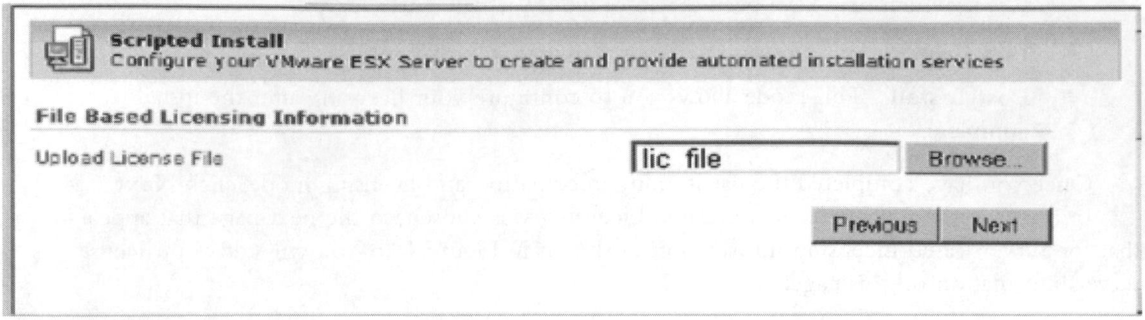

Input the license file, or click the **Browse** button to browse and select the license file. Once you've done so, click **Next**.

Now you can choose **Download Floppy Image** or **Download Kickstart Image**. The differences between these two include the following:

- **Floppy Image**   This provides you with a disk image of a VMware ESX Server boot disk which can be used for unattended, scripted installations of ESX Server.

- **Kickstart Image**   This provides the kickstart image that can be used by third-party deployment tools.

If you selected **Download Floppy Image**, save the image with an .img file extension. If you did not select DHCP in the preceding step because you want to create multiple images for multiple ESX hosts, go back and change the hostname and static IP information and save the floppy images with unique names.

VMware has modified the handling of partition tables so that ESX Server 2.5 automatically clears only the LUNs you specifically designate in the Management Interface.

NOTE

If you are considering booting from your SAN, you should adhere to the following recommendations and work closely with your SAN Administrator:

- Only present the LUN used for the operating system of the ESX Server installation (known as the boot LUN) to the ESX host you are building. Do not present the boot LUN to any other ESX host or server. Do not share boot LUNs between servers.

- During the installation, ensure that you mask off all additional LUNs—like for your vmfs partitions—other than the boot LUN during the installation.

Remote Network Installation

Using a remote network installation to install ESX Server, create a boot floppy image to run the installation instead of scripting the installation. During the installation, you are asked to specify the location of the ESX Server CD-ROM.

To perform a remote network installation with a boot floppy, you need to follow three steps. First, use **dd**, **rawwritewin**, or **rawrite** to create a floppy image called bootnet.img. This file is located on the ESX Server CD-ROM in the /images directory. The second step is to put the boot floppy in your ESX host, and then boot the server. When the installation starts, you will be prompted to choose one of the following selections:

- **HTTP**   This is the preferred installation method. Specify the name of the remote machine where the ESX Server CD-ROM is located, the root directory (/), and HTTP port 8555.

- **NFS**   You must have an NFS server set up. Copy the ESX Server CD-ROM to the NFS server and point the new system to the NFS server.

- **FTP**   You must have an FTP server set up. Copy the ESX Server CD-ROM to the FTP server and point the new system to the FTP server.

The third step is to complete the installation, which is very similar to installing ESX Server normally.

Summary

This chapter should have given you a good understanding of how to quickly scale out your virtual infrastructure using scripted installation methods. You should now be able to create an installation script that is customized for either one specific ESX host or many.

## Chapter 19

An Introduction to ESX Native Tools and How to Use Them

Solutions in this chapter:

- **Esxtop**
- **Vmkfstools**
- **Vmware-cmd**
- **Vmkusage**

☑ **Summary**

Introduction

This chapter is going to review the tools that come native to all ESX servers. It is important that, one, you understand these tools exist, and, two, you know how to use them from the command line and how you can incorporate them into scripts. VMware provides some very powerful tools that are built on native Linux functionality and that are expanded for use within the ESX host and the virtual machines residing on them.

Esxtop

Esxtop is a very simple yet powerful tool which can be used for diagnosing performance issues of the ESX host as well as the virtual machines. In Linux, there exists a comparable command-line tool called *Top* which can be used similarly for Linux OSes to gather performance metrics. VMware has expanded Esxtop to provide metrics specific to virtualization. Esxtop provides real-time monitoring of virtual machine processes (also known as *worlds*). Worlds are simply virtual machine processes run by the VMkernel. VMware has identified three types of worlds, or virtual machine processes, which exist in ESX Server. These are

- Virtual Machine
- System
- Service Console

But before delving too deep into specific processes or the worlds that Esxtop monitors, let's take a quick look at Esxtop when you run it.

Esxtop Overview

Esxtop comes installed natively when you install ESX Server, so there is nothing you need to load. To run Esxtop, you need to access the service console of your ESX host. Once at the service console, type **[root@esx01 root]#** *esxtop*.

The output displayed will be similar to that shown in Figure 19.1.

Figure 19.1 Esxtop Output

```
 9:37am  up 15 days,  4:31, 20 worlds,  load average: 0.05, 0.05, 0.01, 0.00
PCPU:    3.36%,    4.58% :   3.97% used total
LCPU:    2.80%,    0.56%,   1.09%,   3.50%
MEM: 3914752 managed(KB), 1482752 free(KB) :  62.12% used total
SWAP: 4193280 av(KB), 0 used(KB), 4151348 free(KB) :     0.00 MBr/s,    0.00 MBw/s
DISK vmhba0:0:0:    0.00 r/s,    8.35 w/s,    0.00 MBr/s,   0.05 MBw/s
NIC vmnic0:   29.63 pTx/s,   31.82 pRx/s,    0.05 MbTx/s,   0.16 MbRx/s
NIC vmnic2:    0.00 pTx/s,    0.20 pRx/s,    0.00 MbTx/s,   0.00 MbRx/s
NIC vmnic1:    0.00 pTx/s,    0.20 pRx/s,    0.00 MbTx/s,   0.00 MbRx/s

 VCPUID WID WTYPE     %USED %READY %EUSED   %MEM
   128  128 idle      54.69  0.00  54.69   0.00
   130  130 idle      52.21  0.00  52.21   0.00
   131  131 idle      42.26  0.00  42.26   0.00
   129  129 idle      42.26  0.00  42.26   0.00
   142  142 vmm        2.41  0.33   2.41  22.00
   127  127 console    1.86  0.00   1.86   0.00
   146  146 vmm        0.97  0.14   0.97   5.00
   148  148 vmm        0.84  0.56   0.84  11.00
   144  144 vmm        0.60  0.40   0.60   8.00
   143  143 vmm        0.47  0.02   0.47   8.00
   147  147 vmm        0.43  0.02   0.43   1.00
   140  140 driver     0.00  0.00   0.00   0.00
   139  139 reset      0.00  0.00   0.00   0.00
   138  138 reset      0.00  0.00   0.00   0.00
   137  137 helper     0.00  0.00   0.00   0.00
   136  136 helper     0.00  0.00   0.00   0.00
   135  135 helper     0.00  0.00   0.00   0.00
   134  134 helper     0.00  0.00   0.00   0.00
   133  133 helper     0.00  0.00   0.00   0.00
   132  132 helper     0.00  0.28   0.00   0.00
```

Quickly going through the output, note on the top line the time, which in this example is 9:37 A.M. This server has been up 15 days, 4 hours, and 31 minutes and is running 20 worlds. These worlds are not all virtual machines (we will explain each of the different worlds further in the chapter). The load average shows the load the ESX host's CPUs are under. A load average of 1.0 means that the CPU is being fully utilized; thus, an average of 0.5 would mean that the CPU is only being utilized at approximately 50 percent. You can see from the example in Figure 19.1 that the CPUs are hardly being touched on this ESX host, the highest running at 5 percent utilization. However, if you run Esxtop and find that your CPUs are running consistently at 1.0 or above, you may need to adjust the load of virtual machines on that host or increase the number of CPUs on the host itself. The four load averages are collected every five seconds at one-, five-, and fifteen-minute intervals, which give you a snapshot of the overall CPU load of your ESX host during those time slices. The load averages can be used to quickly identify CPU-bound hosts.

The PCPU line and the LCPU line show the number of physical processors, and if hyperthreading is enabled, the number of logical processors and the utilization of each physical and logical processor as well as their averages.

The MEM line shows the total amount of physical memory on the ESX host, the amount of free or nonutilized memory, and the percentage of used memory—in this example, 62.12 percent.

The SWAP line displays a metric you want to pay attention to. The first number shows the amount of swap given to the ESX host, which in the preceding example is 4193280 (KB). Swapping is not necessarily a bad thing. However, excessive swapping can indicate a memory issue and can cause performance degradation. If you see persistently high levels of swapping, which would be shown in the used section, you may need to add physical memory to the ESX host, adjust the amount of memory allocated to your virtual machines, or increase your swap space on the ESX host.

The next section is the disk which will give you the performance data for your disks on the ESX host. If you are experiencing issues related to disk read/write performance or simply want to monitor disk performance, you can review this data. There will be an entry for each LUN per Target per HBA.

The NIC section will give you statistics on the performance of all of your NICs dedicated to virtual machines (Vmnic0 on up). As shown in Figure 19.1, there will be one line per NIC.

Now let's take a look at the different types of worlds or processes Esxtop monitors.

The Virtual Machine World

A virtual machine world is the process under which a specific virtual machine's virtual processor is run. If you are experiencing an issue with a specific virtual machine, this is one place you will want to check out. So what processes are virtual machine world processes? In Figure 19.2, see the highlighted processes.

Figure 19.2 Virtual Machine Processes

```
 9:22am  up 15 days,  4:16, 20 worlds,  load average: 0.04, 0.07, 0.02, 0.01
PCPU:   4.22%,   2.26% :  3.24% used total
LCPU:   3.73%,   0.49%,   1.17%,   1.09%
MEM: 3914752 managed(KB), 1481728 free(KB) :  62.15% used total
SWAP: 4193280 av(KB), 0 used(KB), 4151348 free(KB) :   0.00 MBr/s,   0.00 MBw/s
DISK vmhba0:0:0:    0.00 r/s,   9.36 w/s,   0.00 MBr/s,   0.05 MBw/s
NIC vmnic0:    2.19 pTx/s,   3.58 pRx/s,   0.00 MBTx/s,   0.00 MBRx/s
NIC vmnic2:    0.00 pTx/s,   0.20 pRx/s,   0.00 MBTx/s,   0.00 MBRx/s
NIC vmnic1:    0.00 pTx/s,   0.20 pRx/s,   0.00 MBTx/s,   0.00 MBRx/s

 VCPUID WID WTYPE    %USED  %READY  %EUSED    %MEM
   131  131 idle     58.50   0.00   58.50    0.00
   129  129 idle     58.50   0.00   58.50    0.00
   130  130 idle     38.58   0.00   38.58    0.00
   128  128 idle     37.34   0.00   37.34    0.00
   127  127 console   2.02   0.00    2.02    0.00
   148  148 vmm       0.89   0.30    0.89   14.00
   146  146 vmm       0.86   0.50    0.86    7.00
   142  142 vmm       0.86   1.03    0.86   26.00
   144  144 vmm       0.68   0.26    0.68   10.00
   143  143 vmm       0.62   0.02    0.62   10.00
   147  147 vmm       0.41   0.02    0.41    3.00
   140  140 driver    0.00   0.00    0.00    0.00
```

For quick identification of the type of world each of these processes are, see the WTYPE column. The virtual machine world is denoted by *vmm*. What is not readily evident is which vmm world relates to the specific virtual machine name. However, by examining the VCPUID you can map that number to the VMID found in the MUI. This is shown in Figure 19.3

Figure 19.3 VMID in MUI

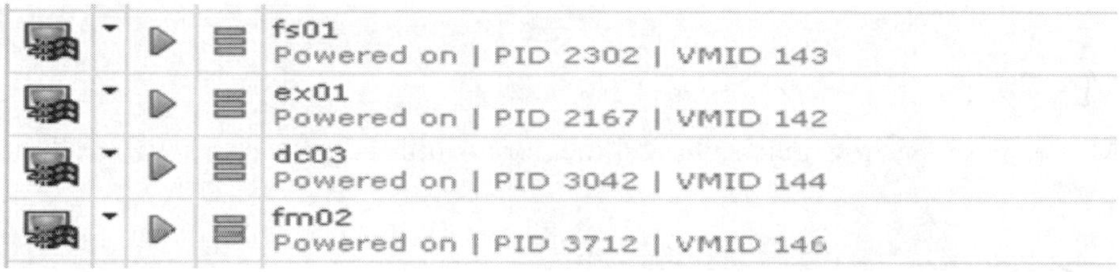

```
fs01
Powered on | PID 2302 | VMID 143

ex01
Powered on | PID 2167 | VMID 142

dc03
Powered on | PID 3042 | VMID 144

fm02
Powered on | PID 3712 | VMID 146
```

NOTE

The PID number shown in Figure 19.3 is the Process ID, which can be seen if you run Top from the service console. You can perform functions such as *kill* using the PID, which is like pulling the plug on your virtual machine. Be careful with this.

System World

System worlds are created to run a number of system services. *Idle worlds* are created for each processor on your ESX host. Idle worlds run an idle loop process, consuming free CPU cycles when the CPUs have nothing else to run. Additionally, *helper worlds* are run for specific system tasks and *driver worlds* are specific drivers within your ESX host.

The Service Console World

The *service console* is itself a world which runs by default on cpu0.

Some Other Helpful Esxtop Metrics

In this section, we discuss other Esxtop metrics that are useful for monitoring the performance of virtual machines.

%USED

The %USED metric identifies how much of a physical processor's utilization is being used by the virtual machine's virtual processor.

%Ready

The %READY metric shows the percentage of time a virtual machine was waiting but could not get scheduled on a physical processor. VMware recommends this number be under 5 percent.

%EUSED

The %EUSED metric shows how much of the maximum physical processor utilization a virtual machine is currently using.

%MEM

The %MEM metric shows how much physical memory is utilized by each virtual machine and world.

vmkfstools

vmkfstools is a powerful command-line tool that comes native to ESX Server. The tool can create and manipulate VMDK files, performing such tasks as importing and exporting disk files, growing and shrinking existing disk files, and committing REDO files. The tool can also create VMFS partitions and has a host of other capabilities. To see the full range and power of the vmkfstools command, from your service console type **man vmkfstools**.

We will next examine some common and very helpful ways to use vmkfstools and its associated arguments.

Viewing Contents VMFS Partition

Similar to the Linux command *ls*, if you want to view the contents of a VMFS volume on your ESX host, type **vmkfstools –l vmfs_label**.

You may specify the HBA number, SCSI target, LUN number, and partition number.

For example, from the service console, type **vmkfstools –l vmhba0:0:0:11**.

Figure 19.4 displays the output from running *vmkfstools –l*. By adding an **h** after the **–l**, the size of the files on the VMFS partition are displayed in a more human-readable format. So the command in the preceding example would look like **vmkfstools –lh vmhba0:0:0:11**.

Figure 19.4 Vmkfstools–l Output

```
[root@esx-server01 root]# vmkfstools -l vmhba0:0:0:11
Name: local        (public)
Capacity 50610115584 (48258 file blocks * 1048576), 10501488640 (10015 blocks) avail
Permission   Uid   Gid        Attr     Bytes (Blocks)  Last Modified Filename
rw-------    0     0          swap 2146435072 ( 2047)  May 27 19:49  SwapFile.vswp
rw-------    0     0          disk 4194304000 ( 4000)  Jun  1 20:03  cluster-01.vmdk
rw-------    0     0          disk 4194304000 ( 4000)  Jun  1 19:54  server-02.vmdk
rw-------    0     0          disk 4194304000 ( 4000)  Jun  1 20:03  server-03.vmdk
rw-------    0     0          disk 4194304000 ( 4000)  Jun  1 20:03  srv-node1.vmdk
rw-------    0     0          disk 4194304000 ( 4000)  Jun  1 20:03  srv-node2.vmdk
rw-------    0     0          disk 4294967296 ( 4096)  Jun  1 20:03  nt4.vmdk
rw-------    0     0          disk  104857600 (  100)  Jun  1 20:03  quorum1.vmdk
rw-------    0     0          disk 2097152000 ( 2000)  Mar  6 21:30  server2k01.vmdk
rw-------    0     0          disk 2097152000 ( 2000)  Jun  1 20:03  server-20.vmdk
rw-------    0     0          disk 4194304000 ( 4000)  Jun  1 20:03  server-05.vmdk
rw-------    0     0          disk 4194304000 ( 4000)  Jun  1 12:29  webserver-01.vmdk
```

Import/Export Files

As mentioned earlier, if you need to import or export .vmdk files onto your VMFS partition, you can use the vmkfstools command. VMware recommends using vmkfstools rather than the Linux command cp to do this. For example, if you need to export a virtual disk from a VMFS partition to a different location on your ESX Server, type

vmkfstools –e /targetdirectory/filename.vmdk /vmfs/volume_label/sourcefile.vmdk

One reason you would want to do this is to move a virtual machine template from the VMFS volume to a directory that contains your template images on your server.

If you need to import a virtual disk file from VMware Server or Workstation, you will first need to scp or ftp the .vmdk file(s) onto a directory of your ESX host (not the VMFS partition) and then run the following command:

vmkfstools –i source_directory_name /vmfs/volume_label/targetfile.vmdk

Adding a New Virtual Disk, Blank Virtual Disk, and Extending Existing Virtual Disks

A very cool use of vmkfstools is its capability to create and modify existing .vmdk files. For example, if you need to create a new blank virtual disk type from the service console, use the following syntax:

vmkfstools –c size vmfs-name:vmdk-name

Example:

vmkfstools –c 2024 m SanRaid1:data01.vmdk

What this allows you to do is add a new 2 GB hard disk which can then be added to existing virtual machines and formatted at the OS level within the VM.

But what if you need to extend or grow an existing virtual disk? For this, you would type the following syntax:

vmkfstools –X new-size vmfs-name:vmdk-name

Example:

vmkfstools –X 12288m SanRaid1:database.vmdk

The preceding command extends the existing database.vmdk from its existing size to 12288 megabytes.

NOTE

The virtual machine will need to be powered off prior to extending the virtual disk. VMware recommends that you make a full backup on the VMDK file prior to completing this task. If you want to extend the partition within the virtual machine itself, you may need to use a utility like Partition Magic for the VM to recognize the additional space added to the disk file. Or you will need to create an additional partition within the virtual machine itself.

Swiss Army Knife...

man vmkfstools

Become familiar with vmkfstools command. To obtain a full list of the arguments associated with vmkfstools, from the service console, type
man vmkfstools

vmware-cmd

The *vmware-cmd* command allows you to perform many different tasks related to virtual machines. If you type **vmware-cmd** from the service console, you will see that vmware-cmd has both Server Operations and VM Operations. Figure 19.5 shows the Server Operations that can be performed on the service console using vmware-cmd. As you can see from the list, you can register and unregister virtual machines and get/set resource variables.

Figure 19.5 Vmware-cmd Server Operations

```
Server Operations:
  /usr/bin/vmware-cmd -l
  /usr/bin/vmware-cmd -s register <config_file_path>
  /usr/bin/vmware-cmd -s unregister <config_file_path>
  /usr/bin/vmware-cmd -s getresource <variable>
  /usr/bin/vmware-cmd -s setresource <variable> <value>
```

For example, if you type

vmware-cmd –l

from the service console, a list of registered virtual machines and the path to the .vmx configuration file will be displayed.

Figure 19.6 shows the VM Operations that can be performed from the service console using the vmware-cmd utility. You can stop, start, reset, and suspend virtual machines, add and commit .redo files (very powerful; especially for backups which will be discussed later in the book), as well as get information about the virtual machine.

Figure 19.6 Vmware-cmd VM Operations

```
VM Operations:
 /usr/bin/vmware-cmd <cfg> getconnectedusers
 /usr/bin/vmware-cmd <cfg> getstate
 /usr/bin/vmware-cmd <cfg> start <powerop_mode>
 /usr/bin/vmware-cmd <cfg> stop <powerop_mode>
 /usr/bin/vmware-cmd <cfg> reset <powerop_mode>
 /usr/bin/vmware-cmd <cfg> suspend <powerop_mode>
 /usr/bin/vmware-cmd <cfg> setconfig <variable> <value>
 /usr/bin/vmware-cmd <cfg> getconfig <variable>
 /usr/bin/vmware-cmd <cfg> setguestinfo <variable> <value>
 /usr/bin/vmware-cmd <cfg> getguestinfo <variable>
 /usr/bin/vmware-cmd <cfg> getid
 /usr/bin/vmware-cmd <cfg> getpid
 /usr/bin/vmware-cmd <cfg> getproductinfo <prodinfo>
 /usr/bin/vmware-cmd <cfg> connectdevice <device_name>
 /usr/bin/vmware-cmd <cfg> disconnectdevice <device_name>
 /usr/bin/vmware-cmd <cfg> getconfigfile
 /usr/bin/vmware-cmd <cfg> getheartbeat
 /usr/bin/vmware-cmd <cfg> getuptime
 /usr/bin/vmware-cmd <cfg> getremoteconnections
 /usr/bin/vmware-cmd <cfg> gettoolslastactive
 /usr/bin/vmware-cmd <cfg> getresource <variable>
 /usr/bin/vmware-cmd <cfg> setresource <variable> <value>
 /usr/bin/vmware-cmd <cfg> addredo <disk_device_name>
 /usr/bin/vmware-cmd <cfg> commit <disk_device_name> <level> <freeze> <wait>
 /usr/bin/vmware-cmd <cfg> answer
```

For example, to add a .redo file to a virtual machine, type the following syntax from the service console:

vmware-cmd <cfg> addredo scsi0:0

NOTE

The scsi0:0 in the preceding command is the actual scsi device name of the virtual machine.

If the command runs successfully, the resultant output would look something like:

Addredo (scsi0:0) = 1

To commit the redo you just added, type

Vmware-cmd <cfg> commit scsi0:0 001

vmkusage

Although not a command-line tool, vmkusage is a great tool for troubleshooting and one you should be aware of. Monitoring the utilization of servers in the past was not the most exciting work. In the past, a server maxed could mean a lot of work for an administrator. Now, allocating more memory, an additional CPU, hard drive, or NIC is a process of minutes not days or weeks. Monitor the performance of your virtual machines to ensure you meet your service level agreements. Use the excellent VirtualCenter for this. You can also use vmkusage, which provides the utilization of your ESX Server as well as all running virtual machines.

To start vmkusage, from the command line of your ESX Server's service console, type

vmkusagectl install

This will create the utilization reports in the /var/log/vmkusage directory. These reports will be updated every five minutes by default. You view the reports with a Web browser by typing **https://esxservername.corp.com/vmkusage**.

Figure 19.7 Vmkusage

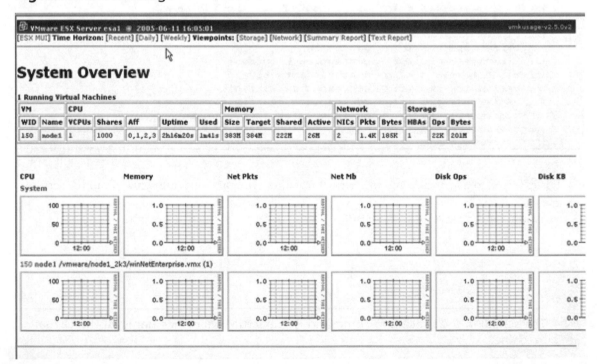

Substitute the URL with the appropriate information in your environment. You will see a window similar to that shown in Figure 19.7.

You can pull very specific utilization reports that you will find important for capacity planning, future demand availability, server sizing, and hardware purchasing. The HTML files and vmkusage graphs are located in /usr/lib/vmware-mui/apache/htdocs/vmkusage.

Summary

These native tools are powerful and you can create many different scripts calling these commands. It is recommended that you become thoroughly familiar with these tools and use them to unlock the power and flexibility of your virtual infrastructure. Of course, be sure to thoroughly test all of your scripts and commands in a test environment prior to using them in production.

## Chapter 20

Scripting and Programming for the Virtual Infrastructure

Solutions in this chapter:

- **VMware Scripting APIs**
- **VMware Virtual Infrastructure SDK**
- **Other VMware SDKs**

☑ **Summary**

Introduction

Simplification of administration and its related overhead is a strategic imperative that most companies are mandating. Although programmatic automation has existed in the Windows and Linux operating systems for some time now, getting a complete solution for system management and automation often requires purchasing expensive third-party, proprietary software that was difficult to learn and sometimes suffered from compatibility issues. Fortunately, VMware has incorporated a variety of interfaces that you can take advantage of to simplify the management of your virtual infrastructure. In this chapter, we will discuss the available APIs and SDKs as they apply to the following VMware products and versions:

- VMware ESX Server 3.0 and 2.5.x

- VMware Server and VMware GSX Server 2.x or later

- VMware VirtualCenter 2.0 and 1.x

So, without further ado, let's jump into scripting and programming techniques for VMware ESX, VMware Server, and VMware VirtualCenter. To help you establish a firm foundation in writing code for VMware products, we will discuss several techniques and technologies in this chapter, specifically:

- VMware scripting APIs

- VMware VirtualCenter SDK

- Other VMware SDKs

VMware Scripting APIs

With the release of the VMware scripting application programming interfaces (APIs), VMware has been offering two components that you can use to develop custom code to manage your VMware ESX, VMware GSX, and VMware Server hosts directly: VmCOM and VmPerl. These APIs have no dependency on any other VMware product, such as VirtualCenter, and are available for use as quickly as you can download them from VMware's site.

VmCOM is a Component Object Model (COM) interface you can use with any language that supports the instantiation of COM objects, such as VB.NET, VBScript, C++, C#, Python, Delphi, and Java, just to mention a few. You must install this interface on a machine with a supported version of the Microsoft Windows operating system. VmCOM is not supported on the Linux platform.

VmPerl is an API that can be utilized through the Perl scripting language. You can install this component on either a Windows-based or a Linux-based admin client.

Designing & Planning...

Choosing an IDE

To efficiently develop, edit, debug, and test your code, you should standardize on an integrated development environment (IDE) that supports the language(s) you plan to write in. Several commercial and open-source products are available, so your decision will really be based on preference. When choosing an IDE, you should look for products that offer file management, integrated building/debugging/testing, deployment, source control, and reference tools to assist with rapid, yet accurate, coding. Some good choices when developing against any of the APIs and SDKs discussed in this chapter are

- **Microsoft Visual Studio (commercial)** For example, most COM developers opt for Microsoft Visual Studio as the preferred IDE since it supports all of the Microsoft languages. With Visual Studio 2005, you get a powerful IDE, code snippets, mobile device support, source control, and code profiling tools. To make coding even easier and faster, you get great features like Intellisense, which helps you with code against methods and properties for objects that you instantiate and provides an "auto-complete" function (Visual Studio only runs on Windows). For those on a budget, a free version is available, called Visual Studio Express, which provides more than enough features to support development against the Scripting APIs. For more information, see http://msdn.microsoft.com.

- **NetBeans IDE (open source)** A fast and feature-rich tool for developing Java software. It includes support for AWT/Swing, Servlets and JSP, and J2EE (EJB and Web services). It also includes a database engine and a J2EE-compliant application server. For more information, visit www.netbeans.org.

- **Eclipse (open source)** Available as a complete SDK, Eclipse is a leading open-source IDE, as well as a suite of tools for building applications based on the Eclipse platform. By adding development components, you can customize the Eclipse platform as an IDE for Java (using JDT), C/C++ (using CDT), or both. It runs on a wide range of operating systems, including Windows, Linux, Mac OS, Solaris, AIX, and HP-UX. For more information, visit www.eclipse.org.

- **ActiveState Komodo (commercial)** For Perl development, the Komodo IDE from ActiveState is a good choice. Not only does it support Perl, but you can use it for Python, Tcl, and Ruby development as well. Komodo is available for Windows, MacOS, and Linux. For more information, visit www.activestate.com.

Continued

> ■ **Sapien Technology's PrimalScript (commercial)** This is one of the more cost-effective, yet powerful, commercial IDEs available. It provides the same scripting language support as Komodo, but also adds support for VBScript, Actionscript, and KiXtart. It also supports Web development efforts in ASP, ColdFusion, JSP, and PHP...a plus if your code is going to have a browser-based UI. For more information, visit www.sapien.com.

Both components are supported by VMware ESX Server as well as VMware Server/GSX. There are some differences when targeting operations against the different VMware server products, so we'll indicate any discrepancies as we discuss the APIs further in this chapter.

What Are the VMware Scripting APIs?

The interfaces for VmCOM and VmPerl are functionally the same. Both interfaces allow developers and savvy administrators to tap into the power of VMware ESX or VMware Server/GSX hosts programmatically. Even more important, they support a wide range of object-oriented languages, allowing just about anyone to immediately write code to simplify the administration and management of their virtual infrastructure. Although the two interfaces are technically different, both provide task automation functionality, such as virtual machine registration, performing power operations on virtual machines, and information gathering and sending to and from the virtual machine's guest operating system. All sessions between the API and the VMware ESX or VMware Server host are secured and use a single TCP port for communication (TCP port 902 is the default), as shown in Figure 20.1.

Figure 20.1 The VMware Scripting API Architecture

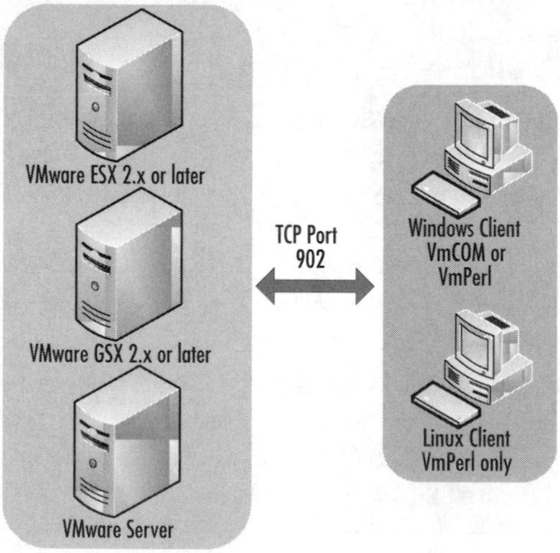

Tip

For Windows installations, you'll also need to install Perl support, such as ActivePerl from ActiveState, to use the VmPerl API. Additional Perl modules may also be required to support certain features needed to work with the API.

VmCOM support is built into Windows by default if you plan on using an interpreted language based on Microsoft's scripting technology (VBScript or JScript). However, if you plan on using a language that requires you to compile your code, such as VB.NET, C#, Java, or Delphi, you will need to install some additional development tools.

Installing the VMware Scripting APIs

Before you can create your own custom scripts to manage your ESX servers, you must install the VMware Scripting APIs on the workstation or server where your scripts will run. The APIs are available at no cost from VMware at www.vmware.com/support/developer/scripting_download.html.

You must log in to the site with your VMware store account and accept the license agreement. You will then be presented with the download links for:

- COM API for Windows
- Perl API for Windows
- Perl API for Linux

To install the scripting API on a Windows client machine, follow these steps:

1. Run the installer package with an account that has administrator rights on the Windows client machine. The naming convention for the installer package is **VMware-VmCOMAPI-x.x.x-yyyyy.exe** (for the VmCOM API) or **VMware-VmPerl-x.x.x-yyyyy.exe** (for the VmPerl API), where "x.x.x" is the ESX Server version the API is for, and "yyyyy" is the build number.

2. Agree to the license agreement by selecting **Yes, I accept the terms in the license agreement.**

3. Click **Next**.

4. Choose the install location by either accepting the default directory or clicking **Change** and browsing to your preferred location.

5. Click **Next**.

6. Click **Install** to begin the copying of files.

7. Click **Finish** when prompted after the install is complete.

To install the scripting API on a Linux client machine, follow these steps:

1. Copy the VmPerl package to the Linux client machine where the scripts will be run.

2. Log on to the machine as root.

3. Untar the installation package. The naming convention for the package is **VMware-VmPerl-x.x.x-yyyyy.tar.gz**, where "x.x.x" is the specific ESX version number and "yyyyy" is the build number.

4. Change to the directory where the extracted files are found, and run the install script **./vmware-install.pl**.

5. Agree to the license agreement by pressing **Enter** when prompted.

6. Enter the installation path for the VmPerl binaries or accept the default destination directory.

7. Enter the installation path for the VmPerl libraries or accept the default destination directory.

Putting the VMware Scripting APIs to Work for You

Once the VMware Scripting APIs have been installed on your management client or server, the next step is to dive in and develop some code to become familiar with the capabilities of the APIs. In this section, we will review the various components for both VmCOM and VmPerl. If you are only familiar with Windows administration, you may feel more comfortable with the VmCOM methods and properties using a scripting language such as Microsoft's VBScript or JScript. If you have a Linux or Unix background, you should feel right at home with the modules or packages exposed by the VmPerl API using the Perl scripting language. You will find the following examples helpful in either case since the functionality of both VmCOM and VmPerl is the same.

Working with the VmCOM API

The VmCOM API exposes five objects that are used to establish, maintain communication, and interact with a VMware ESX server or virtual machine. Two of these objects will serve as primary objects that expose the methods and properties you will use in your scripts to interact with, or gather information from, your hosts and virtual machines. In function, these objects are similar to the VMware::VmPerl::Server and VMware::VmPerl::VM modules provided by the VmPerl API, discussed later in this chapter. They are

- **VmServerCtl**   Used to create a session with an ESX host and expose the services and functionality of the API's server interfaces.

- **VmCtl**   Used to manage and perform operations against a virtual machine on a particular ESX host.

Supporting these primary objects are three other objects that provide a secondary, supporting role. These support objects provide the input or output resources needed to pass to the primary object's properties and methods. They are

- **VmConnectParams** Provides host information and authentication credentials used when establishing a connection to an ESX host.

- **VmCollection**   Provides a collection or array of properties or other interfaces to be passed to the primary objects.

- **VmQuestion**   Provides a interactive interface to respond to questions or error conditions for a virtual machine running on an ESX host.

The process begins by establishing a connection with an ESX or GSX host, or a virtual machine on a particular host using the *Connect()* method of either an instantiated *VmServerCtl* or *VmCtl* object. *VmServerCtl.Connect()* method uses the *VmConnectParams* object to set the target host information and credentials to establish the connection. The *VmCtl.Connect()* method also uses the *VmConnectParams* object, just as the *VmServerCtl* does, in addition to the configuration file name for the target virtual machine. After you have connected to an ESX server host or a virtual machine on that host, you can then call the other methods and properties of the VmCOM component.

As with any COM API, you must expose the VmCOM objects first by either creating an instance of those objects or retrieving an instance of the objects as a returned value for a property. We will discuss this in further detail shortly.

Depending on what your script does, you work with instances of one or more of the following objects:

- VmConnectParams

- *VmCollection*

- *VmServerCtl*

- VmCtl

Before we jump deeper into these topics, we should discuss the development environment within which you will be writing your code. Commonly, VmCOM development is done in a Microsoft development language, be it VBScript or one of the .NET languages (VB.NET, C++, or C#). If you opt to write code in the latter, the IDE best suited for the job is Microsoft Visual Studio.

Although every IDE provides its own set of strengths and benefits, development efforts surrounding COM objects find themselves at home with Microsoft Visual Studio 2005. Two key things that I would like to call out are the ease of including VmCOM in your code and using Intellisense to speed up your development and reduce time spent debugging your code.

If you opt to use Visual Studio 2005 as your IDE, you need to reference the VmCOM Type Library, as shown in Figure 20.2, after creating a new project or solution.

Figure 20.2 Referencing the VMware VmCOM 1.0 Type Library

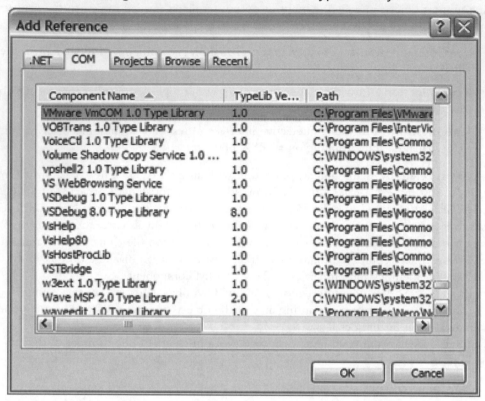

If the library was successfully referenced and included in the project, you should see it listed in the References tree in the Solution Explorer, as portrayed in Figure 20.3. You will also be able to browse the API with VS 2005's Object Browser, as shown in Figure 20.4. Not enough can be said about coding with the appropriate tool for your language. The more feature-rich the tool is, the easier and faster your coding will go.

Figure 20.3 The VMCOMLib Reference in Solution Explorer

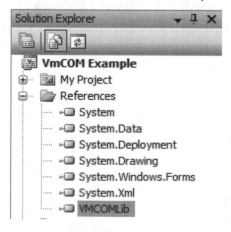

Figure 20.4 Using the Object Browser to View the Methods and Properties of the *VmCtl* Object

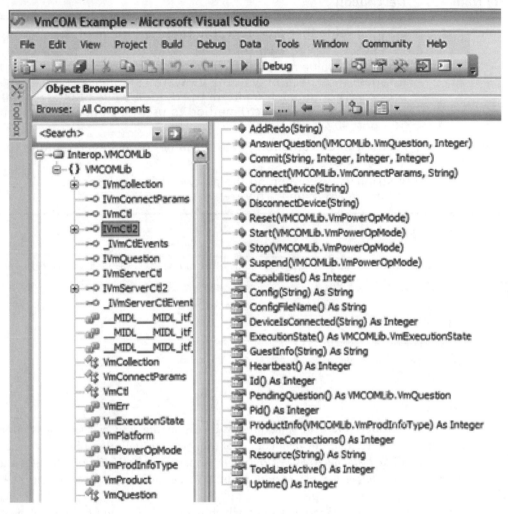

But enough of the formalities…let's move on and take a look at the VmCOM objects.

VmConnectParams

The *VmConnectParams* provides the host information and user credentials required by the *Connect()* method for either the *VMServerCtl* or *VmCtl* object, and exposes properties whose values you can set, as shown in Table 20.1. You can use these properties for data retrieval or modification through your script or application.

Table 20.1 *VmConnectParams* Properties

Property Name	Description
Hostname	A string value that represents the DNS host name of the VMware ESX or GSX host or its IP address.
Port	An integer value representing the TCP port that should be used to establish a connection with the VMware ESX or GSX host. This property is optional. If omitted, the default value of 0 (zero) will be used, telling the *Connect()* method to use the standard management TCP port 902.
Username	A string value containing the username to pass as credentials for the connection.
Password	A string value containing the password for the user set in the *Username* property.

The following demonstrates the instantiation of the *VmConnectParams* object in VBScript and how to set the properties listed earlier.

```
Set objConnParams = CreateObject("VmCOM.VmConnectParams")
objConnParams.hostname = "esxserver1"
objConnParams.username = "adminuser1"
objConnParams.password = "password1"
```

VmCollection

This is a good point to introduce the next object in our discussion, the *VmCollection* object. Although you will never instantiate it directly, there are a couple of properties in the other objects we will discuss that return a *VmCollection*. The *RegisteredVmNames* property of the *VmServerCtl* object and the *Choices* property of the *VmQuestion* object both return a range of elements, or values, as a *VmCollection* object.

A *VmCollection* object has two properties: Count, which is an integer value for the number of elements in the collection; and *Item(index)*, which is a string value that returns the specific element represented by the index value you pass. You can navigate the elements returned by stepping through them as you would an array, or access a specific element by referencing its index. You will see examples of this later in the chapter as we work with those properties that return *VmCollection* objects.

VmServerCtl

The *VmServerCtl* object is used to interact with a specific VMware ESX or GSX host. This objects exposes two properties and three methods, as shown in Table 20.2. One particular property, *RegisteredVmNames*, returns a *VmCollection* object that contains a complete list of virtual machines registered on the host. This property will prove particularly useful as you query for the host's inventory.

Table 20.2 *VmServerCtl* Properties and Methods

Item	Type	Description
RegisteredVmNames	Property	Returns a listing of all registered VMs on the VMware ESX or GSX host as a *VmCollection* object.
Resource	Property	Used syntactically with a particular system resource variable, this property returns the value as a string variant.
Connect	Method	Used to establish a connection with a VMware ESX or GSX host. You must reference a *VmConnectParams* object when calling the method.
RegisterVm	Method	Used to register a VM on a host. You must reference the configuration file name of the VM being targeted.
UnregisterVm	Method	User to unregister a VM on a host. You must reference the configuration file name of the VM being targeted.

NOTE

The VmCOM API limits the total number of concurrent connections supported by the API. Connections established by the *VmCtl* object and the *VmServerCtl* object cannot exceed 62 when using the API. Keep this in mind when you run scripts concurrently to manage VMs and hosts. If you need to perform multiple tasks against a particular virtual machine or host, and you cannot do so in the same connection, try chaining the tasks synchronously, thus freeing connections by destroying instantiated *VmCtl* and *VMServerCtl* objects before establishing new ones.

The following continues from our last code example, adding the instantiation of the *VmServerCtl* object and connecting to the host using the previously defined *VmConnectParams* object.

```
Set objVMServer = CreateObject("VmCOM.VmServerCtl")
objVMServer.Connect objConnParams
objVMList = objVMServer.RegisteredVmNames
for vmIndex = 1 to objVMList.Count
  WScript.Echo VM.objVMList(vmCounter)
  vmCounter = vmCounter + 1
next
```

In this example, we connect to the host according to the property values set in the *VmConnectParams* object earlier, retrieve the collection of registered VMs, and enumerate them, writing their configuration file path as output.

NOTE

Like most methods of the VmCOM component objects, *Connect()* runs synchronously. The script will not continue until the connection attempt has finished successfully, failed, or timed out after two minutes of waiting to connect.

VmCtl

Similar to the *VmServerCtl* object, the *VmCtl* object is used to gather information from or control a virtual machine running on a VMware ESX or GSX host. *VmCtl* exposes quite a few properties and methods, making this object quite powerful. What makes it even more unique than the other VmCOM objects we have discussed so far is that several of the properties and methods use symbolic constant enumerations (SCE) which must be interpreted. As this can get quite complicated, we will review the various properties and methods along with their relationship and dependency on SCEs. You can also reference the VMware Scripting API User's Manual which provides additional information about each method and property we briefly mention in this chapter.

Tables 20.3 and 20.4 outline the properties and methods exposed by *VmCtl*, including the references to the SCEs, while Table 20.5 lists the symbolic constant enumerations and their interpreted values.

Table 20.3 *VmCtl* Properties

Property Name	Description
ExecutionState	Returns the current state of the VM. Returns the SCE *VmExecutionState*.
PendingQuestion	Returns a *VmQuestion* object (a *VmCollection*) with the details of the question if the VM is in a stuck state.
GuestInfo(key)	Accesses the shared variables (discussed later in this chapter).
Config (key)	Accesses the configuration variables defined in the configuration files of the VM.
ConfigFileName	Returns just the name of the configuration file, not the path.
Heartbeat	Returns the heartbeat count generated by the VMware Tools in the guest OS.
ToolsLastActive	Returns an integer representing the number of seconds since the last heartbeat was detected.

Table 20.3 Continued

Property Name	Description
DeviceIsConnected (dev)	Returns a Boolean value concerning the state of the specified device.
ProductInfo(type)	Returns information concerning the VMware product. Returns the SCEs *VmProductInfoType*, *VmProduct*, or *VmPlatform*.
Uptime	Returns the uptime of the Guest OS running in the VM.
PID	Returns the process ID of a running VM.
Resource(name)	Accesses the VM resource variable passed as "name".
ID	Returns the UUID for a running VM.
Capabilities	Returns the access permissions for the current user.
RemoteConnections	Returns the number of users connected to the VM remotely.

Note that *Resource*, *ID*, *Capabilities*, and *RemoteConnections* only apply to virtual machines running on a VMware ESX host. These properties will return an error when attempting to retrieve values from a virtual machine running on a VMware GSX host.

Table 20.4 *VmCtl* Methods

Method Name	Description
Connect(params,name)	Establishes a connection to a VM. You must pass a *VmConnectParams* object and the configuration file name of the VM you are connecting to.
Start(mode)	Powers on or resumes a VM. Utilizes the SCE *VmPowerOpMode* to control the behavior of the operation.
Stop(mode)	Shuts down and powers of a VM. Utilizes the SCE *VmPowerOpMode* to control the behavior of the operation.
Reset(mode)	Shuts down and reboots a VM. Utilizes the SCE *VmPowerOpMode* to control the behavior of the operation.
Suspend (mode)	Suspends a VM. Utilizes the SCE *VmPowerOpMode* to control the behavior of the operation.
AddRedo(diskName)	Adds a redo log to a running VM's virtual disk.
Commit(diskName, level,freeze,wait)	Commits changes in redo logs for a running VM's virtual disk.
AnswerQuestion (question,choice)	Replies to a question for a stuck VM with a specific answer.

Continued

Table 20.4 Continued

Method Name	Description
ConnectDevice(dev)	Connects a specific device to a running VM.
DisconnectDevice(dev)	Disconnects a specific device from a running VM.
SetRunAsUser (uname,pwd)	Runs the VM as a specified user under the credentials passed by the method.
RunAsUser	Returns the name of the user running the VM. Does not return the password.

Note that *AddRedo()* and *Commit()* only apply to virtual machines running on a VMware ESX host. These properties will return an error when attempting to retrieve values from a virtual machine running on a VMware GSX host. Likewise, *SetRunAsUser()* and *RunAsUser()* only apply to virtual machines running on a VMware GSX host, and will return errors if invoked against a VMware ESX host.

NOTE

Similar to *VmServerCtl*, the total number of concurrent connections per VM is limited and cannot exceed two when using the API. To establish new connections to the VM, free up a connection by destroying instantiated *VmCtl* objects first.

Table 20.5 *VmCtl* Symbolic Constant Enumerations (SCE)

SCE Name	Value	Description
VmExecutionState	VmExecutionState_On	VM is powered on.
	VmExecutionState_Off	VM is powered off.
	VmExecutionState_Suspended	VM is suspended.
	VmExecutionState_Stuck	VM is awaiting input from user.
	VmExecutionState_Unknown	VM is in an unknown state.
VmPowerOpMode	VmPowerOpMode_Soft	Runs predefined scripts via the VMware Tools in the Guest OS and attempts to gracefully perform the operation.

Table 20.5 Continued

SCE Name	Value	Description
	VmPowerOpMode_Hard	No scripts are run. Immediately and unconditionally performs the operation.
	VmPowerOpMode_TrySoft	Attempts to perform the operation with the *VmPowerOpMode_Soft* behavior. If it fails to do so, the operation will then be performed as a *VmPowerOpMode_Hard*.
VmProdInfoType	vmProdInfo_Product	Returned as *VmProduct*.
	vmProdInfo_Platform	Returned as *VmPlatform*.
	vmProdInfo_Build	Product's build number.
	vmProdInfo_Version_Major	Product's major version number.
	vmProdInfo_Version_Minor	Product's minor version number.
	vmProdInfo_Version_Revision	Product's revision number.
VmProduct	vmProduct_WS	Product is VMware Workstation.
	vmProduct_GSX	Product is VMware GSX Server.
	vmProduct_ESX	Product is VMware ESX Server.
	vmProduct_UNKNOWN	Product is unknown.
VmPlatform	vmPlatform_WINDOWS	Host platform is an MS Windows OS.
	vmPlatform_LINUX	Host platform is a Linux OS.
	vmPlatform_VMNIX	Host platform is the ESX Server service console.
	vmPlatform_UNKNOWN	Host platform is unknown.

Using our previous example, we can utilize the established connection via *VmServerCtl* and the *VmCollection* of virtual machines on our host to query the uptime for each of the registered VMs using *VmCtl*. The following retrieves the configuration file name for each VM, connects to the VM, and gets the value from the *uptime* property. The results are then echoed as output.

```
For each ConfigFile in objVMList
    Set objVM = CreateObject("VmCOM.VmCtl")
    objVM.Connect objConnParams, ConfigFile
    vmUptime = objVM.Resource("cpu.uptime")
    WScript.Echo "Uptime for VM " & ConfigFile & " is " & VMUptime
Next
```

With VmCOM, you can also write scripts that perform configuration management activities on your hosts and VMs. Focusing on establishing configuration standards, you can ensure that optimal and approved configurations are always maintained without having to use the VMware ESX/GSX MUI to do so. For example, a sample script may ensure that no floppy drives are left connected to the VM. On a host running many VMs, leaving physical devices, such as floppy and optical drives, places unnecessary load on the service console (ESX) or host OS (GSX).

The following demonstrates how you can accomplish this via a simple script. After connecting to the ESX host and retrieving a *VmCollection* of all registered VMs, the script connects to each VM individually, checks the connection status of the floppy device, and disconnects it accordingly.

```
' Set parameters used to connect to the ESX Server.
Set objConnParams = CreateObject("VmCOM.VmConnectParams")
objConnParams.hostname = "esxserver1 "
objConnParams.username = "adminuser1"
objConnParams.password = "password1"

' Establish connection with ESX host
Set objVMServer = CreateObject("VmCOM.VmServerCtl")
objVMServer.Connect objConnParams

' Obtain list of registered VMs on host
Set objVMList = objVMServer.RegisteredVmNames

' Step through list of VMs and connect to each one
' individually. Disconnect floppy drive, if connected
For each ConfigFile in objVMList
    Set objVM = CreateObject("VmCOM.VmCtl")
    objVM.Connect objConnParams, ConfigFile
    vmDevice = "floppy0"
    if objVM.DeviceIsConnected(vmDevice) Then
       objVM.DisconnectDevice(vmDevice)
       vmDeviceStatus = "Now Disconnected"
    Else
       vmDeviceStatus = "Was already disconnected"
    End If
    WScript.Echo "Floppy for VM " & ConfigFile & ":"
    WScript.Echo vbTab & "Status: " & vmDeviceStatus
    WScript.Echo
```

```
Next
objVM = Nothing
objVMServer = Nothing
objConnParams = Nothing
```

Managing Guests with User-Defined Variables

As mentioned earlier, another unique feature within the VMware Scripting API is the ability to pass data between a script and a running virtual machine. This can be accomplished in any direction—either passing information from the script to a running virtual machine or passing information from inside a running virtual machine to a script. The VMware Tools service facilitates the interaction between the script and the virtual machine.

To pass information to or from the running virtual machine, you must set the *GuestInfo* class of variable using the *VmCtl* object. You can define any number of key names and assign any string value to them. The following example assumes that you have already established a connection to a specific VM using the *VmCtl* object. Here we pass specific values to be retrieved later inside the Guest OS.

```
Set objVM = CreateObject("VmCOM.VmCtl")
objVM.Connect objConnParams, "/home/vmware/server1/server1.vmx"
objVM.GuestInfo("Department") = "Accounting"
objVM.GuestInfo("CostCenter") = "5008620"
objVM.GuestInfo("Priority") = "Low"
```

Once these values have been set, the information can be retrieved using the *VMwareService.exe* command for Windows guests or the *vmware-guestd* command for Linux guests. In a similar fashion, you can use those commands to set rather than get values to user-defined variables and retrieve them via VmCOM scripts.

NOTE

When passing information using *GuestInfo*, the data is not persistent. If the virtual machine is powered off and all sessions connected to the virtual machine are closed, the information originally shared with the VM is lost. When the VM is powered on again, all *GuestInfo* variables are again undefined.

Working with the VmPerl API

The VmPERL API provides four Perl modules that are used to establish, maintain communication, and interact with a VMware ESX or GSX server or virtual machine. Two of the modules are functionally equivalent to the *VmServerCtl* and *VmCtl* objects exposed by the VmCOM API, as discussed earlier in this chapter. Both of these modules will serve as the primary modules for your Perl scripts. They are

- **VMware::VmPerl::Server**   Used to create a session with an ESX or GSX host and expose the services and functionality of the API's server interfaces.

- **VMware::VmPerl::VM**   Used to manage and perform operations against a virtual machine on a specific ESX or GSX host.

Also, similar to the supporting objects in the VmCOM API, there are two supporting modules provided by the VmPerl API. These modules are used as the inputs or outputs to the properties and methods exposed by the primary modules. They are

- **VMware::VmPerl::ConnectParams**   Provides host information and authentication credentials used when establishing a connection to an ESX or GSX host.

- **VMware::VmPerl::Question**   Provides an interactive interface to respond to questions or error conditions for a virtual machine running on an ESX or GSX host.

The process begins by establishing a connection with an ESX or GSX host or a virtual machine on a particular host using the *Connect()* method of either the *VMware::VmPerl::Server* or *VMware::VmPerl::VM* objects. The parameter *$connectparams* provides the appropriate input for the *Connect()* method when establishing the connection to a host or virtual machine.

VMware::VmPerl::ConnectParams

The *VMware::VmPerl::ConnectParams* module provides the host information and user credentials required by either the *$server->connect()* or *$vm->connect()*, as well as the methods listed in Table 20.6.

Table 20.6 *VMware::VmPerl::ConnectParams* Methods

Method	Description
$connectparams->get_hostname()	A string value that represents the DNS host name of the VMware ESX or GSX host or its IP address.
$connectparams->get_port()	An integer value representing the TCP port that should be used to establish a connection with the VMware ESX or GSX host. This property is optional.
$connectparams->get_username()	A string value containing the username to pass as credentials for the connection.
$connectparams->get_password()	A string value containing the password for the user set in the *Username* property.

The following demonstrates the instantiation of the *VMware::VmPerl::ConnectParams* object:

```
use VMware::VmPerl;
use VMware::VmPerl::ConnectParams;
use strict;
my $sName = "esxserver1";
my $port = 902;
my $user = "adminuser1";
my $passwd = "password1";
my $connectParams = VMware::VmPerl::ConnectParams::new($sName,$port,$user,$passwd);
```

VMware::VmPerl::Server

The *VMware::VmPerl::Server* module is used for programmatic interaction with, and manipulation of, VMware ESX or GSX hosts running virtual machines. Table 20.7 lists the methods associated with this module. With these methods, you can

- Connect to a server.
- List the virtual machines on that server.
- Register and unregister configuration files for virtual machines.
- Create virtual machine objects
- Disconnect from the server

Table 20.7 *VMware::VmPerl::Server* Methods

Method	Description
$server->connect()	Used to establish a connection with a VMware ESX or GSX host. You must pass *$connectParams* that specifies host information and authentication credentials.
$server->is_connected()	Used to determine if a connection exists.
$server->get_last_error()	Returns an array with information about the last error.
$server->registered_vm_names()	Returns an array with the configuration file name of each virtual machine registered with the host.
$server->register_vm()	Registers a virtual machine with the host. You must pass the configuration file name for the virtual machine.
$server->unregister_vm()	Unregisters a virtual machine from the host. You must pass the configuration file name for the virtual machine.
$server->get_resource()	Gets the value of a particular ESX Server system resource variable. You must pass the variable name. This method applies to ESX Servers only.
$server->set_resource()	Sets the value of a particular ESX Server system resource variable. You must pass the variable name. This method applies to ESX Servers only.

VMware::VmPerl::VM

The *VMware::VmPerl::VM* module is used for controlling interaction with virtual machines on VMware ESX or GSX hosts. Table 20.8 lists the methods associated with this module. Examples of operations provided by this module are

- Connect to a virtual machine.

- Check a virtual machine's state.

- Start, stop, suspend, and resume virtual machines.

- Query and modify configuration file settings.

- Answer status questions from virtual machines.

- Get a basic heartbeat from a virtual machine.

- Pass parameters to and from VMware tools in each virtual machine.

Table 20.8 *VMware::VmPerl::VM* Methods

Method	Description
$vm->connect()	Used to establish a connection with virtual machines running on a VMware ESX or GSX host. You must pass *$connectParams* and the configuration file name for the desired virtual machine.
$vm->is_connected()	Used to determine if a connection exists.
$vm->get_last_error()	Returns an array with information about the last error.
$vm->start()	Powers on a virtual machine. You must pass VM_ POWEROP_MODE for the appropriate behavior for this operation.
$vm->stop()	Powers off a virtual machine. You must pass VM_ POWEROP_MODE for the appropriate behavior for this operation.
$vm->reset()	Powers off and then powers on a virtual machine as a single operation. You must pass VM_POWEROP_MODE for the appropriate behavior.
$vm->suspend()	Suspends a virtual machine. You must pass VM_ POWEROP_MODE for the appropriate behavior for this operation.
$vm->add_redo()	Used to add a redo log to a virtual SCSI disk. You must pass a reference to the target disk for this operation. This method applies to ESX Servers only.
$vm->commit()	Commits all changes in a redo log to a virtual SCSI disk. You must pass a reference to the target disk for this operation along with the LEVEL, FREEZE, and WAIT parameters. This method applies to ESX Servers only.

Table 20.8 Continued

Method	Description
$vm->get_connected_users()	Returns a list of users connected to the host. The list includes connections via a VmCOM or VmPerl API session, MUI, and remote console sessions.
$vm->get_execution_state()	Returns the virtual machine's current state.
$vm->get_guest_info()	Returns the value of a shared variable of the VMware Tools running in a virtual machine, as referenced by the passed key index.
$vm->set_guest_info()	Sets the value of a shared variable of the VMware Tools running in a virtual machine, as referenced by the passed key index.
$vm->get_heartbeat()	Returns the current count for a virtual machine's heartbeat as generated by the VMware Tools.
$vm->get_tools_last_active()	Returns the number of seconds since the last heartbeat was detected by the VMware Tools running inside a virtual machine.
$vm->get_config_file_name()	Returns the name of the configuration file.
$vm->get_config()	Returns the value of a variable from the configuration file of a virtual machine. You must pass the name of the variable to retrieve.
$vm->set_config ()	Sets the value of a variable from the configuration file of a virtual machine. You must pass the name of the variable to set. Note that some variables cannot be changed while a virtual machine is powered on, such as memory size or CPU count.
$vm->get_product_info()	Returns information about the VMware product.
$vm->get_pending_ question()	Returns a *VMware::VmPerl::Question* object with information regarding any pending questions.
$vm->answer_pending_ question()	Used to answer a pending question with an available selection, as indicated by the *VMware::VmPerl:: Question* object.
$vm->device_is_connected()	Used to determine if a virtual device is currently connected. You must pass a reference to the device to target for this operation.
$vm->connect_device()	Connects a currently disconnected virtual device. You must pass a reference to the device to target for this operation.
$vm->disconnect_device()	Disconnects a currently connected virtual device. You must pass a reference to the device to target for this operation.

Continued

Table 20.8 Continued

Method	Description
$vm->get_resource()	Returns the value of a virtual machine resource variable. You must pass a reference of the variable to target for this operation. This method applies to ESX Servers only.
$vm->set_resource()	Sets the value of a virtual machine resource variable. You must pass a reference of the variable to target for this operation. This method applies to ESX Servers only.
$vm->get_uptime()	Returns the uptime of the guest OS in a virtual machine.
$vm->get_id()	Returns the UUID of a virtual machine.
$vm->get_pid()	Returns the process ID of a virtual machine.
$vm->get_capabilities()	Returns the permission of the user used to establish the connection. This method applies to ESX Servers only.
$vm->get_runas_user()	Returns the name of the user running the virtual machine. This method applies to GSX Servers only.
$vm->set_runas_user()	Sets the user credentials for the virtual machine to run under the next time a power-on operation is performed. You must pass the username and password as parameters for this method. This applies to GSX Servers only.

In addition to these methods, the *VMware::VmPerl::VM* module exposes symbolic constants that also provide inputs and outputs to methods in Table 20.8. They are

- **VM_EXECUTION_STATE**   Specifies the state or condition of the virtual machine.
- **VM_POWEROP_MODE**   Specifies the behavior of a power transition operation.
- **VM_PRODINFO_PRODUCT**   Specifies the name of the VMware product.
- **VM_PRODINFO_PLATFORM**   Specifies the host's platform.

VMware::VmPerl::Question

The *VMware::VmPerl::Question* module provides an interface to answer pending questions or error conditions that leave virtual machines in a stuck execution state. As a sub-object to the *VMware:: VmPerl::VM* module, you instantiate the *Question* object by calling the *get_pending_question()* method. Table 20.9 lists the methods associated with this module.

Table 20.9 *VMware::VmPerl::Question* Methods

Method	Description
$question->get_id()	Returns an integer value to identify the question.
$question->get_text()	Returns the text of the question as a string value.
$question->get_choices ()	Returns an array of string values that represent all of the possible answers to the question.

Putting It All Together

With the objects that we have reviewed, you can build simple yet powerful scripts and applications to manage your VMware ESX and GSX Servers and the virtual machines that run on them. Similar to how scripting with WSH and WMI has revolutionized Windows administration similar to what Unix administrators have always enjoyed, you can automate many VMware administration tasks, ensuring that each host and VM has a consistent and managed configuration.

You will really reap the benefits of the VmCOM and VmPerl API as you write scripts and applications to address tasks that were either too complex to perform manually (and subsequently never performed) or too difficult to manage in an infrastructure that frequently changes. In this section, we will review some examples of how the APIs can solve some common problems.

NOTE

For all these examples, and for all of your own development efforts, be sure to have the appropriate Scripting API installed on your development machine, as well as on your test machine, if not the same.

Example 1: Disconnecting Devices from Every Registered VM

Often, VMware administrators put excessive loads on the Service Console by leaving devices that are seldom used connected to the hosted VMs. In particular, administrators should try to disconnect virtual CD/DVD-ROM drives, especially in Windows-based VMs, as well as floppy drives (probably the most unused device), to minimize the overhead these devices place on the Service Console.

For our first example, we will demonstrate a simple administration script using VmPerl to perform this administration task easily, regardless of how many VMs are running on the VMware host.

First, we begin by ensuring that the Perl modules are located and can be used by the script. This is only a consideration that needs to be addressed in Perl scripts running on a Windows-based machine.

```
# This script will disconnect the following devices from the
# running VMs on the target ESX or GSX server:
#      * floppy0
#      * ide1:0
# Add paths when running script on a Windows machine
BEGIN {
  if ($^O eq "MSWin32") {
    @INC = (
      # Set the path to your VmPerl Scripting directory if different
      'C:\Program Files\VMware\VMware VmPerl Scripting
      API\perl5\site_perl\5.005',
      'C:\Program Files\VMware\VMware VmPerl Scripting
      API\perl5\site_perl\5.005\MSWin32-x86');
  }
}
```

Next, we begin instantiating our Perl modules. In this example, we will only need *VMware::VmPerl::ConnectParams*, *VMware::VmPerl::Server*, and *VMware::VmPerl::VM*.

```
use VMware::VmPerl;
use VMware::VmPerl::ConnectParams;
use VMware::VmPerl::Server;
use VMware::VmPerl::VM;
use strict;
```

Then we define our connection parameters and establish a connection with our VMware host. It is always a good practice to code error handling each time you invoke a method. The most basic way to handle any exception is to simply stop the execution of the script with the die directive.

```
# Create a Connect_Params object; no params to new() connects to local machine
my $sName = "esxserver1";
my $port = 902;
my $user = "adminuser1";
my $passwd = "password1";
my $connectParams =
  VMware::VmPerl::ConnectParams::new($sName,$port,$user,$passwd);
# Create a Server object
my $server = VMware::VmPerl::Server::new();
```

```
# Connect to the server using the connect_params
if(!$server->connect($connect_params)) {
   die "Could not connect to local server\n";
}
```

Next, we enumerate the VMs registered with the VMware host and attempt to disconnect the floppy drive and CD-ROM drive from each VM. In this example, we are assuming that only one floppy drive exists as floppy0 and that only one CD/DVD-ROM exists on the IDE bus as ide1:0.

```
# Get a list of registered vmxs
my @list=$server->registered_vm_names();
foreach my $vmx (@list) {
  my $vm = VMware::VmPerl::VM::new();
  if($vm->connect($connect_params, $vmx)) {
    print "\n" . $vm->get_config("displayName");
    if($vm->disconnect_device("floppy0")) {
      print "\n\tFloppy disconnected.";
    } else {
      print "\n\tFloppy not disconnected.";
    }
    if($vm->disconnect_device("ide1:0")) {
      print "\n\tCD-ROM disconnected.";
    } else {
      print "\n\tCD-ROM not disconnected.";
    }
  } else {
    print "\nCould not connect to VM.";
  }
}
```

This script can be easily modified to perform other operations against each VM, such as initiating a snapshot, suspending them, or simply gathering information about each VM as part of a documentation process.

Example 2: Simple GUI to List All Virtual Machines

This example follows a simple workflow, demonstrated in Figure 20.5. First, you capture the basic information as required by the VmConnectParams object in one form. Then you will pass that information to another form that will connect the VMware host and retrieve the list of VMs using the *VmCollection* object. Finally, you will display the configuration file information for each registered VM.

Figure 20.5 Process Diagram for Simple GUI Application

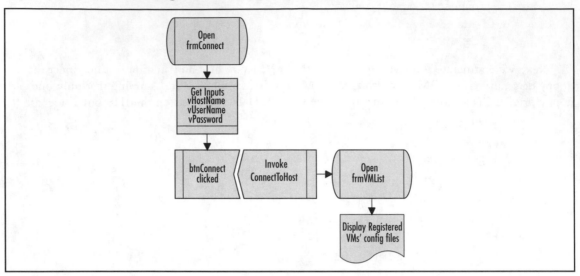

The first step is to create two forms, one called *frmConnect* and the other called *frmVMList*. An example of *frmConnect* is shown in Figure 20.6. This form is composed of three labels, three text boxes (*vHostName*, *vUserName*, and *vPassword*), and one button (*btnConnect*).

Figure 20.6 The Connection Form in Design Mode

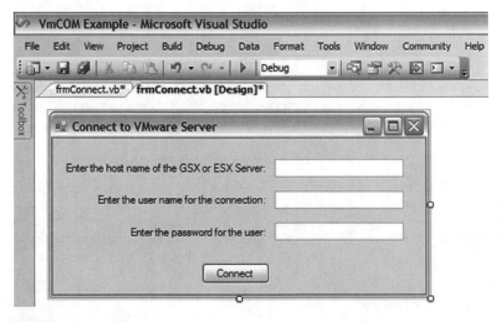

The *btnConnect* control is then used to pass this data to *frmVMList*. This is accomplished by creating a new instance of *frmVMList* and assigning the *ConnectToHost* method to the click event of the control, as shown in the following code fragment.

```
Public Class frmConnect
  Private Sub btnConnect_Click(ByVal sender As Object, ByVal e As _
    System.EventArgs) Handles btnConnect.Click
      Dim VMListForm As New frmVMList
      VMListForm.ConnectToHost(vHostName.Text, vUserName.Text, _
        vPassword.Text)
      VMListForm.Show()
    End Sub
End Class
```

The logic in *frmVMList* captures the value for the host name, username, and password to build to connection parameters. After establishing the connection to the host, we then enumerate all of the VMs registered with the Vmware host and retrieve the configuration file for each one, afterward adding that string value to a *listbox* control visible in the form. The following code shows how this is done.

```
Public Class frmVMList
  Dim objConnParams As New VMCOMLib.VmConnectParams
  Dim objVMServer As New VMCOMLib.VmServerCtl
  Dim objVMList As New VMCOMLib.VmCollection
  Dim ConfigFile As String
  Friend Sub ConnectToHost(ByVal HostName As String, ByVal UserName As _
  String, ByVal Password As String)
    objConnParams.Hostname = HostName
    objConnParams.Username = UserName
    objConnParams.Password = Password
    objVMServer.Connect(objConnParams)
    objVMList = objVMServer.RegisteredVmNames
    For Each ConfigFile In objVMList
      lbxVMs.Items.Add(ConfigFile)
    Next
  End Sub
  Private Sub btnClose_Click(ByVal sender As Object, ByVal e As _
    System.EventArgs) Handles btnClose.Click
      Me.Close()
  End Sub
End Class
```

Figure 20.7 shows a sample output from running our VmCOM sample application. Although this example is basic, you can easily expand on its code base and create your own management application.

Figure 20.7 A Sample Listing Showing the Configuration Files for Each Registered VM

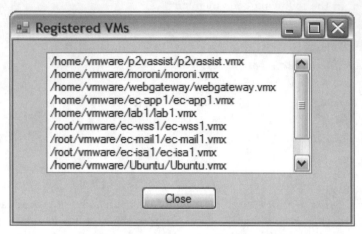

Example 3: Test Automation with VMware

Quality management departments are regularly challenged by the difficulties and expense of configuration testing. To truly certify that software products will run on the wide variety of hardware and software that exists in the field, they must run tests against a daunting variety of configurations. Virtual machines provide a great way to cost-effectively provision the various configurations which the test application runs, including hardware differences (for example, amount of memory, network speed, graphics display resolution, and so on) and software differences (such as OS version, service packs, browsers and their versions, shared libraries, and so forth). However, managing a large library of virtual machines can itself present challenges to the testing process.

You can help realize great benefits by enhancing quality and functional testing further with virtual machines by including automation in the test cycle. By identifying and documenting the testing process and workflow, you can then create automation scripts that quality analysts and managers can run to "initialize" their test environment prior to running a battery of tests, and then release those resources when the test is complete.

The diagram shown in Figure 20.8 demonstrates a process diagram outlining the steps that the automation scripts must take, easily built on Perl or an ActiveX-compatible scripting language. This workflow can involve interaction with other interfaces, such as ADO, WSH, and WMI; however, the Scripting APIs play a big role in the design and execution of this testing process. Although we do not show any script samples here, the operations to be performed are well-documented in the programming and reference guides provided by VMware.

Figure 20.8. Sample Process Diagram for Test Automation with VMware

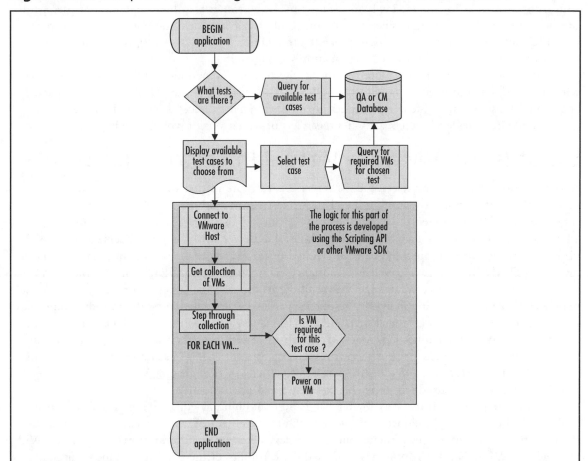

VMware Virtual Infrastructure SDK

Even more powerful than the VMware Scripting APIs, VMware has released Virtual Infrastructure (VI) SDK to give developers a standards-based avenue to manage their VMware investment. Today, there are two versions of the VI SDK tied to the two predominant releases of the VMware ESX Server and VirtualCenter products. In this section, we will review the architecture of the VI SDK 2.0 (for managing ESX 3.0 and VirtualCenter 2.0), as well as the VI SDK 1.1 (for managing ESX Server 2.5.x and VirtualCenter 1.x).

Why continue to discuss the original VI SDK release 1.1? With the release of the Virtual Infrastructure 3 and VI SDK 2.0 in June 2006, VMware is banking on lots of customers upgrading to the latest release to take advantage of the additional benefits and features available. However, the conversion to this major upgrade will take some time, as customer test their upgrade strategies, gain acceptance from the user and business community, and actually perform the upgrades in accordance with their internal change management processes. In addition, VI SDK 1.1 scripts can still be run against the new version if configured for backwards-compatibility.

In the following sections, we will review the architecture and composition of the VI SDK, developing with the SDK 1.1, and developing with the SDK 2.0. Each version of the SDK is discussed separately because of the substantial differences between them; however, the concepts discussed can be incorporated in your development activities regardless of which version you are coding for.

What Is the VMware Virtual Infrastructure SDK?

About the time that VMware released ESX Server 2.x, VMware VirtualCenter started to really become the central tool for managing the virtual infrastructure. Although the Management User Interface, or MUI, continued to be available, it was primarily used for host configuration while administrators chose to manage the virtual machines themselves with the VirtualCenter client. As the virtual infrastructure continued to grow, the MUI also showed its weakness in managing larger farms or arrays of VMware hosts, since each MUI instance can manage one and only one VMware host.

The paradigm change of VI, management shifting its focus to managing in groups in a hierarchal manner rather than managing individual resources was further heightened by the introduction of new infrastructure features such as virtual machine migration, new provisioning techniques and options, and managing virtual machines independently of what VMware host they are running on. Such an extensive and complex management scope provided opportunities to ISVs and savvy administrators and developers to create custom tools to increase the efficiency of managing VI; however, they needed internal hooks into the products to be able to do so in an open manner.

VMware responded to this need by releasing and continuing to enhance the Virtual Infrastructure SDK. With the VI SDK, developers can integrate the management of VMware's server products into their existing data center management solutions or develop a new solution from the ground up. With the release of VI SDK 2.0, VMware has expanded the capability of the SDK to include managed objects and a robust, yet less complex, object model that supports all the previous operations, as well as new ones, such as host configuration, DRS, and HA feature set.

The VI SDK Architecture

The VMware VI SDK is made up of two important elements, the VMware VirtualCenter Web Service and the actual SDK package itself, which contains the supporting binaries needed, samples, and reference and programming guide documentation.

Before starting to develop with the SDK, you must understand its architecture. As shown in Figure 20.9, the VI SDK 1.1 interfaces with the Web service component of VirtualCenter via SOAP calls over HTTP or HTTPS. This interface is the only available Web service for managing virtual machines running VMware ESX hosts. Without VirtualCenter, administrators and developers must utilize the VMware Scripting APIs discussed earlier in this chapter to perform a more limited set of operations against virtual machines.

Figure 20.9 The Virtual Infrastructure SDK 1.1 Architecture

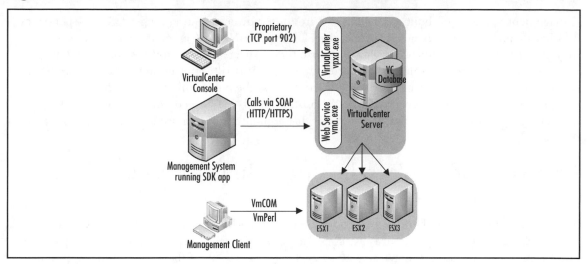

In contrast, Figure 20.10 shows the updated architecture of the VI SDK 2.0, both with and without VirtualCenter implemented. Beginning with the VI SDK 2.0, VMware has standardized the SDK for both ESX hosts and VirtualCenter. In addition, VMware has overhauled the object model and hierarchy of the SDK and included robust host management operations as well. As a result,

Figure 20.10 The Virtual Infrastructure SDK 2.0 Architecture

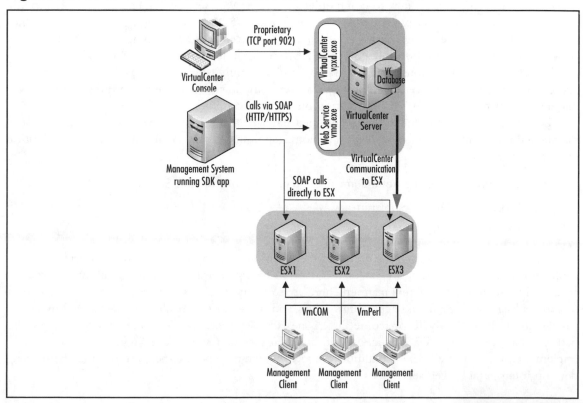

management applications built on VI SDK 2.0 are more powerful and no longer have a dependency on VirtualCenter. That does not mean that the SDK replaces VirtualCenter, though, as enterprises should still implement VirtualCenter to maximize their management capabilities and potential.

The VirtualCenter console, or client, still connects to VirtualCenter using the proprietary VMware communication protocol over TCP port 902, the same as the communication between the VirtualCenter server and the registered ESX hosts. Although the two communication interfaces are different, they both expose the same operations that administrators can use to accomplish the same set of tasks.

Overview of the VMware Virtual Infrastructure Web Service

As previously mentioned, there are two components to the VMware SDK, the Web Service and the SDK package itself. The web service installs as part of the VirtualCenter installation, and as part of the ESX installation (version 3.0 only), and serves as the gateway to all of the advanced management operations that can be performed against VirtualCenter, ESX Server, and virtual machines.

What Are Web Services?

According to the W3C, a Web service is a software system designed to support interoperable machine-to-machine interaction over a network. It has an interface that is described in a format called a Web Service Description Language (WSDL), which is an Extensible Markup Language (XML)-based description on how to communicate with the Web service. Other systems interact with the Web service in a manner prescribed by its interface, or WSDL, by exchanging XML messages that are enclosed in a Simple Object Access Protocol (SOAP) envelope. These messages are typically conveyed using HTTP, and normally comprise XML in conjunction with other Web-related standards. Software applications written in various programming languages and running on various platforms can use Web services to exchange data over computer networks like the Internet in a manner similar to interprocess communication on a single computer.

This interoperability is due to the use of open standards. These standards are defined and maintained by several committees and organizations responsible for the architecture and standardization of Web services, such as:

- Organization for the Advancement of Structured Information Standards (OASIS)
- World Wide Web Consortium (W3C)
- Web Services Interoperability Organization (WS-I)

The latter organization, WS-I, is a charter that promotes interoperability across platforms, applications, and programming languages. Its goal is to be a standards integrator to help Web services advance in a structured, coherent manner. There are so many standards that need to be coordinated to address basic Web service interoperability issues, and the standards are all being developed in parallel and independently. To overcome these issues, the WS-I has developed the concept of a profile, defined as a set of named Web services specifications at specific revision levels, together with a set of implementation and interoperability guidelines recommending how the specifications may be used to develop interoperable Web services.

VMware VI SDK Conformance and Web Service Standards

Both the VMware Infrastructure SDK 1.1 and 2.0 conform to the WS-I Basic Profile 1.0, which expresses a set of assertions about the format and interoperation of the SOAP messages and the WSDL document exchanged between clients and the Web service itself. This profile covers and ensures compliance with the following:

- XML Schema 1.0
- SOAP 1.1
- WSDL 1.1
- UDDI 2.0

One of the advantages of Web services is that they are language-agnostic; any programming language may be used to access the interface. In practice, an adequate Web services toolkit must be available and supported by the chosen language; however, administrators and developers can design management applications based on the SDK with any language and toolkit they choose thanks to the high level of testing and compliance to the above standards.

Operations Available Using the Virtual Infrastructure SDK

The API exposed by the VI Web service provides a powerful set of operations that can be performed when managing your virtual infrastructure. These operations can be categorized into three areas—basic, element management, and virtual computing. The exact set of operations available to you will depend on which version of the VI SDK you are developing against, and what VMware products you are using.

Operations for Basic Web Service Client Interaction

Each version of the VI SDK has standard functionality to facilitate establishing and maintaining connections with the VI Web service. These operations are used regardless of what function or role your applications will have. These basic operations include

- Logging into the Web service
- Logging off from the Web service
- Traversing up and down the object hierarchy
- Grabbing a handle of objects and items exposed by the Web service

Operations for Element Management

Element management consists of the operations used to manage the physical host machine running the VMware ESX Server software. All versions of the VI SDK expose APIs for the following element management operations:

- Virtual machine creation
- Virtual machine deletion

- Virtual machine configuration, including all attributes found in the corresponding VMX file
- Virtual machine power operations, including power on, power off, reset, suspend, and resume
- Virtual machines inventory in a flat namespace
- Virtual disk configuration and management
- Virtual machine guest OS customization
- Physical host and virtual machine performance data collection
- Event and alert management

In addition to these, VI SDK 2.0 also adds the following element management operations that facilitate additional management capabilities for the physical components in the virtual infrastructure:

- Virtual machine inventory with a nested folder hierarchy
- Filtered property collection using the Property Collector
- Host connection and disconnection from VirtualCenter
- Host reboots or shuts down
- Datastore creation and removal from a specific host
- Internet service and firewall configuration for a specific host
- Detection and configuration of storage attached to a host
- Configuration of network interfaces and virtual switches, and configuration for a specific host

Operations for Virtual Computing

Virtual computing consists of the operations used to manage the virtual infrastructure as a whole without targeting any specific host. These operations are more geared towards the virtual machines themselves, providing an API to the features that make VMware VI such a powerful platform. All versions of the VI SDK expose the following virtual computing operations:

- Direct virtual machine management, regardless of which physical host the virtual machines are running on
- Virtual machine migration via VMotion
- Virtual machine provisioning using templates and cloning

The VI SDK 2.0 also adds operations that take advantage of the new features release with VirtualCenter 2.0 and ESX 3.0. These new virtual computing operations are

- Distributed Availability Services (DAS), allowing virtual machines to failover to another host in the event of a host failure.
- Distributed Resource Scheduling (DRS), supporting the migration of virtual machines from one host to another based on resource requirements and desired load-balancing results.

Developing with the Virtual Infrastructure SDK 1.1

The first step to developing with either SDK is to download the appropriate SDK package. The latest package for VI SDK 1.1 when this book was published was build 19058 for VirtualCenter 1.3. The SDK package is distributed as a Zip file that contains two primary directory paths. The first path contains the wsdlProxyGen.exe tool, and the second path contains code samples and automation scripts for building the samples, documentation, and sample vma.wsdl and autoprep-types.xda files.

TIP

It is recommended that you always download and use the latest version of the SDK, available on VMware's site at www.vmware.com/support/developer. Although code that you write against the SDK released alongside a previous release of VirtualCenter may work, it is a good practice to make sure that the SDK is the same version as your VirtualCenter installation or newer.

Central to any interaction or development with a Web service is the consumption of that Web service by the client application. In order to consume the Web service, we must follow three basic steps:

1. Prepare the VI Web service by modifying the configuration file as needed.
2. Generate the proxy class of the VI Web service and consume the Web service source file.
3. Write the code for your management application.

As we walk through these steps, we will demonstrate them in both C# and VB using Microsoft Visual Studio 2005. Even so, this example and walk-through can easily be modified for Java or Perl development. For additional examples of using VI SDK 1.1 in those languages, see the samples included with the SDK Package.

Preparing the Virtual Infrastructure Web Service

Out of the gates, the VMware VI Web service has an initial configuration based on the configuration options selected during the VirtualCenter installation. However, you may find it necessary to modify those configuration settings in order to support your custom management applications. Since the Web service is only used by custom applications with this release of the SDK, any configuration changes made will not impact the functionality of the VirtualCenter client or its interaction with the ESX hosts that are managed by VirtualCenter.

The recommended approach is to test your changes, and then commit them. To do both, you use vma.exe. But first, let's review the configuration options and discuss the syntax for the *vma.exe* command. Code Listing 20.1 is a sample of a vmaConfig.xml file.

Code Listing 20.1 A vmaConfig.xml File

```xml
<vma>
 <service>
  <wsdl>vma.wsdl</wsdl>
  <eventlog rollover="true" file="vma" level="info"
console="true"/>
  <sslport>8443</sslport>
  <externalSchemas>
   <schema>autoprep-types.xsd</schema>
  </externalSchemas>
  <sslCert>C:\Documents and Settings\All UsersApplication
Data\VMware\VMware VirtualCenter\VMA\server.pem</sslCert>
  <sslCAChain>C:\Documents and Settings\All Users\Application
Data\VMware\VMware VirtualCenter\VMA\root.pem</sslCAChain>
 </service>
 <subjects>
  <subject>
   <implementation>VCenter 1.1</implementation>
   <path>/vcenter</path>
   <hostname>localhost</hostname>
   <port>905</port>
   <eventlog level="info"/>
   <ssl>true</ssl>
   <preload>true</preload>
   <index>
    <defaultFarm>Default Farm</defaultFarm>
   </index>
  </subject>
 </subjects>
</vma>
```

Three elements, or sections, make up the Web service configuration: *service, externalSchemas*, and *subjects*. The *service* element, a top-level element, is used to configure the Web service itself. The *externalSchemas* element, a child element of the service, contains a list of all the XSD files that should be included and exposed in addition to the vma.wsdl file. These files are used to customize the VI Web service's schema, and should not be modified. Currently, the only XSD listed is autoprep-types. xsd, which is used to perform customization operations against the guest operating system running in a virtual machine. The *subjects* element, another top-level element, contains child elements, or individual subject elements, that hold configuration attributes used to support connections to other data sources. Only one subject is currently supported, and represents the connection the Web service established with the VirtualCenter Server. Table 20.10 and Table 20.11 describe the configuration attributes for the two top-level elements, service and subjects.

Table 20.10 Service Configuration Attributes

Element	Description
Eventlog	Configures the event logging of the Web service.
Sslport	The port the HTTPS listener is configured to listen on.
sslCert	The certificate file and path.
sslCAChain	The certificate CA chain file and path.

Table 20.11 Subjects Configuration Attributes

Element	Description
Path	Beginning of the VirtualCenter hierarchy.
Hostname	The host name of the VirtualCenter server. Default is "localhost".
Port	TPC port for the proprietary VMware communication with the VirtualCenter server. This is not the same port used for SOAP HTTP-based communication.
Ssl	Boolean parameter for whether the VirtualCenter connection should be secured with SSL.
defaultFarm	The server farm in VirtualCenter that connections will default to.
periodicPerfRefresh Enable	Boolean parameter for performance counters. This attribute is not documented in any of the SDK documentation and does not exist by default. It should only be added if this functionality is needed and will be used.
authorizationEnable	Boolean parameter for the state of managing security with object ACLs. By default, this attribute is not declared in vmaConfig.xml and is enabled. To disable the use of ACLs, add this attribute with the value of false.

Once you have determined what parameters need to be adjusted, you should test those new parameters. You can do this by manually running the VI Web service from a command line. The following steps demonstrate a sample testing process for validating your changes.

1. Make a copy of the vmaConfig.xml file from c:\Documents and Settings\All Users\ Application Data\VMware\VMware VirtualCenter\VMA

2. Edit the copy of vmaConfig.xml with the updated parameters. Among your changes, set eventlog to verbose and console to true.

3. From a command line, change to the directory where the copy of vmaConfig.xml exists.

4. From that directory, run the Web service manually using the following vma.exe statement: <InstallDrive>:\Program Files\VMware\VMware VirtualCenter\vma.exe –config vmaConfig.xml

5. To commit your changes, either copy your modified vmaConfig.xml file to the directory mentioned in step 1 or use the vma.exe command with –update and the appropriate option switches.

6. Restart the VMware VirtualCenter Web Service using the Services MMC snap-in.

Working with the VMware WSDL

With the Web service configured and ready to use, you can now generate a proxy class, or stub, for the VI Web service. This is done by consuming the service source file, or WSDL. You can view the WSDL by browsing the appropriate URL, such as https://esx1.sample.com:8443/?wsdl. The server name and port number will vary, depending on how you have configured your VI Web service.

You can choose to create a proxy using any method. However, you should ensure that any declarations to types defined by the WSDL that conflict with .NET classes are escaped. For example, a stub in the proxy source code for the type CPUPerf (WSDL-defined) with a field called system would normally look like the following snippet:

```
Public System as SystemInfo
```

Since this field will conflict with the .NET predefined class System, it should be escaped by explicitly declaring the field as an XML element attribute and using a name other than "System" in the class declaration, as follows:

```
<System.Xml.Serialization.XmlElementAttribute("System")> _
  Public VMSystem As SystemInfo
```

> **NOTE**
>
> Since our examples here will be based on .NET languages in the Microsoft Visual Studio 2005 IDE, most developers will opt for using the build in a WSDL.exe proxy generator from the command line or including a Web Reference in the project. However, due to misclassifications when running WSDL.exe, these are not valid methods for generating the proxy. For more information, see http://support.microsoft.com/default.aspx?scid=kb;en-us;326790.

The sample application included with the SDK Package demonstrate this workaround, and can be directly included in your projects.

Alternately, VMware provides a proxy generator tool, wsdlProxyGen.exe, which you can use to create the appropriate proxy class for either C# or VB.NET. This tool is a simple GUI that will parse the vma.wsdl file as well as any external schemas referenced, such as autoprep-types.xsd, to create a proper reference source code file. Figure 20.11 demonstrated sample input when using this tool to create a reference file for your project. Using the following steps, you can create your own WSDL proxy to use in your project.

1. Run *wsdlProxyGen.exe* on any Microsoft Windows 2000, XP, or 2003 system.

2. In the Input section, enter or browse to the location of the vma.wsdl file that is included in the SDK Package. For example, the file may be located at C:\VMware-sdk-e.x.p-19058\ SDK\WebService\wsdl\vma.wsdl.

3. In the Output section, enter or browse to the location where you want the resulting output source code file to be located. To reduce steps, you should enter the path to your existing Visual Studio project, if you have created one already. This file should be named appropriately for the language that it will be compiled in, such as *reference.vb* for VB.NET projects, or *reference.cs* for C# projects.

4. Select the appropriate *output language* you want the resulting source code to be in. This, of course, should match the language your project is in.

5. Click **Generate**.

Figure 20.11 VMware's wsdlProxyGen Tool

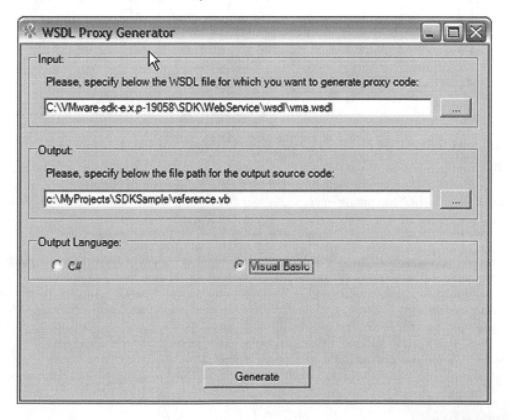

Looking at the resulting file, you will notice important .NET 2.0 namespaces included (if you are developing in Visual Studio .NET 2003, you will see .NET 1.1 namespaces). It is possible that one of the required namespaces, such as System.Web.Services, may not exist as a reference in the project, and will need to be manually added to avoid compilation errors. If you do receive any errors when compiling that state a particular type "is not defined" or that a type "is not a member" in the proxy file you created (as shown in Figure 20.12), add the appropriate reference to the project and attempt to compile again.

Figure 20.12 Compilation Errors Received When System.Web.Services Is Not Imported

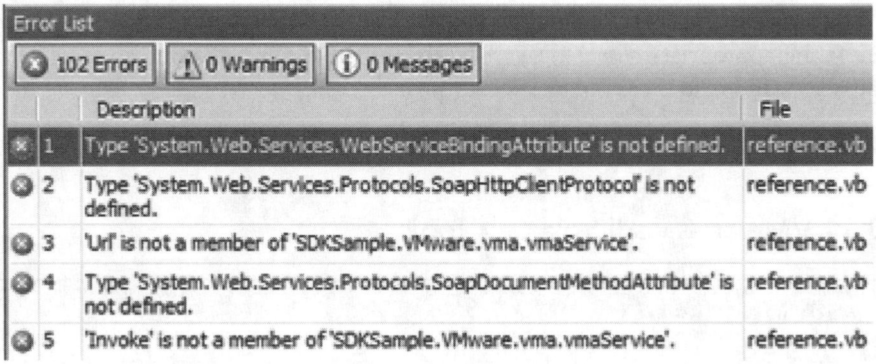

Virtual Infrastructure SDK 1.1 Concepts and Terminology

With all of that preparation out of the way, you are probably ready to jump in and start writing some code. An understanding of the data model and datatypes will allow you to perform the element management and virtual computing operations programmatically. This logical structure of the VI Web service is critical to your success in developing effective and functional applications.

Path Hierarchy

There are several key concepts that must be understood prior to diving into code development against the SDK. The logical presentation of Web service's data and methods is in the structure of a path hierarchy, similar to a file system's hierarchy of directories and files. In this comparison, files are the target of most file system operations, although some operations can be performed against directories as well. Also, directories can contain file or other directories, forming a type of hierarchy that can be traversed. Similarly, the objects exposed by the VI Web service are arranged in a hierarchical structure, as shown in Figure 20.13. This structure can be traversed to accomplish VI management tasks in your applications.

Figure 20.13 The Virtual Infrastructure SDK 1.1 Path Hierarchy

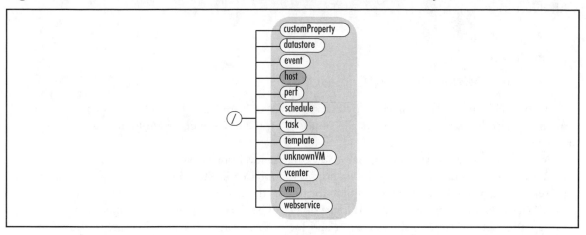

One particular path, /vcenter, can be a particularly large hierarchy. It represents the hierarchy that administrators see using the VirtualCenter client. It can also be one that changes regularly, as administrators reorganize virtual resources into farms and groups. This can cause challenges to your application since targeting a particular host or virtual machine using this path requires that you know its complete path in VirtualCenter. For example, you may have two virtual machines located at the following path:

```
/vcenter/FarmGroup1/VirtualMachineGroup1/VirtualMachineA
/vcenter/FarmGroup1/VirtualMachineGroup2/VirtualMachineB
```

An administrator may choose to relocate VirtualMachineB to a new Virtual Machine Group, VirtualMachineGroup3, resulting in a path as follows:

```
/vcenter/FarmGroup1/VirtualMachineGroup3/VirtualMachineB
```

Without any knowledge of this change, operations that targeted VirtualMachineB would now fail unless the referenced path was altered to reflect the virtual machine's new location. Although it is possible to keep track or identify paths by recursively traversing the entire /vcenter hierarchy to seek out a host or virtual machine, you may choose to use the /host or /vm paths instead. Both /host and /vm are a flat namespace, shortcuts if you will, that contain every host and virtual in the /vcenter hierarchy. Because of its flat nature, you don't have to know its exact path to target it in your application. This can be particularly useful if the only input you have is the host or virtual machine name.

Terminology

While traversing the hierarchy, you will deal with objects and items. Objects are described by an XML document and are the central focus of the VI Web service. This XML document describes the type associated with the object as well as its value. Some objects have child objects that are referenced as nodes in the XML document, and subsequently have their own structure as well. Continuing with our file system analogy, the following is a list of objects exposed by the VI Web service that compare with directories:

- Container

- Farm

- VirtualMachineGroup

All of these objects are containers by nature; however, *Farms* and *VirtualMachineGroups* are special containers with limitations and boundaries imposed on them. Containers are logical assemblies, or arrays, of items.

A container object is the most general and highest-level object type. The *Farm* and *VirtualMachineGroup* objects are also containers, but contain a limited subset of item types. Farms represent the farms in VirtualCenter and are located in the /vcenter path. They can only contain the *VirtualMachineGroup*, *Host*, and *VirtualMachine* objects. The *VirtualMachineGroup* object is also a representation of the same in VirtualCenter and located in /venter. It can only contain the other *VirtualMachineGroup* and *VirtualMachine* objects.

The items, again comparable to files in a file system, are only found within these three object types. They are secured using an ACL, the same security definition you configure in the VirtualCenter client. Each item is identified by a key, which is a unique handle assigned to the item during the session.

The remaining objects, shown in continuation, are all comparable with files in a file system, and are handled similarly:

- Host

- VirtualMachine

- Task

- TaskSchedule

- EventDeclList

- EventCollection

- PerfFilter

- PerfCollection

- Template

In order to work with all of these objects, you will need to get their Handle or vHandle. A handle is a pointer or token that is associated with each object during your connection session. Handles uniquely reference each object; so consequently there can only be one handle per object and only one object per handle. These handles are needed to invoke any operations against the object. Handles are retrieved using the *GetContents* method.

vHandles are similar to handles, but refer to the state of the object at a particular point in time. As objects can change over time, vHandles can be used to determine if any changes have occurred since the last time information was retrieved. vHandles are updated with the *GetUpdates* method and are very efficient since only XML diff documents are sent with the changes, if any, rather than the entire XML document describing the object.

Programming Logic for the SDK

Interaction between your management applications and the Web service will involve certain activities. Which activities you will need to perform will be based on what task you are trying to accomplish. Your application needs to obtain handles to each object that you will perform operations against as referenced by their path. You can then read information about the object through the returned XML document, request updated information about the object, modify and commit any changes (using the *PutUpdates* method), and perform any operations exposed by the Web service.

Your programming logic should also factor in all of the concepts we have discussed so far. For example, if you need to make sure you have the latest information about an object, use the *GetUpdates* method rather than calling *GetContents*. The XML diff document that is returned tends to be much smaller, reducing overall network bandwidth. However, you must have a valid vHandle to be able to call the *GetContents* method.

You should also take the Web service's security model into consideration, as well as how the VM and Host objects are identified. Hosts are referenced using their host name, fully qualified DNS name (FQDN), or IP address, all of which are ways to identify network resources that administrators are familiar with. VMs, however, are not referenced by name or IP, but rather by their universally unique identifier, or UUID. The UUID is a 128-bit hexadecimal number, sometimes called a GUID, and may look something like `564d71c5-d04d-b62e-748a-9020f0ee481e`.

Data Models and Datatypes

Several data models are presented by the Web service, each one focusing on a particular part of VI management. Table 20.12 lists each of these data models exposed by the Web service. Each data model represents a logic structure of datatypes in a hierarchical organization, providing information about ESX hosts, virtual machines, and VirtualCenter-specific items as well.

Table 20.12 Data Models Exposed by the Virtual Infrastructure Web Service

Model	Description
Core Data Model	Describes the hierarchy of the Web service, including the *Container*, *ViewContents*, and *Update* datatypes.
Host Machine Data Model	Describes the ESX host and its configuration. One particular configuration item is whether the host supports the Non-Uniform Memory Architecture, or NUMA. This data model includes the *HostInfo*, *CPUInfo*, *MemoryInfo*, *NetworkInfo*, and *VolumeInfo* datatypes.
Virtual Machine Data Model	Describes the configuration of a virtual machine and its "shares" on the host it is running on. This data model includes the *VirtualMachineInfo*, *GuestInfo*, and *VirtualHardware* datatypes.

Continued

Table 20.12 Continued

Model	Description
Performance Metric Data Model	Describes the performance metrics and counters exposed by the Web service. This model is dependent on the *periodicPerfRefreshEnable* attribute being set in the vmaConfig.xml file. The primary datatype for this data model is *PerfCollector*.
Event Data Model	Describes both ESX host and virtual machine events that are generated and received by VirtualCenter. This data model includes the *EventDeclList* and *EventCollection* datatypes.
Task Data Model	Describes the various tasks that have been created or can be created, as well as those that can be started programmatically. This data model includes the *Task* and *TaskSchedule* datatypes.
Template Data Model	Describes the templates found in the VirtualCenter template repository used to create new virtual machines. This data model only contains a single datatype, *Template*.
Guest Customization Data Model	Describes the configuration items that can be customized when creating new virtual machines from templates. The primary datatype for this data model is *autoprep*. This data model is directly linked to autoprep-types.xsd referenced as an external schema in vmaConfig.xml.

As described earlier, the data models contain information that can be retrieved by your management application. This information is accessed as a datatype that is presented in a hierarchical organization and retrieved as a response to certain methods, such as *GetContents*, *GetUpdates*, *QueryPerfData*, and others.

Datatypes contain one or more fields that further describe the datatype. These fields can be retrieved, modified using the *PutUpdates* method if supported, or linked to other datatypes within the data model's hierarchy. The field values can either be one of the common types, *xsd:int*, *xsd:string*, *xsd: long*, and *xsd:Boolean*, or references to another datatype through a special field, or key.

There are too many datatypes to list in this chapter. However, you can get a complete listing by referencing pages 37–112 of the *Virtual Infrastructure SDK Reference Guide* available for download at www.vmware.com/support/developer/vc-sdk.

Developing Your Management Application

We are now ready to dive into coding management applications. Your applications can perform several functions, such as:

- Systems management
- Performance management

- Provisioning
- Utility computing
- Disaster recovery
- Clustering
- Niche vertical applications

In the previous sections, we discussed all of the core concepts, terminology, and data models. Using that information, we will look at several code examples in both Visual Basic and C#, and we will discuss the process of connecting to the Web service, obtaining the handle for objects, and working with those objects.

The Connection Process

Your application must first connect to the Web service using methods exposed by the stub you created. At this point, you have already created a new project in Visual Studio and have generated the stub, of proxy class, and included it in your project. Code Listings 20.2 and 20.3 demonstrate how to connect to the VI Web service.

Code Listing 20.2 C# Script for Connecting to VI Web Service

```
using System;
using VMware.vma;
protected vmaService vma_;
string url = "https://esx1.sample.com:8443";
string username = "adminuser1";
string password = "password1";
public void Connect(string url, string username, string password) {
  vma_ = new vmaService();
  vma_.Url = url;
  vma_.CookieContainer = new System.Net.CookieContainer();
  vma_.Login(username, password);
}
```

Code Listing 20.3 VB.NET Script for Connecting to VI Web Service

```
Imports System
Imports VMware.vma
Protected vma As VMware.vma.vmaService
Dim url As String = "https://esx1.sample.com:8443"
Dim username As String = "adminuser1"
Dim password As String = "password1"
Public Function Connect(url As string, username As string, password As _string)
```

```
     vma = New vmaService
     vma.Url = url
     vma.CookieContainer = New System.Net.CookieContainer
     vma.Login(username, password)
End Function
```

In the preceding example, we started with some declarations, including the required string variants for the URL for the Web service, the username to use in the connection, and its password. We also declared an instance of the class *VMware.vma.vmaService* as vma. This will be the base class that exposes the Web service.

The properties of the *vmaService* class needed to properly handle a connection to the Web service are *vma.Url* and *vma.CookieContainer*. The CookieContainer is a special system container that will host a collection of cookies collected during our session, a requirement if your application will need to maintain session state. With those properties set, we can then call the Login method, passing the user credentials we established previously. Upon successfully logging in to the VI Web service, the following response is received.

```
<?xml version="1.0" encoding="UTF-8"?>
<env:Envelope xmlns:xsd="http://www.w3.org/2001/XMLSchema"
xmlns:env="http://schemas.xmlsoap.org/soap/envelope/"
xmlns:xsi="http://www.w3.org/2001/XMLSchema-instance">
  <env:Body>
    <LoginResponse xmlns="urn:vma1">
    </LoginResponse>
  </env:Body>
</env:Envelope>
```

Since this is a process that is required for any type of management application that you develop, the remaining examples in this section will assume that vma has already been declared and a session with the VI Web service has already been successfully established.

Handling SSL Certificates

In most cases, you will connect to the Web service through the HTTPS listener instead of HTTP. By default, every VirtualCenter installation comes with a certificate that is used to secure the VI Web service. However, as shown in Figure 20.14, the certificate is not a valid one for production use since it was not issued by a trusted root certificate authority (CA). You can choose to handle this condition one of two ways. First, you can replace the certificate with a valid one from a trusted CA and update the vmaConfig.xml accordingly, as discussed earlier in the chapter. Another option would be to handle the "bad" certificate programmatically in your application. Although the certificate cannot be trusted, it can still be used to encrypt the HTTP data payload transmitted between the management client and the Web service.

Figure 20.14 A Default VMware Test Certificate

The latter option is the most common and still provides adequate security for most situations. The examples found in the SDK package all include a sample workaround which we will discuss briefly. The key component is the CertPolicy.vb or CertPolicy.cs file, which can be copied from any sample and added to your project. Using the System.Security.Cryptography.X509Certificates .NET component and hashtables, the CheckValidationResult function is passed the certificate and assesses its validity. If the function detects any issues with the certificate, it will then display a message box stating any problems that were found, and presenting the management client user the option to continue regardless.

To take advantage of this certificate validation functionality, you can implement ICertificatePolicy. Then you must pass ICertificatePolicy to ServicePointManager.CertificatePolicy before any Web service method calls are made. Include the following code in the client code. Before you make the Web service method call from the client code, the following statement must be executed in C#:

```
System.Net.ServicePointManager.CertificatePolicy = new CertPolicy();
```

In VB.NET the code is as follows:

```
System.Net.ServicePointManager.CertificatePolicy = New CertPolicy
```

In addition to using the CertPolicy distributed in the SDK package, you can create you own CertPolicy that will validate, for example, all certificates. The script shown in Code Listings 20.4 and 20.5 implements ICertificatePolicy and then accepts every request under SSL.

Code Listing 20.4 C# Script for Implementing ICertificatePolicy

```
using System.Net;
using System.Security.Cryptography.X509Certificates;
public class CertPolicy : ICertificatePolicy {
  public bool CheckValidationResult(
     ServicePoint svcPnt
   , X509Certificate cert
   , WebRequest req
   , int certProblem) {
   return true;
  } // end CheckValidationResult
} // class CertPolicy
```

Code Listing 20.5 VB.NET Script for Implementing ICertificatePolicy

```
Imports System.Net
Imports System.Security.Cryptography.X509Certificates
Public Class CertPolicy Implements ICertificatePolicy
  Public Function CheckValidationResult(ByVal _
    svcPnt As ServicePoint, ByVal cert As X509Certificate, _
    ByVal req As WebRequest, ByVal certProblem As Integer) _
     As Boolean Implements ICertificatePolicy.CheckValidationResult
    Return True
  End Function
End Class
```

Obtaining with Object Handles

Once connected, you can now target specific objects in order to get or modify their information or perform operations. The *ResolvePath* method is used to obtain the handle for the object represented by the path, and the *GetContents* method is used to retrieve the XML document that is the value of the object. Code Listings 20.6 and 20.7 continue our sample code:

Code Listing 20.6 C# Script for Obtaining Information with *ResolvePath* and *GetContents*

```
string path = "/vm";
string handle = vma_.ResolvePath(path);
ViewContents contentsXML = vma_.GetContents(handle);
Container objContainer = (Container) contentsXML.body;
```

Code Listing 20.7 VB.NET Script for Obtaining Information with *ResolvePath* and *GetContents*

```
Dim contentsXML As VMware.vma.ViewContents
Dim objContainer As VMware.vma.Container
Dim path As String = "/vm"
Dim handle As String = vma.ResolvePath(path)
contentsXML = = vma.GetContents(handle)
objContainer = CType(contentsXML.body, VMware.vma.Container)
```

In this example, we target /vm of the VI Web service hierarchy. We obtain its handle by invoking *ResolvePath* and passing it the string value of the path as set by vPath. The returned XML document from invoking *ResolvePath* is similar to Code Listing 20.8.

Code Listing 20.8 XML Document Returned by Invoking *ResolvePath*

```xml
<?xml version="1.0" encoding="UTF-8"?>
<env:Envelope xmlns:xsd="http://www.w3.org/2001/XMLSchema"
xmlns:env="http://schemas.xmlsoap.org/soap/envelope/"
xmlns:xsi="http://www.w3.org/2001/XMLSchema-instance">
<env:Body>
  <GetContentsResponse xmlns="urn:vma1">
    <returnval>
      <handle>vma-0000-0000-0008</handle>
      <vHandle>vma-0000-0000-0008@c2f53ca4e000003</vHandle>
      <body xsi:type="Container">
        <item>
          <key>vma-vm-00000000011</key>
          <name>564d0f8b-3bde-1003-fe19-0f77cc31a3dc</name>
          <type>VirtualMachine</type>
        </item>
        <item>
          <key>vma-vm-00000000012</key>
          <name>564d71c5-d04d-b62e-748a-9020f0ee481e</name>
          <type>VirtualMachine</type>
        </item>
        <item>
          <key>vma-vm-00000000014</key>
          <name>564d63db-9aaf-97af-4c47-8562e1dc65e0</name>
          <type>VirtualMachine</type>
        </item>
```

```
      <item>
        <key>vma-vm-00000000015</key>
        <name>564d71b4-d1fc-fdb9-9c4b-125b3ba0b32a</name>
        <type>VirtualMachine</type>
      </item>
    </body>
  </returnval>
  </GetContentsResponse>
  </env:Body>
</env:Envelope>
```

With that handle, we then obtain the contents of the object located at the path using *GetContents*, retrieving its descriptive XML document as a ViewContents datatype, converting the body of the returned document to a collection of relevant items as a Container datatype. In some cases, you will want to retrieve updates from an object to process or evaluate items that have changed. Although you can request the full contents XML document again, doing so may generate a large amount of network traffic and impact application performance. Instead, utilize the *GetUpdates* method to retrieve just the items that have changed, passing with the vHandle of the object to update.

The vHandle is an item that is passed along with the handle in the results of calling the *GetContents* method. In fact, the vHandle is comprised of the handle plus a timestamp. For example, an object may have a handle of vma-0000-0000-0008. Consequently, the vHandle returned with a handle by *GetContents* is vma-0000-0000-0008@c2f53ca4e000003. Every time an item is updated, the vHandle will change, denoting that an update is available. The timestamp is used as a reference point and lets the Web service know if the information that the management client has is older than what is currently available. Code Listings 20.9 and 20.10 demonstrate the use of vHandles in C# and VB.NET, respectively.

Code Listing 20.9 C# Script for Using vHandles

```
while (
  myTask.currentState.Equals(TaskRunState.running) ||
  myTask.currentState.Equals(TaskRunState.scheduled) ||
  myTask.currentState.Equals(TaskRunState.starting)
) {
  VMware.vma.VHandleList vhlist = new VHandleList();
  vhlist.vHandle = new string[] { vc.vHandle };
  UpdateList ul = vma_.GetUpdates(vhlist, true);
  for (int u = 0; u > ul.update.Length; u++) {
    for (int c = 0; c < ul.update[u].change.Length; c++) {
      if (ul.update[u].change[c].target == "currentState") {
```

```
        myTask.currentState =
        (TaskRunState)ul.update[u].change[c].val;
      } else if (ul.update[u].change[c].target ==
        "percentCompleted") {
      myTask.percentCompleted =
        (Single)ul.update[u].change[c].val;
      Console.Write("..." +
        myTask.percentCompleted.ToString());
    }
  }
 }
}
```

Code Listing 20.10 VB.NET Script for Using VHandles

```
While migrateTask.currentState = VMware.vma.TaskRunState.running Or _
  migrateTask.currentState = VMware.vma.TaskRunState.scheduled Or _
  migrateTask.currentState = VMware.vma.TaskRunState.starting
    Dim vhlist As VMware.vma.VHandleList = New VMware.vma.VHandleList
    vhlist.vHandle = New String() {vc.vHandle}
    Dim ul As VMware.vma.UpdateList = vma.GetUpdates(vhlist, True)
    For u = 0 To ul.update.Length - 1
      For c = 0 To ul.update(u).change.Length - 1
        If (ul.update(u).change(c).target = "currentState") Then
          migrateTask.currentState = ul.update(u).change(c).val
        ElseIf (ul.update(u).change(c).target = "percentCompleted") Then
          migrateTask.percentCompleted = ul.update(u).change(c).val
          Console.Write("..." + migrateTask.percentCompleted.ToString())
      End If
    Next c
  Next u
End While
```

Here we pass the vHandleList (an array of vHandles to be updated) to the *GetUpdates* method. This method has a Boolean parameter that defines whether the Web service should wait to send a response until at least one of the vHandles in the vHandleList changes. This blocking action is less intensive than polling for updates on a regular interval and also a more real-time response for change notifications. The diff that returns as an XML document consists of change elements that describe the changes in the update.

Retrieving Items and Performing Operations

The containers consist of items that each have a key, name, type, and ACL. The key is also the handle for the item named. Issuing *GetContents* against an object that is not a container will return an

XML document that contains information relevant to that object type, such as Hosts and virtual machines. In Code Listings 20.11 and 20.12, we demonstrate enumerating all virtual machines in a particular Virtual Machine Group and their CPU and memory performance configuration.

Code Listing 20.11 C# Script for Enumerating VMs in a Particular Group

```
string path = "/vcenter/ESXFarm1/ProductionVMs-Fin";
string handle = vma_.ResolvePath(path);
ViewContents contentsXML = vma_.GetContents(handle);
Container objContainer = (Container)contentsXML.body;
Item[] listVMs = objContainer.item;
for (int i = 1; i <= listVMs.Length-1; i++)
{
  contentsXML = vma_.GetContents(listVMs(i).key);
  VirtualMachine vm = contentsXML.body;
  string Name = vm.info.name
  int cfgNumCPU = vm.hardware.cpu.count
  string cfgCPUShares = vm.hardware.cpu.controls.shares
  int cfgSizeMem = vm.hardware.memory.sizeMb
  string CfgMemShares = vm.hardware.memory.controls.shares
  string msg = vmName + "\t"+ cfgNumCPU + "\t" + cfgCPUShares +
    "\t" + cfgSizeMem + "\t" + CfgMemShares;
  System.Console.WriteLine(msg);
}
```

Code Listing 20.12 VB.NET Script for Enumerating VMs in a Particular Group

```
Dim path, handle, vmName, cfgCPUShares, CfgMemShares, msg As String
Dim i, cfgNumCPU, cfgSizeMem As Integer
Dim contentsXML As VMware.vma.ViewContents
Dim objContainer As VMware.vma.Container
Dim listVMs() As VMware.vma.Item
Dim vm As VMware.vma.VirtualMachine
path = "/vcenter/ESXFarm1/ProductionVMs-Fin"
handle = vma.ResolvePath(path)
contentsXML = vma.GetContents(handle)
objContainer = CType(contentsXML.body, VMware.vma.Container)
listVMs = objContainer.item
For i = 0 To listVMs.Length - 1
  contentsXML = vma.GetContents(listVMs(i).key)
  vm = contentsXML.body
  vmName = vm.info.name
```

```
cfgNumCPU = vm.hardware.cpu.count
cfgCPUShares = vm.hardware.cpu.controls.shares
cfgSizeMem = vm.hardware.memory.sizeMb
CfgMemShares = vm.hardware.memory.controls.shares
msg = vmName & vbTab & cfgNumCPU & vbTab & cfgCPUShares & _
  vbTab & cfgSizeMem & vbTab & CfgMemShares
System.Console.WriteLine(msg)
Next i
```

This example outputs the name, number of virtual CPUs, configured CPU shares, the amount of memory allocated, and the configured memory shares for each virtual machine in the ProductionVMs-Fin Virtual Machine Group. We also take advantage of the virtual machine data model, traversing the various data types in the data model's hierarchy.

We can use a similar set of logic to perform operations against a single object or a group of objects. Code Listings 20.13 and 20.14 demonstrate performing a virtual machine migration operation via VMotion.

Code Listing 20.13 C# Script for Migrating a VM via VMotion

```
string handleHost = vma_.ResolvePath(pathHost);
string handleVM = vma_.ResolvePath(pathVM);
ViewContents contentsXML = vma_.MigrateVM(handleVM, handleHost,
  Level.normal);
```

Code Listing 20.14 VB.NET Script for Migrating a VM via VMotion

```
Dim handleHost, handleVM As String
Dim contentsXML As VMware.vma.ViewContents
handleHost = vma.ResolvePath(pathHost)
handleVM = vma.ResolvePath(pathVM)
contentsXML = vma.MigrateVM(vm, host, VMware.vma.Level.normal)
```

In this example, the handles for both the virtual machine and the target host are retrieved using *ResolvePath*. The *MigrateVM* method is then invoked to initiate the migration process. The request to migrate the virtual machine is returned with a new handle for the task, as well as an XML document that describes the task's details. This particular operation, like many others, can be monitored by using the returned vHandle to retrieve updates on the task's progress. For example, Code Listing 20.15 is a sample result from a *StopVM* operation.

Code Listing 20.15 Results for a *StopVM* Operation

```
<?xml version="1.0" encoding="UTF-8"?>
<env:Envelope xmlns:xsd="http://www.w3.org/2001/XMLSchema"
xmlns:env="http://schemas.xmlsoap.org/soap/envelope/"
xmlns:xsi="http://www.w3.org/2001/XMLSchema-instance">
```

```
<env:Body>
  <StopVMResponse xmlns="urn:vma1">
    <returnval>
      <handle>vma-task-active-0a810</handle>
      <vHandle>vma-task-active-0a810@c2f53ca4e000001</vHandle>
      <body xsi:type="Task">
        <cause>user</cause>
        <entity>vma-vm-00000000012</entity>
        <eventCollector>vma-0000-0000-009b</eventCollector>
        <operationName>Power off VM</operationName>
        <queueTime>2006-07-12T00:56:10-05:00</queueTime>
        <allowCancel>false</allowCancel>
        <currentState>starting</currentState>
      </body>
    </returnval>
  </StopVMResponse>
</env:Body>
</env:Envelope>
```

Updating Interior Nodes

Similar to how the *GetUpdates* method returns a list of changes that are of the Change datatype, you can also work with changes using the *PutUpdates* method. Some of the data values, or interior nodes, returned by *GetContents* or *GetUpdates* can be edited, inserted into, deleted, moved, or replaced. By using the *PutUpdates* method, you can make on-the-fly configuration changes to effectively manage your virtual infrastructure. Code Listings 20.16 and 20.17 demonstrate how to change the priority of a virtual machine by adjusting the shares allocated to its vCPUs.

Code Listing 20.16 C# Script for Changing the Priority of a VM

```
ViewContents vc = vma_.GetContents(vm);
Change change = new Change();
change.target = "hardware/cpu/controls/shares";
change.val = "high";
change.op = ChangeOp.edit;
change.valSpecified = true;
ChangeReqList changeList = new ChangeReqList();
ChangeReq changeReq = new ChangeReq();
changeReq.handle = vc.handle;
changeReq.change = new Change[] { change };
ChangeReq[] changeReqs = new ChangeReq[] { changeReq };
changeList.req = changeReqs;
UpdateList updateList = vma_.PutUpdates(changeList);
```

Code Listing 20.17 VB.NET Script for Changing the Priority of a VM

```
Dim vc As VMware.vma.ViewContents = vma.GetContents(vm)
Dim change As New VMware.vma.Change
change.target = "hardware/cpu/controls/shares"
change.val = "high"
change.op = VMware.vma.ChangeOp.edit
change.valSpecified = True
Dim changeList As New VMware.vma.ChangeReqList
Dim changeReq As New VMware.vma.ChangeReq
changeReq.handle = vc.handle
changeReq.change = New VMware.vma.Change() {change}
Dim changeReqs() As VMware.vma.ChangeReq = {changeReq}
changeList.req = changeReqs
Dim updateList As VMware.vma.UpdateList = vma.PutUpdates(changeList)
```

In this example, we used several datatypes to perform the update operation. *PutUpdates* is passed a *ChangeReqList* as input. This datatype is an array of the *ChangeReq* datatypes containing the handles or vHandles of the objects to be updated. Each change in the set is of the *Change* datatype. This interface allows multiple changes to an object to be performed by using one *PutUpdates* call.

Developing with the Virtual Infrastructure SDK 2.0

With the release of Virtual Infrastructure (VI) 3, VMware has made a considerable departure from the architecture of the ESX Server and VirtualCenter products. Similarly, the latest VI SDK supporting this release has substantially changed. We will review the primary changes and key concepts that you need to know to effectively develop code against the new SDK, as well as introduce some of the new features available in VI 3 and exposed by the SDK.

VMware has made available guides to ease your introduction to the VI SDK 2.0. If you are a seasoned VI SDK developer, these guides will be instrumental in helping you transition to the new SDK. The code references in this chapter are Microsoft-centric, focused on VB.Net or C#. You can reference the programming and reference guides for additional information about developing against the VI SDK 2.0 in Java or Perl.

Features Added to Virtual Infrastructure 2.0

Let's dive in now with a discussion of the differences between the two versions of the SDK, principally regarding what new items or functionality have been added, as shown in Table 20.13. You can perform all of the same operations in VI SDK 2.0 that you could in VI SDK 1.x; however, VMware has made some substantial changes with the new releases. The following is a list of some of those new features.

Table 20.13 New Features Added to Virtual Infrastructure SDK 2.0

Category	Feature	Description
Virtual Infrastructure Management	Web service availability	The VI SDK 2.0 is now available through both the Virtual Infrastructure Web service hosted on the VirtualCenter Management Server as well as the Web service running on the ESX hosts themselves. The latter is provisioned by the *host agent*.
	Host configuration	ESX hosts can now be configured via the SDK.
	All ESX and Virtual Center features available	All of the new features in ESX 3.0 and VirtualCenter 2.0 are available programmatically through the VI Web service.
Object Model	Consolidated inventory hierarchy	All manageable objects and data are now located within a single inventory hierarchy or tree, including hosts, virtual machines, data centers, networks, and datastores.
	Abstraction of resources	The new SDK offers a complete abstraction of VI resources, including physical computer resources, resource pools, and clusters.
	PropertyCollector	A new mechanism that supports filtering of complex resources.
	SearchIndex	A mechanism for searching the inventory hierarchy for a specific managed entity based on one of its properties, such as name, UUID, or IP address.

In addition to the new and enhanced features, VI SDK 2.0 has changed from the perspective of the Web service itself. Hosted by both the VirtualCenter Management Server as well as the ESX server's host agent, the definition of the Web service has also changed substantially.

Preparing the Virtual Infrastructure 2.0 Web Service

The VMware VI 2.0 Web service has an initial configuration based on the configuration options selected during the VirtualCenter installation. You can customize the Web service, just as you can the VI 1.0 Web service, if you find it necessary to modify those configuration settings in order to support your custom management applications. The Web service is available on both the VirtualCenter Management Server and the ESX Server, each with its own configuration location and parameters.

For the VirtualCenter Management Server, you can find the Web service configuration at *C:\Documents and Settings\All Users\Application Data\VMware\VMware VirtualCenter\vpxd.cfg*. On an ESX host, you must modify the */etc/vmware/hostd/config.xml* file. This file is the configuration file for all host agent functions, not just the VI Web service, so you should exercise caution modifying this file in particular. Code Listing 20.18 shows the port configuration for the HTTP/HTTPS proxy.

Code Listing 20.18 Port Configuration for the HTTP/HTTPS Proxy

```
<proxyDatabase>
  <server id="0">
    <namespace> / </namespace>
    <host> localhost </host>
    <port> -1 </port>
  </server>
  <server id="1">
    <namespace> /sdk </namespace>
    <host> localhost </host>
    <port> -2 </port>
  </server>
  <redirect id="2">/ui</redirect>
  <server id="3">
    <namespace> /mob </namespace>
    <host> localhost </host>
    <port> 8087 </port>
  </server>
</proxyDatabase>
```

Table 20.14 describes some of the properties you may want to consider changing to customize the VI Web service to support your management applications. You should create a backup copy of the configuration files, though, before making any changes. Once you have saved the updated version of the configuration file, you must restart the Web service. On a VirtualCenter Management Server, this can be done using the Services control panel applet. On an ESX host, you can restart the host agent with the command *service mgmt-vmware restart*.

Table 20.14 Configuration Information for the VirtualCenter Web Service

Element	Node/Item	Description
ws1x	Enabled	Boolean that defines whether the Web service should support the 1.x SDK calls. Notice that enabling this will disable some functionality in the SDK 2.0 realm. This only applies to the VirtualCenter Web service.
	Datafile	File path to the WS1X file needed to set up the VI SDK 1.x–compatible environment. This only applies to the VirtualCenter Web service.
vpxd	namespace (proxyDatabase)	Relative path of the site being configured, such as "/", "/sdk", or "/mob".
	host (proxyDatabase)	The host that is being proxied. This value should always be the management server. You may want to change the value to the host name if our security policy requires that you remove the *localhost* reference from the local DNS cache.
	port (proxyDatabase)	The port that the HTTP/HTTPS process hosting the management site is listening on.
	Serializeadds	The DAS parameter. Boolean value for whether VirtualCenter should add proposed VMs in a serial manner or concurrently. The default value is *true*. This only applies to the VirtualCenter Web service.
vmacore	TaskMax	Maximum number of concurrently running threads for task-related operations. If you notice that your tasks queue up excessively, you can increase this number. *10* is the default. This only applies to the VirtualCenter Web service.

Working with the VMware VI SDK 2.0 WSDLs

The VMware VI SDK 2.0 Web Service is far more complex than its predecessor. As a result, the WSDLs that describe the interaction with the Web service are much larger in size compared to the WSDL for VI SDK 1.x. There are two options at your disposal for obtaining the necessary stubs to work in your VB.Net or C# code: user-generated stubs or pre-generated, VMware provided stubs.

If you choose to generate your own stubs, you can either run the *Build2003.cmd* or *Build2005. cmd* commands found in the SDK package or run wsdl.exe directly. The following example shows the portion of the build batch files for Visual Studio 2005 included in the SDK package that generates the .CS stubs and compiles them as VimService2005.dll.

```
wsdl /n:VimApi /out:stage\VimObjects.cs ..\..\vimService.wsdl ..\..\vim.wsdl
csc /t:library /out:VimService2005.dll stage\*.cs
```

This sample generates a stub file, **VimObjects.cs**, in the \stage directory. This stub is a merge of *vimService.wsdl* and *vim.wsdl*. You can choose to include VimObjects.cs directly in your source code for your project, or reference *VimService* in your project, being sure to include VimService.dll in your /bin directory. A similar approach would be used for VB.NET, which creates as output the VimObjects.vb stub that you can compile to create VimService2005.dll.

The simpler option would be to use the reference.vb or reference.cs files found in the \SDK directory of the SDK package and include that file in your project, or copy the VimService2005.dll found in the \SDK\samples_2_0\DotNet directory of the SDK package to the \bin directory and reference it in your project.

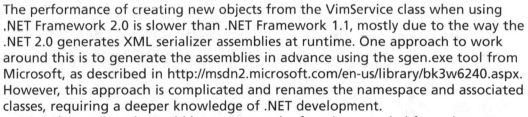

TIP

The performance of creating new objects from the VimService class when using .NET Framework 2.0 is slower than .NET Framework 1.1, mostly due to the way the .NET 2.0 generates XML serializer assemblies at runtime. One approach to work around this is to generate the assemblies in advance using the sgen.exe tool from Microsoft, as described in http://msdn2.microsoft.com/en-us/library/bk3w6240.aspx. However, this approach is complicated and renames the namespace and associated classes, requiring a deeper knowledge of .NET development.

Another approach would be to extract the functions needed from the generated class while still referencing the VimService DLL. This is particularly useful for simpler projects that do not require all of the methods and functions exposed by VimService. One way to perform this extract would be to execute the following steps:

1. Create a new class (in this example, *myClass*) that inherits from the *SoapHttpClientProtocol* class.

2. Open **\stage\VimObjects.cs**, included in the VI SDK 2.0 package.

3. Copy the class *XmlIncludeAttribute*, removing any items you do not need in your project.

4. Include a reference to VimService2005.dll and place "using Vim" in *myClass* for each method retained.

5. Locate each method and copy/paste the code to *myClass*.

Virtual Infrastructure SDK 2.0 Concepts and Terminology

The key to moving forward with your development efforts using VI SDK 2.0 is your understanding of the SDK's architecture. Whether you have experience developing with the previous VI SDK 1.x or you are new to programming against the VI SDK, you will find that the concepts and terminology are critical to the functionality you plan on incorporating into your next management application. In this section, we will discuss the object model and review a few of the critical management objects central to most development efforts.

Data and Managed Objects

Managed objects are composite objects that exist on ESX host and the VirtualCenter 2 management server. They do not exist in the WSDL schema, but are passed indirectly as references, called managed object references, in the WSDL data stream between the Web service and the management client. Data objects, in turn, are also composite objects that are passed by value between the management client and Web service.

Since data objects are actually passed between client and Web service, they are treated in an object-oriented manner. The WSDL schema is not object-oriented itself; however, the class hierarchy of the WSDL can be represented as a hierarchical chain of properties that are exposed by instantiated data objects. The key distinguishing factor for data objects is that they only have properties, or values, not methods. Those values are passed in SOAP messages compliant to the WSDL schema as XML elements serialized by the Web service and client. Operations, in contrast, are components of methods contained in managed objects.

Throughout your coding efforts, you must obtain managed object references. These references are derived from managed object methods, or operations, presented by the WSDL schema. You can learn more about the managed object associated with the reference by:

1. Calling a method associated with the managed object that reports its properties.

2. Calling a method associated with the managed object that returns a data object. The value defined in the data objects can tell you more about the managed object itself.

3. Create a *property collector* filter that can be used to retrieve the properties from or monitor the managed object. Property collectors will be discussed in more detail later in the chapter.

Managed Entity Inventory

Using the VI SDK 2.0, you can manage your infrastructure's virtual machines and host resources using a hierarchical model that represents the inventory, as shown in Figure 20.15. This inventory, as found in VirtualCenter, contains managed entities of various types, including datacenters, resource pools, virtual machines, and hosts. The managed entities are organized and grouped into folders. This hierarchical inventory is in its most complete form when working with the VirtualCenter product. A more limited version of the inventory model is available on hosts.

Figure 20.15 Logical Representation of the Managed Entity Inventory from the VirtualCenter Hierarchy

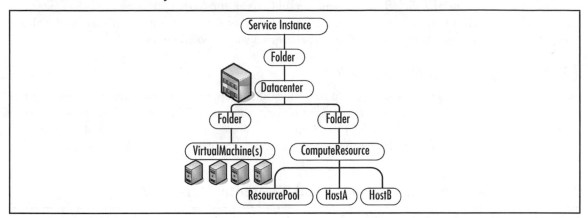

Host Agent versus VirtualCenter Feature Set

VirtualCenter 2 has not changed in function from its predecessor, VirtualCenter 1.x. The product is still designed to help Virtual Infrastructure administrators design, deploy, and manage virtual machines and, new to this release, hosts. The hosts can either be the ESX 3, ESX 2.x, or VMware Server (formerly GSX Server).

The major differences between using the SDK to manage through the Service Instance presented by VirtualCenter and the Service Instance presented by a standalone host are

- **Management of resources**   Refined control of resource pools that scale across more than one host, treating resources as a collective whole rather than that offered by a single physical host. This is also supplemented by VMware DRS and VMware HA, features not available on standalone hosts.

- **Provisioning of new virtual machines**   Deployment of new virtual machines from templates rather than clones. Template deployment also allows guest OS customization.

- **Migration**   Using the VMotion technology that has made VMware ESX an enterprise-ready product, virtual machines can be relocated from one physical host to another. This action can be invoked manually or based on the automation logic facilitated by VMware DRS.

- **Clustering**   A configuration item defining how virtual machines and associated storage failover to available resources on two or more physical hosts. This is the essence of VMware HA.

- **Monitoring**   The ability to configure and report against the data center as a whole. Response to detected conditions can be invoked at a physical or virtual level.

The host agent basically exposes a subset of the VirtualCenter feature set, limited to those operations that can be implemented on a single host. If you mistakenly invoke an operation against a standalone host instead of a VirtualCenter management server, the SDK will throw a *NotSupported* exception. Although this is not a fatal exception, you will want to code for it accordingly while also preventing users of your client from targeting operations against invalid targets.

Data Models and Data Types

All management entities can be grouped into data models that represent the structure they stand for. For example, all power operations, virtual hardware definition, and guest OS information are found in the data model for virtual machines. Table 20.15 and Table 20.16 provide a summary of each data model. Additional information can be found in the documentation accompanying the VI SDK 2.0 package.

Table 20.15 Service Instance, Folder, and Datacenter Data Models

Data Model Name	SDK 1.x Equivalent	Description
Service Instance	Server Farm	This managed object type represents the central entry or access point for the management data and operations. It describes the virtual infrastructure's capabilities, licensing, and discovered host machines. The properties of the Service Instance include the root folder of the managed entity inventory, the session manager, and the property collector.
Folder	Farm Group, Virtual Machine Group	This managed object type represents a folder. This object type is used to organize virtual machines, hosts, and host resources. Folders can be nested, but its contents must be consistent with the *childType* associated with the folder. The key features of the folder managed type.
Datacenter	Farm	This managed object type groups virtual machines and hosts under a top-tier construct. The entire object represents a single management unit contained in the root folder of the associated Service Instance. The key features are virtual machine management methods, managed entity management methods, computer resource management for clusters, datacenter objects, and task information.

Table 20.16 Virtual Machine and Host Resource Data Models

Data Model Name	Sub-Objects	Description
VirtualMachine	VirtualMachineSummary VirtualMachineConfigSpec CustomizationSpecManager Task	Describes the data type used to model a virtual machine. This managed object type contains sub-objects which contain the majority of its properties. Use this object type to: • Define or retrieve basic properties for a virtual machine • View or set virtual machine configuration parameters • Customize the virtual machine during deployment from a template • Perform power operations • List or identify the resources available to, and used by, the virtual machine
HostSystem	HostCapability HostConfigInfo HostConnectInfo HostDatastoreBrowser HostRuntimeInfo HostHardwareInfo	Describes the host machine configuration. Use this data type to manage the physical hosts upon which your virtual machines are running. Use this object to: • Define or retrieve basic properties for a particular host • Retrieve information about the capability of the host's hardware and software
	HostListSummary	• View or set the host configuration properties • View the host's hardware • Connect to the interface to access files in the datacenter
Datastore	DatastoreSummary HostSystem VirtualMachine	Describes data types used to manage physical storage resources. Use this data type to gain access to the catalog of storage devices attached to the host systems in the datacenter. Some of the information available includes the total capacity and free space, as well as the path of the physical storage.

Continued

Table 20.16 Continued

Data Model Name	Sub-Objects	Description
ComputeResource	ComputeResource-Summary EnvironmentBrowser ResourcePool	Describes the model used to hosts as resources with which to run virtual machines. The compute resource exported by the Web service can represent a single host or a cluster of hosts available to run virtual machines. Each ComputeResource contains the following: • List of hosts • List of datastores • List of network objects • Summary information, including resource usage and availability • An environment browser that facilitates access to hardware information, configuration objects, and files stored on the associated datastores.
ResourcePool	ResourceConfigSpec ResourcePoolSummary ComputerResource VirtualMachine	Describes the division of available host resources, whether individual or aggregated, available to run virtual machines. Use this datatype to create divisions of CPU and memory resources that are presented to virtual machines. Those resources can be configured with upper and lower limits as well as with shares, similar to ESX 2.x.
ClusterCompute-Resource	ClusterConfigInfo ClusterDrs Recommendation ClusterDrsMigration HostSystem Task	Describes additional components not exposed by the Compute-Resource data type used by VMware HA and VMware DRS features. The operations and properties available to support DRS and HA include *AddHost_Task* and *MoveInto_Task*, *Recommend-HostsforVm* and *ApplyRecommenda-tion*, *ReconfigureCluster_Task*, and many others.

It is recommended that you keep the Web-based Reference Guide that is included in the SDK package to reference additional information on the previously mentioned datatypes and sub-objects covered in the preceding tables. There are a few datatypes worth mentioning briefly, though, since they support monitoring and managing the virtual infrastructure as a whole. Those datatypes are as follows:

- **SessionManager**   Provides control of sessions, including login and log off operations
- **AuthorizationManager**   Controls access to objects. The access control is defined in a permission object that includes the managed entity reference, user or group name, and role.
- **PropertyCollector**   Used to create property filters that only exist during the user's session. Once the session is destroyed, so are the filters. These filters expose efficient methods that management clients can use to obtain values for properties or target-specific managed objects. In function, the *PropertyCollector* is similar to the *GetContents* and *GetUpdates* methods of VI SDK 1.x.
- **EventManager**   Provides historical information about changes that have taken placed with managed entities.
- **TaskManager**   Similar to *EventManager*, this datatype provides real-time information about tasks in progress, queued, or recently completed.
- **ScheduledTaskManager**   Used to manage scheduled tasks that are not already in progress or queued.
- **AlarmManager**   Used to manage alarms that resulted from defined conditions or situations.
- **PerformanceManager**   Provides an interface that can be used to collect performance statistics for hosts and virtual machines.

Programming Logic for the VI SDK 2.0

Similar to the VI SDK 1.x logic, your management application will follow a standard logical flow regardless of the functionality you have coded it for. You should take into consideration the managed entity inventory hierarchy as previously discussed in this chapter and make good use of property collector filters to minimize traversal times spent traversing through what may be a rather extensive hierarchical structure.

As mentioned before, you will be working with either managed objects or data objects. As input, most operations require a reference to a managed object (called a managed object reference) and possibly a few additional string, integer, or Boolean values. In some cases, you may need to pass a data object in its entirety, usually called a *spec* object. Those operations will either return a data object which contains values for you to work with, or another managed object reference for additional operations invocations.

In most cases, you will code the following steps in the workflow of your application. While reviewing these steps, notice some of the objects referenced and the relationships they have with other objects.

- Establish a session with the Web service. This clearly is the first step for you application. You must obtain a session token by successfully logging into the Web service. This token is used to invoke operations from your client throughout the duration of each user's session.

- Instantiate the *ServiceInstance* managed object. This is a core action that must take place to gain access to the underlying managed and data objects.

- Retrieve the *ServiceContent* data object. This is a very common action that you will perform, and it is accomplished by invoking the *RetrieveServiceContent* operation. This is a prerequisite to instantiating a *PropertyCollector* managed object.

- Once you have made it this far, you can now work with specific managed objects within your inventory. You can target those objects by constructing a *PropertyFilterSpec*. This data object type defines the managed object you wish to target, the properties of that object, and the manner within which you traverse the inventory.

- With a managed object reference for the *PropertyCollector* and the *PropertyFilterSpec* that you constructed, you can then retrieve the properties of the targeted managed object. This is accomplished by invoking the *RetrieveProperties* operation, which will return an *ObjectContent* data object containing all of the information as defined by the *PropertyFilterSpec*.

- Additionally, you can get regular updates for any of those properties by invoking one of several operations. Those operations are *CreateFilter*, *CheckForUpdates*, and *WaitForUpdates*. These operations are similar in function to the *GetUpdates* operation in the VI SDK 1.x, but are more powerful. They require for input the *PropertyCollector* managed object reference, and return either a *PropertyFilter* managed object reference that you can work with later, or the updates you can work with directly in an *UpdateSet* data object.

During all of this, you may run into further complications as you deal with permissions in complex entities such as *Datacenter*, *ComputeResource*, or *ClusterComputerResource*. The complexity is usually related to the parent-child relationships they tend to form in the inventory tree and the corresponding ACLs of those child objects.

Developing Your Management Application

With all those formalities behind us, we're now ready to begin the coding process. The techniques and logic are similar to what you read in the section for VI SDK 1.x. However, with a new object model and some new features, the departure from the previous version is significant enough to spend some time reviewing code samples for some of the popular operations you may perform.

In this section, we will look at some unique tools VMware has provided to assist with SDK development, as well as more deeply explore the operations and processes you will incorporate into your management application.

Managed Object Browser and Other Tools

Before beginning, we should introduce you to an invaluable tool that VMware has included with every ESX host and VirtualCenter: the Managed Object Browser (MOB). We'll also look at a few useful tools in the Visual Studio IDE. The MOB, however, is a Web-based utility that is hosted on the VirtualCenter management server and host agents. To access the MOB, browse to one of the following URLs:

- For VirtualCenter: https://<*your_server*>:8443/mob
- For Host Agents: https://<*your_server*>/mob

> **NOTE**
>
> The TCP port references in the URL (8443 for VirtualCenter and the standard 443 for the host agent) assume that the default ports are being used. If you have changed the ports, please account for this in the URL.

Once you successfully authenticate to the MOB, you will be presented with a page similar to that shown in Figure 20.16. This page represents the instantiation of the *ServiceInstance* object, the main gateway to the exposed managed and data objects. For each object that you view through the MOB, you will see a list of the properties and methods associated with that object.

Figure 20.16 The *ServiceInstance* Object Displayed in the Managed Object Browser

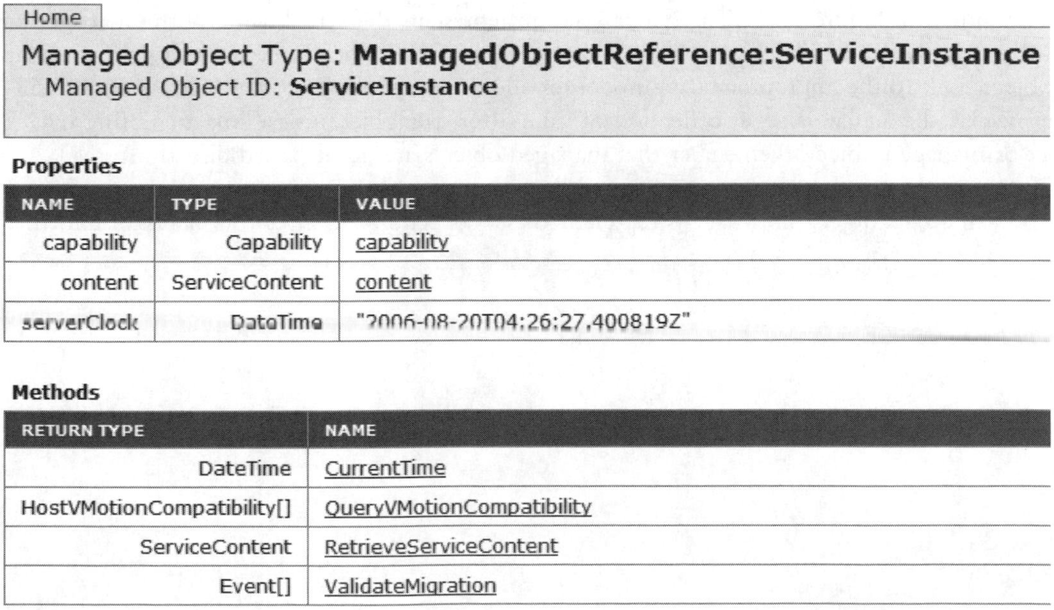

Home

Managed Object Type: ManagedObjectReference:ServiceInstance
Managed Object ID: **ServiceInstance**

Properties

NAME	TYPE	VALUE
capability	Capability	capability
content	ServiceContent	content
serverClock	DateTime	"2006-08-20T04:26:27.400819Z"

Methods

RETURN TYPE	NAME
DateTime	CurrentTime
HostVMotionCompatibility[]	QueryVMotionCompatibility
ServiceContent	RetrieveServiceContent
Event[]	ValidateMigration

In some cases, as defined in the data model for that particular datatype or managed entity, properties are references to another object, usually a data object. The value of such properties is the name of the data object, which is displayed in the Value column as a hyperlink (such as *capability* and *content* in Figure 20.16). Similarly, you can invoke methods by clicking the corresponding sub-object in the Name column, also displayed as a hyperlink.

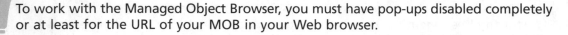

TIP

To work with the Managed Object Browser, you must have pop-ups disabled completely or at least for the URL of your MOB in your Web browser.

Let's explore the power of the MOB by reviewing a simple walk-through. We will gather information about our Web service host by performing the following steps:

1. Connect to the Managed Object Browser by browsing the appropriate URL and entering in valid credentials when prompted.

2. Click the **RetrieveServiceContent** hyperlink under Methods. A new window will open.

3. Click **Invoke Method**.

At this point, you will see the Method Invocation Result displaying various items in table form, as shown in Figure 20.17. The Name column represents the actual name of the managed or data object in the SDK. The Type column tells you more about that object and can help you map the object back to the appropriate data model for additional information. The Value column will either display the actual value or collection of values (for data objects) or a link to another data object or managed object. Remember that managed objects are never passed directly. Instead, a reference to that managed object is returned by operations. In this example, we see the value of the AboutInfo data object. This value is represented as a collection and gives you plenty of information about the Web service.

Figure 20.17 Method Invocation Result from Invoking the *RetrieveServiceContent* Operation

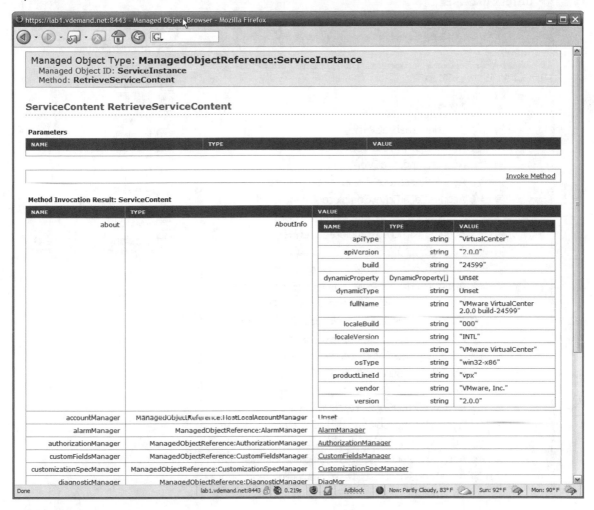

Although not much has been documented about the MOB, it will still serve as a great test or troubleshooting tool. If you need more information about the value you must pass, such as a reference to managed objects that are required as input to an operation call, capture some samples of the returned managed object references to ensure that your input data is compliant with the WSDL schema for all complex types.

Microsoft has also provided some useful tools and functionality in the Visual Studio IDE that you will find handy. As we discussed earlier in the chapter, the Object Browser, as shown in Figure 20.18, can prove to be useful as a quick reference to the various properties, methods, and datatypes of VimService2005. The following figure shows the *VimApi* namespace and associated classes. Highlighting any class will reveal the properties and methods defined by that class, as well as their input and return values.

Figure 20.18 Visual Studio 2005 Object Browser Showing the *VimAPI* Namespace

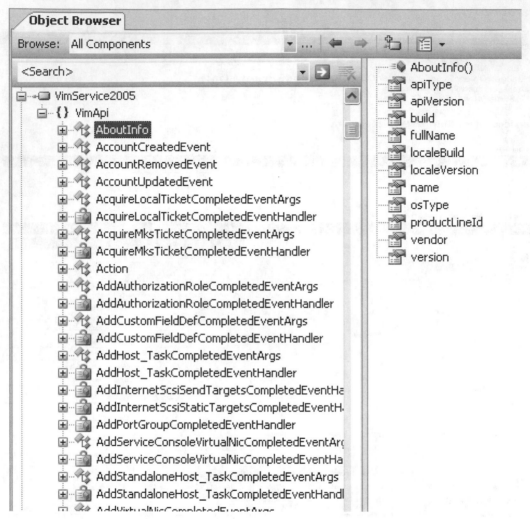

Another great feature about developing in Visual Studio is Intellisense, as shown in Figure 20.19. The IDE is ever mindful about objects that get instantiated, and as you code with those objects, the IDE will present you with the valid methods and properties related to your location of the object-oriented hierarchy, as well as hints on the syntax and datatypes expected. In the following figure, the IDE is aware of that _*service* as an instance of the *VimService* object and is helping to identify valid properties, methods, and events based on what has been typed so far, "_service.QueryVM".

Figure 20.19 Visual Studio 2005's Intellisense Feature Enumerating Properties and Methods of *VimService*

The Connection Process

Now you are ready to start some simple coding exercises. Although we step through some code snippets in this section, you can find complete applications in the samples included with the SDK. Our purpose here is to break down a lot of that complicated code to explore the various operations you may perform in your own management applications.

As the first step, you will need to connect the client to the Web service either using the stub you created or using the one that came with the SDK package. Assuming you have already created a new project, you will want to make a reference to the VimService2005.dll in your project. This will present the *VimApi* namespace for us to use in our code.

To log on to the Web service, perform the following steps:

1. Create a new managed object reference.

2. Create a reference to the Web service URL. Optionally, you can define how to handle cookies as part of the HTTP-based SOAP interaction.

3. Retrieve the *ServiceContent* data object from the service instance.

4. Obtain the session manager reference to be used when invoking the login operation

5. Call the *Login* operation, passing the referenced session manager, username, and password.

Code Listings 20.19 and 20.20 demonstrate a simple logon process and assume you have captured the values of *url*, *username*, and *password* as input or arguments to work with. Remember that the URL to the Web service is https:// <your_server>/sdk.

Code Listing 20.19 C# Script for Logging on to the Web Service

```csharp
using System;
using VimApi;
protected VimService _service;
protected ServiceContent _sic;
protected ManagedObjectReference _svcRef;
public void Connect(string url, string username, string password) {
  _service = new VimService();
  _service.Url = url;
  _service.CookieContainer = new System.Net.CookieContainer();
  _svcRef = new ManagedObjectReference();
  _svcRef.type = "ServiceInstance";
  _svcRef.Value = "ServiceInstance";
  _sic = _service.RetrieveServiceContent(_svcRef);
  if (_sic.sessionManager != null) {
    _service.Login(_sic.sessionManager, username, password, null);
  }
}
```

Code Listing 20.20 VB.NET Script for Logging on to the Web Service

```vbnet
Imports System
Imports VimApi
protected _service As VimService
protected _sic As ServiceContent
protected _svcRef as ManagedObjectReference
Public Function connect(url As string, username as String, password As _String)
  _service = New VimService
  _service.Url = url
  _service.CookieContainer = New System.Net.CookieContainer
  _svcRef = New ManagedObjectReference
  _svcRef.type = "ServiceInstance"
  _svcRef.Value = "ServiceInstance"
  _sic = _service.RetrieveServiceContent(_svcRef)
  if (_sic.sessionManager != null)
    _service.Login(_sic.sessionManager, username, password, null)
  End if
End Function
```

In this example, we reference the *VimAPI* namespace that will facilitate access to the various objects needed in our management application. We declare and instantiate three variables. *_service* serves as a primary object of type *VimService*. *_sic* serves as our *ServiceContent* managed object. *_svcRef* represents an instance of the *ManagedObjectReference* object type. Upon instantiation, we set the appropriate values for the URL and cookie container for the client and invoke the Login operation. You will notice that we must pass the reference to the *sessionManager* managed object as one of the input parameters of the login operation.

Handling SSL Certificates

With VI SDK 2.0, we are faced with the same potential problems surrounding PKI management and certificate issues for your management application that we experienced with earlier SDKs. In most cases, you will connect to the Web service through the HTTPS listener instead of HTTP. The default certificate used by the VI Web service is not a valid one for production use since it was not issued by a trusted root certificate authority (CA). You can choose to handle this condition one of two ways. First, you can replace the certificate with a valid one from a trusted CA and update the vpx configuration as reviewed earlier in this chapter. Another option would be to handle the "bad" certificate programmatically in your application. Although the certificate cannot be trusted, it can still be used to encrypt the HTTP data payload transmitted between the management client and the Web service.

The latter option is the most common and still provides adequate security for situations where the Web service is only accessible on your internal network. The examples found in the SDK package all include a sample workaround which we will discuss briefly. The key component is the CertPolicy. cs file, which can be copied from any sample and added to your project. Using the *System.Security. Cryptography.X509Certificates* namespace and hashtables, the *CheckValidationResult* function is passed the certificate and assesses its validity. If the function detects any issues with the certificate, it will then display a message box stating any problems that were found, presenting the management client user the option to continue regardless.

To take advantage of this certificate validation functionality, you can implement *ICertificatePolicy*. Then you must pass *ICertificatePolicy* to *ServicePointManager.CertificatePolicy* before any Web service method calls are made. Include the following code in the client code. Before you make the Web Service method call from the client code, the following statement must be executed:

```
System.Net.ServicePointManager.CertificatePolicy = new CertPolicy();
```

In addition to using the *CertPolicy* distributed in the SDK package, you can create you own *CertPolicy* that will validate, for example, all certificates. The following sample code implements *ICertificatePolicy* and then accepts every request under SSL:

```
using System.Net;
using System.Security.Cryptography.X509Certificates;
public class CertPolicy : ICertificatePolicy {
  public bool CheckValidationResult(
    ServicePoint svcPnt
  , X509Certificate cert
  , WebRequest req
  , int certProblem) {
    return true;
  } // end CheckValidationResult
} // class CertPolicy
```

Retrieving Property Information

Collecting information from any managed objects requires that you create a *PropertyFilterSpec* data object. This object contains two properties: *propSet*, a set of *PropertySpec* data objects, and *objectSet*, a set of *ObjectSpec* data objects (see Table 20.17).

Table 20.17 Details Concerning the Definition of these Properties as Required for the *PropertyFilterSpec*

Item	Object	Comprised Object Properties
propSet	PropertySpec	• **type** Value that represents the type of managed object being collected.
		• **all** Boolean value that tells the *PropertySpec* to retrieve all available properties of the managed object (is set to TRUE).
		• **pathSet** Comma-separated list of property names identifying the properties whose values should be retrieved for the managed object. This implies that the "all" property was set to FALSE or omitted.
objectSet	ObjectSpec	• **obj** Defines the managed object reference where the collection begins.
		• **skip** Boolean value that tells the *ObjectSpec* whether the object defined in "obj" is part of the selection for property retrieval.
		• **selectSet** (Optional) Is made up of one or more *SelectionSpec* data objects, which in turn contain *TraversalSpec* data objects. Each managed object is a property of the original managed object defined in "obj", and can be traversed or have its properties retrieved as well.
selectSet	SelectionSpec	• **type** Value that represents the TraverseSpec type of managed object for the *TraversalSpec*.

Table 20.17 Continued

Item	Object	Comprised Object Properties
		• **path** The property name that contains the managed object reference as a value. This reference is where the traversal will go next. • **skip** Boolean value that tells the *SelectionSpec* or *TraversalSpec* whether the referenced object is part of the selection for property retrieval. • **selectSet** An array of *SelectSpec* objects defining the next step of the traversal. The *SelectionSpec* can be a *TraversalSpec* if further traversing is necessary.

Mastering the *PropertyCollector*, filters, and inventory traversal will be key to developing efficient and powerful management applications. With this latest release, the frontier is still fairly unexplored, but in time you will develop a strategy that works best for you in your development efforts.

Since property management is such an important area in the new SDK, we will review two examples in C# that should help demonstrate the basic techniques. The first example demonstrates a simple *PropertyFilterSpec* with no traversal. In this example, we will monitor a task by retrieving specific information about it.

We start by declaring *pSpec* as a new instance of *PropertySpec*. Setting the type to "Task", we can focus on managed objects of the desired type. We also set the *all* property to FALSE because we only want to retrieve specific information, "info.state", as defined in the array *pathSet*.

```
PropertySpec pSpec = new PropertySpec();
pSpec.Type = "Task";
pSpec.all = false; pSpec.allSpecified = true;
pSpec.pathSet = new String[] { "info.state" };
```

Next, we declare *oSpec* as a new instance of *ObjectSpec*. By setting the property *obj* to the managed object reference of the specific task that we are focusing on, we define it as the starting point. Since the skip property is not set to TRUE and *selectSet* is not defined, the managed object referenced in *obj* will be checked to see if it matches *pSpec.Type*, or "type", and there will be no traversal to other managed objects. Consequently, this will be the only object that is checked.

```
ObjectSpec oSpec = new ObjectSpec();
oSpec.Obj = taskMgdObjRef;
```

With *pSpec* and *oSpec* defined, we can now construct the *PropertyFilterSpec.* We do so by declaring *_pfsec* as a new instance of *PropertyFilterSpec*, setting its *ObjectSpec* property to *oSpec* and its *PropertySpec* to *pSpec*.

```
PropertyFilterSpec _pfSpec = new PropertyFilterSpec();
_pfSpec.ObjectSet = new ObjectSpec[] { oSpec };
_pfSpec.PropSet = new PropertySpec[] { pSpec };
```

We have everything we need to retrieve the results of the collection. First, we need to declare a *PropertyCollector* managed object reference from the *ServiceContent* data object.

```
ManagedObjectReference _svcRef = new ManagedObjectReference();
_svcRef.type = "ServiceInstance";
_svcRef.Value = "ServiceInstance";
ServiceContent _sic = VimService.RetrieveServiceContent(_svcRef);
ManagedObjectReference pCollector = _sic.PropertyCollector();
```

Next, we invoke the *retrieveProperties* operation, passing it the *PropertyCollector* managed object reference and the *PropertyFilterSpec* that we constructed. The resulting *ObjectContent* is then used alongside a *DynamicProperty* array to store the values retrieved, which we then write to the console. Note that the variable *_service* was declared and defined upon establishing a connection with the Web service.

```
ObjectContent[] ocary = vimService.retrieveProperties(pCollector,
  new PropertyFilterSpec[] { pfSpec });
if (ocary != null) {
  ObjectContent oc = null;
  ManagedObjectReference mor = null;
  DynamicProperty[] pcary = null;
  DynamicProperty pc = null;
  oc = ocary[0];
  mor = oc.obj;
  pcary = oc.propSet;
  Console.WriteLine("Object Type : " + mor.type);
  Console.WriteLine("Reference Value : " + mor.Value);
  if (pcary != null) {
    pc = pcary[0];
    Console.WriteLine(" Property Name : " + pc.name);
    Console.WriteLine(" Property Value : " + pc.val);
  }
}
```

When simple property retrieval isn't wanted or it doesn't fit the situation, you must incorporate object traversal through the entity inventory to collect the information you need. This is particularly true when you do not know where the object you desire to manage is located and you need to traverse the inventory recursively. The following example reviews the steps you will need in order to enumerate all of the virtual machines in the inventory regardless of where they are located. Our objective is to collect the properties *guest.hostName* and *guest.guestFullName*.

We begin by creating a new *PropertySpec* instance, followed by a single *ObjectSpec* property:

```
PropertySpec pSpec = new PropertySpec();
pSpec.Type = "VirtualMachine";
pSpec.all = false; pSpec.allSpecified = true;
pSpec.pathSet = new String[] { "guest.hostName", "guest.guestFullName" };
ObjectSpec oSpec = new ObjectSpec();
oSpec.Obj = refDataCenter;
oSpec.Skip = FALSE;
```

We supposed that the variable *refDataCenter* was declared and defined earlier as a managed object reference to a datacenter managed object. We now define the traversal path. The *TraversalSpec* objects will use the *Datacenter* managed object as a starting point and will cover the six possible paths through the hierarchy, as shown in the following list:

- Folder to childEntity (*folderTSpec*)

- Datacenter to hostFolder (*dc2HostTSpec*)

- Datacenter to vmFolder (*dc2VmTSpec*)

- ComputeResource to resourcePool (*cr2RpTSpec*)

- ComputeResource to host (*cr2HostTSpec*)

- resourcePool to resourcePool (*rp2RpTSpec*)

Code Listing 20.21 demonstrates how the TraversalSpec objects are defined.

Code Listing 20.21 Defining TraversalSpec Objects

```
TraversalSpec dc2HostTSpec = new TraversalSpec();
dc2HostTSpec.Type = "Datacenter";
dc2HostTSpec.Path = "hostFolder";
dc2HostTSpec.SelectSet = new SelectionSpec[]{recursiveSpec};
TraversalSpec dc2VmTSpec = new TraversalSpec();
dc2VmTSpec.Type = "Datacenter";
dc2VmTSpec.Path = "vmFolder";
dc2VmTSpec.SelectSet = new SelectionSpec[]{recursiveSpec};
TraversalSpec cr2RpTSpec = new TraversalSpec();
cr2RpTSpec.Type = "ComputeResource";
cr2RpTSpec.Path = "resourcePool";
TraversalSpec cr2HostTSpec = new TraversalSpec();
cr2HostTSpec.Type = "ComputeResource";
```

```
cr2HostTSpec.Path = "host";
TraversalSpec rp2rpTSpec = new TraversalSpec();
rp2rpTSpec.Type = "ResourcePool";
rp2rpTSpec.Path = "resourcePool";
TraversalSpec folderTSpec = new TraversalSpec();
folderTSpec.Type = "Folder";
folderTSpec.Path = "childEntity";
folderTSpec.SelectSet = new SelectionSpec[]{recursiveSpec,
                                            dc2VmTSpec,
                                            dc2HostTSpec,
                                            cr2RpTSpec,
                                            cr2HostTSpec,
                                            rp2rpTSpec};
```

In order to finalize the declaration of the *PropertyFilterSpec*, we must next define the *ObjectSpec* and referencing *folderTSpec* as the *SelectSet* property. This will be the starting point of the traversal at every possible path, collecting data along the way. At that point, we can construct the *PropertyFilterSpec*, as shown Code Listing 20.22.

Code Listing 20.22 *PropertyFilterSpec*

```
oSpec.SelectSet = new SelectionSpec[]{folderTSpec};
PropertyFilterSpec pfSpec = new PropertyFilterSpec();
pfSpec.PropSet = new PropertySpec[] {pSpec};
pfSpec.ObjectSet = new ObjectSpec[] {ospec};
```

Other Retrieval Mechanisms

In addition to these techniques, you can also retrieve information through several other mechanisms. You can search for managed object by *SearchIndex* API rather than the *PropertyCollector*. There are some inherent differences between the two, as shown in the following list:

- *SearchAPI* returns the first managed entity match, while *PropertyCollector* returns as many items as matched within the scope of its search.

- *SearchAPI* only works with a small group of managed entities, while *PropertyCollector* works with all managed objects.

- SearchAPI is much easier to work with.

The SearchAPI allows a client to query the entity inventory for a specific management object using a variety of search attributes. The common managed objects types retrieved using this mechanism are *VirtualMachine* and *HostSystem*. One thing to keep in mind, though, is that a user cannot find a managed object that it does not have access, so ensuring the proper setting for the ACLs of the objects in question is important. The SearchAPI has the following six operations associated with it:

- FindByDatastorePath
- FindByDnsName
- FindByInventoryPath
- FindByIp
- FindByUuid
- FindChild

You can also retrieve updates for previously collected properties. This is done using one of three operations, as shown in Table 20.18. Each operation has its pros and cons, however, so you must match these characteristics against the goal of your code and the functional and efficiency requirements you may have.

Table 20.18 Three Operations to Get Updates on Properties

Operation	Pros	Cons
RetrieveProperties	Same process as retrieving the original values for the targeted properties.	Retrieves all of the properties as defined in the *PropertyFilterSpec*, whether they have changed or not; least efficient use of network bandwidth.
CheckForUpdates	Efficient use of network bandwidth; only returns properties that have changed.	Runs synchronously, so it returns immediately, whether there were any changes or not.
WaitForUpdates	Efficient use of network bandwidth; only returns properties that have changed.	Runs asynchronously, so it does not return until a change has occurred; will wait or listen indefinitely if change is not detected or *CancelWaitForUpdates* is called.

Performing Advanced Operations

Now that you know how to retrieve information about managed objects and obtain the value of data objects found within your inventory, you are ready to tackle performing management operations against those managed entities. This is where the power of any SDK comes in, as you can build powerful applications that analyze properties of the managed objects and, in turn, invoke the appropriate set of operations as a response.

In this section, we will discuss a few of the common operations that can be accomplished programmatically with the SDK. Reviewing each of the operations is beyond the scope of this chapter; however, both the *Virtual Infrastructure SDK Programming Guide* and the *Virtual Infrastructure SDK Reference Guide* will help tremendously and serve as a great look-up guide when needed.

Power Operations

To control the power state of a particular virtual machine, you can call any of the following operations: *PowerOnVM_Task*, *PowerOffVM_Task* (for "hard" shutdowns), or *ShutdownGuest* (for "cold" shutdowns), *SuspendVM_Task*, and *ResetVM_Task*. Code Listing 20.23 demonstrates the PowerOffVM_Task operation.

Code Listing 20.23 *PowerOffVM_Task*

```
ManagedObjectReference MgdObjRef_VM =
  _service.findByInventoryPath(_sic.SearchIndex(), pathVM);
ManagedObjectReference MgdObjRef_Host =
  _service.findByInventoryPath(_sic.SearchIndex(), pathHost);
ManagedObjectReference MgdObjRef_Task =
  _service.PowerOffVM(MgdObjRef_VM, MgdObjRef_Host);
```

Virtual Machine Migration

The *MigrateVM_Task* operation is used to migrate an existing virtual machine, regardless of power state. Migrating a virtual machine from one host to another is different than moving a virtual machine because the disk files themselves are not migrated, just the ownership of the virtual machine. The operation has the following required and options parameters that are passed when being invoked:

- **VirtualMachine managed object reference**   The reference to the VirtualMachine managed object.
- **Pool**   A reference to a ResourcePool managed object.
- **Host**   A reference to a HostSystem managed object.
- **Priority**   The priority level that you want to set for the migration task.
- **State**   If specified, the migration will only proceed if the power state of the virtual machine matches this parameter.

Code Listing 20.24 demonstrates the MigrateVM_Task operation.

Code Listing 20.24 *MigrateVM_Task*

```
ManagedObjectReference MgdObjRef_VM =
  _service.findByInventoryPath(_sic.SearchIndex(), pathVM);
ManagedObjectReference MgdObjRef_Host =
  _service.findByInventoryPath(_sic.SearchIndex(), pathHost);
```

```
ManagedObjectReference MgdObjRef_RPool =
  _service.findByInventoryPath(_sic.SearchIndex(), pathResourcePool);
ManagedObjectReference MgdObjRef_Task =
  _service.MigrateVM(MgdObjRef_VM, MgdObjRef_RPool, MgdObjRef_Host
  VirtualMachineMovePriority.highPriority,
  VirtualMachinePowerState.poweredOn);
```

Working with Snapshots

New to Virtual Infrastructure 3 is the ability to create multiple points-in-time snapshots and to revert back to other snapshots—a functionality similar to that available in the VMware Workstation product. The operations *CreateSnapshot_Task*, *RevertToSnapshot_Task*, and *RemoveSnaphost_Task* can be used to manage your snapshot processes programmatically. Each operation has its own set of parameters that are passed upon invocation. For example, the *CreateSnapshot_Task* has the following for parameters:

- **Name**   A friendly string value to name the snapshot.

- **Description**   A user-defined string value that describes the snapshot, such as "Pre-SP1 Snapshot #3 Created on 2006/08/20".

- **Memory**   A Boolean value that tells the operation whether a memory dump should be included with the snapshot

- **Quiesce**   A Boolean value that tells the virtual machine, via VMware Tools, to quiesce the file system prior to taking the snapshot. If set to TRUE, the snapshot will be power-down consistent, rather than crash-consistent, as with previous versions of the ESX Server product.

Refer to the Virtual Infrastructure SDK Programming Guide for more information about each of these operations. Code Listing 20.25 demonstrates the *CreateSnapshot_Task* operation.

Code Listing 20.25 *CreateSnapshot_Task*

```
ManagedObjectReference MgdObjRef_VM =
  _service.findByInventoryPath(_sic.SearchIndex(), pathVM);
boolean memoryDump = false;
boolean quiesceFileSys = true;
string snapName = "Pre-SP1 Snapshot #3";
string snapDescription = "Pre-SP1 Snapshot #3 Created on 2006/08/20";
ManagedObjectReference MgdObjRef_Task =
  _service.CreateSnapshot_Task(MgdObjRef_VM, snapName, snapDescription,
  memoryDump, quiesceFileSys);
```

Working with Scheduled Tasks

You can programmatically create scheduled tasks. To do this, you invoke the *CreateScheduledTask* operation and configure the task with the *ScheduledTaskSpec* data objects. This operation has the following parameters:

- **ScheduledTaskManager managed object reference** This reference is derived from the *scheduledTaskManager* property of the *ServiceContent* data object.

- **ManagedEntity managed object reference** The target entity for the action in the task.

- **Spec** The *ScheduledTaskSpec* object.

The *ScheduledTaskSpec* also has various parameters that are defined as properties of the data object. Those properties are

- **Action** Defines the action performed against the targeted managed entity.

- **Scheduler** A *TaskScheduler* data object that is used to define when the action takes place.

- **Enabled** A Boolean property for whether the task is enabled or disabled.

- **Name** A user-friendly name for the task.

- **Description** A user-defined description of the task.

- **Notification** A string value for the e-mail notification associated with the task.

Code Listing 20.26 demonstrates the *CreateScheduledTask* operation.

Code Listing 20.26 *CreateScheduledTask*

```
ManagedObjectReference MgdObjRef_VM =
 _service.FindByInventoryPath(_sic.SearchIndex(), pathVM);
MethodActionArgument[] mActArgumnt = new MethodActionArgument();
MethodAction mAction = new MethodAction();
mActArgumnt.Value = MgdObjRef_VM;
ma.Argument = mActArgumnt;
ma.Name = "MigrateVM";
DailyTaskScheduler dtScheduler = new DailyTaskScheduler();
dtScheduler.Hour = 12;
dtScheduler.Minute = 0;
ScheduledTaskSpec tSpec = new ScheduledTaskSpec();
tSpec.Action = mAction;
tSpec.Scheduler = dtScheduler;
tSpec.Enabled = true;
tSpec.Name = "Migrate virtual machine";
tSpec.Description = "Migrate virtual machine at noon");
tSpec.Notification = "VMAdmin@syngress.com";
_service.createScheduledTask(_sic.ScheduledTaskManager,MgdObjRef_VM,tSpec);
```

For more information, download and review the *VMware Virtual Infrastructure SDK Programming Guide* and the HTML-based *VMware Virtual Infrastructure SDK Reference Guide*.

Other VMware SDKs

In an effort to give developers and administrators even more control over their Virtual Infrastructure, VMware has provided additional SDKs designed to meet specific management needs. In addition to the VMware Scripting APIs and the Virtual Infrastructure SDK, VMware also offers the VMware Guest SDK and the CIM SDK. We will review each of these SDKs briefly.

VMware Guest SDK

Newly introduced with Virtual Infrastructure 3 is the VMware Guest SDK or Guest API. This interface provides access to certain data for the guest operating system running inside a virtual machine. The SDK is facilitated by the VMware Tools, implying that the tools must be installed in order for your management application to be able to hook into the API. In addition, the Guest SDK is a read-only API, intended only to provision a mechanism for data collection.

Using the VMware Guest SDK, you can monitor and collect data for the statistics (shown in Table 20.19) about the virtual machine environment.

Table 20.19 Statistics Available Through the Guest SDK

Item	Statistic
Memory	• The total amount of memory allocated to the guest OS.
	• The amount of memory in use at the time of data collection.
	• The upper limit of memory available to the guest OS, if not equal to the total amount of memory allocated.
	• The number of shares allocated for memory resources.
CPU	• The amount of CPU resources guaranteed.
	• Minimum reserved rate that the virtual machine is allowed to run, even when idle.
	• The number of shares allocated for CPU resources.
	• CPU time scheduled on the hosting ESX Server for the virtual machine's CPU resources.
Miscellaneous	• The runtime since the last power-on event or reset of the virtual machine.
	• The ability of the API to provide accurate data.

The Guest API run-time component exists as a library that is installed with VMware Tools version 3.0 and higher. For Windows guest operating systems, the library file is *vmGuestLib.dll*; for Linux, the library is *libvmGuestLib.so*.

TIP

By default, the run-time component of the Guest API is enabled. Even at idle, this causes the virtual machine to consume CPU cycles, although the amount may be negligible. You may want to consider disabling this component to avoid utilizing unnecessary resources.

To disable the run-time component, edit the config file by either adding the following line or, if it already exists, changing the value as shown in the following:
isolation.tools.guestlibGetInfo.disable = "TRUE"

The run-time component exposes several data types, functions, and a library of Error Messages that you can use to troubleshoot the environment. As a read-only set of API calls, it does not support any operations to perform actions within the virtual machine, such as reconfiguration, power operations, or interaction with other members of the virtual infrastructure. If you need to perform operations, you should utilize the Virtual Infrastructure SDK (preferred) or Scripting APIs.

For more information, please consult the *VMware Guest SDK Programming Guide*.

VMware CIM SDK

Available as 1.0 or 2.0 releases for ESX 2.x or ESX 3, respectively, the VMware CIM SDK is the final offering to developers and administrators for managing components of the virtual infrastructure. This SDK is compliant with Common Information Model (CIM) standards and supports the Storage Management Initiative Specification (SMI-S) schema for storage management. Since the focus of the SDK is on storage, it allows developers and administrators to:

- View and identify logical storage resources using a CIM-compliant application, whether it be "home-grown" or a commercially available tool.

- View allocation of storage resources to virtual machines.

- View the physical layer of the storage presented to the hosts associated with the managed virtual machines.

- Monitor the components responsible for facilitating access to storage, including, but not limited to, host bus adapters, CIM/SMS-S–compliant connectivity devices, and compliant storage servers/arrays themselves.

The CIM SDK is based on standards defined by the DMTF and WBEM bodies, even though it is targeted to storage management and not the overall management of the ESX hosts. The SDK is provisioned by two components as listed next and as illustrated in Figure 20.20:

- **Pegasus CIMOM**   A popular open-source CIMOM application that is installed with, and runs inside, the Service Console of ESX hosts.

- **Set of Managed Object Format (MOF) files**   MOF files that can be compiled and used on management clients to interact with the CIMOM process on the server.

Figure 20.20 The CIM SDK Process for Communication

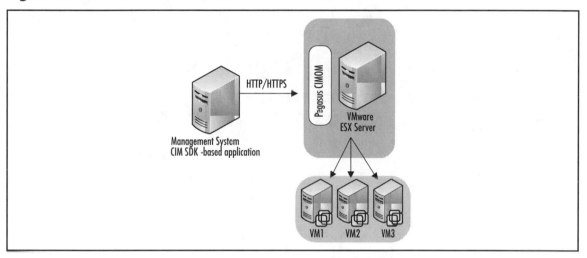

Covering the CIM SDK in detail is beyond the scope of this chapter. If you are interested in developing management applications that take advantage of the SDK for storage management purposes, you will want to make sure you are familiar with CIM concepts and principles as well as the SMI-S schema profile. For more information about the VMware CIM SDK, please see the *VMware CIM SDK Programming Guide*. If you are looking for additional information regarding CIM and SMI-S, visit the following sites:

- **Distributed Management Task Force (DMTF)**   www.dmtf.org
- **Common Information Model (CIM)**   www.dmtf.org/standards/cim/
- **OpenPegasus**   www.openpegasus.org
- **Storage Networks Industry Association (SNIA)**   www.snia.org/home
- **Storage Management Initiative Specification (SMI-S)**   www.snia.org/ smi/tech_activities/smi_spec_pr/spec/

Summary

Beginning with the release of ESX Server 2.x and evolving into the Virtual Infrastructure 3 product line, VMware has uniquely positioned their virtualization technology in such a way that clearly distinguishes them from their competition. Combined with the inherit flexibility and performance that ESX Server and VirtualCenter provide at a functional level, the ability to develop custom management client applications to help administer, manage, and monitor your virtual infrastructure makes their technology the choice for many operations. Even with a limited background in scripting or programming, you can develop programs that will help automate and ease your administration through the VMware Scripting APIs, Virtual Infrastructure SDK, Guest SDK, and CIM SDK.

## Chapter 21

Building a VM

Solutions in this chapter:

- **Creation of Virtual Machines Utilizing Command-Line Tools**

- **Scripting Creation of Virtual Machines in ESX Shell**

- **Scripting Creation of Virtual Machines in Perl Scripts**

- **Cloning Virtual Machines Utilizing ESX Shell Scripts**

- **Cloning Virtual Machines Utilizing VmPerl Scripts**

☑ **Summary**

Introduction

VMware provides many useful command-line tools for the creation and cloning of virtual machines. In this chapter, you will gain a working understanding of these tools and how to leverage them to automate virtual machine creation. At the end of this chapter, you will be able to script the creation and cloning of virtual machines to automate your virtual machine setup.

Creation of Virtual Machines Utilizing Command-Line Tools

VMware ESX Server has tools available for command-line creation and cloning of virtual machines. These tools are available via the service console and require that you access the service console with root-level privileges.

TIP

Remote access to ESX Server by default is disabled for the root account. Create an additional account on your ESX server. Log in with this new account and use the *su – root* command. This command will allow you to assume root level privileges.

Three main steps are involved to create a virtual machine utilizing the command-line tools.

- Creation of a virtual machine configuration file
- Creation of a virtual machine disk file
- Registering the virtual machine with ESX Server

We accomplish the preceding tasks by utilizing the following tools:

- A text editor such as VI
- *vmkfstools*
- *vmware-cmd*

Creation of a Virtual Machine Configuration File

Virtual machine configurations are stored as files with a .vmx extension. The VMX file is just a text file with specific fields that define the virtual machine's configuration. A very short vmx file only needs 14 lines to support a virtual machine that encompasses one CPU, one hard drive, and one network adapter. You could create a VMX file with just three lines but it would be of minimal value. Code Listings 21.1 and 21.2 show sample VMX configurations.

Code Listing 21.1 ESX 2.x VMX Code

```
guestOS = "winnetenterprise"
config.version = "6"
virtualHW.version = "3"
scsi0.present = "true"
scsi0.sharedBus = "none"
scsi0.virtualDev = "lsilogic"
memsize = "512"
scsi0:0.present = "true"
scsi0:0.fileName = "ESX Created VM.vmdk"
scsi0:0.deviceType = "scsi-hardDisk"
ethernet0.present = "true"
ethernet0.allowGuestConnectionControl = "false"
ethernet0.networkName = "VM Network"
ethernet0.addressType = "vpx"
```

Code Listing 21.2 ESX 3.x VMX Code

```
guestOS = "winnetenterprise"
config.version = "8"
virtualHW.version = "4"
scsi0.present = "true"
scsi0.sharedBus = "none"
scsi0.virtualDev = "lsilogic"
memsize = "512"
scsi0:0.present = "true"
scsi0:0.fileName = "ESX Created VM.vmdk"
scsi0:0.deviceType = "scsi-hardDisk"
ethernet0.present = "true"
ethernet0.allowGuestConnectionControl = "false"
ethernet0.networkName = "VM Network"
ethernet0.addressType = "vpx"
```

As you can tell from Code Listings 21.1 and 21.2, the only difference is in the values of the config.version and virtualHW.version entries. These values relate to the version of ESX Server you are running. To check the values for these fields, open up an existing virtual machine's configuration file in a text editor.

NOTE

It doesn't matter whether you use upper- or lowercase, but always make sure to use " " for the values in an (VMX) file.

Once you start a VM using a VMX configuration file like the ones shown in Code Listings 21.1 and 21.2, VMware will generate additional entries in the VMX. These entries identify the virtual machine and set default values for the virtual machine. Examples of these types of entries are shown in Code Listing 21.3

Code Listing 21.3 VMware Autogenerated VMX Entry Examples

```
uuid.bios = "56 4d ee 3c 52 06 a3 de-be 4a 73 9c cc 79 25 2b "
ethernet0.generatedAddress = "00:50:56:a7:42:e2"
powerType.powerOff = "default"
powerType.powerOn = "default"
powerType.suspend = "default"
powerType.reset = "default"
```

NOTE

Configuration files for virtual machines created with VMware ESX Server 2.0 and later use the .vmx extension. Earlier versions of ESX Server used the .cfg extension.

Creating Your Virtual Machine Configuration File

You now have a basic understanding of how a virtual machine configuration file is constructed and are ready to build your own. The steps that follow detail how to create a new virtual machine configuration file.

- Log in locally or connect to your ESX server remotely.
- Log in with an ID that has root privileges (see the Tip in the previous section), as shown in Figure 21.1.

Figure 21.1 Gaining Root Level Access on ESX Server

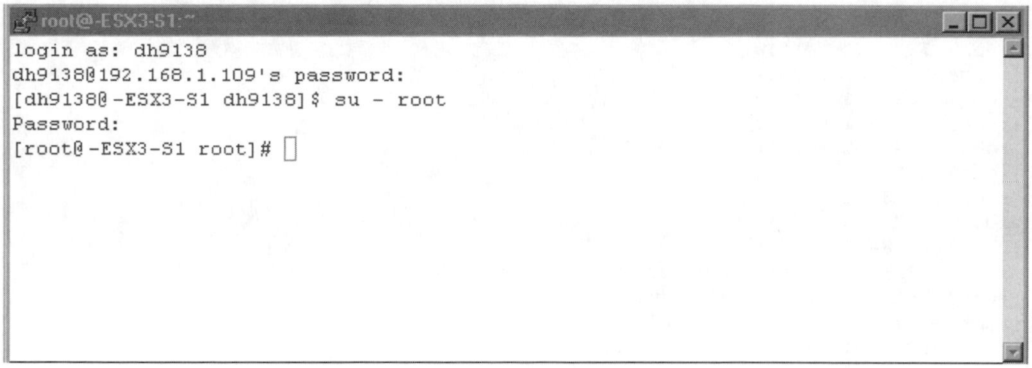

```
root@-ESX3-S1:~                                                    _ □ ×
login as: dh9138
dh9138@192.168.1.109's password:
[dh9138@-ESX3-S1 dh9138]$ su - root
Password:
[root@-ESX3-S1 root]#
```

- Change to the location of where you want to put your new virtual machine. Virtual machine configuration files (VMX) have to be stored in the same location as the other virtual machine files (VSWP, VMDK, and so on). See Figure 21.2.

Figure 21.2 Virtual Machine Storage Location

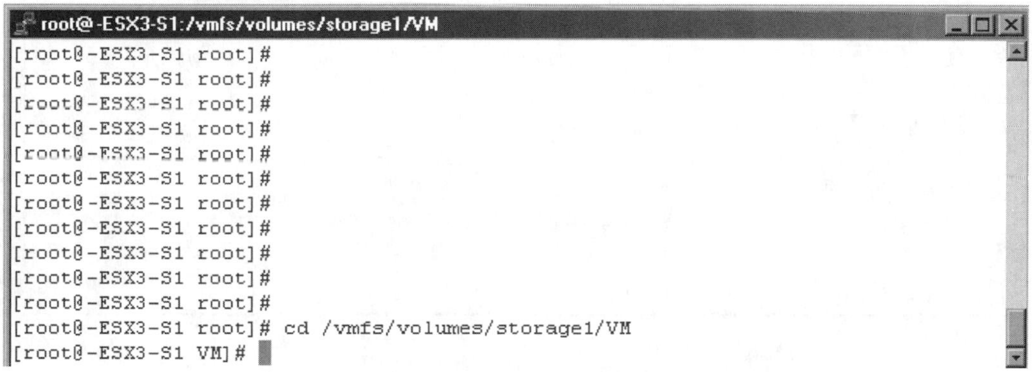

```
root@-ESX3-S1:/vmfs/volumes/storage1/VM                            _ □ ×
[root@-ESX3-S1 root]#
[root@-ESX3-S1 root]#
[root@-ESX3-S1 root]#
[root@-ESX3-S1 root]#
[root@-ESX3-S1 root]#
[root@-ESX3-S1 root]#
[root@-ESX3-S1 root]#
[root@-ESX3-S1 root]#
[root@-ESX3-S1 root]#
[root@-ESX3-S1 root]#
[root@-ESX3-S1 root]#
[root@-ESX3-S1 root]# cd /vmfs/volumes/storage1/VM
[root@-ESX3-S1 VM]#
```

- Create a new directory to store your new virtual machine in newvm and change to that directory (see Figure 21.3).

Figure 21.3 Virtual Machine Working Directory

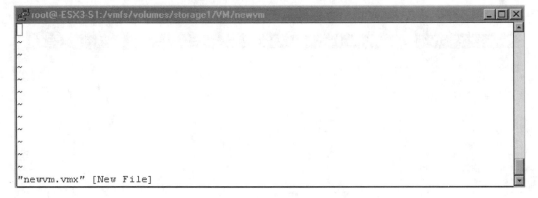

- You are now ready to create your new virtual machine configuration file. We are going to use the built-in text editor VI to create our configuration file. Type **vi newvm.vmx** and press **Enter** (see Figure 21.4).

Figure 21.4 Creating a New Virtual Machine Configuration File in VI

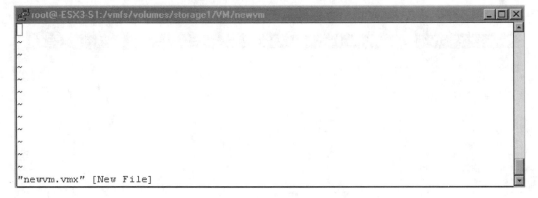

- Press **I** to turn on inserting (you will see the word insert at the bottom of the screen).
- Type in the following example virtual machine configuration file (see Code Listing 21.4).

Code Listing 21.4 Example Virtual Machine Configuration File

```
config.version = "6"
virtualHW.version = "3"
memsize = "256"
floppy0.present = "false"
displayName = "newVM"
guestOS = "winNetStandard"
```

```
ide0:0.present = "TRUE"
ide0:0.deviceType = "cdrom-raw"
ide:0.startConnected = "false"
floppy0.startConnected = "FALSE"
floppy0.fileName = "/dev/fd0"
Ethernet0.present = "TRUE"
Ethernet0.connectionType = "monitor_dev"
Ethernet0.networkName = "VM Network"
Ethernet0.addressType = "vpx"
scsi0.present = "true"
scsi0.sharedBus = "none"
scsi0.virtualDev = "lsilogic"
scsi0:0.present = "true"
scsi0:0.fileName = "newvm.vmdk"
scsi0:0.deviceType = "scsi-hardDisk"
```

- Press the **Esc** key to exit the insert mode, then press and hold **Shift** and press **ZZ** to save and exit (see Figure 21.5).

Figure 21.5 Saving the VMX File in VI

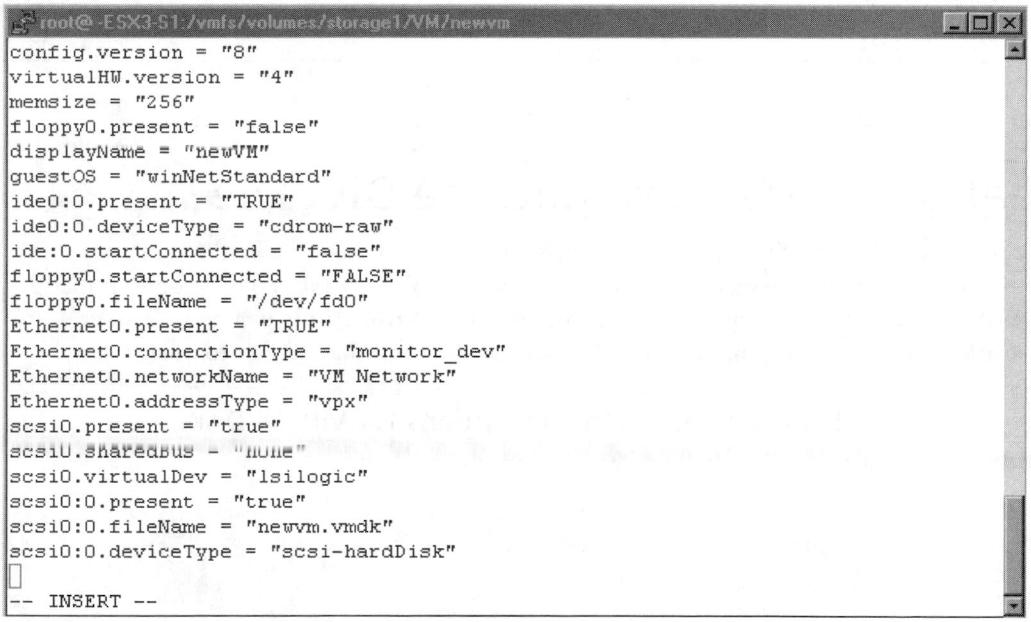

- Type **ls –l** to get a directory listing. You should now see your new virtual machine configuration file (see Figure 21.6).

Figure 21.6 Completed Creation of VMX File

```
root@-ESX3-S1:/vmfs/volumes/storage1/VM/newvm                    _ □ X
[root@-ESX3-S1 root]#
[root@-ESX3-S1 root]#
[root@-ESX3-S1 root]#
[root@-ESX3-S1 root]#
[root@-ESX3-S1 root]#
[root@-ESX3-S1 root]#
[root@-ESX3-S1 root]# cd /vmfs/volumes/storage1/VM
[root@-ESX3-S1 VM]# mkdir newvm
[root@-ESX3-S1 VM]# cd newvm
[root@-ESX3-S1 newvm]# vi newvm.vmx
[root@-ESX3-S1 newvm]# ls -l
total 64
-rw-r--r--     1 root     root           596 Oct   8 13:06 newvm.vmx
[root@-ESX3-S1 newvm]# []
```

You are now ready to go on to the next section to create the virtual disk newvm.vmdk that you will be referencing in your configuration file.

NOTE

Do not log out or close your ESX session just yet. You will continue from this point in the next section.

Creation of a Virtual Machine Disk File

VMware has a command-line utility called *vmkfstools* which can be used for the creation of VMFS file systems and virtual machine disk files. In this chapter, we will only focus on the options that pertain to virtual disks. For a full listing of command options, type **vmkfstools** in a console session or **man vmkfstools**. Code Listing 21.5 lists the *vmkfstools* options that pertain to virtual disks.

Code Listing 21.5 vmkfstools Command Options for Virtual Disks

```
vmkfstools
OPTIONS FOR VIRTUAL DISKS:
vmkfstools -c --createvirtualdisk #[gGmMkK]
           -d --diskformat [zeroedthick|
                            eagerzeroedthick|
                            thick|
                            thin]
           -a --adapterType [buslogic|lsilogic]
```

```
        -w --writezeros

        -j --inflatedisk

        -U --deletevirtualdisk

        -E --renamevirtualdisk srcDisk

        -i --clonevirtualdisk srcDisk

        -d --diskformat [rdm:<device>|rdmp:<device>|
                         raw:<device>|thin|2gbsparse]

        -X --extendvirtualdisk #[gGmMkK]

        -M --migratevirtualdisk

        -r --createrdm /vmfs/devices/disks/…

        -q --queryrdm

        -z --createrdmpassthru /vmfs/devices/disks/…

        -Q   createrawdevice /vmfs/devices/generic/…

        -v --verbose #

        -g --geometry

vmfsPath
```

In our example, we will create a 4 GB virtual disk called newvm.vmdk and assign it a SCSI LSI Logic adapter. In the console, type the following: **vmkfstools −c 4 g newvm.vmdk −a lsilogic**. Then, press **Enter** (see Figure 21.7).

Figure 21.7 Creating the Virtual Disk

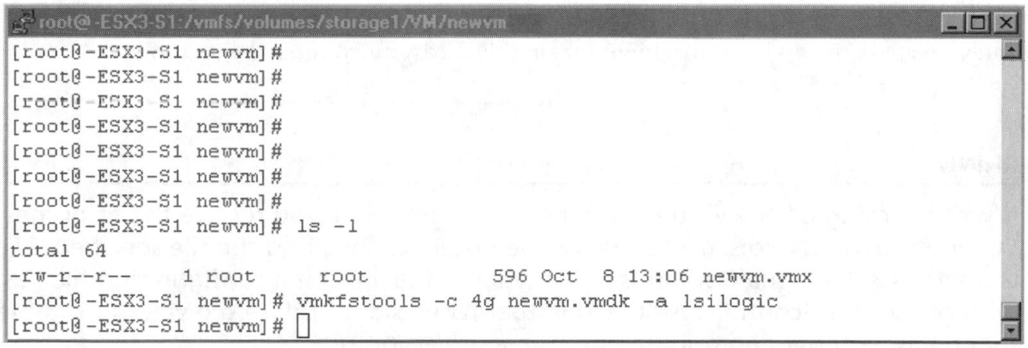

We have now created a virtual disk file newvm.vmdk in the same location as our virtual machine configuration file. The last step is to register this new virtual machine with ESX Server.

Registering Virtual Machines with ESX Server

VMware includes the *vmware-cmd* command tool for performing various operations on virtual machines and the server. In this chapter, we will focus on the virtual machine registration option of this tool *-s register*. For more information on all available tool options, type **vmware-cmd** at the console command prompt.

Type the following all on one line in the console window to register the new virtual machine with the ESX server:

```
vmware-cmd -s register "Your Path"/newvm/newvm.vmx
```

"Your Path" should be in a similar format to */vmfs/volumes/storage1/* (see Figure 21.8).

Figure 21.8 Registering a Virtual Machine with ESX

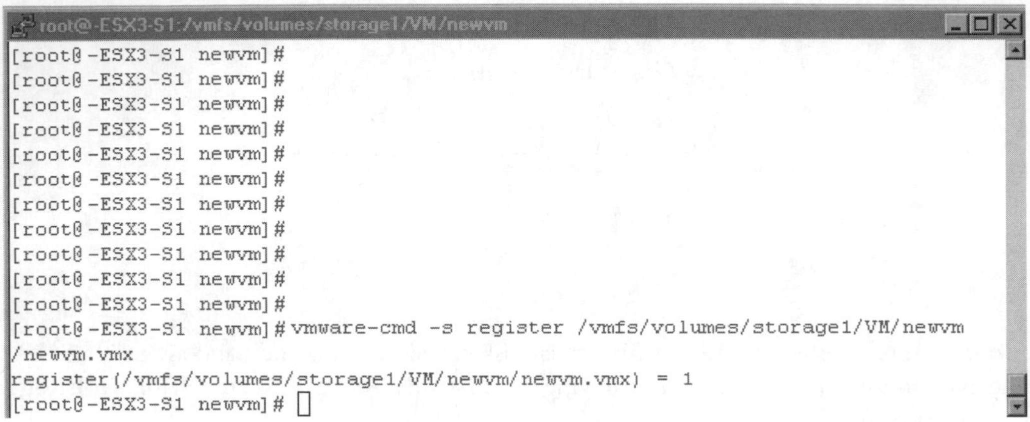

```
[root@-ESX3-S1 newvm]#
[root@-ESX3-S1 newvm]#
[root@-ESX3-S1 newvm]#
[root@-ESX3-S1 newvm]#
[root@-ESX3-S1 newvm]#
[root@-ESX3-S1 newvm]#
[root@-ESX3-S1 newvm]#
[root@-ESX3-S1 newvm]#
[root@-ESX3-S1 newvm]#
[root@-ESX3-S1 newvm]#
[root@-ESX3-S1 newvm]#
[root@-ESX3-S1 newvm]#vmware-cmd -s register /vmfs/volumes/storage1/VM/newvm
/newvm.vmx
register(/vmfs/volumes/storage1/VM/newvm/newvm.vmx) = 1
[root@-ESX3-S1 newvm]# []
```

A returned value of "1" after running this command indicates a successful registration of the virtual machine. Open up the GUI of your ESX server to verify that the new VM is listed. At this point, you are ready to power on the virtual machine and install your operating system. You have successfully created a new virtual machine utilizing the VMware command-line tools.

> ## ! WARNING
>
> If when turning on the virtual machine for the first time you receive the error message "Cannot open disk <diskname.vmdk>:The system cannot find the file specified. Bad value for scsi0:0.virtualDev," this means your virtual machine configuration file has the wrong values for config.version and virtualHW.version. Update the values for these two fields with the appropriate ones for your version of ESX.

Scripting Creation of Virtual Machines in ESX Shell

Scripting the creation of virtual machines is simpler than one might think. We will leverage you new gained experience from previous sections on utilizing the VMware tools to automate the VM creation process. In the previous section, you manually created a virtual machine configuration file and virtual disk. You then registered the virtual machine with ESX Server. We're going to now essentially take all those commands and steps and automate them in a script that you can run repeatedly and customize to build various types of virtual machines.

The VMware ESX shell is simply the service console operating system. This operating system is a custom version of Linux that VMware created. In Linux, you can create a simple text file to automate commands and then execute it. If you are familiar with DOS batch files, then this will be easy for you. Code Listing 21.6 shows an example of scripted VM creation.

Code Listing 21.6 Scripted VM Creation

```
##### VM Creation Script ####################################
#Script Version 1.1
#Author David E. Hart
#Date 10-05-06
#
#--------+
# Purpose|
#--------+--------------------------------------------------=
# This script will create a VM with the following attributes;
# Virtual Machine Name = ScriptedVM
# Location of Virtual Machine = /VMFS/volumes/storage1/ScriptedVM
# Virtual Machine Type = "Microsoft Windows 2003 Standard"
# Virtual Machine Memory Allocation = 256meg
#
#-----------------------------------------+
#Custom Variable Section for Modification |
#-----------------------------------------+--------------------
#NVM is name of virtual machine(NVM). No Spaces allowed in name
#NVMDIR is the directory which holds all the VM files
#NVMOS specifies VM Operating System
#NVMSIZE is the size of the virtual disk to be created
#------------------------------------------------------------
############################################################
### Default Variable settings - change this to your preferences
NVM="ScriptedVM"          # Name of Virtual Machine
NVMDIR="ScriptedVM"       # Specify only the folder name to be
created; NOT the complete path
NVMOS="winnetstandard"    # Type of OS for Virtual Machine
NVMSIZE="4g"              # Size of Virtual Machine Disk
VMMEMSIZE="256"           # Default Memory Size
```

```
### End Variable Declaration
mkdir /vmfs/volumes/storage1/$NVMDIR # Creates directory
exec 6>&1                            # Sets up write to file
exec 1>/vmfs/volumes/storage1/$NVMDIR/$NVM.vmx # Open file
# write the configuration
echo config.version = '"'6'"'         # For ESX 3.x the value is 8
echo virtualHW.version = '"'3'"'    # For ESX 3.x the value is 4
echo memsize = '"'$VMMEMSIZE'"'
echo floppy0.present = '"'TRUE'"'    # setup VM with floppy
echo displayName = '"'$NVM'"'        # name of virtual machine
echo guestOS = '"'$NVMOS'"'
echo
echo ide0:0.present = '"'TRUE'"'
echo ide0:0.deviceType = '"'cdrom-raw'"'
echo ide:0.startConnected = '"'false'"'  # CDROM enabled
echo floppy0.startConnected = '"'FALSE'"'
echo floppy0.fileName = '"'/dev/fd0'"'
echo Ethernet0.present = '"'TRUE'"'
echo Ethernet0.networkName = '"'VM Network'"'   # Default network
echo Ethernet0.addressType = '"'vpx'"'
echo
echo scsi0.present = '"'true'"'
echo scsi0.sharedBus = '"'none'"'
echo scsi0.virtualDev = '"'lsilogic'"'
echo scsi0:0.present = '"'true'"' # Virtual Disk Settings
echo scsi0:0.fileName = '"'$NVM.vmdk'"'
echo scsi0:0.deviceType = '"'scsi-hardDisk'"'
echo
# close file
exec 1>&-
# make stdout a copy of FD 6 (reset stdout), and close FD6
exec 1>&6
exec 6>&-
# Change permissions on the file so it can be executed by anyone
chmod 755 /vmfs/volumes/storage1/$NVMDIR/$NVM.vmx
#Creates 4gb Virtual disk
cd /vmfs/volumes/storage1/$NVMDIR  #change to the VM dir
vmkfstools -c $NVMSIZE $NVM.vmdk -a lsilogic
#Register VM
vmware-cmd -s register /vmfs/volumes/storage1/$NVMDIR/$NVM.vmx
```

NOTE

The standard format for values for the VMX file are to encase them in double quotes, such as memsize = "256". When scripting the creation of the VMX, you need to use single quote, double quote, single quote. So the previous example would be memsize = ' " '256' " '. You must do this for VMX values.

The script in Code Listing 21.6 will create a virtual machine that has the following characteristics:

- A VM called ScriptedVM in a directory named ScriptedVM on storage1
- A VM that will be assigned 256 MB of memory
- A VM that will have a 4 GB SCSI hard drive (lsilogic controller)
- A VM configured for a Windows 2003 standard operating system
- A floppy drive assigned, not connected at startup
- A CD-ROM attached to the ESX server's CD-ROM drive, not connected at startup
- An Ethernet adapter connected to the VM Network, enabled at startup

The *exec* commands in the script are system-level commands in Linux to set up the writing to, and saving of, the script file. It redirects the console screen's output to the script file. The use of the *echo* commands in the script sends the commands to the screen which are redirected to the file for writing. The file is then closed and the virtual configuration file, VMX, is saved. The permissions are changed on the configuration file so any user on ESX can access the virtual machine. Then the script creates the virtual disk and registers the VM with the ESX server.

Use the following process to set up your script on the ESX server:

- Log in locally or connect to your ESX server remotely.
- Log in with an ID that has root privileges (see Figure 21.9).

Figure 21.9 Gaining Root Level Access on ESX Server

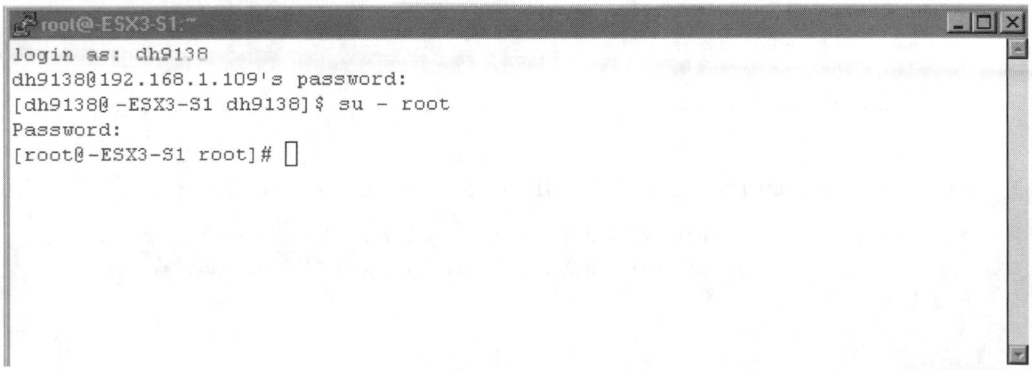

```
login as: dh9138
dh9138@192.168.1.109's password:
[dh9138@-ESX3-S1 dh9138]$ su - root
Password:
[root@-ESX3-S1 root]# []
```

- Change to the location or create a location of where you would like to store your scripts (see Figure 21.10).

Figure 21.10 Script Storage Location

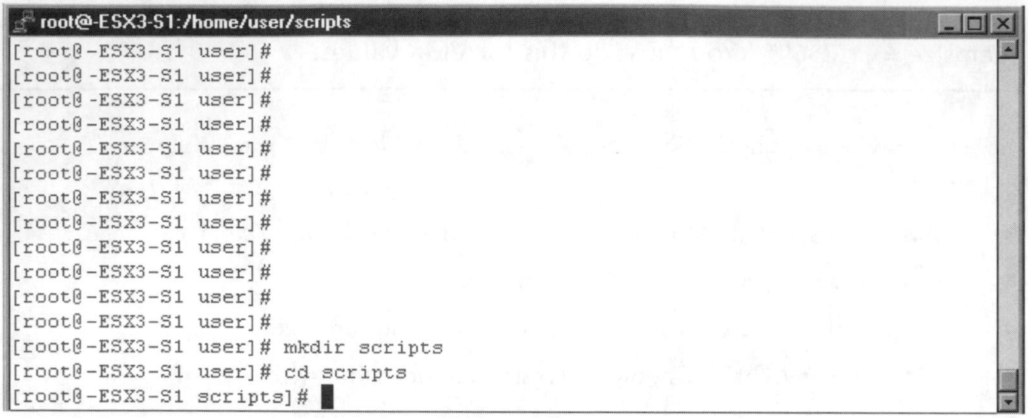

```
root@-ESX3-S1:/home/user/scripts                          _ □ ×
[root@-ESX3-S1 user]#
[root@-ESX3-S1 user]#
[root@-ESX3-S1 user]#
[root@-ESX3-S1 user]#
[root@-ESX3-S1 user]#
[root@-ESX3-S1 user]#
[root@-ESX3-S1 user]#
[root@-ESX3-S1 user]#
[root@-ESX3-S1 user]#
[root@-ESX3-S1 user]#
[root@-ESX3-S1 user]#
[root@-ESX3-S1 user]# mkdir scripts
[root@-ESX3-S1 user]# cd scripts
[root@-ESX3-S1 scripts]#
```

- Type **VI newvm.script** and press **Enter**.

- Press **I** for insert and type in the script as shown in Code Listing 21.6 (see Figure 21.11).

Figure 21.11 Using VI to Create Shell Script

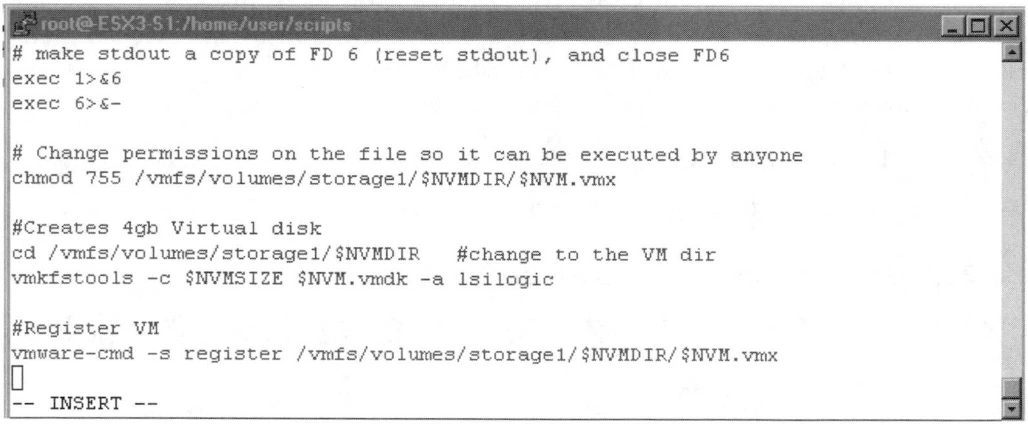

```
root@-ESX3-S1:/home/user/scripts                          _ □ ×
# make stdout a copy of FD 6 (reset stdout), and close FD6
exec 1>&6
exec 6>&-

# Change permissions on the file so it can be executed by anyone
chmod 755 /vmfs/volumes/storage1/$NVMDIR/$NVM.vmx

#Creates 4gb Virtual disk
cd /vmfs/volumes/storage1/$NVMDIR    #change to the VM dir
vmkfstools -c $NVMSIZE $NVM.vmdk -a lsilogic

#Register VM
vmware-cmd -s register /vmfs/volumes/storage1/$NVMDIR/$NVM.vmx
[
-- INSERT --
```

- Press **Esc** and then press and hold **Shift** while pressing **ZZ** to exit and save.

- You should now have a file called newvm.script listed. Before you run the script, you must set permissions on it. To do this, type **chmod 755 newvm.script** (see Figure 21.12).

Figure 21.12 Setting Permissions on Script File

```
root@-ESX3-S1:/home/user/scripts                                    _ □ ×
[root@-ESX3-S1 scripts]#
[root@-ESX3-S1 scripts]#
[root@-ESX3-S1 scripts]#
[root@-ESX3-S1 scripts]#
[root@-ESX3-S1 scripts]#
[root@-ESX3-S1 scripts]#
[root@-ESX3-S1 scripts]#
[root@-ESX3-S1 scripts]#
[root@-ESX3-S1 scripts]#
[root@-ESX3-S1 scripts]#
[root@-ESX3-S1 scripts]#
[root@-ESX3-S1 scripts]# ./newvm.script
-bash: ./newvm.script: Permission denied
[root@-ESX3-S1 scripts]# chmod 755 newvm.script
[root@-ESX3-S1 scripts]# █
```

- Run the script by typing **./newvm.script** (see Figure 21.13).

Figure 21.13 The Execution of Shell Script

```
root@-ESX3-S1:/home/user/scripts                                    _ □ ×
[root@-ESX3-S1 storage1]#
[root@-ESX3-S1 storage1]#
[root@-ESX3-S1 storage1]# cd /
[root@-ESX3-S1 /]# cd home
[root@-ESX3-S1 home]# ls
dh9138   lost+found   user
[root@-ESX3-S1 home]# cd user
[root@-ESX3-S1 user]# ls
scripts
[root@-ESX3-S1 user]# cd scripts
[root@-ESX3-S1 scripts]# ls
newvm.script
[root@-ESX3-S1 scripts]# ./newvm.script
register(/vmfs/volumes/storage1/ScriptedVM/ScriptedVM.vmx) = 1
[root@-ESX3-S1 scripts]# []
```

The virtual machine has now been created and registered with ESX. The next steps are for you to power it on and install the guest operating system. Creating scripts in ESX shell will save you time and effort in creating new virtual machines in your environment.

TIP

VMware ESX shell is just a customized version of Linux. For more information on scripting in shell, reference Linux shell information and examples.

Swiss Army Knife...

Creating Templates with the Scripted VM Creation Script

You can create multiple copies of the Scripted VM Creation script all with unique configurations. Save each of these customized scripts with a descriptive name such as **2003std512 m4 g.script** or **2003ent1 g4 g.script**. You could use the ESX shell command **cp Source.script Target.script** to copy the first script and then use **VI** to customize the second one. Change each script to store its VMs in a staging area and each VM with a unique name. Now when you need to build those types of VMs you have template scripts to do it with. You could even chain together running of these scripts so you can create complete virtual system setups.

   If you are not comfortable with utilizing VI as a text editor, you could also use a text editor such as Notepad on your PC to create your script. Once you have completed your script, highlight the whole script and select **copy**. Connect to your ESX server with a tool like **Putty** and run the **VI** command. Select **I** for input, and then paste in your script. All the script examples in this chapter were created on ESX Server using that method. Alternatively, you could also create the script file locally and then use a tool like WinSCP to copy the file to your ESX server.

Scripting Creation of Virtual Machines in Perl Scripts

VMware ESX Server supports additional scripting languages such as VmPerl. VmPerl is VMware's version of the Perl programming language. VMware has designed VmPerl to provide task automation and simple, single-purpose user interfaces. VmPerl's main purpose is to interact with the virtual machines on ESX Server. You can query status, start and stop virtual machines, as well as manage snapshots. With some creative scripting we can have VmPerl create our virtual machines for us as well. Scripting in VmPerl is not for beginners. If you've never scripted in Perl before then review the sample VmPerl Script and note the code comments in the script. VmPerl is a customized version of Perl, so research the Perl language in general for more information on how to program in Perl. The example script in Code Listing 21.7 was written so it could be easily modified to suit your particular needs. It is a basic VmPerl script with a menu-driven interface. Leveraging the knowledge you've gained in the previous sections will help you understand the script interactions. Novices in scripting should find the next script example very easy to understand and follow. Experienced scripters may find the script rudimentary and know of alternate ways to accomplish similar tasks. Whatever your scripting experience, I hope you find the example scripts in this chapter thought provoking and insightful.

NOTE

VMware in its latest release of ESX Server 3.0 is moving toward more mainstream scripting languages. Scripting APIs such as VmCom and VmPerl are being deprecated. What this means is that VMware prefers that you use a new set of APIs for programming languages such as Java, Visual .NET, and so on. ESX 3.0 will continue to support VmPerl and ESX shell scripting, and all the sample scripts in the chapter have been tested on ESX 3.0.

VmPerl allows for flexibility on how you go about creating your virtual machines. In our example script (see Code Listing 21.7), I used VmPerl's user input and file manipulation commands to accomplish the three primary tasks when creating virtual machines.

- Creating the virtual machine configuration file (VMX)
- Creating the virtual machine disk file (VMDK)
- Registering the virtual machine with ESX Server

NOTE

The script shown in Code Listing 21.7 is meant to be used for educational purposes. Further development in the area of "error checking" and "handling" should be done prior to utilizing it in a production environment. It is meant only to show what can be done with VmPerl.

Code Listing 21.7 Scripted VM Creation with Perl

```
#!/usr/bin/perl -w
use VMware::VmPerl;
use VMware::VmPerl::Server;
use VMware::VmPerl::ConnectParams;
#use strict;
##### VM Menu Driven Creation Script ###########
#Script Version 1.8
#Author David E. Hart
#Date 10-05-06
#
```

```
#----------+
#Purpose   |
#-----------
# This script presents a menu for automatically building
# virtual machine config files (VMX) and Dis files (VMDK)
# This script demonstrates how to automate the setup
# of virtual environments
#---------------------------+
#Custom Variables Section   |
#---------------------------+
#vmname = virtual machine name, will be used for disk as well
#vmmem = amount of memory assigned to VM
#vmos = OS that VM is configured for
#vmdisk = size of VM disk
#######################
main:  # main menu
system("clear");
print "       MAIN MENU \n";
print "-------------------  Virtual Machine Creation ----------- \n";
print "\n";
print "\n";
print "\n";
print "      1) Create a Custom VM \n";
print "\n";
print "      2) Create VM's from Defined Templates \n";
print "\n";
print "      3) View ESX's registered VM's \n";
print "\n";
print "      4) Exit \n";
print "\n";
print "      Your Selection - ";
$menuopt = <>; chomp $menuopt;     # Get user selection
if ($menuopt == 1) { # Get input for custom VM
    system("clear");
    print "What do you want to name your VM? ";
    $vmname = <>; chomp $vmname;  # use chomp to remove
carriage return
    print "How much memory do you want to assign? ";
    $vmmem = <>;chomp $vmmem;
    print "Do you want to run Windows 2003STD as the OS?
(y/n) ";
```

```
    $vmos = <>;chomp $vmos;
  if ($vmos eq "y") {
      $vmos = "winNetStandard";
      } # Only 2 options for this example
  else {
      print "Do you want to run Windows 2003Ent as the OS? (y/n) ";
      $vmos2 = <>;chomp $vmos2;
      if ($vmos2 eq "y") {
        $vmos = "winnetenterprise";
      }
    }
  print "What size hard disk do you want to set up (gb)? ";
  $vmdisk = <>;chomp $vmdisk;
  print "n";
  $x = writevmx();    # Subrouting for creating VMX file
  if ($x -- 1) {
      print "VMX File written successfully n";
      }
  $w = setper();      # Subroutine to set permissions so anyone can use VM
  if ($w == 1) {
    print "Permissions set successfully n";
      }
  $y = createdisk(); # subrouting to create VMDK disk file
  if ($y == 1) {
      print "Virtual disk created successfully n";
      }
  $z = registervm(); # subroutine to register VM with ESX
  if ($z == 1) {
      print "VM registered successfully n";
      }
  print "Press the ENTER key to continue …";
  $pause = <STDIN>;
  goto main
    }
if ($menuopt == 2) { # option to displays the templates
menu1:
  system("clear");
  print "    Defined Templates \n";
  print "    -------------- \n";
  print "\n";
```

```
print "\n";
print "      1) Windows 2003std VM with 256m, 4gb drive \n";
print "\n";
print "      2) Windows 2003ent VM with 1gig, 8gb drive \n";
print "\n";
print "\n";
print "\n";
print "\n";
print "      Your Selection - ";
$menu1opt = <>; chomp $menu1opt;
if ($menu1opt == 1) {
    $vmname = "2003std25m4gb";
    $vmmem = "256"; # change and add on similar sections
    $vmdisk = "4";  # to create templates for your environment
    $vmos = "winnetstandard";
    $x = writevmx();
      if ($x == 1) {
      print "VMX File written successfully \na";
      }
    $w = setper();
      if ($w == 1) {
      print "Permisions set successfully \na";
      }
    $y = createdisk();     # Call subroutines to create VMs
      if ($y == 1) {
      print "Virtual disk created successfully \na";
      }
    $z = registervm();
      if ($z == 1) {
      print "VM registered successfully na";
      }
    print "Press the ENTER key to continue …";
    $pause = <STDIN>;
    goto main
    }
if ($menu1opt == 2) {
    $vmname = "2003Ent1gb8gb";
    $vmmem = "1024";
    $vmdisk = "8";
    $vmos = "winnetenterprise";
```

```
    $x = writevmx();
        if ($x == 1) {
        print "VMX file written successfully na";
        }
    $w = setper();
        if ($w == 1) {
        print "Permissions set successfully na";
        }
    $y = createdisk();
        if ($y == 1) {
        print "Virtual disk created successfully na";
        }
    $z = registervm();
        if ($z == 1) {
        print "VM registered successfully na";
        }
    print "Press the ENTER key to continue …";
    $pause = <STDIN>;
    goto main
      }
   else {
     goto menu1;
   }
  }
if ($menuopt == 3) { # Use a function of VmPerl to display registered VMs
  system("clear");
  my ($server_name, $user, $passwd) = @ARGV;    # Assume running in ESX server
  my $port = 902;    # with appropriate rights
VMware::VmPerl::ConnectParams::new($server_name,$port,$user,$passwd);
VMware::VmPerl::ConnectParams::new(undef,$port,$user,$passwd);
  my $connect_params = VMware::VmPerl::ConnectParams::new();
  # Establish a persistent connection with server
  my $server = VMware::VmPerl::Server::new();
  if (!$server->connect($connect_params)) {
     my ($error_number, $error_string) = $server->get_last_error();
     die "Could not connect to server: Error $error_number: $error_string\n";
   }
  print "\nThe following virtual machines are registered:\n";
  # Obtain a list containing every config file path registered with the server.
  my @list = $server->registered_vm_names();
```

```
    if (!defined($list[0])) {
      my ($error_number, $error_string) = $server->get_last_error();
      die "Could not get list of VMs from server: Error $error_number: ".
        "$error_string\n";
    }
    print "$_\n" foreach (@list);
    # Destroys the server object, thus disconnecting from the server.
    undef $server;
    print "Press the ENTER key to continue …";
    $pause = <STDIN>;
    goto main
}
if ($menuopt == 4) {
  goto end1
  }
sub writevmx {          # Subroutine to Create VM's VMX config file
# $file = '/vmfs/volumes/storage1/perlvm/perlvm.vmx';    # Name the file
    $file = "/vmfs/volumes/storage1/perlvm/". $vmname. ".vmx";
    open(INFO, ">$file");      # Open for output
    print INFO 'config.version = "6"' . "\n";
    print INFO 'virtualHW.version = "3"' . "\n";
    print INFO 'memsize = "'. $vmmem. '"' . "\n";
    print INFO 'floppy0.present = "TRUE"' . "\n";
    print INFO 'displayName = "' . $vmname . '"' . "\n";
    print INFO 'guestOS = "' . $vmos . '"' . "\n";
    print INFO 'ide0:0.present = "TRUE"' . "\n";
    print INFO 'ide0:0.deviceType = "cdrom-raw"' . "\n";
    print INFO 'ide:0.startConnected = "false"' . "\n";
    print INFO 'floppy0.startConnected = "FALSE"' . "\n";
    print INFO 'floppy0.fileName = "/dev/fd0"' . "\n";
    print INFO 'Ethernet0.present = "TRUE"' . "\n";
    print INFO 'Ethernet0.connectionType = "monitor_dev"' . "\n";
    print INFO 'Ethernet0.networkName = "VM Network"' . "\n";
    print INFO 'Ethernet0.addressType = "vpx"' . "\n";
    print INFO 'scsi0.present = "true"' . "\n";
    print INFO 'scsi0.sharedBus = "none"' . "\n";
    print INFO 'scsi0.virtualDev = "lsilogic"' . "\n";
    print INFO 'scsi0:0.present = "true"' . "\n";
    print INFO 'scsi0:0.fileName = "' . $vmname . '.vmdk"' . "\n";
    print INFO 'scsi0:0.deviceType = "scsi-hardDisk"' . "\n";
```

```
      close(INFO);        # Close the file
}
sub createdisk {      # Subroutine to create virtual disk
      $cr = "vmkfstools -c " . $vmdisk . "g " . " /vmfs/volumes/storage1/perlvm/".
$vmname . ".vmdk -a lsilogic";
      system("$cr");
      };
sub registervm {      # Subroutine to register VM with ESX Server
      $rg = "vmware-cmd -s register /vmfs/volumes/storage1/perlvm/" . $vmname . ".vmx";
      system("$rg");
      }
sub setper{    # Subroutine to set permission on VMX file
      $pm = "chmod 755 /vmfs/volumes/storage1/perlvm/" . $vmname . ".vmx";
      system("$pm");
      }
end1:
```

Modifying Scripted VM Creation with Perl

The script shown in Code Listing 21.7, and later in Code Listing 21.11, provides static mapping for VM creation. This is sufficient for an example, but not very practical for real-world scenarios. We will modify the script to support end-user input of VM destination pathing. We will accomplish this by adding a new variable *$vmpath* to our script and adding the appropriate following sections.

- Add new variable *vmpath* to scripts variable notes section

```
#------------------------+
#Custom Variables Section |
#------------------------+
#vmname = virtual machine name, used for disk as well
#vmmem = amount of memory assigned to VM
#vmos = OS that VM is configured for
#vmdisk = size of VM disk
#vmpath = path to VM directory, (must already exist)
####################################################
```

- Add new prompt in Custom VM Creation section, "option 1."

```
print "What size hard disk do you want to set up (gb)? ";
$vmdisk = <>;chomp $vmdisk;
print "\n";
```

```
print "Path to Save VM (ie. /vmfs/volumes/storage1/vm/";
$vmpath = <>;chomp $vmpath;
print "\n";
```

- Add new prompt in Defined Templates section, "option 2."

```
$vmos = "winnetstandard";
print "Path to Save VM (ie. /vmfs/volumes/storage1/vm/";
$vmpath = <>;chomp $vmpath;
print "\n";
```

- Update subroutine "writevmx".

```
$file = $vmpath . $vmname . ".vmx";
```

- Update subroutine "createdisk".

```
$cr = "vmkfstools -c " . $vmdisk . "g " . $vmpath .
$vmname . ".vmdk -a lsilogic";
  system("$cr");
```

- Update subroutine "registerVM".

```
$rg = "vmware-cmd -s register " .$vmpath . $vmname . ".vmx";
system("$rg");
```

- Update subroutine "setper".

```
$pm = "chmod 755 " . $vmpath . $vmname . ".vmx";
system("$pm");
```

The script will now prompt you for VM destination when creating new VMs. Please note that when entering the destination file path, you should include the leading and trailing "/".

When the script in Code Listing 21.7 is executed on the ESX server, a menu will be displayed (see Figure 21.14).

Figure 21.14 The Perl Script VM Creation Menu

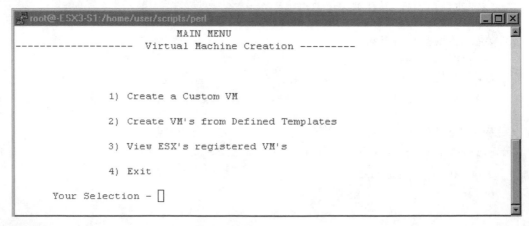

Perl Script Components

Utilizing the script in Code Listing 21.7, you can do the following tasks:

- Create a custom VM with parameters that you supply.
- Create VMs from predefined templates.
- View listing of VMs currently registered on the ESX server.
- Exit the script.

This script was written to be easily customized by you, the reader. Variables have been set up for key VM-related options enabling simple modifications. Let's dissect this script to get a better understanding of VmPerl. Code Listing 21.8 shows the key variables.

Code Listing 21.8 Scripted Creation of VM with Perl Key Variables

```
$vmname = virtual machine name, will be used for disk as well
$vmmem = amount of memory assigned to VM
$vmos = OS that VM is configured for
$vmdisk = size of VM disk
```

These variables in the program are either dynamic or static depending upon which option in the script you choose. The first option presented on the menu shown in Figure 21.14 is Create A Custom VM. This option will prompt you for the variables listed in Code Listing 21.8, as shown in Figure 21.15.

Figure 21.15 Perl Script Custom Creation of VM

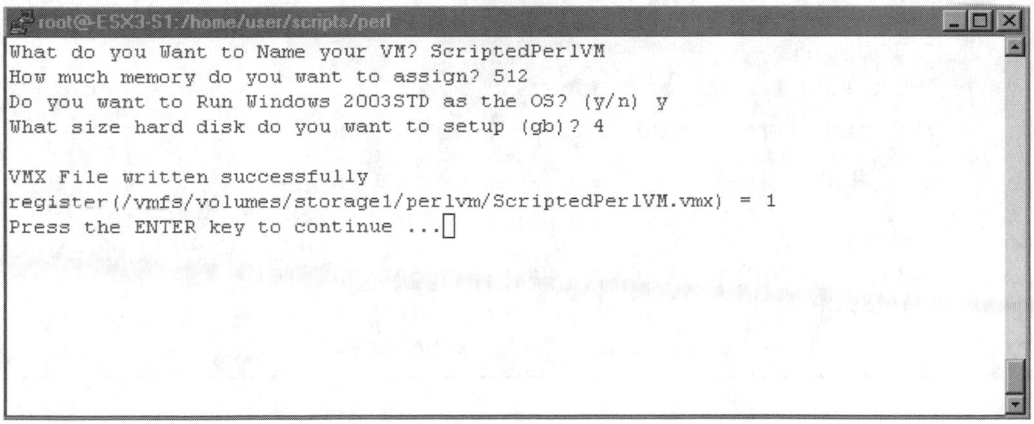

```
root@ESX3-S1:/home/user/scripts/perl
What do you Want to Name your VM? ScriptedPerlVM
How much memory do you want to assign? 512
Do you want to Run Windows 2003STD as the OS? (y/n) y
What size hard disk do you want to setup (gb)? 4

VMX File written successfully
register(/vmfs/volumes/storage1/perlvm/ScriptedPerlVM.vmx) = 1
Press the ENTER key to continue ...
```

If you select the second option, **Create VM's from Defined Templates**, the values are set statically in that section. Code Listing 21.9 shows an example where these values are set in the code.

Code Listing 21.9 Perl Script Static Variables for Template VM Creation

```
if ($menu1opt == 1) {
    $vmname = "2003std25m4gb";
    $vmmem = "256";
    $vmdisk = "4";
    $vmos = "winnetstandard";
```

It's a simple task to add additional menu options for more templates. Adding sections like those in Code Listing 21.9 will enable to you to define a bigger selection of templates for your environment.

Master Craftsman...

VM Procurement Automation

The example script provides basic VM procurement with two templates and a custom VM creation option. Typical production environments have a multitude of system types and requirements. You can modify the script to meet your needs and provide for procurement of VMs for varying situations such as:

- Procurement of new virtual machines for customers
- Procurement of groups of servers
- Automated environment setups (lab testing, and so on)

Because the script is written in VmPerl, which is just a VMware-customized version of Perl, you can leverage Perl's additional features and characteristics. Perl code can be executed from within a Web browser enabling you to create a VM procurement Web site. You could host this new Web site on the ESX server itself, and create a "Self Service" procurement architecture. These are just some suggestions and ideas to get you thinking about the possibilities that VmPerl provides.

The third menu choice option in the script is View ESX's Registered VM's. This section utilizes the VmPerl API to access the ESX server. For more information on the VmPerl API, download the ESX server SDK. This section of the code connects to the local ESX server with your current userid and password on port 902. It then queries ESX Server for a listing of registered VMs. Figure 21.16 shows the output generated by this option.

Figure 21.16 Perl Script Query of ESX Server for Registered VMs

VmPerl Commands

VmPerl by itself cannot create virtual machine files or register virtual machines. To accomplish these tasks, we must use the tools available. The sample VmPerl script utilizes the command "system" to access the following VMware tools:

- *vmkfstools*
- *vmware-cmd*

Do those tools sound familiar? By now you've become quite adept at utilizing these tools for the creation of virtual machines. The latter sections of the code contain the subroutines that handle the virtual machine disk creation *createdisk*, and VM registration *registervm*. It is in these subroutines that we use the tools listed earlier.

Utilizing the example script, and with your working knowledge of the VMware tools from previous sections, you should have a competent understanding of how to create virtual machines from a VmPerl script.

Cloning Virtual Machines Utilizing ESX Shell Scripts

As we've seen in previous sections, VMware provides you with built-in tools to accomplish most virtualization tasks. Cloning is the process of copying an existing virtual machine's virtual disk to a new file for a new virtual machine to use. The source virtual machine is considered to be the template VM. Understand that cloning creates an exact replica of the VM's disk contents. It is very similar to disk imaging. So when this clone is configured and turned on in ESX Server it will come up with all the same attributes as the template VM. To address this, the template VM should be prepared in advanced for cloning. For Microsoft Windows–based servers, you would use *Sysprep* to prepare the template image for cloning. Using template images saves an enormous amount of time when procuring servers for all types of situations. Because the template VM has the operating system preinstalled and configured, setup time for new systems is drastically reduced.

To clone an existing template virtual machine, we will use the VMware utility *vmkfstools*. We will use the *-i* option which instructs *vmkfstools* to import an existing template VM's disk file (VMDK) and copy it. The command syntax is as follows:

```
Vmkfstools -I /pathtoTemplateVM/template.vmdk /pathtoDestinationVM/newvm.vmdk
```

The cloning process does not create a virtual machine configuration file or register the new virtual machine with ESX Server. We will leverage what you've learned in the previous sections to modify the ESX shell script from Code Listing 21.6.

We need to modify the part of the script that calls *vmkfstools* to create the 4 GB virtual disk. We are instead going to use the *-i* command and clone an existing virtual disk. If you've been implementing the scripts in the previous sections, then you will have an example virtual machine disk that we can use for this section. If not, create a quick empty VM via any of the ESX GUI methods: Virtual Client, Virtual Infrastructure Client (ESX 3.0), Web, and so on.

Once you have your source template virtual disk ready, go ahead and edit the code to support cloning (see Code Listing 21.10).

Code Listing 21.10 ESX Shell Script VM Creation Utilizing Cloning

```
##### VM Creation Script Utilizing Cloning        #####
#Script Version 1.2
#Author David E. Hart
#Date 10-05-06
#
#--------+
# Purpose|
#--------+----------------------------------------------------
# This script will create a VM utilizing the cloning option of
# the vmkfstools command tool;
# The New Virtual Machine Configuration will be set as follows
# Virtual Machine Name = ScriptedCloneVM
```

```
# Location of Virtual Machine = /VMFS/volumes/storage1/ScriptedVM
# Virtual Machine Type = "Microsoft Windows 2003 Standard"
# Virtual Machine Memory Allocation = 256 meg
#
#---------------------------------------+
#Custom Variable Section for Modification|
#---------------------------------------+-----------------------
#NVM is name of virtual machine(NVM). No Spaces allowed in name
#NVMDIR is the directory which holds all the VM files
#NVMOS specifies VM Operating System
#-----------------------------------------------------------------
###################################################################
### Default Variable settings - change this to your preferences
NVM="ScriptedCloneVM"          # Name of Virtual Machine
NVMDIR="ScriptedCloneVM"       # Specify only the folder name to be created;
NOT the complete path
NVMOS="winnetstandard"         # Type of OS for Virtual Machine
VMMEMSIZE="256"                # Default Memory Size
### End Variable Declaration
mkdir /vmfs/volumes/storage1/$NVMDIR    # Creates directory
exec 6>&1                               # Sets up write to file
exec 1>/vmfs/volumes/storage1/$NVMDIR/$NVM.vmx   # Open file
# write the configuration
echo config.version = '"'6'"'        # For ESX 3.x the value is 8
echo virtualHW.version = '"'3'"'     # For ESX 3.x the value is 4
echo memsize = '"'$VMMEMSIZE'"'
echo floppy0.present = '"'TRUE'"'    # setup VM with floppy
echo displayName = '"'$NVM'"'        # name of virtual machine
echo guestOS = '"'$NVMOS'"'
echo
echo ide0:0.present = '"'TRUE'"'
echo ide0:0.deviceType = '"'cdrom-raw'"'
echo ide0:0.startConnected = '"'false'"'    # CDROM enabled
echo floppy0.startConnected = '"'FALSE'"'
echo floppy0.fileName = '"'/dev/fd0'"'
echo Ethernet0.present = '"'TRUE'"'
echo Ethernet0.networkName = '"'VM Network'"'    # Default network
echo Ethernet0.addressType = '"'vpx'"'
echo
echo scsi0.present = '"'true'"'
```

```
echo scsi0.sharedBus = '"'none'"'
echo scsi0.virtualDev = '"'lsilogic'"'
echo scsi0:0.present = '"'true'"' # Virtual Disk Settings
echo scsi0:0.fileName = '"'$NVM.vmdk'"'
echo scsi0:0.deviceType = '"'scsi-hardDisk'"'
echo
# close file
exec 1>&-
# make stdout a copy of FD 6 (reset stdout), and close FD6
exec 1>&6
exec 6>&-
# Change permissions on the file so it can be executed by anyone
chmod 755 /vmfs/volumes/storage1/$NVMDIR/$NVM.vmx
#Clone existing Template VM's VMDK into current directory
cd /vmfs/volumes/storage1/$NVMDIR #change to the VM dir
vmkfstools -i /vmfs/volumes/storage1/ScriptedVM/ScriptedVM.vmdk $NVM.vmdk
#Register VM
vmware-cmd -s register /vmfs/volumes/storage1/$NVMDIR/$NVM.vmx
```

When you execute the script, the status of the cloning process will be displayed (see Figure 21.17).

Figure 21.17 Cloning Process

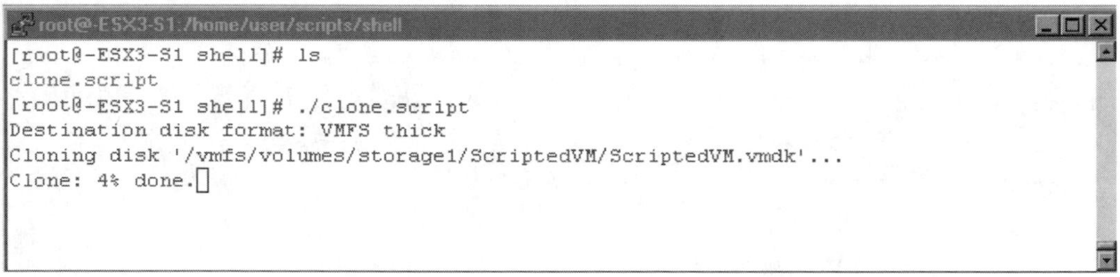

```
[root@-ESX3-S1 shell]# ls
clone.script
[root@-ESX3-S1 shell]# ./clone.script
Destination disk format: VMFS thick
Cloning disk '/vmfs/volumes/storage1/ScriptedVM/ScriptedVM.vmdk'...
Clone: 4% done.
```

When the script finishes, you will have a new cloned copy of the template VM ready for use. Log on to the ESX GUI and validate that the new VM is registered and available.

The ability to script the cloning of existing template VMs allows you to pre-stage your virtual environments for your particular needs. For instance, you could have a Windows Lab of four servers pre-staged. Just run the WindowsLab script and all four VMs are created and ready to go. In the next chapter, you will learn how to perform operations on VMs such as starting and stopping VMs via scripting.

Cloning Virtual Machines Utilizing VmPerl Scripts

You already know the benefits of cloning, but by utilizing the VmPerl scripting language you can build scripted procurement systems. VmPerl provides you more flexibility and more functionality than shell scripting. This allows you to be more creative in your approach to VM creation. We will add the cloning functionality to the example script in Code Listing 21.7. We will also add a new menu option for cloning and a new subroutine. In addition, we will use the VMware command tool *vmkfstools* with the *-i* option for cloning as we did in the previous chapter. Code Listing 21.11 shows the new Perl script with cloning.

Code Listing 21.11 Scripted VM Creation with Perl Utilizing Cloning

```
#!/usr/bin/perl -w
use VMware::VmPerl;
use VMware::VmPerl::Server;
use VMware::VmPerl::ConnectParams;
#use strict;
##### VM Menu Driven Creation Script with Cloning ###########
#Script Version 1.3
#Author David E. Hart
#Date 10-05-06
#
#--------+
#Purpose |
#---------
# This script presents a menu for automatically building
# virtual machine config files (VMX) and disk files (VMDK)
# This script demonstrates how to automate the setup
# of virtual environments and includes cloning of VMs
#------------------------+
#Custom Variables Section |
#-------------------------
#vmname = virtual machine name, will be used for disk as well
#vmmem = amount of memory assigned to VM
#vmos = OS that VM is configured for
#vmdisk = size of VM disk
####################################################
main:  # main menu
system("clear");
print "      MAIN MENU \n";
print "------ Virtual Machine Creation ----- \n";
```

```perl
print "\n";
print "\n";
print "\n";
print "        1) Create a Custom VM \n";
print "\n";
print "        2) Create VM's from Defined Templates \n";
print "\n";
print "        3) View ESX's registered VM's \n";
print "\n";
print "        4) Clone an Existing VM \n";
print "\n";
print "        5) Exit \n";
print "\n";
print "        Your Selection - ";
$menuopt = <>; chomp $menuopt;      # Get user selection
if ($menuopt == 1) { # Get input for custom VM
  system("clear");
  print "What do you Want to Name your VM? ";
  $vmname = <>; chomp $vmname;       # use chomp to remove carriage return
  print "How much memory do you want to assign? ";
  $vmmem = <>;chomp $vmmem;
  print "Do you want to run Windows 2003STD as the OS? (y/n) ";
  $vmos = <>;chomp $vmos;
  if ($vmos eq "y") {
    $vmos = "winNetStandard";
    }   # Only 2 options for this example
  else {
    print "Do you want to run Windows 2003Ent as the OS? (y/n) ";
    $vmos2 = <>;chomp $vmos2;
    if ($vmos2 eq "y") {
      $vmos = "winnetenterprise";
    }
    }
  print "What size hard disk do you want to set up (gb)? ";
  $vmdisk = <>;chomp $vmdisk;
  print "\n";
  $x = writevmx();    # Subrouting for creating VMX file
  if ($x == 1) {
      print "VMX file written successfully \n";
      }
```

```
$w = setper();      # Subroutine to set permissions so anyone can use VM
if ($w == 1) {
   print "Permissions set successfully \n";
      }
$y = createdisk(); # subrouting to create VMDK disk file
if ($y == 1) {
   print "Virtual disk created successfully \n";
      }
$z = registervm(); # subroutine to register VM with ESX
if ($z == 1) {
   print "VM registered successfully \n";
      }
print "Press the ENTER key to continue …";
$pause = <STDIN>;
goto main
   }
if ($menuopt == 2) { # option to display the templates
menu1:
   system("clear");
   print "    Defined Templates \n";
   print "    ---------------- \n";
   print "\n";
   print "\n";
   print "    1) Windows 2003std VM with 256m, 4gb drive n";
   print "n";
   print "    2) Windows 2003ent VM with 1gig, 8gb drive n";
   print "\n";
   print "\n";
   print "\n";
   print "\n";
   print " Your Selection - ";
   $menu1opt = <>; chomp $menu1opt;
   if ($menu1opt == 1) {
     $vmname = "2003std25m4gb";
     $vmmem = "256";   # change and add on similar sections
     $vmdisk = "4";    # to create templates for your environment
     $vmos = "winnetstandard";
     $x = writevmx();
       if ($x == 1) {
       print "VMX file written successfully \na";
       }
```

```
$w = setper();
  if ($w == 1) {
  print "Permissions set successfully \na";
  }
$y = createdisk();       # Call subroutines to create VM's
  if ($y == 1) {
  print "Virtual disk created successfully \na";
  }
$z = registervm();
  if ($z == 1) {
  print "VM registered successfully \na";
  }
print "Press the ENTER key to continue …";
$pause = <STDIN>;
goto main
}
if ($menu1opt == 2) {
$vmname = "2003Ent1gb8gb";
$vmmem = "1024";
$vmdisk = "8";
$vmos = "winnetenterprise";
$x = writevmx();
  if ($x == 1) {
  print "VMX file written successfully \na";
  }
$w = setper();
  if ($w == 1) {
  print "Permissions set successfully \na";
  }
$y = createdisk();
  if ($y == 1) {
  print "Virtual disk created successfully \na";
  }
$z = registervm();
  if ($z == 1) {
  print "VM registered successfully \na";
  }
print "Press the ENTER key to continue …";
$pause = <STDIN>;
goto main
}
```

```
   else {
      goto menu1;
   }
 }
if ($menuopt == 3) { # Use a function of VmPerl to display registered VMs
  system("clear");
  my ($server_name, $user, $passwd) = @ARGV;     # Assume running in ESX server
  my $port = 902;                                 # with appropriate rights
VMware::VmPerl::ConnectParams::new($server_name,$port,$user,$passwd);
VMware::VmPerl::ConnectParams::new(undef,$port,$user,$passwd); my $connect_params =
VMware::VmPerl::ConnectParams::new();
    # Establish a persistent connection with server
    my $server = VMware::VmPerl::Server::new();
    if (!$server->connect($connect_params)) {
      my ($error_number, $error_string) = $server->get_last_error();
      die "Could not connect to server: Error $error_number: $error_string\n";
    }
    print "\nThe following virtual machines are registered:\n";
    # Obtain a list containing every config file path registered with the server.
    my @list = $server->registered_vm_names();
    if (!defined($list[0])) {
      my ($error_number, $error_string) = $server->get_last_error();
      die "Could not get list of VMs from server: Error $error_number: ".
        "$error_stringn";
    }
    print "$_n" foreach (@list);
    # Destroys the server object, thus disconnecting from the server.
    undef $server;
    print "Press the ENTER key to continue …";
    $pause = <STDIN>;
    goto main
}
if ($menuopt == 4) {
    system("clear");
    print " Clone Existing VM.s \n";
    print " ———— \n";
    print "\n";
    print "\n";
    print " 1) Clone ScriptedVM \n";
    print "\n";
```

```perl
print " 2) Clone ScriptedPerlVM \n";
print "\n";
print "\n";
print "\n";
print "\n";
print " Your Selection - ";
$menu4opt = <>; chomp $menu4opt;
if ($menu4opt == 1) {
  $vmname = "ScriptedPerlCloneVM";
  $vmmem = "256"; # change and add on similar sections
  $vmdisk = "4";  # to create templates for your environment
  $vmos = "winnetstandard";
  $vmpath ="/vmfs/volumes/storage1/ScriptedVM/ScriptedVM.vmdk";
  $x = writevmx();
  if ($x == 1) {
  print "VMX file written successfully \na";
  }
$w = setper();
  if ($w == 1) {
  print "Permissions set successfully \na";
  }
$y = clonedisk(); # Call subroutines to create VM's
  if ($y == 1) {
  print "Virtual disk cloned successfully \na";
  }
$z = registervm();
  if ($z == 1) {
  print "VM registered successfully \na";
  }
  print "Press the ENTER key to continue …";
  $pause = <STDIN>;
  goto main
}
if ($menu4opt == 2) {
  $vmname = "ScriptedPerlVMClone";
  $vmmem = "1024";
  $vmdisk = "8";
  $vmos = "winnetenterprise";
  $vmpath ="/vmfs/volumes/storage1/perlvm/ScriptedPerlVM";
  $x = writevmx();
```

```
    if ($x == 1) {
    print "VMX file written successfully \na";
    }
  $w = setper();
    if ($w == 1) {
    print "Permifsions set successfully \na";
    }
  $y = clonedisk();
    if ($y == 1) {
    print "Virtual disk cloned successfully \na";
    }
  $z = registervm();
    if ($z == 1) {
    print "VM registered successfully \na";
    }
  print "Press the ENTER key to continue …";
  $pause = <STDIN>;
  goto main
  }
  else {
    goto menu1;
  }
}
if ($menuopt == 5) {
 goto end1
 }
sub writevmx {        # Subroutine to create VM's VMX config file
#      $file = '/vmfs/volumes/storage1/perlvm/perlvm.vmx';      # Name the file
    $file = "/vmfs/volumes/storage1/perlvm/" . $vmname . ".vmx";
    open(INFO, ">$file");     # Open for output
    print INFO 'config.version = "6"' . "\n";
    print INFO 'virtualHW.version = "3"' . "\n";
    print INFO 'memsize = "' . $vmmem . '"' . "\n";
    print INFO 'floppy0.present = "TRUE"' . "\n";
    print INFO 'displayName = "' . $vmname . '"' . "\n";
    print INFO 'guestOS = "' . $vmos . '"' . "\n";
    print INFO 'ide0:0.present = "TRUE"' . "\n";
    print INFO 'ide0:0.deviceType = "cdrom-raw"' . "\n";
    print INFO 'ide:0.startConnected = "false"' . "\n";
    print INFO 'floppy0.startConnected = "FALSE"' . "\n";
```

```
    print INFO 'floppy0.fileName = "/dev/fd0"' . "\n";
    print INFO 'Ethernet0.present = "TRUE"' . "\n";
    print INFO 'Ethernet0.connectionType = "monitor_dev"' . "\n";
    print INFO 'Ethernet0.networkName = "VM Network"' . "\n";
    print INFO 'Ethernet0.addressType = "vpx"' . "\n";
    print INFO 'scsi0.present = "true"' . "\n";
    print INFO 'scsi0.sharedBus = "none"' . "\n";
    print INFO 'scsi0.virtualDev = "lsilogic"' . "\n";
    print INFO 'scsi0:0.present = "true"' . "\n";
    print INFO 'scsi0:0.fileName = "' . $vmname . '.vmdk"' . "\n";
    print INFO 'scsi0:0.deviceType = "scsi-hardDisk"' . "\n";
    close(INFO);       # Close the file
}
sub createdisk {     # Subroutine to create virtual disk
    $cr = "vmkfstools -c " . $vmdisk . "g " .
" /vmfs/volumes/storage1/perlvm/".
$vmname . ".vmdk -a lsilogic";
    system("$cr");
  };
sub clonedisk {      # Subroutine to create virtual disk
    $cr = "vmkfstools -i " . $vmpath . " " .
" /vmfs/volumes/storage1/perlvm/" . $vmname . "vmdk";
    system("$cr");
  };
sub registervm {     # Subroutine to register VM with ESX server
    $rg = "vmware-cmd -s register
/vmfs/volumes/storage1/perlvm/" . $vmname . ".vmx";
    system("$rg");
  }
sub setper{   # Subroutine to set permission on VMX file
  $pm = "chmod 755 /vmfs/volumes/storage1/perlvm/" . $vmname . ".vmx";
    system("$pm");
  }
end1:
```

The preceding code is highlighted with the changes necessary to support cloning. When the code is executed, you now have a new menu option #4, for cloning of virtual machines. The code currently clones ScriptedVM.vmdk and ScriptedPerlVM.vmdk, created from previous sections.

You can easily modify the code to request the name of the VMs to clone. You could even have the code generate a list of VMs registered with the ESX server and then you would select from this list. The script is provided as an example of how you would go about setting up your own VMs to use as templates and how to automate creating clones of these. Go ahead and expand the sample script to include other options such as "lab setup" where the option clones a series of virtual templates to set up a virtual test environment.

Master Craftsman...

Using Clones to Set Up Virtual Environments

The example script provides basic VM procurement via custom entry, templates, and cloning. Custom VM entry and templates provide you new VMs ready for the installation of an operating system, while cloning provides you with a prebuilt virtual machine ready for use. Create clone templates of your most common server types in your environment for fast deployment in your virtual infrastructure. You can, in essence, set up virtual labs in a matter of minutes versus hours.

Summary

In this chapter, you learned how to use the built-in command-line tools from VMware—namely, *vmkfstools* and *vmware-cmd*—to build and clone virtual machines. You also learned how to use ESX shell scripting to incorporate these tools and automate the VM and cloning process. We showed you how to employ VmPerl for advanced scripting of VM creation and cloning. We then showed you how to use the code examples to build a rough VM creation and cloning architecture for you to expand on. You should now have a good understanding of what you can script on the ESX server as it relates to virtual machine creation.

## Chapter 22

Modifying VMs

Solutions in this chapter:

- **The Virtual Machine VMDK File**

- **The Virtual Machine Configuration vmx File**

- **Virtual Machine Conversion from IDE to SCSI**

- **Dynamic Creation of Virtual Machines**

☑ **Summary**

Introduction

This chapter expands on the virtual machine's creation that was introduced in Chapter 21. To begin, we will discuss the two main components of a virtual machine, the .vmx and the .vmdk files. Then we will look at the hardware and version level of these files, as well as how we can change the files to be able to migrate a virtual machine's disk file from one VMware platform to another.

Virtual machines are made up of two files. The vmx file is the virtual machine's configuration file, while the virtual machine disk format (VMDK) file is the virtual machine's disk file or hard drive. We will examine these files and the different settings that can be used. Afterward, as an example, we will change a virtual machine's IDE disk to a SCSI disk.

To conclude, we will dynamically create a virtual machine using a script, as well as modify the script to build the virtual machine in a few different ways.

TIP

As a best practice, *always* make a backup of the files you are going to edit *before* you edit.

The Virtual Machine VMDK File

When working with virtual machines, there are two main components or files that need to be understood. The first is the VMDK file. But what exactly *is* the VMDK file? A virtual machine disk (VMDK) file is an encapsulation of an entire server or desktop environment in a single file. In a way, it can be seen as the hard drive for a virtual machine.

The VMDK file can have four different forms. Type 0 (monolithic sparse disk), Type 1 (growable; split into 2 GB files), Type 2 (single pre-allocated; monolithic sparse disk), and Type 3 (pre-allocated; split into 2 GB files). Types 1, 2, and 3 use a disk descriptor file, while type 0 does not. To make changes to the VMDK file, you need to be able to open and view the disk descriptor; otherwise, with the type 0 single disk, you would need to edit a very large binary file with a hex editor—an unwise choice. A better option, if you have the VMDK file on a VMFS file system, is to use vmkfstools to easily export the file in a Type 3 format.

For example:

```
Vmkfstools -e /mnt/bigspace/toputfile/thedisk.vmdk vmhba0:0:0:1:thedisk.dsk
```

If you mount a file share to ESX and use the VMware File Manager to copy the VMDK file to this share, ESX uses the preceding command automatically when making the copy.

TIP

VMware does not support the use of VMDK files moved from a VMFS volume to a non-VMFS file system using SCP or FTP without first employing the vmkfstools export command or the file manager in the VMware Management Interface.

We should now have the VMDK file in a Type 1 growable split or a Type 3 preallocated split. You should now see a 1KB VMDK file. This is your disk descriptor file (see Figure 22.1).

Figure 22.1 The Disk Descriptor File

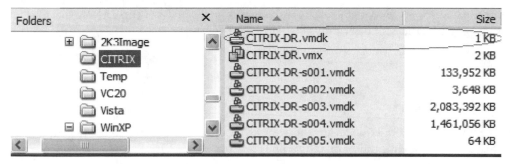

Using a text editor, we can open the disk descriptor file and view its contents. Code Listing 22.1 is one example of a disk descriptor file.

Code Listing 22.1 A Disk Descriptor File

```
# Disk DescriptorFile
version=1
CID=2af6d34d
parentCID=ffffffff
createType="twoGbMaxExtentSparse"
# Extent description
RW 4192256 SPARSE "Windows-s001.vmdk"
RW 4192256 SPARSE "Windows-s002.vmdk"
RW 4096 SPARSE "Windows-s003.vmdk"
```

```
# The Disk Data Base
#DDB
ddb.adapterType = "ide"
ddb.geometry.sectors = "63"
ddb.geometry.heads = "16"
ddb.geometry.cylinders = "8322"
ddb.virtualHWVersion = "4"
ddb.toolsVersion =
```

VMDK Components

In the following subsections, we'll discuss the various parameters, settings, and commands related to VMDKs.

Version=1

The version parameter is the version of the disk descriptor file and not the VMDK file. Currently, in all VMware products, the disk descriptor version is 1.

```
# Disk DescriptorFile
version=1
```

CID=2af6d34d

Every time a VMware product opens up the vmx file, it creates a random 32-bit value and uses that value for the content identification or CID value.

parentCID=ffffffff

This parameter is the parent content identification which is used to specify whether the disk descriptor file is part of a snapshot file. If no snapshot file is being used, the value of this parameter is ffffffff.

file.createType="twoGbMaxExtentSparse"

The createType describes which type of file this is. There are currently 11 different values for this depending on the format of the data. Many values that exist in some products do not exist in others. The three values you see most often, especially with VMware's ESX server, are "twoGbMaxExtent-Sparse", "monolithicSparse", and "monolithicFlat". Performing a manual change would make the disk unusable and has caused my VMware workstation host to crash. If you need to change the type of file, use the tool vmware-vdiskmanager to change the type.

```
# Extent description
RW 4192256 SPARSE "Windows-s001.vmdk"
RW 4192256 SPARSE "Windows-s002.vmdk"
RW 4096 SPARSE "Windows-s003.vmdk"
```

The preceding list shows files (typically VMDKs) that are used to store data blocks for the guest operating system. The values in those lines reveal the access mode of the VMDK, the size in sectors of the VMDK, the type of the extent, and the location of the VMDK data file.

The Size in Sectors Value

The Size in Sectors value is required for a VMware Server to properly initialize the VMDK file. This value must be calculated based on the total byte size of the VMDK file and the number of bytes per sector. The Bytes per Sector is a static value of 512. The equation to calculate this value, as shown next, is quite simple.

Size in Sectors = (VMDK Byte Size – 512) / Bytes per Sector

The Disk Data Base Command

The Disk Data Base command will tell the virtual machine's hardware everything it needs to know to access the VMDK files. This is the actual disk geometry that the VMDK represents as a disk to the virtual machine. In Code Listing 22.2, this disk descriptor represents an IDE virtual disk with 63 sectors on 16 heads with 8,322 cylinders. It is important that the proper disk geometry be chosen to prevent "geometry mismatch" errors on the restored virtual machine (see Table 22.1).

Code Listing 22.2 A Disk Descriptor for an IDE Virtual Disk

```
# The Disk Data Base
#DDB
ddb.adapterType - "ide"
ddb.geometry.sectors = "63"
ddb.geometry.heads = "16"
ddb.geometry.cylinders = "8322"
ddb.virtualHWVersion = "4"
ddb.toolsVersion = "6404"
```

Table 22.1 Disk Geometry

Disk Size	Heads	Sectors
<=1 GB	64	32
>1 GB and <=2 GB	128	32
>2 GB	255	63

Cylinders = (VMDK ByteSize − 512) / (Heads * Sectors * Bytes per Sector)

Three different adapter types can currently be used with virtual machines.

- **ide**   For an IDE drive
- **buslogic**   For a buslogic SCSI controller driver
- **lsilogic**   For a lsilogic SCSI controller driver

One particular thing to notice in this section is the ddb.virtualHW Version. This version number is the VMware platform the virtual machine is running on.

Swiss Army Knife...

Scripting the Backup of Virtual Machine's Configuration Files

In the next section, we will dig into the vmx configuration file for the virtual machines. Before that, however, let's put together a script to take care of one of the most important things we can do with these files: backing them up. This script is what I am using in my VMware ESX servers. They will back up all the configuration files for all the virtual machines, compress them into a tar file along with the vm-list file, and put them on a share on the network. The vm-list file is the list of registered virtual machines on an ESX server. This script runs daily and if I were to lose one of the ESX hosts, I could grab the backup file, register the virtual machines, and I am all set.

```
#!/bin/sh
# Virtual Machine VMX Backup
# Stephen Beaver
DOW=`date +%a` # Day of the week e.g. Mon
mount -t smbfs //server/share /mnt/smb -o
username=username/domain,password=password
SRC_DIR=/home/vmware/ #Directory will all vm configuration files
DST_DIR=/mnt/smb #Destination path which in this case is the mount point
BASE_DIR=/home #Base directory to put the vmlist file
HOST="ESX-Server Name"
echo "src dir ="$SRC_DIR
echo "dst dir ="$DST_DIR
cp -f /etc/vmware/vm-list /home/vmware/vm-list
tar -czvf "$DST_DIR/vm_backup_$HOST-$DOW.tar.gz" "$SRC_DIR"
umount /mnt/smb
exit
```

The Virtual Machine Configuration vmx File

The vmx file is the configuration file that stores all the virtual machine's specific settings in one nice neat place. Code Listing 22.3 is an example of a vmx file.

Code Listing 22.3 A vmx File

```
#!/usr/bin/vmware
config.version = "6"
scsi0:0.present = "TRUE"
scsi0:0.name = "ESX_SAN4:2K900.vmdk"
scsi0:0.mode = "persistent"
scsi0.present = "true"
scsi0.virtualDev = "vmxbuslogic"
memSize = "512"
displayName = "2K900"
guestOS = "win2000Serv"
ethernet0.present = "true"
ethernet0.connectionType = "monitor_dev"
ethernet0.devName = "bond0"
ethernet0.networkName = "FH_Network"
Ethernet0.addressType = "vpx"
Ethernet0.generatedAddress = "00:50:56:9d:4d:10"
Ethernet0.virtualDev = "vmxnet"
floppy0.present = "true"
floppy0.startConnected = "false"
ide1:0.present = "true"
ide1:0.fileName = "/dev/cdrom"
ide1:0.deviceType = "atapi-cdrom"
ide1:0.startConnected = "FALSE"
draw = "gdi"
uuid.bios = "50 1d 07 5c a9 f3 2b dd-8b 3e 83 10 b2 ea 89 0b"
uuid.location = "56 4d b5 45 28 5a b0 20-29 52 da f8 22 74 60 1d"
uuid.action = "keep"
priority.grabbed = "normal"
priority.ungrabbed = "normal"
isolation.tools.dnd.disable = "TRUE"
suspend.Directory = "/vmfs/vmhba1:0:83:1"
autostart = "true"
autostop = "softpoweroff"
tools.syncTime = "FALSE"
```

This vmx file came from one of my virtual machines on a VMware ESX server. Let's take a look at the different settings in the file. As a rule, virtual machines will only read the full vmx file when the virtual machine is powered on. Thus, you should edit the virtual machine's vmx file when the virtual machine is off only. I have come across this scenario while playing around in the lab. There, I had a virtual machine and made a manual change to the configuration file. ESX knew I made a change and so it paused the virtual machine to ask me a question: "The configuration file for this VM has changed. Do you wish to reload the configuration file?" If the virtual machine in my production environment had instead been paused, I would have had a few people to answer to.

```
config.version = "6"
scsi0:0.present = "TRUE"
scsi0:0.name = "ESX_SAN4:2K900.vmdk"
scsi0:0.mode = "persistent"
scsi0.present = "true"
scsi0.virtualDev = "vmxbuslogic"
```

vmx File Components

In this subsection, we'll discuss the various parameters, settings, and commands related to vmx files.

config.version = ""

This is the hardware version level. When we talked about downgrading the disk descriptor file, this is what we must change to control the hardware version so it will work in the different products. What we see next are the settings for the SCSI drive. Scsi0:0 is the virtual machine's boot drive.

Scsi0:0.present = ""

This lets the host know that the virtual machine has a SCSI drive present. This can have an entry of True or False.

Scsi0:0.name = ""

This is the name and path of the VMDK file that the virtual machine will use. In the earlier example, "ESX_SAN4:2K900.vmdk" points to a common name of a LUN on the SAN called ESX_SAN4, and the 2K900.vmdk is the disk file located on the LUN.

Scsi0:0.mode = ""

This setting is the mode of the disk file. The following four disk modes are available.

- **Persistent**   Changes are immediately and permanently written to the virtual disk.
- **Nonpersistent**   Changes are discarded when the virtual machine powers off.
- **Undoable**   Changes are saved, discarded or appended at your discretion.
- **Append**   Changes are appended to a redo log when the virtual machine powers off.

scsi0.present = ""

This setting lets the host know this virtual machine has a SCSI controller. The value can be True for present, and False for no SCSI.

scsi0.virtualDev = ""

This setting determines what SCSI drivers the controller is using. Two different values can be used here.

- **vmxbuslogic**   When using the buslogic SCSI driver
- **vmxlsilogic**   When using the lsilogic SCSI driver

These are also the settings we would change on the vmx file to switch from an IDE disk to a SCSI. The next part of the configuration vmx file is the memory, name, and guestOS, all of which do not need much explanation:

- **memSize = "512"**   How much memory the virtual machine is allocated
- **displayName = "2K900"**   The display name of the virtual machine
- **guestOS = "win2000Serv"**   Which operating system the VM is running

The next part concerns the Ethernet adapter and whether Virtual Center is used to monitor this virtual machine (see the following example).

```
ethernet0.present = "true"
ethernet0.connectionType = "monitor_dev"
ethernet0.devName = "bond0"
ethernet0.networkName = "FH_Network"
Ethernet0.addressType = "vpx"
Ethernet0.generatedAddress = "00:50:56:9d:4d:10"
Ethernet0.virtualDev = "vmxnet"
```

ethernet0.present = ""

This value defines whether the network settings are read and processed. This value can be "true" or "false." If the value is "true," then all other parameters are then processed. If the value is "false," then all other network parameters for that device are ignored.

TIP

ethernet0.startConnected = "true"
    Ethernet0.present = "true" also sets startConnected to "TRUE", though this may not appear in the vmx (another silent default).
    So if you want the device to be present—but not at boot-time—you must use ethernet0.startConnected = "FALSE".

ethernet0.connectionType = "''

This parameter concerns virtual networks. Your choices for this value are "bridged", "hostonly", "nat", "monitor_dev", and "custom". The custom settings are an expert way to use a combination of "connectionType" and "vne.t". A good example of this would be the following:

```
ethernet0.connectionType = "CUSTOM"
```

And the exact number of the VNET you want might look like:

```
ethernet0.vnet = "VMNET0"
```

ethernet0.devName = "''

This parameter is the actual name of the device being used. This could be one of the virtual ethernet cards like vmnic0, or in this case a bond of two ethernet cards together called "bond0".

ethernet0.networkName = "''

This is the name of the virtual switch that the virtual machine will be using for networking. In this example, the virtual switch's name is FH_Network.

Ethernet0.addressType = "vpx"

This parameter is only present when the virtual machine is on an ESX server that is controlled by Virtual Center.

Ethernet0.generatedAddress = "''

This parameter is the MAC address of the virtual machine. In this case, the MAC address is generated by the host application.

VMware has a special range of MAC addresses that are allocated for the virtual machines. The following lists the different ranges of addresses.

- **00:05:69:00:00:00** Automatically assigned by MUI when building a VM without VirtualCenter (ESX <2.0)

- **00:0c:29:00:00:00** Automatically assigned by MUI when building a VM without VirtualCenter as well as the other VMware products (ESX 2.0 +, all VMware)

- **00:50:56:00:00:00 – 00:50:56:3f:ff:ff** Manually configured MACs

- **00:50:56:80:00:00 – 00:50:56:bf:ff:ff** VirtualCenter-generated MACs

Ethernet0.virtualDev = "vlance" or "vmxnet" or "e1000"

This parameter is to define the virtual adapter itself. The choices available are

- **vlance**   This is based on the AMD PCNet 32 and has the most backward compatibility. Take note that if you use vlance with your virtual machine, the VM will only show what it is connected at 10 mb. This is presented for backward compatibility only and does not represent the actual speed with which the VM is communicating. The VM will use all the bandwidth given to it.

- **vmxnet**   This is a VMware custom high-performance vmxnet virtual network adapter which allows for faster networking performance. This is the adapter you should use whenever possible, given it offers better performance than the vlance driver and less overhead.

- **e1000**   This is the Intel pro 1000 adapter, which is the default virtual NIC when choosing a 64-bit guest. It can be manually edited in the config file.

Floppy Drives and CD-ROMs for Virtual Machines

The following parameter is the configuration of the floppy and CD-ROM for the virtual machine. Notice that I have startConnected set to "false" for these devices. As a rule of thumb, I recommend leaving these disconnected until you need them.

```
floppy0.present = "true"
floppy0.startConnected = "false"
ide1:0.present = "true"
ide1:0.fileName = "/dev/cdrom"
ide1:0.deviceType = "atapi-cdrom"
ide1:0.startConnected = "false"
```

Notice that the parameter ide1:0.fileName is currently set to "dev/cdrom." This is the emulation of the CD-ROM device that shows up as a VMware CD-ROM and not the actual physical host CD-ROM device. By changing the fileName and deviceType values, you can also mount ISO images to the virtual machine.

```
ide1:0.fileName = "/iso/nameof.iso"
ide1:0.deviceType = "cdrom-image"
```

Graphics Emulation, Unique Identifiers

VMware products offer two modes for host emulation of the graphics inside the virtual machine: GDI (Graphics Device Interface; the classic Windows graphics mode) and DirectDraw (a mode designed for games and other applications that write directly to the hardware).

```
draw = "gdi"
```

In general, Windows guest operating systems (Windows 95, Windows 98, Windows NT, and Windows 2000) perform better in GDI mode than in DirectDraw mode, while Linux guest operating systems (or any guest operating systems that use an X server) run much better in DirectDraw mode.

WARNING

DirectDraw on Windows 2000 is fairly buggy, so the virtual machine displays a cautionary message if you try to enable it. In addition, some specific issues have been identified on both Windows NT and Windows 2000 hosts when the virtual machine is using DirectDraw mode.

Once you start a virtual machine, the VMware host will then generate another two lines to identify the virtual machine. Whenever you change the path to the vmx-file, either by renaming or moving to a different location, VMware wants to update these lines to reflect that change (see the following example).

```
uuid.location = "56 4d ee 3c 52 06 a3 de-be 4a 73 9c cc 99 15 1f"
uuid.bios = "56 4d ee 3c 52 06 a3 de-be 4a 73 9c cc 99 15 1f"
```

If you've ever moved a virtual machine from one host to another, then when you start the machine you've probably seen a message similar to this:

> The virtual machine's configuration file has changed its location since its last poweron. Do you want to create a new unique identifier (UUID) for the virtual machine or keep the old one?

Your choices are Keep, Create, Always Keep, and Always Create. If you choose **Always Keep** or **Always Create**, then the parameter uuid.action is added to the vmx file (see the following example).

```
uuid.action = "Keep" or "Create"
```

The values you can use here are Keep or Create for Always Keep and Always Create.

Priority, VMware Tools Settings, and Suspend

The "grabbed: HIGH - ungrabbed: NORMAL" setting is useful if you have many background processes or applications and you do not care if they run with fairly low relative priority while a virtual machine is in the foreground. In return, you get a very noticeable performance boost using a virtual machine while another virtual machine is running or while some other processor-intensive task (a compile, for example) is running in the background (see the following example).

```
priority.grabbed = "high" or "normal"
```

The reverse is true of the "grabbed: NORMAL - ungrabbed: LOW" setting. If your host machine feels too sluggish when a virtual machine is running in the background, you can direct the virtual machine to drop its priority when it does not have control of the mouse and keyboard. As with the high setting, this is a heavy-handed change of priority, so the virtual machine (and any background applications inside) runs much more slowly.

```
priority.ungrabbed = "normal" or "low"
```

isolation.tools.dnd.disable = "True" or "False"

This setting is to enable/disable Host/Guest drag and drop interface. The values you can use here are "True" and "False".

suspend.Directory = "/vmfs/vmhba1:0:83:1"

This parameter is the location the host should use to "suspend" a virtual machine. The following example was taken from an ESX server that is attached to a SAN. Notice that the path is made up of the true path vmhba1:0:83:1 and not the friendly name that I set for the LUN: /vmfs/ESX_SAN4/.

Autostart, Autostop, and Time Sync Options

In this section, we'll discuss autostart, autostop, and time sync options that you can be used for configuring a virtual machine. The following example shows autostart and autostop command scripts.

```
autostart = "true" or "false"
autostop = "softpoweroff" or "poweroff"
autostart.order = ""
autostop.order = ""
```

You can configure a virtual machine to automatically begin when the host starts up from a reboot and also to automatically power off or shut down the guest OS when the host is being shut down. When you utilize this option, the autostart and autostop options are added to the virtual machine's vmx file. You can also take this a step further and define the startup and shutdown order of the virtual machines using the autostop.order and autostart.order. By default, it would use order number x10. To give you an example, if you wanted VM1 to be the first virtual machine started and the last virtual machine to shutdown, you would set the configuration this way:

```
autostart.order = "10"
autostop.order = "10"
```

To change this to be the third virtual machine started, change the number from 10 to 30.

```
tools.syncTime = "FALSE" or "TRUE"
```

The tools.syncTime Option

The last option in my vmx file is the tools.syncTime. This option is used to determine if the virtual machine is going to update its time with the host time via the VMware tools or not.

Virtual Machine Conversion from IDE to SCSI

You may find the need to be able to move virtual machines around from one platform to another. For example, I encourage people to utilize VMware Workstation in order to work on a virtual machine while on the go. I have had several instances where a virtual machine was created on VMware Workstation, but unfortunately was not created in legacy mode or had an IDE drive. As a result, when attempting to migrate to ESX, it would fail until some changes were made.

Therefore, here we will examine changing an IDE drive to a SCSI drive. Before we change the settings, we need to get the SCSI drivers in the system first. The easiest way to do this is to add another hard disk to the virtual machine as a secondary drive. Configure this drive to be a SCSI drive. Start the virtual machine with the new drive attached and, the SCSI drivers are now in place, allowing us to continue and really edit the files. When we open the descriptor file for a virtual machine using an IDE drive, it looks like the sample in Code Listing 22.4.

Code Listing 22.4 Descriptor File for a Virtual Machine Using an IDE Drive

```
# Disk DescriptorFile
version=1
CID=2af6d34d
parentCID=ffffffff
createType="twoGbMaxExtentSparse"
# Extent description
RW 4192256 SPARSE "Windows-s001.vmdk"
RW 4192256 SPARSE "Windows-s002.vmdk"
RW 4096 SPARSE "Windows-s003.vmdk"
# The Disk Data Base
#DDB
ddb.adapterType = "ide"
ddb.geometry.sectors = "63"
ddb.geometry.heads = "16"
ddb.geometry.cylinders = "8322"
ddb.virtualHWVersion = "4"
ddb.toolsVersion = "6404"
```

Starting with the ddb.adapterType you can see that this was indeed an IDE drive. There are a total of three different options for this setting. We'll discuss each in this section.

ddb.adapterType = "buslogic"

This entry converts the disk into a SCSI-disk with a BusLogic Controller. This is the standard for Windows 2000 virtual machines.

ddb.adapterType = "lsilogic"

This entry converts the disk into a SCSI-disk with LSILogic Controller. This is the standard for Windows 2003 virtual machines.

```
ddb.adapterType = "ide"
```

This entry converts the disk into an IDE-disk with Intel-IDE Controller.

Next, let's open the SCSI disk that we used to get the drivers in the virtual machine and use it to give us the section, heads, and cylinder values we need.

```
ddb.adapterType = "buslogic"
ddb.geometry.cylinders = "522"
ddb.geometry.heads = "255"
ddb.geometry.sectors = "63"
```

Put this all together and we have a new SCSI disk for our virtual machine.

There is one change left to be done, however. We will need to change the ddb. virtualHWVersion. The ddb.virtualHWVersion is dependent upon which VMware platform you are using. You may need to change the version number to get the virtual machine to start in certain cases, namely moving a virtual machine in to ESX Server.

Change the ddb.virtualHWVersion = "4" and make it ddb.virtualHWVersion = "3". You now have a legacy virtual machine disk file you have converted from IDE to SCSI. You've also brought the virtual machine disk file down to legacy mode so that it can run on ESX.

```
# Disk DescriptorFile
version=1
CID=826d3b6e
parentCID=ffffffff
createType="twoGbMaxExtentSparse"
# Extent description
RW 4192256 SPARSE "Windows-s001.vmdk"
RW 4192256 SPARSE "Windows-s002.vmdk"
RW 4096 SPARSE "Windows-s003.vmdk"
# The Disk Data Base
#DDB
ddb.adapterType = "buslogic"
ddb.geometry.sectors = "63"
ddb.geometry.heads = "255"
ddb.geometry.cylinders = "522"
ddb.virtualHWVersion = "3"
ddb.toolsVersion = "6309"
```

To complete this process we need to make an adjustment in the vmx file in order to change the IDE values to SCSI. Code Listing 22.5 is an example of a disk file that's been configured to use an IDE.

Code Listing 22.5 Configuring a Disk to Use an IDE

```
config.version = "8"
virtualHW.version = "4"
scsi0.present = "TRUE"
memsize = "200"
ide0:0.present = "TRUE"
ide0:0.fileName = "Windows.vmdk"
ide1:0.present = "TRUE"
ide1:0.fileName = "auto detect"
ide1:0.deviceType = "cdrom-raw"
floppy0.fileName = "A:"
ethernet0.present = "TRUE"
usb.present = "TRUE"
sound.present = "TRUE"
sound.virtualDev = "es1371"
displayName = "Windows XP Professional 1"
guestOS = "winxppro"
nvram = "winxppro.nvram"
ide0:0.redo = ""
ethernet0.addressType = "generated"
uuid.location = "56 4d b7 df d7 1d 42 ca-3e 81 5d a3 5e 05 7a f7"
uuid.bios = "56 4d b7 df d7 1d 42 ca-3e 81 5d a3 5e 05 7a f7"
tools.remindInstall = "FALSE"
ethernet0.generatedAddress = "00:0c:29:05:7a:f7"
ethernet0.generatedAddressOffset = "0"
ide1:0.autodetect = "TRUE"
ide1:0.startConnected = "TRUE"
tools.syncTime = "FALSE"
```

To finish the change from IDE to SCSI we need to adjust these lines in the vmx file (see Table 22.2).

Table 22.2 VMX Old and New Settings

From the Old Settings	To the New Settings
config.version = "8"	config.version = "6"
virtualHW.version = "4"	virtualHW.version = "3"
ide0:0.present = "TRUE"	scsi0.present = "TRUE"
ide0:0.fileName = "Windows.vmdk"	scsi0:0.present = "TRUE"
	scsi0:0.fileName = "Windows.vmdk"

Now we have completed downgrading the virtual hardware and also changed a virtual machine from using an IDE drive to a SCSI drive. This virtual machine will now start and run in VMWare ESX server. By using the example of taking a virtual machine from VMware Workstation and getting it to run to VMware ESX Server, we have gone from one extreme of the VMware product line (workstation) to the other extreme (ESX Server).

Scripted Disconnect of IDE Devices

As a general rule, you should always have the CD-ROM and floppy drive disconnect so they don't take away resources from the service console. This is also true if you place a CD-ROM in the physical host's drive, because all the virtual machines will not start to autorun the CD-ROM. VMotion also won't work if either the CD-ROM or the floppy is connected. The script shown in Code Listing 22.6 will disconnect all these devices in virtual machines that are registered on ESX Server. This script was originally posted on the VMware community forum by Stuart Thompson (aka, Mr-T) and Matt Pound, and it includes a few additions by me.

Code Listing 22.6 Disconnecting Devices in Virtual Machines Registered on an ESX Server

```
#!/bin/bash
# IDE / Floppy Disconnect Script
# Script by: Stuart Thompson and Matt Pound
# Edit by: Steve Beaver (Added floppy drive)
vmwarelist=`vmware-cmd -l`
vmwarelist=`echo $vmwarelist | sed -e 's/ /*/g'`
vmwarelist=`echo $vmwarelist | sed -e 's/.vmx/.vmx /g'`
```

```
for vm in $vmwarelist
do
  vm=`echo $vm | sed -e 's/*/ /g'`
  vm=`echo $vm | sed -e 's/ \//*/g'`
  if [ `vmware-cmd "$vm" getstate | sed -e 's/getstate() = //'` = "on" ]
  then
  echo Looking @ $vm
  IDEBUS=`seq 0 1`
  for i in $IDEBUS;
  do
    echo BUS : $i
      IDEDEVICE=`seq 0 1`
    for j in $IDEDEVICE;
    do
        PRESENT=`vmware-cmd "$vm" getconfig ide$i:$j.present | cut -f3 -d " "`
        if [ $PRESENT = "true" ]
        then
          TYPE=`vmware-cmd "$vm" getconfig ide$i:$j.deviceType | cut -f3 -d " "`
          if [[ $TYPE == "atapi-cdrom" || $TYPE == "cdrom-image" ]]
          then
            echo Found CDROM on IDE$i:$j
            vmware-cmd "$vm" disconnectdevice ide$i:$j
          fi
        fi
      done
    done
  fi
done
```

Swiss Army Knife...

vmwarelist=`vmware-cmd -l`

You can change this value to point to a specific path of a virtual machine and have these scripts set up to run on only one virtual machine instead of all virtual machines.

Vmwarelist='/home/vmware/vmserver/vmserver.vmx'

Employing this script as a base, you can choose many options using the vmware-cmd to make a change to all of your registered virtual machines. Take a look at Code Listing 22.7, which shows how you can start all your registered machines.

Code Listing 22.7 Starting All Registered Virtual Machines

```
#!/bin/bash
vmwarelist=`vmware-cmd -l`
vmwarelist=`echo $vmwarelist | sed -e 's/ /*/g'`
vmwarelist=`echo $vmwarelist | sed -e 's/.vmx/.vmx /g'`
for vm in $vmwarelist
do
  vm=`echo $vm | sed -e 's/*/ /g'`
  vm=`echo $vm | sed -e 's/ <0x002F>/*/g'`
  if [ `vmware-cmd "$vm" getstate | sed -e 's/getstate() = //'` = "off" ]
  then
    echo Found $vm that is off, Starting $vm
    vmware-cmd "$vm" start
  fi
done
```

Now, let's take a look at a script to stop those virtual machines that are running.

```
#!/bin/bash
vmwarelist=`vmware-cmd -l`
vmwarelist=`echo $vmwarelist | sed -e 's/ /*/g'`
vmwarelist=`echo $vmwarelist | sed -e 's/.vmx/.vmx /g'`
for vm in $vmwarelist
do
  vm=`echo $vm | sed -e 's/*/ /g'`
  vm=`echo $vm | sed -e 's/ \//*/g'`
  if [ `vmware-cmd "$vm" getstate | sed -e 's/getstate() = //'` = "on" ]
  then
    echo Found $vm that is on, Stopping $vm
    vmware-cmd "$vm" stop trysoft
  fi
done
```

Code Listing 22.8 is one more example of this script, which will reboot all of the running virtual machines. This is very handy if you have installed updates or anything else and want to delay the reboot till later.

Code Listing 22.8 Script for Rebooting All Running Virtual Machines

```
#!/bin/bash
vmwarelist=`vmware-cmd -l`
vmwarelist=`echo $vmwarelist | sed -e 's/ /*/g'`
vmwarelist=`echo $vmwarelist | sed -e 's/.vmx/.vmx /g'`
for vm in $vmwarelist
do
  vm=`echo $vm | sed -e 's/*/ /g'`
  vm=`echo $vm | sed -e 's/ \//*/g'`
  if [ `vmware-cmd "$vm" getstate | sed -e 's/getstate() = //'` = "on" ]
  then
    echo Found $vm that is on, Rebooting $vm
    vmware-cmd "$vm" reset trysoft
  fi
done
```

Dynamic Creation of Virtual Machines

Now that we have looked at what makes up the vmx file, let's generate some scripts to dynamically create virtual machines. First, we'll take a script and modify it so we can create a virtual machine that will use a golden image as its base. We'll then make a couple of changes so we can take advantage of Altiris in the VM creation. We will then modify the script so that a virtual machine will be created and then start the VM with the installation CD mounted to begin the installation.

Code Listing 22.9 shows script that uses a golden image disk file. A golden image disk file is a fully loaded and patched virtual machine vmx file that has had sysprep run on it so it can be cloned.

> **W**ARNING
>
> Please make sure you look through these scripts and make any changes needed to match your environment. Pay attention to the vmhba path and double-check these values with the values in your own environment.

Code Listing 22.9 Using a Golden Image Disk File to Dynamically Create a Virtual Machine

```bash
#!/bin/bash
#Scripting VMware Power Tools: Automating Virtual Infrastructure Administration
#Dynamic Creation of a new Virtual Machine using a Golden Image
#Stephen Beaver
#####USER MODIFICATION#################
#VMNAME is the name of the new virtual machine
#VMOS specifies which Operating System the virtual machine will have
#GLDIMAGE is the path to the "Golden Image" VMDK file
#DESTVMFS is the path to VMFS partition that the VMDK file
#########################################
VMOS="winNetStandard"
VMMEMSIZE="256"
GLDIMAGE="/vmfs/FHVMFS1/Windows_2003_Standard.vmdk"
DESTVMFS="vmhba0:0:0:10"
#####END MODIFICATION#####
LOG="/var/log/$1.log"
echo "Start of Logging" > $LOG
echo "Importing Golden Image Disk File VMDK" >> $LOG
vmkfstools -i $GLDIMAGE $DESTVMFS:$1.vmdk
echo "Creating VMX Configuration File" >> $LOG
mkdir /home/vmware/$1
exec 6>&1
exec 1>/home/vmware/$1/$1.vmx
# write the configuration file
echo #!/usr/bin/vmware
echo config.version = '"'6'"'
echo virtualHW.version = '"'3'"'
echo memsize = '"'$VMMEMSIZE'"'
echo floppy0.present = '"'TRUE'"'
echo usb.present = '"'FALSE'"'
echo displayName = '"'$1'"'
```

```
echo guestOS = '"'$VMOS'"'
echo suspend.Directory = '"'/vmfs/vmhba0:0:0:10/'"'
echo checkpoint.cptConfigName = '"'$1'"'
echo priority.grabbed = '"'normal'"'
echo priority.ungrabbed = '"'normal'"'
echo ide1:0.present = '"'TRUE'"'
echo ide1:0.fileName = '"'auto detect'"'
echo ide1:0.deviceType = '"'cdrom-raw'"'
echo ide1:0.startConnected = '"'FALSE'"'
echo floppy0.startConnected = '"'FALSE'"'
echo floppy0.fileName = '"'/dev/fd0'"'
echo Ethernet0.present = '"'TRUE'"'
echo Ethernet0.connectionType = '"'monitor_dev'"'
echo Ethernet0.networkName = '"'Network0'"'
echo draw = '"'gdi'"'
echo
echo scsi0.present = '"'TRUE'"'
echo scsi0:1.present = '"'TRUE'"'
echo scsi0:1.name = '"'$DESTVMFS:$1.vmdk'"'
echo scsi0:1.writeThrough = '"'TRUE'"'
echo scsi0.virtualDev = '"'vmxlsilogic'"'
echo
# close file
exec 1>&-
# make stdout a copy of FD 6 (reset stdout), and close FD6
exec 1>&6
exec 6>&-
echo "VMX Configuration File Created Successfully" >> $LOG
#Change the file permissions
chmod 755 /home/vmware/$1/$1.vmx
#Register the new VM
echo "Registering .vmx Configuration" >> $LOG
vmware-cmd -s register /home/vmware/$1/$1.vmx
echo "VMX Initialization Completed Successfully" >> $LOG
```

> **NOTE**
>
> Notice that the preceding script uses a golden image file that is local to that machine. If your golden image is located on a network share, you can easily mount that share and import the file from there. To mount a network share you can use the following command:
>
> mount -t smbfs //server/share /mnt/smb -o username=username/domain, password=password

Next, we'll take the same script and make a few changes so it will work with an ESX Server managed with Altiris. At the end of this script, the virtual machine is started and should boot PXE, which Altiris can then take over and use to install the operating system (see Code Listing 22.10).

Code Listing 22.10 Creating a New Virtual Machine to Use with an ESX Server Managed by Altiris

```
#!/bin/bash
#Scripting VMware Power Tools: Automating Virtual Infrastructure Administration
#Creates a new Virtual Machine for use with Altiris
#Stephen Beaver
#####USER MODIFICATION################
#VMNAME is the name of the new virtual machine
#VMOS specifies which Operating System the virtual machine will have
#DESTVMFS is the path to the VMFS partition of the VMDK file
#VMDSIZE is the size of the Virtual Disk File being created ex (500mb) or (10g)
########################################
VMNAME="vm_name"
VMOS="winNetStandard"
VMMEMSIZE-"256"
DESTVMFS="vmhba0:6:0:1 #Must use the vmhba path
VMDSIZE="10g"
#####END MODIFICATION#####
```

```
LOG="/opt/altiris/deployment/adlagent/bin/logevent"
$LOG -l:1 -ss:"Creating VMX Configuration File"
mkdir /home/vmware/$VMNAME
exec 6>&1
exec 1>/home/vmware/$VMNAME/$VMNAME.vmx
# write the configuration file
echo #!/usr/bin/vmware
echo config.version = '"'6'"'
echo virtualHW.version = '"'3'"'
echo memsize = '"'$VMMEMSIZE'"'
echo floppy0.present = '"'TRUE'"'
echo usb.present = '"'FALSE'"'
echo displayName = '"'$VMNAME'"'
echo guestOS = '"'$VMOS'"'
echo suspend.Directory = '"'/vmfs/vmhba0:0:0:5/'"'
echo checkpoint.cptConfigName = '"'$VMNAME'"'
echo priority.grabbed = '"'normal'"'
echo priority.ungrabbed = '"'normal'"'
echo ide1:0.present = '"'TRUE'"'
echo ide1:0.fileName = '"'auto detect'"'
echo ide1:0.deviceType = '"'cdrom-raw'"'
echo ide1:0.startConnected = '"'FALSE'"'
echo floppy0.startConnected = '"'FALSE'"'
echo floppy0.fileName = '"'/dev/fd0'"'
echo Ethernet0.present = '"'TRUE'"'
echo Ethernet0.connectionType = '"'monitor_dev'"'
echo Ethernet0.networkName = '"'Network0'"'
echo draw = '"'gdi'"'
echo
echo scsi0.present = '"'TRUE'"'
echo scsi0:1.present = '"'TRUE'"'
echo scsi0:1.name = '"'vmhba0:0:0:5:$VMNAME.vmdk'"'
echo scsi0:1.writeThrough = '"'TRUE'"'
echo scsi0.virtualDev = '"'vmxlsilogic'"'
echo
# close file
exec 1>&-
# make stdout a copy of FD 6 (reset stdout), and close FD6
exec 1>&6
exec 6>&-
```

```
$LOG -1:1 -ss:"VMX Configuration File Created Successfully"
#Change the file permissions
chmod 755 /home/vmware/$VMNAME/$VMNAME.vmx
#Create the Virtual Disk
$LOG -1:1 -ss:"Creating Virtual Disk"
vmkfstools -c $VMDSIZE vmhba0:0:0:5:$VMNAME.vmdk
$LOG -1:1 -ss:"Virtual Disk Created Successfully"
#Register the new VM
$LOG -1:1 -ss:"Registering VMX Configuration"
#Registering .vmx Configuration"
vmware-cmd -s register /home/vmware/$VMNAME/$VMNAME.vmx
$LOG -1:1 -ss:"VMX Initialization Completed Successfully"
#Starting the Virtual Machine
$LOG -1:1 -ss:"Starting the Virtual Machine"
vmware-cmd /home/vmware/$VMNAME/$VMNAME.vmx start
$LOG -1:1 -ss:"Virtual Machine Started"
$LOG -1:1 -ss:"Passing control to Altiris for PXE boot and install of VM"
```

Let's make one more change to the script so that when the virtual machine first boots up with a brand-new disk, it will boot from the virtual CD-ROM that has an ISO file mounted to it (see Code Listing 22.11).

Code Listing 22.11 Creating a New Virtual Machine That Boots to an ISO

```
#!/bin/bash
#Scripting VMware Power Tools: Automating Virtual Infrastructure Administration
#Creates a new Virtual Machine booting to an ISO
#Stephen Beaver
#####USER MODIFICATION#################
#VMNAME is the name of the new virtual machine
#VMOS specifies which Operating System the virtual machine will have
#GLDIMAGE is the path to the "Golden Image" VMDK file
#DESTVMFS is the path to the VMFS partition of the VMDK file
#VMDSIZE is the size of the Virtual Disk File being created ex (500mb) or (10g)
#ISOIMAGE is the path and file name of the ISO file you are using
#######################################
VMOS="winNetStandard"
VMMEMSIZE="256"
GLDIMAGE="/vmfs/FHVMFS1/Windows_2003_Standard.vmdk"
DESTVMFS="vmhba0:0:0:10"
VMDSIZE="10g"
```

```
ISOIMAGE"/vmfs/ESX_SAN/Windows2000.iso"
#####END MODIFICATION#####
LOG="/var/log/$1.log"
echo "Start of Logging" > $LOG
echo "Importing Golden Image Disk File VMDK" >> $LOG
vmkfstools -i $GLDIMAGE $DESTVMFS:$1.vmdk
echo "Creating VMX Configuration File" >> $LOG
mkdir /home/vmware/$1
exec 6>&1
exec 1>/home/vmware/$1/$1.vmx
# write the configuration file
echo #!/usr/bin/vmware
echo config.version = '"'6'"'
echo virtualHW.version = '"'3'"'
echo memsize = '"'$VMMEMSIZE'"'
echo floppy0.present = '"'TRUE'"'
echo usb.present = '"'FALSE'"'
echo displayName = '"'$1'"'
echo guestOS = '"'$VMOS'"'
echo suspend.Directory = '"'/vmfs/vmhba0:0:0:10/'"'
echo checkpoint.cptConfigName = '"'$1'"'
echo priority.grabbed = '"'normal'"'
echo priority.ungrabbed = '"'normal'"'
echo ide1:0.present = '"'TRUE'"'
echo ide0:0.present = '"'TRUE'"'
echo ide0:0.fileName = '"'$ISOIMAGE'"'
echo ide0:0.deviceType = '"'cdrom-image'"'
echo floppy0.startConnected = '"'FALSE'"'
echo floppy0.fileName = '"'/dev/fd0'"'
echo Ethernet0.present = '"'TRUE'"'
echo Ethernet0.connectionType = '"'monitor_dev'"'
echo Ethernet0.networkName = '"'Network0'"'
echo draw = '"'gdi'"'
echo
echo scsi0.present = '"'TRUE'"'
echo scsi0:1.present = '"'TRUE'"'
echo scsi0:1.name = '"'$DESTVMFS:$1.vmdk'"'
echo scsi0:1.writeThrough = '"'TRUE'"'
echo scsi0.virtualDev = '"'vmxlsilogic'"'
echo
# close file
```

```
exec 1>&-
# make stdout a copy of FD 6 (reset stdout), and close FD6
exec 1>&6
exec 6>&-
#Create the Virtual Disk
echo "Creating Virtual Disk" >> $LOG
vmkfstools -c $VMDSIZE vmhba0:0:0:5:$VMNAME.vmdk
echo "Virtual Disk Created Successfully" >> $LOG
echo "VMX Configuration File Created Successfully" >> $LOG
#Change the file permissions
chmod 755 /home/vmware/$1/$1.vmx
#Register the new VM
echo "Registering .vmx Configuration" >> $LOG
vmware-cmd -s register /home/vmware/$1/$1.vmx
echo "VMX Initialization Completed Successfully" >> $LOG
#Starting the Virtual Machine
echo "Starting the Virtual Machine" >> $LOG
vmware-cmd /home/vmware/$VMNAME/$VMNAME.vmx start
echo "Virtual Machine Started" >> $LOG
```

Summary

Let's review what we've covered. First, we took a solid look at the virtual disk files (*.vmdk). We opened up the disk descriptor file, reviewed its contents, and converted an IDE virtual disk file to a SCSI virtual disk file. We then took an in-depth look at the settings inside the virtual machine configuration files (*.vmx) and finished the IDE-to-SCSI conversion.

I presented a few scripts that covered backing up the configuration files of the virtual machines, and how to build virtual machines. I also discussed a few options for making changes to all (or one) virtual machines at the same time. You can use bits and parts of these different scripts to open the door to various types of automation. Using the native "sed" program, for example, you have the ability to script the edits to any of the files you need. This gives you a wide range of options that can be scripted and automated. The vmware-cmd tool also opens a lot of doors thanks to the different choices available. Run vmware-cmd from the service console to view all the options and syntax

## Chapter 23

Instant Disk: How to P2V for Free

Solutions in this chapter:

- What Is a P2V?
- P2V Techniques
- The "Big Secret" of P2V
- Instant Disk Overview
- Prepping the ESX Host: Setting Up FTP on ESX Host
- Prepping the Source Machine: Install the SCSI Driver
- Continue Prepping the Source Machine: Validate
- The Linux Rescue CD
- At the Command Prompt
- Finding the Hard Drives and Storage
- Virtual Disk Files on the VMFS
- Starting the FTP Process
- Creating a New Virtual Machine and Pointing It to a New VMDK File

☑ Summary

Introduction

Your overall goal is to consolidate that server room full of hardware into a more easily managed and less expensive to operate and maintain integrated system. Some of your current mission-critical servers may be hosted on older hardware that can't be, or are difficult to be, replaced. Virtualization is the answer, but how do you achieve this goal?

What Is a P2V?

A key component when building a virtual infrastructure is establishing a physical to virtual (P2V) migration process. As a guideline, the "do no harm" mantra is a very important concept when performing P2V migrations. What this means is that your source physical server should not be damaged in any way during your P2V process. This permits a fail-back strategy if the P2V does not complete for whatever reason. Some commercial P2V methods add directories into the file system and entries into the Registry. These changes remain, especially if the P2V process does not complete or fails, and can render the source physical server inoperable. No tool you use should ever cause harm to the original server, but amazingly there are tools that do exactly that and yet are out there gaining market share today.

Whether your P2V is successful or not, your original physical server must remain intact with no harm done. Again, you may need to go back to the original server for more reasons than you thought.

For example, suppose the physical server you P2V is a critical production server and you are creating a new development machine from a copy of the real one? If the P2V was unsuccessful, you just need to bring up the original production server and be confident that your process has in no way added directories, Registry entries, or anything that will render the source production server unusable or uncertified.

Another key reason you do not want to "touch" the source server and inject any potentially dangerous changes is illustrated with the following example. Let's say your P2V of a production or dev server is successful but the application owner says that errors exist within the Event log. Having your source server operational, you can turn it back on and parse the logs yourself to see if the problem was preexisting. Since we do a block-by-block transfer in our line of work, it has been our experience that the problem was already there and we simply carried it over into the newly created virtual machine. We have seen this many, many times. Thus, it is a very good idea to go through the logs prior to a migration and note any errors so as to have them corrected prior to the migration.

P2V Techniques

Many different P2V techniques and methods exist, but most involve software that must be purchased. The following subsections provide a brief description of how some of these tools work. This is not meant as a how-to guide for each of these methods, but an explanation of the underlying technology of each P2V process.

VMware P2V Tool

VMware P2V Tool is an easy-to-use, enterprise-class, market-proven tool that can take an image of an existing physical system and create a VMware virtual machine. While this tool is both fast and reliable, its cost as well as the fact that it's restricted to virtualizing only Windows NT 4 to Windows Server 2003 systems does limit its use except in very large enterprises.

The basic process is simple, as shown in Figure 23.1.

Figure 23.1 The Basic Process When Using the VMware P2V Tool

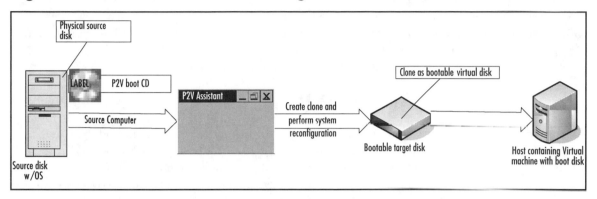

The VMware P2V Tool comes on a self-booting CD-ROM. The disk is placed in the target source computer's CD-ROM player and is run against the selected disk with its installed operating system. The P2V Assistant then creates the clone, performs the system reconfiguration, and now the clone is a bootable virtual disk being hosted on a system with new physical hardware.

Platespin PowerConvert

Currently in release 6.0, Platespin PowerConvert appears to be a much more sophisticated enterprise-class product than VMware's P2V tool. PowerConvert allows any kind of conversion and also supports Microsoft Virtual Server's format. As with VMware's offering, however, Platespin's product is also pricey. For that extra expense though, you get the following:

- The capability to drag and drop virtual machines from older VMware server technology into VMware Infrastructure 3.

- Limiting downtime for production servers running Windows 2000, Windows 2003, and Windows XP operating systems to only a brief (as little as one to five minutes) interruption by allowing the virtual machine to remain live as its OS, applications, and data are migrated to the new VMware Infrastructure 3 hosts.

- The capability to completely automate the Discover, Configure, and Convert functionality.

- The capability to reconfigure the CPU, the disk, and network and memory resources on the new target virtual machines.

- The capability to upgrade multiple virtual machines simultaneously onto new VMware Infrastructure 3 hosts.

In addition to the features previously mentioned, you can add hardware-independent images and Platespin becomes quite a power tool. How is it used? It's fully automated. Choose the source, the destination, and then start the process.

Barts/Ghost

A less-expensive enterprise-class alternative is the use of a boot CD-ROM such as Bart's Network Boot Disk (www.nu2.nu/bootdisk/network), which is free, and a cloning tool such as Symantec's Ghost, which is not. Adding another free tool, Ultimate-P2V (a plug-in for Bart) allows you to clone a physical machine to a virtual machine.

Several versions of tools are available that work in a similar fashion.

The "Big Secret" of P2V

Dozens of different ways exist to move data from a physical server to a virtual one and there are many different philosophies about how to reconfigure the hardware, but we've discovered that the easiest and most reliable method is to let Windows reconfigure itself. Sound too easy?

The Big Secret is that before we copy the source physical server, we install the VMware virtual SCSI driver. This applies to Windows 2000 and 2003. For Windows NT, we install the built-in NT BusLogic driver. But wait, doesn't this go against the "do no harm" mantra? Actually, no. Installing a built-in or supplied driver such as this is very minimal in its effect, but absolutely necessary in any P2V process since the operating system needs to have the SCSI driver in order to read the virtual disks. Initially, we weren't comfortable installing it either, but having installed it now literally thousands of times without any problems to speak of, we can say with confidence that the procedure is quite safe.

Once you install the virtual SCSI driver, you can copy the physical machine to your ESX host any way you like. This chapter explains the easiest way to do this without having to purchase any software. And the method described here is one of the safest and fastest.

After the new virtual machine boots, Windows will fix itself. Linux and Netware will need to be manually fixed. However, after the machine is up and running, you just need to clean up the drivers. By actually learning our methodology and understanding a little about the process, you should be able to achieve great success in your P2V migrations.

Instant Disk Overview

The next thing to do then is to examine the steps of the process. These steps are

1. Install the virtual VMware SCSI driver on the physical source machine.
2. Reboot the physical machine using a Linux boot disk, in rescue mode.

3. Cat (*cat* is like *type* in DOS) the hard drives (**/dev/sd[abcd]** or **/dev/hd**?) and FTP them directly to the /vmfs file system on your ESX host.

4. Reboot the virtual machine, and Windows will redetect the hardware.

5. Install the VMware tools.

6. Remove the old network and other hardware.

7. Optionally shrink or expand the virtual disk.

8. Test.

Once finished, you'll have an Instant Disk.

The Bad News

This Instant Disk method will not work on all machines, only on those physical servers that have modern RAID controllers. Original Compaq Smart Array 2 and Smart Array 3 controllers used special vendor-specific SCSI blocking, which is outside of the norm.

Prepping the ESX Host: Setting Up FTP on ESX Host

Before we start installing drivers and rebooting servers, let's start by making sure the ESX host is ready to be used. We use FTP to directly transfer the image of the hard drive from the physical source server that is being P2V'd onto the VMFS of the ESX host.

Why use FTP? Because FTP is the fastest way to move the raw data from the source server's hard drive. With FTP, we move data nearer to wire speed, or as fast as the physical source server can read it off its hard drives. Isn't secure FTP better? It may be secure, but it is not fast. Secure FTP goes through SSH, which greatly slows down the performance. We chose to use NCFTPPUT. Why, you might ask? We use NCFTPPUT because it will allow us to FTP a stream of data.

Let's start by making sure FTP is running on your ESX host server. If it isn't, you must turn it on. Either do it in the MUI or through the command line. If for security reasons you do not keep FTP running on your ESX Server, then you simply can turn it off.

Through the MUI you would go to the Options tab and then select Security settings. The best choice is to choose Custom. This way, you can turn on FTP without turning on Telnet or other services. Select the FTP check box and save your selection.

From the command line on your ESX host, type **ntsysv**.

Then go to the bottom (using the down arrow) and check the **wu–ftpd** box (see Figure 23.2).

Figure 23.2 Starting the FTP Daemon on the ESX Server

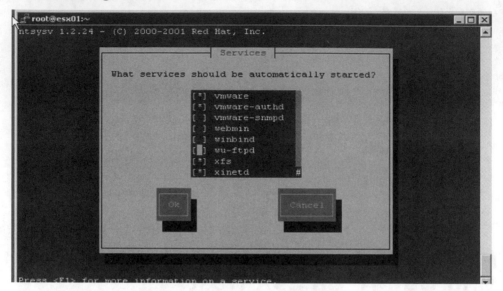

This is the FTP server service. Tab to **OK** and press **Enter** to save the changes.
From the command line, type **service xinetd restart**.
This command will tell the xinetd service to restart, which will then enable FTP.

> **NOTE**
>
> xinetd is the daemon used to manage the Internet daemon running on your ESX Server.

You need to create a user so you can FTP into the ESX host server. By default, ROOT cannot FTP in, and you do not want to change this. It's a good security practice to limit ROOT's access.

Since you need to check permissions and set up a user, it's easier to do all of this from the command line of your ESX host. For example, create a user named **PHD** from the command line, by typing **adduser phd**. Then type **passwd phd**.

You will be prompted to add the password for the user phd. You need to enter the password twice. If done correctly, the process should look something like the screenshot in Figure 23.3.

Figure 23.3 Creating User from the Command Line

```
[root@esx01 root]# adduser ryanharris
[root@esx01 root]# passwd ryanharris
Changing password for user ryanharris
New password:
Retype new password:
passwd: all authentication tokens updated successfully
[root@esx01 root]#
```

Now you need to test the FTP and make sure your user can log in successfully. From the command line of your ESX Server, type **ftp localhost**.

You should be prompted for the User and Password, use "phd" and the password you assigned to phd. Once you can successfully log in, change the directory to the /vmfs folder by typing **cd /vmfs/** *your vmfs partition*.

Ensure you can create new files on your VMFS of choice. For our example, we're going to use **/vmfs/LOCAL**.

You will probably need to change the permissions of the VMFS you want to use, which would be the vmhba*X:X:X:X* name.

To change the permissions on your VMFS partition, you should be at the ESX console, and then cd to your /vmfs folder.

From the command line, type **cd /vmfs**. Then type **ll** (same as ls –l).

Your vmhba folders should be shown, along with a nice name for each. For the VMFS you want to use, we'll change the permissions to 777, which will allow your phd user to write to them. Thus, type **chmod 1777 vmhba*X:X:X:X*** (use the correct name).

Now you need to test the FTP and make sure it works. Create a small test file, then FTP it to the /vmfs/LOCAL. Type the following:

cd /tmp

date > testfile

This is the *date* command and the greater than sign (>), then a new file name, such as testfile. Type **ll**.

You should see the newly created file, called **testfile**. If you were to cat this file, it should contain the current date string. Type **cat testfile**.

Now, from the /tmp folder, you're going to FTP into localhost and try to put this file on the /vmfs. Type **ftp localhost**.

You now want to log in as "phd" and put in the password, so type **cd /vmfs**. Then, type **dir**.

"dir" will give you a directory listing from the FTP command prompt. You should see your available vmfs file systems. You want to cd into the directory you are working with, so type **cd LOCAL** (use your name here; LOCAL is our example).

If this is successful and we do a *pwd* command, FTP will tell us our current folder. This should now be /vmfs/LOCAL. Type **pwd**.

You should get a response like 257 "/vmfs/LOCAL" is the current directory. Now you are going to "put" the testfile to the server. Type **put testfile** and press **Enter** and the local testfile will be transferred to the remote testfile. You'll then receive confirmation that this transfer has occurred and how long it took.

Now if you input a *dir* command again, you should see your testfile on your VMFS. Type **dir** and press **Enter**.

At this point, you have enabled FTP and verified that you can successfully put a file on your VMFS file system. You can delete the test file now. If you want to delete it from the FTP prompt. Type **del testfile**, or you can exit FTP and just delete the file /vmfs using the *rm* command. To exit FTP, type **bye**.

The last thing we want to do to make our work easier is to copy a few programs to our /home/phd folder. This is the home directory that was created when we added the user phd to the ESX host.

When doing our transfer of data form the source server, there are a few programs we need that are not included in a standard Linux rescue image. But all the programs we need already exist on the ESX host itself. Because we use the programs from the ESX host itself, we are limited to which versions of Linux rescue images we can use.

Let's create a p2v folder in our /home/phd folder to put copies of the programs we need to use. Type **mkdir /home/phd/p2v**. We also need to copy ncftpput and mii-tool to our /home/phd/p2v folder, so type **cp /usr/bin/ncftpput /home/phd/p2v**. Then type **cp/sbin/mii-tool /home/phd/p2v**.

Other optional programs like **phdcat** should be copied to your /home/phd/p2v folder. At this point, the ESX host server should be ready for some P2V action.

Prepping the Source Machine: Install the SCSI Driver

Now you are ready to prep and get the physical source machine ready for Instant Disk P2V. You need the VMware SCSI driver, available from www.vmware.com/download/esx/ at the bottom of the page of SCSI Disk Drivers. VMware supplies this driver to be used in a virtual machine, but by installing in your physical first, it makes doing P2Vs very easy.

You need to load this driver onto your source server if you are using Windows 2000, Windows XP, or Windows 2003. You must do this for all machines, whether they are IDE and SCSI machines. The easiest thing to do is put the vmscsi.flp back onto a floppy or extract the contents and put them on a file share. If you copy this vmscsi.flp to your ESX host (or any Linux server), you can easily turn it back into a floppy. A FLP file is just a floppy ISO.

On the ESX host, you just cat the flp image to the floppy device. To do so, type **cat vmscsi. flp > /dev/fd0**. This will write the image in the flp file back to a floppy that you can use to install on the source servers. You can also turn the FLP file back into a real floppy using rawrite (Google it), an open-source utility that allows you to write raw floppy images to floppy drives in Windows.

Installing the SCSI Driver in Windows 2000/2003

When working with Windows 2000 or Windows 2003, you must install the vmscsi.sys driver using the specified method. On the source server, go to the Control Panel and select Add/Remove Hardware (see Figure 23.4).

Figure 23.4 Choose the Add/Remove Hardware Icon in the Control Panel

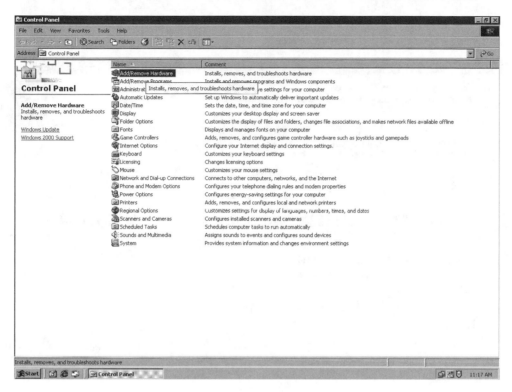

Next, choose **Add/Troubleshoot a Device** (see Figure 23.5).

Figure 23.5 Choose Add/Troubleshoot a Device

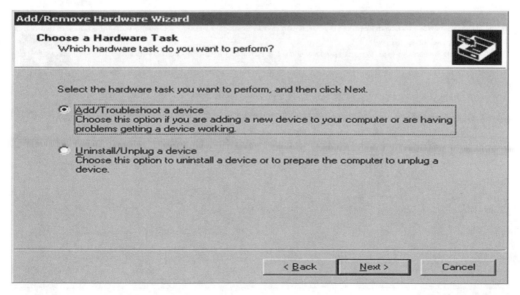

You then want to select **Add a New Device** (see Figure 23.6).

Figure 23.6 Choose Add a New Device

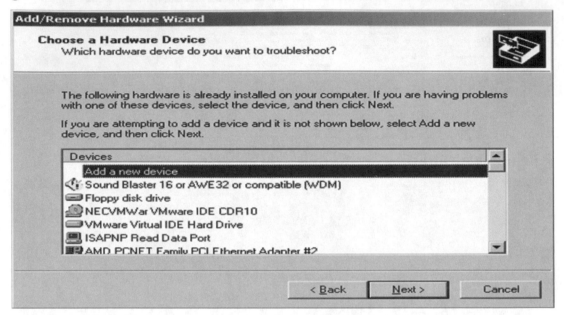

You do not want Windows to search for the new device, so select **No** (see Figure 23.7).

Figure 23.7 Choose the No Option to Select the Device from a Hardware List

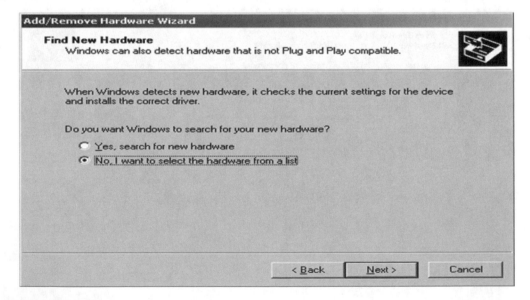

You are presented with a list of different types of hardware to install. You want to select **SCSI and RAID Controllers** (see Figure 23.8).

Figure 23.8 Choose the SCSI and RAID Controllers Option

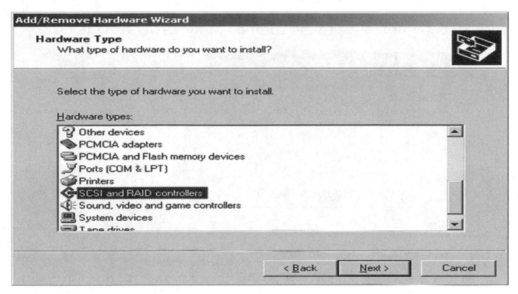

After clicking **Next**, you're shown a list of known SCSI drivers. Here you want to click **Have Disk** (see Figure 23.9).

Figure 23.9 Choose the Have Disk Option

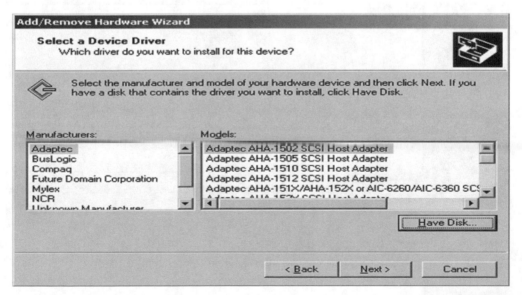

After clicking **Have Disk**, you are asked for the location of the driver you want to install (see Figure 23.10). If you're using the vmscsi.sys driver on a floppy, you just need to insert the floppy and press **Enter**. Or you can browse to a network share and install the vmscsi.sys driver from there.

Figure 23.10 Enter or Browse to the Location of the Driver and Click OK

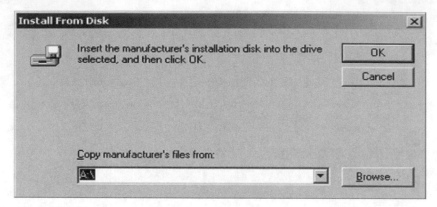

When you browse to the correct path, you are shown the vmscsi.inf file. Select this file and click **Open** (see Figure 23.11).

Figure 23.11 Select the File and Click the Open Button

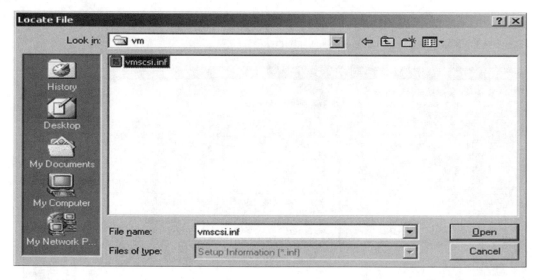

Then you are back to the Install from Disk prompt. Click **OK** (see Figure 23.12).

Figure 23.12 Click OK

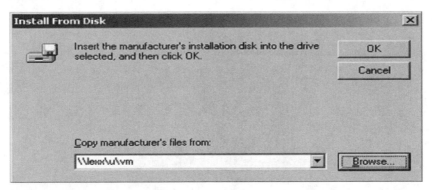

After clicking **OK**, you're asked if you want to install the VMware SCSI Controller. Select it and click **Next** (see Figure 23.13).

Figure 23.13 Click Next to Continue the Installation

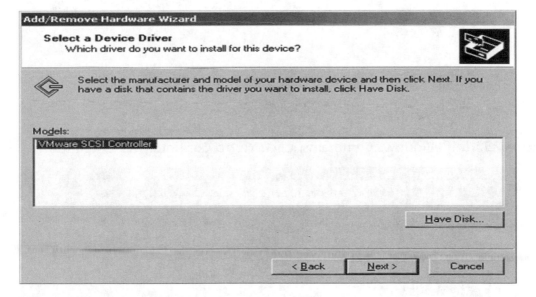

You then are asked to confirm that you want to install the VMware SCSI Controller. Click **Next** (see Figure 23.14).

Figure 23.14 Confirm the Installation

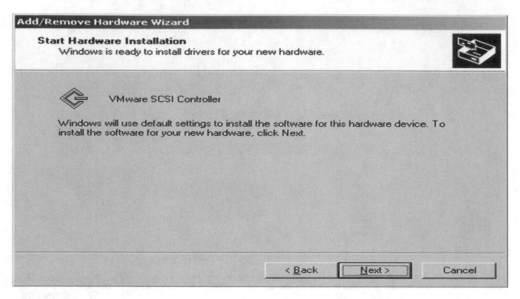

Windows might complain about it not being signed with a digital signature. Click **Yes** to continue (see Figure 23.15).

Figure 23.15 If Windows Complains, Click Yes to Continue the Installation

You're now done installing the vmscsi.sys driver (see Figure 23.16).

Figure 23.16 The Device Driver Is Installed

Afterward, you'll be asked if you want to reboot the server. Say No at this time.

If you're not sure if the vmscsi.sys driver is installed, you can right-click **My Computer**, go to Computer Management, and then click Device Manager (see Figure 23.17). You should see the VMSCSI Controller driver as a non-working device. This is normal since you're not running a virtual machine yet.

Figure 23.17 The VMSCSI Controller Driver Is Seen as a Non-Working Device

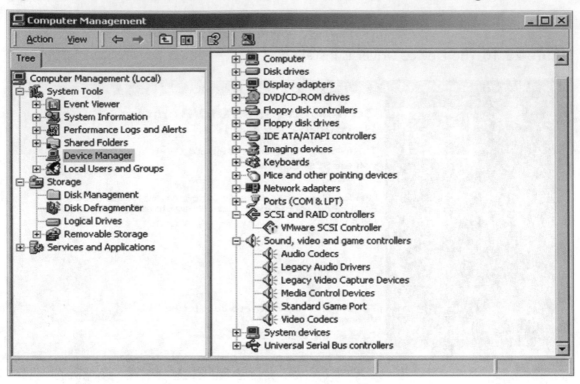

Installing the SCSI Driver in Windows NT

If you are doing a Windows NT P2V, then you need to use the built-in Buslogic SCSI driver from the Windows NT CD-ROM. You will probably need the Windows NT CD-ROM to do this.

Go to the Control Panel and select **SCSI Adapters** (see Figure 23.18).

Figure 23.18 Select SCSI Adapters

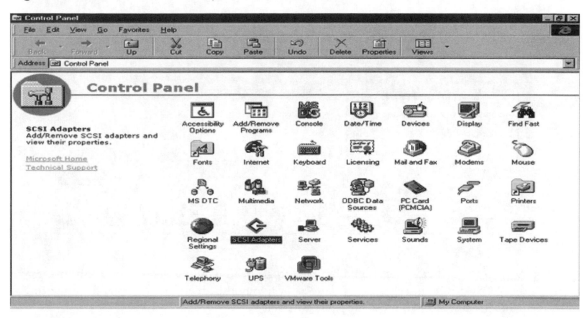

Add the new device. You want to select the **BusLogic MultiMaster PCI SCSI Host Adapters** (see Figure 23.19).

Figure 23.19 Choose the BusLogic MultiMaster PCI SCSI Host Adapters

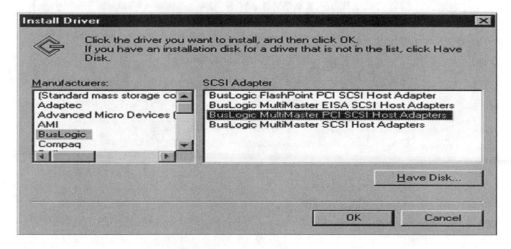

You have to add the ATAPI CD-ROM to the CD-ROM in the Control Panel, also. If you do not add the IDE CD-ROM driver now, and it is not installed, you will have difficulty installing the VMware Tools (see Figure 23.20).

Figure 23.20 Install the ATAPI CD-ROM

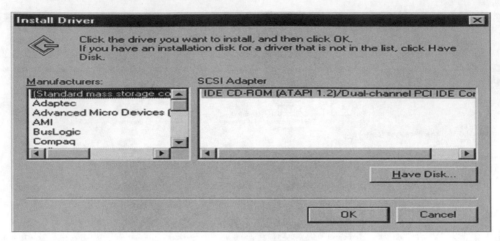

At this point the source server should be ready to go (see Figure 23.21). You may also have various other SCSI drivers installed. Leave these alone. Do not disable or remove any drivers at this time. Remember, cause no harm to your physical server.

Figure 23.21 The Two Adapters You Have Just Added Are Now Started

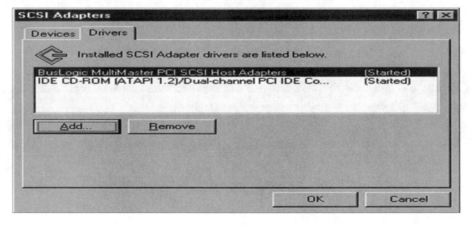

Once you have installed the BusLogic and the IDE CD-ROM drivers you will be asked to reboot. Do not reboot yet.

Continue Prepping the Source Machine: Validate

Once you have the correct SCSI driver installed in your physical machine, there are a few steps left to perform.

1. Run scandisk and make sure your drives have no problems. If you have scandisk errors, this can cause a problem in the new virtual machine.

2. Do not defrag at this time.

3. Note the existing network configuration.

4. Note the way the hard drives are lettered.

5. Note the drive letter of the CD-ROM drive.

Things to be concerned about:

If you are using Windows 2003 and employing the original build that came with your server, you might have to deal with Windows Licensing issues once you move it into a virtual machine. Be prepared with your License Key and the Microsoft Support phone number.

The Linux Rescue CD

Now that the source server has the VMware SCSI driver installed, we can reboot it using a Linux rescue cd and commence with the P2V.

Since we are working with ESX 2.x, we need to use a version of Linux boot CD with it that is binary-compatible. This is because we are going to use ncftpput from the ESX host. We've had good experience using the Fedora 3 Core rescue image or the Red Hat 9 disk 1. Fedora Core 4 is not binary-compatible with the ESX host, so you should download the Fedora Core 3 from http://download.fedora.redhat.com/pub/fedora/linux/core/3/. You can use disk 1 or the rescue image. Download this ISO and burn it to a CD using your favorite software. If you're going to do much older hardware, it's a good idea to burn the CD at a slow speed such as 4x. The Red Hat Linux 9 CD 1 can be downloaded from http://mirrors.kernel.org/redhat/redhat/linux/9/en/iso/i386/. Sometimes with really old hardware you need to use something older, like a Red Hat 7.2 CD.

Booting the Rescue CD

Put the Linux rescue CD into the CD-ROM drive and boot the physical source server from it. At the boot prompt, type **linux rescue** (see Figure 23.22). Unless you're using the FC3 rescue image, it will default to rescue mode.

Figure 23.22 To Enter the Rescue Mode, Press the Enter Key

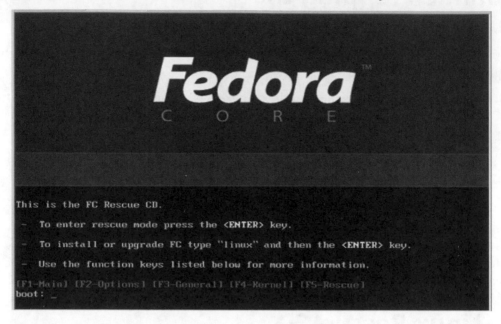

If you have screen issues, where the screen is unreadable after booting, you can try the no frame buffer option. To do so, type **linux rescue nofb**. The Linux kernel will start booting and will auto-detect the hardware.

The first question regards choosing your language. For our demonstration, we've chosen English (see Figure 23.23). At these Linux rescue prompts, you can click **OK** and continue by pressing the **F12** key.

Figure 23.23 Choose What Language You Will Use

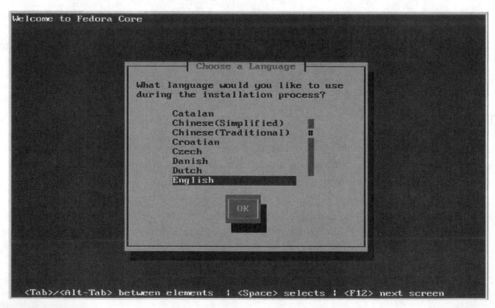

Second question is choose the keyboard type, press **F12** to continue. Or choose your correct keyboard if it's different or nonstandard (see Figure 23.24).

Figure 23.24 Choose Your Keyboard Typ

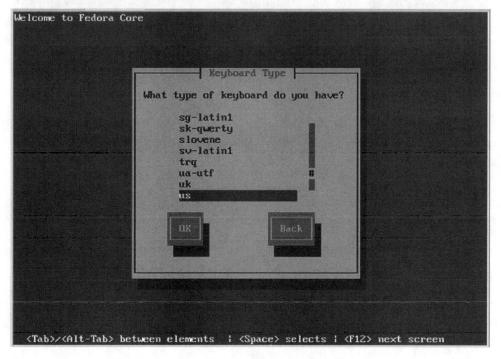

Third question is whether you want to start network services. You should choose **Yes** (see Figure 23.25), or just press **F12**.

Figure 23.25 Start Network Services

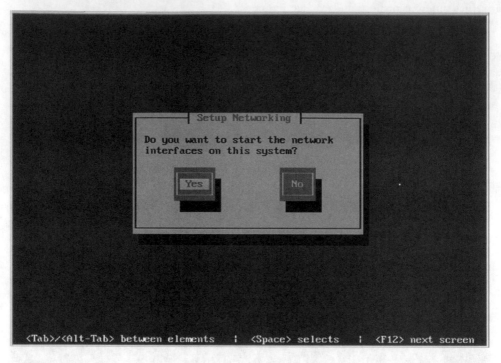

Set up and configure the first network card eth0. If you have DHCP enabled, choose it or enter the IP address. You should use the existing IP address of the physical server (see Figure 23.26).

Figure 23.26 Enable DHCP on the First Network Card eth0

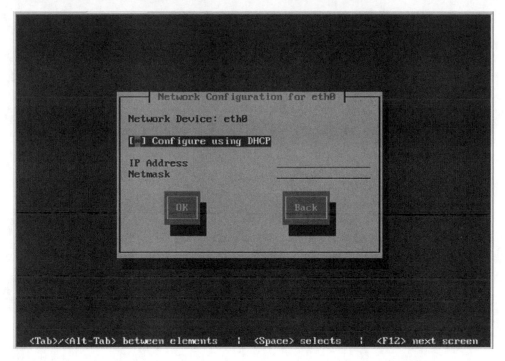

If you have more than one network card, it will ask you to configure them, too. If you do not use DHCP, you will also have to enter a default gateway and DNS servers. We usually just go by IP address. If our network doesn't seem to configure correctly, we'll take a look at it once rescue mode is booted.

Lastly, the rescue image will appear.

Choose **Skip**, which will give you a command-line prompt. Even if this is a Linux P2V, you should still choose **Skip** (see Figure 23.27).

Figure 23.27 Click the Skip Button to Get to the Command-Line Prompt

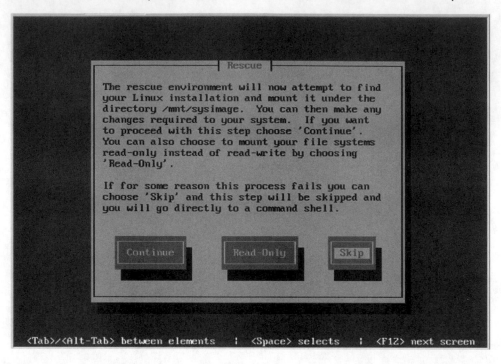

The other options will search for an existing Linux environment and try to mount it, as shown in Figure 23.28.

Figure 23.28 Other Options Will Try to Mount an Existing Linux Environment

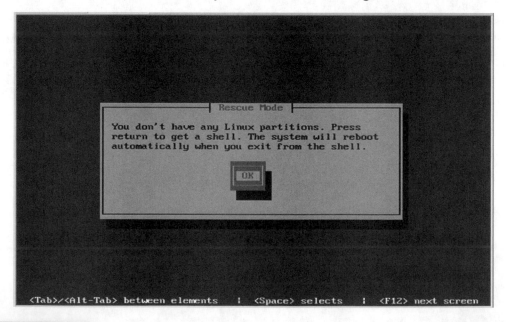

If you choose the Skip button, or if there are no Linux partitions to mount, you will be directed to a shell, as shown in Figure 23.29.

Figure 23.29 You're Now in the Shell

When finished please exit from the shell and your system will reboot.
sh-3.00#

At the Command Prompt

Once you're at the command prompt, you want to make sure your networking is up and working. Try to ping your ESX host by name or IP address. If you did not enter a DNS server or used DHCP, then you will need to use the IP address instead.

If the network is not working, check the network configuration. Typing **ifconfig** will give you a list of your network adapters and their IP addresses. Sometimes with the rescue image it will default to using the highest numbered network adapter in your physical server, while you might be actually using the first one.

You can turn off a network card by typing **ifconfig eth0 down**.

This assumes we want to turn off eth0. If you want to rerun DHCP for an eth device, the command is **pump –i eth1**.

You can set the IP address manually by typing **ifconfig eth1** *xxx.xxx.xxx.xxx*. (For example: **ifconfig eth1 10.10.10.12**.)

This will default to a Class A address, but it should be okay. If your ESX host is not on the same segment as the source server, you will have to add a route to it. We're going to add the route for the ESX host directly, so type **route add <esx host IP> gw <default gateway IP>**. (For example: **route add 136.157.32.121 gw 10.10.10.1**.)

Try to ping your ESX host again. If you're able to ping it, we can move onto FTP. If you can't, then you're still having network problems. If you have more than one network adapter, try using the other one.

Remember, you can check the multiscreens and look for errors. By default, you're on screen 1, which is **Alt + F1**; screens **Alt + F3** and up show kernel output and possible error messages. Screen **Alt + F2** is another command line–like screen F1.

Next, you want to change directory to the /tmp folder (which is writable in the rescue image because it is a RAM drive) and download the contents of the p2v folder from the ESX host. To do so, type **cd /tmp**. Then type **ftp <ESX host IP>**.

You should be asked to log in to the FTP service. Log in as phd and make sure you can successfully connect. You should be in the phd home folder, which is /home/phd. By doing a **dir**, you should see the **p2v** folder. Change directory into the p2v folder by doing **cd p2v** and do a **dir** again. You should see the **ncftpput**, **mii-tool**, **phdcat**, and any other tools you put in this folder.

You'll want to get the contents of this folder. To get all programs, type **mget ***.

You will be prompted to confirm before each file. If you type **prompt** first, it will default to Yes for all files. For example, if you type:

prompt.

mget *.

FTP will transfer the files, placing them in the /tmp folder on your source machine. Remember, this is a RAM drive and does not touch the hard drives in the physical source server at all. *Do no harm!*

You need to make these programs you just downloaded executable by using the *chmod* command. You can *chmod* all the files in the /tmp folder because it's the easiest thing to do. So type **chmod 777 ***.

Now we can check the network connection and make sure we're running full duplex and that everything is the way it should be. By running **mii-tool**, you can check the speed and duplex of the network devices. If they are incorrect, you can change them by using mii-tool. To run mii-tool, you need to. / it. That again is dot slash and then the mii-tool. Or you could completely path the name /tmp/mii-tool. Type:.

/mii-tool.

or

./mii-tool −h

for the help and command options. The dot slash means to run the program from the current folder, which is /tmp. If our path was set up for /tmp, then this wouldn't be necessary. Once the network is all-good, we move onto the hard drives.

Finding the Hard Drives and Storage

Next, you need to find the hard drive devices, which are normally **/dev/sda** (/dev/sdb and so on). But some SCSI controllers do not use standard device names. This means most Compaq RAID cards and some other RAID cards such as Mylex are different from the norm. If you're going to P2V a SAN-attached drive, it should appear as a normal SCSI drive just like local attached storage.

By typing **fdisk −l**, you should get a list of all the known hard drive devices, which should look like the following example:

```
Disk /dev/sda: 41.9GB, 41943040000 bytes
255 heads, 63 sectors/track, 5099 Cylinders
Units = cylinders of 16065 * 512 = 8225280 bytes
Device Boot    Start  End    Blocks      Id     System
/dev/sda1      *      1      5098   40949653+   7       HPFS/NTFS
```

If you have multiple hard drives, then they should all be listed. Compaq, HP, and other RAID controllers may not show when doing the **fdisk –l**. You will need to do the **fdisk –l** against the actual device name. For newer Compaq RAID controllers, try **fdisk –l /dev/ida/c0d0** (c = controller 0; d = drive 0); for older Compaqs, try **fdisk –l /dev/cciss/c0d0** (c = controller 0; d = drive 0).

For Mylex RAID cards, it would be **fdisk –l /dev/rd/c0d0** (c = controller 0; d = drive 0).

For Instant Disk, you are going to copy the whole hard drive, which means every sector, every byte, everything. Because Instant Disk copies the whole drive, the cylinders must be normal. If not, the partition boundaries will not line up and it won't work.

For the **/dev/sda** (or whatever drive), the cylinders must be **16065 * 512 = 8225280**. This is the same for IDE hard drives also since all IDEs should be this value. As mentioned previously, old Compaq computers using Smart Array 2/3s do not use standard cylinders. If your server has these values, then the Instant Disk methodology discussed in this chapter will not work for you. If your source server has dynamic disks or is using some form of software spanning or RAID, you can still use Instant Disk.

For example, your source server is an old NT server with three 4-gigabyte hard drives as a RAID 5. You just need to Instant Disk all the hard drives, and then add all three drives to the new virtual machine. It should work fine. Except that leaving it like this is not the best solution. However, once successfully converted into a virtual machine, you can add another hard drive to it and use a Windows tool to copy the partition from the three-drive RAID 5 onto a normal basic single disk.

The greatest thing here is that you can P2V almost any server, then you can fix it, update it, and convert the hard drives. In fact, you can do anything you want to it.

Linux and Hardware

In Linux, hardware devices are accessed as if they were files. At least the ones we are going to deal with. Your first SCSI hard drive in Linux would be **/dev/sda**. The *a* means drive one, while *b*, as in /dev/sdb, would be drive 2, and so on. For IDE, it would be **/dev/hda** for your first drive.

By accessing this file, you access the hard drive at the hardware level, below the data and partitions. This allows you raw access to the drive. This is the fastest way to get data from the drive.

If you were to **cat /dev/sda**, you would get the raw dumping of that SCSI Hard drive. *Do not do this yet.*

The basic idea is that you **cat /dev/sda > newdisk.vmdk**, which means you are copying the raw hard drive (**/dev/sda**) and putting it into a file called **newdisk.vmdk**, except you're going to copy it across the network and write directly to the VMFS using FTP.

This newly created **newdisk.vmdk** is almost an ESX virtual disk file. The only difference between an ESX .vmdk (.dsk) file and a real hard drive image is a 512 record at the end of the file. This is how ESX knows the file is a virtual disk.

Virtual Disk Files on the VMFS

As mentioned before, there is little difference between a raw hard drive image and an ESX virtual disk file. (In Workstation and GSX, a pre-allocated virtual disk is the same as a raw hard drive, which is the same as an ESX virtual disk without the 512-byte record.)

Because of the format of an ESX virtual disk file, there is very little chance of corrupting a virtual disk (unlike Workstation or GSX) when using virtual cow disks or virtual hard drives split into pieces.

If you were to create a file on a VMFS file system and add the 512-byte record to the end it, it would be a valid ESX virtual disk file.

The following is a little exercise to show you how this works and how ESX manages the VMFS.

Create a small empty virtual disk file. You must path the complete file name. To do so, type **vmkfstools –c 1m /vmfs/LOCAL/test.vmdk**.

This will create an empty 1-megabyte virtual disk file named **test.vmdk**. Change directory to your VMFS file system and do an **ll** (ls –l). You should see the newly created virtual disk file. (For our example, this is **cd /vmfs/LOCAL**.) Then, type **ll**.

You should see output similar to that shown next:

```
-rw------    1      root    root     1049088        Jan 12 23:41 test.vmdk
```

The new virtual disk file you created has a size of 1,049,088 bytes. You created this file as 1 megabyte in size—that is, 1024×1024 bytes = 1,048,576. If we add the 512 bytes—1,048,576 + 512 = 1,049,088—you get the same file size as the newly created file.

If you look at the last 2000 bytes of this file you will see a lot of NULLs and the VMware 512-byte record. Type **tail –c 2000 test.vmdk | cat –vet**.

The **cat –vet** will show us binary characters in a readable format. Notice all the ^@ (NULLS), and then some text that says "This is a VMware ESX server disk image." Those last 512 characters at the end are the VMware ESX 512-byte record. Not a lot of data in it.

Now if you were to echo some text on to the end of this file **test.vmdk**, ESX would know about it and re-add the 512-byte record to keep it as a valid virtual disk file. Once a file is a valid disk, ESX will try and keep it a valid disk. Let's do this. Type **echo THIS IS A TEST OF INSTANT DISK >> test.vmdk**.

The ">>," which is a greater than–greater than sign, means to append data onto the end of the file. Now, if you tail and cat the file again, you will see the original VMware record, followed by the message you echoed, followed again by a new VMware record at the end.

Before we start the FTP process, we need to create an empty virtual disk file in your VMFS that will be the virtual disk drive. By creating a valid disk file first, then FTPing on top of it, the file will remain a valid virtual disk. Because ESX does this for us, you can do an Instant Disk P2V almost anywhere without any special software.

Create a new virtual disk that will represent your physical source server. Our source drive is 40gig, so let's create an empty 40gig drive. You could create a 1 M empty virtual drive, but creating it the same size as your physical source server is a good idea since you can make sure you have enough space to create it. Type **vmkfstools –c 40 G /vmfs/LOCAL/newdisk.vmdk**.

Now that you created an empty virtual disk called **newdisk.vmdk**, you just have to make sure you use the same name when you FTP the source hard drive.

> **NOTE**
>
> If you copied your source hard drive to a local drive or USB drive instead, you can still use the tool from our Web site to convert the file into a valid virtual disk after you copy the file to the VMFS. Read about USB and other methods in the last few pages of this chapter.

Starting the FTP Process

Now we're going to FTP the raw hard drive into your VMFS on your ESX host and create an Instant Disk. If you have the phdcat program, use it instead of cat in the following command. It will give you the amount of data copied and the average speed. Without it, you get no feedback on the source server side.

Type:

cat /dev/sda | /tmp/ncftpput –u <username> -p <password> –c <remote esx host ip> <Full /vmfs

path and new file name>

For example:

cat /dev/sda | /tmp/ncftpput –u phdbot –p "p2v" –c 10.10.10.1 /vmfs/LOCAL/ newdisk.vmdk.

With phdcat: **phdcat /dev/sda | /tmp/ncftpput –u phdbot –p "p2v" –c 10.10.10.1 /vmfs/LOCAL/newdisk.vmdk**

If it is working, you won't see anything until it is done, but you can go check out your /vmfs/ LOCAL on the ESX host and watch the newdisk.vmdk grow bigger.

If you are using phdcat, then you are getting a speed and total amount of data copied. You will see total megabytes copied and average megabytes per second. If you are on a 100 MB network, the max wire speed will be 11 MB a second. If you are on gigabit, you can see speeds much higher, getting 25 MB to 35 MB a second.

By pushing hard drive images to your ESX host, you can really test out your network performance. If you are getting 1 MB/sec or less, then you are running at 10 mb or running half duplex on 100 mb. Or you're copying data from a really old server.

This speed is dependent on the physical source hard drive speed and your network speed. We say this is the fastest method for copying images because it reads the hard drive sequentially, block by block, as fast as it can go.

When using other P2V methods by other vendors to copy the data, they claim they are faster because they only copy the data and not the empty space. But this is not totally true. These other methods open the file system on the physical source server and proceed to copy all the files, one by one. For each and every file on your source server, the hard drive needs to seek and read each file. This can be incredibly slow when you have thousands of files.

If you are getting 10 MB/sec (not bits), which means you are copying 10 MB of real data each second, that is 30+ gigabytes an hour. You can run multiple Instant Disk conversions at the same time and you can really flex your network. But if you are going to do multiple conversions, only write to one VMFS file system at a time. If you have two conversions going to the same VMFS, it will be slower and it will fragment the virtual disk files on the VMFS as the new virtual VMDK files are being created.

After the FTP process is completed, you need to make a new virtual machine using the newly created virtual disk file as a preexisting disk.

Master Craftsman

Instead of Using FTP

Besides using FTP to push the source hard drive image to the ESX host, you can copy the hard drives to another local drive or to a local USB drive.

Why would you do this? Suppose you have a remote location, you can have them attach an external USB drive and walk them through copying the hard drives to the USB drive. Then they mail you the USB drive, and you FTP the images to the ESX host server using Instant Disk.

If you're going to use a USB drive, then you have to use a Linux Rescue image that uses the 2.6 kernel, like the Fedora Core 4 rescue image. If not, by using regular USB, the speed is too slow, topping out at 1 MB/sec if you're lucky. Using the FC4 rescue CD and a USB drive, you can achieve speeds like 25 MB/sec.

You can literally go onsite with a laptop and an external USB drive and image lots of machines, and then come back to your data center and fire up some virtual machines.

Creating a New Virtual Machine and Pointing It to a New VMDK File

It's time now to create the new virtual machine. Here, too, there are a few items you need to make sure you have under control to insure a positive outcome.

Windows VMs

If you are creating a Windows 2003+ machine that normally uses the *lsibuslogic* SCSI driver, you must change it back to the *buslogic* in the configuration. You can always add it back later after the lsi fuson (lsibuslogic) driver has been loaded into the virtual server.

Remember to change the Network Adapter to the **vmxnet** instead of the *vlance* when you create the virtual machine (unless it is a NT4 virtual). Also, before you boot the virtual machine the first time, it's best to put the newly created virtual drive into UNDOABLE mode since it's quicker to commit all your changes than to re-FTP the physical hard drive again if something goes wrong.

When booting Windows 2003+, it may appear to hang for a while. This is normal for the first boot. If it really hangs, just power it off, and then back on.

> **NOTE**
>
> If you're using newer versions of Windows that require activation, they will need to be reactivated after you bring them up as a virtual machine. Be aware of your licensing and Microsoft product codes when starting.

After the virtual machine comes up, you should be able to log in and install VMware Tools. As a prerequisite, the admin password is needed.

After you log in, Windows will continue to redetect hardware and make changes. Keep hitting Yes or Continue. Afterwards, install VMware Tools and you can start some cleanup.

You usually do not have to remove the old devices except for the old network cards. It won't matter if you leave them in, but when you assign the same IP address to the new VMware NIC, it will warn you about it being the same as a disabled NIC. Plus, by leaving the old hardware drivers installed, you can always do a V2P (virtual to physical) conversion.

To remove unused hardware in Windows 2000, go to the Control Panel, select Add/Remove Hardware, choose Remove, then Show Hidden, and delete the old hardware.

In Windows 2003+, they changed it. However, even though it looks more detailed, it's actually quicker and easier. You'll need to open a **cmd** prompt.

Type **set devmgr_show_nonpresent_devices=1**. Then, type **devmgmt.msc**.

Now choose **Show Hidden** from the menu and you should see your hidden hardware. Delete what you want. Since you already installed VMware Tools, you also will see a duplicate vmscsi.sys driver that's not being used. Delete it also.

Post-P2V

Finally, there are a few tasks you should deal with after completing the P2V process. While not a complete list, these tasks might include the following:

- Scandisk
- Defrag
- ZeroFill
- Install the VMware Tools
- Remove any legacy hardware drivers
- Disable legacy services
- NT hal.dll and kernels
- Enable automatic updates on NT
- Determine DSK per drive
- Move/resize any partitions needed
- Resize any drives/dsk

Summary

Hopefully, you are now on the way to virtualizing your server farm after completing this chapter. P2P is a vital and necessary component of your virtualization infrastructure.

## Chapter 24

Scripting Hot Backups and Recovery for Virtual Machines

Solutions in this chapter:

- Anatomy of a VM Backup
- Existing VM Backup Tools
- VMX File Backups
- Backup and Restore Methodology

☑ Summary

Introduction

You probably picked up this book because you need to automate some functions in your virtual infrastructure. Scripting is all about automating our menial tasks. And no menial task begs for automation more than regular backups. Fortunately, VMware provides a rich platform for effective backup and restore solutions that can be controlled through scripts. In this chapter, we will exploit the functionality provided by VMware ESX Server to perform hot (that is, live, while VM is running) backups of our virtual machines. We'll show how to back up the data files and config files. In addition, we'll veer a bit out of the command line and into some consultative topics. We'll discuss the whys and hows of recovery planning for a virtual infrastructure. This will help you decide how you should implement a solution using the scripts and technologies presented in this chapter.

Anatomy of a VM Backup

Before getting into details, it is important to briefly discuss the fundamentals of a VM backup. The feature of virtualization that enables disaster recovery backup is encapsulation. In the VMware ESX world, this is the virtual hard disk, or VMDK. A VMDK file contains the entire contents of a hard disk, the partitions, boot sector, files, everything. A VMDK takes the thousands of files involved in a typical OS and bundles them all together in one VMDK file. We have the ability to create a copy of a VMDK and use this as a complete backup, then treat the backup as we would any file, choosing where to store the file and for how long.

For the purposes of this chapter, we will assume that a VMDK stored on a VMFS volume is a type 2 file, and an exported VMDK is type 1. They are the only file types supported by ESX 2.x. For review, a type 2 file is a preallocated virtual disk, and type 1 is a growable virtual disk split into 2 GB files.

Because the data inside a live VMDK file may be constantly changing, simply making a copy of a VMDK file will result in corruption without some additional technology. Now it is not practical for most organizations to power off a virtual machine prior to backup. Instead a redo log may be placed on the VMDK file prior to making a copy. The VMDK is placed in append mode, and all changes are written to an alternate file. The redo log file has the extension .REDO.

Let's walk through a visual representation of the high-level backup process referencing native tools shipped with ESX to perform the operation. Figure 24.1 is a virtual machine in its simplest form. A VMX file references a single VMDK file on a VMFS volume.

Figure 24.1 Normal State, Persistent Disk

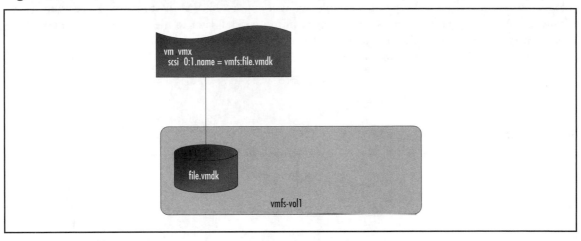

The first step of the process is to create a REDO log on the VMDK. The command *vmware-cmd* provides a quick and easy way to create a redo log (see Figure 24.2):

```
vmware-cmd /home/vmware/vm/vm.vmx addredo scsi0:1
```

Figure 24.2 REDO Is Applied to the VMDK

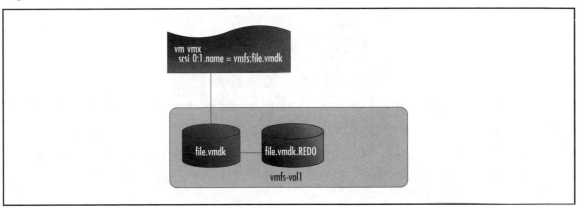

vmware-cmd is a command-line tool that ships with ESX and is for managing virtual machines. We are using one of many functions in this tool, addredo. The only argument to this function is the SCSI address of the VMDK in question. The command refers to the logical SCSI ID assigned to the disk file of the virtual machine, found in the VMX file. Don't confuse this SCSI ID with the physical SCSI ID of your hard disks or SAN LUNs. A number of ways exist to find the SCSI address, including Virtual Center, MUI, or the VMX. This command shows all SCSI lines in the VMX; only devices with the present flag set to TRUE are really there:

```
grep scsi /home/vmware/vm/vm.vmx
```

At this point, changes are being made to the REDO and the VMDK is static. You may now safely make a copy of this file. To keep things simple, we will export this VMDK to an ext3 filesystem (see Figure 24.3). Backup target options are discussed in more detail later in the chapter. The syntax of this command is a bit different than you might expect: vmkfstools –e <target> <source>. The result is a file on the ext3 /vmimages volume in a type 3 format.

```
vmkfstools -e /vmimages/file.vmdk /vmfs/vmfs-vol1/file.vmdk
```

Figure 24.3 VMDK Is Exported

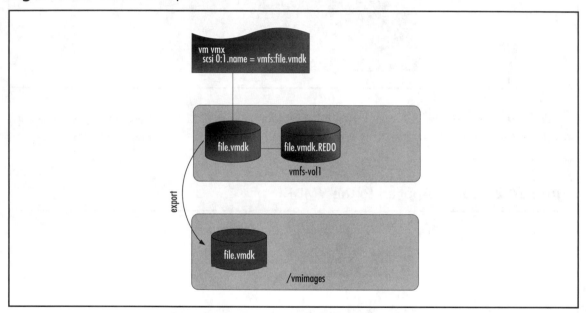

After the export is complete, your next step is to put things back into a normal operating state. This means applying all changes stored in the REDO file back to the VMDK file (see Figure 24.4). Again, *vmware-cmd* is the simplest tool to use.

```
vmware-cmd /home/vmware/vm/vm.vmx commit scsi0:1 0 1 1
```

Figure 24.4 REDO Is Committed

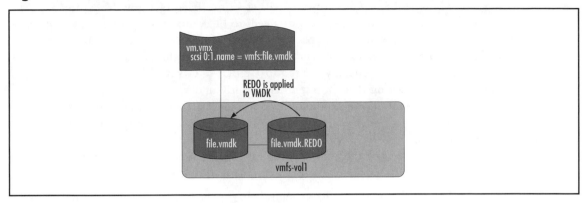

The syntax of this command is

```
vmware-cmd <cfg> commit <disk_device_name> <level> <freeze> <wait>
```

<level> only applies when you have more than one REDO. Actual usage of this option is covered in the "Layered REDO Logs" section of this chapter.

<freeze> is ignored and a freeze 0 is used unless <level> is 1.

<wait> 0 returns when commit begins; 1 returns after the commit is completed.

Limitations

It is important to discuss some of the limitations of this type of backup. The limitations include

- **Crash Consistent State**   The most important thing to understand is that once a redo log is placed on the disk file, the disk file is now in a crash consistent state. The guest operating system is not aware that this has happened. It is as reliable as pressing the power button on the machine, or crash consistent.

- **File-Level Recovery Challenges**   Another limitation of this type of backup is the fact that doing a file-level restore can take a significant amount of time. The entire disk file must be restored and mounted somewhere before you can copy off the file in question. This is a function better left to an agent running inside the guest that is intended as a file-level recovery agent. File-level agents will also help with indexing, versioning and searching. If you must pursue a file-level restore without an agent, the VMware Diskmount utility is your friend. It will save you a significant amount of time mounting VMDK files and looking for the file in question.

- **Wall-Clock Time**   We are talking about a significant amount of data here. Depending on the size of the environment, it may not be practical to copy entire VMDK files around on a regular basis. As your environment grows, you may be looking at a lack of wall clock time to accomplish your backups. Factors that will effect the time your backup takes are the amount of data inside a VMDK, the speed of the disk subsystem, available resources in the service console, and the type of transport used to move the backup data.

- **Performance Considerations** There are performance considerations when running with a redo log. The REDO file grows 16 MB at a time. Each file growth requires a SCSI reservation on the LUN. Also, the redo log needs to be committed after you have a copy of the file. This will rewrite all changes back to the VMDK file. All of this activity requires CPU from the ESX service console and increases activity on the disk subsystem. Resources in the service console are generally limited to 1 CPU, <1 GB RAM, 1 NIC, and 1 SCSI/ RAID device. Considering that this represents a fairly underpowered server, you will run into limitations when trying to do multiple concurrent backups. The available resources will likely limit you to 2–4 concurrent backups before the service console becomes too overloaded. Overloading the service console is very risky. If the service console crashes, so does the ESX server and all the VMs running on it. Use caution, test, and fall on the side of conservatism when planning how many backups to do at once.

- **Frozen Disk Files** While the REDO log is being applied to the VMDK file, the disk is frozen, meaning I/O is halted. If the REDO is small, application of the redo log is relatively quick. If you have been running with a REDO for some time, this frozen state may cause problems. The suggested way to approach this situation is to use a second redo log on the VMDK, while the first is being applied. The method for applying this strategy is covered next.

Layered REDO Logs

As mentioned, while the REDO log is being applied (committed), I/O to the VMDK is frozen. If your REDO file is large enough, users and applications will experience some problems due to the amount of time this takes. A common technique used to mitigate the risk of the commit taking too long is to use two REDO files. The freeze is only necessary while applying the last REDO log. As we pick up the previous walk-though of a backup, we will replace the final commit step with a slightly different process.

First, we add a second REDO log right after our export is completed. The syntax to add this second REDO is exactly like the first (see Figure 24.5):

```
vmware-cmd /home/vmware/vm/vm.vmx addredo scsi0:1
```

Figure 24.5 Second REDO Created

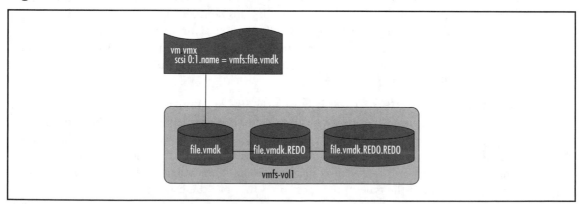

At this point, all transactions are written to the REDO.REDO file. We can commit the first REDO log to the VMDK using the following command.

```
vmware-cmd /home/vmware/vm/vm.vmx commit scsi0:1 1 0 1
```

We give the commit command the following options:

- **<level> = 1**   This tells ESX to only commit one of the two REDO logs.
- **<freeze> = 0**   We will not freeze I/O to the VMDK while the commit is running.
- **<wait> = 1**   Wait for the commit to complete before returning.

As seen in Figure 24.6, we are now in a familiar state with one REDO on the VMDK, except this one is hopefully smaller than the first.

Figure 24.6 First REDO Has Been Applied

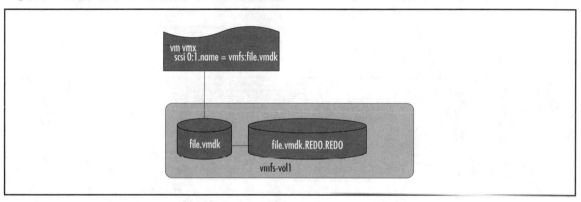

Finally, we will commit the remaining REDO file. Regardless of the freeze option chosen, we are now going to freeze the VMDK.

```
vmware-cmd /home/vmware/vm/vm.vmx commit scsi0:1 0 0 1
```

When complete, this command will leave you as you started. One VMDK and no REDO files (see Figure 24.7).

Figure 24.7 Backup Is Complete; Back to the Normal Operating State

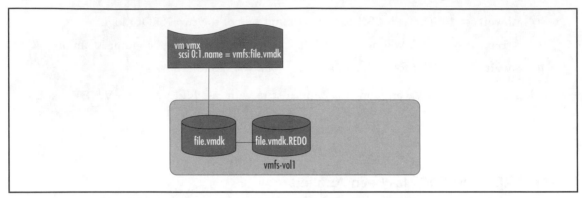

Master Craftsman...

Detecting the Current Mode for a VM Disk

Before you start adding and committing REDO log files to running virtual machines, you need to know what state the current disk file is in. You want to be sure a disk file is in Persistent mode before going to work on starting a hot backup. We've included some code as part of this Master Craftsman tip that you can use to determine the current mode of your disk file.

```perl
#!/usr/bin/perl -w
#
# This script is an example only
# Usage: detectDiskMode.pl <vmxConfigFile> <scsiDisk>
#
# Example: detectDiskMode.pl /home/vmware/vm/vm.vmx scsi0:1
use VMware::VmPerl;
use VMware::VmPerl::ConnectParams;
use VMware::VmPerl::VM;
use strict;
```

```
# User variables
my ($cfg, $disk) = @ARGV;
# Connect to the virtual machine
my $params = VMware::VmPerl::ConnectParams::new();
my $vm = VMware::VmPerl::VM::new();
$vm->connect($params, $cfg);
# Retrieve the mode of the disk in question
my $mode = $vm->get_config("$disk.mode");
if ($mode ne "persistent") {
  print "Warning: $mode\n";
} else {
  print "$mode\n";
} # End if not persistent
$vm->disconnect();
```

Hot VM Backup Sample Script

Using the preceding information, you could put together a quick shell script to run a hot backup. Now, we can pull together all of the concepts shown earlier, except we'll use Perl as the scripting language this time. The following script does exactly what was discussed previously, but processes all disk files for the VM in order. This script has the following objectives:

- The only command-line option is to provide the path to the virtual machine VMX file (required).

- Script will find all VMDK files attached to the virtual machine.

- Process each VMDK, one at a time.

- Apply a REDO log to the VMDK.

- Vmkfstools export on the VMDK.

- Apply a second REDO log.

- Commit the first REDO log.

- Commit the final REDO log.

This script shown in Code Listing 24.1 is an example only and should not be used in a production environment. It lacks user feedback and error checking/reporting.

Code Listing 24.1 Perl Script for Running a Hot Backup of a VM

```perl
#!/usr/bin/perl -w
#
# This script is an example only
# Usage: simpleBackup.pl <vmxPath>
use VMware::VmPerl;
use VMware::VmPerl::Server;
use VMware::VmPerl::ConnectParams;
use VMware::VmPerl::VM;
use strict;
# User variables
my $target="/vmimages";
my $cfg=$ARGV[0];
print "$cfg\n";
# Set up a connection to a virtual machine
my $params = VMware::VmPerl::ConnectParams::new();
my $vm = VMware::VmPerl::VM::new();
$vm->connect($params, $cfg);
# No smooth way to return the number of scsi controllers
# We will cycle through all possibilities checking if it is present
for (my $scsiController=0; $scsiController<=3; $scsiController++) {
  my $presentScsiController = $vm->get_config("scsi$scsiController.present");
  # If it is there, we will continue processing
  if ($presentScsiController eq "true") {
    # Again, cycle through all possible scsi IDs
    for (my $scsiID=0; $scsiID<=15; $scsiID++) {
      my $presentScsiID = $vm->get_config("scsi$scsiController:$scsiID.present");
      if ($presentScsiID eq "true") {
        # Get the path to the vmdk
        my $vmdk = $vm->get_config("scsi$scsiController:$scsiID.name");
        # $vmdk format is now vmfsvol:vmdk
        # Let's break this up into 2 variables
        my ($vmfsvol,$vmdkname) = split (':',$vmdk);
        my $vmdkPath = "/vmfs/$vmfsvol/$vmdkname";
        # Add the first redo
        $vm->add_redo("scsi$scsiController:$scsiID");
        # Do a backup
        `/usr/sbin/vmkfstools -e /$target/$vmdkname $vmdkPath`;
        # Add a second redo
        $vm->add_redo("scsi$scsiController:$scsiID");
```

```
    # Wait a second for the redo to be created
    sleep(1);
    # First commit with same options as vmware-cmd
    $vm->commit("scsi$scsiController:$scsiID", 1, 0, 1);
    # Commit final redo
    $vm->commit("scsi$scsiController:$scsiID", 0, 0, 1);
  } # End If SCSI ID is present
 } # End for SCSI ID Cycle
 } # End If SCSI Controller is present
} # End for SCSI Controller Cycle
# Cleanup
$vm->disconnect();
```

Master Craftsman...

Answer VM Questions from a Script

After some events occur, VMware ESX Server won't continue until you answer a question. ESX requires your answer to the question before the process can resume. For example, if you accidentally try to add a third REDO log, a question is generated. This question has only one answer, OK. Once you answer the question, the process resumes.

The problem here is that your scripts need to be able to answer these questions as they come up. Otherwise, your script will pause indefinitely. The following code can be used in your scripts to answer single option questions. You could also easily modify the script to answer more difficult questions.

```
#!/usr/bin/perl -w
#
# This script is an example only
# Usage: detectQuestion.pl <vmxConfigFile>
#
use VMware::VmPerl;
use VMware::VmPerl::ConnectParams;
use VMware::VmPerl::VM;
```

Continued

```perl
use VMware::VmPerl::Question;
use strict;
# User variables
my ($cfg) = @ARGV;
# Connect to the virtual machine
my $params = VMware::VmPerl::ConnectParams::new();
my $vm = VMware::VmPerl::VM::new();
$vm->connect($params, $cfg);
# Check for a question. Will return undef if
# no questions.
my $question = $vm->get_pending_question();
# If $question is defined, there is an outstanding question
if (defined $question) {
  my $text = $question->get_text();
  my @choices = $question->get_choices();
  if ($#choices == 0) {
    # There is only one choice, easy to answer it
    $vm->answer_question($question,0);
    print "Question answered: $text\n";
  } else {
    print "More than one choice.\n";
    print "Choices: @choices\n";
  } # End if only one choice
} else {
  print "No Questions\n";
} # Endif
# Cleanup
$vm->disconnect();
```

Choosing the Target for VM Backups

At some point, when writing your backup script, you'll need to decide where your backups will go. You'll also need to decide how to get them there. In most cases, you'll choose some type of mass storage device, like a file server, a NAS device, or a SAN array as the target to store your backups. How you get those backups to the chosen target can vary greatly. Considering that the VMware ESX service console is running a modified version of Red Hat Linux, there are a plethora of options available as to where you may target your VM backups. Some protocols copy faster data than others. Some are simpler to use in scripting. Some integrate better with your chosen storage target. We'll cover some of the available options and provide some recommendations on when to use each.

In this section, we'll address the transports available for backups and discuss where the data will be stored. We won't address specific storage types, such as specific SAN arrays or NAS providers. We'll talk about these in more general terms Since we're more concerned here about the transport protocols used to get your backups from ESX to your target storage.

Some of the more common and popular ways of moving backup data are NFS, CIFS, FTP, and copies to VMFS. We'll define each of them here, and then discuss the benefits of each in turn. Each of the following methods is listed in our order of preference. Consider these options when deciding what will be best for your scripting needs.

NFS

Network File System (NFS) is a common file sharing protocol used mainly in Unix and Linux environments. It could be considered the standard file sharing protocol for *NIX systems. NFS works by exporting a file system from one machine and making it available to the network. Other systems use an NFS client to mount the exported file system at a mount point on their local file system. The exported file system is then accessible from the mount point as if it were part of the local file system.

NFS is a fairly simple way to share, or export, a file system from one machine and access it from another. Generally, we like NFS for facilitating all file sharing from the ESX service console, especially for VM backups. NFS is fast, native to the service console, and simple to use in scripts.

Attributes of NFS for VM Backups

In this section, we'll discuss the pros and cons of using NFS for VM backups.

Pros

The pros of using NFS for backups include:

- NFS doesn't require authentication, so you don't have to code in usernames and passwords.
- NFS is very fast over Gigabit Ethernet networks.
- NFS is usually an available option on a NAS device.
- NFS exports mounts directly into the file system on mount points. Very easy to copy data back and forth using native copy commands like *cp* and *vmkfstools*.

Cons

The cons of using NFS for backups include:

- NFS does not have any native support in Windows. Requires Services for Unix. Not recommended.
- NFS is not as secure as other options, due to lack of authentication and data encryption.

CIFS

Common Internet File System (CIFS) is a standard implementation of the SMB (Server Message Block) protocol largely developed by Microsoft. It is essentially the base protocol that Windows uses to copy data between systems. Windows file servers and many NAS devices use CIFS as the protocol to authenticate and transfer data.

Linux uses an open-source implementation called SAMBA to interact with CIFS servers. In order to copy data to a Windows share, you'll need to install the SAMBA client on your ESX service console. CIFS is second on our list of transports because it is a more complicated implementation than NFS. It needs authentication and sometimes requires a two-step process to copy a VM.

Attributes of CIFS for VM Backups

Now we'll discuss the pros and cons of using CIFS for VM backups.

Pros

The pros of using CIFS for VM backups include:

- CIFS is easy to integrate into a Windows sharing environment.
- CIFS is commonly the preferred, or only, protocol supported on an NAS device.
- CIFS can be mounted, via SAMBA, to a local mount point.

Cons

The cons of using CIFS for VM backups include:

- CIFS is more difficult to configure in the service console.
- CIFS requires SAMBA installation and configuration.
- SAMBA has been less stable than NFS in our experience.
- CIFS is not as fast as NFS over GigE.
- CIFS is a very chatty protocol, which decreases performance over latent connections.

FTP

File Transport Protocol (FTP) is a very common protocol for copying data over a network. It is a standards-based protocol that is supported on nearly every modern computing platform. FTP is useful for copying backups to a file server. It is natively supported on the ESX service console. It is pretty easily scripted and has a substantial amount of reference resources available on the Internet.

Attributes of FTP for VM Backups

In this section we'll weigh the pros and cons of using FTP for VM backups.

Pros

The pros of using FTP for VM backups include:

- FTP servers are common and supported natively on most servers.
- FTP copies data quickly over a noncongested network.

Cons

The cons of using FTP for VM backups include:

- FTP often requires a server platform as a target since many NAS devices do not support it natively.
- FTP takes all available bandwidth it can for copying. It may step on other network traffic.
- FTP does not have the capability to mount on the local file system.
- FTP generally requires authentication, but without certificates it sends usernames and passwords in clear text.
- FTP passwords must be coded into your scripts. This is insecure and will break the script if accounts and passwords change.

VMFS

VMware File System (VMFS) is the file system used for virtual machine disk file storage in VMware ESX server. It is a distributed file system, which means it can be accessed by multiple ESX servers at the same time and not corrupt any data. VMFS locks individual files rather than entire volumes. This means many ESX servers can access files from the same VMFS volumes without any trouble.

The nature of VMFS makes it an attractive target for VM backups. A VMFS volume can be designated as a backup target and shared across all of your ESX servers. This way, backups can be directed straight from the source VMFS to the target backup VMFS volume. Since the .vmdk file format doesn't need to change when moving from VMFS to VMFS, you can copy the .vmdk files directly. This simplifies the scripting required to move data around.

Don't be too easily lulled into using VMFS as your backup target. Generally, we prefer to use non–VMFS targets for VM backups. VMFS isn't a good file system for sharing files (for example, there is no support for directories), it only supports a maximum of 192 files, and it has SCSI reservation issues when copying large amounts of data. You're better off using one of the methods discussed earlier for a permanent solution for backup targets.

Attributes of Copies to VMFS for VM Backups

Now we'll discuss the pros and cons of using copies to VMFS for VM backups.

Pros

The pros of using copies to VMFS for VM backups include

- Sharing VMFS volumes between ESX servers is easy.

- Scripting syntax is fairly simple and doesn't require additional mounts or connection syntax as FTP or CIFS might.

- VMFS is often stored on SAN LUNs, which can help facilitate a larger backup strategy. (For example, back up to VMFS, then take a snapshot and/or replicate the SAN LUN.)

Cons

The cons of using copies to VMFS for VM backups include:

- VMFS doesn't scale well in large environments. It's not practical to attach a VMFS to more than 16 ESX servers. You can run into contention issues and SCSI reservation problems when performing a large number of simultaneous backups to a single VMFS.

- VMFS was designed to host large VM disk files, not be a file server.

- VMFS has no support for a directory structure. Organizing backup files in a sensible way is difficult.

- There are limits to the number of files that can be stored in a VMFS volume. Each VMFS extent can hold 192 files. Most often you'll only have one extent, and are therefore limited to 192 total files in the VMFS. This is a big inhibitor for doing a large-scale backup solution with a VMFS target.

Tip

Never use the *cp* command when copying .vmdk files. Always use *vmkfstools*. An undocumented, but useful switch for *vmkfstools* copies a .vmdk in one command and is very fast. This method exports and imports the VMFS in one step. The syntax is as follows:

```
vmkfstools -e /vmfs/vmfsname/target.vmdk -d vmfs/vmfs/vmfsname/source.vmdk
```

If you're going to use VMFS for backup storage, dedicate an LUN to it. Don't combine active VMs on the same VMFS that you're using for backups. You could run into major performance problems due to the large amount of SCSI reservations that can occur on the VMFS volume during copies. These locks, if frequent enough, will be noticed by your VMs and can cause undesirable results.

Existing VM Backup Tools

Now that you know the basics of a hot backup, we hope that you do not set out to write your own backup application without checking out some existing applications. There are many options, both free and commercial, that cover the full spectrum of price and support. Before you sit down and reinvent the wheel, check out some of the wheels that have been created before. We'll go into detail about some affordable (free) options and provide guidance on where to look for commercial solutions.

vmsnap.pl, vmsnap_all, and vmres.pl

VMware ESX 2.x ships with three scripts that work together to create a backup system. *vmsnap.pl* will back up a single virtual machine, while *vmsnap_all.pl* will call *vmsnap.pl* for all virtual machines on the host. *vmres.pl* is the restore portion. The three tools are fully supported by VMware with no additional charges other than the original ESX licensing.

vmsnap.pl has basically the same logic as the simple sample we went through in the beginning of the chapter. It will manage the redo log process for you and copies VMDK files using a *vmkfstools* export. It will also back up your VMX, nvram, and virtual machine log files. The script also handles logging, local or remote. The output destination options include local filesystem and ssh. VMware refers to the ssh destination as an archive server in the documentation.

vmsnap_all.pl is essentially identical to *vmsnap.pl* in functionality, except that it will back up all VMs on an ESX server.

This application has some downsides, however. It does not natively support keeping multiple versions, and will even overwrite files by default. If you have a requirement to keep more than one version of a backup, you need to apply additional scripting and sweep up the output files using a different backup system on a regular basis. Also, *vmsnap.pl* is missing file compression capabilities.

TIP

The three native scripts, *vmsnap.pl*, *vmsnap_all*, and *vmres.pl*, are a good place to start for ideas to apply towards your own scripts. They expose many ESX functions that are useful for other purposes.

vmbk.pl

We have to make mention of *vmbk.pl* in this text. Considering that this Perl script is made freely available by Massimiliano Daneri, and it has a broad range of fantastic features and functionality, we feel obliged to promote his efforts and provide a link to his Web site. You can find the scripts and information at www.vmts.net/.

Basically, *vmbk.pl* employs many of the functions we've described in this chapter. It uses Perl as the scripting engine (our personal favorite). Its main function is to perform hot VM backups. It adds .redo logs to running VMs and exports the .vmdk files using *vmkfstools*. It grabs the VM config files, .VMX and CMOS files, then facilitates the transfer of the backup files via NFS, CIFS, FTP, or through Veritas NetBackup to a backup target—for example, NAS, SAN, or tape. At that point, it commits the .redo log files back to the running VM.

vmbk.pl is a good option to consider as a script, given that you can immediately start using it for backups. It also provides a great place to start if you're looking to incorporate some of these features we've discussed into scripts of your own.

Commercial Options

Many commercial options are available that perform VM backups in various ways. Thus, the following reasons should be considered when deciding whether to use a commercial product versus writing your own scripts:

- You don't have to write your own application. This can save a tremendous amount of time and/or money.

- They carry support contracts. If things break, you have a professional to call. It also helps you keep your job if you have a real disaster.

- The vendors are generally continuing to add features and functions that will make your life easier.

- Scripted solutions generally require significant knowledge of the Linux shell. If your staff is not comfortable here, a Windows GUI option, provided commercially, will make life easier for your admins.

If you're interested in looking at a few options, consider some that we have worked with and feel have good approaches and appropriate pricing models:

- Vizioncore esxRanger www.vizioncore.com/esxrangerPro.html

- esXpress www.esxpress.com/

Swiss Army Knife...

Using Backup Technologies for Other Purposes

In the new world of virtualization, users are continuing to come up with unique uses for the technology. One idea discovered in the field is using backup technologies as version control tools for the support and development of software products. This is a rather simple but useful technique for the software development community.

The idea is that as your software goes through its various versions, an archive backup is written to a file system and stored with the version number referenced in the description. This can be simply one VM, or a complicated multitier environment.

When a customer calls looking for help with an old version of your software, you can restore the complete environment to an alternate virtual infrastructure. Use this duplicate version to facilitate re-creating and solving the problem. In the physical world, this would be a large and possibly expensive task due to the amount of hardware required. In the virtual world, you can do this entirely from your desk or couch with a minimal amount of hardware.

VMX File Backups

Thus far, our focus for backup has been on VMDK files. While VMDK files are critical because they contain your actual data, VMX files are also important. They tend to sit on the local disk of an ESX host, and a copy of the configuration is not located in the VirtualCenter database. Often times, the local copy of the VMX file is your only record of the configuration of each virtual machine. It would be a disaster to lose the local disk and need to figure out each virtual machine's configuration when the heat is on.

TIP

Maintain an inventory of your virtual machines outside of ESX or VirtualCenter. We recommend creating a spreadsheet that has the configuration details for all of your virtual machines. Include every option listed in the VM configuration. With the VMX files stored on the local file system of ESX server, this document will prove invaluable in a disaster.

Things you should document:

- The virtual machine name
- Which ESX host it resides on
- The path to the config files
- The number of CPUs
- The amount of RAM
- Each virtual disk, its SCSI ID, and its path to the VMDK file
- The virtual disk mode settings—for example, Persistent versus Undoable, and so on
- Any other peripherals and their config information
- The startup order in relation to other VMs on the ESX host
- The performance policy settings—for instance, the CPU and RAM shares and Min/Max settings

Many of the products listed in the existing VM backup tools section of this chapter cover VMX backups, but you may be looking outside of the existing tools for your VMX backups. An option would be to install a local backup agent in the service console and configure it to back up the /home directory on a regular basis. If you don't want to shell out for the agent costs just to back up a couple MB of data, then you can easily put together a script to copy the VMX files once a day.

The script shown in Code Listing 24.2 is an example of how to copy VMX files using Perl. This is intended to be a starting point. By default, it will copy to a locally mounted directory on the ESX host. Also included is an example line to copy to another host via SSH.

The script does not do many things that you may wish to cover. You could add /etc/vmware/ to store your ESX configuration files. You could add /var/log to cover the log files in case of system crash or security incident. Also, you may want some versioning on the files to store older VMX files to find out what has changed.

Code Listing 24.2   Perl Script for Copying VMX Files

```perl
#!/usr/bin/perl -w
#
# This script is an example only
# Usage: vmxBackup.pl
use VMware::VmPerl;
use VMware::VmPerl::Server;
use VMware::VmPerl::ConnectParams;
use VMware::VmPerl::VM;
use strict;
# User variables
my $target="/vmimages/vmxBackup";
# Setup a connection to the local ESX host
my $params = VMware::VmPerl::ConnectParams::new();
my $host = VMware::VmPerl::Server::new();
$host->connect($params);
# List of registered virtual machines
my @vmlist = $host->registered_vm_names();
foreach my $vm (@vmlist){
  # Get the displayName of the vm
  # We will use the displayName to title the backup output file
  my $vmo = VMware::VmPerl::VM::new();
  $vmo->connect($params, $vm);
  my $displayName = $vmo->get_config("displayName");
  # Finally, you may have some problems with special characters
  # I recommend removing them to prevent hassles.
  # This line will remove ( and ) and spaces.
  $displayName = ~ s/[\() ]//g;
```

```
# This will tell us what directory the vmx is in.
my @path = split("/",$vm);
my $dir;
my $cnt=0;
until ($cnt == $#path) { $dir = $dir . "$path[$cnt]/"; $cnt++; }
# Here is the actual backup command
my $cmd = `tar cvzpf \"$target/$displayName.tgz\" \"$dir\"`;
# To go remote via ssh, use this command instead
# Remember to set up ssh key auth first
#my $cmd = `tar cvzpf - \"$dir\" | ssh user\@host \"dd of=\"$target/$displayName.
tgz\"\"`;
# Cleanup
$vmo->disconnect();
} # End foreach vm
# Cleanup
$host->disconnect();
```

This script will copy all registered VMX files to the location specified. It will cover all files in the directory with the VMX, such as nvram and log files. Be aware, in its current form, the files will be overwritten each time the script is run. The output is tar gzip format with the filename of the configured display name .tgz.

Swiss Army Knife...

Scripting the Synchronization of VMX Files to Another ESX Host

You may have a need to store VMX files on another ESX host, preregistered. This may be due to a couple of reasons. First, you are replicating the SAN-based VMFS volumes and have warm servers waiting to be used at the DR site. Second, you have a need to recover a failed ESX host very fast—fast enough to warrant the additional complication of managing a sync process. The preceding sample VMX backup script could be slightly modified to cover this situation. Only a couple of simple changes need be made.

Continued

> 1. The tar statement must use SSH, and needs to explode the tarball on the remote side. An example is shown next. Note the capital P options on both sides. This will preserve file paths.
>
> ```
> my $cmd = `tar cvzPpf - \"$dir\" | ssh user\@host \"tar zxPf -"\"`;
> ```
>
> 2. Following the tar command, the VMX needs to be registered. We recommend using *vmware-cmd* to accomplish this.

Incorporating Hot VM Backups into Your Recovery Plan

Up to this point, we have discussed the essential knowledge needed to perform backups and restores with scripts. We also covered a few very useful scripts packaged into applications, some free and some commercial. Where do you go from here? Well, you've now got to assimilate all this technical information and merge it into your backup/restore/disaster recovery strategy. This section is where the rubber meets the road. We're going to dive into why and how you would use hot VM backups as part of your total recovery strategy.

Before we dig in, let's pause and face reality for a moment. Have you ever had an end user give you a high-five after a standard nightly backup job? I didn't think so. No one really cares about backups. No one was ever considered a hero after their backups successfully completed. What does matter, what people love, and what will get you much praise and many free lunches are successful restores. When you restore the sales forecast spreadsheet an end user lost after a week of work, you become the instant hero. Backups are important, restores are critical. The time it takes to restore data matters. The data integrity of restores matters. The amount of data your business can afford to lose and keep on running matters.

With the perspective that restores are what matters most, let's discuss how to incorporate hot VM backups (and restores) into your recovery strategy. When talking about a backup strategy and disaster recovery, it's critically important to start with the end result in mind. You should know now what you need to have happen after a disaster occurs. Without getting into a full out discussion of DR planning topics, let's cover a few basic DR planning topics.

Some key information you need to know about every application or set of data in your environment is its RTO and RPO. Let's define these acronyms.

- **RTO (Recovery Time Objective)**   This is the amount of time that may elapse after a disaster until the application or data needs to be operational. In other words, the RTO is your deadline for recovery.

- **RPO (Recovery Point Objective)**   This is the largest amount of time that may exist between the present and the last recoverable point in time for the application or data. In other words, the RPO is how much data, measured in time, you can afford to lose.

Before you can determine your backup strategy, you should go through and inventory your systems, group them into applications and data sets, and then determine the RTO and RPO for each one. Done correctly, this process isn't really completed by the IT staff. It's a process that is highly dependent on the opinion of those that run your business. If the business says that the CRM database has an RTO of 12 hours and an RPO of five minutes, then your job is now defined. At this point, you can apply strategy and tools to accomplish those objectives. Without those guidelines, it's impossible to create a recovery strategy that is valid to your business.

Often, as you take the guidelines from your business and translate that into tools, human resources, and ultimately expenses, you may get a different answer regarding what the RTOs and RPOs are. Money talks, loud. A few rules of thumb when it comes to determining how redundant to make your systems based on recovery requirements:

- The lower the recovery requirements (RTO and RPO times), the more expensive and difficult the solution to achieve them will be. Zero downtime and zero data loss, for example, generally require completely redundant systems with expensive replication software and high availability clustering. Whereas a slightly less resilient system can be implemented that is good enough with much less investment and generally highly satisfactory results.

- The more complicated your redundancy systems are, the more prone you are to failures. We've often seen "highly available" systems end up with more downtime than less redundant systems. In most cases, it happens because the system became so complex in an effort to be redundant that the human factor mismanaged it.

- The K.I.S.S. factor most often works better than over engineering. K.I.S.S. = Keep It Simple Stupid. A simple system, compared to a complex system with many moving parts, generally has less chance of failing. Simply put, fewer components equates to fewer failures.

Once you and the business come to agreement on what needs to be protected, you'll get the opportunity to dig through the myriad tools and techniques to determine the best way to get it done. You'll then be armed with the data you need to determine what tools, scripts, agents, applications, libraries, arrays, replication, and so on to use for backup and recovery.

Now, the focus of this work is not to teach you how to do disaster recovery planning. However, we thought it very important to frame the concepts of hot VM backups within the discussion about disaster recovery planning. There seem to be misconceptions in the community about what hot VM backups can do. Often, they are given more credit than they deserve. Rarely have we found an enterprise implementation of VMware that can be fully protected by a standalone hot VM backup tool. Now that you've been through this chapter and understand what hot VM backups can do, you can start to figure out where it fits in your plan.

Let's simply state the functionality of hot VM backups by listing what they can and cannot do in the two lists shown in Table 24.1. In this table, the plus column stands for functions that hot backups can do; the minus column stands for functions they cannot do.

Table 24.1 Capabilities of Hot Virtual Machine Backups

Hot Virtual Machines Can...	Hot Virtual Machines Cannot...
Perform zero downtime backups of VMs without a performance hit	Perform file level backups and restore
Capture the entire state of the VM, including boot, sector, OS, and applications.	Create detailed catalogs of backed-up files.
Back up virtual machines without guest OS agents.	Close files and databases before taking a backup. State of backed-up VM is crash consistent.
Be written to disk, tape, or network shares.	

Crash Consistent State

Let's define crash consistent and explain why it matters to you. Have you ever pulled the power from a server while the OS is running? How about hold the power button down for 15 seconds or so? Or, have you ever pulled the fiber cable from a server that boots from SAN? The state that your server is in after it reboots is a crash consistent state. Crash consistent state usually follows an abrupt and immediate power off or freeze of the operating system. The OS and applications were not made aware of the shutdown, so consequently they didn't do any of the things they normally do before powering off. Some of these activities are quite important, such as committing transactions to a database and closing files, writing uncommitted data from memory to files, committing outstanding I/Os to disk, and other items of this sort. When the server comes back up, it has to deal with the sometimes unpleasant and often very messy situation of cleaning up after the crash.

The good news is that most operating systems and applications are aware that crashes occur once in a while. They have mechanisms built into them to recover from this type of disaster. Databases write uncommitted data to transaction logs before it is written to the database. File systems have journaling features that log any changes to a temporary journal before committing them to the main file system. These transaction logs and journals are used to replay data that wasn't committed before the crash back into the main data set.

Keep in mind, however, that crash consistent means that there is a chance that you may have corrupted data, broken file systems, uncommitted transactions, or untold other failures after a crash. We need to throw this warning out there even though in the vast majority of instances with standard applications there are no problems coming out of crash consistent states.

When you perform a hot backup of a virtual machine, you are essentially freezing the disk and taking a snapshot of it. At the exact moment you add a .REDO log to a .vmdk file, the state of the data is frozen, whether or not files are open or closed and databases are running or quiesced. The good news is that VMware takes care to commit any transactions that are in flight to the .vmdk file when the .REDO log is added. In 99+ percent of the cases, you'll have no problem recovering the data in the .vmdk file.

WARNING

We said 99+ percent of the time you'll be able to recover the data in the .vmdk file. That doesn't mean it will meet your usability expectations. If you have an application that doesn't like to be frozen in the middle of a transaction, then you may have a situation where your data is recovered, but useless. The disclaimer is this: test test test this functionality out before you rely on it as part of your disaster recovery plan. That should go without saying, but we've been consulting long enough to know that there isn't much that we leave unsaid and unchecked.

Replication

If you can't afford to lose any data, then hot VM backups are not for you. Neither are file-level backups. You just graduated to an advanced level of backups, called replication. Data replication can be performed at the file system level or at the storage array level. High-end solutions require a lot of bandwidth and can provide synchronous replications of all data. Synchronous replication ensures no data is lost. For situations with less bandwidth, asynchronous solutions queue up replications and trickle them over connections at set times. These can be five minutes behind or 24 hours behind. It's adjustable based on your configuration.

Real-time replication is currently the best solution for zero data loss environments. It's the only way to guarantee that you don't lose a single transaction during a disaster. Replication is reliable and it works, but it comes with a price. Replication solutions are generally many times more expensive than traditional backup methods. However, if you need it, you need it, and you'll be willing to pay for it. If not, then it's time to compromise.

Hot VM Backups as Part of the Recovery Plan

Now, you've taken the earlier advice and considered where this type of backup/restore procedure will fit into your disaster recovery plan. You've considered which of your applications recover well from crash consistent states and which absolutely do not. You've decided that you'll enable journaling on your ext3 and reiser file systems and you'll use transaction logs with your Exchange and SQL servers. Good. Now let's discuss a common approach for using hot VM backups in your plan.

To begin with, it's important to understand that one of the major limitations of a hot VM backup is it has absolutely no knowledge of the files inside the .vmdk file. If you need to recover that sales forecast spreadsheet that is backed up inside a .vmdk file, you're going to have to find it yourself. There is no catalog of files contained inside the guest OS file system that you can refer to.

To achieve file-level restores, you'll need to use a file-level backup tool in addition to your hot VM backup tool.

Let's walk through the steps to determine the correct recovery strategy for your applications and data sets. The five step process shown in Figure 24.8 will help you establish the correct policy for each application.

Figure 24.8 Process to Determine Backup Strategy

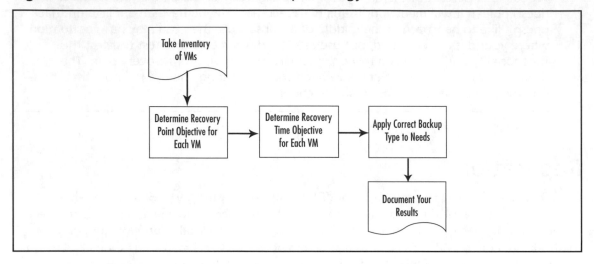

1st Step: Take an Inventory of Your Virtual Machines

You can't plan for recovery unless you know what you have. A wise Electronic Janitor once told me, the majority of IT is inventory. To begin, create a simple spreadsheet that contains a detailed inventory of your virtual machines and the applications running within them. You'll need to record at least:

- The operating system
- Which applications run on each OS
- The location where data is stored

Especially note if some data for your VM is not stored in VMFS volumes. This data will need to be addressed individually.

Now that you've begun this document, you'll be able to use it as a foundation for building out the rest of the recovery plan. Expand the spreadsheet during the next few steps to include RTO and RPO requirements for each virtual machine.

2nd Step: Determine the Recovery Point Objective for Each VM

The recovery point will tell you how often you need to perform a backup of your VM. Answer the following question for each VM:

How much data can I afford to lose?

Once you know how much data you can afford to lose, you can decide the frequency of your backup jobs. If you can afford to lose seven days work, then only back up once a week. If you can afford to lose up to 24 hours of work, then a daily backup is perfect.

3rd Step: Determine the Recovery Time Objective for Each VM

Earlier, we discussed planning for recovery first. At this step, think about the type of recovery that will be required for this application or data set.

Answer the following question for each VM:

How fast does it have to be recovered after a disaster? (RTO)

The time required to recover a VM is often overlooked when applying a blanket backup strategy to systems. If you only have a tape backup of an application, the recovery time will include the process of installing a new operating system, setting up a backup agent, and restoring the application data from tape. This process at a minimum will be several hours. If your RTO is less than those several hours, rethink your tool selection.

Hot VM backups take about as much time to restore as they do to back up. If you're using compression on the backups, then the recovery time will go faster. The compression calculations are not as intense on a recovery as they are on a backup.

4th Step: Apply the Right Backup Job to the Need

Once you have the business requirement for how fast you need to recover, and how much data you can afford to lose, you can use this information to decide on the right backup tool. The tool must back up frequently enough to meet the RPO and be able to provide recovery quick enough to meet the RTO.

At this point, you have gathered enough information to decide which type of backup tool will meet your recovery requirements.

Table 24.2 shows a general comparison between the different backup/recovery tools we've discussed in this chapter. You can use this as a starting point to help decide which tool fits your recovery requirements best, and, ultimately, to determine whether hot VM backups are for you.

Table 24.2 A Comparison of Backup Tools

Backup Type	Min RTO*	Min RPO**	Cost	Complexity
VM hot backup	< one hour	24 hours	Low	Low
Tape backup agent	1–24 hours	24 hours	Medium	Medium
Storage replication	< five minutes	Real time	High	High

* Minimum Recovery Time Objective is an estimate based on experience of the time required to recover typical data using the specified tool. Your situation may vary greatly depending largely on the amount of data to be backed up and recovered.

** Minimum RPO depends on the frequency of backups. For example, daily backups provide a < 24-hour RPO, while weekly backups provide a < seven-day RPO.

Decide here whether a crash consistent copy of the VM will meet your requirements, or whether you need file-level protection and restore capability as well. Your application may require a special agent to perform a proper backup and restore—examples are open file agents, exchange agents, and SQL database agents.

If crash consistent is good enough and the recovery time is acceptable, then a hot VM backup is perfect for you. If you need file-level recovery, then you need file-level backups as well. If your requirements say that you need zero downtime, and your budget supports the need, explore highly available solutions with storage replication.

At this point, you need to prioritize which VMs (applications) are more important than others. The importance of the VM determines its priority in a recovery. You probably can't do all your restores at the same time, and you're more likely to perform recoveries in a serial manner. So, decide which VMs are the most important and categorize them as your top-tier systems. These will be the systems that get restored first after a disaster. Other VMs will be categorized as a lower tier, and will therefore be recovered after the top-tier VMs. Make sure to set expectations with your end users that top-tier systems will be restored first. To change the priority will either cost more money or require a reprioritization of the order in which systems will be recovered.

5th Step: Document Your Results

It is critical to document your plan. Although there seems to be a general aversion to documentation in the IT community, it is nevertheless of utmost importance. If your plan is not documented, you will have a difficult time explaining it to others. If the plan is not documented, you may find yourself in trouble during a disaster. For that matter, make sure your documented plan is stored outside of the system it is protecting. If the plan is stored on the file server, and the file server goes down, you won't have much luck reviewing the plan. Keep a digital and printed copy of the plan at all times. Copies of the plan should be kept in multiple locations in the event a location is inaccessible as part of the disaster.

Hybrid Backup Strategy

For systems that have file-level restore needs, the hybrid approach generally is best. The hybrid backup strategy combines the best attributes of the hot VM backup with the best attributes of the file-level backup. The advantage of the hot VM backup is that the restore is fairly quick and requires little user intervention. Once the server is restored, the last file-level backup can be applied to bring the data back to as current as possible. This approach eliminates the need to reinstall an operating system and tape backup agent. Helping you avoid having to search for OS CD-ROMs, drivers, and agent install disks during a disaster. These are small issues that can waste precious minutes and hours during a disaster.

Let's review a common hybrid backup strategy.

Backup method:

- Take a hot VM backup regularly, such as once per week.
- Take a file-level backup using an agent in the guest OS every day.

Restore method:
To recover the entire server:

1. Perform a restore of the entire VM from the last hot VM backup.
2. Apply the latest file-level restore to that VM.

The advantage here is that you can recover the entire VM very quickly using the hot VM backup, and then bring its files up-to-date with the last file-level restore. This will bring your server up to a state where the OS is fully configured, the backup agent is already loaded and working, and data is current to the last hot backup. This entire effort is achieved with a minimal amount of human intervention. All that is left at this point is restoring data from the last incremental backup. You didn't have to build an OS from scratch, load the backup agent, and then perform a full system restore. You saved yourself hours of work, eliminated countless opportunities for human error, and in the end recovered your data much faster.

Table 24.3 shows an example of what a hybrid backup schedule may look like. It combines the file-level backup agent with hot VM backups, called Full VM Server images. To sum up the following schedule, a full image of the VM is captured once a week with the hot VM backup script—in this case, esxRanger. Then a daily file-level backup is taken using the CommVault agent. (CommVault is a backup software ISV.) Once a week, the repository of VM images is also copied to tape. The retention times listed here are subject to change based on your specific requirements. The times shown in Table 24.3 are merely examples to get you started on your plan.

Table 24.3 Example Backup Schedule

Backup Type	Tool	Media	Schedule	Retention
File-level backup	Example, CommVault	Tape (CommVault Media Server)	Daily	One month
Full VM server image	Example, Hot VM backup script	Disk (Linux NFS export on SAN LUN)	Weekly	One week
Tape backup of full server image files	Example, CommVault	Tape (CommVault Media Server)	Weekly	Two months

This backup schedule is also represented in Figure 24.9.

Figure 24.9 Virtual Machine Backup Process

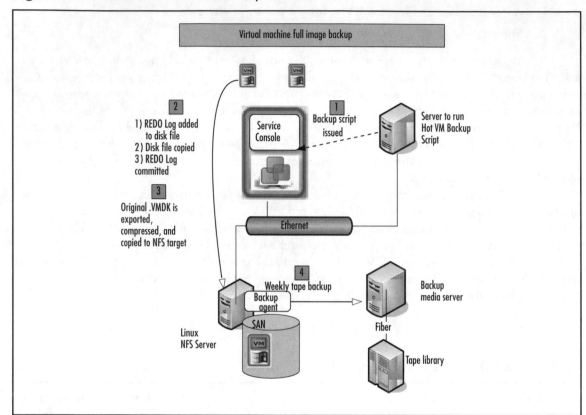

Summary

If you've mastered the topics in this section, you are well on your way to a complete backup solution for your VMware virtual infrastructure. You should be able to confidently script hot backups of your virtual machines and their related config files. You are now armed with information about alternative commercial solutions, and have the knowledge to apply what you've learned to your overall recovery strategy.

## Chapter 25

The Future of Virtualization

Solutions in this chapter:

- The Unofficial Xen Road Map

- Virtual Infrastructure in Tomorrow's Data Center

- The Magic Recipe: Other Hardware and Software Virtualization Trends

☑ Summary

☑ Solutions Fast Track

☑ Frequently Asked Questions

Introduction

Virtualization…virtualization…virtualization. You have likely heard lots about virtualization in the past, and have probably reached your saturation point thanks to all of the chapters in this book. By now, you have either become excited about the possibilities and are sold on the concept, or you are still skeptical about what true value it could have for you or your company. Though all we have talked about is exciting indeed, we have only begun to tap into the potential of what virtualization can really do for enterprises. The promise of a reformed view of data center and infrastructure management will be the focus of many new technologies over the next few years. As server virtualization increases in popularity and becomes more commonplace, companies will look for other synergies within their own infrastructures to accomplish similar goals: simplification, cost containment, if not reduction, and consolidation.

In this final chapter, we will discuss the road map, including its various aspects as officially published by XenSource, along with various generalizations observed in the Xen development life cycle based on customer needs. Next, we will illustrate how Xen fits into a virtual infrastructure, combining it with other virtualization products. We will also invoke some forward thinking as we present some visionary plans from different virtualization companies on where virtualization technology can take your organization in the future.

The Unofficial Xen Road Map

While Xen continues to gain ground and market share among the popular virtualization technologies available, it must also evolve as an enterprise-ready platform that continues to add increased value to companies of all sizes. It will not be enough for the Xen community to provide maintenance releases that address and fix defects or provide support for updated hardware. The demonstration of innovation is what has brought Xen to where it is today. New features and new ways of doing things, as well as the same innovative attitude, will be needed to keep Xen a viable option in the future.

Recognizing this, XenSource is collaborating with the Xen development community in a call for those new features and tools, so as to not just maintain the existing binaries. The main focus for the past few years has been on stability, ensuring that the product survived its infancy without any catastrophic issues. Now, in its adolescence, Xen has an eye fixed on VMware, Microsoft, and others, all with mature products. For Xen to wear the crown as the victor in this race, it must not only meet the needs of its users today, but anticipate what they will need in the future and develop a platform that is extensible and flexible enough to adapt to those changing needs.

Though it would be difficult to list all the activities in which the Xen team is currently engaged or is planning, we can summarize those development activities into focus areas. This informal and unofficial road map for Xen discusses four of those focus areas:

- Performance and scalability
- Operating system support
- Beyond the x86 CPU architecture
- Architecture enhancements

TIP

If you want the inside scoop on what the minds at XenSource are considering for upcoming versions of Xen, check out the Official Xen road map at http://wiki. xensource.com/xenwiki/XenRoadMap. If you'd also like to see what the various developers are working on, you can reference the following site: http://wiki.xensource. com/xenwiki/WhosDoingWhat.

Performance and Scalability

Virtual machines are rapidly taking the place of their dedicated hardware counterparts. Though this pattern continued to accelerate in their push toward lower costs, improved flexibility and speed of provisioning, and maximizing the return on investment in IT infrastructure, acceptance of virtualization has been hampered in production environment concerns with performance and scalability. Development, testing, and less-critical computer systems seem obvious targets for virtualizations, but many still struggle with migrating their more business-critical systems with heavy computing needs to those virtual machines that have been granted a fraction of the underlying hardware resources. In addition to performance and scalability, companies are also concerned about stability and true problem isolation.

As virtual machine monitors progress, the focus on maintaining the quality of raw business value of the hosting guest operating systems and applications will be important. Though reduced infrastructure complexity can be obtained through server consolidation, the ability to process and execute transactions within the time that the business requires cannot be sacrificed. Future versions of Xen will focus on squeezing the most from server subsystems since greater intelligence is built into its hypervisor. Of interest will be improving CPU, memory, and I/O performance.

NUMA-Aware Architecture

Highly parallel computing can take advantage of powerful hardware architectures. Complex systems have been designed with performance optimizing and maximizing components and technologies. In addition, operating systems have been developed to exploit the hardware architecture upon which they run, unlocking their performance-enhancing abilities. However, it would be a shame to migrate those operating systems to virtual machines and lose their potential for high returns and performance, even when running on the same performance-optimized hardware platform.

This can be seen in systems that have been designed with Non-Uniform Memory Architecture (NUMA). NUMA is based on the concept that a CPU can access local memory quicker than it can non-local, or remote, memory. NUMA architectures support scaling in CPUs in symmetric multiprocessing (SMP) architectures since each CPU maintains its own local memory and memory controller logic. Figure 25.1 illustrates memory access in a common NUMA system, along with the three memory paths a processor can take to access data. The most efficient and highest performance (#1) is found when the CPU access data is stored in its cache. This is often done at the same speed as CPU frequency. If a cache miss occurs, the CPU can either access memory in its local bank using its dedicated memory controller (#2) or interface the memory controller of another processor to access data in non–local memory (#3). The last path results in the slowest data access path due to the increased latency and hops.

Figure 25.1 NUMA Data Access Paths

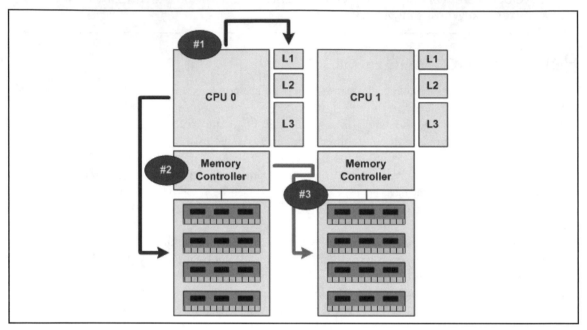

NUMA addresses the problem of memory access caused by the overwhelming effects of high-speed CPU cache, which is incapable of satisfying the needs of operating systems and the applications that run on them. In some cases, multiprocessor systems can be impacted highly by constant "cache misses" due to memory constraints, thus resorting to seeks on lower-speed memory buses. For example, the 64-bit Intel Xeon MP Processor has on die L2 and L3 cache, the latter as high as 8 MB. While the CPU cache is accessible at processor speeds of up to 3.33 GHz, a cache miss will resort to a search in the machine's system memory across the 667 MHz front-side bus. That is five times slower! Machine memory access is further impacted by the fact that all processors share the same memory bus and controller, making environments with high memory activity, such as some virtualization platforms, prone to even poorer memory performance.

On the flip-side, a NUMA gives each CPU a fast bus to its own bank of memory, reducing the occurrence of non-local memory hits and improving memory access by a factor that is roughly the number of processors. However, even with this unique memory architecture, not all data that a processor requires end up in its local bank, requiring access from the memory banks of other processors. As this has the effect of slowing down processors, the overall realized speed of the NUMA system depends on the nature of tasks at any given time.

Supporting NUMA-aware memory virtualization will be important since both AMD's Opteron processor and Intel's Itanium processor utilize NUMA even on smaller two-way systems. Taking this into consideration, the Xen team is challenged with optimizing the memory virtualization supported by the hypervisor to keep memory operations spread across the appropriate memory banks of the scheduled processors. A guest with its virtual memory mapped to physical machine memory addresses in the banks of the processors executing its instructions will perform well. This can be an intelligent, NUMA-aware function of the hypervisor and guest working together since, unlike full virtualization platforms, the guest is aware of the physical memory addresses it uses.

Multicore Processors

RISC platforms have long enjoyed the benefits of processors with more than one execution core, taking advantage of high-performance, multithread execution. Although Intel introduced Hyper-Threading with the later Pentium 4 and same-generation Xeon processors, they did not achieve the same level of concurrency with thread execution as having two identically capable processing cores. This kept the x86 and early x64 platforms at a serious performance disadvantage, barely keeping up with single-server workloads, much less the combined workloads of multiple virtual machines executing on a single server. Enter dual-core processors.

With the introduction of dual-core processors, the future began to look bright for x86 and x64 platforms. The charge was led by AMD with their Opteron offering, which provides greater performance than earlier single-core Opterons, and gives a supporting boost of greater hyper-transport link bandwidth. This was quickly followed by two generations of dual-core processors from Intel, a later release by AMD with an updated Opteron, as well as dual-core offerings in the desktop space with the Core 2 Duo and AMD64 X2 processors.

As 2006 drew to a close, Intel again upped the ante with quad-core processing (two of their dual-core processors on the same chip) with twice the cache size (up to 8 MB of L2) for both their server and desktop line. AMD is bound to follow up with their 4 × 4 architecture, and both companies have plans for true quad-core releases in the future. But what will follow that? Eight- and 16-core solutions?

This is an important factor for the Xen team to consider as CPU schedulers will become increasingly critical. The majority of Xen implementations are, and will be, on two-way and some four-way servers. These servers present a strong value proposition for virtualization since there is no reason to "scale up" versus "scaling out." Unlike large workload servers, such as beefy database servers, virtualization veterans agree that workloads should be spread out across a greater number of servers to achieve a more linear increase in resources with each incremental server unit added to the pool. The increased cost for servers that are eight-way and more is exponentially greater two-way and four-way servers, but performance per CPU actually tends to roll off in a diminishing-returns fashion. Even though Xen supports up to 32-way architectures, it is not unreasonable to think that most of the development efforts to optimize the scheduler sEDF and Credit schedulers currently found in Xen were made with the common two-way server with four execution cores in mind. As two-way systems morph into platforms with 8, 16, and 32 execution cores, software developers will have to code wisely to avoid the law of diminishing returns, as experienced with large n-way systems in the early x86 days.

We will discuss multicore processors later in this chapter. First, we present an overview of Xen's direction on the PowerPC, one of the original multicore CPU architectures in the popular midrange market. We will also discuss the realm of possibilities with Sun Microsystem's UltraSPARC T1. Then we will focus on the multicore road map for both Intel and AMD.

Smart I/O

Users of Xen will acknowledge that CPU and memory performance is so close to native that you almost forget that guests are virtualized—that is, until those same guests need to achieve high-levels of I/O utilization. Although Xen's paravirtualization architecture allows both modified and unmodified guests with good I/O performance, the demands are also ever-increasing, a fact that is bound to tax the existing hypervisor design in many situations, the same way as with a typical physical platform.

Acknowledging the need for improving I/O performance without placing additional overhead on the guest operating system and consuming more of its resources, hardware manufacturers have developed new I/O device architectures that promise to give a server's I/O an injection of nitrous oxide. Notably, Remote Direct Memory Access (RDMA), TCP/IP Offload Engines (TOEs), and new bus technologies such as PCI-Express (PCIe) and InfiniBand enable raw I/O performance at unprecedented levels. However, even these new promising technologies offer challenges to operating systems vendors today. How much more of a challenge will they pose to Xen's architecture then?

Technology Highlight...

Smart I/O Devices: RDMA and InfiniBand

Remote Direct Memory Access (RDMA) is a network interface card feature that lets one computer directly place information into the memory of another computer. The technology reduces latency by minimizing demands on bandwidth and processing overhead.

Conventional hardware architecture (along with the supporting software in the operating system and device drivers) imposes a significant CPU and memory load on a server. Bottlenecks are commonly developed, though to various degrees depending on the system in question, due to the data that must be copied between the kernel and application. Memory bottlenecks can cause a more severe condition as connection speeds exceed the processing power and memory bandwidth of servers, such as in servers with multiple gigabit or even 10Gb interfaces.

RDMA addresses this by implementing a reliable transport protocol in hardware on the NIC and by supporting zero-copy networking with kernel bypass. Zero-copy networking lets the NIC transfer data directly to or from application memory, eliminating the need to copy data between application memory and the kernel. A concept known as *kernel bypass* lets applications issue commands to the NIC without having to execute a kernel call. The RDMA request is issued from user mode to the local NIC and over the network to the remote NIC without requiring any kernel involvement. This reduces the number of context switches between kernel mode and user mode while handling network traffic. This promises to substantially reduce the work performed by Xen's I/O virtualization model.

In comparison, the InfiniBand Architecture (IBA) is an industry standard that defines a new high-speed switched fabric subsystem designed to connect processor nodes and I/O nodes to form a system area network (the next substantial meaning for the acronym SAN). This new interconnect method moves away from the local transaction-based I/O model across busses to a remote message-passing model across channels. The architecture is independent of the host operating system (OS) and the processor platform.

IBA provides both reliable and unreliable transport mechanisms in which messages are queued for delivery between end systems. Hardware transport protocols are defined that support reliable and unreliable messaging (send/receive), and memory manipulation semantics (RDMA read/write) without software intervention in the data transfer path.

The InfiniBand specification primarily defines the hardware electrical, mechanical, link-level, and management aspects of an InfiniBand fabric, but does not define the lowest layers of the operating system stack needed to communicate over an InfiniBand fabric. The remainder of the operating system stack to support storage, networking, IPC, and systems management is left to the operating system vendor for definition. It will be interesting to see how the Xen project's adoption and implementation of InfiniBand evolves over time as this technology becomes more widespread and commonplace.

In response to these types of smart I/O devices, the Xen team will need to enhance or replace the current split device architecture with its frontend and backend drivers. Device channels will need to be optimized in order to not introduce any unnecessary latency to the I/O process. Software-based IOMMUs will need to be retrofitted to work closer and to more tightly integrate with provided hardware IOMMUs, or be eliminated all together. Of course, as software is replaced by hardware, access-control, the mechanism for maintaining safety and isolation, will need to transform and adapt to such conditions as well.

Operating System Support

The operating systems … need we say more? The foundation of any server instance is the operating system upon which the business value applications execute. The hope that one day everyone will run the same operating system or that all operating systems will, in turn, be mutually compatible is a wish in vain. In fact, as Xen's popularity expands with a more diverse selection of customers, the need to support a more diverse selection of operating systems will exist. While this may seem trivial to the open-source community (one that laughs in the face of a challenge), the commercial side of Xen may hit some critical challenges.

Of the greatest importance, XenSource will need to raise the bar a couple of notches with its XenServer product family to meet its ubiquitous goals. While the 3.2 release takes the commercial VMM a step further in that direction, the pace will need to pick up to help Xen compete with other commercial VMM offerings.

Support in Linux Distributions

And while XenSource is up for the challenge, it appears that others are standing in line next to it as well. It reminds me of a scene at the end of a movie when the underdog gains unwavering courage in the face of the opposition—before you know it, he's not alone but finds himself in the company of many others. Playing on that "strength in numbers" idea, Xen is being rewarded for its commitment to open-source Linux. In fact, all of the major Linux distributions have chosen to adopt the VMM as their virtualization technology of choice rather than reinvent the wheel. This accomplishes several things for Xen. First, it gives greater exposure for the VMM since it is distributed with the operating system. Second, it improves the installation and integration experience. No longer will users have to compile the kernel and modules, modify their boot loader, or hack around with dom0 driver integration.

Leading the charge is Novell, who was an early adopter of Xen in its commercial SUSE offering, followed by Red Hat with Fedora Core 6 and RHEL 5, and Sun with an updated release to Solaris 10. It is inevitable that all other distributions will follow suit, although competing technologies such as KVM and UML are fighting for the limelight in the open-source world of Linux. Also, Xen is bound to make a large landing with MacOS users since they have not been provided satisfactory offerings from Microsoft and others that come close to Xen's feature set.

What the Xen team does need to do, however, is make sure consistency is maintained. Recently, Xen issued a public notice stating that companies redistributing their hypervisor should not call it "Xen." Maybe this was done to not associate the tightly quality-controlled release with the derivatives that will grace the distributions, bound to deviate from the stable code based in one form or another. And walking both the "free" world and commercial market, how will Xen continue to maintain demand for its XenServer offering with built-in implementations already lurking in the distributions around the globe?

Furthermore, getting Xen up and running is one thing, but improving the move to modified domUs has proven to be slow as well. To really hit the home run, Xen will need to work with each of the Linux distributions to facilitate a new type of offering… the domU offering. Imagine it: you go to Red Hat's Fedora project page and download the CD/DVD of the latest release of Fedora Core (FC) to install, or download the Xen domU of FC. Finally, as virtual appliances continue to be accepted, the Xen team should work with open-source developers to ensure a Xen appliance is an available download, whether for production or evaluation, allowing Xen customers to further achieve value with the VMM.

Xen and Microsoft

By now, you may have heard about the agreement between Microsoft and XenSource on July 18, 2006. XenSource had announced prior to this agreement that it was going to provide support in its hypervisor for Windows-based guests, using Intel and AMD hardware virtualization technologies in their latest processor offerings. However, the formal agreement signed between Microsoft and XenSource goes much farther than just the ability to run Windows in a domU. In fact, it is the very discussion of hypervisor technology that lies at the base of their agreement.

The two companies have begun to collaborate in the development of virtualization technology that will enable interoperability between XenSource's hypervisor and Microsoft's Windows Server virtualization, an offering that will be available within 180 days of the release of the next Windows server operating system, codenamed "Longhorn Server." The interoperability will allow Xen-enabled guests, or rather modified, paravirtualized guests, to run on Microsoft's upcoming hypervisor.

Two things become important, then, in this new and brave world. First, Microsoft will begin to offer official support for operating systems other than Windows, although the extent of their support is still to be announced. It is expected they will have to support core functionality as it relates to CPU and memory management, networking, and storage. Officially, this new technology will not be a free offering, but will be made available through commercial licensing channels, either from Microsoft, XenSource, or from both. This interoperability between XenEnterprise and Longhorn will create an interesting proposition to IT enterprises.

So maybe the future of operating system interoperability is not that far-fetched. Who would have ever guessed that Microsoft Windows server would also be running RHEL, SLES, BSD derivatives, or even Solaris? But all of this will be possible if the XenSource-Microsoft technology works as planned.

Other HVM Guests

In a similar move to the XenSource-Microsoft agreement, the future looks bright for other operating systems not easily supported in Xen currently. With the first generation of HVM from Intel and AMD proving just how the CPU can assist in virtualization tasks, second- and third-generation HVM processors will undoubtedly allow even more integration and assistance with VMMs for even more guest operating system compatibility. The dreams of many involve the ability to run Novell Netware, Sun Solaris (not just the OpenSolaris flavor), Apple MacOS, and a wider range of Windows operating systems, such as Vista and Longhorn, on top of the Xen hypervisor. And why not? With Smart I/O and improved CPU and memory virtualization through hardware, just about any x86/x64 compatible operating system should be a candidate for its own domU real estate.

Beyond the x86 CPU Architecture

With efforts led by developers at IBM and Intel, Xen is bound to make an explosion on the fronts of other CPU architectures in full-fashion soon. While reasonable performance has been observed, there is still a lot of work to be done to bring the VMM up to the same level as it exists today on x86. In this section, we will review the Xen team's development efforts for popular RISC platform offerings. We will discuss Xen's current capabilities on the road map, if one exists, for the following architectures:

- Intel IA-64 (Itanium and Itanium 2)

- IBM PowerPC

- Sun Microsystems UltraSPARC

IA-64 Feature Sync with x86

IA-64 is the oldest non-x86 port of the Xen VMM. Performance is excellent with very low overhead. While Windows guest VMs are not in the support model yet, multiple SMP Linux domUs are supported. With the age of this port and the evolution of its feature set, Xen for IA-64 has nearly the same functionalities as its x86-based sibling, including

- Virtual block devices use the standard frontend/backend virtual split device model.

- The standard set of control tools and commands are available to manage the Xen environment.

- HVM guests are supported with the Intel-VT capabilities available in the latest generation of Itanium 2 processor.

With most of the hard work accomplished already, the IA-64 port can look forward to development focus on VM life -cycle features, such as save/restore, live migration, and additional functionality since it evolves in the x86 port as well (snapshots, storage management, and so on). Efforts will be placed on stabilizing this platform even further, with emphasis on virtual physical address space for each guest and support for driver domains to enhance performance under heavy I/O workloads.

With the release of Microsoft Windows Server "Longhorn" on the horizon, we can expect that the new relationship with Microsoft will also extend to IA-64 virtualization as well. This may also fuel additional efforts to provide unmodified Windows guest virtualization through existing HVM capabilities up through and including Windows Server Data Center Edition for greater than eight-way Windows guests.

Porting to PowerPC

IBM developers are heavily working on the Xen port for the PowerPC 970 processor. Leading the charge at IBM are Hollis Blanchard and Jimi Xenidis (no pun intended). Based on the POWER4 architecture used in the IBM System p series of midrange servers, the PowerPC 970 was introduced in 2002 to cover the huge gap left by Intel between 32-bit x86 Pentium and Xeon, and Intel's sole 64-bit offering, the IA-64, and today the 970 comes in both single-core and dual-core versions. Although practically abandoned by Apple in favor of Intel's Core 2 Duo, the PowerPC 970FX, 970MP, and 970GX are still extensively used by other IBM partners as well as in IBM's PowerPC-based blade servers, the JS20 and JS21.

NOTE

IBM's PowerPC 970 and 970FX lacked the virtualization feature that has made the POWER architecture so popular. Consequently, it was not possible to run multiple operating systems on a single JS20 blade, for example. Xen brings the ability to virtualize such systems for Linux use, and promises to enhance the virtualization capabilities of the PowerPC 970MP and 970GX even more.

Also note that since Xen requires that guest operating systems be modified, the focus has been to port the hypervisor to stably run Linux for PowerPC in dom0 and domU. Though it is theoretically possible to support other guests as well, there are no plans at the moment to support Windows, AIX, or other operating systems in Xen for PowerPC.

Currently, the port has accomplished the majority of the core functions, including most dom0 functionality and tool compatibility and, most importantly, SMP and virtual I/O device support.

Though lacking the save/restore features and live migration available in x86 versions, Linux for PowerPC domUs are a reality.

The future of the PowerPC port, however, should be focused on the upcoming 2007 release of the POWER6 architecture and the far-away release of POWER7. With IBM moving towards standardizing all of their non-x86 systems on the POWER6 platform, sufficient virtualization may allow AIX and i5/OS to be run inside of a Xen domU, though this may not make much sense given IBM's native capacity to virtualize those platforms already. Although IBM's current ability to micro-partition CPU resources and even build redundant I/O virtualization, called Virtual I/O Servers in IBM's Advanced Virtualization Technology, such functionality is provided at a high cost of resource utilization. What would make sense, however, is to integrate some of the user mode management tool functionality into the Hardware Management Console (HMC) and other IBM virtualization toolsets, making their Advanced POWER Virtualization Xen-aware and compatible.

Porting to the UltraSPARC Architecture

While x64 is gaining popularity among the Sun crowd as a platform for the Solaris operating system, the UltraSPARC processor is still alive and well. It may not make much sense, however, to reach beyond existing x64 support to look at the traditional UltraSPARC IV and IV+ architectures. Though they are capable of large workloads, in the case of virtualizing smaller workloads to aggregate on a single server, even Sun has recognized the potential of x64 with their line of AMD Opteron-based systems.

However, with the introduction in late 2005 of the UltraSPARC T1, or Niagara, processor, Sun leads the entry-level and midrange server market in multicore and multithreaded processors, by count as least. From a core-count perspective, a single T1 processor can contain as many as eight cores. As a multithreaded processor, each core can execute four threads concurrently. The multithreaded nature of the T1 processor helps it overcome the impact of cache misses by moving delayed threads off of the execution queue until data has been fetched and placed into the cache while the remaining threads continue to execute. Even with a small cache size (3 MB of L2), the 1.2 GHz T1 beats a two-way, quad-core 1.9 GHz POWER5 and a four-way, dual-core Intel "Paxville" Xeon MP on several industry benchmarks. With a T1-based system running as many as 32 threads at the same time, one would think that this would be an ideal platform for virtualization.

Ironically, one challenge that may have delayed the acceptance of the T1 processor for virtualization uses is the architecture itself. The T1 was designed to be implemented in a single-processor, or uniprocessor, system. Also, all of the cores share the same floating point unit (FPU). While these may be acceptable limitations for some uses, such as mid-tier application servers and high-traffic Web servers, it may prove to be a hindrance for virtual workloads.

Recognizing these limitations, Sun is preparing the Niagara 2 architecture to run heavier workloads by releasing the T2 processor. It will improve on its sibling by doubling the multithread performance with eight threads per core, increasing the size of its L2 cache, supporting SMP, and providing a dedicated FPU for each core. Later iterations, currently known as Niagara 3, will further increase thread concurrency and cache size, while boosting core count per processor and memory bandwidth. Just imagine a four-way server supporting 128 concurrent threads with the latest in memory and I/O bus technologies; overkill for some applications, yes, but it sounds enticing as a platform for virtual infrastructure. If the Xen team could take advantage of this architecture with a port of the hypervisor, it could end up being one of the most popular platforms for Xen.

In fact, Xen could be the saving grace for Sun's processor architecture since Sun has fallen short in its promise to deliver next-generation computing and virtualization functionality with its latest "container" approach in the Solaris 10 release.

Architecture Enhancements

Evolving Xen for improved performance and scalability, guest support, and additional hardware platforms is bound to be a focus for the development team over the next few years. However, there are some key architectural enhancements they are working on now or will be looking at in the near future, even if in parallel with other key development priorities. Focusing on the hypervisor itself, there is work to be done in the storage arena as well as with resource management and virtual devices.

Control Tools

The team has elaborate plans to greatly improve the control tool stack for Xen. Most of the emphasis will be placed on standardizing the management interfaces and structure of Xen, as well as giving administrators greater insight and control of their Xen infrastructure like never before. While a lot of functionality exists in both native and third-party control tools, Xen needs improved administration and deployment tools as well, specifically in the area of centralized management and storage management.

One of the major initiatives will be to implement standards-based management in Xen, the foundation of which has been defined by the Distributed Management Task Force (DMTF). Included in the plans are the development of a Common Information Model (CIM) object to support life-cycle management of Xen guests as well as certain aspects of Xen hosts, and Web-Based Enterprise Management (WBEM) to provide a simple query/result set mechanism to retrieve management data. It's possible Xen may even become compatible with Carmine, Microsoft's up-and-coming Virtual Server management application. Including such standards for management will allow administrators to utilize their existing enterprise systems' management tools used to manage other components in their infrastructure, such as IBM Tivoli and CA Unicenter, to gain insight into their Xen virtual infrastructure as well.

Much effort will also be made to improve the management of the virtual machine life-cycle. Although Xen currently has *save* and *restore* features, it lacks the more sophisticated functionality needed to compete with other hypervisor products and technologies. It is expected the Xen tools will eventually provide snapshot functionality, improved backup/restore integration with guests, storage management (such as disk provisioning and on-demand disk growth), and improved cloning and provisioning capabilities.

Finally, much work has been done with remote administration, utilizing XML over RPC, or XML-RPC. XenSource has already made great strides with this for their XenSource XenServer Administrator Console application; however, developing a more robust API and exposing it for easier interaction with custom developed code will be important. Rather than utilizing a thick client with TCP socket bindings to the API on the servers, Xen may have a Web service that can be consumed and thus expose a rich set of objects to manage the host and guests. Also replacing the Administrator Console will be a Web-based GUI with similar functionality that supports "anywhere, anytime" management.

Virtual Hard Disk Images and XenFS

Many Xen implementations today take advantage of raw volumes dedicated to a single domU. This configuration is popular because of the performance gains as well as the lower administrative overhead of tracking disks-to-VM. However, the popularity of file-based encapsulation of virtual machines will continue to develop, especially when factoring in the benefits of guest portability and self-containment.

In order for Xen users to shift to this model, the Xen team will have to deliver a more robust and higher-performance solution. The team can choose two paths for the road map: develop a new file-backed model unique to Xen, or incorporate existing virtual hard disk (VHD) technology that is already mature and stable. It is foreseeable that the latter path will be chosen, focusing VHD efforts on VMware's VMDK format, Microsoft's, or some other player, such as QEMU QCOW. QEMU QCOW seems to be the winner, according to XenSource resources, because of its existence as GPL code already, and the closed, or semi-closed, nature of the other two formats. Doing so, however, means dumping the existing *loop* driver and expanding on the *blktap* approach that can already be found in Xen in limited form.

> **NOTE**
>
> QEMU Copy-on-Write (QCOW) has some great advantages. Like other Copy-on-Write systems, actual disk consumption can be substantially lowered with disk image sharing across guests. For example, all guests can boot from the same boot volume but have individual data volumes. QCOW also limits the disk space consumed to what is actually being used. So if you create a 500 GB disk for a guest that only has 20 GB of data stored, the actual space used on the physical mass storage is 20 GB. The adoption of QCOW may help accelerate the implementation of features such as overlay images, which can be used to enable virtual machine snapshots.

Virtual Device Enhancements

As Xen grows in popularity among a more diverse selection of users, the demand for additional virtual device support will continue to put pressure on the Xen development team to extend the functionality further. This is especially true in the area of Xen desktop virtualization, where users will want access to a wider array of devices not commonly found in the data center.

USB will need a large focus from the team. Two factors will drive the development effort. First, USB has become commonplace as a connection interface to computer systems. Though basic support existed in earlier versions of Xen, this functionality has been limited in the current 3.x release to USB host controller ownership assignment to a dedicated guest. And with the advent of USB-over-IP, there are new possibilities for implementing USB support now.

In addition to enhanced USB functionality, the following device enhancements are being considered:

- **Remote console support**   Currently, Xen only supports a virtual serial console to interact with guests without network support, as may be the case while configuring a newly deployed domU. This is suitable for Linux and Windows 2003 (using the Special Administration Console, or SAC), but presents a challenge for guests such as the now-supported Windows 2000 family and Windows XP. Novice Linux users running distribution with X Server may not be familiar with configuring the operating system via a serial console, preferring the Gnome or KDE GUI tools for such tasks. Currently, the only way to gain access to a graphic console is through VNC, RDP, or another protocol, but therein lies the problem for guests without network support. The solution currently being discussed is to implement an in-kernel *fbdev* paravirtual frame buffer driver, which uses a shared memory device channel to make the frame buffer available to domain 0, where it can either be rendered locally, or converted to a network frame buffer protocol. This is already the case for HVM guests today, so this will help bring a consistent look and feel for all guests, HVM-based or not. Another benefit of having the PV frame buffer as a kernel *fbdev* is that it can emulate text mode and display messages during the boot sequence (not just when the operating system is fully booted), providing close-to-native user experience.

- **Advanced graphics**   To support graphic remote consoles and achieve satisfactory performance for two-dimensional graphics, a more complex backend driver for the frame buffer, with copy and fill region commands and a separate hardware cursor, will be required. In HVM guests, video card emulation is used to accomplish this already. However, in the case of paravirtualized guests, the kernel fbdev interface is not rich enough to supply this data, requiring the Xen team to modify X Server to achieve decent graphics performance. Achieving satisfactory performance for three-dimensional graphics requires a substantially higher-level interface than that for two dimensions. With both the X Server and Microsoft window systems moving in the direction of using three-dimensional rendering even for desktop graphics as well as games and CAD/CAM, the Xen team will need to develop frontend drivers that encapsulate and transport OpenGL and Direct3D commands into backend domains where they can be rendered by the actual high-end graphics cards.

- **Smart I/O**   Although we have discussed this already in this chapter, smart I/O device support will be ongoing in upcoming Xen releases. InfiniBand and RDMA technology has basic support in Xen today, as long as they are supported in the dom0 operating system. However, the hypervisor has not been optimized for those devices or other hardware-acceleration devices. The challenge for the Xen team will be to establish a framework for frontend/backend driver architecture that will allow rapid acceptance and support of new hardware technologies in Xen. Rather than waiting for two to three releases to get support, the new framework will allow optimized use of those technologies in domUs by the next release, if not the current one. Even better, wouldn't it be great to have hardware manufacturers provide their own PV driver?

Virtual Infrastructure in Tomorrow's Data Center

Server virtualization has been driven by the need of IT organizations to reduce their server footprint and reclaim space in their at-capacity data centers. Consolidation efforts have, for the most part, been very successful, proving that virtualization is a real and viable solution to the "server sprawl" problem. However, it is not enough to just consolidate; you must optimize the infrastructure as well. Accomplishing this requires more than just replacing physical servers with their virtual equivalents. Infrastructure optimization must look at all data center components as a whole, and will vary depending on the size of the company. We will look at future trends that will drive the possibilities of virtualization, and also examine possible solutions for both the small and medium-sized business (SMB), as well as large enterprises.

Technology Trends Driving Improvements in Virtualization

While the benefits are easy to realize in SMB-sized companies, larger enterprises are often the greatest beneficiaries of virtualization. While the debate concerning larger companies has been over "scale-out" or "scale-up" strategies for enterprise-class server systems, those companies must now compound that issue with another one: physical or virtual. Xen is well poised to play an important role in enterprise data centers, and will continue to fortify that position with enhancements and additions to future releases along its road map. To make an educated choice, enterprises must consider the relationship between:

- Xen
- The underlying hardware
- The corporate strategy for application and infrastructure deployment

Hardware Economies of Scale

Virtualization's introduction to larger corporate entities was often in support of development and test initiatives, and was rarely considered for production use. This was understandable since the CPU architecture with the most growth, x86, had a fairly low performance ceiling. Even with the introduction of hyper-threaded technology (not to be confused with multithreaded), a conventional two-way or four-way server could only host a handful of virtual machines, each with some degree of performance loss. At the same time, midrange server offerings provided hardware-level partitioning, such as IBM's LPAR technologies found in the Unix and mainframe offerings, but the costs were astronomical compared to x86. So the question became one of choosing between larger yet more expensive midrange servers that could scale up, and smaller commodity servers implemented in a scaled-out fashion but with a lower price tag overall. Companies rapidly converted to x86 for both Windows and Linux, migrating their business applications to take advantage of lower Total Cost of Ownership (TCO) and better Return on Investments (ROIs).

The economy of scale is being achieved now with new dual-core and quad-core servers with extensions for hardware-virtualization assistance. The current release of Xen enables modified and unmodified guests to perform at near-native levels. The trend is not transforming from "scale-out" to "scale-out and virtualize." A rack of two-way servers working together as a virtual host farm can account for dozens of virtualized server instances, and an unprecedented level of density. The high-density accomplishments that companies are achieving are helping reduce infrastructure complexity. At the same time, overcrowded data centers are reclaiming precious square footage thanks to consolidation efforts and the lowered cost of environmental issues, such as power and cooling.

Multicore and Multithreaded Computing

CPU manufacturers have pushed their processor architectures to their limits over the past few years. As clock speeds have increased, thermal envelope limitations and the need to do more with less has led their engineers to devise creative ways to develop high-performing processors to satisfy future needs while maintaining backwards compatibility.

The most common way to extract more from the CPU is to layer more than one core on the processor die. Dual-core processors have existed in the IBM PowerPC and Sun UltraSPARC line for some time, but such technology was only recently made available on the x86 platform. Both Intel and AMD have played rounds of leapfrog with their releases of dual-core processors. As both companies have shifted their focus on delivering quad-core options to their customers, neither has delivered a true die with four distinct cores—yet. While the race is on to reach true quad-core status, they are setting their sites on what lies beyond quad-core. Table 25.1 lists the 2007 and 2008 road map for both Intel and AMD.

Table 25.1 The CPU Road Map for 2007/2008

	Platform	Codename	Feature	Release Date
Intel	Desktops	Ridgefield	45-nm version of the Core 2 Duo based on the Penryn architecture	Second half, 2007
		Yorkfield	45-nm quad-core, still on two dies	First half, 2008
		Bloomsfield	45-nm quad-core, on single die	2008
	Servers	Tigerton	65-nm Core 2–based quad-core chip update to the Intel Xeon MP with new front-side bus	Second half, 2007
		Dunnington	45-nm, up to eight-core processor for two-way systems	2008
		Harpertown	Updated version of Dunnington eight-core only, with 12 MB of L2 cache	2008
		Gainestown	Up to eight-core, based on new Nahalem architecture, including integrated memory controller, support for DDR3 RAM, and integrated graphics	2008

Table 25.1 Continued

	Platform	Codename	Feature	Release Date
		Beckton	Intel Xeon MP version of the Gainestown; may feature larger cache as well	2008
AMD	Desktops	Altair	65-nm quad-core on a single die based on the Griffin architecture	Second half, 2007
		Antares	65-nm dual-core based on Barcelona	Second half, 2007
		Fusion	Similar to Antares, except with integrated graphics (ATI-based)	Second half, 2007
	Servers	Deerhound	65-nm quad-core on a single die; introduction of L3 cache and HyperTransport 3.0	Second half, 2007
		Shanghai	45-nm up to quad-core with Direct Connect Architecture 2.0, PCI-express 2.0, DDR3 support, larger cache, and 10 Gb NIC	First half, 2008

Even more important to Xen, the 2008 processor releases from Intel and AMD will include improved CPU and memory virtualization (version 2.0). They will also introduce native hardware-based I/O virtualization as well as improved TCP offload for improved network throughput, in preparation for the shift to 10 Gb Ethernet as the data center connectivity standard.

Historically, the typical enterprise application life cycle includes a major release every three to four years. So it can be expected that the load and demand placed on the hardware by application workloads will not see a major jump upwards for some time. At this point, it appears that the raw processing power of computer hardware will more than stay ahead of the application loads that will run on top of them, increasing the amount of underutilization of resources. This will further drive the adoption of virtualization technologies, such as Xen, as the primary and preferred platform for all but the most intensive workloads.

While x86 CPU manufacturers continue to drive additional cores into their offerings, other Xen platforms are doing the same, as well as allowing each core to execute more than one thread concurrently.

This multithreaded approach, though not as efficient as with core count increases, still allows the underlying server platform to satisfy a higher degree of concurrent scheduling for Xen guests. And the more instructions that Xen can schedule, the higher the load it can support and the better performing the guests will run.

Multithreaded processors will appear to the Ring-0 software as individual processors, one for each potentially executing thread, and thus will be queued for execution in the same manner that single-threaded execution cores are. For example, a single-core processor that supports two concurrent threads will appear to Xen as two distinct processors, allowing Xen to schedule two instructions from its guests simultaneously. A key difference, however, with multithreading is that each thread is handled by a "logical processor" rather than a physical one, as is the case with multicore architecture. Executing in the same physical environment, each thread will share CPU cache, memory, and I/O bandwidth, and, in some cases, the CPU-allocated FPU and memory controller, causing the per-thread increase to be less efficient in gain than a per-core increase.

Looking ahead, as hardware manufacturers continue to introduce features that assist in, or directly perform, virtualization tasks, the lines between full virtualization and paravirtualization will change. The combination of multiple cores executing multiple threads concurrently while providing offloading assistance of I/O and virtualization overhead make "100 percent virtualization" achievable, even in large enterprises. Operating systems will become virtualization-aware, containing hypervisor-like logic that will take advantage of hardware VT feature sets. Even more, the need for complexly developed code to serve as an intermediary between the operating system and hardware will diminish over time as the hypervisor and operating system become one.

Solutions for Small and Medium-Sized Businesses

Virtualization has been a boon in the SMB arena. Companies without the budget for large and lavish data centers can easily sustain the servers needed to run their business applications on a small footprint of infrastructure. They are capable of truly realizing the benefits of virtualization because the typical workload per application (messaging, CRM, finance, and so on) is smaller than that of a larger enterprise. Placing Xen at the heart of the virtual infrastructure will help SMB-sized companies accelerate their return on technology investments, even with the flagship product.

While consolidation may not be that important for the typical SMB, cost-effective and optimized infrastructure is. Creative solutions based on Xen can help businesses contain costs while meeting business needs and addressing real business problems. Two such solutions demonstrate how virtualization can really change the paradigm of servers: integrated computing and the data center in a box.

Integrated Computing

Integrated computing is a term for tightly coupled services that form the framework for business activities. Tied to business processes, each service is a software-based technology that can be leveraged by SMBs to run their business effectively. Consider the example shown in Figure 25.2.

Figure 25.2 Integrated Computing Representation

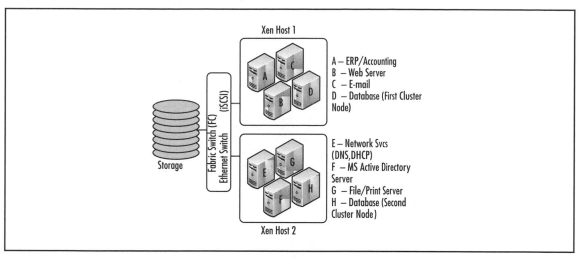

In this configuration, the SMB has two physical hosts, Xen Host 1 and Xen Host 2, which are connected to low-cost, SAN-based storage, either fibre-connected or iSCSI. Each physical host is running Xen, open-source or the commercial product, and hosts four guests. Xen Host 1 has guests A thru D, while Xen Host 2 is hosting guests E thru H. Also notice that the database servers on each (Guests D and H) form a cluster, a high-availability requirement for the SMB's business-critical application. Not shown in the figure are the network connections, two per host, requiring four gigabit Ethernet ports. Although small, this configuration demonstrates just how virtualization can simplify a potentially complex infrastructure of systems and connectivity.

Data Center in a Box

No scenario is too small for virtualization. In the future, virtualization technologies like Xen will be commonplace and will be the norm rather than the exception. Except for extreme cases of resource requirements, the typical installation of an operating system will be in a virtual machine instead of on a physical server. Such cases will be rare in the SMB space, where virtual machines are capable of serving just about every workload presented by the business. When this becomes the standard, the paradigm of what data center infrastructures look like and their bite into the selling, general, and administrative (SG&A) expenses budget will change. As long as you need at least two servers, Xen can help you simplify and reduce costs. Another practical example of how virtualization can change what you think about systems architecture, we will take a look at an extreme approach to data center consolidation—the data center in a box, as illustrated in Figure 25.3.

Figure 25.3 Data Center in a Box

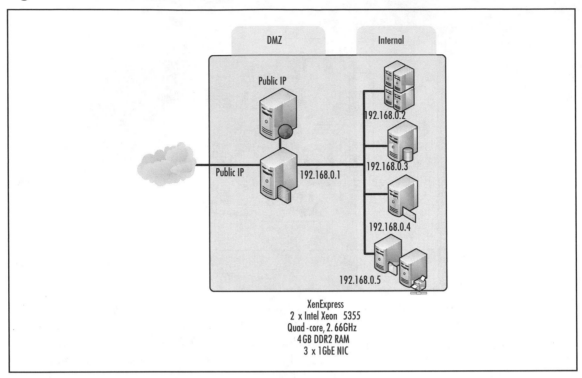

In this example, all the IT services that support an SMB's operation run on a single physical server with plenty of hardware resources running XenSource's XenExpress. Using Xen's virtualization technology, several servers are being hosted on this single server. What makes this different than other scenarios is the combination of services being hosted. They make up an entire data center ecosystem, including software-based firewalls and routers forming a perimeter DMZ, the Web server, internal applications, the database, e-mail, and file/print servers. Behind the scenes, a single privileged domain, dom0, contains the backend drivers for all the underlying hardware devices, while several domUs host a variety of Linux and Windows guests and their respective applications.

Large Enterprises

Large enterprises have the opportunity to benefit most from server virtualization. Relief is needed as floor space, power, and cooling have reached an all-time high, bringing many data centers to their maximum capacity. Add to that the increasing requirements for reliability, availability, security, and compliance, and the need for a change becomes clear. We will next discuss how virtualization addresses these problems.

Reliability and Availability

Reliability and availability are inseparable. For that reason, the points we discuss here apply to both. Although reliability is not the only factor that can impact application availability, it is key to running a consistent and predictable business operation. Applications that enable core business processes thus become the weak link in the chain, crippling the business with unexpected outages and lost revenues. The call for increased reliability, and availability as we will discuss shortly, has led to heavy investments in redundant hardware and software. In many cases, less critical applications are not implemented with high levels of redundancy or tend to be run in less reliable environments, creating pockets of risk throughout the organization.

Virtualization addresses reliability through three key areas: fault containment, simple recovery, and built-in failover capabilities. Focusing on Xen, fault containment is achieved through the use of unprivileged domains, or domUs, that isolate and ensure the safety of each guest operating system from faults in other running guests. The lack of fault propagation gives Xen guests the same degree of reliability as the underlying hardware. Since fewer servers must be deployed, enterprises can allocate funding in their budget to build up their host hardware to a substantially more robust level. Figure 25.4 gives an example of the level of fault tolerance that can be accomplished at the hardware layer. Every guest hosted on that hardware benefits from the same level of hardware reliability, regardless of criticality or tolerance for outages. In essence every server is highly reliable and highly available.

Figure 25.4 Components of a Highly Available Xen Host

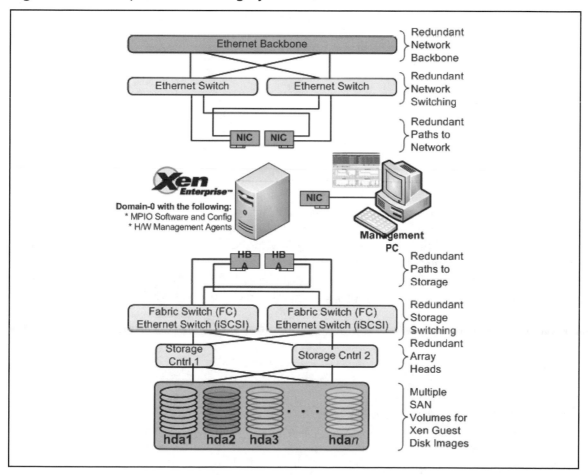

Security

Security is another frontier where virtualization will help large enterprises. Conventional security implementations factor in layers of protection, ranging from firewalls and intrusion detection systems (IDSs) at the network layer to Access Control Lists (ACLs) to antivirus/antispyware software to protect the running kernel from malicious code. In fact, all of these areas have a basic component in common: privilege. The risk would be substantially mitigated if it was limited to user-space access, but most IT security risks exist because they take advantage of direct or indirect vulnerabilities to access through privileged operations. On a traditional server or desktop system, this is difficult to stop because it is not possible to police Ring-0 operations without integration into the kernel of the operating system, often requiring expensive third-party hardware and software. But, theoretically, this is not a problem for the virtual infrastructure.

Since guests run their kernel operations in a privileged ring other than Ring-0, it is possible to develop code in the VMM to analyze and assess the safety and viability of all privileged calls being made by guests. Virtualization provides strong isolation while allowing organizations to encourage best security practices and even undo any changes made. Let's take a look at the future of the VMM, or hypervisor, and the role it may play in securing the IT landscape with the following:

- Embedded IDS

- Network interposition

- Attack-resistant virtual hardware

- VM (guest) recovery

With an embedded IDS, the VMM can be used to inspect network traffic going to, or coming from, virtual machines. This is particularly effective in split device driver models, such as that found in Xen, but may be tricky in models providing more direct access in guests. However, an embedded IDS in the VMM would benefit from centralized management and consistent rules and policies across all hosted VMs. As multicore processor designs continue to develop, the VMM IDS can be given a dedicated CPU core (or fraction of one) to guarantee sufficient compute resources to carry out its task. With the potential cost savings from not having to purchase elaborate hardware-based IDSs or host IDSs, embedded IDSs will further enhance the business case for virtualization.

Another future security enhancement of the VMM is the interposition to enhance security. The goal of VMM network interposition is to only allow safe and correction communication. It is becoming increasingly difficult to identify network traffic caused by malicious users or processes. However, most organizations should be able to profile the expected traffic patterns for their applications in a manner similar to configuring access in a firewall. This "good traffic" profile can even be learned over time, dynamically generating a set of policies that can be used to discern good from bad traffic. If network communication is attempted that does not fit the correct profile as defined by the policy, those packets are dropped or contained for further analysis.

One of the pros of virtualization is the use of a consistent hardware set across all virtual machines, regardless of the operating systems running inside the VM. In all cases, software and code logic is used to present the hardware environment to the guest operating systems. This code either lives inside the VMM itself or is part of the hardware-assist virtualization technologies. Future developments in the virtual hardware should include modifications that can be used to prevent attacks.

Technology Highlight...

The Collective: A Virtual Appliance Computing Infrastructure

Computers today run billions of operations per second, dazzle us with video and sound, store libraries of data, and quickly exchange data with millions of other computers. Yet, computers and software are still difficult to deploy and maintain. Applications and user data are tied to individual computers, making it harder to deal with hardware failures. When users move around, they must remember to bring their computers with them. And, keeping software up-to-date on each computer is a challenge; too many computers suffer security compromises because people fail to apply available updates or correctly configure protections.

Research is being performed at Stanford University to create a new system architecture, called the Collective, that will address those issues. Based on VMM technology hosted on the x86 architecture (to support both Windows and Linux), the Collective attempts are focused on user compute environments, but can easily be adapted to meet the needs of enterprise server landscapes. In the Collective system architecture, virtual appliances, and their updated versions, are deposited in repositories. Individual computers run a universal appliance receiver that retrieves the latest copies of virtual machines from repositories upon request. In other words, the computers operate as a cache of appliances. The system uses a number of optimizations to minimize the cost of the storage and transfer of appliances. This approach allows a small number of professional staff to create fully tested, integrated environments that are made available quickly to all users anywhere on the network.

As part of their research, the researchers have made several major findings, including the following:

- **Efficient migration of appliances** X86 appliances, complete with operating systems, application programs, and possibly user data, can be very large. It has been found that the storage and transfer of appliances can be effectively optimized using the techniques of caching, demand paging, memory ballooning to reduce the memory state, and Copy-on-Write disks to capture changes. The time to transfer an appliance on a DSL link (384 kbps) is typically less than 20 minutes.

- **Virtual appliance networks** Generalizing the concept of virtual appliances to include a virtual network enables the encapsulation of network management knowledge and sets of related services.

- **The Collective Virtual-appliance Language (CVL)** Researchers have developed a language for describing the composition of virtual appliances to create virtual networks of appliances. The language uses the concept of inheritance

Continued

to allow appliances to be individually configured and customized while retaining the ability to be upgraded automatically.

- **Livewire: An intrusion detection system for virtual machines** Through the Livewire prototype, the researchers demonstrated that virtual machine technology can be used to build an intrusion detection system (IDS) that is both difficult to evade and difficult to attack. Like a host-based IDS, it has excellent visibility since it can access all the states of the computer being watched. Like a network-based IDS, it is not vulnerable to being disabled by the attacker.

- **Terra: A virtual machine-based platform for trusted computing** The researchers have developed a flexible architecture for trusted computing, called Terra. Terra allows applications to run in an "open box" VM with the semantics of a modern open platform, or in a "closed box" VM with those of dedicated, tamper-resistant hardware. They have developed attestation primitives to cryptographically identify the contents of closed-box VMs to remote parties and showed how to implement them efficiently.

- **Remote timing attacks** The researchers demonstrated the first remote timing attack where a private key can be extracted from a Web server. Patches to eliminate such a vulnerability were developed and applied to the OpenSSL library. Our paper on the topic won the best paper award at the 2003 Usenix Security conference.

- **C Range Error Detector (CRED): A dynamic buffer overrun detector** The researchers have developed a practical detector that finds all buffer overrun attacks as it directly checks for the bounds of memory accesses. Unlike the original referent object–based bounds-checking technique, CRED does not break existing code because it uses a novel solution to support program manipulation of out-of-bounds addresses. Finally, by restricting the bounds checks to strings in a program, CRED's overhead is greatly reduced without sacrificing protection in the experiments they performed. CRED is implemented as an extension of the GNU C compiler version 3.3.1, and has been tested on over 20 open-source programs, comprising over 1.2 million lines of C code. The software is publicly available at http://sourceforge.net/projects/boundschecking.

The most intriguing aspect of future VMM–enhanced security will be virtual machine recovery. Future VMMs will be able to record the various executions inside a VM, similar to how a digital video recorder (DVR) such as TiVo or Microsoft's Media Center continually record television programs. This record/playback capability further enhances the snapshot ability found in many VMMs today, and is useful for various areas such as development and testing cycles, as well as debugging or troubleshooting production applications. However, it is particularly useful in security incident management. Using rollback and replay of virtual machine execution, it then becomes possible to perform deep and accurate forensics to identify the techniques used in an attack, as well as recover from attacks by removing intrusion damage and backdoors from the virtual machine.

Compliance

Compliance is a very impactful area that challenges corporate enterprises policies and processes today. The list of acronyms that account for the several millions of dollar spent each year continues to grow, and includes Sarbanes-Oxley (SOX), Gramm-Leach-Bliley (GLB), SAS70, PCI, and HIPAA, just to name a few of the U.S. domestic challenges. Couple those with international compliance laws such as Australia's APRA, the Data Protection Act (DPA), and Freedom of Information Act 2000 (FIA2000) in the UK, compliance can become a nightmare for global enterprises.

One way that virtualization can assist large enterprises with the compliance struggles extends beyond the data center to the desktop. Virtual desktop solutions have actually existed for some time with solutions based on Microsoft's Terminal Server and Citrix Presentation Server for server-hosted desktop user environments. However, using virtualization to carve up a robust server into multiple isolated desktop environments is more appealing under the scope of compliance. These solutions are maturing steadily and will soon be the standard for the typical corporate PC; however, the future of virtual desktops will solve many of the compliance problems encountered by large enterprises, including the following:

- Resolving issues with insufficient controls for change management.

- Resolving issues with abnormal transactions not being identified in a timely manner and/or the violation of security policies within the network.

- Centrally managed security patch processes or removal of the need to patch as a whole because of VMM security layers.

- Moving sensitive data normally stored on a PC into the data center.

- Securing desktop environments with the same level of protection and policies as in the corporate office, even for remote or offshore users, since the desktop never actually leaves the data center.

The Magic Recipe: Other Hardware and Software Virtualization Trends

While we have discussed server virtualization in general to a great degree in this book, server virtualization alone will not allow you to realize the maximum potential of the virtual infrastructure. Many of the same issues that exist within the server landscape also exist in other critical areas as well, such as underutilization (or wasted) resources, too much hardware, difficulty managing disparate hardware sets within the infrastructure, and so on.

This section discusses how to further consolidate, centralize, and optimize the hardware infrastructure on which virtual machines will run. We will briefly discuss increasing server densities with blade servers, virtual storage presentation, and application virtualization.

Increasing Density Further with Blade Servers

Although server virtualization allows IT organizations to achieve higher densities (in other words, servers per rack) than possible before, server density can be increased even further by deploying blade servers. All of the major hardware manufacturers offer an x86-based blade infrastructure that promises to accomplish the same goals of infrastructure consolidation and centralization, although their approach varies. In all cases, though, blade servers accomplish higher densities for both physical and virtual hosts.

If we compare the standard 42U server rack, the highest density that can be achieved using typical rack-mounted servers is 42 servers (using 1U servers). However, supporting this density can require a substantial cost penalty in infrastructure, factoring in the cabling, power, and core and edge switch port connections (network and SAN) to support that quantity of servers. In comparison, the same rack can accommodate up to four blade server chassis for up to 64 servers, more than a 50-percent increase in density. At the same time, the supporting infrastructure is substantially reduced through the use of integrated chassis switching for Ethernet networking and SAN connectivity. Since only uplinks to the core data center infrastructure are needed, cabling is substantially reduced, as well as the port count consumed on core enterprise switches, further reducing costs.

Blade servers are not perfect for all scenarios, though, since they are limited in expansion options. Each brand of blade servers has a specific set of I/O expansion that is available, and adoption of newer technologies tend to be available for blade servers long after the release of their standard PCI equivalents for the typical nonblade server. For most implementations, especially for deployments of VMMs such as Xen, blade servers can be an ideal hardware platform.

Storage Virtualization

The prominent gains from operating a virtualized server infrastructure include rapid provisioning, transparent and consistent hardware presentation, and the pooling of resources to maximize utilization without waste. However, many companies are not able to fully realize these benefits without also doing something about their physical storage and network. Storage and network virtualization is subsequently growing in popularity as a means to truly virtualize the entire IT infrastructure landscape.

Storage virtualization refers to the process of abstracting logical storage from physical storage. The presentation of the storage to virtual hosts, such as XenEnterprise hosts, is comprised of a location-independent address space. This is accomplished using controller logic that remaps the presented address to the actual physical address. This remapping allows for new storage configurations that help optimize the utilization and placement of data that is stored in a SAN. For example, a volume presented to a Xen host can exist across multiple physical arrays, optimizing I/O performance and spindle count. At the same time, the storage controller provisioning the virtualized storage to the hosts can analyze and trend I/O patterns and migrate volumes from one tier (Fibre-Channel storage) to another (SATA storage) without any interruption of service and without the knowledge of the host itself. Storage virtualization can also be used to make data storage more robust and resilient by using techniques such as replication and pooling.

Network Virtualization

Network virtualization is a method of combining the available resources in a network by splitting up the available bandwidth into channels, each of which is independent from the others, and each of which can be assigned (or reassigned) to a particular server or device in real time. Each channel is independently secured, and every subscriber has shared access to all the resources on the network from a single computer.

Network management can be a tedious and time-consuming business for a human administrator. Thus, network virtualization is intended to improve the productivity, efficiency, and job satisfaction of the administrator by performing many of these tasks automatically, thereby disguising the true complexity of the network. Files, images, programs, and folders can be centrally managed from a single physical site. Storage media such as hard drives and tape drives can be easily added or reassigned. Storage space can be shared or reallocated among the servers. Network virtualization is also intended to optimize network speed, reliability, flexibility, scalability, and security. Network virtualization is said to be especially effective in networks that experience sudden, large, and unforeseen surges in usage. By tackling these issues and providing increased flexibility, network virtualization can further increase a Xen's (and other VMM's) value proposition to both small and large enterprises.

Summary

Virtualization is still at "buzz word" status today. As a technical concept that is helping organizations improve efficiency and substantially reduce infrastructure costs, it is gaining in popularity with IT organizations of all sizes. With the current offerings of virtualization technologies, such as XenSource's XenServer product family, and hardware assists available in current multicore processors, the popularity of virtual infrastructures is growing as companies acknowledge and desire the benefits they promise.

In the future, though, virtualization will play a more prominent role in the data center. Fueled and supported by HVM improvements and development efforts of hardware manufacturers, enhancements within the VMMs themselves, and the inclusion of other infrastructure components in the overall virtual landscape, virtual will prove to be better than "real." Xen is well poised to play an instrumental role, but will need to expand on an already impressive feature set with a road map that delivers on the true potential of virtualization.

Both small to medium-sized businesses and larger enterprises will base a large portion, if not all, of their future technology investments on products that will propel the "virtual first" methodology for infrastructure management and delivery.

Solutions Fast Track

The Unofficial Xen Road Map

☑ The performance and scalability of Xen guests will improve as the hypervisor takes advantage of CPU and memory virtualization in NUMA-aware architectures with multicore processors

☑ I/O virtualization will improve and Xen will shift I/O management even more back to the guests, further reducing the overhead on the hypervisor with direct smart I/O devices such as RDMA NICs and InfiniBand.

☑ Xen will continue to support additional x86-compatible operating systems through guest modification, as well as a wider range of HVM-based guest platforms.

☑ Although primarily targeted to run on the x86 architecture, Xen is currently being ported to the IBM PowerPC and Intel IA-64 architectures. These platforms will align with the feature set and functionality currently available on x86. There is also potential for ports to other platforms, such as Sun's UltraSPARC T1/T2.

☑ Along with growing support for new hardware technologies, the Xen hypervisor itself will grow with rich features, such as improved control tools, an open file system to support virtual hard disk images and QCOW, and virtual device enhancements.

Virtual Infrastructure in Tomorrow's Data Center

☑ Hardware economies of scale are driving improvements in virtualization. In particular, multicore and multithreaded processors promise to break the boundaries that currently limit guest performance and viability.

☑ Small and medium-sized business will benefit from virtualization due to integrating computing and a substantially reduced infrastructure, requiring a minimal investment in hardware to deploy a wide range of business applications.

☑ Larger enterprises will be turning to virtualization to improve reliability and availability, security, and compliance through improved demonstrable controls and audit trails.

The Magic Recipe: Other Hardware and Software Virtualization Trends

☑ Blade servers can help further increase the density achieved in virtual and physical server deployments. They also help lower infrastructure costs by centralizing and reducing the cabling and switch ports needed for both Ethernet networking and SAN connectivity.

☑ Storage virtualization, the abstraction of logic storage from physical storage, supports server virtualization by reducing the management overhead and increasing utilization of storage devices in a manner transparent to VMMs.

☑ Network virtualization can help further secure and improve the performance of network traffic within a virtual infrastructure by providing independently secured and isolated channels as a backbone for virtual machine communication with the rest of the public and private network.

Frequently Asked Questions

Q: What processor architecture does Xen support today?

A: The current release of the Xen hypervisor, release 3.0.4, supports all available x86 processor architectures in the 686 (P6) family, up to and including the latest multicore offerings from Intel and AMD. Experimentally, Xen has also been ported with limited functionality to the IBM PowerPC 970 (not the POWER4/4+ or POWER5) and the Intel IA-64 (Itanium and Itanium 2) architectures. The Xen hypervisor is also future-ready to support upcoming quad-core and eight-core offerings.

Q: Which processor is recommended for Xen implementations?

A: The base premise for virtualization is to reduce the physical infrastructure by hosting the maximum number of guests on a single physical server without adversely impacting application performance and response. Based on this, it is recommended you host your Xen VMM on either Intel's Core 2 multicore architecture (Intel Core 2 Duo E, Q, X, and QX 6000-series for desktops, and Intel Xeon 5100 and 5300 series for servers) or AMD's dual-core offerings (AMD64 X2 for desktops and AMD Opteron Rev F for servers).

Q: Who is responsible for the direction and road map of the Xen VMM?

A: XenSource Inc. is responsible for setting the direction of the VMM's development efforts. While providing the majority of resources to the project, development efforts are supplemented by the open-source community, as well as IBM, Intel, HP, and others. Ian Pratt, the recognized father of Xen, in particular, maintains the official road map, as well as the "who's working on what" pages on the Xen Wiki, available at http://wiki.xensource.com/xenwiki/.

Q: Does the development of future virtualization technologies pose a threat to computer hardware manufacturers?

A: Although at face value, virtualization can pose a threat to reduced sales of hardware units, there are opportunities for hardware manufacturers to provide value-added solutions, products, and services to support virtualization. This is particularly important since software-based VMMs rely on partnerships with such companies to help develop and support their products.

Q: What is the future vision of the data center?

A: In an ideal situation, server, storage, and network hardware resources will be pooled together and centrally managed to provision, support, and monitor virtual machine instances. Knowing which physical server is running a particular guest or which array contains its data will be irrelevant. Guests will migrate as needed based on policies defined by administrators, maximizing and optimizing the use of pooled compute resources.

Q: What other companies are important to the development and growth of Xen?

A: Due to the x86-inherent nature, both Intel and AMD partnerships and code contributions to the hypervisor project are important to Xen's future. Also, IBM has played a substantial role, exclusively developing many features and components found in Xen today. However, the relationship with the various Linux distributions (such as Red Hat and Novell) will be important, and the recently forged relationship with Microsoft will prove key to the hypervisor's growth and acceptance in the IT community.

Index

A

access denied errors, 400
ActiveState Komodo, for Perl development, 671
Address Space Identifier (ASID), 641
administration agent installation, in Automated
        Deployment Services (ADS)
    account information, 291
    certificate installation, 290
    license agreement, 289
    setup wizard, 288–289
Administrator Console
    division, 537
    installation, 527
        on Linux, 535
        on Windows (XP/2000/2003), 528–535
    Java-based GUI application, 524, 527, 536
    master password in, 535
    system requirements for, 527–528
    usage of, 535–536
    xe CLI installation in, 524
ADS Administration Agent service, 358
ADS Agent Certificate Installation, 358
ADS Agent Logon Settings, 359
ADS Capture Image Job, 374
ADS Deployment Agent Builder, 266
ADS Sequence Editor
    actions performed by, 293
    boot to hard disk, 297
    disk partitioning, 295
    image deployment, 296
    sequence files, 294
ADS Setup Splash Screen, 357
ADS_VSMT_1.1.exe file, 357, 359
AMD IOMMU technology, 640
AMD Opteron-based systems, 897
AMD SVM, 641
AMD-V, with virtual extensions, 640
application programming interfaces (APIs), 670
application virtualization, 25–26
attach in virtual server, 228
authentication warning, 396

Automated Deployment Services (ADS), 356
    administration agent installation
        account information, 291
        certificate installation, 290
        license agreement, 289
        setup wizard, 288–289
    client server requirements for, 267
    configuration of
        client installation, 281–285
        multicast enabling, 285–287
    driver installation, 292
    host server requirements for, 266–267
    installation of, 356–357
        Controller services, 275
        database selection, 275
        Deployment Agent, 269
        image repository location, 277
        installation media, 281
        license agreement, 273–274
        MSDE installation, 270–272
        NBS support, 275
        opening source files, 269
        options, 268, 273
    management requirements for, 267–268
    services by
        Controller service, 265
        Image Distribution Service (IDS), 266
        Network Boot Service (NBS), 266

B

BackEnd layer, in Xen, 618
backup strategy process, 880–882
backup system. vmsnap.pl, 871
Bart's Network Boot Disk, 826
Basic authentication box, 395
BIOS clock, 410
BIOS configuration, in virtual machine
    for floppy disk drives, 233–234
blade servers, 912
Blktap. *See* Copy-on-Write
Block-attach, 638

Bonding, for multiple network interfaces, 625
  configuring and implementation, 626–627
Broadcom NetXtreme Gigabit Ethernet, 338
business continuity plans (BCPs), 28

C

capture.cmd Output, 373
capture term, in virtual server, 229
ccsd daemon, 631
chaining, in differencing disks, 253–255
80386 chipset, 17
CID=2af6d34d parameter, 798
CIM SDK, 752–753
Citrix Presentation Server, 911
CLI. *See* Command-line interfaces
client installation, for ADS
    Administrator Console for, 282
    controller service selection, 282–284
    IP address changing, 282–283
client-server requirements, for ADS, 267
"cluster.conf," 635
clvmd, LVM metadata distribution, 630
COM API for Windows, 673
COM (Component Object Model), 319
COM Interface, in Virtual Server, 320
Command-line interfaces, 524, 593
Command-name, 525
Common Information Model (CIM), 898
Common Internet File System (CIFS), 868
Compaq Smart Array 2 and Smart Array 3
    controllers, 827
compliance and virtualization, 911
COM ports, in virtual machine,
    101, 121–122, 124
ConfigureDHCPServer method, 338
config.version = "", 802
constrained delegation, configuration for, 398
Controller service, by ADS, 265
conventional security implementations factor, 908
CookieContainer system, 714
Copy-On-Write method, 619
  for storage optimization
    Blktap, 622
    DmUserspace, 623
    UnionFS, 623–624

Core Data Model, 711
CPU architecture, and OS, 16–18
CPU road map for 2007/2008, 902–903
CPU virtualization, in Xen
  exceptions, 435
  hypercalls, 435
  scheduling, 436–437
  time, 437–438
CreateDynamicVirtualHardDisk method, 334
CreateVirtualMachine method, 330, 333
CreateVirtualNetwork method, 337
CreateVirtualNetwork.vbs, 360
Createvirtualnetwork.vbs script, 411
CreateVM.cmd, 378–379
Cscript, 328

D

DAS (Distributed Availability Services), 702
Data Protection Act (DPA), 911
data replication, 879
ddb.adapterType = "buslogic," 808
ddb.adapterType = "lsilogic," 809
ddb.virtualHWVersion, 809
deployment agent
  in ADS, 269
  capture process, 375
DeployVM.cmd, 381
DHCP (Dynamic Host Configuration
    Protocol), 356
DHCPVirtualNetworkServer property, 338
differencing virtual hard disks
  chaining in, 253–255
  compression using NTFS, 250–252
  creation, 250
  logical architecture of, 249
  merging of, 254–256
  and parent disks, 249, 253
  undo disk, 256–257
Directory Security tab, 394
disk bound, 228
disk data base command, 799
disk descriptor for IDE virtual
    disk, 799
Distributed Availability Services (DAS),
    for virtual machines, 702

Distributed Management Task Force
(DMTF), 898
Distributed Replicated Block Device (DRBD),
629–630
Distributed Resource Scheduling (DRS), for
virtual machines migration, 702
DmUserspace. *See* Copy-on-Write
domU management, controls for, 572
drbdadm, for DRBD, 631
driver domains, 618
driver worlds, for ESX host, 661
DRS (Distributed Resource Scheduling), 702
DSI (Microsoft Dynamics System Initiative), 46
dual-core and quad-core servers, 901
dynamically expanding virtual hard disks
compaction, 238, 246
converting, 247
creating new, 238
default size, 237
disadvantage of, 238
pre-compaction, using Microsoft Virtual Disk
Pre-Compactor
attaching ISO to CD/DVD drive, 240
prerequisite for, 242
switches for, 243
zeroing file list, 241
Dynamic Host Configuration Protocol (DHCP),
356, 408
Dynamic Host Configuration Protocol server,
549, 607

E

ebtables filtering tool, 627
echo commands in script, 767
Eclipse, 671
Elastic Computing Platform (ECP), 568
End User License Agreement, 605–606, 651
Enomalism
administrative tools, 573
fast track solutions for, 583–584
installation of, 569–570
overview of, 568–569
for VMCasting, 574
Xen management with, 570
Enomalism Virtualized Grid (EVG), 568

enterprise-class server systems, 901
Enterprise Unique Identifier (EUI), 622
esx01, 650
ESX 3.0, 652
ESX host and FTP setting, 827
esx01:loadesx, 650
ESX server, 648
Esxtop, 658–660
vmkfstools, 662
ESX Server root level Access gaining, 759
ESX shell script VM creation by cloning,
783–784
Esxtop, 658, 659, 661–662
ethernet0.addressType = "vpx," 804
ethernet0.connectionType = "", 804
ethernet0.devName = "", 804
Ethernet0.generatedAddress = "", 804
ethernet0.networkName = "", 804
ethernet0.present = "", 803
Ethernet0.virtualDev = "vlance" or "vmxnet"/
"e1000," 805
EULA. *See* End User License Agreement
Event Data Model, 712
events
in virtual machines, 346
in virtual server, 344–345
exec commands in script, 767

F

Fast track solutions, 164
creating
virtual disk and virtual server, 164
hardware to the server, addition, 164
installation
non-Windows OS, 165
virtual machine tools, 165
Windows OS, 165
FAT volumes, 362
Fedora Core 6 and Xen installation
add/remove software, 477
allocation of memory and CPU, 485
choice virtualization method, 482
choosing Fedora core installation type, 469
choosing minimal installation, 472–476
configuring network card, 471

Fedora Core 6 and Xen installation (*Continued*)
creating new virtual system, 481–482
defining LVM layout, 470
defining size of your root file
system, 470–471
defining storage space, 484
installation of MediaNote, 483
package selection, 477–479
proceeding with installation, 486–487
virt-manager
new host running in, 487–488
use of, 479–481
file.createType = "twoGbMaxExtent
Sparse," 798
fixed-size virtual hard disks
converting, 248–249
creating, 248
disadvantage of, 248
Floppy.vfd, 235
fragmentation, 238
Freedom of Information Act 2000
(FIA2000), 911
FrontEnd layer, in Xen, 618
FTP process, 851

G
GatherHW.cmd script, 412
GatherHW Command Prompt,
365–366
GatherHW.exe, 364
GetContents method, 710–711
GetUpdates method, 710–711
Global Network Block Devices
(GNBDs), 619
grabbed: NORMAL - ungrabbed: LOW
setting, 807
Gramm-Leach-Bliley (GLB), 911
Guest Customization Data Model, 712
GuestInfo, in virtual machine, 685
guest operating system, 100, 166
GuestOS object, 339
GuestOS.Shutdown method, 340
Guest SDK, 751–752
Guests Only network, 337
GUID, 711

H
hard disks, 112–113, 167
hardware
assisting processors, 24
validation error, 368
virtualization software, list of, 39–42
Hardware Virtual Machine (HVM), live
migration of, 637
helper worlds, for ESX host, 661
Hercules, 369
high-performance computing (HPC)
paravirtualization system, 628
HostAdapter property, 338
Host bus adapters (HBAs), 547
network interface card, 620
Host Machine Data Model, 711
host server
development, in virtual machines, 123–125
requirements, for ADS, 266–267
HwgenerateP2V, 368
hybrid backup strategy, 882–883
hyper-threaded technology, 901

I
IA-32 CPU architecture, 17, 21
IA-64 feature Sync with x86, 895–896
IA-64 virtualization, 896
IDE Devices, scripted disconnect of, 811–814
IDE-disk with Intel-IDE controller, 809
IDE virtual hard disks, 229
idle worlds, for ESX host, 661
IISRESET Command, 397
Image Distribution Service (IDS), by ADS, 266
Imgdeploy.exe errors, 413–414
InfiniBand and RDMA technology, 900
InfiniBand enable raw I/O performance, 891
in-kernel *fbdev* paravirtual frame buffer
driver, 900
installation of, Automated Deployment
Services (ADS)
Controller services, 275
database selection, 275
Deployment Agent, 269
image repository location, 277
installation media, 281

license agreement, 273–274

MSDE installation, 270–272

NBS support, 275

opening source files, 269

options, 268, 273

installing non-windows OS, 143

non-microsoft operating systems, 143

installing virtual machine additions, 137, 139–140

completing setup of, 141

configuring and, 138

Instant Disk method, 827

Instruction Set Architecture (ISA), 20

integrated computing, 904–905

integrated development environment (IDE), 671

Integrated Drive Electronic (IDE), 236

Intel Core Duo mobile processors, 465

Intel Virtualization Technology (Intel VT), 24

Internal Server Error 500, 397–400

International Organization for Standardization (ISO) 9660, 113

Internet Information Server, 308

Internet Information Services (IIS) Manager, 393

Internet Storage Name Server (iSNS), 621

I/O virtualization, in Xen

device I/O rings, 447–448

driver domains, 451–452

event channels, 448–449

hypercalls, 446–447

I/O devices and split device drivers, 449–451

software and hardware IOMMUs, 452–454

iSCSI, 237, 468

initiators and target setting, 620–622

integration with Xen, 619–622

usage, 621

IsHeartBeating property, 339

isolation.tools.dnd.disable = "True" or "False," 807

Iterative Pre-copy, 636

IVMVirtualServer interface

accessing, 323

methods, 325

properties, 326

K

KDE GUI tools, 900

Kerberos Constrained Delegation (KCD), 309, 312

Kickstart configuration file, 648

L

Lawrence Livermore National Laboratory (LLNL), 628

LCPU line, 659

Lightweight Directory Access Protocol (LDAP), 549

Linux

and hardware, 849

rescue CD, 841

Linux distributions support, 894

Live migrations, through *xm* command, 524

loadesx, 650

Local area network (LAN), 611

local deployments, in openQRM, 547

Logical unit numbers (LUNs), 619

Logical Volume Manager (LVM), 550, 619, 631

LPT port, in virtual machine, 102, 122–124

LsaLogonUser() failed! error, 390–397

M

Managed Object Browser (MOB), 734–735

management application development, for virtual infrastructure

connection process, 713–714

functions, 712–713

interior nodes updation, 722–723

items retrieval and operations performance, 720–722

object handles

C# Script, for obtaining information, 716

C# Script, for using vHandles, 718–719

VB.NET Script, for obtaining information, 717

VB.NET Script, for using vHandles, 719

XML document return, 717–718

SSL Certificates handling, 714–716

management interface, in virtual server, 308–319

master boot records (MBRs), 414

Master password, in Administrator Console, 535

Media Access Control (MAC), 362

Media Access Control (MAC) address, for network devices, 117–118

MEM line, ESX host physical memory, 660

memory, 101

memory virtualization, in Xen
address translation, 443–445
allocation, 439–441
page tables and segmentation, 441–443

Microsoft Dynamics System Initiative (DSI), 46

Microsoft Management Console 3.0, 308

Microsoft Operations Manager (MOM), 46

Microsoft's Knowledge Base Article ID 891609, 400

Microsoft's up-and-coming Virtual Server management application, 898

Microsoft Virtual Disk Pre-Compactor, 239–243

Microsoft Virtual PC 2004
applications of, 55–56
vs. Virtual Server 2005, 52–55

Microsoft Virtual Server 2005 COM Interface Reference, 323

Microsoft VSMT directory, 364

Migration Script Generation, 369, 371

MOB (Managed Object Browser), 734–735

modern RAID controllers, 827

Modified Guests installation, 591

MOM (Microsoft Operations Manager), 46

Mozilla Public License (MPL), 549

MS SQL Server Desktop Engine (MSDE), 270

Multicore processors, 891

MULTICS time-sharing system, 16

MySQL installation, for openQRM, 555

N

Nagios, for system administrators, 549

navigation, in virtual machines, 135

NBD (Network Block Devices), 619

NetBeans IDE, for Java software development, 671

NET Framework 1.1, 268, 727

Netmask field, 651

network adapters, in virtual machine, 116–118

network-based deployments, in open QRM, 547

Network Block Devices (NBDs), 619

Network Boot Service (NBS), 266, 408

network changes, in Virtual Server settings, 402–405

Network File System (NFS), 867

network interface card (NIC), 124, 402, 527

network virtualization, 25, 912–913

new unique identifier (UUID), 806

NIC (Network interface card), 124, 527

non-uniform memory architecture (NUMA), 889

Norton Ghost, 264

NTFS, 362

NTFS compression, for differencing disk, 251–252

NUMA data access paths, 890

O

OASIS (Organization for the Advancement of Structured Information Standards), 700

o2cb.init, for for ocfs2-tools, 634

OCFS. *See* Oracle Cluster File System

openQRM
dashboard, 557
data center management tools, 547
deployments in, 547–548
evaluation of, 552
installation, 552
for IT professionals, 547
management solutions, 583
partition's profile creation, 563–564
plug-ins and licensing, 549–551
provisioning with, 565
resources in, 562
scenario deployment, 551
system requirements, 553–554
Xen guests, booting environment for, 548
Xen management with
with Xen integration, 561
Xen Plug-in works, 560–561

Xen Plug-in installation, 558–559
Xen VE in, 560
3.1.x Server installation, 554–557
operating system-level virtualization softwares, list of, 43–44
Oracle Cluster File System, 628
initial release of, 634
Organization for the Advancement of Structured Information Standards (OASIS), 700

P

packet filtering, 627
PAE (Physical Address Extensions), 465
paravirtualization, with Xen, 428–430
parentCID=ffffffff parameter, 798
parent virtual disk, 249, 253
Pascal notation, 325
PCI-Express (PCIe), 891
PCPU line, 659
Pentium 4 662 and 672, 465
Pentium D 9x0, 465
Pentium 4 Extreme Edition 955 and 965, 465
Performance Metric Data Model, 712
Perl API, 673
Perl script components, 779–781
physical server migration
creation of migration scripts
script generation, 368–372
validation of hardware, 367–368
creation of virtual machine on virtual server host, 378–381
data capturing of disks of physical server, 372–377
deployment of disk, 381–384
process of capturing physical machine, 361–364
hardware inventory for, 364–366
virtualization of environment
creation of virtual network, 360–361
installation of Virtual Server Migration Toolkit (VSMT) software, 357–360
planning and installation of ADS server, 356–357

physical to virtual (P2V) migration process, 824
Big Secret, 826
of existing systems, 606–607
post, 853
techniques, 824
PlateSpin PowerConvert, 51, 825
Popek and Goldberg virtualization requirements, 19–20
Poseidon, 369, 380
POWER4 architecture, 896
PowerConvert virtualization tool, 51
PowerPC 970, 896
PowerRecon virtualization tool, 51
Pre-Boot eXecution Environment (PXE), 267, 407
Project ConVirt, 574
installation, 575–577
overview, 575
solutions for, 584
Xen management with
dashboard, 577–578
server operation, 579
server pool operations, 578
VM operations, 579–580
property retrieval information
mechanisms for retrieval, 746–747
PropertyFilterSpec, 742–745
TraversalSpec Objects definition, 745–746
protection rings, in CPU architecture, 16–18
PutUpdates method, 711
P2Vdrivers.xml file, 362
P2V (physical-to-virtual) process, 50
PXE boot, 357, 362, 372
PXE-enabled device, 266
PXE servers, 409

Q

802.1Q, 624
QEMU Copy-on-Write (QCOW), 899
QEMU processor, 622
Qlusters, Inc., 546, 550
QRM-HA, in openQRM server, 550

R

RAID1 software, 367
Real Application Cluster (RAC), for Xen clustering, 628

reboot prompt, 141
Recovery Point Objective (RPO), 876
Recovery Time Objective (RTO), 876
Red Hat Enterprise Linux 4 (Red Hat ES 4)
    installation, 591–592
RedHat Fedora Core, 619
Red Hat Linux Enterprise 5 (Red Hat 5)
    installation, 598–599
redo log file, 856
reference.cs, for C# projects, 707
reference.vb, for VB.NET projects, 707
regcert command, 411
Remote Direct Memory Access (RDMA), 891
Remote Installation Services (RIS), 357, 372
Remote Network installation, 655
Remote offices, 170
removable disks, in virtual server
    CD/DVD drive
        attach, 228
        capture, 229
        IDE architecture, 229
        ISO images and, 229
        properties, modification of, 230
    floopy disk drive
        BIOS configuration, 233–234
        creating, 232
        modification in, 231
        read-only, 235
Removing virtual machine additions, 142
Replication, definition of, 590

S

safearray, 331
SAN, 237
SAN LUNs., 857
Sapien Technology's PrimalScript, 672
Sarbanes-Oxley (SOX), 911
Scripted installation
    creation, 648–649
    of ESX Server, 654
scripted VM Creation, 765
scripted VM creation script by creating
    templates, 770
Scripts for
    accessing virtual server using

listing properties, 329–331
    setting properties, 331–332
attached floppy images listing, 348–349
attaching DVD image to virtual machine, 349
attaching scripts to
    virtual machine event, 346
    virtual server event, 344–345
creating virtual machines, 332–333
guest OS information retrieving, 338–340
MAC addresses list of, 348
registered virtual machines listing, 350
save all running virtual machines, 346–347
start all saved virtual machines, 347–348
state of virtual machine
    listing properties, 341–343
    virtual disk creation, 333–334
    virtual network creation, 337–338
scripts, in virtual machine, 118–119
script storage location, 768
SCSI adapters
    in Microsoft Windows OS, 134
    in virtual machines, 115–116
SCSI controller, 414–415
SCSI controllers, 237
SCSI-disk with LSILogic controller, 809
SCSI driver installation
    in Windows 2000/2003, 830–838
    in Windows NT, 838–840
Scsi0:0.mode = "", 802
Scsi0:0.name = "", 802
Scsi0:0.present = "", 802
scsi0.virtualDev = "", 803
SearchPaths property, 330–331, 331
Server Message Block (SMB), 868
server sprawl problem, 901
server virtualization, 22–23
Setspn, 316
shell script
    creation using VI, 768–769
    execution of, 769
Simple Object Access Protocol (SOAP), 700
Small Computer Systems Interface (SCSI), 236
Small office/home office (SOHO), 162
smart I/O devices, 892–893
SOAP (Simple Object Access Protocol), 700

SSHLogin, for administrators, 549
states, in virtual machine, 342–344
StdOut.Write method, 336
storage area network (SAN), 101
storage virtualization, 24–25, 912
Supervisor Mode (Ring 0), 18
suspend.Directory = "/vmfs/vmhba
    1:0:83:1," 807
SWAP line, 660
switches, for dynamic virtual hard disks, 243
switches in, Cscript, 328
Switches, in xe CLI, 525
Symantec Ghost, 414
symmetric multiprocessing (SMP)
    architectures, 889
Symposium on Operating Systems Principles
    (SOSP), 422
Sysprep, 264, 294
System Center Virtual Machine Manager, 308

T
Task Data Model, 712
TCP/IP Offl oad Engines (TOEs), 891
TCP port 902, 672, 700
TCP port 8002, for incoming migration, 636
TCP Segmentation Offl oad (TSO), 406
Template Data Model, 712
TFTP (Trivial File Transfer Protocol), 549
third-party tools, for virtualization, 51
tools.syncTime Option, 807
Top, for Linux OSes, 658
total cost of ownership (TCO), 901
Trivial File Transfer Protocol (TFTP),
    266, 549
troubleshooting
  ADS service, 410–411
  automated deployment services, 407–410
  migration process, 413–417
  Virtual Server Migration Toolkit, 411–413
  Virtual Server performance issues, 406–407
  Virtual Server 2005 R2
    access denied errors, 400
    Internal Server Error 500, 397–400
    LsaLogonUser() failed! error, 390–393,
      390–397

  Virtual Server settings
    disappearing settings, 401–402
    network changes, 402–405
tunefs.ocfs2 utility, 635

U
UltraSPARC processor, 897
UNDOABLE mode, 852
undo disks, 256–257
UnionFS. *See* Copy-on-Write
unmodified Guests installation, 597–598
USB ports, in virtual machines, 125
UUID, 711

V
VBD (virtual block device), 619
VBScripts, 320, 326, 333
vendor-specifi c SCSI blocking, 827
version parameter of disk descriptor
    file, 798
vHandles, 710
VimAPI Namespace, 737–738
virtual 8086, 17
virtual block device (VBD), 619
Virtual disk files on VMFS, 850
Virtual disks (VDIs), 608
virtual environment, definition of, 547
virtual floppy disks
  BIOS configuration, 233–234
  creating, 232
  modification in, 231
virtual hard disk
  settings, 104
  types, 100
virtual hard disk images and XenFS, 899
virtual hard disks
  differencing type
    chaining in, 253–255
    compression, 250–252
    creation, 250
    merging of, 254–256
  dynamically expanding
    compacting, 238–246
    converting, 247
    creating new, 238

virtual hard disks (*Continued*)
 fixed-size
  converting, 248–249
  creating, 248
 image format specification, 253
 size of, 237
 storage architecture for, 236–237
 storing, 258
virtual hard disk (VHD) technology, 899
virtual infrastructure SDK 2.0
 data and managed objects, 728
 data models and types, 730–733
 development
  features, 723–724
  web service preparation, 725–726
 entity inventory, 728–729
 host agent *vs.* virtual center, 729–730
 programming logic for, 733–734
Virtual IP (VIP), 25
virtualization
 advantages in
  disaster recovery, 49–50
  production servers, 47–48
  test and development areas, 49
 tools
  PowerConvert, 51
  PowerRecon, 51
  Virtual Server 2005 Migration Toolkit, 50
 types
  application, 25–26
  network, 25
  server, 21–23
  storage, 24–25
 uses of
  business continuity and disaster recovery, 28
  for development teams, 29–30
  proof of concept (POC), 29
  technology refresh, 27–28
  virtual desktops, 29
 working principle, 52
  CPU architecture and OS, 16–18
Virtual LAN (VLAN), 25, 624–625
virtual machine additions for Linux
 CD/DVD properties, 155
 designing and planning, 160

destination folder, 151
finishing the installation, 153
installation startup, 149
installing the RPM package, 159
installing with YaST, 160
license agreement, 150
Linux status page, 154
mounting CD, 156
ready to install, 152
starting install, 157
virtual infrastructure, 161
vmadd-full-0.0.1-1.rpm, 158
VMAdditions for Linux, 149
Virtual Machine Additions ISO
  (VMAdditions.iso), 340
Virtual Machine Control Block (VMCB), 640
Virtual Machine Control Structure, 640
virtual machine, creating
 CD/DVD properties, 146
 create
  new virtual machine status page, 145
  virtual machine page, 144
 SuSE Linux 10 Desktop, 148
 SuSE Linux install screen, 147
Virtual Machine Monitor (VMM), 16, 24, 628
 file, 796
 functions of, 19, 20
 IA-32 (x86) architecture, 21
 Ring-0 presentation, 18
 virtualization requirements, 19
Virtual Machine Remote Console (VMRC),
  85–89, 400
virtual machines
 autostart and autostop command scripts, 807
 backup process for, 884
 cloning by ESX shell scripts, 782–784
 cloning by VmPerl scripts, 785–792
 configuration vmx file, 801–802
 conversion from IDE to SCSI, 808
 creation by command line tools, 756
 disk file creation, 762–763
 dynamic creation of, 814–821
 enhancements of, 899–900
 with ESX Server registering, 763–764
 in ESX Shell scripting creation of, 764–769

file in VI creation, 760
floppy drives and CD-ROMs for, 805
graphics emulation, unique identifiers, 805–806
performance and scalability, 889
saving VMX File in VI, 761
scripted VM Creation modification with Perl, 777–778
scripting creation in Perl scripts, 770–777
storage Location, 759
VMDK file, 796–798
VMX File creation of, 762
working directory, 760
Virtual Machine State Diagram, 342
Virtual machines (VMs), 524
    administration web page
        section selection, 102–103
        settings creation, 103
    CD/DVD in, 113–115
    COM ports in, 101, 121–122
    configuration
        additions, 109–110
        file, 107–109
        properties, 106–107
    controlling, 135
    disconnecting devices, 691–693
    floppy disk drive in, 101, 120–121
    GuestInfo in, 685
    GUI list, 693–696
    hard disk, 100, 112–113
    hardware installation, 123–125
    LPT ports in, 102, 122–123
    memory in, 100
    migration, 748–749
    navigation use in, 135
    network adapters in, 116–118
    parameters for, 582
    planning and placement
        CPU, 588–589
        memory, 588
        network, 589–591
    process, 660
    scripts in, 118–119
    SCSI adapters in, 115–116
    scsi0:0 in, 665
    test automation with, 696–697

virtual infrastructure SDK
    architecture, 698–700
    developing SDK 1.1, 703–706
    operations availability, 701–702
    programming logic for, 710
virtual infrastructure SDK 1.1
    path hierarchy, 708–709
    terminology, 709–710
virtual infrastructure web service, 700–701
virtual network adapter, 104
vmware-cmd and, 664–666
Windows OS installation
    booting from floppy disk, 128–130
    operating system loading, 126–128
    virtual hardware, 125–126
virtual network, 337–338
virtual network object (objVN), 338
Virtual Network VM0, 361
Virtual PC 2004, 239
Virtual Private Network (VPN), 25
virtual server
    accessing, using scripts
        properties listing, 329–331
    COM object connection, 326–328
    creation, 100–102
    disappearing settings, 401–402
    events in, 344–345
    hosts, 308, 315, 317
    migration toolkit, for server deployment, 100
    removable disks in
        CD/DVD drive, 228–230
        floppy disk drive, 232–235
Virtual Server 2005
    vs. Microsoft Virtual PC 2004, 52–55
    vs. Virtual Server 2005 R2, 56
Virtual Server Administration Web site, 308
Virtual Server Administrative Web site, installation
    configuring components, 79–81
    connection with virtual server, 84–85
    customer information, 77
    license agreement, 76
    post-installation summary, 83
    setup for, 75
    setup type selection, 78–79

Virtual Server COM API, 319–320
Virtual Server COM Interface Reference
    IVMVirtualServer node, 324
    server properties, 326
    virtual server methods, 325
Virtual Server Deployment Scenarios, 391–392
Virtual Server management site, configuration of
    domain needs, 310
    Microsoft Virtual Server 2005 installation
        feature selection, 311
        firewall exception setting, 313
        Kerberos Constrained Delegation and, 312
        setup type, 310
Virtual Server 2005 Migration Toolkit, 50
Virtual Server Migration Toolkit (VSMT)
    installatation of
        accepting license, 300
        completing, 302
        component selection, 301
        installation selection, 300
        Setup Wizard, 299
    software, 357, 360
Virtual Server Programmer's Guide, 320
Virtual Server 2005 R2, 166, 308, 401, 405
    installation of
        Administrative Web site installation, 76–85
        configuring components, 69–71
        customer information, 67
        default location and search path settings,
            89–92
        license agreement, 66
        post-installation summary, 74
        preinstallation tasks, 64
        resource allocation settings, 92–95
        running setup, 64
        setup screen, 65
        setup type selection, 68–69
        system requirements, 63
        Virtual Machine Remote Console (VMRC)
            configuration, 85–89
Virtual Server SDK
    COM Interface Reference, 323
    default view, 321
    sections in, 322
    uses, 321

Virtual Split Devices Model, 618, 642
virtual VMware SCSI driver, 826
Visual Studio 2005, 675
VLAN, 357
vma.exe command, 703
VM backup
    anatomy of, 856–859
    CIFS for, 868
    FTP for, 868–869
    limitations of, 859
    NFS for, 867–868
    sample script, 863–865
    target for, 866–867
    Tools for, 870–871
    VMFS for, 869–870
vmbk.pl, 871–872
VMCB (Virtual Machine Control Block), 640
VmCollection, 675, 678
VmCOM. *See* VM Component
        Object Model
VM Component Object Model, 670
    development, 675
    limitations, 679
    script writing, 684
    in Windows, 673
    working with, 674–675
VmConnectParams, 675
    properties, 677–678
    in VBScript, 678
VMCS. *See* Virtual Machine Control Structure
VmCtl API, 674
    methods, 681–682
    object browser use of, 677
    properties, 680–681
    Symbolic Constant Enumerations (SCE),
        682–683
    use of, 680
VMDK. A VMDK file, 856
VMDK components, 798–800
vm-install, in XenVMs, 526
vmkfstools command-line utility, 762
vmkfstools export, 871
vmkfstools, for ESX server, 662–664
vmkusage, for troubleshooting, 666
VMM (Virtual Machine Monitor), 628

VmPerl API, 670, 685–686
  methods, 687
  for programe interaction, 687
VmPerl Commands, 781
VMRCEnabled property, 332
VMRC Server Port, 401
VMRC (Virtual Machine Remote Control), 109
VMScript.exe, 412
VmServerCtl API, 674
  properties and methods, 679
  use of, 678
vmsnap_all.pl, 871
vmsnap.pl, 871
vmware-cmd command tool, 763
VMware ESX Server, 856
VMware ESX Server 3.0, 670
VMware ESX Server tools, 756
VMware ESX Server 2.5.x, 670
VMware ESX shell, 765
VMware File System (VMFS), 869
VMware GSX Server 3, 412
VMware GSX 2.x, 672
VMware P2V Tool, 824–825
VMware scripting APIs, 670
  ActiveState Komodo, 671
  architecture of, 672
  data movement in, 685
  Eclipse for, 671
  installation
    in Linux client machine, 674
    in Windows client machine, 673
  Microsoft Visual Studio for, 671
  Sapien Technology's PrimalScript, 672
VMware SDKs
  CIM SDK, 752–753
  Guest SDK, 751–752
VMware Server 1.0 platform, 412
VMwareService.exe, 685
VMware's VMDK format, 899
VMware tools, 781
VMware VirtualCenter 2.0, 670
VMware VirtualCenter 1.x, 670
VMX configurations, 757
VMX file backups, 873–875
vmx file components, 802

VMX old and new settings, 811
VNCLogin, for administrators, 549
VSHostNet switch, 361
VSMT Installation Setup Type, 360
vssrvc service, 316
"vstandard" SCSI adapter properties, 415–417
VT-support virtualization, on laptops, 466
VT-x technology, for x86 processor, 639

W
Web-Based Enterprise Management
      (WBEM), 898
Web Service Description Language
      (WSDL), 700
Web Services, definition of, 700
Windows Guests installation, 602
Windows NT Server 4.0 Service
      Pack 6a, 362
Windows Script Technologies, 327
Windows Server 2003
  domain functional levels, 309
  Enterprise Edition, 270
  Web Edition, 268
Windows Server 2003 Service Pack 1, 400
Windows Server Virtualization, 308
Windows VMs, 852
Windows XP, as virtual machine, 488–492
Windows XP. Novice Linux, 900
Windows XP Professional, 308
Windows XP Service Pack 2, 400
WinImage, 232
writable virtual floppy disk, 235
Wscript. *See* Cscript
wsdlProxyGen.exe, 706–707
WSDL (Web Service Description Language), 700

X
x86-based blade infrastructure, 912
x86 CPU architecture, 895
Xen
  cluster building
    RedHat Cluster Suite, 628
    solution, 643
  CoW solutions for, 622–624
  CPU virtualization

Xen (*Continued*)
  exceptions, 435
  hypercalls, 435
  scheduling, 436–437
  time, 437–438
defined, 422–424
disk access in, 619
features, 424
installation of
  configuration, 513–518
  on free Linux distribution, 468–488
  methods, 510–513
  planning, 465–468
  selection of platform, 464–465
  system requirements, 465
  on Windows XP, 488–492
  XenServer product family, 492–509
I/O virtualization
  device I/O rings, 447–448
  driver domains, 451–452
  event channels, 448–449
  hypercalls, 446–447
  I/O devices and split device drivers,
    449–451
  software and hardware IOMMUs,
    452–454
iSCSI integration with, 619–622
memory virtualization
  address translation, 443–445
  allocation, 439–441
  page tables and segmentation, 441–443
networking concepts
  bonding creation, 625–627
  routing, 627
  VLANs bridging, 624–625
product family, 424–426
virtualization in, 639
virtualization model
  architecture overview, 427
  domains, 430–434
  paravirtualization, 428–430
  processor architecture, 428
Virtual Machine Monitor (VMM), 628
Xenstore, 454–457

Xen and Microsoft, 894–895
Xen code base, 423
Xen host components, 907
XenHosts
  command-name, 525
  execution, 525
  options for, 527
  shutting down and rebooting of, 526
  working with, 537–538
Xen hypervisor, 424
XenMan
  image store in, 581–582
  solutions for, 584
  for Xen virtualization platform, 574
XenoServers Project, 422
Xen Plug-in openQRM
  building, 558
  sample configuration, 559
Xen PV Tools
  End User License Agreement (EULA), 606
  from Media Drop-Down, 605
Xen road map, 888
XenServer Administrator Console, 425
XenServer product family, installation of
  binaries and LVM, 510–513
  client installation, 501–505
  host installation, 494–501
  of Initial Virtual Machine, 505–509
  overview of XenServer, 492–493
  server requirements, 493
  versions, 493
XenSource, 422
Xenstore, 454–457
XenVMs
  backup and recovery solutions,
    638–639
  booting, 526, 600
    sequence for, 601
  deploying and configuring
    additional operations, 541
    cloning, 540–541
    installation, 539–540
    performance monitoring, 542
  execution, 525

exporting of, 608–611
importing of, 610–611
installation and cloning of, 526
migration, 635–637, 643
Red Hat ES 4 installation, 591
windows tab installation in, 603
Xeon MP 7000, 465

Xeon MP Processor, 890
xinetd daemon, 828
xm CLI
    live migrations accomplishment, 611
    for Xen management, 525
XML File, 366
XVM, 428